RUSSIAN FOREIGN RELATIONS AND INVESTMENT LAW

RUSSIAN FOREIGN RELATIONS AND INVESTMENT LAW

William E Butler

John Edward Fowler Distinguished Professor of Law, Pennsylvania State University
Director, The Vinogradoff Institute, Dickinson School of Law
Academician, National Academy of Sciences of Ukraine and
Russian Academy of Natural Sciences

OXFORD
UNIVERSITY PRESS

OXFORD
UNIVERSITY PRESS

Great Clarendon Street, Oxford OX2 6DP

Oxford University Press is a department of the University of Oxford.
It furthers the University's objective of excellence in research, scholarship,
and education by publishing worldwide in

Oxford New York

Auckland Cape Town Dar es Salaam Hong Kong Karachi
Kuala Lumpur Madrid Melbourne Mexico City Nairobi
New Delhi Shanghai Taipei Toronto

With offices in

Argentina Austria Brazil Chile Czech Republic France Greece
Guatemala Hungary Italy Japan Poland Portugal Singapore
South Korea Switzerland Thailand Turkey Ukraine Vietnam

Oxford is a registered trade mark of Oxford University Press
in the UK and in certain other countries

Published in the United States
by Oxford University Press Inc., New York

First published 2006

British Library Cataloguing in Publication Data
Data available

Library of Congress Cataloging in Publication Data
Data available

Typeset by RefineCatch Limited, Bungay, Suffolk
Printed in Great Britain
on acid-free paper by
Biddles Ltd, King's Lynn

ISBN 0–19–928165–3 978–0–19–928165–7

1 3 5 7 9 10 8 6 4 2

PREFACE

This book addresses as a unified whole a body of material which is not so regarded in Russian legal doctrine or by the Russian legal system, or for that matter in most legal systems. The legal rules under discussion cut across the categories of natural persons, juridical persons, States, and international organizations. They share common addressees who are non-Russian, or transactions (to adapt a concept from private international law) with a 'foreign element', or a legal system which is non-Russian. In the broadest sense of the word, these rules concern 'foreign relations' (which term will be used throughout this volume to mean collectively 'foreign relations law, including investment law').

Oddly, comparative lawyers have not seized the opportunity to pursue comparative foreign relations law. This work is intended as a modest step in that direction by concentrating upon the approach of a country whose position in the international community and whose legal traditions are quite different from those of, for example, the United Kingdom and the United States, to regulating relations with the international community in the largest sense of the word—people, companies, foreign States, and regional and international entities.

In part, foreign relations law is an expression of a country's approach to or attitude towards the international community and its legal system. It is evidence of the extent to which the international legal system has been accommodated or integrated into the national and sub-national legal systems. Foreign relations law also may be evidence of State practice with respect to the affirmation, or creation, or acceptance, and so on of individual rules of international law. In some cases individual provisions of foreign relations law may constitute claims of States vis-a-vis the existing legal regime.

For the legal practitioner (and by that term here we mean the private practitioner in law firms and the legal advisor to governments and international institutions) foreign relations law comprises the body of rules and doctrines that determine the legal status and regulate the behaviour of 'foreigners' within national legal orders, and the national legislation and other forms of State practice that reflect or regulate the interface between the national legal system and the international community of States and international institutions. One could, in principle, approach the subject from the vantage point of either the national legal system concerned, or the international legal system. In this study we adopt chiefly the former approach, emphasizing the domestic Russian legal regulation of its foreign relations. We do not, however, consider the legal status of foreigners in wartime, except in passing.

Against the fabric of more than ten centuries of recorded Russian history, the subject of this book touches upon the very identity of the Russians as a distinct people, society, culture, and entity. It is surprising how sparingly cultural historians use legal instruments of identity and affiliation (subjecthood, citizenship, statelessness, foreignness) in the Russian context to particularize or reinforce (or not) a formal association between an individual and the larger community(ies) with which he is linked.[1]

For background on the Russian legal system, readers will find my *Russian Law* (2nd edn, Oxford University Press, 2003) indispensable.

A special word of thanks is extended to Consultant Plus, the outstanding electronic legal data base in the Russian Federation, without whom the preparation of this volume would have been incalculably more difficult. Footnotes have been kept to a minimum, and where transliteration is necessary, the Library of Congress abbreviated version is used.

status juris: 15 August 2006

W E Butler
May 2006

[1] For a recent and outstanding study, see N. V. Riasanovsky, *Russian Identities: A Historical Survey* (2005).

CONTENTS—SUMMARY

ANNEXES

CONTENTS

ANNEXES

TABLE OF RUSSIAN LEGISLATION

(Including Subjects of the Russian Federation)

1991

1992

1993

1994

1995

1996

1997

1998

1999

2000

2001

2003

2005

2006

TABLE OF USSR LEGISLATION

TABLE OF JUDICIAL MATERIALS

2005

TABLE OF TREATIES OF THE RUSSIAN FEDERATION

1995

1996

1997

1998

2004

TABLE OF DOCUMENTS OF THE UNION OF BELARUS AND THE RUSSIAN FEDERATION

LIST OF ABBREVIATIONS

БМД	Бюллетень международных договоров [Bulletin of International Treaties]
БНА РФ	Бюллетень нормативных актов Российской Федерации [Bulletin of Normative Acts of the Russian Federation]
CIS	Commonwealth of Independent States
IGO	International Governmental Organization
ILO	International Labour Organization
NGO	Nongovernmental organization
ПСЗ	Complete Collected Laws of the Russian Empire
RSFSR	Russian Soviet Federated Socialist Republic
САПП РФ	Собрание актов Президента и Правительства Российской Федерации [Collection of Acts of the President and Government of the Russian Federation]
СЗ РФ	Собрание законодательства Российской Федерации [Collection of Legislation of the Russian Federation]
USSR	Union of Soviet Socialist Republics

Part I

LAW AND FOREIGN RELATIONS

1

TOWARDS A CONCEPT OF FOREIGN RELATIONS LAW

'Foreign relations law' has received its greatest doctrinal elaboration in the United States, where it has been the subject of a major *Restatement*, now in its third edition,[1] pioneering treatises,[2] law school casebooks[3] and nutshells.[4] There is no uniform view as to what 'foreign relations law' encompasses. The *Restatement* subdivides the subject-matter into two categories. The first is 'international law as it applies to the United States'. This category is largely outside the purview of the present work with respect to Russia except insofar as Russian constitutional and other legislation expressly mentions or draws upon public international law within the Russian legal system. To do otherwise would require a work on Russian approaches to international law, and in this writer's view that would be quite a different undertaking. **1.01**

The second category singled out in the *Restatement* with respect to the United States is 'domestic law that has substantial significance for the foreign relations of the United States or has other substantial international consequences'. This category is primarily the concern of the present work with regard to the Russian Federation, except that in the present work the term 'foreign relations' is more broadly understood than in both the *Restatement* and American doctrinal writings generally. It is not merely the 'foreign relations' of the Russian Federation in the sense of the legal regime for participation in international relations with other **1.02**

[1] See American Law Institute, *Restatement of the Law Third: The Foreign Relations Law of the United States* (1987). 2 vols. plus Supps. Hereinafter: the *Restatement.*

[2] L Henkin, *Foreign Affairs and the United States Constitution* (1972).

[3] C A Bradley and J L Goldsmith, *Foreign Relations Law. Cases and Materials* (2003).

[4] P R Trimble, *International Law: United States Foreign Relations Law* (2002).

States or entities in the international community, or in international law-making processes, but also in the 'foreign relations' of Russia as expressed, for example, by the Russian legal regime with respect to non-Russian natural and juridical persons on the territory of the Russian Federation (legal status of aliens), the jurisdiction of Russian courts in cases involving a foreign element, the duties owed by Russian agencies and officials to foreigners, the duties owed by foreigners in Russia to the Russian Federation, and so on. Not included here, although arguably they could be, are relations of Russian citizens with the 'abroad'; the exclusion is justified on the basis that although there is Russian legislation that regulates some of these relations (for example, whether Russians may take hard currency abroad and under what circumstances), mostly the legal regime of Russian citizens outside the Russian Federation is regulated by the law of the country in which they are situated and therefore the subject falls more properly within the foreign relations law of that country.[5] Not an entirely satisfactory reply, but for the purposes of this study, it will need to suffice.

1.03 However helpful the preceding discussion may be for orientating the reader about the scope of this volume, it would be considered by many Russian jurists to be unsatisfactory in principle from the standpoint of Russian legal science. The very title of this study suggests the existence of a *branch* of Russian law (not merely Russian legislation) which encompasses a cohesive set of legal relations distinct from other branches of Russian law, although there may be elements of overlap. The present writer has already addressed a major sub-branch of Russian foreign relations law, namely foreign investment law.[6] Here, however, we are concerned with the aggregate of legal norms of the Russian Federation and subjects of the Russian Federation, including the interpretation and application thereof in Russian judicial and arbitral practice, and international legal principles and rules which are an integral part of the legal system of the Russian Federation that

[5] Russian policy, however, tends to see these 'compatriots' who have become foreign citizens as falling into a special category. Under the 1999 Federal Law 'On State Policy of the Russian Federation With Respect to Compatriots Abroad', as amended, these individuals when present in the Russian Federation '. . . enjoy rights and bear duties equally with citizens of the Russian Federation, except for instances established by the Constitution of the Russian Federation, international treaties of the Russian Federation, federal constitutional laws, and federal laws' (Article 13). *СЗ РФ* (1999), no. 22, item 2670; (2002), no. 22, item 2031; (2004), no. 35, item 3607; (2005), no. 1(I), item 25.

[6] W E Butler, *Foreign Investment Law in the Commonwealth of Independent States* (2002). Although this volume is the only detailed comparative analysis of succeeding generations of foreign investment law within each of the twelve members of the Commonwealth of Independent States, there is substantial consensus among Russian jurists that 'foreign investment law' is a proper subject for autonomous analysis. See S S Starikov, 'Foreign Investments in Subjects of the Russian Federation', *Sudebnik*, IX (2004), 10. The issue of 'autonomy' of analysis is complicated by the existence of general Russian (and other CIS) investment legislation, which may also extend to foreign investors. Placed in the larger context of foreign relations law, however, foreign investment relations take on quite a different aspect.

regulate the relations of the State, constituent entities of the State, and Russian juridical persons and citizens in their relations with foreign States, international organizations, and foreign juridical persons and citizens. The argument advanced is that these principles and rules, although they may repose primarily in general legislation or in specialized legislation dedicated to components of what is here regarded as foreign relations law, it is appropriate to treat these at the doctrinal level as a single whole conceptually linked by the role they perform in regulating the foreign relations of Russia in the largest sense of the word.

This is not a traditional approach to the division of Russian law into branches. It **1.04**
may be that this approach can survive only in the form of an analytical prism. Nonetheless, the legal relations are real and cohesive, and more central to the place of Russia in the international community than at any time in her past. It is, moreover, constructive from the perspective of policy decisions, including foreign policy, to have a total appreciation of the aggregate of legal rules involved in the regulation of foreign relations. These rules are simultaneously an instrument of foreign relations and a complex of foreign relations obligations owed to other actors, whether they directly engage the responsibility of the State or not. Many Russian international lawyers, though, would consider the title of this volume to relate to public international law and not to aspects of Russian law. Lukashuk wrote: 'The law of foreign relations is the branch of international law whose principles and norms regulate official relations whose participants are States and international organisations.'[7]

From the standpoint of this study, the legal regime or status of foreigners is a **1.05**
component of foreign relations law and refers to the aggregate of norms or rules regulating their legal position. In the absence of a conception of foreign relations law, legal doctrine has vacillated between treating the legal status of foreigners as part of State or administrative law, or as part of public international law, or as part of private international law. Soviet and Russian doctrinal writings addressed the legal regime of foreigners in the standard textbooks on public international law, and the norms concerning their legal capacity and procedural rights in works on private international law and civil law. Boguslavskii expressed the general frustration with the issue: 'It is evident that the entire aggregate of norms regulating the legal status of foreigners in any country, including the USSR, can not be relegated to any single branch of law. Some norms are relegated to one of the branches, and others, to another, and the aggregate of these norms also comprises a complex legal institution – the "legal status of

[7] I I Lukashuk, *Международное право: Особенная часть* [International Law: Special Part] (3rd edn, 2005), II, p. 69. However, Lukashuk acknowledges that 'the law of foreign relations is sometimes understood as the aggregate of the norms of internal law regulating the effectuation of the foreign relations of a State' (p. 69).

foreigners". The State-law, international legal, and other legal relations are closely intertwined.'[8]

1.06 The same controversies and dilemmas arise when addressing lesser issues arising with respect to the legal status of foreigners. Take, for example, the rules of labour legislation concerned with the labour activity of foreigners based on the conclusion of a labour contract. The Labour Code itself (Article 11) extends the provisions of the Code to labour relations with the participation of foreigners, which would seem to dispose of the branch affiliation of those rules. Indeed, Article 11 seemed to fill a gap since the 1971 Code of Laws on Labour of the RSFSR made no mention of regulating the labour of foreigners in the RSFSR,[9] as a result of which many Soviet jurists considered that private international law encompassed the relevant norms. Boguslavskii included labour relations with the participation of foreigners in his cours on private international law, observing that 'the general concepts and provision of international private law apply to labour relations with a foreign element'.[10]

1.07 A number of Russian jurists have suggested the creation of a sub-branch of private international law exists, called private international labour law.[11] All the authors concerned, in making these observations, overlook or underplay the role of international treaties in determining labour relations with a foreign element; that is, rules of public international law which are an integral part of the Russian legal system.

A. Historical Background

Pre-Revolutionary period to 1917

1.08 The earliest surviving documents of Russian legal history—the peace treaties of the early tenth century between Kievan Rus and Byzantium and the earliest known Russian legislative codes, the Russkaia Pravda—contain rules regulating

---

[8] Boguslavskii, *Статус иностранцев в СССР* [Status of Foreigners in the USSR] (1984), p. 20.

[9] The late I Ia Kiselev observed: '. . . the legal regulation of labour relations with foreign participation is a new orientation for the labour law of the Russian Federation which was virtually nonexistent in Soviet labour law and which has still not finally formed to this day'. I Ia Kiselev, *Труд с иностранным участием (правовые аспекты)* [Labour with Foreign Participation (Legal Aspects)] (2003), p. 7.

[10] Boguslavskii, *Международное частное право. Элементарний курс* [International Private Law. Elementary Cours] (2002), p. 229.

[11] See N I Marysheva (ed.), *Международное частное право. Краткий курс* [International Private Law. Concise Cours] (2003), pp. 229–30; V P Zvekov, *Международное частное право: Учебник* [International Private Law. Textbook] (2nd rev. edn, 2004), p. 521.

the legal status of foreigners. For the most part, however, the legal status of foreigners in Russia was regulated by a combination of legislative acts, historical tradition, and the existence of precedents formed by reactions to the realities of political and economic contacts and policies.

The Russian language contains a wealth of terms to express the relationship between those identified as 'Russian' and those who on one ground or another are classified as 'other' or 'different'. A 'foreigner' is literally a person from 'another country' (ино|странец), or from another land (ино|земец; also чуже|земец), or from 'another tribe' (ино|племенник), or from 'another city or community' (ино|городец), also used to refer to a non-Cossack peasant living in a Cossack community, or of 'another clan' or non-Russian national minority (ино|родец), or of 'another faith' or creed (ино|верец). The term немец could in the narrow sense mean a 'German' or, more broadly, any foreign European, and often was used in the word combination 'unbaptized foreigner' (некрещенный немец). Persons of the Islamic faith were commonly referred to as 'Tatars' or 'Murzy' in Russian legislation.

The numbers of foreigners who visited Muscovy up to the reign of Peter the Great can only be estimated. Some estimates are spectacularly improbable. Paul of Aleppo wrote that in the seventeenth century the Tsar had 30,000 German soldiers distributed throughout his various regiments and formations.[12] Those who have recently examined Russian archival sources suggest that with minor exceptions throughout the seventeenth century the number of foreigners present from Western Europe varied between 1,000 and 2,500, including all auxiliary personnel and families. The principal minor exception was the years 1631 to 1634, when large numbers of Poles entered Russian territories as mercenaries.[13] These figures would not include non-European individuals, for whom no figures are available as yet. Among traders, the overwhelming majority was Dutch, followed by English, and smaller numbers from Hamburg, Lubeck, and Bremen.

Medieval Muscovy was renowned throughout Europe for its remoteness and self-imposed isolation.[14] The memoirs of European adventurers, diplomats, merchants, missionaries, and soldiers were the primary source of knowledge

[12] Paul of Aleppo, *Путешествие Антиохийского патриарха Макария в Россию в половине XVII века* [Journey of the Patriarch of Antioch, Makarii, to Russia in the Mid-Seventeenth Century] (1898), vyp. 3, p. 12.

[13] A V Demkin, *Западноевропейское купечество в России XVII в.* [Western European Merchantry in Russia of the Seventeenth Century] (1994), I, pp. 26–8; S P Orlenko, *Выходцы из западной Европы в России XVII века: правовой статус и реальное положение* [Emigrants from Western Europe to Russia of the Seventeenth Century: Legal Status and Real Position] (2004), pp. 44–52.

[14] M T Poe, *The Russian Moment in World History* (2003), pp. 28–37.

about Muscovy; even the cartouches of atlases contained the rudiments of information sufficient for many to form an initial impression of that land. Russian legislation made no provision whatsoever concerning the rights of foreigners to enter the realm even though dozens, if not hundreds, of individuals—and on rare occasion thousands—crossed the Muscovy frontier on various missions and pretexts. Except for those categories of foreigners actively recruited to come to Russia or individuals expressly invited, foreign visitors seem to have been regarded as an unwelcome necessity. Those admitted seem to have fallen into the categories of diplomat, traders, and specialists in trades or crafts that the Russian authorities wished to attract. Family members and servants were usually admitted together with the foreigner. Clergy required special authorization, Protestant pastors commonly being required to swear an oath of fealty to the Muscovy sovereign.

Russian archives for the period give a general picture of the applicable procedures.[15] Upon arrival at a frontier point of Muscovy the foreigner would be subjected to an 'interview' by representatives of the local administration. In his explanations the foreigner would declare the purpose of his arrival in Muscovy and relate his prior service in other lands. It was desirable and, as time passed, even essential for letters of recommendation to be presented. If the local administration lacked sufficiently precise instructions about admitting particular categories of foreign specialists, the record of the interview and explanations would be sent to Moscow while the foreigner waited at the frontier point for a response. As a rule, a foreigner would be issued, while waiting, money for maintenance at treasury expense, the amount of which depended upon the rank of the foreigner. Depending upon what the Moscow authorities decided, the foreigner either received an escort to travel to Moscow[16] or was turned away.

Surviving records suggest a highly utilitarian approach to the admission of foreigners. If their skills were required at a particular time, admission was swift; if not, admission was denied. Policy fluctuations occurred frequently, especially with respect to military personnel. Edicts sent to Novgorod in 1636 and to Pskov in 1639 stipulated that foreign military personnel were not required at the time because Muscovy was not at war with anyone, or that only very senior military

[15] Russian State Archive of Ancient Acts, fond 150 (Matters Concerning Visits of Foreigners to Russia), cited by Orlenko, *Выходцы из западной Европы в России XVII века: правовой статус и реальное положение* [Emigrants from Western Europe to Russia of the Seventeenth Century: Legal Status and Real Position] (2004), pp. 104–5.

[16] Although the escort was supposedly without charge to the foreigner, adjutants [приставы] assigned to accompany honoured guests expected and received generous gifts. See H F Graham (ed. & transl.), *The Moscovia of Antonio Possevino, SJ* (1977).

officers should be admitted, or in 1647 to Pskov that only junior military officers and ordinary soldiers should be admitted.[17]

Foreign merchants could come and go freely to attend trade fairs in the frontier cities, or winter in Archangel by reason of the weather. But commercial visits into the interior of Russia were limited to those foreigners who had rendered special services to Muscovy and had received a special authorization. English merchants enjoyed the privileges of free trade from the time of the Embassy of Sir Giles Fletcher in the reign of Tsar Ivan IV through The Muscovy Company; this privilege was limited from 1649, when King Charles I was executed. Swedish merchants obtained privileges of free trade with designated areas under peace treaties with Muscovy. In practice, Swedish subjects also were admitted to Muscovy in order to visit relatives.

The New Trade Statute of 22 April 1667 required that trading foreigners were to be permitted to arrive in Moscow and other cities only if they had an appropriate instrument from the Grand Sovereign with a red seal. Others, the Statute provided, were allowed only to trade in the cities of Archangel and Pskov.[18] Towards the end of the seventeenth century the exceptions to the general rule proliferated. Other foreigners besides the Swedes began to frequent Novgorod and Pskov. There is evidence that by the 1680s entry to Muscovy could be obtained simply by presenting a 'pass' certifying identity and explaining the purpose of the intended visit. The phenomenon of tourism began to manifest itself, as demonstrated by three Italians who arrived for the sole purpose of seeing the country. They were admitted, indeed received by V V Golitsyn, but later suspected of espionage, detained, and subsequently released after detailed information was received from the Polish authorities concerning their persons. Even political asylum began to be practised on a larger scale: during the Regency of Sofia Alekseevna (who ruled during the minority of Peter the Great and his brother) instruments were issued to grant asylum to French protestants fleeing repression at home. Although it was intended these refugees should enter State service, such service was not a precondition of entry.

By 1689, however, there was a return to the previous system of authorizing entry. An Edict of 29 October 1689 prohibited entry by foreigners to Russia without the prior agreement of Moscow.[19] Privileges were returned under an

[17] Cited in Orlenko, *Выходцы из западной Европы в России XVII века: правовой статус и реальное положение* [Emigrants from Western Europe to Russia of the Seventeenth Century: Legal Status and Real Position] (2004), pp. 105–6.

[18] *ПСЗ* (1st series), I, No. 408, pp. 85–6.

[19] *ПСЗ* (1st series), III, No. 1358, pp. 46–7.

instrument of 5 January 1691 to Swedish subjects who wished to visit relatives in Russia.

The fluctuations of Russian policies with respect to the legal status of foreigners reflected the conundrums associated with a foreign presence in Muscovy. When Russia needed foreign military personnel or required technical assistance in engineering, crafts, trades, and the like, policies of admittance were rather liberal. When campaigns were instigated by the senior Russian Orthodox clergy, especially during 1652 to 1654, against 'heretics', all foreigners were viewed as potential subverters of the faith; proselytizers dedicated to undermining the true church. These apprehensions led to requirements, for example, that foreigners not be seen in Russian clothing, lest they deceive the faithful as to who they truly were. Security concerns were relevant. Foreigners might be a source of espionage, and foreign embassies in particular were shadowed or escorted so that members of the retinue did not see or visit fortifications (unless, on occasion, the Russian hosts wanted to demonstrate the quality of their fortifications, in which case the foreign diplomats were shown them as part of their reception). Given the significant numbers of foreigners in Russian military service, however, including in senior command positions, the policies with respect to foreigners being a security risk were at best ambivalent.

Suspicion did extend, at least in the perception of foreigners, to those in State service who wished to return to their homeland. More than one had to remain longer than he wished because of concern that his departure would be misunderstood as a security risk.

Becoming a Russian was not a matter regulated by legislation in the seventeenth century. Being a Russian subject was closely intertwined with the Russian Orthodox faith. An 'unbaptized foreigner' who converted to Russian Orthodoxy also passed to the protection of the Tsar of Muscovy and simultaneously renounced his relationship to any other monarch. A foreigner baptized in the 'Greek faith' lost the right to return to his motherland and thus de facto became a Russian subject. Foreigners who did not convert to Russian Orthodoxy therefore retained the right to leave Russia and go back home. Documents from the seventeenth century suggest that the concept of 'Russian subjecthood' at the time originated with those foreigners who had come to Russia and wished to pass 'under the hand of the sovereign of Muscovy' without changing their confession of faith. Petitions to achieve this status are known at least as early as 1648.[20]

[20] See A S Muliukin, *Приезд иноземцев в Московское государство. Из истории русского права XVI–XVII вв.* [Arrival of Foreigners in the Muscovite State. From the History of Russian Law of the Sixteenth and Seventeenth Centuries] (1909), pp. 152–3.

The Petrine era marked a new attitude towards foreigners in Russia. In December 1695 the Tsar instructed that foreigners arriving at the Russian frontier to enter State service be admitted without delay. On the eve of his departure to Western Europe on his Grand Embassy the Tsar issued an Edict (1696) requiring that all foreigners, on whatever business they arrived, be admitted to Moscow provided their interview was 'genuine'. By a Manifesto of 16 April 1702 the Tsar not only offered free access to foreigners but actually sought to recruit them by promising various rights, privileges, and freedom of confession. This was done, the Manifesto recited, so that his 'subjects might learn knowledge up to now unknown and become more skillful in matters of trade'.[21] After the explanation of the reasons for the new status of foreigners, the Manifesto enumerated the guarantees and rights which foreigners in Russia would enjoy. Foreigners who wished to enrol for service in the Russian armed forces, merchants, and artists who intended to come to Russia were to be provided with a certificate from the Russian General Commissar in Germany, showing this upon arrival at the Russian frontier to the local official in charge, after which they would be accompanied free of charge with their suite and baggage to Moscow. The Manifesto guaranteed freedom of worship, both private and public, to foreigners—a considerable change with respect to a most sensitive issue in Russia.

The Manifesto further provided for the formation of a privy college of the military council, which was responsible for all affairs concerning the foreigners amongst military personnel. The privy council was to be guided when considering cases by 'God's laws' and then by 'Roman civil law and other people's customs'.

From the Petrine era onwards the numbers of foreigners seeking admittance to Russia increased significantly. A massive, underpopulated territory, Russia eventually sought not only greatly needed artisans and military personnel, but also settlers who would cultivate the land. Catherine II in a Manifesto of 4 December 1762 encouraged foreigners to come to Russia for this purpose.[22] Germans arrived in significant numbers in response to her appeal to 'colonise' especially the southern regions of Russia.[23] The incentives were considerable: large land grants, loans, and reduction of financial and other obligations to the State.[24] Some regard it as a mistake of that era that colonists were encouraged to

[21] *ПСЗ* (1st series), I, No. 1910. [22] *ПСЗ* (1st series), XVI, No. 11720.

[23] See R P Bartlett, *Human Capital: The Settlement of Foreigners in Russia, 1762–1804* (1979).

[24] The financial incentives were also a burden and form of limitation on the legal status of the Germans who arrived. Movement away from the colony to take other work, or even marriage, normally required authorization (a passport) so as to reduce avoidance of debt obligations. A Guardianship Chancellery for Foreigners was created at St. Petersburg in 1763 to receive colonists and escort them to their place of settlement. By 1765 it was necessary to form a Guardianship

form their own settlements with their own special charters or statutes, forming a 'State within a State'.[25] When in 1871 the Russian authorities sought to equate the colonists with the legal status of rural inhabitants, many emigrated from Russia in response. Efforts also were made to integrate foreign settlers into the Russian community. By a set of Rules dated 8 November 1860 on the procedure for settling foreign emigrants in the Crimea, the authorities encouraged them to be dispersed among local Russians rather than to be concentrated in dense settlements.[26]

On the other hand, political considerations of the day could worsen the legal status of foreigners. From the French Revolution in 1789 onwards the Russian authorities were apprehensive about foreigners entering Russia, especially the French. Frenchmen who did not wish to become subjects of the Russian Empire but whom the Russian Government considered it possible to accept as subjects were subject to banishment from Russia. By a Manifesto of 1 January 1807 the rights of foreigners to engage in trade were severely restricted. Foreign merchants could resell or exchange their goods only with a Russian merchant and were prohibited from engaging in retail trade. Not until 7 June 1860 were foreigners granted equal rights with Russian subjects in the fields of trade, agriculture, and industry.[27]

Taking the nineteenth and early twentieth centuries as a whole, the legal status of foreigners in Russia was regulated by a series of enactments often inconsistent with one another and certainly at cross purposes. In principle, foreigners of all nations might freely enter Russia (except Jews, excluding those from Central Asia). Foreign Jews might be authorized to enter Russia so long as (a) they intended to build plants and factories (except distilleries), on condition that such construction was completed within three years and, if not, that they return abroad and, if they succeeded, that they become subjects of Russia; (b) craftsman registered by Jewish manufacturers in order to perform manufacturing work.

From the nineteenth century foreigners were required to have for admittance to Russia national passports or travel books viséd by Russian embassies, missions,

Office for Foreigners at Saratov to assist in organizing the settlement of foreigners there. The Office also had judicial powers. Its files for the first ten years were destroyed during the Pugachev Rebellion. On the routine thereafter (the Office opened six days a week from 08:00 to 14:00 hours), see I R Pleve (ed.), *Журнал заседаний общего присутствия Саратовской Конторы опекунства иностранных* [Journal of Sessions of the General Office of the Saratov Guardianship Office for Foreigners] (Saratov, 1995), I, pp. iii–viii.

[25] See Iu A Dmitriev and K A Korsik, *Правовое положение иностранцев в Российской Федерации* [Legal Status of Foreigners in the Russian Federation] (1997), p. 11.

[26] *ПСЗ* (2nd series) (1860), No. 36298, art. 3.

[27] See, respectively, *ПСЗ* (1st series), XXIX, No. 22418; *ПСЗ* (2nd series), XXV, No. 35880.

or consulates abroad.[28] Although such passports would gain admission to Russia for its carrier, they did not give the right to move about the territory of the Russian Empire. The Statute on Passports (Article 129) provided that 'every foreigner who has arrived in Russia with a legal passport must appear in the first gubernia city en route at the local governor and, having submitted to him his passport with which he arrived, receive in place thereof a passport for residence in and travel in the Empire'. In practice the national passports were not collected; rather an inscription was made on them and sealed to the effect that 'On the basis of this passport a special Russian permit has been issued' (Article 132). These residence and travel permits were valid for a period of one year. When that period had expired, the foreigner was required to obtain a new passport from the governor of that gubernia where he was situated at the moment.

Foreigners would not be admitted to Russia if they (1) had been prohibited from entering by the Government of Russia; (b) were considered to be unreliable (politically) in the opinion of Russian embassies, missions, or consulates; or (c) were gypsies, organ-grinders, peddlers of pharmaceutical materials and plaster figures, and, in general, idlers. Clergy from Turkey required, in addition to a passport from the Russian ambassador in Constantinople, a residence and travel permit from the Holy Synod. Jews were limited as noted above.

There were limitations neither of time nor of place on foreigners who had been admitted to the Russian Empire, excluding Jews and, in adjacent frontier regions, China and Korea. Jews, when admitted, were confined to strictly determined localities unless they had received an authorization to engage in trade or they were foreign bankers or the heads of large trade houses.

Once in Russia, foreigners were subject to Russian law and enjoyed the defence and protection of such law. They were granted the right of faith and religious services. They could enter into transactions, bequeath their property to foreigners and Russian subjects, acquire inheritance by operation of law and by will on the same basis as subjects of the Russian Empire, and adopt foundlings. The right of authorship was recognized for foreigners to the same extent as for Russian authors. The national regime for granting patents and equivalent privileges extended to foreigners. Certain property rights of foreigners were limited, however. In stipulated western regions of the Russian Empire foreigners were prohibited from acquiring ownership in immoveable property beyond the limits of ports or cities. Inheritance of immoveable property by foreigners in those territories also was permitted only by operation of law (and not by will) on condition

[28] See M Lloyd, *The Passport. The History of Man's Most Travelled Document* (2003), pp. 118–19; V. Kruglov, «Паспорт: это слишком серьезно?» [The Passport: Is It Too Serious?], *antiq.info*, no. 23 (2004), pp. 8, 61.

that the inheriting was between spouses or by direct descending line, and provided that the heir settled in Russia before 14 March 1887. Otherwise, the foreign heir was required to sell the inheritance property to a Russian subject within three years, and if this was not done, the property was to be sold at auction. In addition to the western European territories of Imperial Russia, foreigners were prohibited from acquiring immoveable property in the Turkestan Territory and were restricted in the properties that could be acquired in the Crimea or in the Russian territories of Poland.

Leaving aside restrictions on Jews, foreigners were equated with Russian subjects as regards the right of production for trade and crafts and the leasing and equipping of plants and factories with the exception, for foreigners, of gold production and mining in the Maritime Province and adjacent islands, navigation on the Caspian Sea, cabotage trade generally in Russia, and being skippers of vessels. The civil service was, as a rule, closed to foreigners except for training and instructional positions. Learned degrees could be acquired by foreigners on an equal basis with Russians. Other exceptions favouring foreigners included appointment to posts in the medical and pharmaceutical sector, aides to inspectors of university students, teachers in law schools and other higher educational institutions, and positions in the Imperial Public Library in St. Petersburg. When foreigners were appointed to positions that did not require taking an oath as a subject of Russia, they did swear an oath of loyalty to service. Foreigners in service had the right to pensions and lump-sum benefits.

City and zemstvo elective offices were not open to foreigners. Nor could foreigners be employed as bailiffs, sworn attorneys, or notaries, subject to minor exceptions for specific posts in designated ports.

On the territory of the Russian Empire the applicable law was Russian. Foreign law could be applied only when an action was performed or transaction was concluded in a foreign State under the laws existing there but corresponding to those for similar transactions in Russia, or in the event of the inheriting of moveable property by subjects of States which had concluded treaties with Russia (among them: Germany, Spain, Italy, Sweden, and France). The principle of national regime applied to foreigners with respect to the right of judicial defence. However, a special rule did operate with respect to foreign plaintiffs in Russian courts who were not in Russian service bringing suit against a Russian respondent and not possessing immoveable property in Russia. Under this rule, the foreigner would be required to offer security for court costs against the possibility that his suit would be rejected. This rule was amended in 1896 to allow such security to be waived when the foreign plaintiff held the citizenship of a country with which Russia had concluded a treaty that exempted Russians from posting such security in the foreign jurisdiction concerned. Denmark,

France, Germany, and Switzerland did conclude such treaties between 1871 and 1896. Foreign judicial decisions were not subject to enforcement in Russia unless a treaty between Russia and the respective foreign State was in force providing for mutual recognition and enforcement.

As regards the criminal law, foreigners were subject to the national regime. However, a special punishment did exist applicable only to foreigners convicted of a crime in Russia: banishment abroad in an administrative proceeding. Banishment was undertaken by the ministry of internal affairs. Members of the foreign nobility who happened to be convicted of a crime in Russia also were relieved from corporal punishment, thus creating a discriminatory distinction based on rank rather than citizenship or subjecthood.

The Russian Empire never endeavoured to consolidate the regulation of the legal status of foreigners into a unified legislative act determining the rights and duties of foreigners.

Soviet period, 1917–91

Most Soviet jurists proposed a periodization of the development of Soviet legislation on the legal status of foreigners by linking such development with the successive generations of USSR and union republic constitutions.[29] In the early years after the Revolution of October 1917, the emphasis was more on class origin than on citizenship of a foreign State. The 1918 RSFSR Constitution and the constitutions of the other republics granted to foreigners residing in Russia or their respective countries the full plenitude of political rights, provided that those foreigners belonged to the working class or to the peasantry which did not employ hired labour. The 1918 Constitution provided (Article 20) that 'Proceeding from the solidarity of the toiling people of all nations, the RSFSR grants all the political rights of Russian citizens to foreigners residing on the territory of the Russian Republic for labour occupations and belonging to the working class or the peasantry not using hired labour and recognizes for local soviets the right to grant to such foreigners without any difficult formalities the rights of Russian citizenship'.[30] Foreigners were granted the right of suffrage on the same basis as Soviet citizens (Article 64). **1.09**

Other legislative acts embodied the same principle of equalizing foreigners with Soviet citizens on a class basis. Under the Statute on Social Security for Toilers of

[29] See, for example, *Статус иностранцев в СССР* [Status of Foreigners in the USSR] (1984), pp. 8–9; L V Lazarev, et al. *Иностранные граждане (правовое положение)* [Foreign Citizens (Legal Status)] (1992), p. 12.

[30] *СУ РСФСР* (1918), no. 51, item 582.

31 October 1918, foreigners had the right to social security equally with Soviet citizens provided that the sources of their existence were their own labour without the exploitation of another's labour.[31] Foreigners in this period could be employed in the Russian Soviet civil service or in State enterprises, and if they were, they were subject to the same rules as citizens of the RSFSR.

It followed that if foreigners enjoyed the rights of Soviet Russian citizens, they should bear the duties of citizenship. The 1922 Code of Laws on Labour made possible the enlistment of Russian citizens for labour to combat natural disasters or cope with a shortage of labour force. No distinction was drawn on the basis of citizenship, which meant foreigners were in principle subject to the same duty.[32] However, foreigners were excluded from types of labour duties associated with national security, such as the construction of fortifications.

This approach to the legal status of foreigners led one Soviet civilist and private international lawyer to conclude that the Russian Soviet legislator had '. . . completely abolished the concept of foreigner with respect to foreign workers and peasants who settled [in Russia] for labour occupations, granting them not only civil, but also political rights'.[33] As for foreign citizens from the non-labour classes, one Soviet jurist put the position as follows: 'the absence in Soviet law of this period of special norms relative to the political rights of these foreigners was understood by practice to mean that the privileges established for the toiling classes did not extend to them. In accordance with this the status of foreigners from the non-labour classes in the RSFSR was determined by analogy with the respective categories of Soviet citizens from the non-labour classes, which completely corresponded to the class approach established in the Soviet State after the October Revolution to determine the extent of rights of the said categories of the population'.[34]

Working class origin or not, foreigners in the RSFSR soon found themselves the subject of individual decrees limiting their activities in comparison with Soviet citizens. Compulsory military service, a legal duty of Soviet citizens, was not imposed on foreigners, although those who wished to volunteer to take part in the defence of revolutionary conquests might do so. Foreign students were not eligible for stipends in higher technical educational institutions if they did not assume the obligation upon graduation to place themselves at the disposition of economic agencies of the RSFSR and serve in their specialization until their

[31] *СУ РСФСР* (1918), no. 89, item 906.

[32] *СУ РСФСР* (1922), no. 70, item 903.

[33] A G Goikhbarg, *Частное международное право* [Private International Law] (1928), p. 70.

[34] N V Mironov, *Правовое регулирование внешних сношений* [Legal Regulation of Foreign Relations] (1971), pp. 100–1.

period of employment equalled their period of study on stipend. Foreigners were excluded from fishing and taking marine resources in the White Sea and Northern Arctic Ocean.[35]

Gradually the legislative acts pertaining to the legal status of foreigners multiplied in number and scope, including decrees on the right of asylum, entry to the RSFSR from abroad, departure abroad, and banishment of foreigners. The civil-law status of foreigners in the RSFSR was set out in the 1922 Civil Code. Priority was given to the law of treaties insofar as they regulated these questions. Insofar as they did not, the rights of foreigners were made dependent upon individual laws and decrees, including their right to freedom of movement about Russian territory, the opening and acquisition of trade and industrial enterprises, and the acquisition of rights to a thing in structures and land plots. Limitations of this nature and scale had to be introduced by agreement with the People's Commissariat for Foreign Affairs. The principle of national regime thus applied with the exceptions indicated. The Civil Code further stipulated that 'sex, race, nationality, confession of faith, and origin' had no influence on the extent of civil rights. However, the RSFSR did not emulate the practice of Ukraine and Belorussia, who adopted unified or consolidated normative acts regulating the legal status of foreigners.

It is worthy of note that in introducing the sanction of banishment for foreigners on 29 August 1921, the provisions of RSFSR legislation were virtually identical to those of Imperial Russia. Banishment might be administrative or judicial and originate either with local or central officials. The national passport of the foreigner which served as the basis for a residence permit was taken back and the notation added that the 'said citizen has been banished from the limits of the RSFSR and has no right to reside in Soviet Russia' if his presence were 'incompatible with the principles and way of workers-peasants' life'.

With the formation of the Union of Soviet Socialist Republics by the Treaty of the Union on 30 December 1922 and adoption of the USSR Constitution in 1924, Russian legislation became less important. The USSR was granted jurisdiction over 'basic legislation in the domain of Union citizenship and with respect to the rights of foreigners' (Article 1[10]). The Statute on Union Citizenship, confirmed on 29 October 1924, in pursuance of the Constitution, provided that foreign citizens residing on the territory of the USSR for labour occupations and belonging to the working class or to the peasantry not using hired labour enjoyed all the political rights of citizens of the USSR (Article 2). A special law called for by the 1924 Constitution on the status of foreigners was

[35] For this restriction, which in effect emulated those of the pre-Revolutionary period, see W E Butler *The Soviet Union and the Law of the Sea* (1971).

never enacted. In 1925 foreign toilers residing on the territory of the USSR and enjoying political rights were granted the right to use land for agricultural purposes equally with Soviet citizens. Commencing in September 1926, USSR legislation introduced the distinction between foreigners who were 'permanently residing (domiciled)' in the USSR and those who were 'temporarily residing'.

The 1936 USSR Constitution reflected the transition to a socialist society in that country, which in turn had certain implications for the legal status of foreigners. Foreign citizens were excluded from the constitutional duty to perform military service. Only citizens of the USSR were permitted to be members of the command or crew of aircraft (1961 Air Code of the USSR) or merchant ships (1968 Merchant Shipping Code of the USSR).[36] The benefits accorded to foreigners in the Soviet Union commonly depended upon their being 'permanently residing' and were regulated piecemeal in individual enactments. Soviet pension legislation permitted pensions to be assigned to foreign citizens and their families if two-thirds of the necessary labour experience to receive a pension had been attained at a job in the USSR.[37] The right of foreigners to enjoy medical assistance equally with Soviet citizens also required the foreigners to have a 'permanent place of residence' in the Soviet Union; other foreigners were accorded medical assistance in accordance with instructions issued by the USSR Ministry of Public Health.

Foreigners were subject to criminal responsibility in the USSR under the criminal law in force at the place of commission of the crime. This meant in accordance with the union republic criminal code in force on the territory of the union republic where the crime was committed, for the all-union criminal legislation in force was incorporated verbatim into the union republic criminal codes.

Although a number of proposals were made in support of a single all-union codification act regulating the legal status of foreigners,[38] this transpired only after the adoption of the 1977 USSR Constitution and constitutions of the union

---

[36] See W E Butler and J B Quigley, Jr., *Merchant Shipping Code of the USSR (1968)* (1970). Article 41.

[37] For the Statute on the Procedure for the Assignment and Payment of State Pensions, confirmed by Decree of the Council of Ministers of the USSR of 4 August 1956, see *СП СССР* (1957), no. 1, item 1.

[38] See, among others, A I Mikulski, «О понятии и видах режимов иностранцев» [On the Concept and Types of Regimes of Foreigners], *Советский ежегодник международного права 1974* (1974), p. 188; V D Iavorskii, «Конституционное регулирование статуса иностранцев и лиц без гражданства в СССР» [Constitutional Regulation of Status of Foreigners and Stateless Persons in the USSR], in *Проблемы социалистической законности на современном этапе коммунистического строительства* [Problems of Socialist Legality at Contemporary Stage of Communist Construction] (Kharkov, 1978), p. 71.

republics in 1978.[39] The USSR Constitution, emulated by the union republic constitutions, elevated the legal status of foreigners to an issue of constitutional stature, providing in Article 37: 'The rights and freedoms provided for by a law shall be guaranteed to foreign citizens and stateless persons, including the right to have recourse to a court and other State agencies for defence of personal, property, family, and other rights belonging to them. Foreign citizens and stateless persons situated on the territory of the USSR shall be obliged to respect the Constitution of the USSR and comply with Soviet laws'.

The Law of the USSR 'On the Legal Status of Foreign Citizens in the USSR', adopted on 24 June 1981 (hereinafter: 1981 Law) and in force as from 1 January 1982,[40] remained in force in the Russian Federation until the entry into force of the 2002 Law.[41] The 1981 Law proves to have been the first and sole normative legal act in Russian history which undertook to regulate on a comprehensive and integrated basis the principal questions of the legal status of foreigners. Although the USSR Constitution was its point of departure, the 1981 Law also incorporated or reflected Soviet practice, including treaty practice, and eliminated certain gaps in legislation. The 2002 Law, notwithstanding its title, is but a pale reflection of the 1981 version. Boguslavskii noted at the time that in comparison with 'capitalist countries', whose laws on foreigners were principally concerned with detailed regulation of residence and movement of foreigners, the 1981 Law placed its 'centre of gravity' in the socio-economic domain in granting to foreigners many of those rights enjoyed by Soviet citizens.[42] In that spirit the 2002 Law of the Russian Federation has moved to the centre of gravity of the market economies.

The 1981 Law consisted of five sections. The first, 'General Provisions', defined the concept of a 'foreign citizen in the USSR' and addressed the right of asylum. Section Two was devoted to the basic rights, freedoms, and duties of foreign citizens; among them the right to leisure, health, social security, housing, education, labour, and others. Provisions also addressed taxation, recourse to courts, military service, and the right of suffrage. In Section Three there were general provisions on the right of exit and entry, later repealed. Section Four was concerned with administrative and criminal responsibility of foreign citizens,

[39] All sixteen were translated, together with the constitutions of the autonomous republics, in W E Butler, *Collected Legislation of the USSR and Union Republics* (1979–91), a loose-leaf service.

[40] *Ведомости Верховного Совета СССР* (1981), no. 26, item 836; transl. in W E Butler, *International Legal Materials*, XX (1981), 1211–16.

[41] However, Chapter 3 of the 1981 Law lost force as from 22 August 1996 with the entry into force of the Federal Law 'On the Procedure for Exit from the Russian Federation and Entry to the Russian Federation'. *СЗ РФ* (1996), no. 34, item 4029.

[42] M M Boguslavskii (ed.), *Статус иностранцев в СССР* [Status of Foreigners in the USSR] (1984), p. 18.

including deportation. The final Section Five dealt with stateless persons, diplomatic and consular personnel, and others.

The 1981 Federal Law followed the 1977 USSR Constitution by expanding the concept of 'foreigner' to encompass stateless persons. Prior to then, Soviet legislation had used the term 'foreigner' and 'foreign citizen' as synonyms. As a result of introducing the 1977 USSR Constitution, consequential amendments were made in other Soviet legislative acts to substitute the term 'foreigner' with 'foreign citizen'.[43] This terminology generally met with approbation in Soviet legal doctrine.[44]

[43] See, for example, the 1968 Fundamental Principles of Legislation of the USSR and Union Republics on Marriage and Family, as amended by Edict of the Presidium of the USSR Supreme Soviet on 9 October 1979. *Ведомости Верховного Совета СССР* (1979), no. 42, item 696; transl. W E Butler, *Soviet Legal System: Legislation and Documentation* (1978), pp. 451–62.

[44] See, among others, L N Galenskaia, *Правовое положение иностранцев в СССР* [Legal Status of Foreigners in the USSR] (1982), p. 7 (although the author preserved the term 'foreigner' in the title of her monograph). Estonia and Latvia have introduced the category of 'non-citizen' and issued passports to individuals who are not considered to be stateless but also who are not ethnic Estonians or Latvians.

2

SOURCES OF RUSSIAN FOREIGN RELATIONS AND INVESTMENT LAW

The sources of Russian law generally[1] are also the sources of Russian foreign relations and investment law, albeit with some adjustments of emphasis. Technically, the sources of Russian law are rules or norms created, sanctioned, or recognised by the Russian State or subjects of the Russian Federation and their agencies and officials within their respective competences in a duly established procedure. Insofar as these rules or norms prescribe general rules of conduct they are called 'normative legal acts'. Although the Russian legislator has never defined the term 'normative legal act', the Plenum of the Supreme Court of the Russian Federation by Decree No 19 of 25 May 2000 explained that an 'act issued in the established procedure by a duly empowered agency of State power, **2.01**

[1] See W E Butler, *Russian Law* (2nd edn, 2003), pp. 83–109 for a discussion of the sources of Russian law. This Chapter adapts and in some respects enlarges upon the discussion in *Russian Law* with particular reference to foreign relations law.

agency of local self-government, or official establishing legal norms (or rules of behaviour) binding upon an indefinite group of persons intended for repeated application and operating irrespective of whether specific legal relations provided for by the act have arisen or terminated' is a normative legal act.

2.02 From this definition it follows that not all sources of law originate in the State itself. With respect to the sphere of foreign relations this proposition has two implications. First, although it is unlikely that rules of Russian jus [право] will directly concern foreign relations law, subsidiary sources of law such as 'customs of business turnover' emanating from non-State bodies and local normative legal acts adopted by or originating within non-State entities (for example, commercial organisations with foreign investments) may be of considerable importance in the domain of foreign relations and investment issues especially. Second, international treaties of the Russian Federation and general principles of international law (including rules of customary international law) are an integral part of the Russian legal system (see below) and, at a minimum, in one way or another have been 'sanctioned' by the Russian State.

2.03 The Russian legal system does attach importance to a formalistic hierarchy of the sources of law. The normative legal acts which in this study are classified as sources of foreign relations law pose challenging issues for that hierarchy and are controversial within general discussions of sources of Russian law. We pursue that discussion below from the vantage point of foreign relations concerns.

A. Jus [право]

2.04 Russian law has distinguished since its earliest days between law (jus) that originates somewhere other than with the prince of the day or the State, and a law (lex) enacted or introduced by the prince or the State. Whether the former be of divine origin, or the natural order of the universe, or the laws of societal development, or the fabric of Russian (or Slavic) socio-cultural values, or otherwise is the subject of a lively debate of the utmost importance for the future of a Russian civil society.[2]

2.05 For the purposes of this study it can be said that jus may serve as the source of foreign relations law insofar as incorporated in general principles of international law or in international treaties of the Russian Federation, most notably in human rights covenants. Russian constitutional provisions and legislative acts appertaining to the very definitions of human rights or to the status of refugees,

[2] See W E Butler, '*Jus* and *Lex* in Russian Law: A Discussion Agenda', in D J Galligan and M Kurkchiyan (eds.), *Law and Informal Practices: The Post-Communist Experience* (2003), pp. 47–60.

migrants, asylum seekers, and other aliens may be considered to crystallize norms of Russian jus which exist independently of their positivist expressions.

B. Soviet Law

Treaties, international documents, and legislation of the former Soviet Union have a significant role—declining, to be sure—in Russian foreign affairs law. The RSFSR was the largest and principal moving force behind the formation of the Union of Soviet Socialist Republics in 1922 and had been the locus of the Russian revolutions during 1917. With the formation of the USSR, however, the RSFSR became a minor actor in foreign relations of all types (although not completely excluded). When a compromise was reached in 1944 regarding membership of the Soviet union republics in the United Nations, only Ukraine and Belorussia[3] were chosen to have full membership in their own right, and RSFSR interests were represented by the USSR. With the secession of the RSFSR from the USSR in early December 1991, the Russian Federation returned as a fully fledged member of the international community for the first time since December 1922. **2.06**

Prior to formal secession from the USSR by means of denouncing the Treaty of the Union concluded on 30 December 1922, however, the RSFSR had taken a number of measures to disengage from USSR legislation and, therefore, sources of law. In its Declaration of State Sovereignty of 12 June 1990, the RSFSR had established 'the supremacy of the RSFSR Constitution and laws of the RSFSR throughout the territory of the RSFSR; the operation of acts of the USSR which are contrary to the sovereign rights of the RSFSR shall be suspended by the Republic on its territory'.[4] No attempt was made to declare USSR legislation 'invalid', or to repeal it. No mention was made in this formulation of international legal obligations of the USSR and their relevance to the sovereignty of the RSFSR. **2.07**

In pursuance of the Declaration, the RSFSR adopted on 24 October 1990 the Law on the Operation of Acts of Agencies of the USSR on the Territory of the RSFSR.[5] According to this Law, recognition would be accorded to the operation of laws and other acts of the highest agencies of State power of the USSR, edicts **2.08**

[3] For the view that Belorussia and Ukraine did not properly ratify the United Nations Charter, see P P Kremnev, 'On Ukrainian and Belorussian Membership in the United Nations and Entry of the United Nations Charter into Force', *Sudebnik*, IX (2004), 456–92.

[4] *Ведомости СНД и ВС РСФСР (1990)*, no. 2, item 22; translated in W E Butler, *Basic Legal Documents of the Russian Federation* (1992), pp. 35–7.

[5] Transl. in Butler, *Basic Legal Documents of the Russian Federation* (1992), pp. 49–50.

and other acts of the President of the USSR, acts of the Council of Ministers and of ministries and departments of the USSR only insofar as they were adopted within the powers transferred by the Russian Federation to the USSR in accordance with the Declaration and certain other enactments. Provided that USSR enactments met this test, they were of direct application on the territory of the RSFSR; if they violated the sovereignty of the Russian Federation, they were subject to suspension by the RSFSR Supreme Soviet or by the RSFSR Council of Ministers. However, if USSR enactments did not meet the criteria set out above, they would enter into force in the Russian Federation only after having been ratified by the RSFSR Supreme Soviet, RSFSR Council of Ministers, or empowered State agencies of the RSFSR respectively. The acts of agencies of the USSR issued prior to 24 October 1990 operated on the territory of the RSFSR unless they were suspended by the RSFSR Supreme Soviet or the RSFSR Council of Ministers.

2.09 Although the Law of 24 October 1990 made no specific mention of international treaties or other international documents, it could be argued that insofar as treaties and agreements were ratified by a law of the USSR or consented to by decrees of the Government or, in the case of interdepartmental treaties, by decisions of the relevant USSR agencies, they were covered by the Law. No evidence has been found to suggest that the Law of 24 October 1990 was invoked to disengage from international legal obligations of any kind whatsoever. Nor is the author aware of any USSR foreign affairs legislation that became the subject of suspension under this Law. Alternatively, the provisions of the Law simply did not extend to international treaties of the Soviet Union.

2.10 The issue of Soviet legislation was addressed in the decree of the RSFSR dated 12 December 1991 ratifying the Agreement on the Creation of the Commonwealth of Independent States (point 2):

> For the purposes of creating conditions necessary for the realisation of Article 11 of the said Agreement, to establish that the norms of the former USSR shall apply on the territory of the RSFSR until the adoption of respective legislative acts of the RSFSR in that part which is not contrary to the Constitution of the RSFSR, legislation of the RSFSR, and the present Agreement.[6]

2.11 Article 11 of the said Agreement was so formulated as to be virtually meaningless, such that one wonders whether a drafting error was made in the final text: 'From the moment of signature of the present Agreement, the application of the norms of third States on the territories of the States which have signed it,

[6] *BBC PФ* (1991), no. 51, item 1798; transl. in Butler, *Basic Legal Documents of the Russian Federation* (1992), p. 51.

including the former USSR, shall not be permitted.'[7] For all of the ambiguity of Article 11, in practice the formulation of the Decree on ratification of 12 December 1991 has been used.

In sum the legislation of the former USSR may apply on the territory of the Russian Federation unless (i) it has been expressly repealed or suspended; or (ii) it is contrary to the Constitution of the Russian Federation and other Russian legislation adopted after 12 June 1990; or (iii) it has become obsolete. Special provision was made in individual instances for USSR legislation to continue to be operative even though Russian enactments were in force. An example was the Fundamental Principles of Civil Legislation of the USSR and Republics adopted 31 May 1991 and stipulated to enter into force on 1 January 1992. Because the USSR had been dissolved before the date of its entry into force,[8] it did not become legally binding. However, the Russian Federation by a Decree of the Supreme Soviet adopted 14 July 1992 did introduce it into operation as from 3 August 1992. The provisions of the Fundamental Principles concerned with foreign economic relations, especially Part VII, would for our purposes constitute part of foreign relations law. **2.12**

It should be noted that the Family Code of the Russian Federation recognises legal relations established under pre-revolutionary Russian and Soviet legislation, and also relations arising under international treaties of the Russian Empire, irrespective of whether those treaties remain in force or not. **2.13**

C. Legislation

Constitution of Russian Federation

Within the sphere of legislation, the 1993 Constitution is the most important source of foreign affairs law in the Russian Federation. The Constitution has 'the highest legal force, direct effect' and is applicable throughout the entire territory of the Russian Federation (Article 15, Constitution). **2.14**

The supremacy of the Constitution as a source of law originates in two considerations. First is the method of enactment. The Constitution of the Russian **2.15**

[7] The Agreement was signed at Minsk on 8 December 1991; transl. in Butler, *Basic Legal Documents of the Russian Federation* (1992), pp. 3–6.

[8] See W E Butler (transl.), *The Fundamental Principles of Civil Legislation of the USSR and Republics* (1992). This is assumed to be the case, that is, assumed that all former union republics of the USSR completed the ratification of the Agreements on the formation of the Commonwealth of Independent States and the USSR had technically ceased to exist by 1 January 1992. I have seen no empirical evidence that all ratifications were duly completed or that they were completed by 31 December 1991.

Federation was adopted by an all-people's referendum held on 12 December 1993. It therefore was and remains the only example of post-Soviet legislation in the Russian Federation adopted by the people as a whole rather than their elected representatives. Second is the content of the Constitution. Its text contains the rules of law most fundamental to the status of the individual, the structure of the State, and so on. The view is consequently taken that all laws and other legal acts must not be contrary to the Constitution, and all agencies of State power, local self-government, officials, citizens, and their associations must comply with it. Special measures have been incorporated in the text of the Constitution to preclude its being treated as 'ordinary legislation'. Distinctions are drawn between chapters that may not be changed except in the procedure established by the Constitution, and some chapters are more fundamental than others: Article 16(2) of the Constitution, for example, provides that no other provisions of the Constitution may be contrary to that chapter.

2.16 The Constitution being the highest form of legislative law, all other enactments are subordinate legislation (avoiding the use of the term 'delegated', for in the Russian legal system subordinate acts may be issued without delegation so long as they are 'on the basis and in execution of' the acts of superior agencies or agencies at the same level as the issuing organ). This concept sits uneasily with the terminological legacy of Imperial Russia and the Soviet Union, for never before in Russian history has a constitution been placed above monarch and State. The term that needs to be developed (but has not) is 'subconstitutional', better reflecting the proposition that all enactments, whether from the Federal Assembly, President, Government, or other State agencies, must conform to the constitution first and foremost.

2.17 Numerically speaking, legislation is the paramount source of law in the Russian Federation. The hierarchical relationship of normative legal acts is partly expressed in the more than forty denominations in the Russian language for enactments, but the hierarchy itself is confused and complicated.

2.18 The federated structure of the Russian Federation aggravates the complications. What has been said of the 1993 Russian Constitution applies respectively to the constitution or other fundamental constitutive act of each of the subjects of the Russian Federation.

Federal Assembly

2.19 The 1993 Constitution of the Russian Federation confers on the bicameral Federal Assembly of the Russian Federation the right to adopt (a) constitutional laws, the specific subjects of which are enumerated in the Constitution; and (b) federal laws. The same applies to the respective legislative bodies of the subjects of the Russian Federation, down to and including the legislative bodies of the cities of Moscow and St. Petersburg. A law also may be, and on occasion has been, adopted by referendum.

Constitutional laws are superior, in the hierarchy of sources of law, to federal laws. A qualified majority is required to enact the former, whereas a simple majority suffices for the last. In addition, the chambers of the Federal Assembly may adopt decrees on matters relegated specifically to their respective jurisdictions. Each chamber also has its own Reglement[9] to govern its internal proceedings, including those relating to foreign affairs. **2.20**

The Federal Assembly also confirms, by way of federal laws, such normative acts as the statute, code, fundamental principles, appeal, declaration, statement, or message. Whether each of these is normative or not will depend upon the specific content. **2.21**

President of Russian Federation

Under Article 88 of the 1993 Russian Constitution, the President of the Russian Federation issues edicts and regulations. These must be consistent with the Constitution and with both types of federal laws. In practice edicts are used for the most important Presidential enactments, and a number are concerned with the legal status of foreigners. **2.22**

Government of Russian Federation

Executive power in the Russian Federation resides with the Government, which enacts decrees 'on the basis of and in execution of' the Constitution, federal laws, and normative edicts of the President. Decrees are, as a rule, normative, and regulations, as a rule, are not. The President of the Russian Federation has the power to repeal governmental decrees and regulations that fail to conform to the Constitution, federal laws, or presidential edicts. **2.23**

Enactments of the Government are superior to all others adopted by agencies of State administration and many decisions of subjects of the Russian Federation. **2.24**

Ministries and Departments

The denominations of ministerial and departmental enactments are highly diverse. In practice, the nomenclature within a particular ministry or department is determined by the statute thereon. To a considerable extent the terminology of the Soviet era largely survives. Decrees, instructions, instructive regulations, **2.25**

---

[9] The 1998 Reglement of the State Duma is translated in Butler, *Russian Public Law: The Foundations of a Rule-of-Law State: Legislation and Documents* (2005), pp. 265–360.

orders, and others are among the terms used; ministers or chairmen of State committees or federal services commonly issue an order or an instruction.

2.26 It is not uncommon for ministries or federal services and the heads thereof to issue joint enactments. A number of these apply to the legal status of foreigners.

Subjects of the Russian Federation

2.27 The constitutive documents of the subjects of the Russian Federation and other normative legal acts adopted by their agencies and officials contain analogous terminology. The hierarchy of normative legal acts within subjects of the Russian Federation also is, as a rule, analogous throughout the country.

Local self-government

2.28 The agencies of 'local self-government' bear different names in various localities throughout the Russian Federation, although the term 'soviets' is still widely employed. They adopt, as a rule, decisions within the limits of rights and powers granted to them by legislation of the Russian Federation. In the City of Moscow an entirely new terminology has attended the creation of new urban governmental and administrative structures. The Moscow City Duma adopts laws; the Mayorate, decrees; and the Mayor, decisions. In St. Petersburg the appellations differ slightly but the same differentiations are preserved.

2.29 Insofar as decisions of local self-government regulate matters within their exclusive jurisdiction, the enactment operates autonomously on the territory concerned. Consistent with the hierarchy of normative legal acts, those agencies of local self-government must be consistent with the enactments of superior agencies of subjects of the Russian Federation and superior agencies of federal agencies of State power and administration.

D. Treaties of the Federation

2.30 On 31 March 1992 the Russian Federation concluded three treaties, collectively known as the Treaty of the Federation, as a means of controlling the centrifugal forces at work in Russia following the dissolution of the USSR. These documents, in making substantial concessions to the subjects of the Russian Federation, delimited the subjects of jurisdiction and powers between federal agencies of State power and the agencies of power of the various subjects of the Russian Federation. They are expressly mentioned in Section Two, Concluding and Transitional Provisions, of the 1993 Russian Constitution.[10]

[10] The texts are translated in W E Butler, *Russian Public Law* (2005), pp. 627–45.

After 1993 and until late 2001, the Russian Federation quietly concluded a substantial network of mostly bilateral treaties with each of the subjects of the Russian Federation on a vast range of matters. From November 2001 the federal authorities actively discouraged further treaties of this nature and sought the termination of those concluded by mutual agreement. **2.31**

Some of these treaties will have dealt with issues of foreign relations law as defined in this study. Most of them were not gazetted in the central media, although some appeared as unnumbered annexes in the principal official gazette. Moreover, some subjects of the Russian Federation concluded agreements between themselves or with foreign States without involving the Russian Federation as a party (for example, the Autonomous Republic Crimea, in Ukraine, in September 1997 signed a Treaty on Friendship and Cooperation, with Kalmykia, a subject of the Russian Federation).[11] **2.32**

The place of these treaties in the hierarchy of sources of law in Russia is controversial. Depending upon their subject matter, they may be a source of rules of particular branches of law. A compelling argument can be made that these treaties and agreements may override inconsistent provisions of federal laws, although there are serious conceptual problems with this view. **2.33**

E. Judicial and Arbitration Practice

Judicial practice has become in post-Soviet Russia a vital component of the legal process, and the doctrine of judicial precedent is finding increasing favour in many Russian legal circles. In actuality, judicial practice was not ignored in the Soviet legal system and at various times played a creative and unusual role in the development of law. The publication of judicial practice has been an important component of Soviet and Russian legal life since the nineteenth century. **2.34**

Although Soviet legal doctrine took a hard line against judicial precedent in principle as being undemocratic, there never was a rule of Soviet law which prohibited or rejected judicial precedent as such. Evidence is accumulating that the Constitutional Court of the Russian Federation holds its decisions in high esteem when encountering analogous questions in different cases.[12] **2.35**

---

[11] See L I Volova, *Международные договоры в правовых системах федеральных государств* [International Treaties in the Legal Systems of Federal States] (Rostov-on-Don, 2004), p. 80. Volova writes: 'The constitutions and charters of subjects of the Federation do not contain norms establishing the procedure for the conclusion of treaties between themselves and the need for their ratification by some agency'. Ibid., p. 81.

[12] See the discussion in Butler, *Russian Law* (2nd edn, 2003), pp. 93–6.

2.36 Arbitral awards are published and commented upon in the Russian Federation, with due measures taken to protect the identity of the parties, to a greater extent than perhaps any other country in the world. It would be an overstatement to say that published awards constitute precedents binding upon arbitrators considering disputes in the International Court of Commercial Arbitration or the Maritime Arbitration Commission in Moscow. On the other hand, arbitrators there are familiar with the compendium of arbitral practice and it is open to counsel to draw the attention of arbitrators to prior awards. This body of material is an invaluable guide as to how arbitrators in the past have dealt with legal issues arising and may therefore in the future also be persuaded to do the same.

F. Customs of Business Turnover

2.37 These are a species of customary law and, in the domain of Russian civil law, originate in the Civil Code of the Russian Federation (Article 5) but are also mentioned, *inter alia*, in the 1999 Merchant Shipping Code of the Russian Federation and the 1993 Law on International Commercial Arbitration. They comprise rules of behaviour formed and extensively applied in any domain of entrepreneurial activity and have not been created or provided for by legislation. Generally they are fixed in commercial or entrepreneurial documents, including industry manuals or standards. They may not be applied if they are contrary either to legislation or to the provisions of a contract binding upon the parties; that is, they may not override legislation or contractual provisions agreed by the parties.

Customs of business turnover may exist at any level: local, regional, national, or international, and they may appertain to branches of industry, or to spheres of activity, or be inter-branch in nature. Foreign investors encounter customs of business turnover from time to time, as do shipping companies entering Russian ports.

2.38 The term is broadly construed to encompass commercial customs, business customs, trade customs, and so on. That these have not been provided for by 'legislation' means not merely laws, but normative legal acts of presidential, governmental, and departmental origin. Such customs must be stable and generally recognised in the respective domain of entrepreneurial activity and may be oral or written. Examples of customs of business turnover include Incoterms, published collections of the customs of commercial seaports, and model contracts published for general information (Article 427, Civil Code). The existence of a custom is a matter of proof. They are dispositive, and parties may therefore exclude them or incorporate contractual provisions which are contrary to them. Such customs need not be of general application within their own sphere; that is, they could apply exclusively to foreigners and stateless persons.

G. Normative Acts of Non-State Entities

Russian legal doctrine, following the Soviet era, continues to treat certain non-State enterprises and organizations as being vested with the right to enact normative legal acts. These are called 'local' [локальный] acts. Classic examples, and among those most likely to affect foreign citizens and stateless persons, are found within an enterprise or economic society or partnership: collective labour contracts, charters, and other acts adopted by the owners or the executive of an organization, sometimes with the participation of the workers or their representatives. The Labour Code of the Russian Federation makes specific reference to such local acts: 'An employer shall adopt local normative acts concerning norms of labour law within the limits of its competence in accordance with law and other normative legal acts, collective contracts, and agreements' (Article 8).[13] Normative legal acts pursuant to the Labour Code extend to all workers or to individual categories of workers in the enterprise. They may be adopted for a determined or an indeterminate period. **2.39**

Russian juridical persons either operate under or themselves confirm local normative acts. In the case of a joint-stock society, for example, it is the founding stockholders who prepare and confirm the charter of the society, which is then subject to State registration. The stockholders are thereby empowered to 'legislate': the 'charter is a local normative act, the operation of which is determined by State registration of the society'.[14] The stockholders or the management of the society concerned confirm or adopt individual internal statutes regulating, for example, the management organs of the juridical person. **2.40**

H. Acts of the Union State

The Russian Federation and the Republic Belarus are at an advanced stage of forming a Union State pursuant to a Treaty of 8 December 1999. The Union State has its own organs: the High State Council, the Parliament of the Union State, the Council of Ministers, the Court of the Union State, and the Counting **2.41**

[13] *СЗ РФ* (2002), no. 1(I), item 3; transl. in W E Butler, *Labour Code of the Russian Federation* (2004), pp. 20–1.

[14] M V Teliukina, *Комментарий к Федеральному закону «Об акционерных обществах» (постатейный)* [Commentary to Federal Law 'On Joint-Stock Societies' (Article-by-Article)] (2005), p. 80.

Chamber. These agencies all adopt normative legal acts within the competence laid down by the Treaty of 8 December 1999: laws, fundamental principles of legislation, decrets, decrees, directives, resolutions, recommendations, and opinions.[15]

2.42 It remains to be seen how the Union State will approach the issue of citizenship and the legal status of foreigners. Citizens of the Russian Federation and Belarus will doubtless become citizens of the Union State, if that proves to be the appropriate designation of affiliation for natural persons to the Union State. While there are certain analogies between the Union State in gestation and species of federalism, with respective implications for the legal regime of foreigners, it is by no means certain that those analogies are appropriate in this instance. One way or another, however, as the Union State comes into being there will be an impact upon the foreign relations law of the Russian Federation.

I. Documents of Commonwealth of Independent States

2.43 During the first fifteen years of its existence the Commonwealth of Independent States has adopted or otherwise generated more than 10,000 normative documents. The forms include treaties under various designations, decisions of CIS organs, and protocols. Their publication is irregular even though many matters addressed by these documents are of considerable legal importance. Insofar as the normative documents are treaties, pursuant to the 1993 Constitution of the Russian Federation (Article 15) they are an integral part of the Russian legal system. The great majority would certainly qualify as interdepartmental agreements. Large numbers concern matters of foreign relations; some would contend that they all address matters of foreign relations because of the very nature of the CIS.

J. Generally-Recognized Principles of International Law

2.44 Generally-recognized principles and norms of international law are, according to Article 15(4) of the 1993 Russian Constitution, an integral part of the legal system of the Russian Federation. This language, with slight adjustments, has been incorporated in the 1995 Law on Treaties (Article 5). The formal recognition of generally-recognized principles and norms of international law to enjoy this stature in the Russian legal system is among the momentous changes of the twentieth century in the development of Russian law.

[15] See Butler, *Russian Law* (2nd edn, 2003), pp. 99, 670–4.

There is disagreement in Russian doctrinal writings as to whether 'generally-recognized' principles encompass rules *jus cogens* only, or also include rules of customary international law. In its Decree on the Application by Courts of General Jurisdiction of Generally-Recognized Principles and Norms of International Law and International Treaties of the Russian Federation, adopted 10 October 2003, the Plenum of the Russian Supreme Court declared that 'by generally-recognized principles of international law should be understood the basic imperative norms of international law adopted and recognized by the international community of States as a whole, deviation from which is inadmissible'. Such norms would fall into the category of norms *jus cogens*. The Plenum of the Supreme Court gave two examples of imperative norms: the principle of universal respect for human rights and the principle of the good-faith fulfilment of international obligations. **2.45**

General principles of international law are recognized in Russian legal doctrine as acting as a 'limitation' on the competence of States in establishing the regime of foreigners. For example, 'in accordance with these principles the discrimination against foreigners for indicia of race, sex, confession of faith, and so on is prohibited' even though 'no rights and duties of foreigners have been consolidated expressly in norms of international law'.[16] The domestic legislation of a State concerning foreigners must 'take into account' its international obligations, and to legislate or act outside the framework of those obligations would '. . . signify a violation of generally-recognized principles of international law'. **2.46**

Russian doctrinal writings have identified the 1966 Covenant on Civil and Political Rights as containing rules which are deemed to be generally-recognized, and there is support for regarding the 1948 Universal Declaration of Human Rights, technically merely a resolution of the United Nations General Assembly and therefore having only recommendatory force, as containing norms of general international law because the State practice of the international community has so deemed them to be. **2.47**

The precise place of generally-recognized norms of international law within the Russian legal system is not determined by the 1993 Russian Constitution. The status of such norms appears to fall into two distinct categories depending upon the subject-matter of the norms. The 1993 Russian Constitution placed human rights at the very foundation of the legal system, providing that the basic rights and freedoms contained in the 1993 Constitution must not be construed as a **2.48**

[16] Iu A Dmitriev and K A Korsik, *Правовое положение иностранцев в Российской Федерации* [Legal Status of Foreigners in the Russian Federation] (1997), p. 30. This is not exactly so. Foreign citizens and stateless persons are human beings, and their rights originate in their status as such, as recognized in Article 1 of the 1966 human rights covenants, rather than in domestic legislation.

denial of or impingement on other generally-recognized rights and freedoms of man and citizen, and that laws repealing or abridging the rights of man and citizen may not be adopted (Article 55). The 1993 Constitution further provides (Article 17) that 'The rights and freedoms of man and citizen shall be recognized and guaranteed in the Russian Federation according to generally-recognized principles and norms of international law and in accordance with the present Constitution'. This formulation places international law ahead of the Constitution and, in so doing, imparts to international law a special status in the Russian legal system that is not accorded to other generally-recognized norms of international law. This formulation also would appear to extend to all generally-recognized principles and norms of international human rights law and not merely, in the language of the Plenum of the Russian Supreme Court, to the 'principle of universal respect for human rights'.

K. International Treaties

2.49 The Russian Federation has taken a fundamentally different approach to the sources of international law and to the role of treaties in domestic Russian law since the dissolution of the former Soviet Union.[17] The 1993 Russian Constitution provides (Article 15[4]) that 'generally-recognized principles and norms of international law and international treaties of the Russian Federation' are an integral part of the legal system of the Russian Federation. This formulation, unprecedented in Russian legal history, (a) accepts generally-recognized principles and norms of international law as part of Russian law, and (b) places such norms and principles side by side with norms of Russian municipal law. This formulation may imply that such norms and principles are incorporated into domestic Russian law and overridden by rules of Russian law later in time or *lex specialis*. It further follows that applicable law clauses in contracts which choose Russian law automatically incorporate the general rules of international law and the norms of international treaties of the Russian Federation.

2.50 The Union of Soviet Socialist Republics acceded to the 1969 Vienna Convention on the Law of Treaties with effect from 29 April 1986.[18] The 1995 Federal Law on International Treaties of the Russian Federation is intended to reflect fully the 1969 Vienna Convention and the new stature of international treaties in the Russian legal system under Article 15 of the 1993 Russian Constitution. Some

[17] See W E Butler, *The Law of Treaties in Russia and the Commonwealth of Independent States: Text and Commentary* (2002).

[18] See A N Talalaev, *Венская конвенция о праве международных договоров. Комментарий* [Vienna Convention on the Law of International Treaties. Commentary] (1997).

account is taken in the 1995 Law on Treaties of the 1986 Vienna Convention on the Law of Treaties Between States and International Organizations or Between International Organizations. The Russian Federation is not a party to the 1978 Vienna Convention on the Legal Succession of States with Respect to Treaties.

The 1995 Law on Treaties incorporates and adapts to Russian circumstances the definition of a treaty contained in the 1969 Vienna Convention. The distinction among inter-State, intergovernmental, and interdepartmental treaties, introduced by the 1978 USSR Law on the Procedure for the Conclusion, Execution, and Denunciation of International Treaties of the USSR,[19] has been carried over to the 1995 Law on Treaties. Inter-State treaties are those concluded in the name of the highest agencies of State power—the State in the person of the President, in the name of the Russian Federation. Intergovernmental treaties are those concluded in the name of the Government of the Russian Federation, whereas those concluded in the name of federal agencies of executive power are treaties of an interdepartmental character. Whether a particular treaty falls into one or the other of the three categories is a matter partly for the 1993 Russian Constitution, the jurisdiction of the State agencies concerned, and policy decisions taken by the governments concerned. **2.51**

The provision in Article 15(4) of the 1993 Russian Constitution that international treaties of the Russian Federation take precedence over an inconsistent law was known to Soviet law but in Russia has been elevated for the first time to a rule of constitutional stature. The rule is repeated verbatim in dozens of other federal laws and codes, although by reason of its constitutional stature and generality, such repetition would appear to be superfluous. A literal interpretation of the provision requires that it extend to all treaties of the Russian Federation, including intergovernmental and interdepartmental. The Plenum of the Supreme Court of the Russian Federation in a Decree of 10 October 2003 has concluded otherwise: '. . . consent to the bindingness of an international treaty for the Russian Federation must be expressed in the form of a federal law if other rules have been established by the said treaty than by the federal law . . .' (point 5). It follows, declared the Plenum, that 'the rules of an international treaty of the Russian Federation in force, consent to the bindingness of which was adopted in the form of a federal law, shall have priority in application with respect to laws of the Russian Federation' (point 8). Treaties of the Russian Federation whose binding force was consented to not in the form of a federal law, which would be intergovernmental or interdepartmental treaties, **2.52**

[19] *Ведомости Верховного Совета СССР* (1978), no. 28, item 439; transl. in *International Legal Materials*, XVII (1978), 1115–22.

have priority only with respect to subordinate normative acts issued by the agency of State power that concluded the said treaty.[20]

L. Doctrine

2.53 The teachings and writings of jurists are not regarded as formal sources of law in the Russian Federation, although they may be used in court proceedings and pleadings. However, insofar as doctrinal writings are a subsidiary source of international law, they would be recognized in Russia as such in the domain of foreign relations law.

M. Publication and Entry into Force of Foreign Affairs Legislation and Treaties

2.54 The publication and entry into force of legal normative acts are usually closely interrelated. Publication is associated with the 'presumption of knowledge of the law'; if a legal normative act has been brought to the information of the general public in a duly established procedure—ordinarily printing the act in a designated official gazette—no one may plead ignorance of the law as a pretext for failure to comply with its prescriptions. Publication in printed form also may establish the official text of the enactment, provide a precise benchmark in time from which the normative legal act takes effect, and enable the legislator to communicate most effectively with those to whom his enactments are addressed.

2.55 The 1993 Russian Constitution provides that laws are subject to official publication, that unpublished laws shall not be applied, and that any normative legal acts affecting the rights, freedoms, and duties of man and citizen may not be applied unless they have been published officially for general information (Article 15[3]). In practice this principle has rested uneasily with long-established Russian administrative traditions with the result that access to Russian normative legal acts, although incommensurably improved in comparison with the Soviet period, nonetheless falls short of full disclosure. The Federal Law on State Secrecy of 21 July 1993, as amended,[21] does not make specific provision for the security classification of normative legal acts or part thereof, but in enumerating (Article 5) in a general way the information

[20] The Decree is translated in Butler, *Russian Public Law* (2005), pp. 60–1.

[21] *Российская газета*, 21 September 1993; *СЗ РФ* (1997), no. 41, item 4673; no. 41, item 8220, 8235.

comprising a State secret, it is evident that some information would inevitably be contained in normative acts issued by the President, by the government, or by other agencies of executive power.

Legislative Acts

The 1994 Law on the Procedure for the Publication and Entry into Force of Federal Constitutional Laws, Federal Laws, and Acts of Chambers of the Federal Assembly, as amended,[22] provides that only those which have been officially published shall be applied on the territory of the Russian Federation. Confusion has arisen over the dates of adoption, approval, and signature of federal laws and federal constitutional laws. The 1994 Law provides that the 'date of adoption' of a federal law is considered to be the date on which the State Duma adopted the law in its final version. In practice the 'final version' of a federal law is actually in existence only after an editorial commission of the Federal Assembly incorporates the emendations required as a result of the final reading of the draft law; these may be stylistic, or may record changes that the deputies accepted but left to be reduced to final wording by the editorial team. As for federal constitutional laws, the date of adoption is considered to be the day when it was approved by the chambers of the Federal Assembly in the procedure established by the Russian Constitution. The date, however, by which a federal law or federal constitutional law is commonly referred to is neither of the two dates mentioned above, but rather the date of signature by the President of the Russian Federation. The official number of the law is assigned when the law appears in the official gazette. This can lead to anomalies when the President succeeds in having adjustments made to the final text of a law and delays formal signature for an extended period—which has happened in practice. **2.56**

Official publication must occur in the case of federal constitutional laws or federal laws within seven days after signature by the President and within ten days, in the case of acts of the chambers of the Federal Assembly, after adoption. First official publication is considered to be the publication of the full text in *Российская газета*, a newspaper published six days each week, the *Собрание законодательства Российской Федерации*, published weekly but approximately two weeks after the cover date, or, from October 1999, *Парламентская газета*, a newspaper issued by the Federal Assembly. Additional publication in other printed media, television, radio, circulation to State agencies, officials, enterprises, institutions, or organizations, on-line, or in machine-readable form are acceptable. They also may be published as separate **2.57**

---

[22] *СЗ РФ* (1994), no. 8, item 801; (1999), no. 43, item 5124; transl. in Butler, *Russian Public Law* (2005), pp. 67–9.

pamphlets or brochures, and frequently are. Federal laws also are subject to obligatory publication in a computer database prepared by the Scientific-Technical Centre for Legal Information, 'Система' [System], whose machine-readable text has the status of an official text.[23] Publication by commercial legal data bases does not constitute official publication.

2.58 Entry into force occurs simultaneously throughout the entire territory of the Russian Federation upon the expiration of ten days after official publication unless a different procedure for entry into force is established by the laws themselves or acts of the chambers. The practice varies widely: some laws or codes enter into force many months or even years after signature. Certain portions of a law may enter into force on one date, and other articles or sections at a later date. Frequently a law enters into force on the date of official publication, in which case the date of first official publication becomes significant.

2.59 The Constitutional Court of the Russian Federation has ruled on the date of official publication of laws in connection with a case arising out of the adoption of the Federal Law of 7 March 1996 'On Making Changes in the Law of the Russian Federation on Excises'. This Law confirmed a new version of the Law on Excises which according to its provisions entered into force from 1 February 1996 and introduced excise tax on goods imported from CIS countries, whereas previously such goods had been exempt.

2.60 On 15 March 1996 the State Customs Committee circulated the text of the law by teletype to the heads of regional customs administrations, instructing them to recover excise tax with respect to all affected goods as from 1 February 1996. Observing that this Law was retroactive in operation and disadvantageous to the taxpayers concerned, the Constitutional Court held that the enactment was in plain violation of Article 57 of the 1993 Russian Constitution. Invoking Article 4 of the 1994 Federal Law on the procedure for the publication of laws, the Court observed that it was to be determined whether first publication occurred in the *СЗ РФ* or in *Российская газета*. The relevant issue of the *СЗ РФ* was dated 11 March 1996, whereas *Российская газета* was dated 13 March 1996. However, the Constitutional Court noted that the cover date of *СЗ РФ* was the date on which the issue was signed to press, and not the actual date of publication (which had to have been later than the cover date and therefore the taxpayers to whom the law was addressed could not have had knowledge of the law on that date). Therefore the newspaper date was that of

[23] On-line publication is authorised by Edict of the President of the Russian Federation on the Procedure for the Publication and Entry into Force of Federal Laws, adopted 5 April 1994, as amended. *СЗ РФ* (1994), no. 15, item 1173; no. 16, item 1881; (1995), no. 49, item 4777; transl. in Butler, *Russian Public Law* (2005), pp. 70–1.

first publication, and the Law, not providing any other date for entry into force, could only enter into force not earlier than 24 March 1996, when ten days had elapsed from the moment of official publication.[24] Each issue of the official gazette will bear scrutiny on this basis; the day on which an issue is signed to press, that is, officially approved for printing, can be days or weeks after the cover date.

Presidential, Governmental, and Departmental Acts

Under the 1993 Russian Constitution, the President of the Russian Federation issues edicts and regulations (Article 90[1]), and the government issues decrees and regulations (Article 115). The publication of these is regulated by the 1996 Edict of the President of the Russian Federation on the Procedure for the Publication and Entry into Force of Acts of the President of the Russian Federation and of the Government of the Russian Federation and Normative Legal Acts of Federal Agencies of Executive Power, as amended,[25] and by the Federal Constitutional Law on the Government of the Russian Federation of 17 December 1997, as amended (Article 23).[26] **2.61**

Acts of a normative character adopted by the President enter into force simultaneously throughout the territory of the Russian Federation upon the expiry of seven days after their first official publication. Decrees of the Government affecting the rights, freedoms, and duties of man and citizen enter into force not earlier than the day of their official publication. Other decrees of the Government enter into force from the day of their signature unless the decrees themselves provide another procedure for their entry into force. Other Presidential acts and regulations of the Government enter into force from the day of signature thereof. **2.62**

Whereas all federal laws are subject to publication without exception, accessibility to Presidential edicts, governmental decrees, and departmental acts is affected by the Law on State Secrecy. Edicts and regulations of the President and decrees and regulations of the Government which contain information constituting a State secret or information of a confidential character are not subject to publication. These would ordinarily enter into force upon signature unless provided otherwise in the enactment itself. **2.63**

[24] For the text of the decision, see T G Morshchakova (ed.), *Конституционный Суд Российской Федерации: Постановления, Определения. 1992–1996* [Constitutional Court of the Russian Federation: Decrees, Rulings. 1992–1996] (1997), pp. 459–65.

[25] *СЗ РФ* (1996), no. 22, item 2663; (1997), no. 20, item 2242; (1998), no. 33, item 3967; transl. in Butler, *Russian Public Law* (2005), pp. 72–4.

[26] *СЗ РФ* (1997), no. 5, item 571; (1998), no. 1, item 1; (2004), no. 25, item 2478; no. 45, item 4376; transl. in Butler, *Russian Public Law* (2005), pp. 181–97.

2.64 Departmental normative acts, subject to exceptions such as certain acts of the Central Bank of the Russian Federation, require registration with the Ministry of Justice of the Russian Federation as a condition of their validity. A departmental act will not be registered if in the view of Ministry of Justice specialists the act is contrary to law. The Ministry routinely rejects numerous draft enactments on these grounds. Those departmental acts or parts thereof containing information constituting a State secret or information of a confidential character which have not undergone State registration, or those registered but not published in the established procedure, have no legal consequences on the grounds that they have not entered into legal force. Accordingly, they may not serve as a ground for regulating legal relations or applying sanctions to citizens, officials, or organisations for the failure to comply with the prescriptions contained therein; nor may they be referred to when settling disputes. Departmental acts enter into force simultaneously throughout Russian territory upon the expiry of ten days after the date of official publication unless a different period is specified therein, whereas those which by reason of State secrecy or the confidential information contained therein are not officially published enter into force from the date of their State registration and the conferment of a registration number on them, unless the acts themselves specify a later date.

2.65 The 1997 Rules for the Preparation of Normative Legal Acts of Federal Agencies of Executive Power and the State Registration Thereof were confirmed by Decree of the Government of the Russian Federation, as amended.[27] Normative legal acts are issued by federal agencies of executive power in the form of decrees, orders, regulations, rules, instructions, and statutes. The Rules expressly prohibit normative legal acts being issued in the form of letters and telegrams (excluding the Russian Central Bank, which is not a federal agency of executive power). The amendments of 11 December 1997 excluded deputy ministers and other deputy heads of federal agencies of executive power from signing, and therefore confirming, normative legal acts. Internal procedures have been introduced to expedite the process of evaluating departmental enactments.

2.66 Under the Rules, the Ministry of Justice registers not only normative legal acts affecting the rights, freedoms, and duties of man and citizen or those having an interdepartmental character, but also acts establishing the legal status of organizations. Ministries and departments seeking the registration of a normative legal act must submit an original and five copies of the draft act because, if registered, the act must also be published in the *Бюллетень нормативных актов федеральных органов исполнительной власти* [Bulletin of Normative Acts of Federal Agencies of Executive Power] and copies supplied to the

[27] *СЗ РФ* (1997), no. 33, item 3895; no. 50, item 5689; (1998), no. 47, item 5771; (1999), no. 8, item 1026; (2000), no. 41, item 4081.

Scientific-Technical Centre for Legal Information (System) and the Institute of Legislation and Comparative Law attached to the Government of the Russian Federation. If the act contains information comprising a State secret or of a confidential character, only one original and one copy are submitted. The Ministry of Justice has up to 15 days, with possible extensions for a further ten days, to complete its expert legal evaluation of the draft normative act. If draft normative acts contain a violation of the established procedure for submission thereof or provisions contrary to law, they are returned to the issuing agency for rectification and possible resubmission. Non-normative acts; that is, acts not containing a legal norm, may proceed to issuance without State registration, a fact which also is confirmed by the Ministry of Justice and recorded in a separate published list.

Nevertheless, there are numerous acts whose form is not mentioned in the 1997 Rules but which meet the definition of normative legal acts subject to State registration and official publication. Within this group are acts containing ecological, sanitary-epidemiological, hygienic, fire prevention, product safety, and analogous rules. In Russian legal doctrine these have been called 'normative legal acts with technical content': State standards, construction norms and rules, State sanitary-epidemiological rules, and the like. In practice some are registered and others are not. In a case which went to the Supreme Court of the Russian Federation a citizen alleged that certain provisions of an Order of the Ministry for Communications and Informatisation on the procedure for introducing technical means to conduct operational and search operations were illegal because they violated his right to secrecy of telephone conversations. The claimant contended that the Ministry Order contained references to orders of certain ministries and departments that were unregistered and not officially published. The respondents averred that the unpublished orders were of a 'technical' nature, non-normative, and did not require State registration. The Supreme Court accepted this distinction in rejecting the claimant's arguments.[28] The reasoning of the Supreme Court is not persuasive against the definition of a normative legal act set out in its Decree No. 19 of 25 May 2000.[29] **2.67**

Departmental acts not subject to registration in the view of the Ministry of Justice may be published in designated official gazettes. Many ministries and **2.68**

[28] *Бюллетень Верховного Суда РФ* [Bulletin of Supreme Court of Russian Federation] (2001), no. 4, pp. 10–11.

[29] See Ia Partsii, «О лицензировании отдельных видов деятельности» [On Licensing Individual Types of Activity], *Хозяйство и право*, no. 1 (2002), pp. 31–40.

federal services have adopted regulations or orders naming particular departmental publications as the official gazette for this purpose.[30]

International treaties

2.69 The 1994 Federal Law on the Procedure for the Publication of Federal Laws provides that 'international treaties ratified by the Federal Assembly shall be published simultaneously with the federal laws concerning their ratification' (Article 3). The 1995 Law on Treaties elaborates the provision to require that official publication is to follow the entry of the treaty into legal force, that such publication is upon the recommendation of the Ministry of Foreign Affairs of the Russian Federation, and that publication is to be in the *Собрание законодательства Российской Федерации* (Article 30). For all practical purposes these provisions extend only to inter-State treaties of the Russian Federation.

2.70 In practice the requirement of 'simultaneous' publication is not complied with. Sometimes this is expressly provided; for example, the Federal Law on the Ratification of the Convention on the Protection of Human Rights and Basic Freedoms and the Protocols Thereto, of 30 March 1998, was published on 6 April 1998 with the emendation that the 'Convention and Protocols thereto will be published upon their entry into force for the Russian Federation'.[31]

2.71 Treaties which have entered into legal force, except treaties of an interdepartmental character, are subject to publication in the *Бюллетень международных договоров* [Bulletin of International Treaties], issued monthly by the Administration of the President of the Russian Federation.[32] From time to time the texts of treaties are published in the newspaper *Российская газета*, which, although an official gazette, does not enjoy that status for treaties. Interdepartmental treaties of the Russian Federation are to be published in the official organs of the ministries or departments which concluded those treaties.

2.72 The courts of general jurisdiction of the Russian Federation may apply directly only those treaties officially published in the *Собрание законодательства Российской Федерации* or in the *Бюллетень международных*

[30] An example is Regulation No. 13-p of 19 February 2002 issued by the Ministry of Transport of the Russian Federation. Ministry acts are subject to publication in the newspaper *Транспорт России* [Transport of Russia]. See *Российская газета*, 16 March 2002.

[31] *СЗ РФ* (1998), no. 14, item 1514.

[32] The basis for publication of the journal is the Edict of the President of the Russian Federation on the Procedure for the Publication of International Treaties of the Russian Federation, adopted 11 January 1993, as amended. *СЗ РФ* (1993), no. 3, item 182; (1995), no. 49, item 4777. Some believe the Edict de facto lost force with the entry into force of the 1995 Law on Treaties, a position difficult to sustain in light of the fact that the Edict was amended after the entry into force of that Law.

договоров. Interdepartmental treaties published in the 'official publications' of the relevant departments also will be recognized by Russian courts. As for the former Soviet Union, however, of which the Russian Federation is the 'State-continuer', only treaties of the USSR published '. . . in the official publications of the Supreme Soviet of the USSR and Council of Ministers (or Cabinet of Ministers) of the USSR' will apparently be applied in the Russian courts. These publications would be, at a minimum, the *Ведомости Верховного Совета СССР* [Gazette of the Supreme Soviet of the USSR] and the *Соврание постановлений* [Collection of Decrees] of the Council or Cabinet of Ministers of the USSR. Whether this would extend to the classified versions of these gazettes is another matter, or to the Digests of laws published for the USSR and union republics. The Plenum of the Russian Supreme Court correctly notes that the '. . . collections of international treaties of the USSR' published treaties, '. . . but this publication was not official'. Official communications of whether a particular treaty is in force or not for the Russian Federation are subject to publication in the same procedure as the treaties themselves.[33]

Treaties concluded between subjects of the Russian Federation and the Russian Federation itself, or treaties between subjects of the Russian Federation, find no mention in the legislation regulating the publication and entry into force of normative legal acts. The great majority appear to be unpublished, or if published, are commonly in the newspapers of the subjects of the Federation concerned. Some appeared in *Российская газета*. What would qualify as an official text should these treaties be required in a judicial proceeding remains unclear. **2.73**

Official gazettes

The *Собрание законодательства Российской Федерации* [Collection of Legislation of the Russian Federation] is published weekly as the official serial publication in which there are published 'federal constitutional laws, federal laws, acts of chambers of the Russian Federation, edicts and regulations of the President of the Russian Federation, decrees and regulations of the Government of the Russian Federation, decisions of the Constitutional Court of the Russian Federation concerning an interpretation of the Constitution of the Russian Federation and concerning the conformity to the Constitution of the Russian Federation of laws, normative acts of the President of the Russian Federation, Soviet of the Federation, State Duma, Government of the Russian **2.74**

[33] See point 5, Decree on the Application by Courts of General Jurisdiction of Generally-Recognized Principles and Norms of International Law and International Treaties of the Russian Federation, transl. in Butler, *Russian Public Law*, p. 60.

Federation, or individual provisions of the enumerated acts' (Article 7, 1994 Federal Law on Procedure for the Publication and Entry into Force of Federal Constitutional Laws, Federal Laws, and Acts of Chambers of the Federal Assembly).[34]

2.75 Both the internal structure of this gazette and the forms of citation and layout of normative acts are regulated by the 1994 Federal Law. The gazette is divided into five sections. Section One contains federal constitutional laws and federal laws, and in practice the texts of international treaties when they appear in this gazette. Section Two consists of the acts of chambers of the Federal Assembly. In Section Three the edicts and regulations of the President of the Russian Federation appear. Section Four publishes the decrees and regulations of the Government of the Russian Federation. Section Five reproduces the decisions of the Constitutional Court subject to publication in this gazette.

2.76 Section Two is divided into two parts. The first contains decrees of the chambers of the Federal Assembly adopted with regard to questions relegated by Articles 102 and 103 of the 1993 Russian Constitution to the jurisdiction of the chambers. Part Two consists of other acts of the chambers of the Federal Assembly. Sections Three and Four also are subdivided into two parts; in each case Part One consists of normative acts, whereas Part Two contains acts of a non-normative character.

2.77 Acts placed within the gazette are given a consecutive item number; annexes to acts are placed under the same number as the act itself. The full name of the federal constitutional or federal law is given, the date of its adoption by the State Duma and the date of its approval by the Soviet of the Federation, the name of the official who signed it, the place and date of signature, and the registration number, which consists of an abbreviation of the type of law and the number assigned; for example, No. 6–ФЗ indicates that the enactment is a Federal Law, No. 5. The numeration commences anew each calendar year, so that the number of the law without a date is not helpful. International treaties are given an item number when published in the gazette but do not have a registration number as a federal law. Only the law on ratification of the treaty has a registration number.

2.78 When changes and additions are made to a federal constitutional law, federal law, or act of a chamber of the Federal Assembly, the new version may be published in an integrated text containing all the changes and additions, or a law instructing the changes and additions to be inserted may be adopted, as the Federal Assembly may choose. In practice both approaches are extensively used.

[34] For an extensive list of official gazettes, see Butler, *Russian Law* (2nd edn; 2003), pp. 689–92.

For many years the Federal Assembly published two gazettes, one official and the other not. The *Парламентская газета* [Parliamentary Newspaper] since October 1999 has been recognized as an official gazette for federal constitutional laws, federal laws, and decrees of chambers of the Federal Assembly whose publication is required by the parliament. Through the year 2003 the Federal Assembly also published the *Ведомости Федерального Собрания Российской Федерации* [Gazette of the Federal Assembly of the Russian Federation], but this serial, issued weekly, did not enjoy the status of an official gazette.

Normative legal acts of federal agencies of executive power are subject to official publication in the *Бюллетень нормативных актов федеральных органов исполнительной власти* [Bulletin of Normative Acts of Federal Agencies of Executive Power], presently published weekly. **2.79**

The monthly *Бюллетень международных договоров* [Bulletin of International Treaties] has the status of an official gazette for the texts of international treaties of the Russian Federation. It also publishes some of the federal laws on the ratification of treaties, but these are not regarded as official texts. **2.80**

Part II

FOREIGN ECONOMIC RELATIONS LAW

3

FOREIGN TRADE LAW

Although the period of perestroika during the late years of the former Soviet Union was accompanied by the abolition of the State monopoly of foreign trade originally introduced in the Russian Federation in April 1918, the Russian Federation has found it difficult to disengage substantially from State intervention in foreign commerce. After some years of what specialists have described as an era of indecision in the domain of foreign trade, the Russian Federation sought to clarify the role of the State in foreign trade by enacting the 1995 Federal Law on the State Regulation of Foreign Trade Activity.[1] This enactment was superseded by the 2003 Federal Law on the Fundamental Principles of State Regulation of Foreign Trade Activity, as amended.[2] **3.01**

The 2003 Federal Law refers to the 'foundations' or 'fundamental principles' of State regulation because both the Russian Federation and the subjects of the Russian Federation have powers and jurisdiction in the domain of foreign trade. The delimitation of jurisdiction and powers between the federal centre and the subjects of the Russian Federation is regulated by the 1999 Federal Law **3.02**

[1] *СЗ РФ* (1995), no. 42, item 3923; (1997), no. 28, item 3305; transl. in W E Butler, *Foreign Investment Law in the Commonwealth of Independent States* (2002), pp. 556–79.

[2] *СЗ РФ* (2003), no. 50, item 4850.

on the Coordination of International and Foreign Economic Relations of Subjects of the Russian Federation.[3]

3.03 For the purposes of this study, Russian foreign trade legislation is important not merely because foreign natural and juridical persons may import and export goods, products, and services to and from the Russian Federation while acting, so to speak, externally; but also because the 2003 Federal Law on Foreign Trade Activity provides that the regime established therein proceeds from the principle of national regime, subject to exceptions: 'Any Russian persons and foreign persons shall possess the right to effectuate foreign trade activity' (Article 10). State regulation of foreign trade in products of military designation or with respect to goods, information, work, services, and results of intellectual activity that might be used when creating a weapon of mass destruction, means for the delivery thereof, and other types of armament and military technology are regulated by federal laws on military-technical cooperation of the Russian Federation with foreign States and on export control.

A. Basic Principles of State Regulation

3.04 The 2003 Federal Law on Foreign Trade Activity enumerates no less than thirteen basic principles of State regulation of foreign trade activity. Collectively they summarise the foundations of Russian foreign trade policy. They are: (1) defence by the State of the rights and legal interests of those who participate in foreign trade activity and those who produce and consume goods and services; (2) equality and nondiscrimination of those who participate in foreign trade activity unless provided otherwise by a federal law; (3) unity of the customs territory of the Russian Federation; (4) reciprocity in relation to another State(s) or group of States; (5) ensuring the fulfilment of obligations of the Russian Federation under international treaties and effectuation of the rights arising from those treaties; (6) selecting measures of State regulation of foreign trade activity which are not more burdensome for the participants of foreign trade activity than is necessary to ensure the effective achievement of the goals which State regulatory measures intended; (7) glasnost in working out, adopting, and applying measures of the State regulation of foreign trade activity; (8) substantiation and objectivity of the application of measures of State regulation of foreign trade activity; (9) excluding unjustified interference of the State or State agencies in foreign trade activity and causing prejudice to participants of foreign trade activity and the economy of the Russian Federation; (10) ensuring the defence of Russia and the security of the State; (11) ensuring the right to

[3] *СЗ РФ* (1999), no. 2, item 231; transl. in Butler, *Foreign Investment Law in the Commonwealth of Independent States* (2002), pp. 579–84.

appeal in a judicial or other proceeding against the illegal actions or failure to act of State agencies and officials and the right to contest normative legal acts of the Russian Federation which impinge upon the right of a participant of foreign trade activity to engage in such activity; (12) unity of the system of State regulation of foreign trade activity; and (13) unity of application of the methods of State regulation of foreign trade activity throughout the entire territory of the Russian Federation.

Russian trade policy is regarded as an integral part of the economic policy of the Russian Federation. Its purpose is to create favourable conditions for Russian exporters, importers, producers, and consumers of goods and services. Russian trade policy is structured on the basis of compliance with generally-recognized principles and norms of international law and obligations arising out of international treaties of the Russian Federation. There are four methods of State regulation of foreign trade activity: (1) customs tariff regulation; (2) nontariff regulation; (3) prohibitions against and limitations on foreign trade in services and intellectual property; and (4) measures of an economic and administrative character which facilitate the development of foreign trade activity. Other methods of State regulation of foreign trade activity are not permitted. 3.05

Powers of federal, subject of federation, and local agencies

As noted above, powers in the domain of foreign trade activity are shared between the federal agencies of State power and agencies of State power of subjects of the Russian Federation. The powers of federal agencies of State power in the domain of foreign trade activity include the following: (1) forming the conception and strategy for developing foreign trade links and the basic principles of trade policy of the Russian Federation; (2) defending the economic sovereignty and economic interests of the Russian Federation and Russian persons; (3) State regulation of foreign trade activity, including customs tariff and nontariff regulation and the conformity of goods to obligatory requirements in connection with their being brought into and out of the Russian Federation; (4) the establishment of safety requirements and criteria for the life and health of citizens and the property of natural or juridical persons or municipal property, the environment, and the life or health of fauna and flora which are binding throughout the territory of the Russian Federation; (5) determination of the procedure for bringing in and taking out of the Russian Federation fissionable nuclear substances; poisonous or explosive substances; dangerous wastes; virulent or narcotic means; psychotropic substances and precursors thereof; biologically active materials such as donor blood, internal organs, and other materials; genetically active materials such as mushroom cultures, bacteria, viruses, seeds, flora and fauna under threat of extinction or parts or derivatives thereof; and other goods which may impact unfavourably on human life or health, the environment, or flora 3.06

and fauna; (6) determination of the procedure for bringing in and taking out precious metals and stones; (7) coordination of international cooperation of the Russian Federation in the domain of outer space activity and control over the working out and realization of international space projects of the Russian Federation; (8) establishment of indicators for statistical reports of foreign trade activity which are binding throughout the territory of the Russian Federation; (9) the conclusion of international treaties of the Russian Federation in the domain of foreign trade activity; (10) the founding, maintenance, and liquidation of trade representations of the Russian Federation in foreign States; (11) participation in the activity of international economic organizations and the realization of decisions taken by those organizations; (12) determination of the procedure for taking out of the Russian Federation goods of which a component part is information comprising a State secret; (13) information provision for foreign trade activity on the territory of the Russian Federation; and (14) the creation of insurance and pledge funds in the domain of foreign trade activity.

3.07 The powers of agencies of State power of subjects of the Russian Federation in the domain of foreign trade activity include: (1) conducting negotiations and concluding agreements concerning the effectuation of foreign economic links with subjects of foreign federated States, administrative-territorial formations of foreign States, and, provided the consent of the Government of the Russian Federation is obtained, with agencies of State power of foreign States; (2) maintaining representatives attached to trade representations of the Russian Federation in foreign States from the budgets of subjects of the Russian Federation by agreement with the Ministry of Foreign Affairs of the Russian Federation and the relevant federal agency of executive power; (3) opening representations in foreign States with a view to realizing agreements concerning the effectuation of foreign economic links; (4) forming and realizing regional programmes for foreign trade activity; (5) information provision for foreign trade activity on the territory of a subject of the Russian Federation; and (6) creating insurance and pledge funds in the domain of foreign trade activity on the territory of the subject of the Russian Federation.

3.08 The exercise of these powers is coordinated by preparing draft plans and programmes to develop foreign trade activity that affects the interests of subjects of the Russian Federation and are within their competence. The initiative originates in the subject of the Russian Federation, which at its discretion and leisure may prepare such a document and within thirty days submit the document for an official opinion, which must be given by the Ministry of Trade and Economic Development of the Russian Federation. The failure to submit an official opinion is construed as no objection to the programme.

The types of 'international and foreign economic relations' which subjects of the

Russian Federation may engage in are defined in the 1999 Federal Law on the Coordination of International and Foreign Economic Relations: '. . . relations to be effectuated in the trade and economic, scientific-technical, ecological, humanitarian, cultural, and other domains . . .' (Article 1). The agreements negotiated and concluded by subjects of the Russian Federation may not include provisions contrary to the 1993 Russian Constitution, generally-recognized principles and norms of international law, international treaties of the Russian Federation, federal legislation, treaties of the Federation, or the legal interests of another subject of the Russian Federation. Each subject of the Russian Federation has the right to determine the procedure for concluding such agreement, having regard to the requirement that the drafts of the agreements must be duly agreed.

The scheme depends upon mutual notifications. The agencies of State power of a subject of the Russian Federation must inform in good time the appropriate federal agencies of executive power that they are entering into negotiations to conclude an agreement in the domain of international and foreign economic relations. The draft agreement must be submitted not less than a month before signature to the Ministry of Foreign Affairs of the Russian Federation and, when necessary, to other federal agencies of executive power. The recipient federal agencies have twenty days to comment, and if there are disagreements about the draft, conciliation procedures are set in motion to resolve the differences of opinion. **3.09**

Example: Bashkortostan. The Republic Bashkortostan on 6 March 2001 adopted a Law on the Development of Foreign Trade Activity in the Republic Bashkortostan, amended on 14 March 2003, 1 January 2004, and 23 December 2004.[4] This enactment determines the powers of agencies of State power of the Republic in the domain of foreign trade activity, and as such is narrower in scope than similar legislation of other subjects of the Russian Federation. The relevant powers include: (1) conducting negotiations and concluding agreements to effectuate foreign economic links with subjects of foreign federal States, administrative-territorial formations of foreign States, and, with the consent of the Russian Government, with agencies of State power of foreign States; (2) maintaining Bashkortostan representatives attached to trade representations of the Russian Federation in foreign States at the expense of Bashkortostan; (3) opening representations in foreign States to realize agreements on foreign economic ties (the representative must be a citizen of the Russian Federation); (4) giving authorizations to open in Bashkortostan the representations of subjects of foreign federal States and administrative-territorial formations of foreign **3.10**

[4] *Ведомости Государственного – Собрания – Курултая, Президента и Правительства Республики Башкортостан* (2004), no 18(192), item 1053.

States; (5) forming and realizing Bashkortostan programmes for the development of foreign trade activity; (6) sending proposals within its competence and comments on draft normative legal acts of the Russian Federation concerning the right to effectuate foreign trade activity and official opinions on foreign trade activity affecting the interests of Bashkortostan; (7) ensuring control over foreign trade activity in Bashkortostan; and (8) providing information on foreign trade activity in Bashkortostan.

3.11 The President of Bashkortostan is empowered to sign agreements on foreign economic links in the name of the Republic and to represent the Republic in negotiations with foreign federal States and administrative-territorial formations of foreign States, and to appoint and recall representatives of Bashkortostan abroad, whereas the Government of Bashkortostan takes decisions to develop foreign trade activity and to negotiate and sign intergovernmental foreign economic agreements. If there is a violation of such an agreement, the Government informs the Ministry of Foreign Affairs of the Russian Federation.

3.12 The Republic Bashkortostan maintains its own data base of foreign trade information which includes entries for Russian and foreign citizens who engage in foreign trade activity in the Republic, or who have received quotas and licenses; international trade treaties of the Russian Federation and foreign economic agreements of Bashkortostan; Russian, Bashkortostan, and foreign legislation concerning foreign trade; information on the activities of Bashkortostan representations abroad and foreign representations in Bashkortostan; customs statistics for Bashkortostan; the situation in the goods markets; violations in the domain of foreign trade activity; a list of goods whose bringing in to or taking out of Bashkortostan is prohibited.

3.13 The Government of Bashkortostan is empowered, *inter alia*, to grant credits to participants of foreign trade activity and arrange a system of guarantees and insurance for export credits, organize trade exhibitions and fairs or related specialized symposia or conferences, and to carry on advertising campaigns and other measures promoting exports of goods, services, and intellectual property.

3.14 *Example: City of St. Petersburg.* The City of St. Petersburg is one of two cities in the Russian Federation (Moscow being the other) which enjoys constitutional stature as a subject of the Russian Federation. On 29 December 2000 the Legislative Assembly of St. Petersburg adopted a Law on Agreements Regulating International and Foreign Economic Ties of St. Petersburg.[5] This enactment determines the procedure for the conclusion, fulfilment, and suspension of the

[5] *Вестник Законодательного Собрания Санкт-Петербурга* (2001), no. 2. This Law replaced the Law of St. Petersburg of 2 July 1997 'On the Procedure for the Conclusion of Treaties of St. Petersburg'.

operation and termination of agreements regulating international and foreign economic links of St. Petersburg irrespective of their name (memorandum, protocol, exchange of letters, or other). The Law provides that such agreements are '. . . international treaties and may be concluded only with regard to questions relegated by the Constitution of the Russian Federation and federal legislation to the competence of subjects of the Russian Federation' (Article 1[2]).

The St. Petersburg Law imitates the 1995 Federal Law on International Treaties by distinguishing between agreements concluded in the name of St. Petersburg, in the name of the Administration of St. Petersburg, and in the name of branch and territorial agencies of the Administration of St. Petersburg. In addition, the Legislative Assembly of St. Petersburg itself may conclude agreements in its own name with counterpart organs of foreign States, subjects of foreign federal States, and international organizations combining the agencies of power of similar nature. The analogy with treaties is pursued at the level of the expression of consent, which may take the forms of signature of an agreement, an exchange of documents comprising the agreement, accession to the agreement, confirmation of the agreement, or otherwise as the parties may have stipulated (Article 3). The Governor of St. Petersburg may sign agreements *ex officio*; other persons may sign agreements on the basis of powers issued by the Governor. **3.15**

Certain agreements require the decision of the Legislative Assembly of St. Petersburg for confirmation (the equivalent of ratification) or dissolution (the equivalent of denunciation): those agreements whose fulfilment requires changes of laws of the City or the enactment of news laws, or agreements containing rules not corresponding to the requirements of St. Petersburg laws; agreements of St. Petersburg to participate in international organizations if the decisions of those organizations would be binding upon agencies of State power of St. Petersburg; agreements containing obligations requiring financing from the St. Petersburg budget which were not provided for in the budget or which transcend a single financial year; agreements on the provision or receipt of loans, credits, or change of financial obligations of St. Petersburg; certain guarantee agreements; and agreements where the parties have so stipulated. The originals of agreements are kept by the Administration of St. Petersburg. Agreements which have entered into force and were subject to confirmation by the Legislative Assembly are to be officially published in the official gazette of the said Assembly; others are subject to publication in the procedure determined by the Administration of St. Petersburg. **3.16**

The St. Petersburg requirements on publication are based on the general provisions of Russian legislation that agreements concerning international and foreign economic relations concluded by subjects of the Russian Federation are subject to being registered in the procedure established by the Government of the **3.17**

Russian Federation and are subject to publication. However, in a remarkable provision which reverses the presumptions of the 1969 Vienna Convention on the Law of Treaties, 'agreements concerning the effectuation of international and foreign economic relations concluded by agencies of State power of a subject of the Russian Federation shall, irrespective of form, name, and content, not be international treaties' (Article 7, 1999 Federal Law on the Coordination of International and Foreign Economic Relations). It follows that federal agencies of State power do not bear responsibility for such agreements unless those agreements have been concluded with agencies of State power of foreign States with the consent of the Government of the Russian Federation or official guarantees have been given with regard to a specific agreement of a subject of the Russian Federation by the Government of the Russian Federation.

3.18 If an agreement concluded by a subject of the Russian Federation is alleged to be contrary to the Russian Constitution, federal laws, generally-recognized principles and norms of international law, and international treaties of the Russian Federation, or impinges the legal interests of another subject of the Russian Federation, or has been concluded in violation of the procedure established by the 1999 Federal Law on the Coordination of International and Foreign Economic Relations, the agreement may be contested in a judicial proceeding, and pending resolution of the issue, a court may suspend the operation of the agreement.

3.19 Subjects of the Russian Federation are entitled to legal and other advice or consultations from federal agencies of State power in developing their international and foreign economic relations, in organizing and conducting negotiations, drafting and performing obligations under the agreements, and in defending the rights and legal interests of subjects of the Russian Federation in foreign States. Although so far few in number, representations of subjects of the Russian Federation have been opened in foreign States with the endorsement of the Russian Ministry of Foreign Affairs and consent of the authorities of the foreign State concerned. Russian natural persons employed by or staffing these representations do not enjoy diplomatic privileges and immunities. Only Russian citizens may head these representations, but this does not preclude foreigners from being retained in a position other than the head.

Basic provisions on State regulation

3.20 Russian regulation of foreign economic relations proceeds from the assumption that Russian and foreign persons are the normal participants in foreign trade activity. The Russian Federation itself, subjects of the Russian Federation, and municipal formations, engage directly in foreign trade only when federal laws so establish.

Role of President of Russian Federation

Under the 2003 Federal Law on Foreign Trade Activity, the President of the Russian Federation is given virtually unlimited powers in this domain. Only three are enumerated: (1) determine the basic orientations of trade policy of the Russian Federation; (2) determine the procedure for bringing in and taking out of the Russian Federation precious metals and stones; and (3) establish prohibitions and limitations in the foreign trade of goods, services, and intellectual property for the purposes of the participation of the Russian Federation in international sanctions. The fourth reads: 'effectuate other powers'. **3.21**

Role of Government of Russian Federation

The powers of the Government of the Russian Federation in regulating foreign trade activity are at once vaster and more limited as befits the more subordinate role of Government in the Russian constitutional system. **3.22**

Its principal powers, of which there are thirteen, are quite specific: (1) ensure that the Russian Federation carries on a unified trade policy, take measures to realize that policy, adopt respective decisions and ensure they are fulfilled; (2) take special protective measures, anti-dumping measures, and compensatory measures with regard to foreign trade in goods and other measures to defend the economic interests of the Russian Federation; (3) establish customs tariff rates within the limits determined by the Customs Tariff of the Russian Federation; (4) introduce quantitative limitations on the export and import of goods in accordance with international treaties and federal laws and determine the procedure for applying those limitations; (5) establish an authorization procedure for the export and/or import of individual types of goods which may have an unfavourable impact on the security of the State, human life or health, the property of natural or juridical persons or State or municipal property, the environment, flora and fauna, and determine the list of individual types of goods to which this procedure extends; (6) determine the procedure for licensing in the sphere of foreign trade and the procedure for forming and keeping a federal licence bank; (7) determine the list of goods over whose export and/or import observation is to be established; (8) determine the procedure for observation over the export and/or import of individual types of goods; (9) take decisions within its competence to conduct negotiations and sign international treaties of the Russian Federation; (10) take decisions concerning the introduction of retaliatory measures with respect to foreign States of limitations in the foreign trade of goods, services, and intellectual property; (11) determine the procedure for bringing in and taking out of the Russian Federation fissionable nuclear substances; (12) establish the procedure for bringing in and taking out of Russia goods in which a component part is information comprising a State secret; and (13) confirm the goods nomenclature of foreign economic activity. **3.23**

3.24 However, instead of exercising 'other powers', as in the case of the President of the Russian Federation, the Government is empowered only to effectuate other powers placed on it by the Constitution of the Russian Federation, federal laws, and edicts of the President of the Russian Federation in the domains of State regulation of foreign trade activity and State control.

Other federal agencies of State power

3.25 It is in fact contemplated in the 2003 Federal Law on Foreign Trade Activity that the Government of the Russian Federation will endow the Ministry of Trade and Economic Development and other agencies of State power with individual functions, including the conclusion of international trade treaties and other treaties of the Russian Federation in the domain of foreign economic relations. Subjects of the Russian Federation are to be involved in working out the said proposals for treaty provisions if they would affect their interests.

3.26 The procedure for developing and submitting proposals concerning the conclusion of international trade treaties and other treaties is regulated by the 1995 Law on International Treaties of the Russian Federation.[6] Foreign trade negotiations and the drafting of legislation on foreign trade matters can be delicate, and the 2003 Federal Law on Foreign Trade Activity endeavours to strike a balance between transparency, confidentiality, and secrecy. Transparency is intended to happen at the initial stages. If a normative legal act is involved, the relevant federal ministry is to request comments on proposals or drafts if their economic interests may be affected by the contemplated enactment. It sometimes follows from an international treaty that the competent agencies of other State(s) or group of States should comment pursuant to the treaty, and it is common practice to invite foreign organizations and entrepreneurs to do the same.

3.27 Under certain conditions a decision may be taken not to consult either within or outside the Russian Federation because: (1) the measures provided for by the draft normative legal act must not be known until it enters into force, and to conduct consultations would or could lead to the failure to achieve the purposes sought by the normative legal act; and (2) the conducting of consultations would delay adoption of the normative legal act of the Russian Federation affecting the right to effectuate foreign trade activity and this could seriously prejudice the interests of the Russian Federation. These circumstances do not, however, extend to special defensive measures, anti-dumping measures, or to compensatory measures. In all instances the confidentiality of information comprising a

[6] Transl. with commentary in W E Butler, *The Law of Treaties in Russia and the Commonwealth of Independent States* (2002).

State, commercial, or other secret protected by law must be preserved and such information used only for the purposes for which it was provided.

Foreign trade in goods

Russian legislation undertakes to determine exhaustively the means and methods which may be used by way of State regulation in the domain of goods, services, and intellectual property. To a considerable extent these are renvoi provisions. **3.28**

So far as trade in goods is concerned, the Russian Federation uses customs tariffs and charges in accordance with the Customs Code of the Russian Federation as a principal method of regulating foreign commerce. The methods of nontariff regulation include quantitative limitations that may be introduced only in exceptional instances by the Government of the Russian Federation as follows: (1) provisional limitations or prohibitions of the export of goods in order to prevent or reduce a critical shortage on the Russian domestic market, such goods being incorporated in a List confirmed by the Government of Russia; (2) limitations on the import of agricultural goods or aquatic biological resources brought into the Russian Federation in any form if such is necessary to: (a) reduce the production or sale of an analogous good of Russian origin; (b) reduce the production or sale of a good of Russian origin which may be directly substituted by an imported good if the Russian Federation does not have significant production of the analogous good; (c) removal from the market of a temporary surplus of an analogous good of Russian origin or a good of Russian origin by providing such surplus good to groups of Russian consumers free of charge or at below-market prices; and (d) limit the production of products of animal origin dependent upon a good of imported origin if the production of an analogous good in the Russian Federation is relatively insignificant. Such quantitative limitations must be nondiscriminatory and applied irrespective of the country(ies) concerned unless a federal law provides otherwise. However, when quantitative limitations on an import lead to a distribution of shares of import of a good among interested foreign States, the previous import of the good from those States is taken into account; provided, however, that these requirements do not extend to States with whom the Russian Federation has no mutual treaty obligations to provide a most-favoured-nation regime. Nor do these limitations extend to border trade, customs unions, or free trade zones. **3.29**

If quotas are introduced on goods, the Government of the Russian Federation determines the method of distributing the quotas and, where appropriate, establishes the procedure for an auction or competition for quotas. Quotas are to be distributed on the principle of the equality of participants of foreign trade turnover and nondiscrimination from the standpoint of forms of ownership, place of registration, and position in the market. **3.30**

3.31 Licensing in the domain of foreign trade is introduced under the following circumstances: (1) the introduction of provisional quantitative limitations on export or import of individual goods; (2) the realization of an authorization procedure for the export and/or import of individual types of goods which may unfavourably impact upon the security of the State, life or health of citizens, property of natural or juridical persons, State or municipal property, environment, or life or health of flora and fauna; (3) granting of an exclusive right for the export and/or import of individual types of goods; and (4) fulfilment by the Russian Federation of international obligations. Transactions for the export and/or import of individual types of goods concluded without a license for which an exclusive right to export or import has been granted are void.

3.32 Licensing also may be introduced as part of the mechanism of 'observation' over the export or import of individual types of goods for the purpose of monitoring the dynamics of export and/or import. Authorisations to import or export the affected goods are issued upon application by any participants of foreign trade activity within three working days from the date of application. Other documents besides the application for an authorization are not required.

3.33 Special defensive measures, anti-dumping measures, and compensatory measures may be introduced in accordance with federal laws with respect to imports of goods in order to defend the economic interests of Russian goods producers.

3.34 In order to protect the interests and rights of consumers and to counteract the unfair practice of distorting information about goods being imported into the Russian Federation, including a reduction of their value, the Russian Government has the right to introduce 'pre-unloading inspection' with respect to certain goods for a period not exceeding three years. The importer of the good bears the costs of such inspection, which may, however, be offset in whole or in part by a reduction of customs duties on such goods. The agency which conducts such inspections is chosen on a competitive basis by the Government of the Russian Federation. Pre-unloading inspections must be carried out in compliance with the principles of glasnost and openness, the objective application of procedures and criteria on a equal basis to all importers of the good, verification of the quality and quantity of the good in accordance with Russian legislation, provision to importers of information concerning the criteria for meeting legislative requirements, and confidentiality of the information received during such inspections. Goods which are subject to pre-unloading inspection may be imported only upon presentation of a certificate confirming that the inspection has been completed; the inspection period should not exceed, as a rule, three working days.

3.35 National regime operates in the context of foreign trade regulation somewhat differently from the way in which we have used that term in connection with the legal status of foreign citizens. Excluding customs duties, differential rates of taxes and charges may not be imposed on goods by reason of their country of origin. As for technical, pharmacological, sanitary, veterinary, phytosanitary, and ecological requirements, these apply to goods originating in a foreign State just as they would apply to analogous goods of Russian origin assuming, as a rule, that these States have respective international treaties with the Russian Federation. Moreover, goods originating in a foreign State or groups of foreign States are to be granted a regime no less favourable than the regime for analogous goods of Russian origin with respect to sale, offer for sale, purchase, carriage, distribution, or use on the domestic market of the Russian Federation, although this is not understood to extend to differential payments connected with carriage based on the type of transport used rather than the origin of goods.

All payments recovered in the Russian Federation in connection with the import and export of goods, excluding customs duties and other taxes, must not exceed the approximate cost of services rendered. Such payments include those relating to quantitative limitations, licensing, currency control, statistical services, conformity to obligatory requirements, expert examination and inspection, quarantine, sanitary service, and fumigation. **3.36**

An integral part of Russian foreign trade regulation is the principle that the freedom of international transit operates along rail, water, air, and motor vehicle routes which are most suitable for such transit without distinction of flag, place of registration, place of origin of a vessel, place of putting in, place of departure, point of destination, dispatch, or any circumstances relevant to the ownership of the goods concerned, the vessel, or other means of transport unless provided otherwise by federal laws. Customs legislation of Russia, however, may require that certain goods enter, pass through, or exit from Russia via determined sites on the State boundary of the Russian Federation, or follow determined routes. **3.37**

All of the foregoing provisions concerning limitations, freedoms, and concomitant measures are subject to considerations of national interests of the Russian Federation. Subject therefore to international treaties of the Russian Federation and federal laws, measures of a non-economic nature that affect foreign trade in goods may be introduced on condition that such measures are essential: (1) in order to comply with public morality and legal order; (2) in order to protect human life or health, the environment, or the life or health of flora and fauna; or (3) relate to the export or import of gold or silver; (4) apply to the defence of cultural valuables; (5) are needed to prevent the exhaustion of nonrenewable natural resources and accompany limitations of internal production or consumption; (6) are needed to acquire and distribute goods in general or local deficit; (7) are needed to fulfil international obligations of the Russian Federation or to ensure the defence and security of the Russian Federation; and (8) are needed to **3.38** ensure compliance with normative legal acts which are not contrary to international treaties concerning: (a) the application of customs legislation; (b) the submission of documents of conformity to customs agencies together with cargo customs declarations; (c) environmental protection; (d) obligations under Russian legislation to take out or destroy goods not meeting technical, pharmacological, sanitary, veterinary, phytosanitary, or ecological requirements; (e) the prevention and investigation of crimes or court proceedings and the execution of court decisions with respect to such crimes; and (f) the grant of an exclusive right. However, these measures may not apply to goods originating in foreign States or groups thereof with which the Russian Federation has no treaty obligations to provide a regime no less favourable than the regime granted to other States or groups of States.

Foreign trade in services

3.39 The rendering of services, which qualifies as foreign trade, is conceptualized rather differently from goods. Under the 2003 Federal Law on State Foreign Trade Activity, the following qualify as foreign trade in services: (1) services rendered from the territory of the Russian Federation to the territory of a foreign State; (2) services rendered from the territory of a foreign State to the territory of the Russian Federation; (3) services rendered on the territory of the Russian Federation to a foreign customer of the services; (4) services rendered on the territory of a foreign State to a Russian customer of the services; (5) services rendered by a Russian performer who has no commercial presence on the territory of the foreign State through his presence or the presence of persons empowered to act in his name on the territory of the foreign State; (6) services rendered by a foreign performer who has no commercial presence on the territory of the Russian Federation through his presence of the presence of persons empowered to act in the name of the foreign persons on the territory of the Russian Federation; (7) services rendered by a Russian performer through a commercial presence on the territory of a foreign State; and (8) services rendered by a foreign performer through a commercial presence on the territory of the Russian Federation. Unless provided otherwise by an international treaty of the Russian Federation, foreign trade in services may be limited through the introduction of prohibitions and limitations affecting all or certain sectors of services with respect to the means of rendering services, but only on the basis of federal laws or other normative legal acts of the Russian Federation.

3.40 The principle of national regime is more restrictive than in the case of foreign trade in goods, and the measures that may be introduced in the national interest, although they overlap in some measure with those applicable to trade in goods, differ in certain respects, including: (1) measures directed to ensure the integrity and stability of the financial system, defence of the rights and legal interests of investors, depositors, policyholders, and those who perform financial services; (3) measures needed to ensure the equal and effective establishment or collection of taxes with respect to foreigners who perform services; (4) measures relating to the realization of double taxation treaties; and (5) measures of defence against interference in the private life of individuals with respect to processing and disseminating information of a personal character and confidential information concerning individuals and personal accounts.

Foreign trade in intellectual property

Intellectual property is not categorized as a service, and the types of measures **3.41**
that may be introduced to limit foreign trade in intellectual property are narrower than is the case with goods or services.

Prohibitions and limitations

The specific prohibitions and limitations with respect to foreign trade are dic- **3.42**
tated by the purpose for which they are to be introduced. If they are required in connection with Russian participation in international sanctions pursuant to the United Nations Charter, the President of the Russian Federation enacts them by way of edict.

The Government of the Russian Federation may introduce, upon the recommen- **3.43**
dation of the Central Bank, limitations in order to support the balance of payments of the Russian Federation. Among the particular relevant circumstances are: (a) to stop a serious threat of or reduction in the hard currency reserves of the Russian Federation; and (b) to achieve a reasonable rate of increase in the hard currency reserves if they are small. Currency regulation and control measures may be introduced in accordance with relevant provisions of the Agreement with the International Monetary Fund and Russian currency legislation.

Retaliatory measures in foreign trade are within the province of the Government **3.44**
of the Russian Federation. They may be introduced against a foreign State which: does not fulfil international treaty obligations with respect to the Russian Federation; undertakes measures that violate the economic interests of the Russian Federation, subjects of the Russian Federation, or municipal persons or Russian persons or the political interests of Russia, including closing the access of Russian persons without justification to the markets of the foreign State or otherwise discriminating against Russian persons; does not provide adequate and effective defence of the interests of Russian persons, for example, against the anti-competition activity of other persons; or fails to take reasonable actions against the unlawful activity of natural or juridical persons of the foreign State on the territory of the Russian Federation. These measures of retaliation must be introduced in accordance with generally-recognized principles and norms of

international law, international treaties of the Russian Federation, and within the limits necessary to defend the economic interests of those adversely affected.

3.45 For a brief period the 1998 Federal Law on Measures for the Defence of Economic Interests of the Russian Federation When Effectuating Foreign Trade in Goods[7] was directed towards enumerating special protective measures, anti-dumping measures, compensatory measures, and import and export limitations applicable when economic interests of the Russian Federation were threatened. These provisions have been superseded by the 2003 Federal Law on Special Defensive, Anti-Dumping, and Compensatory Measures in the Event of the Import of Goods,[8] except for the stipulation that a special duty on agricultural goods might be introduced during the calendar year in which the duty is introduced, the duty not to exceed one-third of the usual customs duty on such goods. The definition of 'agricultural good' is broad, extending to such items as furs, cotton, and others.

3.46 Whereas the limitations and prohibitions addressed above are mostly directed towards protecting the Russian Federation and the general public, the 2003 Federal Law on the Defence of Economic Interests is concerned primarily with the interests of Russian goods producers in connection with increased imports, dumping imports, or subsidized imports, and the procedures for introducing and applying defensive measures against these practices. The application of defensive measures must be preceded by an investigation in order to determine whether in fact imports have actually increased and whether this increase constitutes serious prejudice or threat thereof to the relevant branch of the Russian economy, or whether dumping or subsidized imports[9] are occurring and whether these constitute material harm or threat thereof to the respective branch of the Russian economy. The Government of the Russian Federation has fourteen days from the day of the registration of a report by the investigating agency which recommends the introduction, application, revision, or repeal of a special defensive measure, anti-dumping measure, or compensatory measure to decide or not to act on the recommendation submitted.

3.47 Arbitrazh courts have jurisdiction over disputes connected with the special defensive measures, including cases to contest normative legal acts and non-normative legal acts, decisions, and actions or failure to act of State agencies and officials.

---

[7] *СЗ РФ* (1998), no. 16, item 1798. [8] *СЗ РФ* (2003), no. 50, item 4851.

[9] Subsidies are calculated according to the Rules for Calculation of the Amount of Specific Subsidy of a Foreign State (or Union of Foreign States) and on Recognition as Having Lost Force Certain Acts of the Government of the Russian Federation Regulating Questions of the Application of Special Defensive, Anti-Dumping, and Compensatory Measures in Event of Import of Goods, confirmed by Decree of the Government of the Russian Federation, No. 546. *СЗ РФ* (2004), no. 42, item 4139.

Frontier trade

Also known as 'border' trade, frontier trade is conducted as a rule literally on the frontier of the Russian Federation with certain adjacent neighbouring countries on the basis of an international treaty. Commonly, the basis on which such trade is carried on includes an especially favourable regime, usually to satisfy the permanent local population and juridical persons situated on the frontier. The frontier regime does not extend to situations in which the most-favoured-nation regime operates. **3.48**

Accordingly, the Russian persons engaging in frontier trade must have a permanent location or place of residence on the strip of territory classified as 'frontier territory' and the trade which occurs is solely to meet the requirements for goods and services within the frontier territories. International treaties of the Russian Federation with the respective neighbouring foreign State normally determine the conditions under which frontier trade may be conducted. **3.49**

Special economic zones are addressed separately below (see Chapter 4). **3.50**

Barter trade

Although barter contracts are regulated by the Civil Code of the Russian Federation (Chapter 31), insofar as they comprise part of foreign trade they are regulated by the 2003 Federal Law on State Foreign Trade Activity (Chapter 10). Barter is not a means of circumventing prohibitions and limitations that may be introduced with respect to goods, services, or intellectual property as part of State foreign trade regulation. Any prohibitions and limitations applicable to foreign trade in goods, services, or intellectual property also extend automatically to barter. **3.51**

Barter transactions in foreign trade may be entered into only on condition that such transactions make provision for the exchange of goods, service, work, or intellectual property which are equal in value, or the duty of the respective party to pay any difference in value should the barter involve the exchange of goods, services, work, or intellectual property of unequal value. **3.52**

A document formalizing a foreign trade barter transaction must indicate: the date of concluding and the number of the transaction; the nomenclature, quantity, quality, and price of the goods concerned; and the periods and conditions for export and import. If the barter transaction involves the delivery of sets of equipment, there are additional requirements. In the case of services, work, or intellectual property there must be a list with their value specified and the periods for rendering the services, fulfilling the work, or transferring the exclusive rights to intellectual property or granting the right to use intellectual property, together with a list of documents to be submitted to the Russian person as confirmation **3.53** of the fact that everything agreed has been delivered, performed, or transferred. A key document in any barter transaction is the so-called 'passport' of a foreign trade barter transaction, which includes information on the use of monetary and/or other means of payment. The barter transaction 'passport' must be submitted to Russian customs agencies when declaring the goods crossing the customs boundary of the Russian Federation.

Export control

3.54 Within the framework of export control established by the 1999 Federal Law on Export Control,[10] the definition of foreign economic activity is exceedingly broad, and encompasses foreign trade, investment, and other activity, including production cooperation, in the domain of the international exchange of goods, information, work, services, and results of intellectual activity. The complex of measures regulate the procedure for effectuating foreign economic activity insofar as the respective goods, information, work, services, and results of intellectual activity can be used in the creation of weapons of mass destruction, means of delivery thereof, and other types of armaments and military technology. Weapons of mass destruction are nuclear, chemical, bacteriological or biological, and toxic weapons; and means of delivery are missiles and pilotless flying apparatus capable of delivering a weapon of mass destruction.

3.55 Foreign persons may qualify as Russian participants, also called 'Russian persons' for the purposes of legislation, in the relevant foreign economic activity inasmuch as such persons include juridical persons created in accordance with Russian legislation, having a permanent location on Russian territory, or individual entrepreneurs registered on Russian territory, and natural persons having a permanent or primary place of residence on the territory of the Russian Federation, and have the right to engage in foreign economic activity under Russian legislation. Nonetheless, to the extent that they do not fall into this category, 'foreign persons' for the purposes of export control also are juridical persons and organizations in other organizational-legal form whose civil-law capacity is determined according to the law of the foreign State in which they are founded, natural persons whose civil law capacity and dispositive legal capacity is determined under the law of a foreign State of which they are a citizen, and stateless persons whose dispositive legal capacity is determined under the law of a foreign State in which they have a permanent place of residence.

3.56 The purposes of export control in the Russian Federation are to defend the interests of the Russian Federation, to implement the requirements of international treaties of the Russian Federation with respect to the nonproliferation

[10] *СЗ РФ* (1999), no. 30, item 3774.

of weapons of mass destruction and means of delivery thereof and to exercise control over the export of military technology and dual-purpose technologies, as well as to further the integration of the Russian economy into the world economy. Lists of controlled goods are confirmed by edicts of the President of the Russian Federation upon the recommendation of the Government of the Russian Federation.

Foreign economic transactions which involve the transfer of controlled goods and technologies to a foreign person must be concluded when there is a written obligation of the foreign person that the said goods and technologies will not be used to create a weapon of mass destruction or means of delivery. Additional requirements may be imposed by the Government of the Russian Federation, including the right to verify the use by a foreign person of the goods and technologies received in accordance with the obligation assumed. All such transactions are subject to licensing. General licences may be issued for the export of individual types of controlled goods to foreign States who adhere in their domestic and foreign policy to generally-recognized principles and norms of international law in the domain of the nonproliferation of weapons of mass destruction; under a general licence the quantity of goods is specified, but the specific recipient is not. Only a Russian juridical person may be issued a general licence. **3.57**

Russian persons are prohibited from concluding or performing a foreign economic transaction with goods, information, work, services, and results of intellectual activity or to participate in such a transaction in any other way if they reliably know that those items will be used by a foreign State or foreign person to create a weapon of mass destruction or means of delivery. Whether a particular foreign economic transaction meets the requirements of Russian legislation in this respect is determined by a State expert examination as part of the export control process. The Rules for Conducting State Expert Examination of Foreign Economic Transactions with Goods, Information, Work, Services, and Results of Intellectual Activity With Respect to Which Export Control is Established were confirmed by a 2001 Decree of the Government of the Russian Federation, as amended.[11] **3.58**

Normative legal acts of the Russian Federation in the domain of export control, including departmental enactments, are subject to official publication. Information concerning these normative legal acts is distributed to all interested Russian participants and citizens free of charge. **3.59**

[11] *СЗ РФ* (2001), no. 17, item 1713.

4

FOREIGN INVESTMENT LAW

A. Overview

4.01 Foreign natural and juridical persons who become foreign investors in the Russian Federation enjoy special rights, duties, and guarantees under Russian legislation. These comprise the subject of the present Chapter.[1]

4.02 Although the principal legislative act regulating relations connected with State guarantees of the rights of foreign investors who make investments on the territory of the Russian Federation is the 1999 Federal Law on Foreign Investments in the Russian Federation, many subjects of the Russian Federation have adopted their own foreign investment laws to augment or elaborate the 1999 Federal Law. Depending upon the territory where the foreign investment is to be made, the investor will need to determine whether there is relevant applicable legislation of the subject of the Russian Federation. Also of relevance is the 1999 Federal Law on Investment Activity in the Russian Federation Effectuated in the Form of Capital Investments.[2]

4.03 Moreover, the Russian Federation has a growing network of bilateral investment treaties (see Annex 6 below) and gradually is acceding to the important multilateral treaties that regulate investing and protect investors. Under the 1993 Russian Constitution, these treaties have precedence over inconsistent provisions of Russian legislation, as do generally-recognized principles of international law.

4.04 The principle of national regime is the basic point of departure for determining the legal regime for the foreign investor and foreign investing. The 1999 Federal Law on Foreign Investments provides that both the legal regime of the activity of foreign investors and the use of profit received from investments '. . . may not be less favourable than the legal regime of activity and the use of profit received from investments granted to Russian investors', subject to exceptions established by federal laws to the extent this is necessary to defend the foundations of the constitutional system, morality, public health, and the rights and legal interests of other persons and the defence of the country and security of the State. As for 'more favourable', the legislator has declared a policy of limiting such exceptions of 'an incentive character' to promoting the 'interests of the socio-economic development of the Russian Federation'.

[1] For a comparative analysis of the foreign investment laws of all CIS countries, see W E Butler, *Foreign Investment Law in the Commonwealth of Independent States* (2002).

[2] *СЗ РФ* (1999), no. 9, item 1096; (2000), no. 2, item 143; transl. in Butler, *Foreign Investment Law in the Commonwealth of Independent States* (2002), pp. 597–612. Also see: S S Shcherbinin, *Комментарий к закону «Об инвестиционной деятельности в Российской Федерации, осуществляемой в форме капитальных вложений»* [Commentary to Law on Investment Activity in the Russian Federation Effectuated in the Form of Capital Investments] (2003).

Foreign investor

Under the 1999 Federal Law on Foreign Investments, there are six categories of foreign investor: (1) foreign citizens, whose civil law capacity and dispositive legal capacity are determined in accordance with the legislation of the State of citizenship and who have the right in accordance with the legislation of the said State to effectuate investments on the territory of the Russian Federation; (2) stateless persons who reside permanently beyond the limits of the Russian Federation and whose civil law capacity and dispositive legal capacity are determined in accordance with the legislation of the State where they permanently reside and who have the right in accordance with legislation of that State to effectuate investments on the territory of the Russian Federation; (3) foreign juridical persons, the civil law capacity of whom is determined in accordance with the legislation of the State in which they were founded and who have the right in accordance with the legislation of that State to effectuate investments on the territory of the Russian Federation; (4) foreign organizations which are not juridical persons (e.g. the classic Anglo-American partnership) and whose civil law capacity is determined in accordance with the legislation where they are founded and which have the right in accordance with the legislation of that State to effectuate investments on the territory of the Russian Federation; (5) international organizations which, in accordance with an international treaty of the Russian Federation, have the right to effectuate investments on the territory of the Russian Federation; and (6) foreign States, which may become investors in Russia in accordance with the procedure determined by federal laws. **4.05**

So far as foreign citizens are concerned, there appears to be no criterion of residence required in a particular country. Citizenship is itself the crucial point of nexus for foreign investment purposes, and foreign investment legislation does not address issues of dual or multiple citizenships. Stateless persons under the 1999 Federal Law on Foreign Investments are required to have a permanent residence abroad, but there is no definition of what such residence comprises or whether it is determined by Russian criteria or the legislation of the State where the stateless person resides. There is, as is common in Russian legislative practice, an assumption that foreign countries share a legal concept of 'permanent residence'. However, it would appear that a stateless person permanently resident abroad who invests in Russia and then qualifies as being 'permanently residing' in the Russian Federation is no longer a foreign investor. **4.06**

No restriction is placed on the State of which an individual may be a citizen or permanently resident, nor is a change of citizenship apparently relevant so long as the individual remains a foreign citizen. The requirement that a foreign citizen or stateless person 'have the right in accordance with the legislation of the State of his citizenship or permanent residence' to invest in Russia must not be construed **4.07** too literally. No foreign country expressly authorizes its citizens or permanent residents to invest in Russia. At best, they may authorize citizens to invest abroad, but even that is uncommon. In the Anglo-American family of legal systems it is uncommon for individuals who wish to carry on business activity to register with a State agency for that purpose; the right to do so is assumed. The same applies to a foreign organization which is not a juridical person, for the foreign jurisdiction concerned is likely to confer general legal capacity on such entities rather than specifically authorize them to invest in the Russian Federation.

4.08 Foreign juridical persons are the most common foreign investors in the Russian Federation. They become investors either by founding themselves or co-founding with Russians one of the types of juridical person available under Russian civil legislation for this purpose. Juridical persons created and registered in the Russian Federation are classified as a 'commercial organization with foreign investments' from the day on which a foreign investor possesses not less than 10% of the participatory share(s) or contribution(s) to the charter or contributed capital of the said commercial organization. If such foreign investors 'reinvest' their profit, the Russian commercial organization also enjoys the legal defence, guarantees, and privileges established by the 1999 Federal Law on Foreign Investments. These do not extend, though, to subsidiaries or dependent societies of a commercial organization with foreign investments.

4.09 A Russian commercial organization receives the status of a commercial organization with foreign investments from the day that the participants of the foreign investor enter the composition of the said commercial organization and consequently the legal defence, guarantees, and privileges established by the 1999 Federal Law on Foreign Investments. The status of a commercial organization with foreign investments is lost from the day that the foreign investors withdraw from the participants (if there are several foreign investors, all must withdraw, it being unclear whether the minimum 10% criterion continues to operate for those who remain). The formulation of the investment requirement makes clear that joint-stock societies are not included within this concept, for stocks are neither participatory shares [доля] nor contributed [пай] capital. This is perhaps understandable, since the ownership of stocks may change several times in the course of a day in sufficient volume to alter the foreign investment and foreign investors in a juridical person.[3]

4.10 A foreign investor which does not wish to create a Russian juridical person as an investment vehicle may choose instead to create a 'branch' pursuant to the 1999

[3] This distinction was at issue in the Yukos bankruptcy litigation. See *In Re Yukos Oil Company, Debtor* 321 BR 396 (2005) (US Bankruptcy Court SD Texas, Houston Division) in W E Butler (ed.), *Russia and the Republics: Legal Materials* (2005–5).

Federal Law on Foreign Investments. A branch is not a juridical person in its own right. It performs part or all of the functions, including the function of representation, in the name of the foreign juridical person which created it on condition that the said foreign juridical person pursues purposes and activities of a commercial character and provided that the creating organization bears direct property responsibility for obligations assumed by it in connection with conducting its activities on the territory of the Russian Federation. The decision to create and liquidate a branch is taken by the head organization.

Control by the Russian Federation over the creation, activities, and liquidation of a branch takes the form of accreditation, which may be refused only on grounds of defence of the constitutional system, morality, public health, the rights and legal interests of other persons, or ensuring the defence of the country and security of the State. A branch operates on the basis of a Statute which specifies the name of the branch and its head organization; location in Russia; legal address of the head organization; purposes for creation and types of activity to be undertaken; the composition, amount, and periods for investing capital in the basic funds of the branch; and procedure for management of the branch. The investing of capital in the basic funds of a branch is valued by the head organization on the basis of internal prices or world prices, but in the currency of the Russian Federation. A branch has the right to engage in entrepreneurial activity in the Russian Federation from the day of accreditation and terminates such activity on the day it is deprived of accreditation. **4.11**

International organizations such as The World Bank or the European Bank for Reconstruction and Development also make investments on a substantial scale. Russian international legal doctrine considers an international organization to be an 'inter-State' or 'intergovernmental' organization established on the basis of an international treaty and operating as subjects of public international law. In Russian practice, the term international organization would not reach what is commonly styled an NGO, or international nongovernmental organization. **4.12**

In the absence of a treaty, an international organization is subject to the same legal regime as other foreign investors. There are no special general rules regulating the legal relations in which international organizations may be participants in Russia. Individual investment projects, however, involving international organizations, are sometimes the subject of individual presidential edicts or governmental decrees, and international organizations enjoy a special tax regime, as a rule, that can be beneficial for investment projects. **4.13**

Foreign investment

Privileges and special status are sometimes directed towards the particular investment rather than the investor. Russian legislation defines a 'foreign **4.14** investment' in general and then distinguishes between a 'direct foreign investment' and a 'priority investment project'. Foreign investment is defined as a process; the investing of foreign capital in 'an object of entrepreneurial activity' on the territory of the Russian Federation. The investing is 'in the form of objects of civil rights', provided that these have not been withdrawn from or limited in turnover in Russia in accordance with federal legislation. Examples of such objects of civil rights are money, securities (whether in foreign or Russian currency), other property, property rights having the monetary value or exclusive rights to the results of intellectual activity, services, and information.

4.15 A direct foreign investment comprises the acquisition by a foreign investor of not less than a 10% participatory share or contributed capital in the charter capital of a commercial organization created or newly formed on the territory of the Russian Federation in the form of an economic partnership or society pursuant to civil legislation of the Russian Federation. It also includes the investing of capital in the basic funds of a branch of a foreign juridical person created on the territory of Russia, or the foreign investor acting as the finance lessor of equipment specified in certain sections of the Goods Nomenclature of Foreign Activity of the Commonwealth of Independent States, provided the equipment has a customs value of not less than one million rubles.

4.16 A priority investment project involves a direct investment whose total volume is valued at not less than one billion rubles or the equivalent in foreign currency or in which the minimum participatory share is one hundred million rubles.

4.17 Reinvestment also is a form of investing that carries guarantees and privileges. The effectuation of capital investments in objects of entrepreneurial activity on the territory of the Russian Federation from the revenues or profit of a foreign investor or commercial organization with foreign investments which have been received by them from the foreign investments constitutes reinvesting.

4.18 Relations connected with investment activity in the form of capital investments by foreign investors on the territory of the Russian Federation also are regulated by the 1999 Federal Law on Investment Activity in the Russian Federation Effectuated in the Form of Capital Investments.[4]

Guarantees

4.19 The 1999 Federal Law on Foreign Investments contains eleven principal guarantees to foreign investors. Most of them have a renvoi character; that is, they are mentioned in the foreign investment law but their substance is to be found in other legislation.

[4] Transl. in W E Butler, *Russian Company and Commercial Legislation* (2003), p. 828.

Legal defence

This guarantee consists of two parts. The first is an assurance that a foreign investor is granted the full and unconditional defence of the rights and interests set out in the 1999 Federal Law on Foreign Investments, other federal laws and normative legal acts, and international treaties of the Russian Federation. The means of legal defence available are in effect the national regime of such means of defence available to Russian investors, subject to any special requirements or privileges for foreigners. **4.20**

The second part is the right to compensation for losses caused to the foreign investor by the illegal action or failure to act of State agencies, agencies of local self-government, and officials of those agencies. Compensation is determined in accordance with civil legislation of the Russian Federation, which is a reference to the Civil Code (Article 15). Losses are defined by the Civil Code as '. . . expenses which the person whose right has been violated made or must make in order to restore the violated right, loss or damage of his property (real damage) and . . . revenues not received which this person would have received under ordinary conditions of civil turnover if his right had not been violated (lost advantage)'. **4.21**

Use of various forms of investing

This guarantee consists of assuring foreign investors that they have the right to effectuate foreign investments on the territory of the Russian Federation in any forms that are not prohibited by Russian legislation. The valuation of capital invested in the charter or contributed capital of a commercial organization with foreign investments is undertaken in accordance with Russian legislation. **4.22**

This formulation, as noted above, employs terminology which excludes the purchase and sale of stocks from the requirement of valuation. **4.23**

Transfer of rights and duties to another

This guarantee is directed towards reinforcing the normal rights granted to natural and juridical persons under the Civil Code of the Russian Federation to transfer or assign rights and duties or demands and debts. The legislator has in view especially Chapter 24 of the Civil Code, addressing the change of persons in an obligation. The 1999 Federal Law on Foreign Investments goes out of its way to specifically acknowledge the legality of a transaction under which, pursuant to a contract of guarantee or insurance, a foreign State or State agency is subrogated to the rights of a foreign investor, having made payments to the foreign investor or other designated beneficiary under the guarantee or insurance contract. **4.24**

This foreign investment guarantee is broadly drawn and must be read against potential limitations on the transfer or assignment of rights, duties, demands, and **4.25** debts that may be contained in concession, special economic zone, production sharing, or other legislation involving particular types of foreign investment.

Contributory compensation in event of nationalization or requisition

4.26 Strictly read, this guarantee protects the 'property of a foreign investor or commercial organization with foreign investments' against 'compulsory seizure, including nationalization or requisition . . .' unless provided otherwise by a federal law or international treaty of the Russian Federation. The formulation of the guarantee approaches disingenuity for several reasons. First, the term 'property' is used, rather than ownership, and this leaves open the possibility of a construction that would encompass only tangible property, excluding intangibles. Second, there are at least eleven terms in the Russian language for forms of the 'taking' of property: nationalization, requisition, seizure, expropriation, sequestration, confiscation, withdrawal, withholding, socialization, monopolization, and taking. None are synonymous, and it is doubtful those unnamed are covered. Third, the provision offers 'contributory compensation', which is the same word in Russian used to provide compensation to pensioners for inflation. It is not the same as full compensation, for which a different word is applicable. Fourth, read against the guarantee of repatriation of contributory compensation received, difficulties could arise with regard to the scope of the right of repatriation.

4.27 Enforcement of a Russian judicial decision by bailiffs for the recovery of tax arrears will not be regarded, as a matter of Russian law, as falling under this guarantee for foreign investors.

Unfavourable changes

4.28 The guarantee here, which extends to foreign investors and commercial organizations with foreign investments, is lengthy, complex, and subject to exceptions and qualifications. If new federal laws or other normative legal acts of the Russian Federation change the amounts of customs duties on imports, or federal taxes, or contributions to State extrabudgetary funds, or if changes and additions made to federal laws and other normative legal acts of the Russian Federation in force lead to an increase of the aggregate tax load on the activity with regard to the realization of priority investment projects, or they establish a regime of prohibitions and limitations with respect to foreign investments in comparison with that operating on the day when the financing of a priority investment project commenced from foreign investments, these new enactments or changes and additions do not apply for the period of recoupment of the investment project, but not exceeding seven years from the date such financing from foreign investments commenced.

4.29 The exceptions are several. The guarantee against customs duties does not apply to measures relating to defence of the economic interests of the Russian

Federation when effectuating foreign trade in goods. The guarantee against federal taxes and extrabudgetary funds does not extend to excises and value-added tax on goods produced in Russia, nor to contributions to the Pension Fund of the Russian Federation. And commercial organizations with foreign investments enjoy this guarantee only if the said organization has more than 25% foreign investment or is realizing a priority investment project. In exceptional instances the Government of the Russian Federation may extend the guarantee to certain specified priority investment projects in designated areas of activity. Moreover, the guarantee does not extend in general to changes and additions made to legislative acts of the Russian Federation or newly adopted legislation introduced for the purpose of defending the foundations of the constitutional system, morality, public health, rights and legal interests of other persons, and ensuring the defence and security of the State.

The criteria for evaluating changes of conditions for the recovery of customs duties on imports, federal taxes, and contributions to State extrabudgetary funds and the regime of prohibitions and limitations for effectuating foreign investments in Russia which are unfavourable are determined by the Government of the Russian Federation. If the foreign investor or commercial organization with foreign investments fails to perform obligations connected with this guarantee, the privileges may be revoked and monies paid pursuant to the privileges are subject to being refunded to the Russian Federation. **4.30**

Settlement of disputes

This is largely a renvoi guarantee, for it provides that a dispute of a foreign investor which has arisen in connection with the effectuation of investment and entrepreneurial activity on the territory of the Russian Federation shall be settled in accordance with international treaties of the Russian Federation and federal laws in a court or arbitrazh court, or in international arbitration or in an arbitration court. The reference to a court or arbitrazh court has in view Russian courts. A system of arbitration courts exists in the Russian Federation within the system of arbitrazh courts. International arbitrations may be commenced either in the Russian Federation or abroad. **4.31**

The reference to the availability of these means of dispute settlement does not mean that any party to a foreign investment dispute has consented to the jurisdiction of any particular court or arbitration tribunal as and when a dispute arises. This guarantee merely makes available in principle these options for dispute settlement to the foreign investor subject to the special jurisdictional requirements for each court or tribunal. Nor does this provision indicate in any way that the Russian Federation has consented to any form of jurisdiction in the event of being named a defendant or respondent to a suit by a foreign investor. **4.32**

4.33 Nor does this guarantee override procedural formalities in Russian arbitrazh courts. A foreign juridical person which is a foreign investor, for example, must prove in order to claim guarantees under the Foreign Investment Law that it is a foreigner by submitting documents to this effect. It is not sufficient, as confirmed by the Information Letter of the Supreme Arbitrazh Court of the Russian Federation of 18 January 2001, No. 58, that the documents confirming the status of a foreign juridical person be attested by a foreign consular service. Such documents must be legalized by diplomatic or consular services of the Russian Federation in the foreign State where the documents were made. Otherwise the documents are not admissible as evidence in the case and do not confirm the legal status of the foreign juridical person.

Use of revenues, profit, and other amounts

4.34 After the payment of taxes and charges provided for by Russian legislation a foreign investor is guaranteed the right to the free use of revenues and profits for the purpose of reinvesting or for other purposes not contrary to Russian legislation. Such free use includes the right to repatriate revenues and other lawfully received monetary amounts in foreign currency in connection with investments previously effectuated by him. 'Revenues' includes proceeds in the form of profit, dividends, interest, and other revenues; monetary amounts in the performance of obligations of a commercial organization with foreign investments or a foreign juridical person which open a branch in Russia with regard to contracts and other transactions; monetary amounts received by a foreign investor in connection with the liquidation of a commercial organization with foreign investments or a branch of a foreign juridical person, or with the alienation of invested property, property rights, and exclusive rights to the results of intellectual property; and contributory compensation received in connection with nationalization or requisition of a foreign investment or part thereof.

4.35 The national currency of the Russian Federation remains a nonconvertible currency, although many of the foreign currency controls that hindered foreign investors have been attenuated or removed. This guarantee needs to be read especially against potential or existing foreign exchange controls. Money-laundering controls in place in the Russian Federation also are of relevance to this guarantee, and the foreign investor may be required to relate particular funds in his bank accounts to particular transactions or sources of revenue.

Unhindered export of property or information in documentary or electronic form

4.36 Property and information brought into the Russian Federation by a foreign investor in documentary or electronic form as a foreign investment may be re-exported without quotas, licensing, or the application of other nontariff measures by the foreign investor. Evidence will be required to establish that what is being re-exported is what was imported, and the law is silent as to whether upgraded or supplemented information, for example, qualifies under this guarantee.

Acquisition of securities

This guarantee essentially reinforces the position under Russian civil legislation that a foreign investor has the right to acquire stocks and other securities of Russian commercial organizations and State securities in accordance with Russian securities legislation. The legal definition of 'securities' under Russian legislation is broader than in many countries and includes, in addition to stocks and bonds, such items as bills of exchange, bills of lading, and cheques. Participatory shares and shares in Russian juridical persons are not securities under Russian law. **4.37**

Participation in privatization

This guarantee is, upon close reading, virtually devoid of substance. As formulated, a foreign investor may participate in the privatization of objects of State and municipal ownership by means of the acquisition of the rights of ownership to State and municipal property or participatory share(s) or contribution(s) to the charter or contributed capital of the organization being privatized. However, this participation is on the conditions and in the procedure established by Russian privatization legislation, which actually excludes foreign participation in individual instances when this is deemed undesirable for policy reasons. **4.38**

Right to land plots and other immoveable property

There is no real guarantee in this formulation, which says that the acquisition by a foreign investor of the right to land plots, other natural resources, buildings, installations, and other immoveable property is effectuated in accordance with legislation of the Russian Federation and of subjects of the Russian Federation. A Russian juridical person which is a commercial organization with foreign investments may lease a land plot, provided that the right to lease is acquired at a public sale, competition or auction and unless Russian legislation provides otherwise. **4.39**

The limitations on the ownership of immoveables by foreign citizens, stateless persons, and foreign juridical persons are discussed in Chapter 6 below. In substance this guarantee is a renvoi reference to those limitations. **4.40**

Privileges

With respect to customs duties, privileges are granted to foreign investors and commercial organizations with foreign investments only if they are undertaking a priority investment and only if customs legislation makes privileges available in this event. Subjects of the Russian Federation and agencies of local **4.41** self-government may within the limits of their competence grant privileges and guarantees to a foreign investor at the expense of their respective budgets or extra-budgetary funds.

B. Special Economic Zones

4.42 Special economic zones have enjoyed a chequered history since the days of perestroika in the former Soviet Union. Initially they were viewed as a mechanism for creating a mini-market economy within a Soviet planned economy. When an independent Russian Federation decided to introduce a market economy on a nationwide scale, special economic zones nonetheless offered a mechanism for creating an economic and legal infrastructure even more favourable than the national regime and a possible laboratory for experimenting with various market institutions.

4.43 The initiative for free economic zones came from below. On 14 July 1990 the Supreme Soviet of the RSFSR adopted the Decree 'On the Creation of Free Entrepreneurship Zones' which accepted the 'proposals' of the cities of Leningrad and Vyborg and of the Maritime Territory (including the city of Nakhodka) and the regional soviets of Kaliningrad, Sakhalin, and Chita to declare their territories to be free entrepreneurship zones.[5] Between July 1990 and July 1991 twelve free economic zones were created by a series of governmental decrees and regulations issued by the Chairman of the Supreme Soviet; that is, these zones were created by subordinate normative legal acts. The great majority of these zones experienced difficulties that most found to be insuperable. The fact that so many were created by subordinate normative legal acts meant that the privileges conferred on them constituted exceptions to superior laws and other legislative acts. State agencies, especially the Ministry of Finances, refused to recognize these exemptions and privileges. So long as the tax privileges were doubtful, as they proved in practice to be, foreign investors had no interest. By 1996 eighteen free economic zones had been formally established on fifteen territories which collectively comprised about one-third of the territory of the Russian Federation.

4.44 The 2005 Federal Law on Special Economic Zones in the Russian Federation[6]

[5] *Ведомости Верховного Совета РСФСР* (1990), no. 7, item 107. This Decree was clarified procedurally in a subsequent Decree bearing an identical title and adopted 13 September 1990. Both are translated in W E Butler, *Basic Documents of the Russian Legal System* (1992), pp. 289–91. For a candid account of the political difficulties encountered by proponents of free or special economic zones, see V V Ivechko and L V Samoilova, *Свободные экономические зоны в зарубежных странах и России: Учебное пособие* [Free Economic Zones in Foreign Countries and Russia: Instructional Manual] (Kaliningrad, 1999), pp. 58–88.

[6] *СЗ РФ* (2005), no. 30(II), item 3125; (2006), no. 23, item 2383.

represents an attempt to bring order and attractiveness to an idea which generated a certain amount of chaos in practice and disappointment of expectations that such zones would become a major instigator of economic growth and foreign investment. It is disingenuous in providing that 'legislation of the Russian Federation on special economic zones consists of the present Federal Law, edicts of the President of the Russian Federation, decrees of the Government of the Russian Federation, and normative legal acts adopted in accordance with them' (Article 1). Most zones in existence were created by presidential edict or government decree, and each zone authority has enacted dozens, if not hundreds, of normative legal acts regulating zone activities. The 2005 Federal Law on Special Economic Zones abolished existing special economic zones and free economic zones created before its entry into force except two: the Kaliningrad Region Special Economic Zone and the Magadan Region Special Economic Zone (Article 40).

The Kaliningrad and Magadan special economic zones continue to be exceptions to the 2005 Federal Law on Special Economic Zones. The Special Economic Zone in the Kaliningrad Region is regulated by the 2006 Federal Law on the Special Economic Zone in the Kaliningrad Region and on the Making of Changes in Certain Legislative Acts of the Russian Federation,[7] and not by government decree. In numerous basic respects the Kaliningrad Special Economic Zone differs from the model introduced by the 2005 Federal Law on Special Economic Zones. The existence of the Kaliningrad Special Economic Zone is to be twenty-five years, and it is unclear whether that period is measured by the 2006 law or from the moment when it was established. The Magadan Zone, created in 1999, has a life until the year 2014 and, as in the case of Kaliningrad, differs from the new model being introduced.[8] **4.45**

The Government of the Russian Federation, however, on 21 December 2005 created special economic zones in the City of Moscow (technical-introductory type),[9] City of Tomsk (technical-introductory type),[10] City of St. Petersburg (technical-introductory type),[11] City of Dubno, Moscow Region (technical-introductory type),[12] Griazinskii District in Lipetsk Region (industrial production type),[13] and Elabuzhsk District in the Republic Tatarstan (industrial production type).[14] **4.46**

---

[7] *СЗ РФ* (2006), no. 3, item 280. This Federal Law replaces the Federal Law on the Special Economic Zone in the Kaliningrad Region of 22 January 1996. *СЗ РФ* (1996), no. 4, item 224. Normative legal acts adopted to realize the Federal Law of 22 January 1996 and in force on the day of the entry into force of the 2006 Federal Law remain in force insofar as not contrary to the 2006 Federal Law.

[8] *СЗ РФ* (1999), no. 23, item 2807; (2005), no. 52(I), item 5575; no. 52(II), item 5602.

[9] *СЗ РФ* (2005), no. 52(III), item 5742.

[10] *СЗ РФ* (2005), no. 52(III), item 5746.

[11] *СЗ РФ* (2005), no. 52(III), item 5743.

[12] *СЗ РФ* (2005), no. 52(III), item 5744.

[13] *СЗ РФ* (2005), no. 52(III), item 5745.

[14] *СЗ РФ* (2005), no. 52(III), item 5747.

4.47 The general administration of special economic zones is entrusted to the Federal Agency for the Administration of Special Zones, which is within the jurisdiction of the Ministry of Economic Development and Trade of the Russian Federation. The powers of the Federal Agency include: (1) conducting competitions and concluding State contracts for placing orders for the delivery of goods, rendering of services, and fulfilment of work, including scientific research, experimental construction design, and technological work for State needs, such needs including those of the Federal Agency; (2) exercising the powers of owner with respect to federal power necessary to ensure the performance of the functions of federal agencies of State power, including property transferred to federal State unitary enterprises and federal State institutions within the jurisdiction of the Federal Agency; (3) administering special economic zones in the procedure and within the limits established by Russian legislation; (4) selecting applications for the creation of special economic zones of the same type;[15] (5) organizing the data bank of land plots allotted for the creation of special economic zones and immoveables on the territory of such zones; (6) monitoring the realization of agreements on the creation of economic zones; (7) registering juridical persons and individual entrepreneurs as residents of a special economic zone; and (8) formalizing upon the application of a resident invitations for the entry of foreign citizens to the Russian Federation in order to effectuate labour activity; and others. These powers are elaborated in the Statute on the Federal Agency for Administration of Special Economic Zones, confirmed by a 2005 Decree of the Government of the Russian Federation, as amended.[16]

Configurations of special economic zones

4.48 Conceptually, a special economic zone is a portion of the territory of the Russian Federation determined by the Government of Russia on which a special regime operates for entrepreneurial activity. Three types of special economic zones may be created: (1) industrial production special economic zones; (2) technical-introductory special economic zones; and (3) tourist-recreational special economic zones.

---

[15] Such applications are submitted by the highest executive agencies of State power of subjects of the Russian Federation jointly with the executive-administrative agencies of municipal formations to the Ministry of Economic Development and Trade of the Russian Federation. See the Statute on Holding a Competition for the Selection of Applications to Create Special Economic Zones, confirmed by a 2005 Decree of the Government of the Russian Federation, No. 563. *СЗ РФ* (2005), no. 38, item 3821. The competitions are arranged according to the Rules for the Formalization and Filing of an Application to Create a Special Economic Zone, confirmed by a 2005 Decree of the Government of the Russian Federation, No. 564. *СЗ РФ* (2005), no. 38, item 3822.

[16] *СЗ РФ* (2005), no. 35, item 3611; no. 48, item 5049. The Reglement of the Federal Agency for the Administration of Special Economic Zones was confirmed by Order No. 24, 6 October 2005, of the Ministry of Economic Development and Trade of the Russian Federation. See ConsultantPlus for the text.

The industrial production zone may be created on parcels of territory not exceeding twenty square kilometers; industrial production is understood in the 2005 Federal Law on Special Economic Zones to mean the production and/or processing of goods or products and the realization thereof. **4.49**

The second type of zone, the technical-introductory zone, may be created on not more than two parcels of territory which in aggregate are not larger than three square kilometers. This type of zone is concerned with the creation and realization of a scientific-technical product and bringing it to industrial application, including manufacture, testing, realization of experimental lots and the creation of software products, collection systems, the processing and transfer of data, computer systems, and services relating to the introduction and servicing of such products and systems. Tourist-recreational zones are created on territories whose dimensions are determined by the Government of Russia. **4.50**

There are additional spatial limitations. A special economic zone may not be situated on the territories of several municipal formations, nor may the territory of such a zone encompass the entire territory of any administrative-territorial formation (except tourist-recreational zones). Housing may not be sited on the territory of a special economic zone (excluding tourist), nor may the following activities be engaged in on the territory of such a zone: (1) the extraction of minerals and metallurgical production as enumerated in the All-Russian Classificator of Types of Economic Activity; (2) the processing of minerals or scrap of ferrous and nonferrous metals; or (3) the production and processing of goods subject to excise tax, except for motor vehicles and motorcycles – all subject to exceptions for tourist-recreational zones. The Government of the Russian Federation when creating a special economic zone determines the types of activity authorized for that territory. And the resident of a special economic zone may not have branches and representations outside the territory of the zone. **4.51**

Moreover, special economic zones may be created only on land plots which are in State and/or municipal ownership, although for tourist-recreational zones there may be elements of private ownership. In the case of technical-introductory zones there may be an exception for land plots in the possession or use of educational and/or scientific research institutions. The same exception extends to objects situated on the land plots. **4.52**

Creation of special economic zones

Only the Government of the Russian Federation has the right to create a special economic zone, a decision which is formalized by a decree. This effectively removes the creation of zones from the President of the Russian Federation. The initiative to create a zone formally comes from below: the highest executive **4.53** agency of State power of a subject of the Russian Federation jointly with an executive-administrative agency of a municipal formation files a substantiated application with the Government of the Russian Federation, making a case that the creation of a special economic zone would help resolve tasks of federal, regional, and local significance. The procedure for making such an application is determined by the Government of the Russian Federation, which may hold a competition to select an application for confirmation, pursuant to the 2005 Statute and Rules for Holding a Competition for the Selection of Application to Create Special Economic Zones.

4.54 Once the Government adopts a decision to create a special economic zone, an agreement is concluded within thirty days. The agreement must determine: (1) the amount and periods for financing the creation of the engineering, transport, and social infrastructure of the special economic zone from the budgets of the federal, subject of the Russian Federation, and local levels; (2) the plan for public amenities and respective material-technical equipping of the special economic zone and adjacent territories; (3) the complex of measures for working out the long-term development plan for the zone and the procedure for financing them; (4) the participatory shares of the Russian Federation, subject of the Russian Federation, and municipal formation in the common participatory share ownership in objects of the engineering, transport, and social infrastructure of the zone; (5) the procedure for the operation and maintenance, including capital repair, of infrastructure objects of the zone in common participatory share ownership; (6) the procedure for the possession, use, and disposition of infrastructure objects in common participatory share ownership after the existence of the zone is terminated; (7) the obligations of agencies of State power of the subject of the Russian Federation with regard to granting tax privileges to zone residents; (8) the procedure for forming the supervisory council of the zone; (9) the obligations with regard to delegating powers with regard to the administration and disposition of land plots and other immoveables within the territory of the zone; (10) the obligations of the municipal formation to delegate rights to administer and dispose of land plots and other immoveables in municipal ownership within the territory of the zone; and (11) other conditions provided for by the 2005 Federal Law on Special Economic Zones.

4.55 The existence of a zone may be terminated if this is necessary for the security interests of Russia, or if within three years from the date of creating the zone not a single agreement has been concluded for the industrial production or technical-introductory activity, or such agreements have been dissolved, or if for three years in succession the residents of the zone have not conducted any activity. The Government of Russia decides whether to terminate the existence of a zone or not.

Management of Special Economic Zones

The 2005 Federal Law on Special Economic Zones contemplates a unified approach to zone management from the federal level. A supervisory council of each zone will coordinate the activities of the three levels of State involvement in the zone, oversee the fulfilment of the agreement to create the zone and the expenditure of budget resources allotted, and consider and confirm long-term development plans for the zone. **4.56**

The members of the supervisory council will be drawn from each level of State involvement in the zone, representatives of zone residents, and other organizations. If the zone is concerned with the introduction of technology, the supervisory council also may include representatives of educational and scientific research organizations which operate within the boundaries of the municipal formation on whose territory the special economic zone is situated. The powers of the supervisory council are determined by the Statute on the Supervisory Council of a Special Economic Zone, confirmed by the Government of the Russian Federation.[17] **4.57**

The management organs of a special economic zone: (1) register juridical persons and individual entrepreneurs as zone residents and keep the resident register; (2) issue extracts from the resident register at the request of residents or interested persons; (3) submit a report on the results of the functioning of the zone annually not later than 1 July following the end of the reporting year to the relevant federal agency of executive power; (4) effectuate control over the performance by zone residents of the agreement to conduct industrial production or technical-introductory activity; (5) publish not less than once a quarter in printed and electronic mass media determined by the Government of Russia information concerning land plots not leased or other State and/or municipal property; (6) formalize at the request of zone residents invitations to foreign citizens to enter the Russian Federation to effectuate labour activity; (7) fulfil the functions of customer for the preparation of documentation on planning the territory of the zone and creating engineering, social, and other infrastructure from the budgets of all State levels; (8) manage and dispose of immoveables on the territory of the zone and in State and/or municipal ownership in the procedure established by the agreement on the creation of the zone; (9) ensure the expert examination of draft documentation; (10) issue authorizations for construction and receive technical conditions for accessing networks of engineering and technical provision and transfer them to citizens and juridical persons **4.58**

[17] See the Statute on the Supervisory Council of a Special Economic Zone, confirmed by a 2005 Decree of the Government of the Russian Federation, No. 758 as amended 4 August 2006. *СЗ РФ* (2005), no. 51, item 5544.

effectuating construction or reconstruction; and (11) exercise other powers provided for by the 2005 Federal Law on Special Economic Zones.

Legal status of zone residents

4.59 A commercial organization, excluding a unitary enterprise, registered in accordance with Russian legislation on the territory of the municipal formation within whose boundaries the zone is located, and which has concluded with the management organs of the zone an agreement on conducting industrial production activity, is deemed to be a resident of an industrial production special economic zone. The definition of a resident in a technical-introductory zone is identical except that an individual entrepreneur, as well as a commercial organization, may be a resident, and in a tourist-recreational zone the same, except that State unitary enterprises are excluded. A commercial organization may have foreign investments under the Civil Code of the Russian Federation, although the 2005 Federal Law on Special Economic Zones makes no special reference to foreigners and stateless persons.

4.60 Management organs of the zone register commercial organizations and individual entrepreneurs as residents within three days after the signature with them of an agreement to conduct industrial production or technical-introductory activity. A registration certificate is issued to the resident, and the tax and customs agencies are notified of the registration and supplied with a copy of the agreement on conducting activity.

4.61 A resident may be deprived of that status only in a judicial proceeding in the instances provided by the 2005 Federal Law on Special Economic Zones. Deprivation of resident status automatically terminates the agreement on conducting activity in the zone. The fact of deprivation is recorded in the zone register and notification is also sent to tax and customs agencies.

State control on zone territory

4.62 In addition to the supervisory council, which operates as an agency of a special economic zone, State control or supervision is exercised by other federal agencies of executive power in accordance with the 2001 Federal Law 'On Defence of the Rights of Juridical Persons and Individual Entrepreneurs When Conducting State Control (or Supervision)'.[18] Except for tax and customs control, verifications must be of a 'planned integrated' nature carried out by agreement with the management organs of the special economic zone on the basis of decisions adopted by the management organs. The subject of the verification and period

[18] *СЗ РФ* (2001), no. 33(I), item 3436.

when it will be conducted must be specified. A verification may not exceed two weeks in duration.

If violations of law are discovered during a verification, the resident concerned is issued a 'prescription' under receipt to eliminate the violations specified. An extraordinary verification may be undertaken by the State control agencies concerned two months or more after the prescription is issued. If the violation has not been eliminated, the resident may be deprived of his status as resident by decision of a court upon the application of the control agency concerned. Extraordinary verifications nonetheless require the consent of the zone management organs. **4.63**

During a verification a resident has the right to be present and give explanations regarding questions relevant to the subject of the verification, receive information provided for by normative legal acts of the Russian Federation, familiarize himself with the results of the control measures and indicate agreement or disagreement with the acts drawn up by the officials of the State control agencies, and appeal the actions or failure to act of officials of State control agencies in an administrative or judicial proceeding. **4.64**

Tax and customs agencies perform control functions in accordance with Russian legislation. Two or more material violations by a zone resident of tax or customs legislation may result in deprivation of the status of resident if the said agencies petition a court to impose such a sanction. **4.65**

Agreements to conduct activity in zone

The key document around which the special economic zone is conceptualized is an agreement, or contract, to conduct industrial production or technical-introductory activity in the zone. The agreement is concluded between a zone resident and the zone management organs. Under such an agreement the zone resident is obliged within the period stipulated in the agreement to conduct the agreed activity on the territory of the special economic zone and to make investments in the amount and within the periods provided for by the agreement. The management organs of the special economic zone are obliged within the period provided for by the agreement to conclude with the resident a lease contract for a land plot within the zone and to effect the cadastre recording of the land plot at the expense of the resident for the period of operation of the agreement unless the resident stipulated a briefer period. **4.66**

The minimum investment in rubles is the equivalent at the exchange rate of the Central Bank of Russia of ten million euros, excluding the value of intangible assets, on the day of concluding the agreement. Of this sum, one million euros must be invested at the ruble equivalent on the day of submitting the application **4.67** during the course of not more than one year from the day of concluding the agreement. These amounts are separate from the lease payments to be made for leasing the land plot from the management organs of the zone.

4.68 Model or standard lease agreements and agreements to conduct activities in the zone are confirmed by the federal agency of executive power which effectuates the normative legal regulation in the domain of creating and the functioning of special economic zones. The documents needed to conclude an agreement to conduct activity in a special economic zone differ slightly, depending upon the type of zone. Basically, however, they comprise the following: (1) information on the proposed activity of the applicant which corresponds to the type of special economic zone; (2) information of the land plot needed for the proposed activity; and (3) information on the proposed amounts of capital investments, including those to be made within a year from the day of concluding the agreement to conduct activity in the zone. To the application must be appended: (1) a copy of the certificate of State registration of the juridical person; (2) a copy of the certificate of registration with the tax authorities; (3) a copy of the constitutive documents; (4) a business plan according to the form established by the federal agency responsible for special economic zones; and (5) a positive opinion on the business plan prepared by a bank or credit organization according to the criteria established by the federal agency responsible for special economic zones. Within ten working days from receipt of the foregoing documents the management organs of the special economic zone send one of the following decisions to the applicant: (1) to conclude an agreement on conducting activity in the zone; or (2) to refuse to conclude such an agreement with reasons given.

4.69 A refusal to conclude an agreement is permitted only in the event of the failure to submit the documents specified or if there is no land plot available on the territory of the zone which meets the conditions specified in the application, or if the activity proposed by the applicant does not conform to the types of activity authorized for the economic zone, or if the capital investments proposed do not satisfy the minimums established by Russian legislation for this purpose, or if the business plan does not meet the conditions specified in the application. A refusal to conclude an agreement may be appealed to a court.

4.70 If a positive decision to conclude an agreement with the applicant has been taken, the management organs of the special economic zone prepare a draft contract for the application which takes effect from the moment of signature. The form of the contract must be (a) in writing, and (b) comprise a single document (which is a departure from the Civil Code of the Russian Federation). The period of validity may not exceed the termination of the existence of the special economic zone. A resident of a zone who wishes to alter the conditions of the agreement may submit a proposal to do so to the management organs of the zone, together with a business plan and bank or credit organization opinion on the plan. The management organs must accept or reject the proposed change within ten working days from the day of receipt of the application to alter the contract.

An agreement to conduct activity in a special economic zone terminates: (1) upon the expiry of the period for which it was concluded; (2) in the event of dissolution of the agreement; (3) in the event of termination of the lease of the land plot unless the lease contract is dissolved by reason of purchase of the plot; (4) if the resident of the zone is deprived of that status; or (5) in the event of termination before time of the existence of the special economic zone. Dissolution may be by agreement of the parties or in court upon the demand of one party by reason of a material violation of the agreement by the other party, a material change of circumstances, and on other grounds permitted by the 2005 Federal Law on Special Economic Zones. **4.71**

The 2005 Federal Law on Special Economic Zones defines in some detail what would be considered to be a material violation: (1) the failure to submit draft documentation to the management organs of the zone for expert evaluation and agreement; (2) the failure to make capital investments in the amounts and within the periods provided for by the agreement on conducting activity in the zone; and (3) the effectuation of entrepreneurial activity on the territory of the special economic zone which is not provided for by the agreement on conducting activity in the zone. The resident may seek dissolution of the contract to conduct activity in the zone if the management organs refuse to conclude a lease contract for the land plot or for State and/or municipal property. The parties have the right to determine other circumstances which may be deemed by them to be material violations in the agreement to conduct activity. Equally, the management organs of the zone may dissolve an agreement to conduct activity in court if the expert evaluation of the draft documentation is negative and within a reasonable period the documentation is not reworked, in which event the expenses of the resident are not compensated. **4.72**

The consequences of termination of the agreement to conduct activity in the zone are several. First, the person who concluded the contract loses the status of resident of the economic zone. But he may continue to engage in entrepreneurial activity on the territory of the special economic zone on the general grounds (that is, without the preferences which the status of resident gives). Someone who has lost the status of resident has the right to dispose of moveable and immoveable property belonging to him which is on the territory of the zone at his discretion, subject to any customs regulations, in accordance with Russian civil legislation. In the event of termination of the agreement to conduct activity in the zone before time by reason of a material violation, the resident of the zone **4.73** must pay a fine in the amount determined in the agreement. The lease of land and/or State or municipal property concluded with the resident also terminates together with the termination of the contract to conduct activity in the zone.

Taxation

4.74 Residents of a special economic zone are subject to taxation in the Russian Federation in accordance with legislation on taxes and charges. However, a free customs zone operates in a special economic zone under which foreign goods are placed and used within the zone without the payment of customs duties or value-added tax, or without the application to those goods of prohibitions and limitations of an economic character established by Russian legislation on the State regulation of foreign trade activity. Russian goods are placed and used in the zone on conditions applicable to being carried out in accordance with the customs regime for export with payment of excises and without payment of export customs duties.

4.75 The sources of the goods under the customs regime of a free customs zone are threefold: (1) those brought into the customs territory of the Russian Federation from foreign States; (2) those brought in to the territory of the special economic zone from another part of the customs territory of the Russian Federation; and (3) those on the territory of the special economic zone and acquired from persons who are not residents of the special economic zone. The Government of the Russian Federation has the right when adopting a decision to create a special economic zone to establish a List of prohibited operations with goods situated on the territory of the special economic zone.

Guarantees for residents of special economic zones

4.76 The 2005 Federal Law on Special Economic Zones attempts to address the fundamental flaw of earlier special economic zones in the Russian Federation: taxation. The solution is expressed in terms of a guarantee against an unfavourable change of legislation of the Russian Federation on taxes and charges:

> acts of legislation of the Russian Federation on taxes and charges, laws of subjects of the Russian Federation on taxes and charges, and normative legal acts of agencies of local self-government on taxes and charges which worsen the position of resident taxpayers of special economic zones, except for acts of legislation of the Russian Federation on taxes and charges concerning the taxation of goods subject to excise, shall not apply with respect to residents of special economic zones during the period of operation of the agreement on conducting industrial production or technical-introductory activity (Article 38).

4.77 An equivalent provision in the Tax Code of the Russian Federation would strengthen the guarantee, but the fact remains that the law latest in time governs.

On more than one occasion the Russian authorities have introduced new legislation without due regard to pre-existing privileges and exemptions in taxation for special economic zones.

Settlement of disputes

Disputes connected with the creation of termination of the existence of a special economic zone or a violation by a resident of the conditions in an agreement on conducting activity on the territory of the zone or other disputes arising from relations regulated by the 2005 Federal law on Special Economic Zones are subject to resolution in a judicial proceeding in accordance with legislation of the Russian Federation (Article 39). **4.78**

C. Concession Agreements

Concession arrangements have been an element of Russian foreign investment policies since the early days of the New Economic Policy of the Soviet era, actually predating the formation of the Union of Soviet Socialist Republics.[19] Those actually formed during the 1920s were mostly phased out by the late 1930s, although some in the fishing industry survived until the 1950s.[20] With the transition to a market economy from the late 1980s, Soviet and post-Soviet policymakers revisited the possibility of concessions, but for a variety of reasons concession initiatives were not successful. **4.79**

On 21 July 1993 the Supreme Soviet of the Russian Federation adopted a law on concession contracts to be concluded with foreign investors, but it was vetoed by the President of the Russian Federation. In furtherance of the same idea, the State Duma of the Russian Federation in April 1996 adopted at first reading a draft federal law on concession contracts to be concluded with Russian and foreign investors.[21] A second reading, scheduled for 1998, did not proceed, and work languished for several years until ultimately the Federal Law on Concession Agreements of 21 July 2005 was enacted.[22] This contractual arrangement should be distinguished from the Concession Contract provided for by Chapter 54 of the Civil Code of the Russian Federation. **4.80**

---

[19] See J B Quigley, *The Soviet Foreign Trade Monopoly* (1974)

[20] On early Soviet concession legislation, see V V Gsovski, *Soviet Civil Law* (1948), I, pp. 22, 363.

[21] See I Z Farkhutdinov and V A Trapeznikov, *Инвестиционное право* [Investment Law] (2006), pp. 145–6.

[22] *СЗ РФ* (2005), no. 30(II), item 3126.

Definition of concession agreement

4.81 A concession agreement is a species of 'mixed contract', that is, it contains elements of various contracts provided for by the Civil Code and other federal laws. In addition to the 2005 Federal Law on Concession Agreements, the rules of civil legislation on those contracts whose elements are incorporated in a concession agreement also apply to the relations of the parties unless it arises otherwise from the 2005 Federal Law on Concession Agreements or from the essence of the concession agreement.

4.82 The concession agreement in its 2005 manifestation is limited to immoveable property. The concessionaire is obliged under the concession to create and/or reconstruct the immoveable property determined by the agreement, the right of ownership to which belongs or will belong to the party granting the concession, and then to use or operate the object of the concession for the period stipulated by the agreement. 'Reconstruction' for these purposes means introducing new technologies, mechanization, and automation of production, modernization and replacement of morally obsolete and physically worn out equipment with new more productive equipment, or a modification of the technological or functional designation of the object of the concession agreement or individual parts thereof, and other measures to improve the characteristics and operational properties of the said object.

Limitations

4.83 There are a number of imperative and dispositive limitations built into the concession scheme. Among the imperative requirements, the object of the concession agreement must be in the ownership of the party granting the concession and free of the rights of third persons. The object of the concession agreement may not be pledged or alienated, and the rights of the concessionaire under the concession agreement may not be pledged. Changing by agreement or otherwise the special-purpose designation of the object being created or reconstructed is not permitted. The rights of possession and use of the concessionaire in the object of the concession agreement and any immoveable property provided to the concessionaire as part of the arrangement are subject to State registration as an encumberment of the rights of ownership of the party granting the concession. The concessionaire carries the object of the concession on a separate balance sheet and depreciates that object.

4.84 The dispositive default clauses are numerous. Unless the concession agreement provides otherwise, the products and revenues received by the concessionaire as a result of activities provided by the concession agreement are the ownership of the concessionaire. However, property created or acquired by the concessionaire when performing the concession agreement and not the object of the concession agreement also is in the ownership of the concessionaire unless agreed otherwise. Exclusive rights to the results of intellectual activity obtained by the concessionaire at his expense when performing the concession agreement belong to the party granting the concession unless established otherwise by the concession agreement.

Expenses for the performance of obligations under the concession agreement are borne by the concessionaire unless provided otherwise by the concession agreement. If the party granting the concession does agree to assume part of the expenses or to provide guarantees to the concessionaire, the amount of these expenses must be specified in the conditions of the competition for the right to conclude a concession agreement or in the decision to conclude a concession agreement without holding a competition, as well as in the concession agreement itself. The concessionaire bears the risk of accidental perishing or damage to the object of the concession agreement unless provided otherwise by the concession agreement. By agreement of the parties, the duty to insure the object of the concession agreement may be placed on the concessionaire at his expense. **4.85**

Objects of concession agreement

The 2005 Federal Law on Concession Agreements gives an exhaustive enumeration of what may be the object of a concession agreement. Immoveable property is the *sine qua non*, provided that such property comprises a part of: (1) highways and engineering installations of the transport infrastructure, including bridges, overpasses, tunnels, motor vehicle stops, admittance points for motor vehicles, and payment points for drivers of goods vehicles; (2) objects of railway transport; (3) objects of pipeline transport; (4) sea and river ports, including hydroengineering installations of ports and objects of the production and engineering infrastructure thereof; (5) sea-going and river vessels, ships of river-sea navigation, and ships performing icebreaker escort or hydrographic and scientific research activity, ferryboats, floating and dry-docks; (6) aerodromes or buildings and/or installations intended for the takeoff, landing, taxiing, and mooring of aircraft; (7) objects of the production and engineering infrastructure of airports; (8) objects of a unified system for the organization of air traffic; (9) hydroengineering installations; (10) objects for the production, transfer, and distribution of electric power and heat; (11) systems of the municipal infrastructure and other objects of the municipal economy, including objects of water, heat, gas, and electric power supply, drainage, purification of sewage waters, processing and utilization or burial of domestic wastes, objects intended to illuminate territories of urban and rural settlements, and objects intended for the public amenities of territories; (12) underground and other common use transport; (13) objects to be used for treatment-prophylactic and medical activities and the organization of the leisure of citizens, and tourism; and (14) objects **4.86** of public health, education, culture, sport and other objects of socio-cultural and socio-domestic designation.

Parties to concession agreement

4.87 The concessionaires under a concession agreement may be: (1) a foreign or Russian individual entrepreneur; (2) a foreign or Russian juridical person; (3) a simple partnership operating without the formation of a juridical person under a contract of simple partnership or contract on joint activity and composed of two or more foreign and/or Russian juridical persons.

4.88 The party granting the concession may be: (1) the Russian Federation, represented by the Government of the Russian Federation or federal agency of executive power empowered by it; (2) a subject of the Russian Federation, represented by an agency of State power of the subject of the Russian Federation; or (3) a municipal formation, represented by an agency of local self-government.

4.89 A change of persons under a concession by way of assignment of a demand or transfer of a debt may be permitted by the party granting the concession from the moment when the object of the concession enters into operation. If the rights and duties of a concessionaire which is a juridical person pass in the event of a reorganization to another juridical person, the transfer must be on condition that the juridical person reorganized or newly created as a result of the reorganization meets the requirements established by the decision to conclude the concession agreement.

Period of concession agreement

4.90 Russian legislation imposes no minimum or maximum period for the duration of a concession agreement. It is left to the parties to agree this period, having regard to the period needed for the creation and/or reconstruction of the object of the concession agreement, the amounts of investment, and the period needed to recoup those investments, as well as other obligations of the concessionaire under the agreement.

Payments under concession agreement

4.91 What Russian legislation calls the 'concession payment' is to be made during the period of use or operation of the object of the concession agreement. It may be made at one time for the entire duration of the concession, or at periodic intervals as agreed. The amounts of payment, form, procedure, and periods for making it are established by the concession agreement in accordance with the decision to conclude the agreement. Three methods of payment are stipulated in the 2005 Federal Law on Concession Agreements, which may be used individually or combined: (1) a lump-sum payment made periodically or once to the budget of the respective level; (2) a participatory share of the products or revenues received by the concessionaire as a result of activities carried on under the concession agreement; or (3) transfer to the party granting the concession in ownership the property in the ownership of the concessionaire.

Rights and duties of concessionaire

A concessionaire has the right to dispose of the object of the concession agreement in the procedure determined by the 2005 Federal Law on Concession Agreements and the concession agreement. He also has the right to perform the concession agreement with his own forces and/or by involving other persons. If other persons are involved, the concessionaire is responsible for their actions as though they were his own. The concessionaire has the right to use without paying compensation to do so and in the procedure established by the concession agreement, on condition of complying with confidentiality clauses, the exclusive rights to the results of intellectual activity received by the concessionaire at his expense when performing the concession agreement for the purpose of performing his obligations under the concession agreement. **4.92**

The duties of the concessionaire are several: (1) to create and/or reconstruct the object of the concession agreement and commence the use or operation thereof within the periods agreed; (2) to use or operate the object of the concession agreement for the purposes and in the procedure established by the concession agreement; (3) to carry on the activities provided for by the concession agreement and not terminate or suspend them without the consent of the party granting the concession; (4) to ensure when effectuating the activity provided by the concession agreement the possibility of consumers to receive the respective goods, work or services; (5) to provide to consumers the privileges established by federal laws, laws of the subject of the Russian Federation, or normative legal acts of agencies of local self-government, including privileges for the payment of goods, work, and services as established by the concession agreement; and (6) to maintain the object of the concession agreement in proper condition and perform at his own expense capital and current repairs and bear maintenance expenses unless established otherwise by the concession agreement. **4.93**

Supervision rights of party granting concession

Representatives of the respective agencies granting the concession have the right of unhindered access to the object of the concession agreement and to documentation relating to the activities provided by the concession agreement. Supervisory control for these purposes on the part of the grantor of the concession is to ensure that the conditions of the concession agreement are being **4.94** complied with and investments being made as agreed, technical-economic indicators of the object of the concession agreement being conformed to, and activities under the agreement being carried out in accordance with its conditions.

4.95 The representatives of the grantor of the concession do not have the right to interfere in the economic activities of the concessionaire or divulge information classified as confidential or a commercial secret under the concession agreement. It is open to the parties to the concession agreement to establish more precisely the procedure for exercise of the control functions.

Minimum contractual conditions

4.96 Under the Civil Code of the Russian Federation (Article 432) a contract is considered to be concluded when agreement regarding all the material conditions of the contract has been reached in the form required. Conditions concerning the subject of the contract, conditions which are named in a law or other legal acts as material or necessary for contracts of the particular type, and all conditions relative to which agreement must be reached according to one of the parties are 'material'. The 2005 Federal Law on Concession Agreements stipulates (Article 10) that a concession agreement must include the following material conditions: (1) obligations of the concessionaire with regard to the creation and/or reconstruction of the object of the concession agreement and compliance with the periods to do so; (2) obligations of the concessionaire with regard to effectuating the activities provided for by the concession agreement; (3) the period of operation of the concession agreement; (4) the composition and description, including technical-economic indicators, of the object of the concession agreement; (5) the procedure for granting to the concessionaire the land plots earmarked for the activities provided for by the concession agreement and the period for concluding contracts of lease or sublease of these plots with the concessionaire if this is necessary to carry out the activity provided for by the concession agreement; (6) the purposes and period of use or operation of the object of the concession agreement; and (7) other material conditions provided for by federal laws.

4.97 A concession agreement is concluded in written form and enters into force from the day of signature thereof.

4.98 Whereas the foregoing conditions are material and imperative, the 2005 Federal Law on Concession Agreements also enumerates by way of example other clauses that might be included in a concession agreement so long as they are not contrary to legislation of the Russian Federation or the conditions of the competition to conclude a concession agreement. These include: (1) the volume of production of goods, fulfilment of work, or rendering of services when performing activities under the concession agreement; (2) the procedure and conditions for establishing and changing prices or tariffs, or supplements thereto, for goods, work, or services under the concession agreement; (3) the volume of investments to be made in the creation and/or reconstruction of the object of the concession agreement; (4) the period for handing over for operation the object of the concession agreement to be created or reconstructed, together with the technical-economic indicators; (5) obligations of the concessionaire with regard to realization of the goods, work, or services on the internal market within the period established by the concession agreement; (6) obligations of the concessionaire with regard to the realization of goods, work, and services at regulated prices or tariffs and in accordance with established supplements to the said prices or tariffs; (7) obligations of the concessionaire with regard to providing privileges, including payment privileges, established by legislation; (8) means of securing the performance of obligations by the concessionaire under the concession agreement, including insurance of the risk of loss or damage to the object of the concession agreement; and (9) obligations of the party granting the concession with regard to financing part of the expenses for the creation and/or reconstruction of the object of the concession agreement or expenses for the use or operation of that object.

The Government of the Russian Federation confirms model concession agreements with regard to all the objects of a concession agreement enumerated in the 2005 Federal Law on Concession Agreements. **4.99**

The duration of a concession agreement is specified in the agreement itself but determined in the conditions for holding a competition to conclude a concession agreement. The 2005 Federal Law on Concession Agreements requires that the model concession agreements confirmed by the Government of Russia be used for all agreements and allows changes to be introduced only in accordance with the 2005 Federal Law if the changes engage conditions stipulated by the conditions of the competition. Otherwise, changes in the concession agreement may be made by decision of a court on the grounds provided for by the Civil Code of the Russian Federation. **4.100**

Termination or dissolution of concession agreement

A concession agreement may be terminated upon the expiry of its period of operation; by agreement of the parties; or on the basis of a court decision in the event of dissolution by one of the parties before time. **4.101**

The consequences of terminating a concession agreement are several. First, the concessionaire must transfer to the grantor of the concession the object of the concession agreement and other property provided for by the concession agreement within the period stipulated in the agreement. Second, the object of the **4.102** concession agreement being transferred to the grantor must be in the condition stipulated by the concession agreement and suitable for effectuating the activity provided by the agreement and meeting the requirements established by the 2005 Federal Law on Concession Agreements. Moreover, the object of the concession agreement must not be encumbered by the rights of third persons.

4.103 Third, the transfer of the property must be on the basis of an act of transfer or other transfer document signed by the parties to the concession agreement. Unless provided otherwise by a federal law or the concession agreement, the transfer of the property to the grantor shall be considered to be performed after the acceptance of this object and such property and signature by the parties of the respective transfer document. An evasion by a party to the concession agreement of the signature of the transfer document shall be considered a refusal by this party to perform duties under the concession agreement. The termination of the right of possession and use of the concessionaire to the object of the concession agreement and other immoveable property shall be subject to State registration in the procedure provided by Russian legislation.

4.104 A court may dissolve a concession agreement at the demand of a party to the concession in the event of a material violation of the conditions of the concession agreement by the other party, or a material change of circumstances from which the parties proceeded when concluding it, or on other grounds provided for by the 2005 Federal Law on Concession Agreements, other federal laws, or the concession agreement itself. Unlike the Civil Code of the Russian Federation, which contains provisions on dissolution, the 2005 Federal Law on Concession Agreements elaborates precisely what constitutes a material violation: a violation of the periods for the creation and/or reconstruction of immoveable property; use or operation of the object of the concession agreement for purposes not established by the concession agreement or a violation of the procedure for the use or operation thereof; the failure of the concessionaire to perform obligations with regard to the effectuation of activity provided by the concession agreement; the termination or suspension by the concessionaire of activity provided for by the concession agreement without the consent of the grantor of the concession; and the failure to perform or improper performance by the concessionaire of obligations established by the concession agreement to grant privileges to citizens and other consumers, including services relating to water, heat, gas, electric power supply, drainage, and common use transport.

4.105 An action or failure to act of the grantor of the concession or concessionaire which are material conditions of the concession agreement may also be determined by the concession agreement to be material violations. The failure of a reorganized or newly-created juridical person-concessionaire to meet the requirements established by the decision to conclude a concession agreement also are grounds for dissolution of the concession agreement.

Guarantees for concessionaires

A concessionaire is guaranteed by the 2005 Federal Law on Concession Agreements that his rights and legal interests will be defended under the 1993 Russian Constitution, the said federal law, and other federal laws and normative legal acts. 'Other' federal laws would include, first and foremost, the 1999 Federal Law on foreign investments in the Russian Federation. There is a certain overlap between the foreign investment law and law on concession agreements which will need to be considered against the background of each transaction. **4.106**

The concessionaire has the right to compensation of losses caused to him as a result of the illegal actions or failure to act of State agencies, agencies of local self-government, or officials of those agencies in accordance with the Civil Code of the Russian Federation. The 2005 Federal Law on Concession Agreements specially singles out for mention foreign juridical persons which are concessionaires; they, together with all other concessionaires, are guaranteed equal rights provided for by legislation of the Russian Federation and a legal regime of activity precluding the application of measures of discriminatory character and other measures obstructing concessionaires in freely disposing of their investments and the products and revenues received as a result of effectuating the activity provided by the concession agreement. **4.107**

The concessionaire is guaranteed against unfavourable changes of legislation which may occur during the period of operation of the concession agreement. 'Legislation' includes that of the Russian Federation, subjects of the Russian Federation, and agencies of local self-government which worsen the position of the concessionaire such that he in significant degree is deprived of that which he had the right to count on when concluding the concession agreement. The guarantee is grounds for enabling the parties to the concession agreement to change the conditions of the agreement in order to ensure the property interests of the concessionaire which existed on the day of signature of the concession agreement. The procedure for making such changes should be provided for in the concession agreement. However, this guarantee does not extend to a change in a technical reglament or other normative act of the Russian Federation regulating the protection of the subsoil, environment, or public health of citizens. **4.108**

The 2005 Federal Law on Concession Agreements provides that disputes between the grantor and concessionaire are to be settled in accordance with legislation of the Russian Federation (Article 17). Under the 1999 Law on Foreign Investments in the Russian Federation, as amended, international **4.109** arbitration is one of the possible alternatives for the settlement of a dispute between a foreign investor and the grantor of a concession (Article 10).[23]

Procedure for conclusion of concession agreement

4.110 The 2005 Federal Law on Concession Agreements consists primarily of procedural requirements which will lead to the conclusion of a concession agreement. The intended keys are transparency and competition. There are two types of competition: open (anyone may submit an application to take part in the competition) and closed (invited persons may take part in the competition in accordance with a decision concerning the conclusion of a concession agreement). Closed competitions are arranged where the intention is to conclude a concession agreement with respect to an object of a concession agreement, the information on which is a State secret or which has strategic significance for ensuring the defence capacity and security of the Russian Federation. In the event of a closed competition, the grantor, the competition commission, and the participants in the competition must comply with the requirements of Russian legislation on State secrecy.

4.111 When an open competition is held, the information provided for in the 2005 Federal Law on Concession Agreement must be placed on the official internet site of the grantor of the concession. An official site may be established by the Government of the Russian Federation on which information is placed concerning all open competitions.

4.112 A central document is the decision concerning the conclusion of a concession agreement. The Government of the Russian Federation adopts such a decision with respect to objects of a concession agreement which belong to the Russian Federation by right of ownership, except that if the said objects have strategic significance, the Government adopts the decision on behalf of the President of the Russian Federation. If objects of a concession agreement are in the ownership of a subject of the Russian Federation, an agency of State power of the subject of the Russian Federation adopts the decision, and the same is true respectively of an agency of local self-government. The decision concerning the conclusion of the concession agreement determines what will be the competition documentation, including the conditions of the concession agreement; the procedure for the conclusion of the concession agreement; and the membership of the competition commission, which administers the competition for the right to conclude the concession agreement.

[23] Transl. in Butler, *Russian Company and Commercial Legislation* (2003), p. 818.

A competition can be avoided only after the deadline has lapsed for the submission of proposals and less than two proposals have been submitted, or less than two proposals meet the criteria for competition proposals. In this event the competition is declared by the competition commission to be unconstituted and deposits are refunded to the participant(s) who submitted a proposal. The grantor then has the right to consider a proposal submitted by only one participant in the competition and, if it meets the criteria of the competition, to adopt a decision to conclude a concession with this participant in accordance with the conditions contained in the competition proposal. **4.113**

In the interests of transparency the competition commission must within five working days from the day of signature of the protocol on the results of holding the competition or adoption by the grantor of a decision to announce that the competition was unconstituted publish the results of the competition, designating the name of the winner or the decision to declare the competition unconstituted. Publication must be in the official gazette where the competition was announced and on the official internet site. The participants in the competition also must be notified within five working days about the results; such notification may be in electronic form. Any participant in the competition has the right to seek explanations of the results of the competition, and the grantor must submit the explanations in written form within thirty days from the day of receiving such request. **4.114**

If the decision to conclude a concession agreement is positive, the grantor sends within five working days from the day of signature by competition commission members of the protocol on the results of the competition to the winner a copy of the said protocol, draft concession agreement, and decision to conclude a concession agreement. The final concession agreement must be signed within ninety working days from the day of signature of the protocol on the results of holding the competition. If the winner refuses or avoids the signature of the concession agreement within the ninety-day period, the grantor has the right to turn to the proposal which was second best in the competition. The winner who does not sign a concession agreement loses his deposit. **4.115**

D. Production Sharing

The concept of production sharing agreements was introduced to the Russian Federation and other CIS by western natural resource industries from the late Soviet period onwards. Eventually, formal legislation was enacted as part of the package of foreign investment inducements and presently takes the form of the **4.116**

1995 Federal Law on Production Sharing Agreements, as amended.[24] Production sharing relates to the prospecting, exploitation, and extraction of mineral raw materials on the territory of the Russian Federation and also within or on the continental shelf and exclusive economic zone of the Russian Federation. A production sharing agreement regulates the relations that arise in the process of the conclusion, performance, and termination of such agreements and determines the basic conditions of such agreements.

4.117 Oil and gas companies have been the most visible in concluding production sharing agreements with the Russian Federation, but they also exist in the domains of gold and diamond mining, among others.

4.118 Relations not regulated by the Federal Law on Production Sharing Agreements, including those arising in the course of using land and other natural resources and the special limitations imposed by legislation on the right of ownership to precious metals, natural precious stones, radioactive raw materials and other metals and products, are regulated by subsoil and other relevant Russian legislation. Although the production sharing agreement is a special type of contract, it is not regulated by the Civil Code of the Russian Federation directly and explicitly; however, the rights and duties of the parties to a production sharing agreement having a civil-law character are determined by the Federal Law on Production Sharing as *lex specialis* and civil legislation.

4.119 A production sharing agreement is defined by the Federal Law on Production Sharing Agreements as a '. . . contract in accordance with which the Russian Federation grants to a subject of entrepreneurial activity', named an 'investor', exclusive rights on a compensated basis and for a determined period for the exploration, exploitation, and extraction of mineral raw material on the subsoil plot specified in the agreement and to conduct work connected therewith, and the investor is obliged to conduct the said work at his expense and risk. The agreement determines the necessary conditions connected with the use of the subsoil, including the conditions and procedure for sharing the products produced among the parties provided that these are consistent with Russian legislation.

4.120 Individual federal laws establish the lists of subsoil plots which may be granted by the Russian Federation on a production sharing basis. The Government of the Russian Federation may determine these lists, but so too may those who under the Russian Constitution have the right of legislative initiative. Not more than 30% of the mineral reserves exploited and taken into account on the State balance sheet may be authorized for production sharing.

[24] *СЗ РФ* (1996), no. 1, item 18; transl. in Butler, *Foreign Investment Law in the Commonwealth of Independent States* (2002), pp. 634–55.

The parties to a production sharing agreement are the Russian Federation, in whose name the Government of the Russian Federation or agencies empowered by it act in the agreement, on one side, and the investors, who are juridical persons or associations of juridical persons created on the basis of a contract on joint activity and not having the status of a juridical person and who invest their own or borrowed means, including property and/or property rights. If an association of juridical persons not having the status of a juridical person acts as the investor in the agreement, the participants of that association have joint and several rights and bear joint and several duties under the agreement. The license for the use of a subsoil plot is, in this event, issued to one of the participants of the association of juridical persons. **4.121**

Production sharing agreements usually are concluded with the winner of an auction held for the purpose of the agreement. The participation of Russian juridical persons in the realization of the production sharing agreement must be provided for by the auction conditions in participatory shares established by the Government of the Russian Federation. The decision to sign an agreement on the part of the State is adopted by the Government of the Russian Federation. **4.122**

A production sharing agreement must provide for the formation of a management committee which has responsibility for coordinating the activity relating to the performance of work under the agreement. Such a committee is composed of an equal number of representatives from each party. The precise numerical composition, the rights and duties of the management committee, and its work procedure are all determined by the production sharing agreement. However, the procedure for appointing representatives of the State to the management committee in the name of the State are determined by the 2006 Decree of the Government of the Russian Federation, No. 133.[25] Such representatives are appointed by the Government of the Russian Federation upon the recommendation of the federal agency of executive power which performs the functions of empowered agency within the framework of the realization of production sharing agreements. The appointee is chosen from among federal civil servants or civil servants of a subject of the Russian Federation. The State representatives on the management committee are to form a consolidated opinion with regard to the agenda of a session of the management committee. The 'expression by representatives of the State of different opinions with regard to questions on the agenda of a session of the management committee requiring the adoption of a decision is not permitted' (point 7, Decree No. 133). **4.123**

The State and the investor share the products produced in accordance with the **4.124**

[25] *СЗ РФ* (2006), no. 12, item 1304.

agreement, which must provide for the conditions and procedure of determining the total amount of products produced and the value thereof, determining the part of the products produced which are to be transferred to the ownership of the investor in order to compensate his expenditures for the fulfilment of work under the agreement, the maximum level of compensation not exceeding 75 per cent, and in the case of the continental shelf, 90 per cent, of the total volume of products produced. The expenditures subject to compensation to the investor are determined by an agreement in accordance with Russian legislation. The agreement also must stipulate the transfer to the State of the part of the products produced or value equivalent thereof[26] and the receipt by the investor of products produced belonging to it. If an auction is held, the auction conditions must specify that an agreement is to be concluded in accordance with the said conditions.

4.125 The participatory share of the products produced which belong to the investor do so by right of ownership. The investor has the right to export mineral raw material received under the production sharing agreement from the customs territory of the Russian Federation without quantitative limitations unless provided otherwise by Russian foreign trade legislation. The State participatory share of the products produced is realized in accordance with federal laws.

4.126 An investor has the right of free access and use on a contractual basis to pipeline transport and other types of transport and objects for the keeping and processing or refining of mineral raw materials without any discriminatory measures.

4.127 A special procedure for the calculation and payment of taxes and charges established by the Tax Code of the Russian Federation is applicable to production sharing. The investor when performing the agreement makes one-off payments for use of the subsoil when events stipulated in the agreement ensue and for the use of a licence (or bonus), payment for geological information on the subsoil, annual payments for the contractual aquatory and seabed plots to be paid as the agreement requires, a fee for participating in a competition or auction, a fee for the issuance of a licence, regular payments (rentals) for use of the subsoil, compensation to the State for expenses for the prospecting and exploitation of minerals, and compensation for damage caused as a result of performing work under the production sharing agreement to native peoples of the Russian Federation.

4.128 An investor has the right to transfer in whole or in part his rights and duties under the production sharing agreement to any juridical or natural person only

[26] The State under production sharing arrangements is entitled to compensation for expenses made to explore for and exploit minerals. The Rules for determining the amounts due were confirmed by Decree of the Government of the Russian Federation, No. 764, on 12 December 2004. See *СЗ РФ* (2004), no. 51, item 5179.

with the consent of the State, provided that these persons have sufficient financial and technical resources and management experience needed to fulfil work under the agreement. Such transfer must be in written form by means of drawing up a special act which is an integral part of the agreement in the procedure and within the periods determined by the agreement and accompanied by a reformalised licence for use of the subsoil within 30 days from the date of signing the said act. With the consent of the State an investor may use the property and property rights belonging to it as a pledge in order to secure obligations under contracts concluded in connection with the performance of the production sharing agreement in compliance with the requirements of civil legislation of the Russian Federation.

The conditions of a production sharing agreement retain their force throughout **4.129** the entire period of operation of the agreement. Changes in the agreement are permitted only by consent of the parties or upon the demand of one party in the event of a material change of circumstances in accordance with the Civil Code of the Russian Federation. Any changes made in the agreements by agreement of the parties are introduced into operation in the same procedure as the original agreements.

If the Russian Federation or a subject of the Russian Federation or agencies of **4.130** local self-government adopt legislation which worsens the commercial results of the investor's activity within the framework of the production sharing agreement, changes are to be made in the agreement which ensure that the investor receives the commercial result which would have been received if the relevant legislation had not been changed. The production sharing agreement contains procedures for making such changes. However, changes in legislation concerning the standards, norms, or rules for the safe conduct of work, protection of the subsoil and natural environment, and health of the population, including for the purpose of bringing such standards, norms, or rules into conformity with generally-recognized international practice, do not fall under this provision.

Under the Federal Law on Production Sharing Agreements, the investor is **4.131** guaranteed the defence of property and other rights acquired and effectuated by it in accordance with the production sharing agreement (Article 18). This formulation would appear to grant the investor fewer rights than he enjoys under the 1999 Federal Law on Foreign Investments unless the provision is construed to incorporate the guarantees of that enactment. Disputes between the State and the investor connected with the use, termination, and validity of agreements are to be settled in accordance with the production sharing agreement in a court, arbitrazh court, or arbitration court, the last including international arbitration tribunals.

4.132 The Russian Federation may agree to waive immunity with respect to judicial immunity, the preliminary securing of a suit, and the execution of a judicial decision or arbitral award in accordance with Russian Federation legislation (Article 23).

Part III

LEGAL STATUS OF ALIENS

5

FOREIGNERS AND STATELESS PERSONS IN RUSSIA

The 1993 Constitution of the Russian Federation, as already noted, follows the general pattern of Russian legal history and extends to foreigners and stateless persons the principle of 'national regime', subject to exceptions established by a federal law or by an international treaty of the Russian Federation (Article 62[3]). The concept of 'exception' can take one of three forms: (a) foreigners are excluded from exercising rights of Russian citizens; (b) foreigners enjoy preferences or privileges in comparison with Russian citizens; or (c) whether foreigners enjoy rights or must perform duties may depend upon the existence of reciprocity between Russia and the foreign country concerned. In addition, distinctions are drawn among foreigners which turn upon the visa regime under which they have entered the Russian Federation. **5.01**

Although the definition concerned purports to apply only to the Federal Law in which it is set out, the 2002 Federal Law on the Legal Status of Foreign Citizens in the Russian Federation, translated as an Annex to this volume (hereinafter: 2002 Federal Law on the Legal Status of Foreign Citizens), contains definitions **5.02** of the terms 'foreign citizen' and 'stateless person' which have found general acceptance and use in Russian legislation and in Russian legal doctrine. A 'foreign citizen' is defined with reference to Russian citizenship; that is, a 'natural person who is not a citizen of the Russian Federation and who has evidence of the existence of citizenship (or subjecthood) of a foreign State'. A stateless person, on the other hand, is defined with reference to the citizenship of all States: a 'natural person who is not a citizen of the Russian Federation and who has no evidence of the existence of citizenship (or subjecthood) of a foreign State' (Article 2).[1] The 2002 Federal Law on Citizenship of the Russian Federation differs slightly in its definition of a 'foreign citizen': a 'natural person who is not a citizen of the Russian Federation and has the citizenship "or subjecthood" of a foreign State' (Article 3); the definition of a stateless person is identical to that in the 2002 Federal Law on the Legal Status of Foreigners.[2] However, the 2003 Federal Law on the Fundamental Principles of State Regulation of Foreign Trade Activity, as amended, contains quite a different, even laconic, definition: a foreign person is: 'a natural person, juridical person, or organization which is not a juridical person under the law of a foreign State who is not a Russian person' (Article 2).[3]

5.03 Although the 2002 Federal Law on the Legal Status of Foreigners says that it determines the 'legal status of foreign citizens in the Russian Federation and regulates relations between foreign citizens and State agencies and officials arising in connection with the presence of foreigners on Russian territory', in fact that formulation is misleading against the recent background of Soviet legal history. The 1981 USSR Law on the Legal Status of Foreigners, replaced by the 2002 Federal Law, undertook to virtually codify the entire scope of the rights and duties of foreigners in the Soviet Union. In comparison, the 2002 Federal Law on the Legal Status of Foreigners is a technical piece of legislation preoccupied with the details of admitting and registering foreigners to the Russian Federation.

5.04 Nonetheless, this 2002 Federal Law on the Legal Status of Foreigners is the fundamental legislative act regulating foreigners in Russia. It reinforces the principle of 'national regime' subject to exceptions without making any specific reference to the 1993 Russian Constitution. And within the framework of traditional Russian legal doctrine and legislation the 2002 Federal Law on the

---

[1] The terminology has been criticized on a number of occasions, especially where Russian legislation imposes limitations on foreign citizens that do not extend to, for example, stateless persons or to refugees.

[2] *СЗ РФ* (2002), no. 30; item 3032; (2003), no. 27(I), item 2700; no. 46(I), item 4437; (2004), no. 35, item 3607; no. 45, item 4377.

[3] *СЗ РФ* (2003), no. 50, item 4850.

Legal Status of Foreigners creates the most comprehensive administrative law framework regulating the presence of foreigners in Russia ever undertaken, although in this study that framework is regarded as a component of foreign relations law.

A. Freedom of Exit, Movement, and Entry

The 1993 Constitution of the Russian Federation (Article 27[2]) provides that 'each' may depart freely from the limits of the Russian Federation. This right extends by virtue of its formulation to foreign citizens and stateless persons. The procedure for exit (including transit) is regulated by the Federal Law on the Procedure for Exit from the Russian Federation and Entry into the Russian Federation of 15 August 1996, as amended.[4] The procedure for exit is distinguished from the procedure for crossing the State boundary of the Russian Federation, which also is regulated by the Law of the Russian Federation on the State Boundary of the Russian Federation, as amended. **5.05**

Foreign citizens and stateless persons are obliged when exiting the Russian Federation to present valid documents attesting their identity and recognized by the Russian Federation to do so, together with a visa, unless provided otherwise by a treaty of the Russian Federation. **5.06**

Stateless persons are thus assimilated for these purposes to foreign citizens unless provided otherwise by Russian federal laws or treaties. However, stateless persons or refugees granted permanent residence in the Russian Federation may apply, in the event they should lose their documents, in the same procedure as Russian citizens for restoration thereof, including to Russian representations abroad. **5.07**

Departure from the Russian Federation may be refused to foreign citizens or stateless persons under five circumstances set out in the 1996 Federal Law on the Procedure for Exit from the Russian Federation or Entry into the Russian Federation, as amended, as follows: (1) detention on suspicion of the commission of a crime or being brought to responsibility as an accused, until a decision is taken in the case or the judgment of a court has entered into legal force; (2) being convicted for the commission of a crime on the territory of the Russian Federation until the sentence is served or there is relief from punishment; (3) evasion of duties imposed by a court until the duties have been performed or agreement of the parties has been reached; (4) until obligations with regard to the payment of taxes provided for by legislation of the Russian **5.08**

[4] *СЗ РФ* (1996), no. 34, item 4029.

Federation have been fulfilled; and (5) being brought to administrative responsibility in accordance with legislation of the Russian Federation for the commission of an administrative violation on the territory of the Russian Federation, until the punishment has been executed or there has been relief from punishment.

5.09 The identity of a foreign citizen in the Russian Federation is attested by the passport[5] issued by his country of citizenship or other document established by a federal law or recognized in accordance with an international treaty of the Russian Federation. For stateless persons the situation is rather more complicated. An acceptable form of identification in Russia for a stateless person is a document issued by a foreign State as recognized in accordance with an international treaty of the Russian Federation as an acceptable evidence of identity. Otherwise, Russian documents suffice; namely an authorization for temporary residing, residence permit, other documents provided for by a federal law or recognized under a treaty concluded by the Russian Federation. Whether a person has a visa or other document to enter a foreign State from the Russian Federation is a duty of the transport company or carrier unless provided otherwise by a treaty of the Russian Federation.

5.10 There are certain situations not regarded as departure by a foreign citizen or stateless person from the Russian Federation: crossing while holding a valid visa the State boundary of the Russian Federation on to another part of Russian territory and transiting across the territory of a foreign State under the regime of transit passage, or when travelling on Russian flag vessels across the exclusive economic zone of the Russian Federation or the high seas without putting in to foreign ports.

5.11 The basic principle of Russian law is that foreign citizens may exit and enter the Russian Federation when they have a visa issued under valid documents attesting their identity and recognized by the Russian Federation in this capacity, unless provided otherwise by an international treaty of the Russian Federation. The rights and duties of foreigners in Russia turn not solely upon their physical presence on Russian territory, although that is a factor, but also upon the classification of the legal regime under which they are present. Distinctions are

[5] This passport is to be distinguished from the internal identity document held by all Soviet and Russian citizens, also called in Russian and English a 'passport'. This internal passport is not used, as a rule, for travel by Russians abroad, although in individual cases it may substitute for a foreign passport when treaties between the Russian Federation and the receiving country so provide, usually on a reciprocal basis. This is usually the document contemplated when Russian legislation or treaties mention the 'other document established by a federal law or recognized in accordance with an international treaty of the Russian Federation'. On the internal passport system, see M Matthews, *The Passport Society: Controlling Movement in Russia and the USSR* (1993).

drawn between a 'temporary sojourn', 'temporary residing', and 'permanent residing' based upon a residence permit. We examine each distinction in sequence.

Temporary sojourn

Most foreigners entering the Russian Federation will do so for a 'temporary' stay. Although the duration of the stay may turn on the visa issued, that is not necessarily the case. Some foreigners enter without a visa, in which case their sojourn may not last more than ninety days unless provided otherwise by the 2002 Federal Law on the Legal Status of Foreigners. If a visa was issued but not extended, the foreign citizen must leave Russia upon the expiry of the visa. Special provisions for extension operate when the foreign citizen after entry concluded a labour or independent-work contract or contracted for military service in Russia. **5.12**

Temporary residing

The Russian Government maintains a quota for issuing authorizations to foreigners to temporarily reside in the country. The quota is confirmed annually,[6] having regard to the demographic situation in various subjects of the Russian Federation and opportunities for the arrangement of employment. In addition to the quotas and outside that system, authorizations may be issued by the Russian Government to a foreign citizen who was born in the territory of the RSFSR, or who held citizenship of the USSR in the past, or who was born on the territory of the Russian Federation, or to a foreign citizen who lacks the capacity to labour and has a son or daughter who has Russian citizenship and dispositive legal capacity, or who has one parent lacking the capacity to labour but is a Russian citizen, or is married to a citizen of the Russian Federation with a place of residence in Russia, or who has made investments in the Russian Federation in an amount established by the Government of Russia, or who has enlisted in military service—in this instance for the period of military service, or in other instances provided by a federal law. **5.13**

A foreign citizen or stateless person who has reached eighteen years of age may obtain an authorization for temporary residing either within or outside the established quota. If the applicant is in Russia when applying, the application must be made in person. The application will not be considered if the foreign citizen certifies his identity with a document issued in connection with his employment or professional activity, such as a seaman's passport, or if the **5.14**

[6] The quota for the year 2004 was 20,633 foreign citizens, with distribution stipulated by subjects of the Russian Federation. The quota for 2005 was 24,745.

identity document is valid for less than six months. Strict rules govern completion of the application forms, including use of the Russian language and no abbreviated words.

5.15 Together with four photographs and the application form, the foreign citizen must submit: documents certifying his identity and citizenship; a document issued by an empowered agency of his State of permanent residing confirming the presence or absence of a record of conviction; a residence permit or other document issued by an empowered agency of a foreign State which confirms that the foreign citizen is residing outside the State of which he is a citizen; a document confirming that the applicant has means enabling him and his family to live in the Russian Federation at the minimum level of sustenance or a document confirming his lack of labour capacity (examples of such documents are references concerning incomes, tax declarations, labour book, pension certificate, or evidence of receiving other social benefits or alimony, bank deposit book, certificate of right to inheritance, and so on); marriage certificate; birth certificate of child and identity document of child who has not reached eighteen years of age or passport if he has such; documents of consent for children of fourteen to eighteen years of age concerning their moving to Russia for temporary residing (the child's signature must be attested by a notary); HIV certificate; and a document issued by an empowered agency of the foreign State or public health institution in Russia confirming that the applicant and members of his family are not narcotics addicts and do not have contagious diseases specified in a List confirmed by the Government of Russia.[7] Those who apply for temporary residing outside the quota system, depending upon their situation, must supply additional documents specified in normative legal acts. Any documents supplied in languages other than Russian as part of an application must be accompanied by a notarially attested translation into Russian.

5.16 The maximum period for consideration of a completed application should not exceed six months, and another month is allowed for notifying the applicant of the decision. This formulation allows for some applicants to be considered for a longer period. If a positive decision is taken with regard to the application and the applicant is not in Russia, the applicant is issued a visa to come to Russia, in which case the foreign citizen must apply to actually receive the authorization within three working days of arrival. The authorization for residing is issued for

[7] The List of Contagious Diseases Representing a Danger for Surrounding Persons and Being Grounds for Refusal to Issue to or for Annulment of Authorization for Temporary Residing to Foreign Citizens and Stateless Persons, or Residence Permit, or Authorization for Work in the Russian Federation was confirmed by Decree of the Government of the Russian Federation on 2 April 2003, No. 188. In addition to HIV, diseases include leprosy, tuberculosis, and syphilis. *СЗ РФ* (2003), no. 14, item 1286.

a period of three years; however, the recipient of such authorization must undergo annual re-registration at the internal affairs agency.

Those who apply for temporary residing will pay a fee to receive the application form, and if such authorization is granted, State duty will be imposed upon the issuance of such authorization.[8] Applicants will be fingerprinted when the authorization is issued. 5.17

When the authorization for temporary residing is issued to a foreign citizen, the official of an internal affairs agency who is issuing the authorization must explain to the recipient '. . . the legal status of a person who has received an authorization for temporary residing, the grounds for annulment thereof provided by Article 7 of the [2002 Federal] Law, and also the duty annually to undergo re-registration in an internal affairs agency'. The grounds for refusing an authorization for temporary residing or for the annulment of such an authorization are extensive: favouring the forcible change of the constitutional system of Russia or by other actions threatening the security or Russia or citizens thereof; financing or planning terrorist or extremist acts assisting the commission or committing such acts, or otherwise supporting such activities; within five years before filing an application for an authorization was administratively deported or otherwise deported from Russia; submitted forged or false documents or information about himself; is convicted by a court of a grave or especially grave crime or crime whose recidivism is deemed to be dangerous; has an uncancelled or unremoved record of conviction for the commission of a crime or especially grave crime in or outside Russia; within one year has been brought to administrative responsibility twice or more for violating legislation regulating the sojourn of foreign citizens in Russia; is unable to provide evidence of the ability to support himself and family in Russia without resorting to State assistance unless he lacks the capacity to labour; within three years after entry into Russia has no dwelling premise in Russia on the grounds provided by Russian legislation; has left Russia to reside permanently in a foreign State; is outside Russia for more than six months; married a Russian citizen to receive an authorization for temporary residing and later that marriage was deemed by a court to be invalid; is addicted to narcotics or has no certificate confirming the absence of HIV infection or certain other contagious diseases. 5.18

[8] The amounts of State duty recovered for visas, residence permits, and the like are now determined by the Tax Code of the Russian Federation as amended 2 November 2004. Under Article 333.28 of the Tax Code, State duty of 400 rubles is to be paid for issuing an authorization for temporary sojourn or for extending such an authorization. The State duty is 100 rubles for authorizations for temporary residing or residence permits.

Permanent residing

5.19 Foreigners who have an authorization for temporary residing may, not later than six months before the expiry of the said authorization, apply to receive a residence permit provided they have lived in the Russian Federation for at least one year under the said authorization. Although the residence permit is valid for five years and may be extended indefinitely for five-year periods, only a stateless person receives a permit valid for five years; foreign citizens receive such a permit for not more than five years but the actual period will not exceed the validity of the document certifying their identity (i.e. passport). The grounds for refusing a residence permit are virtually identical to those for the authorization for temporary residing.

5.20 The application procedure to obtain a residence permit is similar to that for an authorization for temporary residing. Foreign citizens and stateless persons who have valid identity documents recognized by the Russian Federation and a Russian residence permit may enter and exit the Russian Federation on the basis of those documents without a visa. State duty is recovered for the issuance of a residence permit (or a duplicate residence permit in the event of loss) in the amount of 1000 rubles under Article 333.28 of the Tax Code of the Russian Federation.

Visa regime

5.21 Foreigners enter the Russian Federation on the basis of a 'visa', unless provided otherwise by an international treaty of the Russian Federation. A 'visa' is defined as an 'authorization for entry into the Russian Federation, sojourn in the Russian Federation, or transit passage through the territory of the Russian Federation . . .' for the period of validity of the visa.[9] A foreign citizen may apply for a visa either personally or through a duly empowered representative. Empowered Russian State agencies having the right to formalize, issue, extend, restore, or annul a visa are: (a) a diplomatic or consular representation of the Russian Federation; (b) the Ministry of Foreign Affairs of the Russian Federation or a representation of the said Ministry on the territory of the Russian Federation, including at admittance points on the State boundary of the Russian Federation; or (c) the Ministry of Internal Affairs of the Russian Federation or territorial agency thereof.

[9] Article 25^1, 1996 Federal Law on the Procedure for Exit from the Russian Federation and Entry into the Russian Federation; Point 4, Statute on the Establishment of the Form of Visa, Procedure and Conditions for the Formalization and Issuance Thereof, Extension of Period of Operation Thereof, Restoration Thereof in the Event of Loss, and also the Procedure for the Annulment of a Visa, confirmed by Decree of the Government of the Russian Federation, No. 335, of 9 June 2003.

The period for the formalization of a visa established by legislation is not more than 20 working days from the date the foreign citizen applies, the date of application being considered the day on which all the documents required are duly formalized and presented. In practice visas are normally issued more rapidly, including on the same day of application, if a higher fee is paid. Russian legislation allows periods longer than 20 working days to be operated with respect to countries which do not issue visas to Russian citizens within a 20-day period '. . . on the basis of the international principle of reciprocity'.[10] Foreign citizens who are passengers on board cruise vessels which have authorization to carry passengers and arrive in Russian sea and river ports open to international passenger traffic may be present on the territory of the Russian Federation for 72 hours without a visa in the procedure established by the Government of the Russian Federation. **5.22**

A visa may be refused in the instances set out by the 1996 Federal Law on the Procedure for Exit from the Russian Federation and Entry into the Russian Federation. There are seven such instances: (1) refusal is necessary for the purpose of ensuring the defence capacity or security of the State, public order, or protection of public health; (2) during a previous sojourn in Russia the foreign citizen or stateless person was subjected to administrative deportation or was deported, in which case a period of limitations of five years operates from the day of deportation; (3) the foreign citizen or stateless person has an uncancelled or unremoved record of conviction for the commission of a grave or especially grave crime on the territory of the Russian Federation or beyond the limits of Russia but recognized as such in Russia; (4) the foreign citizen or stateless person has not submitted documents necessary to receive a visa, but only until they are submitted; (5) the foreign citizen or stateless person has not submitted a medical insurance policy valid on the territory of the Russian Federation, with certain exceptions for designated categories of diplomatic, consular, and other personnel; (6) when applying for a visa or when crossing the State boundary the foreign citizen or stateless person could not confirm that he had means for residing on the territory of the Russian Federation or subsequent departure from the Russian Federation or submit guarantees of such means; and (7) a decision of the undesirability of sojourn or residing in the Russian Federation has been taken with respect to a foreign citizen or stateless person (Article 27). **5.23**

If the entry of a foreign citizen was limited for the reasons set out in subpoints (2) and (7) above, a notation is made by the border guard agencies on his identity document: 'Entry not authorised' pursuant to the Decree of the Government of the Russian Federation, No. 382 'On Placing a Notation on **5.24**

---

[10] Point 11, ibid.

Prohibition of Entry into Russian Federation of Certain Categories of Foreign Citizens and Stateless Persons'.[11] A notation is made when there is one of the following decisions of: (1) a judge, concerning administrative deportation beyond the limits of the Russian Federation of a foreigner who violated the rules for sojourn in Russia or the regime of the State boundary or the regime at admission points on the State boundary; (2) an official of border control agencies, concerning administrative deportation beyond the limits of the Russian Federation of a foreigner who violated the regime of the State boundary or regime at admission points on the State boundary; or (3) an official of the Ministry of Internal Affairs of Russia or territorial agency thereof, concerning deportation from Russia of a foreigner who did not leave Russia within the established period after reduction of his period of temporary sojourn, or annulment of his authorisation for temporary residing in Russia (or residence permit), or after a warning of the undesirability of his presence in Russia. The notation indicates the grounds for prohibition of entry, the name of the agency placing the notation, the signature and full name of the official, and the date of placing the notation. The agency which makes the notation sends to the Federal Security Service the information necessary to record persons whose entry has not been permitted to Russia.

5.25 The empowered State agency which refuses a visa is not obliged to explain the reasons. The procedure for the interaction of the Ministry of Foreign Affairs, Ministry of Internal Affairs, Ministry of Defence, and Federal Security Service when deciding whether to issue, extend, restore, annul, or formalize a visa, as well as the procedure for the use of 'visa information',[12] is established jointly by those agencies. Although the relevant agencies have considerable discretion to decide visa issues, their discretion is limited by the 1996 Federal Law in comparison with that enjoyed by agencies of the former USSR. The reasons for denial of a visa may be divided into imperative and dispositive. Reasons (4) to (6) above are dispositive, and it is within the ability of the applicant to overcome the shortcomings of his application and eliminate the reasons for the rejection.[13]

5.26 In addition, entry may be refused to a foreign citizen under the 1996 Federal Law on the Procedure for Exit from the Russian Federation and Entry into the Russian Federation if the foreign citizen or stateless person: (1) at the admittance point on the State boundary of the Russian Federation has violated the

---

[11] *СЗ РФ* (2003), no. 27(II), item 2805.

[12] 'Visa information' is a legal term defined as the 'data specified on a visa, and also information concerning the formalization, issuance, extension of the period of operation, restoration, or annulment of a visa . . .'. See point 14, ibid.

[13] See V V Komarov, «Новые федеральные законы Российской Федерации и правовой статус иностранных граждан» [New Federal Laws of Russian Federation and the Legal Status of Foreign Citizens], *Юрист*, no. 2 (1997), p. 42.

rules for crossing the State boundary, customs zone, or sanitary norms until the violation is eliminated; (2) has used false documents or communicated information known to be false about himself or about the purpose of his sojourn in the Russian Federation; (3) has an unremoved or uncancelled record of conviction for the commission of an intentional crime on the territory of the Russian Federation or beyond its limits deemed to be such in accordance with a federal law; (4) two or more times within three years has been brought to administrative responsibility in accordance with legislation of the Russian Federation for the commission of an administrative violation on Russian territory; (5) during his previous sojourn in Russia did not surrender his migration card when departing from Russia; or (6) during his previous sojourn in Russia evaded the payment of a tax or administrative fine or did not compensate expenses connected with administrative deportation beyond the limits of the Russian Federation or with deportation, until the said payments are made in full.

Visas may be single-entry, double-entry, or multi-entry.[14] There are five categor- **5.27**
ies of visa, each of which we discuss below.

Diplomatic

A diplomatic visa is issued on the basis of a decision of the Ministry of Foreign **5.28**
Affairs to a foreign citizen which is sent to the issuing Russian diplomatic or consular representation. The basis for the decision is a note verbale from the foreign affairs department or the diplomatic or consular institution of the sending foreign State or representation of an international organization in the Russian Federation. The presumption is that the relevant foreign citizen has a diplomatic passport from his own country and occupies the position of head of State or government, members of the families thereof, and accompanying persons, such visas being single or double entry and valid for up to three months unless provided otherwise by a treaty of the Russian Federation; diplomatic agents of a diplomatic mission or consular officials of a consular mission, and personnel of representations of international organizations in the Russian Federation whose diplomatic status is recognized by Russia and members of their families, visas for this group being single-entry or double-entry and valid for a period of up to three months but subject to extension for up to one year by issuance of a multi-entry visa; and foreign diplomatic and consular couriers, for whom visas may be single-entry or double-entry for up to three months or multi-entry for a period of up to one year.

Russia reserves the right, however, to issue a diplomatic visa to foreign citizens **5.29**

[14] Article 25^2, 1996 Federal Law on Procedure for Exit from Russian Federation and Entry into Russian Federation.

who do not have a diplomatic passport but nonetheless Russia recognizes their diplomatic status, and vice versa. A foreign citizen who has a diplomatic passport but whose diplomatic status is not recognized by the Russian Federation may be given an official or an ordinary visa.

Official

5.30 An official visa is also issued on the basis of a decision of the Ministry of Foreign Affairs to a foreign citizen which is sent to the issuing Russian diplomatic or consular representation on the basis of a note verbale submitted by the same entities as in the case of a diplomatic visa. The presumption is that the foreign citizen concerned has an official passport from his own country and is a member of an official foreign delegation, including family of the said member and accompanying persons, the visa being single-entry or double-entry for a period of up to three months. Official visas also are issued to administrative-technical and service personnel of diplomatic representations or consular missions of foreign States or representations of international organizations and family of the said persons, the visa being single-entry or double-entry for up to three months but subject to extension for up to one year. Military servicemen of the armed forces of a foreign State and family members who travel to Russia not as military attaches of diplomatic missions are issued an official multi-entry visa for up to one year.

5.31 A foreign citizen who does not have an official passport but is deemed by the Russian Federation to have official status may be issued an official visa. If a foreign citizen has an official passport but the Russian Federation does not recognize his official status, he may be issued an ordinary visa.

Ordinary

5.32 Most visas issued by the Russian Federation fall into this category. There are seven varieties of ordinary visa: private, business, tourist (including tourist group), education, work, humanitarian, and asylum (the present classification of visas was introduced by the 2003 amendments to the 1996 Federal Law on Exit from the Russian Federation and Entry into the Russian Federation).

5.33 An ordinary private visa is issued for a period of up to three months to foreign citizens who are travelling to Russia on the basis of an invitation for entry into the Russian Federation as guests of the inviting person or organization. Under the 2002 Federal Law on the Legal Status of Foreigners (Article 16) petitions for an invitation for entry are considered by internal affairs agencies at the request of individual Russian citizens or juridical persons (including commercial organizations with foreign investments). The host individual or organization must provide guarantees of material, medical, and housing provision for the foreign citizen during his sojourn in Russia. Visas of this nature are issued to a foreign citizen who travels to Russia for urgent medical treatment or as a result of the grave illness or death of a close relative. Ordinary private visas may be single-entry or double-entry.

An ordinary business visa is issued to a foreign citizen who travels to Russia for business reasons and may be single-entry or double-entry for a period of up to three months or may be multi-entry for a period of up to one year. A foreigner who travels under a multi-entry business visa may not stay longer than 180 days without interruption; that is, without leaving the country. Visas of this nature are formalized either on the basis of an invitation for entry as regulated by the 2002 Federal Law on the Legal Status of Foreigners, or by a decision of the Ministry of Foreign Affairs sent to the diplomatic or consular representation of Russia, or in exceptional instances by a decision of the head of a diplomatic or consular representation on the basis of the written application of the foreign citizen for such a visa. **5.34**

An ordinary tourist visa is issued for a period of up to one month to a foreign citizen travelling to Russia as a tourist and may be single-entry or double-entry. A tourist group visa is valid for the same period but requires a minimum of five persons and not more than 50 who comprise an organized tourist group. All members of the group must travel on the same means of transport, and simultaneously enter and exit the country together at the same border point as a group. The group visa also may be issued with the authorization of the Ministry of Foreign Affairs when difficulties are encountered in issuing individual visas. Whether individual or group, tourist visas are issued on the basis of a duly formalized contract for rendering tourist services (or tourist voucher) and confirmation of the acceptance of the foreign tourist by the organization acting as a tour operator. The Ministry of Foreign Affairs of Russia maintains a list of tourist organizations approved to accept foreign tourists. **5.35**

An ordinary educational visa is issued to a foreign citizen who comes to the Russian Federation for study in an educational institution on the basis of an invitation by a diplomatic or consular representation of the Russian Federation for a period of up to three months with the possibility of subsequent extension by the territorial internal affairs agency at the place where the foreign citizen is registered in Russia by means of issuing a multi-entry visa for the period of operation of the contract for study concluded in accordance with Russian legislation, the visa being valid for not more than one year for each subsequent visa. **5.36**

An ordinary work visa is issued to a foreign citizen who travels to Russia for the purpose of engaging in labour activity on the basis of an invitation by a diplomatic or consular representation of Russia for a period of up to three months with the possibility of extension by the territorial internal affairs agency at the place where the foreign citizen is registered in Russia. In the event of extension, **5.37** a multi-entry visa is issued for the period of the labour contract concluded or civil-law contract for the fulfilment of work or rendering of services, but not exceeding one year for each subsequent visa (see Chapter 6). The purpose of the foreigner entering the Russian Federation is specified in accordance with the 'List of Trips' used when formalising invitations and visas for foreigners confirmed by joint orders of the Ministries of Foreign Affairs, Internal Affairs, and Federal Security Service on 27 December 2003. The List contains Section 6: 'Foreigners Entering for Purpose of Effectuating Labour Activity' (Code 006).

5.38 An ordinary humanitarian visa is issued to a foreign citizen who travels to Russia to engage in scholarly, cultural, socio-political, sport, or religious links and contacts, pilgrimages, philanthropic activity, or to deliver humanitarian assistance. Visas of this category may be single or double-entry for a period of up to three months or multi-entry for a period of up to one year. Those who have a one-year multi-entry visa can not stay for more than 180 days before leaving for the first time. This visa is formalized on the basis of an invitation or in exceptional instances by the head of a diplomatic representation or consular mission of Russia on the basis of the written application of the foreign citizen.

5.39 An ordinary visa issued for entry into Russia for the purpose of seeking asylum is issued to a foreign citizen for a period of up to three months on the basis of a decision of the Ministry of Foreign Affairs to deem the said citizen to be a refugee in Russia. Such a visa may only be a single-entry.

Transit

5.40 Transit visas are issued to a foreign citizen who wishes to cross the territory of the Russian Federation or to evacuate a foreign citizen who arrived in Russia in a procedure not requiring a visa (passenger on a cruise ship, citizen of a country with which Russia has an agreement for visa-free entry, or passenger making a visa-free transit of up to 24 hours; for example, change of aircraft). The transit visa is issued for a period of up to 10 days. However, if the foreign citizen is making a transit by air, the visa is issued for up to three days. A transit visa is not required for a foreign citizen flying above the territory of the Russian Federation without making a landing. If the foreign citizen is transiting Russian territory by motor vehicle, the visa is issued for the period necessary to make transit passage by the shortest route on the assumption that the person will travel 500 kilometres per day.

5.41 A transit visa bearing the code TP1 is single-entry, whereas that coded TP2 may be single or double-entry. Such a visa is issued on the basis of travel tickets or a confirmed guarantee that such tickets will be acquired on the territory of Russia and there is a visa for entry to a State neighbouring Russia or a visa of the State of destination, or a passport of that State, or a reasoned request and documents confirming the need to stop over, unless provided otherwise by a treaty of the Russian Federation. The last grounds may be used when a transit visa is issued giving the right to a stop over or to evacuate a citizen who arrived in Russia under a visa-free regime.

A foreign citizen in transit across Russian territory whose diplomatic or official status is recognized by Russia is issued respectively a diplomatic or official visa which may be single or double-entry unless provided otherwise by a treaty. **5.42**

Temporarily residing person

A visa for a temporarily residing person is issued for a period of four months to a foreign citizen who has been authorized entry into the Russian Federation for temporary residing on the basis of a territorial agency of the Ministry of Internal Affairs of the Russian Federation. Visas of this category may be only single-entry. If a person who has received such a visa is unable to take advantage of it within the established period but the reasons for issuing it continue to exist, he may, upon his written application, receive a new visa of the category which is valid for two months from the date of issue. **5.43**

The period of sojourn under an ordinary business or humanitarian single, double, or multi-entry visa is established by the Ministry of Foreign Affairs by agreement with the competent federal agencies of executive power. **5.44**

Having been granted a visa for temporary residing, the respective foreign citizen does not have the right at his own wish to change the place where he temporarily resides within the subject of the Russian Federation, or to choose a place to reside beyond the limits of the said subject of the Russian Federation. Furthermore, a person authorized to reside temporarily is subject to fingerprint registration in the Russian Federation. **5.45**

Special arrangements are in place for citizens of the Baltic States who previously held citizenship of the USSR. Under a 2001 Decree of the Government of the Russian Federation, No. 4, 'On the Procedure for Entry into the Russian Federation, Sojourn on its Territory, and Exit from the Russian Federation of Stateless Persons Who Were in Citizenship of the USSR and Residing in the Latvian Republic, Lithuanian Republic, and Estonian Republic',[15] are issued a visa on the basis of a 'passport of a noncitizen' issued by the Latvian Republic, or a 'travel document of a stateless person' issued by the Lithuanian Republic, or under a 'passport of a foreigner' issued by the Estonian Republic. The grounds for issuance of a Russian visa in these instances is a written recourse to a diplomatic or consular mission of the Russian Federation, although the general **5.46**

[15] *СЗ РФ* (2001), no. 2, item 190.

procedure is applicable to these individuals if they seek to travel to Russia in order to engage in labour activity.

Documents for receipt of visa

5.47 In order to receive a Russian visa, a foreign citizen is required, as a rule, to submit four documents. The first is a valid passport (diplomatic, official, ordinary) or other document certifying identity which is recognized in that capacity by the Russian Federation. Second is a visa questionnaire (excepting heads of foreign States and governments), usually with one photograph (but in certain instances, two). Third is a medical insurance policy valid on Russian territory, except for diplomatic and consular personnel, their guests, and a number of other exempt categories of individuals. The insurance policy must satisfy the requirements of the Statute on Medical Insurance of Foreign Citizens Temporarily in the Russian Federation, confirmed by Decree of the Government of Russia on 11 December 1998, No. 1488.[16] Fourth is a certificate indicating that the foreign citizen does not have HIV if the visa is to be issued for more than three months, but also subject to exceptions specified in the Federal Law on HIV infection. This certificate is formalized in accordance with requirements confirmed by Decree of the Government of Russia of 25 November 1995, No. 1158.[17]

5.48 The passport submitted by the applicant must satisfy certain criteria. There should be no doubt as to its genuineness or that it actually belongs to the applicant, nor should it contain notations, reservations, entries, amendments or corrections not certified by the competent authorities of the respective foreign State, nor should pages have been removed or torn. There must be at least two unused pages designated for visas. As a rule, the passport should be valid for a period of at least six months beyond the period for which a visa is sought. Where an ordinary private visa is applied for in order to receive urgent treatment or in consequence of the grave illness or death of a relative, the passport should not expire earlier than the visa to be granted. In the case of an educational or work visa, the passport must be valid for at least 1½ years from the date of issue of the visa.

5.49 The visa questionnaire is submitted in accordance with a form established jointly by competent agencies of executive power. The applicant may complete

[16] *СЗ РФ* (1998), no. 51, item 6305.

[17] *СЗ РФ* (1995), no. 49, item 4800. Pursuant to an unpublished Letter of the relevant authorities dated 6 March 1996, foreign citizens who arrive in Russia for employment from States whose citizens require a visa to enter Russia, the HIV testing should be done in their country of permanent residing. Refugees, forced resettlers, and citizens of CIS countries are not required to undergo HIV testing.

the questionnaire in Russian, or in the State language of the country where the Russian embassy or consulate is located, or in the English language. If the visa is applied for at an admission point of the State boundary of Russia, the questionnaire must be completed in Russian or in English. The questionnaire may vary from one country to another; for citizens of the United States, for example, the Russian questionnaire resembles in detail that which Russian citizens are required to complete by United States authorities. Most Russian visas are now issued in machine-readable form.

Extension of visa

Visas issued to foreign citizens and stateless persons are extended in accordance **5.50** with an interdepartmental instruction of 30 April 1997, confirmed by Order No. 272 of the Federal Border Service, insofar as such extensions take place at frontier posts and there are no representatives present of the consular service of the Ministry of Foreign Affairs. The grounds for extension are exemplary: natural disasters delaying the movement of a train, ship, motor vehicle, or aircraft; need to repair a means of transport occasioned by an accident or breakdown; illness of the foreign citizen if in a doctor's opinion further travel by the person taken ill would be dangerous for life or health; delays in transit when transferring from one type of transport to another at the point of transit. The circumstances must be confirmed by documentary materials issued by agencies of local self-government, public health, internal affairs, or transport officials. A fee is recovered for extension depending upon whether the visa is extended for up to ten days or longer.

Visa-free regime

Citizens of the former republics of the Soviet Union have, as a rule, a special **5.51** visa regime in the Russian Federation, up to and including no requirement to obtain a visa whatsoever. Belarus, Kazakhstan, Kyrgyzia, and Tadzhikistan concluded an agreement with the Russian Federation on 30 November 2000 which authorised a visa-free regime for citizens of the said countries to travel to Russia; this exception has been suspended with respect to citizens of Tadzhikistan.[18] On the same date, bilateral agreements were concluded between the Russian Federation and Moldova (not officially published) and the Russian Federation and Uzbekistan (not officially published) to the same effect. Azerbaidzhan[19] and Ukraine[20] also have bilateral agreements to the same effect. With Georgia the

[18] *СЗ РФ* (2003), no. 37, item 3566.
[19] *БМД*, no. 10 (1998).
[20] *БМД*, no. 2 (1999).

arrangements are more complex. A 2001 Regulation of the Government of the Russian Federation, No. 708-p, 'On Establishment of a Visa-Free Regime for Crossing the Russian-Georgian State Boundary At the Control-Admittance Point of Upper Lars-Kazbegi', permits Georgian citizens who permanently reside on the territory of the Kazbeg District of Georgia to visit the territory of the Republic North Osetia-Alania for a period of up to ten days without a visa.[21] Otherwise, Georgian citizens require a visa to visit the Russian Federation. Armenia also has a visa-free arrangement with Russia. Turkmenistan citizens require a visa for Russia unless they are under diplomatic or official passports or are crew members of civilian aircraft, ships, trains, or official couriers.

5.52 Special regimes also exist for citizens or certain citizens of China, Croatia, Cuba, Japan, Macedonia, Mongolia, Poland, Serbia and Montenegro, and Vietnam.[22]

Migration cards

5.53 In the aftermath of a number of terrorist incidents in the Russian Federation it was decided to introduce more controls on the movement of foreign citizens and stateless persons about the country. Migration cards were the chosen instrument 'for control over the temporary sojourn on the territory of the Russian Federation . . .'.[23] The migration card serves as the basis for the registration of foreign citizens who have entered the Russian Federation; registration must be effected within three working days from the day of arrival in the Russian Federation. The migration card forms are distributed to incoming passengers on aircraft, buses, and railways or at border points. Each foreigner completes the form in two copies and submits these together with his passport or identity document and visa to the border guard personnel at the point of entry in the arrival halls. One copy of the migration card form is retained by the border guard and the second is returned with the passport and visa for submission upon exit from the Russian Federation. The border guard agency will retain the second migration card form at this time.

5.54 Within three working days the foreign citizen then submits his passport, visa, and migration card to the internal affairs agency at his place of sojourn. Hotels which accommodate foreigners will arrange this registration routinely;

---

[21] *СЗ РФ* (2001), no. 22, item 2263.

[22] A useful chart of visa requirements is set out in A N Golovistikova, *Иностранцы и граждане России: особенности правового положения, регистрация, учет* [Foreigners and Citizens of Russia: Peculiarities of Legal Status, Registration, and Recording] (2006), pp. 39–44.

[23] Statute on the Migration Card (point 2), confirmed by Order of the Ministry of Internal Affairs of the Russian Federation, and others, of 11 November 2002. The consequential changes in federal legislation were introduced by amendments of 10 January 2003 to the 1996 Federal Law on Exit from the Russian Federation and Entry into the Russian Federation. See Article 25^9.

foreigners having their own apartments or staying with friends register personally at the territorial agency of the internal affairs agency of executive power. If the foreigner changes his place of sojourn, re-registration is required within three working days at the new place of sojourn.

On 16 August 2004 the migration card system was reformed to some extent and new Rules for Use of the Migration Card introduced with effect from 1 January 2005.[24] A modified form was introduced; migration cards issued before 1 January 2005, however, continued to be valid, as did the form used for their issuance. The differences between the old and new forms of migration card were minimal. The Russian Federation and Belarus concluded an Agreement on 5 October 2004 to use a migration card of the same model.[25] On 18 July 2006 the system was elevated to the status of a Federal law pursuant to the Federal Law on the Migration Recording of Foreign Citizens and Stateless Persons in the Russian Federation. **5.55**

There are special provisions for foreign seamen who go ashore in Russian ports, and exceptions for diplomatic and consular personnel and their families, heads of foreign States and governments, members of parliamentary and governmental delegations, and executives of international organizations and members of their families. **5.56**

Should the period for which a foreign citizen is authorized for sojourn or temporary stay be reduced, the foreign citizen must leave the Russian Federation within three days. If an authorization for temporary residing or a residence permit is annulled, the exit must be completed within fifteen days. An individual who does not comply with these conditions is subject to deportation by internal affairs agencies, but at his own expense; however, if the individual was hired in violation of the procedure for the recruitment and use of foreign workers, the agency which invited him or the diplomatic or consular representation of the foreign State of which the said individual is a citizen, or others designated by the 2002 Law must bear the expense (Article 31). **5.57**

For reasons that are ambiguous, deportation under Article 31 of the 2002 Law differs from 'administrative deportation' under Article 34 of the same enactment, which, although dedicated to the 'procedure' for deporting foreign citizens, overlaps in substance with Article 31. Those being administratively deported are subject by decision of a court to being confined in special internal affairs or security agency premises or in special institutions until the deportation is carried out. **5.58**

[24] See Decree No. 413 of 16 August 2004, 'On Migration Card', which confirmed the Rules for Use of the Migration Card. *СЗ РФ* (2004), no. 34, item 3553.

[25] Ratified by the Russian Federation on 9 January 2006. See *БМД*, no. 3 (2006), p. 79.

Recording of sojourn and residing

5.59 The 2002 Law calls for the creation of a centralized system for recording foreign citizens and stateless persons who are temporarily sojourning or who are temporarily or permanently residing in the Russian Federation. The system has been organised on the basis of the Decree of the Government of the Russian Federation, No. 186, confirming the Statute on the Creation, Keeping, and Use of the Central Data Bank for the Registration of Foreign Citizens Temporarily Sojourning and Temporarily or Permanently Residing in the Russian Federation.[26] This is essentially an internal process in which the foreign citizen is not directly involved. Depending upon what basis he has arrived in Russia and for what purpose (for example, to study, work, perform military service, or for diplomatic or consular duties) the respective federal agency of executive power concerned with these matters will submit data to the centralized recording system. As for the migration cards themselves which are collected at entry and exit points, they are entered in the local and central electronic data banks for processing purposes. Later, the hard copy versions, after local analysis, are transferred to the superior internal affairs agency together with the results of the analysis. As a rule, the period of keeping these materials at immigration control posts should not exceed one month.

5.60 A foreign citizen, however, who is illegally in Russia and who is brought to responsibility for this is independently subject to recording, photographing, and fingerprinting, all this data being placed in the centralized recording system.

5.61 Although mechanisms are in place to prevent unsanctioned access to the central data bank, the agencies who have routine access to the data bank are extensive in number, including federal agencies of State power and their territorial agencies or structural subdivisions, agencies of State power of subjects of the Russian Federation, the Administration of the President of Russia, the apparatus of the Government of the Russian Federation, the chambers of the Federal Assembly of the Russian Federation, the Central Bank of the Russian Federation, the Counting Chamber of the Russian Federation, the Central Election Commission of the Russian Federation, and the General Procuracy of the Russian Federation. Information from the system is provided to nonusers of the central data bank, including natural persons, in a procedure determined by the Ministry of Internal Affairs by agreement with the Federal Security Service and Ministry of Foreign Affairs. It is the intention of the central data bank scheme to contain

[26] *СЗ РФ* (2005), no. 15, item 348. The data bank is a specialised interdepartmental automated information subsystem containing information on foreigners and intended for the joint use of interested federal agencies. As such, it is a constituent part of the federal interdepartmental information system for ensuring supervision over the 'migration situation' in Russia. The suppliers of information bear responsibility for its completeness and reliability.

information concerning absolutely all foreigners who arrive in the Russian Federation.

Freedom of movement

In comparison with the former Soviet Union, which placed severe limitations on the movement of foreigners about the country, the Russian Federation has adopted a far more permissive attitude. In principle, foreign citizens may move about Russia freely for personal or business purposes on the basis of a visa or other documents issued to them, or documents formalized in accordance with the 2002 Federal Law on the Legal Status of Foreigners. Exceptions are territories, organizations, or objects for which a special authorization is required for entry or which are closed administrative-territorial formations. **5.62**

The territories requiring special authorisation are enumerated on a List confirmed by Decree of the Government of the Russian Federation on 4 July 1992, as amended.[27] In all, there are territories where visits by foreign citizens are regulated in 19 subjects of the Russian Federation. **5.63**

Entry of foreign citizens to a territory of the Russian Federation 'with a regulated visit' is agreed by the receiving organizations or agencies of State administration of the Russian Federation or relevant subject of the Russian Federation with the Ministry of Security of the Russian Federation or its agencies in the subjects of the Russian Federation where the receiving organization is located. The Ministry of Security adopts a decision to permit a foreign citizen to visit such territories by agreement with the interested ministries and departments or their territorial agencies. In the event of a disagreement, the decision is taken by the State Technical Commission attached to the President of the Russian Federation. Maps are published on which the territories with regulated visit are indicated; the maps are distributed, *inter alia*, to foreign embassies and consulates in Russia. The List is amended from time to time. Some of the restrictions are quite extensive; for example, the City of Komsomolsk on Amur, the Chukotsk Autonomous National Area, areas of the Russian Arctic, and so on. **5.64**

A closed administrative-territorial formation is a city, settlement, or other population centre within whose limits are located industrial enterprises for the development, manufacture, keeping, or utilisation of weapons of mass destruction, the processing of radioactive or other materials, and military and other objects for which a special security regime has been established, including special conditions for citizens to reside. These are regulated by the 1992 Law of the Russian Federation 'On the Closed Administrative-Territorial Formation', as **5.65**

[27] *САПП РФ* (1992), no. 2, item 37.

amended.[28] A systematised list of closed administrative-territorial formations was confirmed by a 2001 Decree of the Government of the Russian Federation, No. 508.[29] Access to a closed formation (for example, the location of a plant which produces military products for the Ministry of Defence) would be obtained through that Ministry, agreed with the relevant agency of the Federal Security Service pursuant to a 1998 Decree of the Government of the Russian Federation confirming the Statute on Ensuring a Special Regime in a Closed Administrative-Territorial Formation on Whose Territory Objects of the Ministry of Defence of the Russian Federation Are Located.[30] There are 42 closed administrative-territorial formations located on the territories of 22 subjects of the Russian Federation.

5.66 The freedom of movement of foreign citizens and stateless persons is restricted on territories of the Russian Federation where an 'extraordinary' or a 'military' situation has been introduced pursuant to the 2001 Federal Constitutional Law 'On an Extraordinary Situation', as amended.[31] Depending upon the circumstances, foreigners may be prohibited completely from visiting the affected areas, or visit subject to special permission, or leave the area concerned. A 'military situation' is a special legal regime introduced in the Russian Federation or part thereof in the event of aggression or a threat of aggression against Russia. On the basis of the 2002 Federal Constitutional Law 'On a Military Situation', the President of the Russian Federation introduces such a special legal regime, whose aim is to create conditions to repulse or prevent an attack against the Russian Federation. The rights of foreign citizens and stateless persons may be limited, including the right of entry or exit, or freedom of movement, or choice of place of residence. Individual areas may be closed to foreigners completely or subject to special authorisation.[32]

5.67 Quarantine or other special measures or regimes may be introduced in accordance with the 1999 Federal Law on Sanitary-Epidemiological Well-Being of the Population, as amended.[33] Visits to restricted places by foreigners may be prohibited or limited to persons with special passes issued by empowered public health officials or agencies.[34]

5.68 Closed military cantonments are off limits to foreign citizens and stateless persons unless they have enlisted in military service under contract. The 1998

[28] *Ведомости СНД и ВС РФ* (1992), no. 33, item 1915.

[29] *СЗ РФ* (2001), no. 29, item 3019.

[30] *СЗ РФ* (1998), no. 27, item 3180.

[31] *СЗ РФ* (2001), no. 23, item 2277.

[32] *СЗ РФ* (2002), no. 5, item 375.

[33] *СЗ РФ* (1999), no. 14, item 1650.

[34] These agencies and officials are designated in the Statute on the State Sanitary-Epidemiological Service of the Russian Federation, confirmed by Decree of the Government of the Russian Federation, No. 554, as amended. *СЗ РФ* (2000), no. 31, item 3295.

Federal Law on the Status of Military Servicemen, as amended,[35] makes provision for closed military cantonments which are located often within large population centres. Access to them is based on a system of passes. Closed military cantonments exist in virtually every subject of the Russian Federation; there are at least several hundred. A List was confirmed by a 2000 Regulation of the Government of the Russian Federation, No. 752-p, as amended.

Counter-Terrorism Operations territories are authorised under the 2006 Federal Law 'On the Struggle Against Terrorism'. These are defined as territories or objects within which the legal regime of a counter-terrorist operation has been introduced and a list of provisional limitations within which the said regime operates. A foreigner would require the authorisation of the respective operational headquarters to enter such a territory.[36] **5.69**

The procedure for establishing or creating ecological disaster zones has yet to be formalised in Russian legislation after the repeal of the 1991 Law of the RSFSR on the Protection of the Natural Environment. In practice such zones have been established, for example, in the City of Karabash, Cheliabinsk Region. There is as yet no special procedure for regulating or limiting the access of foreign citizens and stateless persons to such zones. **5.70**

Special economic zones may have special limitations on entry by foreigners and stateless persons. Foreigners who are representatives of zone residents, investors, and persons invited to discuss possible cooperation in the Kaliningrad Special Economic Zone, enjoyed a simplified procedure for the formalization of visas, including the receipt of visas directly at the admittance point to the zone. However, to protect the security interests of the Russian Federation, the federal agencies of executive power have the right to introduce limitations for foreign citizens and stateless persons affecting both entry and duration of stay.[37] **5.71**

Foreign diplomatic and consular personnel and foreign journalists accredited in Russia have the right of movement on the basis of reciprocity. **5.72**

B. Migrants

Official Russian sources estimate there were from twelve to sixteen million persons living in the Russian Federation in 2005 who fell into the category of illegal immigrants; a figure which, if correct, would mean that these individuals constituted 10% of the Russian population and a larger percentage of the work **5.73**

---

[35] *СЗ РФ* (1998), no. 22, item 2331. [36] *СЗ РФ* (2006), no. 11, item 1146.

[37] Article 19, 2006 Federal Law on the Special Economic Zone in the Kaliningrad Region. *СЗ РФ* (2006), no. 3, item 280.

force.[38] The great majority originated in the 'near abroad', that is, the union republics of the former Soviet Union; some were from the 'far abroad', that is, other countries outside the Commonwealth of Independent States such as North Korea, China, or even Turkey.

5.74 Generally speaking, these 'migrants' fell into the legal category of 'foreign worker' from the standpoint of determining the legal status of foreigners. There is no legal definition of 'migrant' in Russian legislation; the various expressions used in international treaties of the Russian Federation, including International Labour Organization Conventions and the 1994 Agreement of the CIS on Cooperation in the Domain of Labour Migration and Social Defence of Migrant Workers,[39] are regarded for analytical purposes as rough synonyms of 'foreign worker' used in the 2002 Federal Law on the Legal Status of Foreigners.[40]

5.75 The agency of executive power primarily responsible for the affairs of migrants is the Federal Migration Service of the Russian Federation.[41] The Federal Migration Service is within the jurisdiction of the Ministry of Internal Affairs of the Russian Federation and carries on its activities either directly and/or through a network of territorial agencies and other organizations and subdivisions within its system. Among the powers with which the Federal Migration Service is endowed are: the formalization and issuance of entry visas to foreigners and documents for residing and temporary sojourn in Russia, or annulment of the said authorizations or residence permits; the registration of foreigners temporarily sojourning in the Russian Federation; the formalization of invitations to foreigners for entry into Russia and the recording of formalized invitations issued by juridical persons; the issuance of authorizations to recruit and use the labour of foreign workers for employers and customers or work or services; the issuance of work permits to foreigners; carrying out the State fingerprint registration of foreigners; and pursuing cases concerning administrative violations of foreigners within its competence.

5.76 Also involved in migration affairs is the Interdepartmental Commission for Putting in Order the Entry and Sojourn on the Territory of the Russian Federation Foreign Citizens and Stateless Persons, created on 30 March 2005 by

---

38 See C J Chivers, in *The New York Times*, 3 March 2006, p. A4, cols. 1–2.

39 *СЗ РФ* (1996), no. 47, item 5299.

40 See G S Skachkova, *Труд иностранцев в России; правовое регулирование* [Labour of Foreigners in Russia: Legal Regulation] (2006), pp. 5–6, who comments on some of the distinctions in the terminology.

41 The present powers of the Federal Migration Service are determined by the Edict of the President of the Russian Federation of 19 July 2004, as amended, 'Questions of the Federal Migration Service', which also confirmed the Statute on the Federal Migration Service. *СЗ РФ* (2004), no. 30, item 3150; no. 41, item 4023.

Joint Order No. 3769/227/244/183/20 of the Ministry of Foreign Affairs, Ministry of Internal Affairs, Ministry of Public Health and Social Development, Federal Security Service, and Foreign Intelligence Service.[42] The principal concern of the Interdepartmental Commission is to interact and coordinate migration policies. Among its powers is the preparation of proposals relating to the regime of sojourn and movement of foreigners on the territory of Russia; regulation of the procedure for trips of foreigners in Russia to work; formation of the list of persons whose entry into Russia is prohibited and, when necessary, to make changes therein; and the preparation of proposals for normative documents regulating the procedure for the entry and sojourn of foreigners on Russian territory.

On 6 March 1998 an Agreement was concluded among CIS countries on **5.77** cooperation in the struggle against illegal migration.[43] The Agreement recites that illegal migration is a threat to public and national security and economic stability and promotes criminality on the territories of the parties. 'Illegal migrants' are defined as the citizens of third States (that is, citizens of countries who are not parties to the Agreement) and stateless persons who have violated the rules of entry, exit, sojourn, or transit across the territories of the parties, or citizens of parties to the Agreement who have violated the rules for sojourn on the territory of one of the parties established by national legislation. Illegal migrants according to the Agreement are subject to deportation to the State of exit in accordance with legislation of the receiving State unless provided otherwise by other treaties.

C. Refugees

There is no constitutional right to being recognised as a refugee in the Russian **5.78** Federation except insofar as political asylum is the reason for seeking refugee status. The Federal Migration Service of the Russian Federation has responsibility for organizing the recording, registration, admission, and temporary placement of persons who are petitioning for asylum or for recognition as having refugee status. The Service helps refugees find temporary employment in Russia and undertakes the procedures for determining or confirming the identification of foreigners who petition to be recognised as refugees and are situated in Russia.

Under the 1998 Agreement concluded within the framework of the CIS on **5.79** cooperation in the struggle against illegal migration, persons who have arrived

[42] *БНА РФ*, no. 21 (2005).

[43] Ratified by the Russian Federation on 12 July 2000. *СЗ РФ* (2000), no. 29, item 3006.

on the territory of one of the parties in order to seek asylum or the status of a refugee, provided they have petitioned in the established procedure for such status, do not fall within the purview of the Agreement.

5.80 The 1993 Law on Refugees (Article 1), as amended,[44] defines a 'refugee' as a person who is not a citizen of the Russian Federation and who, by virtue of wholly justified apprehensions of becoming a victim of persecution by reason of race, confession of faith, citizenship, nationality, affiliation with a certain social group, or political convictions, is outside the country of his civil affiliation and cannot take advantage of the protection of that country or does not wish to use such protection as a consequence of such apprehensions. Or the individual concerned has no citizenship and is outside the country of his previous usual place of residence as a result of similar events and cannot or does not wish to return there as a consequence of such apprehensions. The personal law of a refugee is the law of the country which has granted asylum to him (Article 1195, Civil Code of Russian Federation).

5.81 There is no definition of 'persecution' in Russian legislation. Based on practice it would appear that persecution includes a threat to life; causing of physical suffering; creation of economic hardship; and deprivation of the possibility of employment, engaging in one's profession, receipt of an education, or other limitation of freedom traditionally guaranteed in a democratic society, such as freedom of speech, assembly, religion, or movement, insofar as these measures or actions harm the interests, inviolability, and dignity of the person so as to be considered improper under international norms or standards existing in the Russian Federation.[45]

5.82 *Examples:* (1) The Lenin District Court in Perm on 19 November 1996 vacated, upon the appeal of M, a decision of the migration service refusing M the status of a refugee. The court drew to the attention of the territorial migration service agency that the applicant could be deemed a refugee by virtue of his political convictions and State activities, such as membership in the People's Democratic Party of Afghanistan, participation in combat actions against the Muhadjin, study in the USSR, employment in State institutions of the former government of Afghanistan in Kabul, and threats and persecution by the Muhadjin after the change of government in April 1992.

5.83 (2) A district court in Rostov on Don in a decision of 12 July 1999 upon the

[44] Transl. in Butler, *Russian Public Law* (2005), pp. 132–52.

[45] The examples given here and elsewhere in this Chapter are summarised or adapted from A N Golovistikova, *Иностранцы и граждане России: особенности правового положения, регистрация, учет* [Foreigners and Citizens of Russia: Peculiarities of Legal Status, Registration, and Recording] (2006), pp. 199–201, 221–4.

application of D indicated that it was evident from the evidence submitted that the applicant had left his country of citizenship because of the danger of forcible actions against him by reason of his association with the Government of Afghanistan and service in the police, during which he was wounded and disabled. These facts were confirmed by testimony of the applicant and written evidence from the mass media and from the United Nations refugee officials.

(3) The distinction between 'persecution' and 'discrimination' was analysed in this connection by a district court in Moscow, which on 15 February 2002 adopted a decision in the case of B against the Moscow Regional Migration Service. The applicant, from Iraq, asserted that he was subjected to persecution in Iraq because of his ethnic affiliation. The judge observed that various attitudes towards ethnic minorities exist in various countries. However, in the judge's view persons who encountered 'less favourable treatment' as a result of such distinctions were not necessarily the 'victims of persecution'. In the judge's view discrimination may become persecution when it 'causes material prejudice to the particular persons' or groups of persons; when, for example, it leads to serious limitations in such basic rights as the right to earn a living or access to education. In this case the court did not consider the discrimination to which the applicant referred as the equivalent of persecution. **5.84**

An individual who appears at the Russian frontier seeking refuge is escorted to places of temporary confinement under the 1995 Provisional Instruction on Accompanying Foreign Citizens and Stateless Persons Seeking Refuge on the Territory of the Russian Federation to Places of Temporary Confinement attached to Immigration Control Posts and Centres for Temporary Placement of Immigrants, confirmed jointly by Order of the Ministry of Internal Affairs and Federal Migration Service. If the foreign citizen has crossed the State boundary illegally, he must appear at a border agency, regional subdivision for migration affairs, or territorial internal affairs agency and petition within twenty-four hours of the illegal crossing for refugee status. To avoid prosecution, the crossing must have been forced; in order, for example, to seek a hospital at the nearest population centre, or to avoid persecution by armed persons. If circumstances prevent the filing of the petition promptly (for example, illness), it must be submitted immediately after the foreigner is in a state to do so. In practice, justifiable reasons for delay in filing the petition are not only illness, but also ignorance of Russian laws concerning the procedure for filing the petition; provided, however, that the circumstances of the case do not show that he should have been aware of the procedure (for example, by living among the diaspora of his compatriots after the illegal crossing). **5.85**

If a foreigner illegally crossed the State boundary without being forced to do so by circumstances but could have crossed at an admittance point and did not **5.86** take advantage of the possibility to do so, his actions will be regarded as an administrative violation under Article 18.1 of the Code of the Russian Federation on Administrative Violations, for which a fine may be imposed with or without administrative deportation. Even under these circumstances, however, if the person submits a petition within twenty-four hours to be recognised as a refugee, it is within the discretion of the authorities not to pursue the administrative violation.

5.87 A person is recognised to be a refugee pursuant to the following procedure: (a) recourse with a petition to be recognised as a refugee; (b) preliminary consideration of the petition; (c) adoption of a decision to issue or not a certificate to consider the petition in substance; (d) issuance of a certificate (or not); (e) consideration of the petition in substance; (f) adoption (or not) of a decision to grant recognition as a refugee; and (g) issuance of a certificate of refugee or notification of such recognition. The ultimate decision regarding refugee status is based on a questionnaire completed by the applicant, the formalization of a survey sheet based on individual interviews, and on verification of the reliability of information received concerning the applicant and his family members, the circumstances of their arrival in Russia and the grounds for being on Russian territory. Additional interviews may be conducted if necessary in order to clarify facts. Fingerprint registration is obligatory.

5.88 The petition to be recognised as a refugee may be filed in person or through an empowered representative. If application is made to a Russian diplomatic or consular mission abroad, the applicant must not be a citizen of the country where the Russian embassy or consulate is located. *Example:* If a United States citizen applies to the Russian embassy in Washington D C to be deemed a refugee, the application would be refused. The application must be made to a Russian embassy or consulate outside the United States.

5.89 Representations of the Federal Migration Service of Russia have been established and attached to Russian embassies in accordance with the 2001 Decree of the Government of the Russian Federation, No. 424 'On the Procedure and Conditions of Activity of Representations of the Ministry for Federation Affairs and Nationality and Migration Policy of the Russian Federation Abroad'.[46] The Russian Federation has created such migration representations in Armenia, Kyrgyzia, Latvia, Tadzhikistan, and Turkmenistan.

5.90 A migration mission represents the Federal Migration Service in the receiving State and promotes the implementation of Russian migration policies. Pursuant to the 1996 Statute on the Representation of the Federal Migration Service of

[46] *СЗ РФ* (2001), no. 23, item 2375.

Russia attached to an Embassy of the Russian Federation Abroad,[47] the head of the migration representation receives and gives preliminary consideration to petitions from foreign citizens and stateless persons seeking refugee status in Russia and sends them on for final decision to the Federal Migration Service in Moscow.

While the petition for refugee status is being considered, the applicant and his family are accommodated in places of temporary confinement, the status and powers of which institutions are set out in the 1998 Statute confirmed by Decree No. 679 'On Confirmation of the General Statute Concerning the Place of Temporary Confinement of Persons Petitioning for Recognition as Refugees'.[48] In these places the applicants for refugee status are accommodated, supplied with food and domestic servicing, given a medical examination and first aid, if necessary, given assistance in applying to official representations of the States of their citizenship, enabled to petition for refugee status, and accorded protection of their persons and belongings. Individuals accommodated in these centres must remain there until their request for refugee status is considered. They do not have the right to come and go or to leave. They are required to live in compliance with the rules for internal order confirmed by the Federal Migration Service; failure to do so may result in an administrative fine and/or administrative deportation. **5.91**

The decision to recognize an individual as being a refugee is taken by the Federal Migration Service of Russia or territorial agency thereof. A person recognized to be a refugee who is aged 18 or above is issued a certificate which serves as an identity document in Russia. The certificate is valid throughout the entire territory of the Russian Federation and issued in the procedure laid down by the 1995 Decree of the Government of the Russian Federation, No. 1227, 'On a Refugee Certificate', as amended.[49] **5.92**

A person is recognized to be a refugee for a period of three years. If the circumstances which obliged him to become a refugee persist in the State of his civil affiliation, his refugee status may be extended on a year by year basis. **5.93**

Refusal to consider petition on recognition as refugee

The 1993 Law on Refugees contains an exhaustive list of grounds for refusing to consider a petition for refugee status in substance (Article 5). We consider them in the sequence they are set out in Russian legislation. **5.94**

First, consideration may be refused if a criminal case has been instituted for the **5.95**

[47] *Российские вести*, no. 97 (1996). [48] *СЗ РФ* (1998), no. 27, item 3196.
[49] *СЗ РФ* (1995), no. 51, item 5070; (2001), no. 18, item 1861.

commission of a crime on the territory of the Russian Federation against the person seeking refugee status. A criminal case may be 'instituted' by law enforcement officials enumerated in the Code of Criminal Procedure of the Russian Federation (Article 46) or by the victims of certain crimes by private accusation. Excluded from this category are crimes committed abroad where the prosecution is nonetheless instituted by Russian law enforcement agencies, or where crimes prosecuted by foreign law enforcement agencies are alleged to have been partly committed in Russia. *Example:* Estonian law enforcement agencies institute a criminal case against an Estonian citizen for inciting nationality hatred or on any other ground. This proceeding would not be grounds for refusal to consider a petition in substance for recognition of refugee status. However, this would not be so if the prosecutions involved, for example, war crimes or crimes against peace.

5.96 Second, if the person seeking refugee status was previously refused recognition as a refugee because he failed to meet the criteria of the Law on Refugees on condition that the situation in his country of citizenship or ordinary place of residence has not changed. *Example:* A citizen of Iraq active during the 1990s in the ruling political party was refused consideration of his petition for refugee status in substance because his petition was based entirely on economic considerations. Given the fall of the Saddam Hussein regime, if the person were to reapply for refugee status in Russia a new evaluation would have to be undertaken to determine the individual's apprehension of persecution by the new regime.

5.97 Third, if the foreign citizen was given a substantiated refusal of recognition as a refugee in any of the States-parties to the 1951 United Nations Convention on the Status of Refugees and/or 1967 Protocol thereto,[50] provided that the legal norms for recognition of a refugee in the particular State are not contrary to legislation of the Russian Federation. *Example:* A citizen of Iran arrived in Russia from Azerbaidzhan, where he was refused recognition as a refugee, and petitions to be so recognized in Russia. The Iranian citizen would be refused consideration of his petition in substance because Azerbaidzhan is a party to the 1951 Convention on refugees and the 1967 Protocol and the legislation of Azerbaidzhan on refugees is not contrary to Russian legislation. The result would have been otherwise if Azerbaidzhan legislation had been contrary to Russian legislation, or the State where he first petitioned for recognition as a refugee had not been a party to the 1951 Convention or 1967 Protocol, or if the State where he first petitioned for recognition as a refugee had ratified the 1951

[50] The Convention entered into force for the Russian Federation on 1 February 1993. *БМД*, no. 9 (1993), pp. 6–31.

Convention or 1967 Protocol but with reservations which limited its geographic operation to certain States and the foreign citizen seeking refugee status was not a citizen of those States.

Fourth, if the person has the citizenship of a third State whose defence the foreigner may take advantage of, or has the right to sojourn on legal grounds on the territory of a third State, provided there are no substantiated apprehensions of becoming a victim of persecution in the third State as determined in Russian legislation on refugees. Consideration of a petition in substance will be refused to foreign citizens who, in addition to holding the citizenship of the State where they fear persecution, also have the citizenship of another State (dual citizenship). *Example:* A citizen of Lebanon seeks refugee status in Russia, being apprehensive of persecution in Lebanon for his religious beliefs, but also has French citizenship, where no such persecution is likely. Under Russian legislation this foreigner would be refused consideration of his petition in substance. The same would apply to a foreigner who had a right of permanent or temporary residence in a State of which he is not a citizen. *Example:* A citizen of India who had a right of residence in the United Kingdom would not have his petition for refugee status in Russia considered in substance. To qualify for such consideration, he would need to fear persecution in both India and the United Kingdom. The same would apply to a stateless person who had a right of permanent or temporary residence in a country where he did not fear persecution. **5.98**

Fifth, if the person arrived from a foreign State on whose territory it was possible for him to have been recognized as a refugee. This provision extends as a rule to persons who arrived in transit from any State that is party to the Convention on Refugees or the 1967 Protocol provided that the rules for the recognition of refugee status in that State are not contrary to Russian legislation. *Example:* A citizen of Kuwait who arrives in the Russian Federation via Azerbaidzhan would be refused consideration of his petition in substance in Russia because Azerbaidzhan is a party to the Convention and Protocol on refugees and Azerbaidzhan legislation on refugees is not contrary to Russian legislation. **5.99**

Russian judicial and migration practice is of interest in this connection. *Example:* A was refused consideration of a petition in substance by the migration service on the grounds that he had been in a country prior to arrival in Russia where he could have been recognized as a refugee. The district court in Krasnoyarsk Territory determined that in February 1992 the applicant had left Uzbekistan with his family and come to Russia in March 1993. Uzbekistan was not a party to either the 1951 Convention on Refugees or the 1967 Protocol; therefore the petitioner could not have been recognized a refugee in Uzbekistan. The decision of the migration service was reversed. **5.100**

The same would apply if the legislation of a country which was a party to the **5.101**

1951 Convention and 1967 Protocol was contrary to Russian legislation. *Example:* The migration service in Orel Region refused to consider a petition in substance of a foreign citizen who left Afghanistan and arrived in Russia from Tadzhikistan, where he could have received the status of refugee. The court determined that by Decree of the Government of Tadzhikistan, No. 323, of 26 July 2000, a list of States was established whose residing in which before arrival in Tadzhikistan was grounds for refusal to recognize as a refugee. Afghanistan was among the countries included in the List. Moreover, according to evidence from United Nations refugee sources, the procedure for determining the status of refugee, including the initial stage of registering a petition concerning recognition as a refugee, was suspended in February 2000 and did not operate before 2002. Accordingly, the Tadzhikistan authorities during this period did not take decisions with regard to petitions on recognition as a refugee. The court ruled that since for nearly two years the petitioner could not be deemed a refugee on the territory of the third country, the decision of the migration service in Orel was illegal.

5.102 Moreover, if a person arrived in Russia from the territory of a State which was a party to the 1951 Convention and 1967 Protocol but when ratifying or acceding had limited the geographic operation of those documents to citizens or permanent residents of particular States, and the foreign citizen petitioning for consideration in substance of refugee status was not a citizen or permanent resident of this State, the State would not as a rule grant refugee status in general or to the category of persons in which the petitioner fell. *Example:* A appealed to a Moscow district court in 2001 against a decision of the migration service refusing to consider a petition in substance for refugee status. A was a citizen of Rwanda who had been before coming to Russia on the territories of Zaire, Tanzania, Kenya, and Djibouti. In reversing the migration service the court determined that, although Djibouti was a party to the 1951 Convention and 1967 Protocol, the status of refugee could be granted in Djibouti only to foreign citizens from countries directly adjacent to Djibouti, and Rwanda was not so adjacent.

5.103 The same result would apply if a foreign citizen arrived in Russia from the territory of a foreign State, but during the transit there was no actual possibility to petition there for refugee status.

5.104 Sixth, if a foreign citizen does not wish to return to the State of which he is a citizen or previous ordinary place of residence by reason of apprehension that he will bear punishment for illegal exit or another violation of law committed there, he may be deemed a refugee not merely because of apprehension of punishment, but because prosecution is one of the means of persecuting the foreign citizen for reasons of race, nationality, political convictions, and so on.

Example: By decision of the St. Petersburg City Court, a citizen of Jordan had his appeal against the St. Petersburg Migration Service rejected with regard to granting him the status of a refugee. The Jordanian had come to Russia from Lebanon without returning to his country of citizenship. The court established that he did not return to Jordan by reason of political views but because he feared prosecution for specific military actions and the socio-economic situation generally in Jordan. These were determined not to be sufficient reasons to be granted refugee status in the Russian Federation.

Seventh, if a foreign citizen was forced illegally to cross the Russian State **5.105**
boundary with the intention to petition for recognition as a refugee and did not petition to be so recognized, this will ordinarily preclude a petition being considered in substance. The Russian courts have sometimes been understanding when delays in filing the petition occur.

Eighth, when the foreign citizen refuses to communicate information about **5.106**
himself and/or the circumstances of his arrival on Russian territory, which in effect means the person declines to complete the questionnaire for refugee status or does not answer all questions, refusal to consider the petition for refugee status in substance will happen routinely.

Ninth, a foreign citizen being married to a Russian citizen and in accordance **5.107**
with Russian legislation having the right to receive authorization for permanent residing in the Russian Federation plays a formal role as grounds for a petition for refugee status receiving consideration in substance, although the rationale of the legislator is not entirely clear. In practice this criterion is irrelevant, because marriage to a Russian has nothing whatsoever to do with obtaining a residence permit in the Russian Federation.

Tenth, refugee status would be refused if a person had a residence permit in **5.108**
Russia, that is, an authorization for permanent residing on the territory of the Russian Federation.

Rights of refugee

Under the Law on Refugees a foreign citizen or stateless person recognized to be **5.109**
a refugee and who has arrived with members of his family has the following rights:

(1) the receipt of services of an interpreter and receipt of information concerning his rights and duties, and also other information;
(2) the receipt of assistance in the formalization of documents for entry to the territory of the Russian Federation if the particular persons are situated beyond the limits of the Russian Federation;
(3) the receipt of assistance in the provision of travel and carriage of baggage to

the place of sojourn in the procedure determined by the Government of the Russian Federation. The procedure is laid down by the 1998 Decree of the Government of the Russian Federation 'On the Procedure for Rendering Assistance to a Person Who Has Received a Certificate on the Consideration of a Petition Concerning Recognition as a Refugee in Essence and to a Refugee to Provide Travel and Carriage of Baggage to the Place of Sojourn';[51]

(4) the receipt of nourishment and use of municipal services in the centre of temporary accommodation in the procedure determined by the Government of the Russian Federation until departure for a new place of sojourn;

(5) protection by representatives of the territorial agency of the federal agency of executive power for internal affairs at the centre of temporary accommodation for the purposes of ensuring the security of the particular persons;

(6) the use of a dwelling premise provided in the procedure determined by the Government of the Russian Federation from the housing fund for temporary settlement. The procedure is established by a 2001 Decree of the Government of the Russian Federation 'On the Housing Fund for Temporary Settlement of Persons Recognised as Refugees and Use Thereof'.[52] A person recognized as a refugee and members of his family lose the right to use of the dwelling premise from the housing fund for temporary settlement in the event of the acquisition, receipt, or rental of other housing. Under Russian sanitary regulations a centre for temporary settlement includes, as a rule, an admittance point, reception point, medical clinic, laboratory, housing block, laundry, and food centre;

(7) medical and medicinal assistance equally with citizens of the Russian Federation, unless provided otherwise by international treaties of the Russian Federation. The assistance is provided under an unpublished joint Order of the Ministry of Public Health, State Committee for Sanitary and Epidemiological Supervision, and Federal Migration Service of 7 February 1995, No. 26/14/30, which confirmed the Procedure for the organization of medico-sanitary assistance and ensuring of sanitary-epidemiological well-being of foreign citizens and stateless persons seeking asylum on the territory of the Russian Federation. This document also extends to refugees and persons seeking the status of refugee;

(8) the receipt of assistance in being sent for professional training or arrangement of employment equally with citizens of the Russian Federation in accordance with Russian legislation, except for instances provided for by legislation of the Russian Federation and international treaties of the Russian Federation;

---

[51] Such assistance is provided under 1998 Decree of the Government of the Russian Federation, No. 485. *СЗ РФ* (1998), no. 22, item 2458.

[52] *СЗ РФ* (2001), no. 16, item 1604.

(9) work by hire or engagement in entrepreneurial activity equally with citizens of the Russian Federation in accordance with Russian legislation, except for instances provided for by legislation of the Russian Federation and international treaties of the Russian Federation;
(10) social defence, including social security, equally with citizens of the Russian Federation in accordance with Russian legislation, except for instances provided for by legislation of the Russian Federation and international treaties of the Russian Federation;
(11) the receipt of assistance in the arrangement of children of a person recognized as a refugee in State or municipal preschool and general educational institutions, educational institutions of primary professional education, and also in the transfer thereof to educational institutions of secondary professional and higher professional education equally with citizens of the Russian Federation in accordance with Russian legislation and normative legal acts of subjects of the Russian Federation, unless provided otherwise by international treaties of the Russian Federation;
(12) assistance of the Federal Migration Service in receiving information concerning the relatives of a person recognized as a refugee residing in the State of his civil affiliation (or previous ordinary place of residence);
(13) recourse to the territorial agency of the Federal Migration Service at the place of sojourn of the person and members of his family for the purposes of formalizing a travel document for exit of the particular persons beyond the limits of the territory of the Russian Federation;
(14) recourse with an application concerning the granting of the right for permanent residence on the territory of the Russian Federation in accordance with legislation of the Russian Federation and international treaties of the Russian Federation;
(15) participation in social activity equally with citizens of the Russian Federation, except for instances provided for by legislation of the Russian Federation and international treaties of the Russian Federation;
(16) voluntary return to the State of his civil affiliation (or his previous ordinary place of residence);
(17) exit to a place of residence in a foreign State; and
(18) use of other rights provided for by legislation of the Russian Federation and international treaties of the Russian Federation, and also legislation of subjects of the Russian Federation.

Those granted refugee status receive a lump-sum monetary benefit under the **5.110**
1998 Decree of the Government of the Russian Federation 'On the Amount of Lump-Sum Monetary Benefit and Procedure for Payment Thereof to Person Who Has Received Certificate on Consideration of Petition Concerning Recognition as a Refugee on the Territory of the Russian Federation in Essence',

No. 484.[53] A person who has received a certificate for consideration of a petition in substance as a refugee receives a benefit of 100 rubles, as does each member of his family who has not reached eighteen years of age. The benefit rises to 150 rubles for indigent individuals, pensioners, disabled persons, and larger families. Application is made upon receiving the certificate to the regional migration subdivision, and if refugee status is received through application to a Russian embassy or consulate, the benefit is received after arrival in the Russian Federation.

5.111 The benefit application must be acted upon within one day by the regional migration subdivision and is processed by the Savings Bank of Russia pursuant to an unpublished Order of the Ministry of Internal Affairs of Russia, 6 November 2002, No. 1087, 'On Measures With Regard to the Realisation of the Agreement between the Ministry of Internal Affairs of Russia and Sberbank of Russia'. If the person granted a certificate is ultimately refused refugee status, the benefit received need not be refunded to the issuing agency unless it was obtained by having intentionally communicated false information or having submitted documents known to be false.

5.112 So far as labour rights are concerned, refugees have rights analogous to foreigners who have the status of permanent residing in the Russian Federation. Refugees do not require a work permit in order to be hired for work. Under the Letter of the Federal Obligatory Medical Insurance Fund of 3 November 1999 and pursuant to the Law on Refugees (Article 8(1)[7]), a refugee and members of his family have the right to medical and medicinal care and assistance equally with Russian citizens unless provided otherwise by a treaty.

5.113 Refugees may join trade unions and other social organizations and associations, but may not be members of political parties or engage in campaigning which precedes elections or a referendum.

5.114 A foreign citizen granted refugee status in the Russian Federation may make application for a travel document under which he may travel outside Russia and return, provided that he does not travel to the State of which he is a citizen or had a previous place of residence, or to a State in which the situation is unsafe for him and his family. The travel document also serves as an identity document, but it will not engage the Russian Federation in his defence by Russian embassies and consulates abroad. The document will be valid for a period not exceeding three months.

---

53 *СЗ РФ* (1998), no. 22, item 2457.

Duties of refugee

Persons recognised to be refugees also have to perform duties associated with that status. These duties are as follows: **5.115**

(1) comply with the Constitution of the Russian Federation, federal laws, and other legal acts of the Russian Federation and laws and other normative legal acts of subjects of the Russian Federation;
(2) arrive in good time at the centre of temporary accommodation or other place of sojourn determined by the Federal Migration Service or territorial agency thereof;
(3) comply with the established procedure for residing and fulfil the established requirements of sanitary-hygienic norms for residing at the centre of temporary accommodation;
(4) communicate within seven days to the territorial agency of the Federal Migration Service information concerning a change of surname, forename, and composition of the family, family status, acquisition of citizenship of the Russian Federation, or citizenship of another foreign State or receipt of authorization for permanent residing on the territory of the Russian Federation;
(5) communicate the intention to change place of sojourn on the territory of the Russian Federation or depart for a place of residence beyond the limits of the territory of the Russian Federation;
(6) remove himself from the records at the territorial agency of the federal agency of executive power for the migration service in the event of a change of place of sojourn, and within seven days from the day of arrival at the new place of sojourn be recorded at the territorial agency of the federal agency of executive power for the migration service. The recording of a person recognized as a refugee in the territorial agency of the Federal Migration Service is grounds for registration of the particular person and members of his family at the territorial agency of the federal agency of executive power for internal affairs at the new place of sojourn; and
(7) undergo annual re-recording within the periods established by the territorial agency of the federal agency of executive power for the migration service in accordance with the 1999 Instruction on Conducting Annual Re-recording of Persons Recognised as Refugees on the Territory of the Russian Federation, confirmed by Order of the Federal Migration Service.

There are two bases on which a person may lose the status of a refugee: 'loss' and 'deprivation'. One may lose the status of refugee: **5.116**

(1) after receipt of an authorization for permanent residence on the territory of the Russian Federation or in the event of the acquisition of citizenship of the Russian Federation;

(2) if voluntarily the refugee has taken advantage anew of the protection of the State of his civil affiliation;
(3) if having been deprived of citizenship the refugee has acquired it anew;
(4) if the refugee has acquired the citizenship of a foreign State and taken advantage of the protection of the State of his new civil affiliation;
(5) if voluntarily the refugee has based himself in the State which he left or beyond the limits of which he arrived as a consequence of apprehension of persecution with regard to the circumstances by reason of which he became a refugee;
(6) if the refugee may no longer refuse the use of protection of the State of his civil affiliation, whose territory he was forced to leave with regard to the circumstances for which he became a refugee if those circumstances no longer exist; or
(7) if the refugee has no determined citizenship and may return to the State of his previous ordinary residence in connection with the fact that the circumstances for which he became a refugee no longer exist in the particular State.

5.117 A refugee may be deprived of the status of a refugee if he: (1) was convicted under the judgment of a court which has entered into legal force for the commission of a crime on the territory of the Russian Federation; or (2) communicated information known to be false, or presented false documents serving as grounds for recognition as a refugee, or permitted another violation of the provisions of the Federal Law on Refugees.

5.118 A refugee who has lost the status of such or who has been deprived of such status must surrender to the Federal Migration Service or territorial agency thereof the refugee certificate. A person petitioning for recognition as a refugee, or a recognized refugee, or a person who has lost the status of a refugee or been deprived of the status of a refugee, may not be returned against his will to the territory of the State of his civil affiliation (or his previous usual place of residence) so long as in the particular State the circumstances for which refugee status was sought continue to exist.

5.119 A refugee who fails to comply with certain recording and registration procedures, including annual re-registration as a refugee in accordance with the 1999 Order of the Federal Migration Service, No. 5, confirming the Instruction on Conducting Annual Re-Recording of Persons Recognised as Refugees on the Territory of the Russian Federation, is subject to administrative responsibility under the Code on Administrative Violations of the Russian Federation (Article 18.12).

5.120 Russian legislation does not define 'members of a single family' for the purposes of refugee legislation. In practice, the Federal Migration Service is inclined to consider as members of a family all close relatives (spouse, children, grandparents, brothers, sisters) provided that they resided together and kept a common household in the State which they left. Persons under eighteen years of age are deemed to be refugees automatically when their parent(s), guardian, or other member of the family who is aged eighteen or over is deemed to be a refugee and voluntarily assumes responsibility for them. Even though only one family member feared persecution in the country which they departed, in the interests of preserving the family all members will be given refugee status.

Example: A Moscow court on 10 May 2001, considering an appeal of K against the Moscow Immigration Control Administration, determined that an Afghan female came to Russia in 1993 together with her brother and his family, consisting of a wife and children. The Immigration Control Agency refused her refugee status but granted the same to her brother and his family. In determining whether she comprised part of her brother's family, the Moscow court looked to the application of Afghan customary law and concluded that 'an unmarried woman in Afghanistan cannot live alone; she must live in a family where there is a male who is the head of the family. A woman in Afghanistan is completely dependent on and maintained by the head of the family, who bears responsibility for her. A single woman in Afghanistan has no rights and guarantees of safety'. The court further observed that the life of the applicant in Afghanistan and in Russia was inextricably linked with the family of her brother, with whom she lived. They kept a common household and budget. She was a housewife, not otherwise employed, and dependent on her brother. The court reversed the decision of the Immigration Control Agency and recognized K as a refugee. **5.121**

The Russian Federation is a party to the 1951 Convention on the Status of Refugees and 1967 Protocol Thereto,[54] and to the 1993 Agreement on Assistance to Refugees and Forced Resettlers.[55] **5.122**

D. Political Asylum

The 1993 Russian Constitution provides (Article 63) that political asylum shall be granted to foreign citizens and stateless persons in accordance with generally-recognized norms of international law.[56] Under the 1997 Statute on the Procedure for Granting Political Asylum by the Russian Federation, as amended,[57] **5.123**

[54] *БМД*, no. 9 (1993).

[55] Ratified by the Russian Federation on 22 November 1994. *БМД*, no. 2 (1995).

[56] Transl. in Butler, *Russian Public Law* (2005), p. 17.

[57] *СЗ РФ* (1997), no. 30, item 3601; (2003), no. 49, item 475; transl. in Butler, *Russian Public Law* (2005), pp. 162–5.

political asylum may be granted to foreign citizens and stateless persons on the basis of generally-recognized principles and norms of international law in accordance with the 1993 Russian Constitution and the said Statute, having regard to the State interests of the Russian Federation. Asylum is granted to persons seeking asylum and protection against persecution or against a real threat of becoming a victim of persecution in the country of their civil affiliation or country of their ordinary place of residence by reason of socio-political activity or convictions which are not contrary to democratic principles recognised by the international community nor to norms of international law. The persecution, as a rule, in such instances is being directed against the person who is petitioning for asylum to be granted to him. The legal form of granting asylum is an edict of the President of the Russian Federation.

5.124 A person to whom political asylum has been granted enjoys on the territory of the Russian Federation the rights and freedoms and bears duties equally with citizens of the Russian Federation, except for instances established for foreign citizens and stateless persons by a federal law or by an international treaty of the Russian Federation. Their labour rights are analogous to those persons who have the status of permanently residing in the Russian Federation.

5.125 Asylum granted extends to family members of the person who received asylum, provided that they concur with the petition. The consent of family members under the age of fourteen is not required.

5.126 Foreign citizens and stateless persons are not eligible to be granted asylum if: (1) the person is persecuted for an action (or failure to act) deemed in the Russian Federation to be a crime, or is guilty of the commission of actions contrary to the purposes and principles of the United Nations; (2) the person has been brought as an accused with regard to a criminal case or with respect to whom there is a judgment of guilty of a court on the territory of the Russian Federation which has entered into legal force and is subject to execution; (3) the person has arrived from a third country where he is not threatened with persecution; (4) the person has arrived from a country with which the Russian Federation has an agreement concerning visa-free crossing of boundaries, without prejudice to the right of the particular person to asylum in accordance with the Law of the Russian Federation on Refugees; (5) the person has provided information known to be false; or (6) the person has the citizenship of a third country where he is not persecuted.

5.127 A person granted political asylum loses the right to asylum in instances of: (1) return to the country of his civil affiliation or country of his ordinary place of residence; (2) exit for residence in a third country; (3) voluntary refusal of political asylum on the territory of the Russian Federation; or (4) acquisition of citizenship of the Russian Federation or citizenship of another country. A person may be deprived of political asylum granted by the Russian Federation to him for considerations of State security, and also if this person engages in activity contrary to the purposes and principles of the United Nations, or if he committed a crime and with respect to him there is a judgment of guilty of a court which has entered into legal force and is subject to execution. Loss of political asylum is a matter for the Commission for Questions of Citizenship attached to the President of the Russian Federation upon the recommendation of the Ministry of Internal Affairs of the Russian Federation on the basis of opinions of the Ministry of Foreign Affairs and the Federal Security Service. Deprivation of political asylum is by edict of the President of the Russian Federation.

A person wishing to receive political asylum on the territory of the Russian **5.128** Federation is obliged within seven days upon arrival on the territory of Russia or from the moment of the arising of circumstances not allowing this person to return to the country of his civil affiliation or country of his ordinary place of residence to have recourse personally to the Ministry of Internal Affairs, chief administration, and administration of internal affairs of a subject of the Russian Federation at the place of his sojourn with a written petition which, if there are sufficient grounds for the consideration thereof, is sent to the Ministry of Internal Affairs of the Russian Federation. Petitions concerning the granting of political asylum on the territory of the Russian Federation are not accepted for consideration when the grounds are present that would preclude asylum being granted. The Ministry of Foreign Affairs of the Russian Federation annually draws up a list of countries with developed and stable democratic institutions in the domain of the protection of human rights and submits it to the Commission for Questions of Citizenship attached to the President of the Russian Federation and to the Ministry of Internal Affairs of the Russian Federation.

A reference of the established form is issued for the period of consideration of **5.129** the petition of the person who has applied which, together with his document certifying identity, serves as confirmation of legal sojourn on the territory of the Russian Federation. After the adoption of the decision with regard to the petition, the reference is taken back by the agency which issued it. The circumstances testifying to the circumstances giving rise to the petition for political asylum and the necessary autobiographical information must be set out in the petition submitted in the name of the President of the Russian Federation to grant political asylum on the territory of the Russian Federation.

The Ministry of Internal Affairs of the Russian Federation considers petitions **5.130** received, and asks for opinions of the Ministry of Foreign Affairs of the Russian Federation and Federal Security Service of the Russian Federation, after which all materials are sent to the Commission for Questions of Citizenship attached to the President of the Russian Federation together with its own opinion concerning the possibility and advisability of granting political asylum by the Russian Federation to the person. The Commission for Questions of Citizenship attached to the President of the Russian Federation considers petitions and materials thereto and makes its own proposals with regard to each petition to the President of the Russian Federation for the adoption of a decision by him.

5.131 The period for the consideration of petitions in the Ministry of Internal Affairs of the Russian Federation, Ministry of Foreign Affairs of the Russian Federation, and Federal Security Service of the Russian Federation must not exceed one month in each of those agencies.

5.132 An Edict of the President of the Russian Federation on granting political asylum by the Russian Federation to a person enters into force from the day of signature thereof. The Federal Migration Service within a seven day period from the day of issuance of the Edict of the President of the Russian Federation informs the petitioner about the granting of political asylum by the Russian Federation through its territorial agencies concerning the decision adopted. In the event that the petition is rejected, this decision is communicated to the person and his further sojourn in Russia is regulated by legislation of the Russian Federation determining the procedure for the sojourn of foreign citizens and stateless persons on the territory of the Russian Federation.

5.133 A certificate of the established form is issued at the place where the person petitioned for political asylum to the Russian Federation to the petitioner and to members of his family. Internal affairs agencies of the Russian Federation on the basis of a certificate concerning the granting of political asylum by the Russian Federation formalize a residence permit for the persons granted asylum.

5.134 Insofar as a foreign citizen or stateless person in seeking political asylum from the Russian Federation crosses the State boundary illegally (that is, without valid documents or proper authorisation) they are specifically exempted from prosecution under the Criminal Code of the Russian Federation for this particular act (Article 322, Note).[58]

Temporary asylum

5.135 Russian legislation also has introduced the concept of 'temporary asylum' for foreign citizens and stateless persons who arrive temporarily on the Russian Federation. This status gives such foreigners a number of special rights and guarantees against deportation to the State of their citizenship or previous

[58] See Butler, *Criminal Code of the Russian Federation* (4th ed.; 2004), pp. 252–3.

ordinary place of residence. Temporary asylum is granted when (a) there are grounds to deem the person a refugee but the application submitted by such person is confined to requesting the possibility to sojourn temporarily on the territory of the Russian Federation; or (b) there are no grounds to confer the status of refugee, but humane considerations dictate that the foreigner concerned not be deported. Temporary asylum may be granted to individuals who left their country by reason of hunger, epidemic, or extraordinary natural or technogenic calamities, internal armed conflicts, and the like. Such asylum is granted until the reasons for granting it have been eliminated or disappeared. In Russian practice, temporary asylum has been granted most often to Afghans who fled the conflict unleashed there by the Taliban.

The procedure for granting temporary asylum in Russia is regulated by the 2001 Decree of the Government of the Russian Federation 'On Granting Temporary Asylum on the Territory of the Russian Federation', No. 274.[59] The regional migration subdivision grants temporary asylum upon the written application of the foreigner and members of his family who have arrived with him. The application sets out the personal data of the individual and the circumstances which led them to seek temporary asylum. The applicants are subject to mandatory fingerprinting and medical examination under pain of being brought to administrative responsibility for a violation of immigration rules if they refuse either. While their application to be granted temporary asylum is being considered, they are issued a card concerning the consideration of the application on granting temporary asylum; on the basis of this card they may be registered at the territorial internal affairs agency where they are situated. **5.136**

A decision to grant temporary asylum is made after a verification of the information concerning the applicants and the circumstances under which they arrived in Russia, or when there are humane reasons for granting such asylum. The decision must be taken within three months from the day of filing the application and is granted for a period of up to one year, subject to extension year by year by decision of the regional migration subdivision at which the foreigner is registered. Extension will not be given if the circumstances which caused the foreigner to seek temporary asylum have disappeared. **5.137**

A foreigner granted temporary asylum has the same rights and duties as a person who is issued a certificate concerning the consideration of a petition for recognition as a refugee in essence except for the right to receive a lump-sum monetary benefit. A certificate concerning the granting of temporary asylum on the territory of the Russian Federation is issued on the basis of the decision to grant **5.138**

[59] *СЗ РФ* (2001), no. 16, item 1603.

temporary asylum; this certificate serves as an identity document while the recipient is in Russia and is the basis for registration with the territorial internal affairs agency. Issuance of the certificate must be completed within two weeks of adoption of the decision to give temporary asylum.

5.139 Persons aged eighteen or above receive a certificate, and family members under that age are entered on the certificate of a parent or guardian. The certificate contains the following information: (a) name of the regional migration subdivision which issued the certificate; (b) date of issuance, number, and period of validity of the certificate; (c) full name of the possessor; (d) birth date; (e) citizenship or indication of statelessness; (f) sex and marital status; (g) personal file number of possessor; (h) signature of possessor; (i) period of extension, if applicable; (j) information on any persons below eighteen years of age; and (k) information on registration at internal affairs agency. Public health agencies may, at the request of the holder, indicate blood type, and if the holder marries or children are born, the Registry for Acts of Civil Status may make an appropriate notation on the certificate.

5.140 A certificate may be deemed invalid if there are amendments, erasures, or other types of forgery; the photo of the holder is missing or reaffixed; necessary entries, seals, and stamps are missing; notations and entries not provided for by Russian legislation are present; inaccuracies or errors in entries are detected; there is damage which harms the integrity of the document or parts thereof; or the document is lost or the holder is deprived of or has lost temporary asylum.

5.141 A foreigner loses temporary asylum if the circumstances which served as grounds for granting it have been eliminated, or he has received a residence permit in the Russian Federation, or he has returned to his place of residence outside the Russian Federation. Deprivation of temporary asylum follows if the foreigner is convicted by judgment of a court for the commission of a crime on the territory of the Russian Federation which has entered into legal force, or he has communicated information known to be false or submitted false documents which served as grounds for granting temporary asylum, or has committed other violations of the Law on Refugees. The grounds for deprivation of temporary asylum are, therefore, identical to those for loss of the status of refugee.

5.142 A foreigner who loses or is deprived of temporary asylum must leave the Russian Federation within one month from the day of receipt of notification by the regional migration subdivision. Appeal against the decision suspends the duty of the foreigner to leave Russia until the appeal is decided. If a foreigner granted temporary asylum has been convicted of a crime in Russia, upon the completion of serving punishment he is subject to deportation unless provided otherwise by an international treaty of the Russian Federation.

Appeal against a decision of a regional migration subdivision lies to a court or to the Federal Migration Service. In the event of appeal to a court, the procedure for considering the matter is regulated by the Code of Civil Procedure of the Russian Federation (Chapter 25). The Federal Migration Service has a special appellate commission which considers appeals against decisions of regional migration subdivisions.[60] The Appellate Commission of the Federal Migration Service must consider an appeal filed in the established procedure within one month. A foreigner who appeals first to the Federal Migration Service may, if he loses, then appeal to a Russian court within one month from the day of receipt of a copy of the decision of the Appellate Commission; however, the reverse process is not possible. **5.143**

A decision of the Appellate Commission enters into force from the day of adoption and is sent or handed to the appellant and the regional migration subdivision against whose decision the appeal was made. If the decision requires the regional migration subdivision to satisfy the demand of the appellant, this must be done within seven days from the day of receipt. **5.144**

E. Forced Resettler

Generally speaking, a forced resettler is beyond the purview of this book. The definition of a forced resettler most widely used is set out in the 1993 Law on Forced Resettlers: a Russian citizen forced to leave a place of residence in a foreign State who has come to the Russian Federation, or a Russian citizen forced to leave a place of residence on the territory of one subject of the Russian Federation who has arrived on the territory of another subject of the Russian Federation.[61] **5.145**

However, a foreign citizen or stateless person permanently residing on the territory of the Russian Federation on legal grounds and who has been forced to change his place of residence as a consequence of coercion or persecution committed with respect to him or members of his family in other forms, or as a consequence of a real danger of being subjected to persecution by reason of race or nationality, profession of faith, language, or affiliation to a certain social **5.146**

[60] For the Statute on the Appellate Commission of the Ministry for Affairs of the Federation and Nationality and Migration Policy, confirmed by Order of the said Ministry on 25 May 2001, No. 51, see *Российская газета*, no. 130 (2001).

[61] *Ведомости СНД и Верховного Совета Российской Федерации* (1993), no. 12, item 427; *СЗ РФ* (1995), no. 52, item 5110; (2000), no. 33, item 3348; (2002), no. 52(I), item 5132; (2003), no. 52(I), item 5038; (2004), no. 35, item 3607; transl. in Butler, *Russian Public Law* (2005), pp. 153–61. See generally on this issue M Flynn, *Migrant Resettlement in the Russian Federation: Reconstructing 'Homes' and 'Homelands'* (2004).

group, or of political convictions which became occasions for conducting hostile campaigns with respect to a specific person or group of persons or mass violations of public order, also qualifies as a forced resettler. The category of forced resettler also extends to a citizen of the former Soviet Union who resided permanently on the territory of a union republic and who received the status of refugee in the Russian Federation and lost this status because he was acquiring Russian citizenship but was not properly arranged for while being a refugee.

5.147 A foreign citizen or stateless person who left his place of residence in the Russian Federation under the circumstances set out above must submit a petition personally or through an empowered representative to be recognised as a forced resettler to the territorial agency of the migration service at his new place of residence. A person applying for being deemed a forced resettler has the right before leaving the place of residence to petition the federal agency of the migration service or territorial agency of the migration service at the place of proposed resettlement to send the said petition to the Federal Migration Service or territorial agency of the migration service at the place of proposed resettlement. A decision concerning registration of a petition should be adopted by the territorial agency of the migration service within three days from the day of receipt of the petition. In the event of an urgent mass arrival on the territory of the Russian Federation of persons who have left their place of residence under the circumstances constituting forced resettlement, these persons are to be received in the procedure determined by a decree of the Government of the Russian Federation. The registration of petitions of these persons is to be effectuated immediately.

5.148 A certificate concerning the registration of his petition is issued or sent in the event of a positive decision concerning registration of the petition to each person applying to be deemed a forced resettler. Information concerning members of the family who have arrived and not attained eighteen years of age is entered on the certificate of one of the parents. The form of the certificate and the procedure for the issuance thereof are determined by the Government of the Russian Federation. The certificate is grounds for granting rights to the person and placing the duties provided for by law on him. If a person who has applied to be deemed a forced resettler is refused registration of the petition, notification in written form specifying the reasons for refusal and the procedure for appeal of the decision adopted is sent or issued to him within five days from the day of adoption of the decision.

5.149 Once a person receives the certificate concerning registration of the petition to be deemed a forced resettler, that individual has certain rights and duties which apply solely to foreign citizens and stateless persons who fall into this category. The rights are as follows: (1) receipt of a lump-sum monetary benefit for each member of the family in the procedure and amounts determined by the Government of the Russian Federation, but not lower than 100 rubles; (2) receipt of a referral of the territorial agency of the migration service to reside in a centre for the temporary accommodation of forced resettlers in the absence of the possibility to autonomously determine their place of residence or place of sojourn on the territory of the Russian Federation; (3) assistance in the provision thereof with travel and carriage of baggage to the place of temporary settlement in the procedure determined by the Government of the Russian Federation. In so doing, indigent persons (single pensioner, single disabled person, family consisting only of pensioners and/or disabled persons, single parent (or person replacing him) with a child or children up to eighteen years of age, family with three or more children up to eighteen years of age) who have received a certificate concerning registration of the petition have the right to contributory compensation of expenses for travel and carriage of baggage from the place of registration of the petition to the place of temporary settlement on the territory of the Russian Federation in the procedure determined by the Government of the Russian Federation; (4) reside in a centre of temporary accommodation for forced resettlers, receive nourishment according to established norms and use of municipal services in accordance with the procedure determined by the Government of the Russian Federation until resolution of the question to deem them to be forced resettlers; and (5) the receipt of medical and medicinal assistance in State and municipal public health institutions in accordance with legislation of the Russian Federation.

The duties of a foreign citizen and members of his family who have received a certificate concerning registration of a petition to deem him a forced resettler are three: (1) comply with the established procedure for residing therein when in a centre for temporary accommodation of forced resettlers; (2) undergo obligatory medical examination in accordance with legislation of the Russian Federation; and (3) communicate to the Federal Migration Service and territorial agency thereof the reliable information necessary to adopt a decision concerning the granting thereto of the status of forced resettler. **5.150**

Once a person has the certificate concerning the registration of the petition to deem him a forced resettler, he commences the procedure by which a decision is to be adopted to deem him a forced resettler. The decision to deem a person a forced resettler must be adopted by the respective territorial agency of the migration service within three months from the day of registration of the petition, irrespective of whether it is possible for the person to autonomously arrange himself in the particular locality. The territorial agency of the migration service has five days from the day of adoption of the decision to issue or send notification in written form concerning the results of consideration of the petition. **5.151**

5.152 A decision to deem a person a forced resettler is grounds for granting him guarantees established by the Russian legislation.

5.153 A respective certificate is issued to the person deemed to be a forced resettler. Information concerning members of the family who have not attained eighteen years of age deemed to be forced resettlers is entered in the certificate of one of the parents. The certificate is valid throughout the entire territory of the Russian Federation.

5.154 The status of forced resettler is granted for five years. When circumstances prevent the arrangement of the forced resettler in a new place of residence, the period of operation of his status is extended by the territorial agency of the migration service for each subsequent year upon the application of the forced resettler.

5.155 Federal agencies of executive power, agencies of executive power of subjects of the Russian Federation, and agencies of local self-government adopt within the limits of their powers measures with regard to the provision of arrangement of the forced resettler and members of his family at the new place of residence on the territory of the Russian Federation. These powers vary depending upon the level of State administration concerned. Federal agencies of executive power, agencies of executive power of subjects of the Russian Federation, and agencies of local self-government within the limits of their powers are to:

(1) provide to a forced resettler a full list of population centres recommended for permanent residing and information concerning the conditions of residing and the possibility for the arrangement of employment in these population centers;
(2) include a forced resettler in accordance with housing legislation of the Russian Federation on the list of citizens to receive housing irrespective of the period of residing in the particular locality;
(3) render assistance to a forced resettler, in the event he joins a housing cooperative, assistance in individual housing construction, including the granting (or acquisition) of a land plot and acquisition of construction materials in the established procedure;
(4) grant to a forced resettler who needs an improvement of housing conditions uncompensated subsidies for the construction (or acquisition) of a dwelling in accordance with legislation of the Russian Federation;
(5) assist forced resettlers in the organization of compact settlements on the territory of the Russian Federation in the construction of housing and creation of engineering and social infrastructure and jobs at sites of compact settlements;
(6) provide by way of priority to a single forced resettler (aged or disabled) needing constant care a place in an institution of social defence of the population;

(7) render assistance in placing children of a forced resettler in State or municipal preschool and general educational institutions, institutions of primary and vocational education, and also in the transfer thereof by way of priority to respective institutions of secondary vocational and higher vocational education; and
(8) consider recourses in written form of a forced resettler and give replies to them in written form in the procedure and within the periods determined by legislation of the Russian Federation.

Federal agencies of executive power and agencies of executive power of subjects of the Russian Federation within the limits of their powers are to: **5.156**

(1) promote the realization of the rights of a forced resettler to employment, vocational training (or retraining), and raising of qualifications in accordance with legislation of the Russian Federation;
(2) register a forced resettler as an unemployed person in the event it is impossible to arrange labour in accordance with legislation of the Russian Federation irrespective of the period of residing in the particular locality on the territory of the Russian Federation;
(3) render assistance to a forced resettler at his request in receiving documents necessary for the restoration of labour experience in accordance with legislation of the Russian Federation;
(4) provide orphan children and children left without the care of parents of forced resettlers places in children's homes;
(5) render assistance to a forced resettler at his request to return to his previous place of residence.

Federal agencies of executive power and agencies of executive power of subjects of the Russian Federation are within the limits of their powers to render assistance to a forced resettler in the: (1) return of property left by them on the territory of the Russian Federation in their ownership. If the return of property to a forced resettler is impossible, contributory compensation should be paid in accordance with legislation of the Russian Federation; and (2) organisation in accordance with international treaties of the Russian Federation of the carriage of property in the ownership thereof on the territory of a foreign State. If the return of property is impossible, contributory compensation is to be paid to a forced resettler in accordance with international treaties of the Russian Federation and normative legal acts of the Russian Federation. **5.157**

Those who achieve the status of forced resettler are the beneficiaries of certain rights and subject to certain duties which attend that status. The rights, including significant social and economic rights, are as follows: **5.158**

(1) to autonomously choose a place of residence on the territory of the Russian

Federation, including in one of the population centres proposed to him by the territorial agency of the migration service. A forced resettler may, in accordance with the established procedure, reside with relatives or other persons on condition of their consent to joint residing, irrespective of the amount of dwelling space occupied by the relatives or other persons. A forced resettler loses the right to reside in a dwelling premise from the housing fund for temporary settlement of forced resettlers if he receives (or acquires) another dwelling or completion of construction of an individual dwelling, loss or deprivation of the status of a forced resettler, and also if he is absent without justifiable reasons for more than six months;

(2) in the absence of the possibility autonomously to determine his new place of residence on the territory of the Russian Federation, to receive from the Federal Migration Service or territorial agency of the migration service in the procedure determined by the Government of the Russian Federation a referral to reside in a centre of temporary accommodation for forced resettlers or in a dwelling premise from the housing fund for temporary settlement of forced resettlers; and

(3) receive assistance in the provision of their travel and carriage of baggage to the new place of residence or whereabouts in the procedure determined by the Government of the Russian Federation. In so doing, indigent persons (single pensioner, single disabled person, family consisting only of pensioners and/or disabled persons, single parent (or person replacing him) with a child or children up to eighteen years of age, families with three or more children up to eighteen years of age) have the right to contributory compensation of expenses for travel and carriage of baggage from the place of temporary settlement to the new place of residence or whereabouts on the territory of the Russian Federation in the procedure determined by the Government of the Russian Federation.

5.159 The duties of a forced resettler include: (1) to comply with the Constitution of the Russian Federation and laws; (2) to comply with the established procedure for residing in a centre of temporary accommodation for forced resettlers and dwelling premise from the housing fund for temporary settlement of forced resettlers; (3) in the event of a change of place of residence, before departure to be removed from the record at the territorial agency of the migration service and within one month be placed on the record at the territorial agency of the migration service; and (4) to undergo annual re-recording within the periods established by the territorial agency of the migration service.

5.160 A forced resettler who fails to comply with the recording and registration procedures, including annual re-registration as a forced resettler in accordance with the 1999 Order of the Federal Migration Service, No. 5, confirming the Instruction on Conducting Annual Re-Recording of Persons Recognized as

Refugees on the Territory of the Russian Federation, is subject to administrative responsibility under the Code on Administrative Violations of the Russian Federation (Article 18.12). The duty to re-register is commonly announced through the local mass media.

In addition, and unlike foreign citizens and stateless persons in any other category except that of foreign investor, the forced resettler receives certain guarantees: (1) a forced resettler may not be returned against his will to the territory (or population centre) which he left under the circumstances which made him a forced resettler, nor may a forced resettler be resettled without his consent to another population centre; and (2) decisions and actions (or failure to act) of federal agencies of executive power, agencies of executive power of subjects of the Russian Federation, and agencies of local self-government and officials of the said agencies with regard to execution of the present Law may be appealed to the superior agency or to a court within stipulated time periods. **5.161**

6

RIGHTS OF FOREIGNERS

It has been usefully observed that the rights and freedoms enjoyed by foreign citizens and stateless persons in the Russian Federation may be subdivided into three groups: (a) personal rights and freedoms; (b) political rights and freedoms; and (c) socio-economic and cultural rights and freedoms. We shall follow that scheme in this chapter, subject to minor departures. We address them in this sequence, although it must be said the sequence is relatively new to Russian legal doctrine. During the Soviet era, with its emphasis upon the collective and the State, categories (a) and (c) would have been reversed. The present sequence is consistent with the 1993 Russian Constitution. **6.01**

A. Personal Rights and Freedoms

6.02 Within this category fall those rights and freedoms linked with the individual as inalienable and attaching to each human being by virtue of and from the moment of birth (whenever that is deemed to have occurred). Rights of this category exist irrespective of an individual's affiliation with the citizenship or subjecthood of any State.

Right to life

6.03 As a matter of positive Russian law, these rights extend to foreigners by reason of the Russian Federation being a party to the 1966 International Covenant on Civil and Political Rights and by virtue of the fact that the rights laid down in that Covenant have been expressly reiterated in the 1993 Russian Constitution. The Constitution commences the enumeration of rights in their logical sequence, the first mentioned being: 'Each shall have the right to life' (Article 20[1]). It is accepted by Russian legal doctrine that the words 'each' and 'no one' signify that the right belongs to all persons situated on the territory of the Russian Federation, including, therefore, foreign citizens and stateless persons. Although the death penalty exists in the Russian Constitution and Criminal Code of the Russian Federation and in principle could be applied to foreign citizens or stateless persons, the application of the death penalty has been suspended by the President of the Russian Federation in connection with the accession of the Russian Federation to the European Convention on Human Rights. Abortion is permitted in the Russian Federation for medical reasons in accordance with regulations issued by the Ministry of Public Health of the Russian Federation.

Dignity of person

6.04 Foreign citizens and stateless persons enjoy the constitutional right to dignity of the person (Article 21). No one may in this connection be subjected to torture, force, or other cruel treatment or to a punishment humiliating human dignity, nor may they be subjected without their voluntary consent to medical, scientific, or other experiments. Dignity has been well described as the recognition that a person has value as an '. . . essence endowed with reason and possessing a will and feelings irrespective of what he thinks of himself and what others may think of him'.[1]

[1] Iu A Dmitriev and K A Korsik, *Правовое положение иностранцев в Российской Федерации* [Legal Status of Foreigners in the Russian Federation] (1997), p. 41.

Personal inviolability

The constitutional right to freedom and personal inviolability (Article 22) extends to foreign citizens and stateless persons, together with Russian citizens. Inviolability extends to the person and to intimate life, health, honour, and dignity and to corporal, moral, and mental inviolability. Freedom means the right of each person to dispose of his free time at his discretion without being under observation or protection. These notions are elaborated in ensuing provisions of the 1993 Russian Constitution that address noninterference in personal and family life. Private life in this context refers to those spheres of personal existence not under the control of the State. Personal inviolability means a person is at liberty to commune or communicate with whom he chooses, including by correspondence, telegraph, telephone, fax, or other means of communication, or to keep diaries and other personal writings. Divulgences made to a clergyman, medical doctor, notary, or advokat are protected insofar as they are regulated in individual legislative acts. **6.05**

The 2001 Code of Criminal Procedure of the Russian Federation, 2002 Code of Civil Procedure of the Russian Federation, and 2003 Code of Arbitrazh Procedure of the Russian Federation prohibit representatives in a civil case or defenders in a criminal case from being summoned to court and questioned about circumstances that became known to them in their capacity as representatives or defenders. Under the 1997 Federal Law on the Freedom of Conscience and on Religious Associations, a clergyman may not be brought to responsibility for a refusal to give testimony with regard to circumstances which became known to him from confession (Article 3[7]).[2] A notary is obliged to keep secret information which became known to him in connection with the effectuation of his professional activity; however, a court may relieve a notary from that duty of secrecy if a criminal case is initiated against the notary in connection with the performance of a notarial action (Article 16).[3] **6.06**

Defence of honour and good name

The constitutional right to defend one's honour and good name (a right which a number of foreign citizens have taken advantage of in Russian courts) is elaborated in the Civil Code of the Russian Federation (Article 152). Damages may be **6.07**

[2] *СЗ РФ* (1997), no. 39, item 4465; (2000), no. 14, item 1430; (2002), no. 12, item 1093; no. 30, item 3029; (2003), no. 50, item 4855; (2004), no. 27, item 2711; transl. in W E Butler, *Russian Public Law* (2005), p. 118.

[3] Fundamental Principles of Legislation of the Russian Federation on the Notariat. *Ведомости Съезда народных депутатов и Верховного Совета Российской Федерации* (1993), no. 10, item 37; *СЗ РФ* (2003), no. 50, item 4855; (2004), no. 27, item 2711; no. 35, item 3607; no. 45, item 4377; transl. in Butler, *Russian Public Law* (2005), p. 752.

awarded for losses caused, including lost advantage (Article 15), and for moral harm. When determining the amounts of contributory compensation due for moral harm the court takes into account the degree of fault of the offender and other circumstances deserving of attention (Article 151).[4]

Privacy of information

6.08 The collection, keeping, use, and dissemination of information concerning the private life of a person is not permitted other than with his consent under the 1993 Russian Constitution (Article 24). The term 'person' in the formulation has the effect of extending this constitutional protection to foreign citizens and stateless persons. The presumption of the formulation is that any such collection, keeping, use, and dissemination of information must be effectuated by legal means. Exceptions to this rule are established by federal legislation and likewise extend to Russian citizens and foreigners, among them the Federal Law 'On Operational-Search Activity in the Russian Federation', as amended; the 1991 Law 'On the Police', as amended; 1995 Federal Law 'On Federal Security Service Agencies', as amended; 1996 Federal Law 'On Foreign Intelligence', as amended; and others. The enactments creating the said exceptions also provide for and extend to foreigners the right to appeal against the unlawful actions of personnel of law enforcement officials to the superior official, procurator, or a court. Agencies of State power and agencies of local self-government and their officials must ensure to each, including foreigners, the opportunity to familiarise himself with documents and material directly affecting his rights and freedoms unless provided otherwise by a law.

Inviolability of dwelling

6.09 The right to inviolability of personal life extends to the inviolability of the individual's dwelling, including the dwelling of a foreigner who is on Russian territory. No one has the right to penetrate into a dwelling against the will of the persons residing therein other than in the instances established by a federal law or on the basis of a judicial decision (Article 25, 1993 Russian Constitution). The penetration of a dwelling is possible in accordance with Russian law in order to elicit whether a crime has been committed, obtain information concerning persons suspected of the commission of a crime as part of operational-search work, suppress crimes and other violations of law, and execute judgments and other judicial decisions. Under the Code of Criminal Procedure of the Russian Federation, an investigator or inquiry official may penetrate a premise when performing a search or seizure, or inspecting the site of an incident and

[4] Transl. in W E Butler, *Civil Code of the Russian Federation* (2003).

arresting property or making an inventory thereof with the sanction of a judge or procurator. To the extent that Russian legislation has not satisfactorily determined the procedures for such entry into a premise, foreigners will be affected by the gaps and ambiguities as much as any Russian citizen.

Freedom of movement

The constitutional principle of the freedom of movement on the territory of the Russian Federation (Article 27, 1993 Russian Constitution), based on Article 12 of the 1966 International Covenant on Civil and Political Rights, is rather disingenuous. The Constitution provides that 'each who is legally on the territory of the Russian Federation' has the right to freely move about and choose a place of sojourn and residence.[5] The term 'each' here means the right extends to foreigners and stateless persons. For a foreigner to be 'legally on the territory' of Russia will require that he has entered the Russian Federation with the proper visa and/or other required documents and has remained in Russia in compliance with registration requirements. The right to 'freely move about', although phrased in absolute terms, is in practice territorially limited to exclude areas declared by the Russian Federation to be off limits to foreigners (see Chapter 5). The choice of a 'place of sojourn' or 'residence' likewise is limited by the same prohibitions against the presence of foreigners; even where certain prohibitions may be lifted in individual instances for foreigners to visit a particular territory, the question of sojourn or residence for any extended period would be out of the question. The 1992 Decree 'On Confirmation of List of Territories of Russian Federation with Regulated Visit for Foreign Citizens', as amended, although introduced plainly for reasons of State security, was not expressly contemplated in the Russian Constitution. **6.10**

The 1993 Law on the Right of Citizens of the Russian Federation to Freedom of Movement and Choice of Place of Sojourn and Residence Within the Limits of the Russian Federation[6] gives effect to these constitutional provisions. **6.11**

The freedom of movement of a foreign citizen or stateless person present in the Russian Federation on the basis of 'temporary residing' also is limited in the **6.12**

[5] A 'place of sojourn' is understood to be a temporary location such as a hotel, sanatorium, house of leisure, boarding house, camping ground, tourist base, hospital, or similar premise or a dwelling premise which is not the place of residence of the individual. A 'place of residence', on the other hand, is a dwelling house, apartment, employment dwelling, dormitory, specialized home for the disabled, pensioners, veterans, and the like or any other dwelling premise in which a citizen permanently or primarily resides as owner, lessee, or tenant. For the necessary documents associated with either status, see Chapter 5 above.

[6] *Ведомости Съезда народных депутатов и Верховного Совета Российской Федерации* (1993), no. 32, item 1227; *СЗ РФ* (1996), no. 34, item 4029. The distinction between place of sojourn and place of residence is consolidated in this Law.

sense that this person may not change his place of residing at his own wish. The authorization for temporary residing will specify the region of the Russian Federation in which the individual is permitted to live and/or work. A violation is grounds for annulment of the authorization and issuance of an exit visa.

6.13 It should be noted that a foreign citizen or stateless person does not enjoy a constitutional right to enter the Russian Federation, although each enjoys the constitutional right to depart from Russia in accordance with the 1996 Federal Law on the Procedure for Exit from the Russian Federation and Entry to the Russian Federation, as amended. Only Russian citizens who have left Russia have the constitutional right to return.

Freedom of conscience

6.14 The 1993 Constitution guarantees to 'each' (Article 28) freedom of conscience; freedom of religious belief, including the right to propagate any religion individually or jointly with others, or not to propagate; to freely choose, have, and disseminate religious and other convictions and to act in accordance with them. These constitutional guarantees are elaborated and clarified in the 1997 Federal Law on the Freedom of Conscience and on Religious Associations, as amended[7] and in other Russian legislation enumerated in the said Federal Law, together with normative legal acts of subjects of the Russian Federation.

6.15 Foreign citizens and stateless persons legally on the territory of the Russian Federation enjoy the right to freedom of conscience and freedom of religious belief equally with citizens of the Russian Federation and likewise bear responsibility established by Russian legislation for a violation of legislation on the freedom of conscience and religious belief. Federal law may limit the right of man and citizen to freedom of conscience and freedom of religious belief only to the extent this is necessary for the purpose of defending the foundations of the constitutional system, morality, health, and the rights and legal interests of man and citizen and of ensuring the defence of the country and security of the State.

6.16 No one is obliged to communicate his attitude towards religion and may not be subjected to coercion when determining his attitude towards religion, nor coerced to propagate or not propagate religion, nor to participate or not participate in religious services or other religious rites and ceremonies, nor to study religion. To the extent in practice that foreign citizens experience legal difficulties in Russia arising out of their religious faith, these are more likely to arise in connection with the organisation and activities of religious associations (see Chapter 8 para. 8.19).

[7] Translated in W E Butler, *Russian Public Law* (2005), pp. 116–31.

Freedom of thought and speech

The freedom of thought and speech are guaranteed to 'each' as well. Russian jurists have distinguished between 'thought' and 'speech' as follows: freedom of thought is the right of a person to determine his attitude towards phenomena and events in the world surrounding him, whereas freedom of 'speech' is the right of a person to make 'his thoughts and convictions the weal of society'.[8] **6.17**

The limitations on this freedom established by the 1993 Constitution apply equally to foreigners: propaganda or agitation inciting social, racial, nationality, or religious enmity and hatred are not protected and propaganda of social, racial, nationality, religious, or linguistic supremacy is prohibited. While there is a general freedom to freely seek, receive, transmit, produce, and disseminate information by any legal means, information falling within the category of a State secret is not protected.[9] It follows that no one may be forced to express an opinion or convictions or to renounce them. **6.18**

B. Political Rights and Freedoms

The rights and freedoms which fall into this category are not regarded as 'natural rights' inalienable to the individual. They do not arise from birth; on the contrary, their existence depends upon affiliation by citizenship with a particular State. As a rule, therefore, political rights are reserved to Russian citizens and foreigners and stateless persons are specifically excluded from exercising them. **6.19**

Only citizens of the Russian Federation, it follows, have the right to assemble peacefully without weapons, hold assemblies, meetings, demonstrations, processions, and engage in picketing (Article 31, 1993 Russian Constitution), or participate in the administration of the affairs of the State either directly or through representatives, elect or be elected to agencies of State power and agencies of local self-government, or take part in a referendum, or have equal access to State service, or to take part in the dispensing of justice (Article 32, 1993 Russian Constitution), or to have recourse personally or to send individual and **6.20**

[8] Dmitriev and Korsik, *Правовое положение иностранцев в Российской Федерации* [Legal Status of Foreigners in the Russian Federation] (1997), p. 50.

[9] The proper scope of State secrecy has been the subject of judicial consideration in the Russian courts. For the Law on State Secrecy, see *Российская газета*, 21 September 1993; *СЗ РФ* (1997), no. 41, pp. 8220–35.

collective appeals to State agencies and to agencies of local self-government (Article 33, 1993 Russian Constitution).[10]

6.21 These constitutional limitations are carried over to individual legislative acts regulating elections or referendums. Under the 2002 Federal Law on the Legal Status of Foreign Citizens (Article 12), foreign citizens in the Russian Federation do not have the right to elect or to be elected to federal agencies of State power and agencies of State power of subjects of the Russian Federation, or to take part in a referendum of the Russian Federation or subjects of the Russian Federation. However, foreign citizens permanently residing in Russia do have the right to elect and to be elected to agencies of local self-government and to vote in a local referendum on condition that there is an international treaty of the Russian Federation with the country of which the foreigner is a citizen.[11] To date the Russian Federation has no such treaties. However, a special legal regime is being created for Belarus citizens in the Russian Federation. Under the Charter of the Union of Belarus and Russia, signed 23 May 1997, a citizen of the Union permanently residing in the other State-party has the right to elect and be elected to agencies of local self-government on the territory of that State.[12]

6.22 Foreign citizens are prohibited or limited in serving in the Russian civil service either at the federal level or in the subjects of the Russian Federation. The 1995 Federal Law 'On the Foundations of State Service', as amended, prohibits foreigners from working in State service, that is, performing '. . . duties with regard to a State office . . . for monetary remuneration to be paid at the expense of means of the federal budget or means of the budget of a respective subject of the Russian Federation'. Individual normative acts regulating the police, tax police, firemen, federal security service, foreign intelligence service, and the courts specifically exclude foreign citizens from service in those agencies.

6.23 The prohibitions with respect to Russian courts extend only to State courts; that

[10] Russian legislation attaches special meaning to the concepts of an 'appeal', or 'application' or a 'proposal', or a 'petition', but there is no obvious reason why foreign citizens should be excluded from exercising these rights of Russian citizens. The exclusion is the more baffling when one bears in mind that the 1993 Russian Constitution grants to 'each' the right to judicial defence, including the right to 'appeal' decisions and actions or omissions to act of agencies of State power or local self-government, social associations, or officials to a court (Article 46). Also a foreign citizen or stateless person may 'petition' to be admitted to Russian citizenship.

[11] See the 2002 Federal Law 'On Basic Guarantees of Electoral Rights and Rights to Participate in a Referendum of Citizens of the Russian Federation', as amended. *СЗ РФ* (2002), no. 24, item 2253.

[12] The Charter was published in *Российская газета*, 24 May 1997.

is, courts of ordinary jurisdiction,[13] arbitrazh courts,[14] military courts,[15] justices of the peace,[16] and the constitutional courts[17] and include judges, people's assessors, and arbitrazh assessors. The 1993 Law on International Commercial Arbitration expressly permits foreigners to be elected to the panel of arbitrators of the International Court of Commercial Arbitration,[18] and in practice some fifty or so foreign citizens presently serve as members of that Court. The Maritime Arbitration Commission likewise may include foreigners, although in practice this is less common. In principle, the same applies to arbitration courts in the Russian Federation which operate outside the domain of international commercial arbitration.[19]

Notaries, whether they work in a State notarial office or engage in private practice, may not be foreigners or stateless persons.[20] However, under changes introduced in 2002, 'a person' may become an advokat, a formulation that encompasses foreign citizens.[21] But foreign citizens who become advokats are not permitted to provide legal advice on the territory of the Russian Federation with regard to matters connected with State secrets of the Russian Federation. Foreigners also may be auditors in Russia. Foreigners may not engage in private detective or protection activities under the 1992 Law on Private Detective and Protection Activity in the Russian Federation, as amended.[22] And Russian citizenship is required to become a patent attorney under the 1992 Law **6.24**

[13] Article 8, Federal Constitutional Law on the Judicial System of the Russian Federation; transl. in Butler, *Russian Public Law* (2005), p. 363.

[14] Article 8, Federal Constitutional Law on Arbitrazh Courts in the Russian Federation. Transl. in Butler, *Russian Public Law* (2005), p. 544.

[15] Article 2, Federal Constitutional Law on Military Courts of the Russian Federation. Transl. in Butler, *Russian Public Law* (2005), p. 573.

[16] Article 5, Federal Law on Justices of the Peace; transl. in Butler, *Russian Public Law* (2005), p. 526.

[17] Article 8, Federal Constitutional Law on the Constitutional Court of the Russian Federation; transl. in Butler, *Russian Public Law* (2005), p. 456.

[18] See Article 11(5). Transl. in Butler, *Russian Public Law* (2005), p. 596.

[19] See Article 2 of the 2002 Federal Law on Arbitration Courts in the Russian Federation, which defines an 'arbitration judge' as a 'natural person selected by the parties or appointed in a procedure agreed by the parties to settle the dispute in an arbitration court'. Transl. in Butler, *Russian Public Law* (2005), p. 609.

[20] Article 2, Fundamental Principles of Legislation of Russian Federation on Notariat; transl. in Butler, *Russian Public Law* (2005), p. 747.

[21] Article 2, Federal Law 'On Advocate Activity and the Advokatura in the Russian Federation'; transl. in Butler, *Russian Public Law* (2005), p. 776.

[22] *Ведомости СНД и Верховного Совета Российской Федерации* (1992), no. 17, item 888; *СЗ РФ* (2002), no. 12, item 1093; (2003), no. 2, item 167; no. 24, item 2449; no. 27(I), item 2700; (2005), no. 24, item 2313; transl. in Butler, *Russian Public Law* (2005), pp. 901–8.

'On Trademarks, Service Marks, and Names of Places of Origin of Goods', as amended.[23]

6.25 The right of association is guaranteed to 'each' under the 1993 Russian Constitution (Article 30). This was construed to mean for many years in Russian legal doctrine that foreign citizens and stateless persons could be members of Russian political parties.[24] However, the 2001 Federal Law on Political Parties, as amended, limited the right of association in political parties to Russian citizens (Article 2) and also forbids gifts or donations to political parties or regional divisions thereof by foreign citizens and stateless persons (Article 30).[25] Moreover, although foreign citizens and stateless persons have equal rights under the 1995 Law on Social Associations with Russian citizens in the sphere of relations regulated by that Law—and they may be, if legally in the Russian Federation, founders, members, and participants of social associations, including being elected honorary members or participants—they are excluded if: (1) a decision has been adopted on the undesirability of their sojourn or residing in the Russian Federation in the procedure established by Russian legislation; (2) they are included on a List relating to money laundering; (3) the activity of the social association was suspended in connection with extremist activity; (4) it has been established by decision of a court which has entered into legal force that the indicia of extremist activity are contained in the actions thereof; or (5) the person is confined in places of deprivation of freedom by judgment of a court.

6.26 The right of association extends to noncommercial organizations under the 1996 Federal Law on Noncommercial Organisations (Article 15). Foreign citizens and stateless persons legally in the Russian Federation may be founders, participants, or members of noncommercial organizations unless provided otherwise by international treaties of the Russian Federation or federal laws. The exceptions established are identical to those enumerated above in the 1995 Federal Law on Social Associations.

---

[23] *Ведомости СНД и Верховного Совета Российской Федерации* (1992), no. 42, item 2322; *СЗ РФ* (2001), no. 1(I), item 2; no. 53(I), item 5030; (2002), no. 50, item 4927; no. 52(I), item 5132; transl. in W E Butler (ed.), *Intellectual Property Law in Russia* (4th edn, 2005), pp. 76–124.

[24] See Dmitriev and Korsik, *Правовое положение иностранцев в Российской Федерации* [Legal Status of Foreigners in the Russian Federation] (1997), p. 58: 'Thus, foreign citizens, according to the Constitution of the Russian Federation, have the right to association, including membership in political parties'.

[25] Transl. in Butler, *Russian Public Law* (2005), p. 75.

C. Social and Economic Rights and Freedoms

The transition to a market economy in the post-Soviet era has served to substantially enlarge the social and economic rights and freedoms of foreigners and stateless persons in the Russian Federation. The right of a person to the free use of his abilities and property for the purpose of entrepreneurial activity and other activities not prohibited by a law is guaranteed to 'each' under the 1993 Russian Constitution (Article 34). The Civil Code of the Russian Federation elaborated the position: 'The rules established by civil legislation shall apply to relations with the participation of foreign citizens, stateless persons, . . . unless provided otherwise by a federal law' (Article 2[1]).[26] Entrepreneurial activity is defined in the Civil Code in the same Article as '. . . autonomous activity effectuated at one's own risk directed towards the systematic obtaining of profit from the use of property, the sale of goods, the fulfilment of work, or the rendering of services by persons registered in this capacity in the procedure established by law . . .'. Under the 1999 Federal Law on Foreign Investments, citizens of foreign States and stateless persons may engage in entrepreneurial activity in Russia, provided they have the right in accordance with the legislation of their respective States of citizenship or permanent residence to effectuate investments on the territory of the Russian Federation.[27] **6.27**

However, in some instances foreign citizenship or statelessness is immaterial. What matters is permanent place of residence. For the purposes of currency control, 'nonresidents' are natural persons having a permanent place of residence beyond the limits of the Russian Federation, including those temporarily situated in the Russian Federation (Article 1(6), 2003 Law on Currency Regulation and Currency Control).[28] **6.28**

Legal regulation of labour of foreigners

A correlative right of the right to freely use one's abilities is the right to dispose of one's capability to labour and to choose one's nature of activity and profession, as laid down in the 1993 Russian Constitution (Article 37). A foreigner who exercises his right in Russia to engage in labour activity acquires under the 2002 Law on the Legal Status of Foreigners the status of a 'foreign worker', defined as a 'foreign citizen temporarily sojourning in the Russian Federation and effectuating labour activity in the established procedure'. **6.29**

[26] W E Butler, *Civil Code of the Russian Federation* (2003).

[27] Article 2. Transl. in W E Butler, *Russian Company and Commercial Legislation* (2003), p. 812.

[28] *СЗ РФ* (2003), no. 50, item 4859.

6.30 Accordingly, the 1991 Law on the Employment of the Population in the Russian Federation, as amended, provides that in determining the legal, economic, and organizational foundations of State police for promoting employment of the population, Russian legislation concerning employment also extends to foreign citizens and stateless persons unless provided otherwise by federal laws and international treaties of the Russian Federation.

6.31 Also in force, but substantially obsolete and superseded by the 2002 Federal Law on the Legal Status of Foreigners, is the 1993 Edict of the President of the Russian Federation 'On the Recruitment and Use in the Russian Federation of Foreign Work Force', as amended.[29] While a number of federal agencies of the Russian Federation are concerned with the employment of foreigners, of special relevance is the Federal Migration Service and the Statute regulating its activities[30] (see Chapter 5 above).

6.32 The size of the foreign labour force in the Russian Federation is in principle determined by a system of annual quotas. The 2002 Law on the Legal Status of Foreign Citizens (Article 18) provides that the quota for the issuance to foreign citizens of invitations for entry into the Russian Federation for the purposes of the effectuation of labour activity annually is confirmed by the Government of the Russian Federation upon the proposals of executive agencies of State power of subjects of the Russian Federation, having regard to the demographic situation in the respective subject of the Russian Federation and the possibilities of a particular subject with regard to the arrangement of foreign citizens in employment. In making proposals, priority is to be given to using Russian labour resources and the situation of the labour market.

6.33 The first quotas were established in autumn 2002 for the year 2003. Since this was the first year of quotas, they were generous in size, doubtless taking into account the number of foreign citizens already employed. The total quota for 2003 was 530,000 invitations for entry into the Russian Federation. The enabling legislation also determined the procedure for determining future quotas.[31] Commencing from 2003, proposals have been submitted not later than 1 August of the preceding year for quotas in the forthcoming year. The Ministry of Labour of the Russian Federation, jointly with the Ministry of Internal Affairs and the Ministry of Economic Development, submits to the Government of Russia a draft decree considered by the Governmental Commission for Migration Policy to fix the quotas for the next year, having regard to the proposals

[29] *САПП РФ* (1993), no. 51, item 4934; *СЗ РФ* (1994), no. 2, item 77; (2002), no. 40, item 3905.

[30] *СЗ РФ* (2004), no. 30, item 3150; no. 41, item 4023.

[31] Decree of 30 October 2002, No. 782. *СЗ РФ* (2002), no. 44, item 4394.

from the subjects of the Russian Federation. The total quota established for a particular year is distributed among the subjects of the Russian Federation.

For the year 2004 the total quota was reduced by more than half, to 213,000 invitations.[32] The level was maintained at virtually the same level, 214,000, for 2005.[33] Once the Government of Russia confirms the annual quota, the distribution of invitations among the subjects of the Russian Federation is accomplished by joint Order of the Ministry of Labour, Ministry of Internal Affairs, and Ministry of Economic Development of Russia. Various schemes have been undertaken to improve the coordination of the distribution process, including 'hot lines' and data banks. The quota for 2005, for example, was distributed first among seven federal districts, with a reserve quota of 20,190 invitations to be used for adjustments. The seven federal districts then each subdistributed their quotas among the subjects of the Russian Federation within their jurisdiction. The distributions over the three-year period showed considerable variation from one year to another. **6.34**

The right of foreigners and stateless persons in Russia to conclude a labour contract is provided for by the Labour Code of the Russian Federation (Article 11), which says that the rules established by the said Code, laws, and other normative legal acts containing norms of labour law, extend to the labour relations of foreign citizens, stateless persons, and organisations created or founded by them or with their participation and to workers of international organisations and foreign juridical persons unless provided otherwise by a federal law or international treaty of the Russian Federation. It follows that foreigners who engage in 'labour activity' may do so either as employers or workers. **6.35**

In their capacity as workers, foreigners conclude a labour contract with the employer unless special rules apply (see below). It must be stressed, however, that so-called 'special rules' of labour legislation impose within the general framework of the Labour Code a differentiated approach to the regulation of the labour relations of foreigners, together with the rules of general applicability. **6.36**

The role of international treaties of the Russian Federation as a source of Russian law has been discussed in Chapter 2 above. With respect to the employment of foreigners, they are of special importance. The Labour Code of the Russian Federation (Article 10) replicates the language of the 1993 Constitution of Russia to the effect that generally-recognized principles and norms of international law and international treaties of the Russian Federation are an integral part of the Russian legal system. If an international treaty contains other rules than provided for by laws and other normative acts containing norms of **6.37**

[32] *СЗ РФ* (2003), no. 45, item 4384.

[33] *СЗ РФ* (2004), no. 49, item 4915.

labour law, the rules of the international treaty apply.[34] Russian legal doctrine holds that: '. . . law-application in so doing is structured on the principle of the direct application of international norms, including also in instances when other rules have been established by them than provided for by a national law, or national legislation does not regulate at all determined legal relations in the sphere of labour'.[35]

6.38 Among the relevant treaties cited by Russian labour lawyers as being relevant to the labour rights of foreign citizens and stateless persons in Russia are the 1966 International Covenant on Economic, Social, and Cultural Rights (ratified by the USSR) and the various United Nations conventions prohibiting discrimination in labour and employment, against women, and on the basis of race. The International Labour Organization conventions to which the Russian Federation is a party are enumerated in Annex 7 below.[36]

6.39 Regional labour standards originating in the Council of Europe (Russia joined in 1996) and CIS are relevant to Russia. Although the Russian Federation is not associated with the European Union, acts of the European Union exert a certain influence on Russian labour legislation and standards insofar as Russia endeavours to harmonise with European Union standards. The 1994 Agreement of the CIS on Cooperation in the Domain of Labour Migration is directed towards the basic orientations of cooperation in the domain of labour activity and social defence of workers and members of their families who permanently reside on the territory of a party and who are employed in enterprises, institutions, and organisations of all forms of ownership on the territory of another party. The Agreement does not extend to refugees and forced resettlers, nor to performing artists and others who arrive to work for brief periods, nor to individuals who enter to receive education. Bilateral agreements are concluded among CIS countries on the basis of this 1994 Agreement to fix quotas for the recruitment of, in this case, foreigners from the near abroad for work in Russia. Provisions exist for the mutual recognition of diplomas and certificates, and

[34] See W E Butler, *Labour Code of the Russian Federation* (Moscow, 2004). This includes relevant treaties concluded by the USSR, to which the Russian Federation is a party as the legal-continuer of the former Soviet Union. See Article 2, Federal Law 'On International Treaties of the Russian Federation', transl. in Butler, *The Law of Treaties in Russia and the Commonwealth of Independent States* (2002), pp. 21–4.

[35] V I Anishina, *Применение российскими судами международных трудовых норм Учебно-методическое пособие* [Application by Russian Courts of International Labour Norms: Instructional-Methods Manual] (2003), p. 9.

[36] Although Russia is a party to some sixty ILO conventions (of 185), it remains nonetheless obliged with respect to the others to inform the ILO about national legislation and practice regarding unratified conventions and to indicate what measures are being taken to implement or ratify those conventions.

the conferment of titles and skills without legalisation. Labour experience is mutually recognised by the parties in one another's countries.

The 1994 Agreement goes further than the Labour Code of the Russian Federation in a number of respects, and its provisions are further elaborated by bilateral treaties. For example, a foreign worker from a CIS country in Russia who is made redundant has not only the rights of Russian workers to compensation and privileges, but also has the right to return to his home country at the expense of the employer. Some bilateral treaties give foreign workers from CIS countries in Russia special privileges with regard to the import and export of personal effects. Pension rights are regulated by the 1992 Agreement on Guarantees of Rights of Citizens of States-Participants of the CIS in the Domain of Pension Security[37] and bilateral treaties. **6.40**

The basic principles applicable to labour migration within the framework of the CIS have been set out in a recommendatory enactment adopted by the Inter-Parliamentary Assembly of State-Participants of the CIS on 13 May 1995 and entitled: 'Migration of Labour Resources in Countries of the CIS'.[38] The Recommendation makes extensive use of the conflicts of law principle *lex loci laboris*. The entry of citizens to the territory of the State where employment is arranged, their sojourn there, and exit, are effectuated in accordance with the legislation in force on the territory of the receiving State and relevant treaties. Accordingly, empowered agencies may require the termination of labour relations before time and the return of the migrant worker to his own State if he violates legislation of the receiving State. Labour migration is defined as: (a) the exit of a citizen abroad to obtain paid work under a contract; (b) the entry of citizens of other States to obtain paid work on the territory of States of which they are not citizens; and (c) border labour migration where migrant workers residing in one State commute to another on a daily basis in order to work. The Recommendation requires that limitations on entry of migrant workers be introduced only when the situation on the domestic labour market so requires, for reasons of national security, to ensure the sanitary-epidemiological well-being of the population, or with respect to certain categories of persons who have committed crimes against peace, mankind, or other grave crimes provided for in the receiving State. **6.41**

The Recommendation prohibits discrimination against migrant workers based on nationality, race, gender, and religion. Migrants have the right to be hired, paid, and dismissed on the same basis as Russian citizens. In an interesting **6.42**

[37] *БМД*, no. 4 (1993).

[38] The text appears in the information bulletin of the Council of the Heads of States and Council of the Heads of Governments of the CIS, *Содружество*, no. 8 (1995).

departure from the usual rules on the law applicable to employment injuries, the applicable law is that of the State whose legislation extends to the migrant worker at the moment the injury or impairment of health occurs.

6.43 Certain CIS countries have concluded special agreements on a common market and social policy within a single economic space. On 26 February 1999 Belarus, Kazakhstan, Kyrgyzia, and the Russian Federation concluded the Treaty on the Customs Union and Single Economic Space which required the States-parties to ensure the free movement of citizens within that space. The parties made provision for a unified legal regime with regard to employment, remuneration, and other conditions of labour which presupposed the possibility to: (a) freely move about the territory of the parties while engaged in labour activities; (b) grant to citizens of the parties permanently residing on the territory of any of the parties the legal status maximally approximate to the status of citizens of the receiving country; (c) be in one party while engaging in labour activity in accordance with legislation regulating the employment of citizens of that receiving State; and (d) remain on the territory of a party after completing labour activity in that receiving State. All of these possibilities, however, are to be the subject of separate treaties among the parties.

6.44 Within the framework of the CIS there are a number of special multilateral treaties which affect labour standards of foreigners and stateless persons: the 1994 Agreement on Cooperation in the Domain of Labour Protection;[39] 1994 Agreement of the CIS on the Mutual Recognition of Rights to Compensation of Harm Caused to Workers by Injury, Vocational Illness, or Other Impairment of Health Connected with the Performance by Them of Labour Duties;[40] and the 1994 Agreement of the CIS on the Procedure for Investigation of Accidents in Production Occurring to Workers When Situated Outside the Territory of the State of Residing.[41]

6.45 Bilateral treaties of Russia concerning the labour of foreigners fall into two categories: (a) those concluded within the framework of the CIS; and (b) those concluded with countries who are not members of the CIS. Within the first category is the 1999 Treaty on the Creation of the Union State concluded by Russia and Belarus and ratified by the Russian Federation on 2 January 2000. Under this Treaty (Article 18) issues of migration are within the joint jurisdiction of the Union State and the States-parties to the Treaty. The Action Programme relating to the realization of the Treaty on the Union State stipulated that in the medium-term and long-term perspective, the inter-State migration

---

[39] *БМД*, no. 1 (1996).

[40] *Российская газета*, 30 March 1996.

[41] *БМД*, no. 1 (1996).

of the labour force is one of the basic parameters for the development of the Union State.[42]

The Russian Federation also has agreements on labour activity and social defence of migrant workers with Kyrgyzia (28 March 1996, with Protocol of 22 September 2003); Ukraine (15 January 1993); Moldova (27 May 1993); Belarus (24 September 1993); Armenia (19 July 1994); Tadzhikistan (16 October 2004). The recent agreements are more detailed than those dating from the early 1990s. Under the 2004 Agreement with Tadzhikistan, for example, Tadzhiks in the Russian Federation may engage in temporary labour activity on the basis of (a) contracts for the fulfilment of work or services concluded between juridical or natural persons of the Russian Federation and juridical persons of the State of permanent residing with which the worker is in labour relations; (b) civil-law contracts for the fulfilment of work or rendering of services concluded with customers of work or services of the Russian Federation; or (c) labour contracts concluded with employers arising from contracts concluded within the framework of the Agreement of 16 October 2004. However, Tadzhiks in Russia must obtain a work permit and meet certain health and skills requirements. The rights to leisure for foreign workers under this Agreement depend in some measure upon which category they fall into. **6.46**

On the other hand, the 1998 Agreement between Russia and Kazakhstan on Social Guarantees of Citizens of the Russian Federation and Republic Kazakhstan Residing and/or Working on the Baikonur Complex provided that Russian citizens are provided social guarantees in accordance with Russian legislation and Kazakh citizens, in accordance with Kazakhstan legislation, subject to individual exceptions.[43] **6.47**

As would be expected, most bilateral agreements of the Russian Federation with countries outside the CIS were concluded with the former socialist countries and China. These follow a general pattern. Consisting of fifteen to twenty articles, they provide for a most-favoured-nation regime and address such issues as: the requirement for foreign workers to obtain work permits in Russia with an expiry date; the period for working for a determined employer; annulment of the work permit if the foreigner performs other work for remuneration; the procedure for covering travel expenses of the foreign worker from and to his home country; living and labour conditions; social and medical insurance; **6.48**

42 These policy objectives were presaged by, for example, the Decision of the Supreme Council of the Community of Belarus and Russia of 22 June 1996 'On Equal Rights of Citizens to Arrangement of Employment, Payment of Labour, and Provision of Other Socio-Labour Guarantees'. Under this Decision Belarus citizens may engage in labour activity in Russian organisations without any special permits or authorisations.

43 *БМД*, no. 6 (2001).

medical servicing; taxation, remuneration, legal defence, and the like. Among such agreements are those with Poland (15 March 1994);[44] Vietnam (29 September 1992);[45] China (3 November 2000);[46] Lithuania (29 June 1999);[47] Slovakia (13 February 1995);[48] Germany (17 May 1993);[49] and Switzerland (2 September 1993).[50]

6.49 Absent the special provisions of international treaties of the Russian Federation, the rights of foreign citizens and stateless persons to take up employment in Russia turn on the visa regime applicable to them (see Chapter 5 above); that is, the regimes and grounds of their being physically present in the Russian Federation. Those present in Russia on the basis of *temporary sojourn*—defined by the 2002 Federal Law on the Legal Status of Foreign Citizens (Article 2)—arrived in Russia on the basis of a visa or in a procedure not requiring receipt of a visa and not having a residence permit or authorization for temporary residing. These individuals may engage in labour activity: (a) if this is compatible with the purposes of their sojourn in Russia; (b) if they conclude a labour contract in the general authorization procedure; (c) if the employer has received an authorization to recruit foreign work force in the established procedure; (d) if the foreigner has received confirmation of the right to work in Russia in the established procedure; and (e) if the labour relations with such foreigners are of a fixed-term character. The period of labour relations will be in effect determined by the period of validity of the visa, and if no visa is required, ninety days, unless provided otherwise by the 2002 Law on the Legal Status of Foreigners. If the visa is extended, so too may labour relations be extended.

6.50 A person temporarily residing in Russia is an individual who has received an authorization for *temporary residing* (Article 2, Federal Law on Legal Status of Foreign Citizens). This authorization represents confirmation of the foreign

[44] *Дипломатический вестник*, no. 7–8 (1994). Labour law also was addressed in the 1996 Russo-Polish Treaty on Legal Assistance and Legal Relations With Regard to Civil and Criminal Cases, which contains a special Section V on labour law. Article 44(1) allows the parties to a labour contract to choose the law applicable to the contract; in the event of the failure to choose, the law of the country where the work is or was fulfilled is the applicable law. See *СЗ РФ* (2002), no. 7, item 634.

[45] *Российская газета*, 6 July 1996. This Agreement imposes age limits on Vietnamese (ages 18 to 40; specialists, up to age 50) and, inter alia, addresses issues of payment of remuneration in money or in kind.

[46] *БМД*, no. 7 (2001).

[47] *БМД*, no. 5 (2000). Under this Agreement the Parties determined yearly quotas for labour migrants which, if not fully used, do not carry over to the next year.

[48] *БМД*, no. 10 (2004).

[49] *Дипломатический вестник*, no. 11–12 (1993). This Agreement deals with so-called 'guest workers'. Work permits are issued as a rule for twelve months, with possible extension up to eighteen months.

[50] *Дипломатический вестник*, no. 17–18 (1993).

citizen's right to reside temporarily until he has received a residence permit; as a rule, the authorization takes the form of a notation on the identity document of the foreign citizen. In the absence of such a document, the authorization takes the form of a separate document (see Chapter 5 above). The authorization specifies the region of Russia in which the foreign citizen may and must live. A person temporarily residing does not require an authorization to work in order to engage in labour activity in Russia.

A foreign citizen or stateless person who enjoys the status of *permanent residing* in Russia may engage in labour activity on the same grounds and in the same procedure as Russian citizens, subject to the exceptions established by Russian legislation which reserve certain vocations or professions to Russian citizens (discussed above). Under the 2002 Federal Law on the Legal Status of Foreigners, a person who has received a residence permit is deemed to have the status of permanent residing (see Chapter 5 above). A person who permanently resides in Russia does not need an authorization to work in order to engage in labour activity. **6.51**

As noted in Chapter 5 above, the identity of a foreign citizen in the Russian Federation is attested by the passport issued by his country of citizenship or other document established by a federal law or recognized in accordance with an international treaty of the Russian Federation. For stateless persons the situation is rather more complicated. An acceptable form of identification in Russia for a stateless person is a document issued by a foreign State as recognized in accordance with an international treaty of the Russian Federation as an acceptable evidence of identity. Otherwise, Russian documents suffice; namely an authorization for temporary residing, residence permit, or other documents provided for by a federal law or recognized under a treaty concluded by the Russian Federation. **6.52**

One of the identity documents recognised in the Russian Federation is that issued to a seaman issued in accordance with ILO Convention No. 108, to which Russia is a party (see Annex 7 below). Fishing vessels flying the Russian flag have various requirements for the types of documents which may certify the identity of a foreign seaman serving on the Russian vessel, depending upon whether the vessel is one of foreign navigation or not. Under the 2004 Rules confirmed by Order of the State Committee of Fisheries of the Russian Federation, No. 112,[51] the document certifying the identity of a foreigner is the seaman's document issued in accordance with ILO Convention No. 108. **6.53**

Treaties of the Russian Federation concluded with neighbouring States **6.54**

[51] *БНА РФ*, no. 14 (2004).

concerning visa-free travel by citizens of the relevant parties to the treaties routinely contain a lengthy list of documents that will be accepted as satisfactory identity documents. The 2000 Agreement between the Governments of Belarus, Kazakhstan, Kyrgyzia, Russia, and Tadzhikistan on Mutual Visa-Free Trips of Citizens[52] contains five annexes enumerating for each State-party the documents under which citizens may travel freely within or from one State party to another. Although the lists vary slightly, from ten to twelve documents qualify for this purpose for each country. Among them are passports of various categories, birth certificates for persons under sixteen years of age, military identity documents, flight and railway identification documents, and a seaman's passport.

Civil-law 'labour' contracts

6.55 Many foreigners (and their employers) prefer to engage in labour activity under an entirely separate legal regime: the civil-law contract for the fulfilment of work or rendering of services. A number of standard civil-law contracts are available for this purpose: independent work contract (including domestic independent-work, construction independent-work, independent-work for the fulfilment of design and survey work, State contract for the fulfilment of independent work for State needs); contracts for the fulfilment of scientific-research work and experimental design and technological work; contract for the compensated rendering of services; contracts of carriage (including carriage of cargo, passenger, and organisation of carriages); transport expediting contract; contract of keeping agency contracts; contract for trust management of property; and contract of simple partnership. These contracts are all regulated by, principally, the Civil Code of the Russian Federation and by other civil legislation. Under Russian legislation on author's rights, foreigners may conclude contracts to create works of art, literature, translation, and so on and be fully protected in their rights under these contracts.

Authorization procedure to recruit and use foreign labour

6.56 Irrespective of whether a foreign citizen disposes of his capacity to labour by a labour or civil-law contract, his employer—whether a juridical or natural person or an individual entrepreneur—must have an authorization received in the established procedure for the recruitment and use of foreign workers. It follows

[52] *СЗ РФ* (2003), no. 37, item 3566. By Decree of the Government of the Russian Federation of 31 May 2005, No. 341 'On Mutual Trips of Citizens of the Russian Federation and Citizens of the Republic Kazakhstan' it was established that in addition to the documents enumerated in Annex No. 2 of the Protocol to the Agreement of 30 November 2000, the internal passports of Russian and Kazakhstan citizens and certain birth certificates could be used to cross the Russo-Kazakh border. See *СЗ РФ* (2005), no. 23, item 2273.

that if the employer must have such an authorization, the worker can be lawfully employed only when such an authorization exists; that is, the foreign worker has a right to engage in labour activity only when the employer has a valid authorization. This requirement concerns only foreign workers who temporarily sojourn in the Russian Federation; it does not concern foreigners who temporarily or permanently reside in Russia. Nor does it concern other categories of foreigners enumerated in Article 13(4) of the 2002 Federal Law on the Legal Status of Foreign Citizens.

A fixed-term contract is commonly concluded with foreign citizens in this **6.57** category, since their sojourn in Russia is limited by the term of their visa. If the visa is extended, so too may the labour contract be. When workers enter Russia under a visa-free regime, the period of their sojourn is determined in the invitation issued. In individual instances these matters are decided by international treaties of the Russian Federation.[53]

However, for foreign workers who fall under the authorization regime, a num- **6.58** ber of documents must be obtained by the employer. First, the employer must obtain an Opinion on the advisability of recruiting and using foreign work force. Next, the employer applies to agencies of the Ministry of Internal Affairs for authorization to recruit and use foreign workers. On the basis of the authorization received, an invitation is issued for the entry of a foreign worker to the Russian Federation for the purpose of effectuating labour activity. Simultaneously with the invitation for entry of a foreigner, the employer must obtain an authorization to hire each individual foreigner; a document issued on the basis of the authorization issued to the employer. Having obtained all the said authorizations, the employer then has the right to conclude a contract with the worker for, as a rule, the period of sojourn in Russia. The procedure is complex, for besides the three basic documents required, the employer also must, under Article 18(8) of the 2002 Federal Law on the Legal Status of Foreign Citizens, comply with several other formalities, such as registering the foreign worker at his place of sojourn, notification of tax agencies, and others.

Turning to the first step, an opinion on the advisability of recruiting and using **6.59** foreign workers is issued in accordance with the 2003 Instruction on the Organization of Work With Regard to the Preparation and Issuance by Territorial Agencies of the Ministry of Labour of Russia on Questions of Employment of the Population of Opinions Concerning the Advisability of Recruitment and

[53] In the 1996 Agreement between Russia and Kyrgyzia the duration of a labour contract is fixed at two years with possible extension for one additional year. *СЗ РФ* (1998), no. 48, item 5858.

Use of Foreign Workers, confirmed by Order of the Ministry, No. 575,[54] which, under a State reorganization implemented in 2004, is called the Federal Service for Labour and Employment and falls within the Ministry of Public Health and Social Development of the Russian Federation. The opinion is issued either by the territorial agency of the Federal Service autonomously or by having regard to proposals of State agencies and employment agencies, in either instance taking into account local employment market data where it is proposed to bring in foreign workers. The priority right of Russian citizens to employment is weighed, as is the possibility of training or retraining unemployed Russian citizens.

6.60 In seeking the opinion, an employer must submit: (a) an application in the established form; (b) copies of the registration certificate if the applicant is a juridical person; and (c) copies of the registration certificate if the applicant is an individual entrepreneur or identity document if the applicant is a natural person. If a foreign organisation acts in the name of the employer which is not registered in the Russian Federation, the employment centre verifies documents in the Russian language confirming the fact of its registration and taxpayer number conferred on the employer in the State of registration. The employment centre, having verified the entire application for the correctness of submission, then prepares a proposal with regard to the application on the basis of applications in the centre from people seeking work and the reasons for the unfilled jobs. The centre considers the possibility of filling jobs with Russian citizens, including from other cities or even subject of the Russian Federation, or of retraining redundant workers for these vacant positions. If the employer submitted his application a month or more in advance of seeking the opinion, the agency has not more than seven days to respond, and in any event should not exceed fourteen days. If the application is rejected, reasons must be given for the rejection.

6.61 Within three days after preparing its proposal regarding the employer's application, the employment centre sends its proposal and the application form to the territorial employment agency (copies are kept, and if necessary duplicates issued, for three years). If the application is made directly to the regional territorial agency, essentially the same procedures are followed and analyses of the labour market undertaken. An exception to these procedures exists for proposals to hire foreign citizens as crew members on Russian flag vessels, in which event the employer applies to the federal agency of executive power concerned with transport.[55]

---

[54] *Российская газета*, 22 August 2003.

[55] Also see the Statute on the Procedure for Issuance of Authorisations for Recruitment and Use of Foreign Workers as Crew of Russian Sea-Going Vessels, confirmed by Decree of the Government of the Russian Federation, No. 21, of 16 January 2003. *СЗ РФ* (2003), no. 4, item 324.

In order to obtain an authorisation for the recruitment of foreign workers, an employer or a customer of work or services applies to the territorial administration of the Federal Migration Service where he is located with the following documents: (a) application; (b) proposal or opinion of the respective agencies of executive power of the Russian Federation substantiating the advisability of recruitment and use by the employer of foreign work force; and (c) draft labour contract or other documents confirming the preliminary arrangement with foreigners or foreign partners concerning the intention to recruit and conditions of recruiting foreign workers. The conditions, payment for, and protection of labour and their social security and social insurance are determined by Russian legislation, having regard to any relevant international treaties of Russia. If defence enterprises or institutions are involved, the consent of the Ministry of Defence also must be obtained. **6.62**

The decision to issue an authorization is taken by the Federal Migration Service within thirty days from the day the documents are filed by the employer. If an expert examination needs to be undertaken as part of considering the application, an extra fifteen days is allowed for the decision. If the application is rejected, a reasoned refusal must be issued to the employer within five days. As a rule, authorizations are issued for a period of up to one year. Upon the employer's reasoned request, the authorization may be extended, but for not more than one year. A charge is imposed both for the authorization and any extensions. **6.63**

An authorization is not transferable or assignable, nor may the foreign worker hired for specific work be transferred to another. An authorization specifies: (a) the name of the issuing agency; (b) the name and address of the employer to whom the authorization is issued and information concerning his State registration; (c) the territory on which the authorization is valid; (d) the number and vocational profile of the workers to be recruited; (e) the country of their origin or usual residence; (f) the grounds for issuance of the authorization; and (g) the period of operation of the authorization and other incidental data. The authorization is signed and sealed by an officer of the Federal Migration Service. Employers who have been issued an authorization are obliged within one month to send to the Federal Migration Service information about the conclusion of labour or other contracts concluded with the foreign workers. **6.64**

If an employer violates the conditions specified in the authorization or other Russian legislation, as a result of which the rights of foreign workers are impinged, the Federal Migration Service may suspend the authorization until the violations are eliminated or instruct that the violations be eliminated within a specified period upon penalty of annulment of the authorization. If individuals perish or their health is impaired as a result of an employer's actions or failure to act, the authorization may be revoked at once. If the employer winds **6.65** up or there is a reduction of staff, the authorization loses force irrespective of the period for which it was issued. Under the Tax Code of the Russian Federation (Article 333.28), State duty in the amount of 3,000 rubles is payable for each foreign worker to be recruited. If the employer needs confirmations of the right to engage in labour activity to be issued to foreign citizens in situations where an authorization is not required, payments to cover expenses are recovered from the employer.

6.66 It follows from the 'authorization of employer' system to recruit foreign workers that the foreign citizen himself must receive a document, called a work authorization for foreigners, or a work permit. Article 18(6) of the 2002 Law on the Legal Status of Foreign Citizens simply provides that 'the procedure for issuance of an authorization for work and list of documents to be submitted simultaneously with an application concerning issuance of an authorization for work shall be confirmed by the Government of the Russian Federation'. The Government of Russia confirmed that procedure in the form of Decree No. 941 and the Statute on the Issuance to Foreigners of Authorizations for Work. At present, having regard to certain reorganizations within the Russian State structure, these authorizations are issued by the Federal Migration Service, which is part of the Ministry of Internal Affairs of the Russian Federation.

6.67 A foreigner who is at least eighteen years of age may have an authorization to work. Such authorizations also may be issued to an individual entrepreneur (see below) who engages in entrepreneurial activity without the formation of a juridical person. Otherwise, it is the employer or customer of work or services who seeks the authorization to work for the employee. An application filed with the territorial agency of the Federal Migration Service consists of the following: (a) full name and date of birth of the foreigner; (b) citizenship or State of permanent or primary residence of the foreign citizen; (c) address of permanent residence of the foreigners; (d) period during which the foreigner will effectuate labour or entrepreneurial activity; (e) information concerning existence of authorization for work (with submission of original) for foreigner registered as individual entrepreneur and acting as employer or customer for work or services; (f) type of activity; (g) place of work; (h) information concerning employer or customer; (i) information on the existence of an authorization for the recruitment and use of foreign workers (with submission of the original); and (j) information concerning the conditions of recruitment and use of a foreign worker, or information concerning forthcoming entrepreneurial activity of foreigner. The application must be in the Russian language without any use of abbreviations, and the information provided must be exhaustive.

6.68 With this, the foreign citizen then submits an application with a coloured photograph and (a) a copy of the certificate(s) of a specialist concerning recognition of the document on vocational education received by the foreign worker in a foreign State, or certificate of equivalence of such document to a Russian diploma if Russian legislation or an international treaty of Russia requires such documents; (b) a copy of the certificate of registration of the foreigner in Russia as an individual entrepreneur; and (c) a copy of a special authorization for entry of the foreigner to a territory which is on a List confirmed by the Government of Russia, if applicable. Identity documents of the foreign citizen also must be submitted and must be valid for at least six months. Any documents issued by foreign States must be legalised unless international treaties of Russia provide otherwise, and if the documents are in a foreign language, a notarially attested translation into Russian must be provided. The application is then subject to verification by the receiving agency and a decision taken to issue, or not, the authorization. A separate decision is taken with respect to each application.

The grounds for refusal are unreliable or distorted information in the documents submitted or the presence of circumstances set out in the 2002 Federal Law on the Legal Status of Foreigners (Article 18), as follows if the foreign citizen: (1) favours the forcible change of the foundations of the constitutional system of the Russian Federation or by other actions creates a threat to the security of the Russian Federation or citizens of the Russian Federation; (2) finances and plans terrorist (or extremist) acts, renders assistance in the commission of such acts or commits them, and likewise by other actions supports terrorist (or extremist) activity; (3) within five years preceding the day of filing an application concerning issuance of an authorization for work was subjected to administrative deportation beyond the limits of the Russian Federation or deportation; (4) submits forged or false documents or communications information about himself known to be false; (5) is convicted by judgment of a court which has entered into legal force for the commission of a grave or especially grave crime, or a crime the recidivism of which was deemed to be dangerous; (6) has an uncancelled or unremoved record of conviction for the commission of a grave or especially grave crime on the territory of the Russian Federation or beyond the limits thereof deemed to be such in accordance with a federal law; (7) repeatedly (two or more times) within one year was brought to administrative responsibility for a violation of legislation of the Russian Federation with respect to ensuring the regime of sojourn (or residing) of foreign citizens in the Russian Federation; (8) departs from the Russian Federation to a foreign State for permanent residing; (9) is beyond the limits of the Russian Federation for more than six months; or (10) is ill with narcotics addiction, or has no certificate concerning the absence in him of the disease caused by human immuno-deficiency virus (HIV-infection) or suffers from one of the contagious diseases which represent a danger for surrounding persons. A list of such diseases 6.69

and the procedure for confirming the existence or absence thereof shall be confirmed by the Government of the Russian Federation.

6.70 The period for consideration should not exceed thirty work days from the day of filing the application. The Federal Migration Agency has ten days to inform the applicant of the decision. Under the Tax Code of the Russian Federation (Article 333.28) State duty in the amount of 1,000 rubles is recovered for issuing a foreigner with an authorization to work. The employer or customer of work or services must transfer the authorization for work to the foreign applicant before he commences labour activity on the territory of the Russian Federation. Once the authorization for work expires, the foreign citizen has three days to leave the Russian Federation. Under Article 18(5) of the 2002 Law on the Legal Status of Foreign Citizens the employer will have been required to make a pledge deposit in a special account opened with the Ministry of Internal Affairs to cover the cost of the foreigner's travel if the foreigner does not leave Russia in accordance with his visa; that deposit is refunded once the foreigner departs on his own volition in accordance with law.

6.71 Having received an authorization for the recruitment of foreign workers, the employer or customer of work or services then sets about arranging an invitation for entry of the foreign worker to the Russian Federation. The invitation will be issued upon petition of the employer by the Ministry of Internal Affairs of the Russian Federation or territorial agency thereof. One of the grounds for the issuance of a visa to a foreigner is an invitation to engage in labour activity in Russia under the Law on the Procedure for Exit from the Russian Federation and Entry into the Russian Federation (Article 25). The Ministry issues the invitation pursuant to the Statute on the Formalization of an Invitation to the Russian Federation of Foreign Citizens and Stateless Persons, confirmed by Decree of the Government of the Russian Federation, No. 1142, of 1 October 1998.[56]

6.72 Where provided by an international treaty, an invitation may be grounds for entry into the Russian Federation without a visa. The invitation issued by the Ministry of Internal Affairs is then formalized by the Ministry of Foreign Affairs. Application forms for invitations are documents of strict accountability under Russian law. The form of the application form, the procedure for recording and keeping these forms, and the procedure for the interaction of federal agencies of executive power when formalizing and issuing invitations is regulated by departmental normative legal acts. Under a 2003 Regulation of the Government of the Russian Federation, No. 390-p,[57] the Ministry of Internal

[56] *СЗ РФ* (1998), no. 41, item 5020; (1999), no. 40, item 4862; (2002), no. 41, item 3983; (2003), no. 13, item 1240; no. 17, item 1622.

[57] *СЗ РФ* (2003), no. 14, item 1295.

Affairs of the Russian Federation issued on the same date Order No. 72 'On Organization of the Activity of Internal Affairs Agencies of the Russian Federation With Regard to the Formalization and Issuance of Invitations for Entry into the Russian Federation of Foreign Citizens and Stateless Persons and the Recording and Keeping of Invitation Forms'.[58] The Ministry of Foreign Affairs issued Order No. 1833 'On Confirmation of Rules for the Formalization of Invitations for Entry into the Russian Federation of Foreign Citizens and Stateless Persons'.[59]

The Ministry of Foreign Affairs issues Series KC–2 invitations upon the petition **6.73** of: (a) federal agencies of State power; (b) diplomatic representations and consular institutions of foreign States in the Russian Federation; (c) international organizations and their representations in Russia, and representations of foreign States attached to international organizations located in Russia; or (d) agencies of State power of subjects of the Russian Federation. The Ministry of Internal Affairs, pursuant to the 2002 Federal Law on the Legal Status of Foreign Citizens (Article 16), issues invitations upon the petition of: (a) agencies of local self-government; (b) juridical persons; (c) citizens of the Russian Federation; or (d) foreign citizens and stateless persons permanently residing in Russia.

Invitations are to be formalised within not more than thirty days from the day **6.74** of application. Pursuant to the Tax Code of the Russian Federation (Article 333.28), State duty is recovered for the issuance of an invitation (200 rubles) and for making changes in a formalized invitation (100 rubles).

The types of visas issued by the Russian Government and the conditions of issuance are discussed in Chapter 5 above.

Cooperative societies and peasant (or farmer) economy

There exists a third legal 'sphere' outside civil and labour law under which **6.75** foreigners may engage in labour activity under Russian law. Under the 2003 Federal Law 'On the Peasant (or Farmer) Economy', foreign citizens and stateless persons who have dispositive civil-law capacity have the right to create, equally with Russian citizens, a peasant or farmer economy.[60]

Foreigners may also engage in labour activity as members or shareholders of **6.76** various types of cooperative society, as well as concluding labour contracts or civil-law contracts enumerated above with the cooperative society. The possibilities here depend upon the legislation regulating each type of cooperative. The position with respect to the agricultural cooperative society is ambiguous,

[58] *БНА РФ*, no. 18 (2003). [59] *БНА РФ*, no. 14 (2004).
[60] *СЗ РФ* (2003), no. 24, item 2249.

for example. The 1995 Federal Law 'On Agricultural Cooperative Societies', as amended,[61] imposes in its provisions on membership no requirement of Russian citizenship. However, in the provisions regulating agricultural production cooperatives, a reference is made to members being a citizen of the Russian Federation and nothing is said about foreigners whatsoever. If this formulation is construed against foreigners (as would be the ordinary construction of the provision), it is inconsistent with the 1996 Federal Law on Production Cooperatives, as amended, which provides (Article 7) that foreign citizens and stateless persons may be members of the cooperative equally with Russian citizens. No other limitations are imposed on foreigners in the law.[62]

6.77 Neither the 1992 Law 'On Consumer Cooperative Societies'[63] nor the 2001 Federal Law 'On Credit Consumer Cooperatives of Citizens'[64] imposes the requirement of Russian citizenship for membership.

Individual entrepreneur

6.78 Under the Civil Code of the Russian Federation (Article 23), foreign citizens may register as an individual entrepreneur and carry on entrepreneurial activity without the formation of a juridical person. The 2002 Federal Law on the Legal Status of Foreigners (Article 13) also permits a foreign citizen registered as an individual entrepreneur to act as a customer of work or services.

Currency control

6.79 Under the 2003 Law on Currency Regulation and Currency Control,[65] natural persons, juridical persons, and enterprises and organizations that are not juridical persons—all of which have a permanent place of residence or location beyond the limits of the Russian Federation—and foreign diplomatic and other official representations, together with international organizations and their branches and representations, are classified as 'nonresidents' for the purposes of currency regulation and control. Nonresidents have the right without limitation to transfer, bring in, and send currency valuables to the Russian Federation in compliance with customs rules. They also may sell and purchase foreign currency for currency of the Russian Federation in the procedure established by the Central Bank of the Russian Federation.

[61] *СЗ РФ* (1995), no. 50, item 4870; (1997), no. 10, item 1120; (1999), no. 8, item 973; (2002), no. 12, item 1093; no. 28, item 2790; (2003), no. 2, items 160 and 167; no. 24, item 2248.

[62] *СЗ РФ* (1996), no. 20, item 2321; (2001), no. 21, item 2062; (2002), no. 12, item 1093; no. 28, item 2790.

[63] *Ведомости Верховного Совета Российской Федерации* (1992), no. 30, item 1788; *СЗ РФ* (1997), no. 28, item 3306; (2000), no. 18, item 1910; (2002), no. 12, item 1093; no. 28, item 2790.

[64] *СЗ РФ* (2001), no. 33(I), item 3420.

[65] *СЗ РФ* (2003), no. 50, item 4859.

Natural persons who are nonresidents have the right to transfer, take out, and send from the Russian Federation currency valuables previously transferred, brought in, or sent to the Russian Federation within the limits specified in their customs declaration or other document which confirms the transfer, bringing in, or sending to the Russian Federation; foreign currency in cash, however, may be taken out without declaration if the amount does not exceed the equivalent of US$3,000, and with a written customs declaration if the amount does not exceed the equivalent of US$10,000. Evidence need not be submitted to the customs agencies confirming that the cash foreign currency being taken out was previously transferred, brought in, or sent to the Russian Federation or acquired in the Russian Federation. Amounts in excess of US$10,000 require the special authorization of the Central Bank of the Russian Federation. On 29 June 2006 the Government of the Russian Federation approved the repeal of the last formal limitations on the movement of Russian currency with a view to making the ruble a convertible currency with effect from 1 July 2006. Foreign investors which have formed juridical persons or legal entities in Russia will benefit particularly from these changes. The compulsory sale of foreign currency for rubles is eliminated, as is the need for special foreign currency accounts. Money laundering regulations, however, remain in operation. **6.80**

Military service

The Russian Armed Forces have moved from the draft of conscripts as the principal means of recruiting military personnel to a contractual system, emulating the example of other leading military powers. Although foreign citizens may not be called up to military service or alternative civilian service,[66] they may be hired under contract for work in the Armed Forces of the Russian Federation, other forces, military formations, and agencies as civilian personnel pursuant to the 2002 Federal Law on the Legal Status of Foreigners. Foreign citizens who elect employment of this nature are in effect engaging in labour activity under the norms of Russian administrative law which regulate military service. The Labour Code of the Russian Federation (Article 349) makes this clear: workers who have concluded a labour contract concerning work in military units, institutions, military educational institutions of higher and secondary vocational education, and other organisations of the Armed Forces of the Russian Federation and federal agencies of executive power in which military service is provided for by Russian legislation, are subject to labour legislation 'with the peculiarities **6.81**

[66] *СЗ РФ* (2002), no. 30, item 3030; (2004), no. 3, item 3607. In determining who may or may not be sent for alternative civilian service, this Federal Law provides (Article 3) that citizens who are not subject to being conscripted for military service are not eligible for civilian service. This formulation has the effect of excluding foreigners, since they are not subject to conscription.

provided by federal laws and other normative legal acts'.[67] Although labour legislation is permissive, the possibility of foreigners enlisting under contract in the Armed Forces is sufficiently new that general military legislation has not been consequentially amended to take this fully into account and model contracts for performing military service by foreigners have not been developed.

6.82 The concept of military service is a broad one in the Russian Federation. As defined in the 1998 Federal Law on Military Duty and Military Service, as amended,[68] military service is a 'special type of federal State service' performed in the Armed Forces of the USSR, border guard, internal forces of the Ministry of Internal Affairs, civil defence forces, engineering and road construction military formations attached to federal agencies of executive power, the Foreign Intelligence Service of the Russian Federation, Federal Security Service, federal agency for special communications and information, federal State protection agencies, federal agency for ensuring the mobilization training of agencies of State power of the Russian Federation, military subdivisions of the State Fire Service of the Ministry for Extraordinary Situations of Russia, and special formations created during wartime. Foreigners may undergo military service in the Armed Forces of the Russian Federation and in certain—but not all—other forces, military formations, and agencies.

6.83 The 2003 Federal Law on the System of State Service of the Russian Federation, as amended 11 November 2003,[69] provides that foreigners may enter military service in accordance with a federal law (Article 18^1). Consequently, the legal foundations of State service laid down in this law extend to foreign citizens. The amendments to this law, with corresponding changes to other legislative acts,[70] elaborated the rights of foreigners to enlist under contract in the Armed Forces of the Russian Federation.

6.84 The 1998 Law on Military Duty and Military Service contains a special provision (Article 37) that military servicemen who are foreigners participate in the

---

[67] Transl. in W E Butler, *Labour Code of the Russian Federation* (2004).

[68] *СЗ РФ* (1998), no. 13, item 1475; no. 30, item 3613; (2000), no. 33, item 3348 no. 46, item 437; (2001), no. 7, items 620 and 621; no. 30, item 3061; no. 52(I), item 4924; no. 53(I), item 5025; (2002), no. 7, item 631; no. 21, item 1919; no. 26, item 2521; no. 30, items 3029 and 3030; (2003), no. 1, item 1; no. 8, item 709; no. 27(I), item 2700; no. 46(I), item 4437; no. 52(I), item 5038; (2004), no. 8, item 600; no. 18, item 1687; no. 18, item 1687; no. 25, item 2484; no. 27, item 2711 no. 35, item 3608; no. 49, item 4848; (2005), no. 10, item 763; no. 14, item 1212.

[69] *СЗ РФ* (2003), no. 22, item 2063; no. 46(I), item 4437.

[70] For example, the 1996 Federal Law on Defence (Article 12), which added foreigners who volunteer for military service to the categories of individual who make up the Armed Forces; the 1997 Federal Law 'On Internal Forces of the Ministry of Internal Affairs of the Russian Federation' (Article 15) excluded Russian citizenship as a requirement for enlistment; the 1998 Federal Law 'On the Status of Military Servicemen' equates in rights foreign military servicemen in the Russian Armed Forces with Russian citizens.

fulfilment of tasks under conditions of a military situation or in armed conflicts 'in accordance with generally-recognized principles and norms of international law, international treaties of the Russian Federation, and legislation of the Russian Federation'. Commanding officers are prohibited from giving orders to foreigners which do not relate to military duties or which are directed towards a violation of Russian legislation. The contract on military service is concluded in writing with the foreign citizen by the Ministry of Defence of Russia (Article 32) or federal agency of executive power in which military service is provided for by the Law on Military Duty. The initial contract may be concluded with a foreigner who is aged from eighteen to thirty years old (which differs from Russian citizens, who may join up to age forty). The contract enters into force from the day of signature.

Not all military positions are open to foreign citizens, however. A close reading **6.85** of the legislation suggests that foreigners might be recruited as soldiers, sailors, sergeants, and sergeant-majors, but not as officers. The Order of the Ministry of Defence of Russia, No. 062 'On Confirmation of the List of Military Offices of Soldiers and Sergeants Subject to Being Filled by Foreign Citizens-Military Servicemen', dated 25 December 2003, has not been officially published in its initial version, although 2005 amendments thereto were published.[71]

Foreigners working under contract in the Armed Forces of Russia will be subject **6.86** in relevant part to the Statute on the Procedure for Undergoing Military Service, confirmed by a 1999 Edict of the President of the Russian Federation, as amended.[72] The concept of 'undergoing military service' includes appointment to military service, conferment of military rank, and other circumstances or events which determine the legal status of military servicemen.

Under this Statute, a foreigner wishing to serve in the Russian Armed Forces **6.87** should submit an application together with: (a) a document confirming identity and citizenship; (b) a completed and signed questionnaire of the established form; (c) a handwritten autobiography; (d) an attested copy of his labour book; (e) attested copies of documents confirming vocational or other education; (f) attested copies of marriage certificate and birth certificates of citizens; (g) photograph; (h) copy of birth certificate; and (i) employment reference from last place of work or study. All documents issued on the territory of a foreign State must be accompanied by a notarially certified translation. Commissions

[71] *Российская газета*, 19 July 2005. The Unified Method for Selection of Candidates for Military Service Under Contract, confirmed in 2003 by Order of the Deputy Minister of Defence of Russia, is known only because of reports in the mass media; it has not been officially published, although it would affect foreigners.

[72] *СЗ РФ* (1999), no. 38, item 4534; no. 42, item 5008; (2000), no. 16, item 1678; no. 27, item 2819; (2003), no. 16, item 1508.

attached to military commissariats determine whether a foreigner meets the requirements for persons who enlist in military service under contract, including the medical and professional psychological requirements for specific specializations.[73] Also relevant is the 2003 Instruction on the Procedure for Conducting Military Doctor Examination in the Armed Forces of the Russian Federation, confirmed by Order of the Ministry of Defence, as amended.[74] A copy of the decision of the commission that the foreigner meets the requirements for military service under contract must be issued at his request within three days from adoption of the decision.

6.88 The foreigner is then sent to a military unit where, by decision of the commander, he may again undergo medical and psychological examinations and verification of his physical, educational, and professional readiness before being offered a contract. A personal interview with the commander is part of this process, after which he decides to conclude or not a contract with the foreigner. A new contract, if one is to be offered, is concluded not later than three months before the existing contract expires.

6.89 The selection of foreign citizens for military service under contract thus involves two stages: first at the level of the military commissariats and then at the level of the military unit. The final decision rests with the commander of the unit, who may for specific objective reasons reject a candidate who has been approved at the level of the military commissariat. However, a rejected candidate may enlist in another military unit if the military commissariat sends his personal file for consideration. Contracts usually are concluded for a period of five years, but may be shorter if the maximum age for military service is reached earlier. The period of commencing military service is deemed to be the day on which the contract entered into force.

6.90 A contract for military service may not be concluded with persons (a) with respect to whom a judgment of guilty has been rendered and punishment assigned; (b) with respect to whom an inquiry or preliminary investigation is being conducted or a criminal case with regard to whom has been transferred to a court; or (c) who have a record of conviction not removed nor cancelled for the commission of a crime for which punishment has been served in the form of deprivation of freedom. Nor may a contract be concluded with a person who by decision of a court has been deprived of the right to occupy military office for a determined period.

---

[73] Foreign recruits are medically examined under the Statute on Military Doctor Medical Examination, confirmed by Decree of the Government of the Russian Federation, No. 123, of 25 February 2003, as amended. *СЗ РФ* (2003), no. 10, item 902; (2004), no. 4, item 279.

[74] *Российская газета*, 2 October 2003; *БНА РФ*, no. 35 (2004).

A foreign citizen who has been refused conclusion of a contract for military service has the right to appeal this decision to a superior agency, procuracy, or a court. 6.91

A foreign citizen who concludes a contract for military service may be assigned a probation period of three months, during which his conformity to the requirements will be verified. If the foreigner does not complete the probation period satisfactorily, he is discharged on the grounds established by the Law on Military Duty and Military Service. Should, however, the foreigner be successful in completing the probation period and basic training, he then takes an oath as follows: 'I, [full name] give an obligation to comply with the Constitution of the Russian Federation, strictly fulfil the requirements of military charters and the orders of commanders and superiors, and worthily perform military duty' (Article 40). The oath in and of itself is not regarded as imposing any additional rules or duties on the foreign citizen who swears it; that is, in comparison with the basic duties and obligations following from applicable military legislation, but it does add a different source of duty to those arising from the contract itself. 6.92

Foreigners who enlist in Russian military service under contract are required to be registered and recorded in accordance with the 2002 Federal Law on the Legal Status of Foreign Citizens (Articles 5 and 28) and the 2003 Decree of the Government of the Russian Federation 'On Periods of Temporary Sojourn in the Russian Federation of Foreign Citizens Enlisting in Military Service Under Contract and the Procedure for the Registration and Recording Thereof', No. 793.[75] The period of sojourn is determined by proceeding from the time needed to formalise enlistment and is determined by the Ministry of Defence of the Russian Federation by agreement with the federal agency of executive power in which military service is contemplated. In implementation of this Decree, two further documents were adopted: the 2004 Order of the Ministry of Defence of the Russian Federation, No. 101, 'On the Period of Temporary Sojourn in the Russian Federation of Foreign Citizens Enlisting in Military Service Under Contract'[76] and the 2004 Order of the Ministry of Internal Affairs 'On Organisation of the Activity of Internal Affairs Agencies of the Russian Federation With Regard to the Registration of Foreign Citizens Enlisting in Military Service Under Contract', No. 553.[77] 6.93

Order No. 101 provides that the period for the formalization of enlistment may not exceed ninety days from the day of recourse of the foreign citizen to the military commissariat of a subject of the Russian Federation with a view to enlistment. Order No. 553 clarifies the registration procedure for internal affairs 6.94

[75] *СЗ РФ* (2004), no. 2, item 120.
[76] *БНА РФ* no. 18 (2004).
[77] *БНА РФ*, no. 41 (2004).

agencies in closed or special regime territories of the Russian Federation. A foreigner applying for registration in any event must submit: (a) his identity document; (b) his migration card duly stamped by the border authorities of the Russian Federation; and (c) a copy of the application to enlist for military service under contract attested by the seal of the military commissariat.

6.95 Foreign military servicemen in the Russian Armed Forces do not acquire any special rights to dwelling premises, nor the right to receive land plots, nor the right to study in Russian military educational institutions.[78] Their family members do not qualify for housing, sanatorium or resort treatment, paid travel to places where leave is spent, or maintenance for children who attend State preschool institutions.

6.96 Permitting foreigners to enlist in the Armed Forces of the Russian Federation was accompanied by changes in the 2002 Federal Law on Citizenship of the Russian Federation.[79] Citizens from the Independent States, that is, States which were union republics of the former Soviet Union, have the right to apply for Russian citizenship in a simplified procedure. Foreigners from other countries do not qualify for this preference.

6.97 The possibility of foreigners enlisting in the Russian Armed Forces also is addressed by certain bilateral treaties concluded with the Russian Federation, notably with Kyrgyzia.[80]

Service as seaman on Russian flag vessel

6.98 Foreign citizens employed as members of the crew of Russian flag vessels are governed both by relevant Russian legislation and quite a large complex of international treaties of the Russian Federation. As for Russian legislation, the principal legislative acts are two: the 1999 Merchant Shipping Code of the Russian Federation, as amended;[81] and the 2001 Code of Internal Water Transport of the Russian Federation, as amended.[82] Both enactments contain provisions regulating labour relations on the vessel which are based on the conclusion by crew members of a labour contract with the shipowner. The 1999 Merchant

[78] Foreign technical personnel are trained by the Ministry of Defence under international treaties of the Russian Federation. See the Decree of the Government of the Russian Federation, No. 308, 'On the Rendering by the Ministry of Defence of the Russian Federation to Foreign States of Services for the Training of National Military Cadres and Technical Personnel', as amended. *СЗ РФ* (2000), no. 16, item 1704; (2001), no. 20, item 2022.

[79] *СЗ РФ* (2002), no. 22, item 2031; (2003), no. 46(II), item 4447; (2004), no. 45, item 4377.

[80] *СЗ РФ* (2004), no. 12, item 1036.

[81] *СЗ РФ* (1999), no. 18, item 2207; (2001), no. 22, item 2125; (2003), no. 27(I), item 2700; (2004), no. 15, item 1519.

[82] *СЗ РФ* (2001), no. 11, item 1001; (2003), no. 14, item 1256; no. 27(I), item 2700; (2004), no. 27, item 2711.

Shipping Code provides that the procedure for hiring members of the crew of the vessel and their rights and duties, conditions of labour and payment, and the procedure and grounds for dismissal are determined by legislation of the Russian Federation on labour, the Merchant Shipping Code itself, the charters for service on vessels and on discipline, the general and branch tariff agreements, collective contracts, and labour contracts (Article 57; the provisions of the Code of Internal Water Transport are analogous: Article 28).

The Merchant Shipping Code stipulates that no member of the crew may be hired without the consent of the master of the vessel, even though the master does not have the right to hire and dismiss, which belongs to the shipowner. However, the master does act in this situation as the representative of the shipowner-employer, by whom the master is entrusted with management of the vessel and to maintain order on the vessel. The shipowner is required to provide members of the crew with safe labour conditions, health protection, rescue equipment, uninterrupted supply of food and water, proper premises, and cultural and domestic servicing. The shipowner also has to insure earnings and other amounts due to crew members, including repatriation expenses, and the life of crew members. **6.99**

Confirmation of the position that Russian labour legislation regulates the labour of foreign crew members on Russian flag vessels is found in the provisions of the Merchant Shipping Code which provide that the legal status of members of the crew of a vessel and the relations between crew members connected with the operation of the vessel are determined by the law of the flag State of the vessel, unless provided otherwise by a contract regulating relations between the shipowner and crew members who are foreigners (Article 416). The same Article further stipulates that the law chosen by the parties to the labour contract as the applicable law must not lead to a worsening of the labour conditions of crew members of the vessel in comparison with the norms of law of that State by which those relations would be regulated in the absence of an agreement concerning the applicable law. Thus, although a choice of law is possible in a labour contract relating to a Russian flag vessel, Russian legislation constitutes the minimum standard for labour relations under the contract. **6.100**

The Labour Code of the Russian Federation, it should be said, makes provision for certain special rules that apply to workers on all types of transport, including maritime, and these too would be applicable to foreign members of the crew of a Russian flag vessel. Collective contracts are likely to be relevant here more than would normally be the situation with foreigners employed by Russian land-based enterprises. A certain amount of USSR legislation continues in force in this domain. **6.101**

Foreign natural persons as employers

6.102 Under the 2002 Federal Law on the Legal Status of Foreigners (Article 13), a natural person who has received an authorization in the established procedure to recruit and use foreign workers and uses the labour of foreign workers on the basis of a labour contract concluded with them is an employer. A foreigner registered as an individual entrepreneur also may be an employer.

Foreigners engaging in individual types of labour activity

6.103 As noted above, the Labour Code of the Russian Federation and other legislative acts establish certain limitations and preferences for foreign citizens and stateless persons who engage in labour activity in the Russian Federation. Those collectively comprise what may be characterized as part of the general legal regime for foreigners in the Russian Federation. However, the 2002 Law on the Legal Status of Foreign Citizens also contains renvoi norms (Articles 13–15) referring to rules regulating in detail the peculiarities of the legal status of foreigners engaging in individual types of activity. We turn to those rules here.

Municipal service

6.104 The 2002 Law on the Legal Status of Foreign Citizens provides (Article 14(1)[1]) that a foreign citizen does not have the right to 'be in municipal service'. The 1998 Federal Law 'On the Foundations of Municipal Service in the Russian Federation', as amended,[83] provides (Article 7) that Russian citizens who meet the minimum qualifications laid down may be municipal employees. However, foreigners may, without filling municipal posts of municipal service, perform duties relating to the technical provision of activity of agencies of local self-government because these persons are not considered to be municipal employees.

State service

6.105 The 2002 Law on the Legal Status of Foreign Citizens contains a renvoi norm with respect to foreigners being in State service: 'The relation of foreign citizens to State service shall be determined by a federal law' (Article 14(1)[1]). In fact, State service in the Russian Federation is regulated by a number of federal laws. The original position set out in the 1995 Federal Law on the Foundations of State Service of the Russian Federation (Article 3)[84] was unequivocal: Russian citizens only could be a State employee. The formulation left open whether a Russian citizen having dual citizenship could be a Russian civil servant. In the

[83] *СЗ РФ* (1998), no. 3, item 224; (1999), no. 16, item 1933; (2002), no. 16, item 3029.

[84] *СЗ РФ* (1995), no. 31, item 2990; (1999), no. 8, item 974; (2000), no. 46, item 4537; (2003), no. 22, item 2063; (2004), no. 31, item 3215.

absence of an express provision to the contrary, it was presumed this was possible.[85] Moreover, when addressing the requirements for persons who entered State service under contract, the 1995 Law did not impose a requirement of Russian citizenship. And, under amendments introduced to this Law in 2004, the enlistment of foreigners in the Russian Armed Forces was permitted.

The 2004 Federal Law on State Civil Service of the Russian Federation[86] named Russian citizenship as one of the obligatory prerequisites for being a State employee (Article 13). This Law further stipulated (Article 16) that a Russian citizen may not be hired for State service and a civil servant may not remain in State service in the event of: (a) withdrawal from citizenship of the Russian Federation or acquisition of the citizenship of another State; or (b) the existence of citizenship of another State(s) unless provided otherwise by an international treaty of the Russian Federation. This law is more precise, in comparison with earlier legislation, in clarifying the requirement of citizenship for State service in Russia. Given the aforementioned provisions with regard to military and law enforcement service being open to foreign citizens, the legal status of foreigners in this respect is the subject of various provisions depending upon the types of State service. **6.106**

We have already noted above in some detail the possibilities for foreigners to join the Armed Forces of the Russian Federation under contract. Given the limitations on foreigners in State service, it would appear that foreign citizens may not be hired as State employees to perform civilian tasks in the Armed Forces. However, Russian legislation does not proscribe foreigners being hired as civilian personnel under a labour contract with a view to effectuating technical provision for the activity of federal agencies of executive power and not having the status of civil servants in this connection. Even this exception may be subject to certain further exceptions, as will be seen below. **6.107**

Rules somewhat different from those relevant to military service are applicable to foreign citizens and stateless persons who seek employment in Russian law enforcement agencies. Foreign citizens are categorically prohibited from service in internal affairs agencies, the 1992 Statute on Service in Internal Affairs Agencies confirming Russian citizenship as a requirement for service.[87] The 1991 Law on the Police prohibits foreigners from being police personnel within **6.108**

---

[85] At one time, for example, the oligarch Boris Berezovsky held a senior position in the Russian State system while having both Israeli and Russian citizenship.

[86] *СЗ РФ* (2004), no. 31, item 3215.

[87] *Ведомости Верховного Совета РФ* (1991), no. 2, item 70; *САПП РФ* (1993), no. 52, item 5086; *СЗ РФ* (1998), no. 30, item 3613; (1999), no. 29, item 3698; (2001), no. 1(I), item 2; no. 51, item 4836; no. 52(I), item 4924; no. 53(I), item 5030; (2002), no. 27, item 2620; no. 30, item 3033; (2004), no. 35, item 3607; (2005), no. 14, item 1212.

the system of the Ministry of Internal Affairs.[88] Russian citizenship also is a requirement for service in customs agencies under the 1997 Federal Law on Service in Customs Agencies in the Russian Federation, as amended.[89]

Special status of foreign citizens in certain types of labour activity

6.109 As a rule, foreign citizens have a special status when engaging in certain types of labour activity connected with the security or national defence of the Russian Federation. These limitations arise principally from the 2002 Federal Law on the Legal Status of Foreign Citizens (Article 14). Article 14(1)(3) of the 2002 Law provides that foreign citizens do not have the right to be a *member of the crew of a warship of the Russian Federation or other vessel to be operated for noncommercial purposes or a flying apparatus of State or experimental aviation.*

6.110 The prohibition against foreign citizens being a member of the crew of a Russian warship or other vessel operated for noncommercial purposes originates in considerations of national security.[90] A warship is defined in the United Nations Convention on the Law of the Sea (Article 29), to which the Russian Federation is a party[91] and which is an integral part of the Russian legal system, as: 'a vessel belonging to the Armed Forces of any State having external marks distinguishing such ships by nationality and under the command of an officer who is in the service of the government of the State and whose surname is entered in the respective list of military servicemen or document equivalent thereto and having a crew subordinated to regular military discipline'.

6.111 Among other ships in the ownership of the Russian Federation and operated by it solely for governmental noncommercial purposes are customs vessels, border guard ships, fishery protection vessels, quarantine vessels, and others. It follows that foreign citizens may only be crew members of commercial vessels.

---

[88] *Ведомости Верховного Совета РСФСР* (1991), no. 16, item 503; *Ведомости Верховного Совета Российской Федерации* (1993), no. 10, item 360; no. 32, item 1231; *СЗ РФ* (1996), no. 2, item 2964; (1999), no. 14, item 1666; no. 49, item 590; (2000), no. 31, item 3204; no. 46, item 4537; (2001), no. 1(I), item 15 no. 31, item 3172; no. 32, item 3316 no. 52(I), item 4924; (2002), no. 12, item 1093; no. 27, item 2620; no. 53(I), item 5030; (2003), no. 2, item 167; no. 27(I), item 2700; no. 28, item 2880; no. 50, item 4847; no. 52(I), item 5038; (2004), no. 30, item 3087; no. 35, item 3607; (2005), no. 13, item 1978; no. 14, item 1212; no. 19, item 1752.

[89] *СЗ РФ* (1997), no. 30, item 3586; (2000), no. 33, item 3548; no. 46, item 437; (2001), no. 53(I), items 5025 and 5030; (2002), no. 27, item 2620; no. 30, items 3029 and 3033; (2003), no. 1, item 15 no. 27(I), item 2700; (2004), no. 27, item 2711; no. 35, item 3607; no. 49, item 4876; (2005), no. 14, item 1212.

[90] See the 1992 Law on Security, as amended. *Ведомости Верховного Совета Российской Федерации* (1992), no. 15, item 769; (1993), no. 2, item 77; *САПП РФ* (1993), no. 2, item 5086; *СЗ РФ* (2002), no. 30, item 3033; (2003), no. 27(I), item 2700; (2005), no. 10, item 763.

[91] *СЗ РФ* (1997), no. 48, item 5493.

As for aviation, the 1997 Air Code of the Russian Federation, as amended,[92] distinguishes among three types: civil, State, and experimental. Civil aviation is further subdivided into commercial civil aviation and aviation used on an uncompensated basis, called aviation of common use. State aviation is that used for military, border, police, customs, and other State service or to fulfil defence mobilization tasks. The use of State aviation for commercial purposes is regulated by the Government of the Russian Federation. Experimental aviation encompasses that used to conduct experimental construction design, scientific-research, and tests of aircraft; the use of this category of aviation also is regulated by the Government of Russia. It follows that foreign citizens may be members of the crew of aircraft used 'for the purpose of meeting the requirements of citizens and the economy', which would be principally privately-owned aircraft used for corporate or personal purposes. **6.112**

The 2002 Federal Law on the Legal Status of Foreign Citizens expressly prohibits foreign citizens from being the captain of a civil aviation aircraft. This prohibition needs to be read against those provisions of the Air Code which regulate the crew of an aircraft. The crew of an aircraft is divided by the Air Code into the flight crew and the cabin crew (Article 56). Only citizens of the Russian Federation may be members of the flight crew unless provided otherwise by a federal law. It would therefore follow that foreign citizens might be members of the cabin crew. However, the 2002 Federal Law on the Legal Status of Foreign Citizens only prohibits foreign citizens from being the captain of an aircraft of civil aviation and imposes no limitations on the possibility of foreign citizens having other positions in the flight crew. It would seem that the 2002 Law is in effect a federal law which 'provides otherwise' in the meaning of Article 56 of the Air Code and therefore foreigners may be members of a flight crew other than the captain. **6.113**

Under the 2002 Federal Law, foreign citizens may not be *hired for work at objects and in organizations whose activity is connected with ensuring the security of the Russian Federation.* In furtherance of this provision the Government of the Russian Federation confirmed the List of Objects and Organizations in Which Foreign Citizens Do Not Have the Right to be Hired.[93] There are three types of such objects and organizations: (1) objects and organizations of the Armed Forces of the Russian Federation and other forces and military formations; (2) structural subdivisions for the protection of State secrecy and subdivisions effectuating work connected with the use of information comprising a State secret and agencies of State power and organisations; and (3) organizations **6.114**

---

[92] *СЗ РФ* (1997), no. 12, item 1383; (1999), no. 28, item 3483; (2004), no. 35, item 3607 no. 45, item 4377; (2005), no. 1(I), item 30.

[93] Decree of 11 October 2002, No. 755. *СЗ РФ* (2002), no. 41, item 3996.

within which there are radioactively dangerous and nuclear dangerous production entities and objects at which the development, production, operation, keeping, transporting, and utilization of nuclear weapons and radioactively dangerous materials and manufactures takes place.

6.115 Turning to the first type, the limitations established by Decree 755 concern individuals classified as civilian personnel who work under a labour contract; they would be prohibited from being employed at objects and organizations on the List. As for the second type, although Decree 755 appears to be categorical in prohibiting foreign citizens from working in structural subdivisions and subdivisions as designated, there are circumstances under which foreigners may work with information comprising a State secret pursuant to the 1998 Statute on the Procedure for Admittance of Persons Having Dual Citizenship, Stateless Persons, and Also Persons From Among Foreign Citizens, Emigrants, and Re-Emigrants to State Secret.[94] Individuals having dual citizenship are given access to State secrets classified as 'secret' in the procedure for officials and citizens of the Russian Federation, but only after security clearance by the Federal Security Service. Stateless persons may be given access to information comprising a State secret on the basis of a decision of the Government of the Russian Federation, but as a rule are not in any event given access to information of special importance or top secret information.

6.116 Foreigners may be given access to a State secret on the basis of an international treaty which makes provision for the foreign State to protect information transferred to it which comprises a State secret of the Russian Federation. Foreign citizens are given access only to that information with respect to which procedures have been complied with under the 1997 Statute on the Preparation for Transfer of Information Comprising a State Secret to Other States.[95] The Statute provides that the 'transfer of information to other States' means bringing the said information by a foreign State or empowered representative thereof by some means (transfer, sending, familiarization, provision of access). In each instance the transfer of information is effectuated by decision of the Government of the Russian Federation on the basis of an expert opinion of the Interdepartmental Commission for the Defence of State Secrecy.

6.117 Foreign citizens given access to a State secret in the procedure established by the Statute of 22 August 1998, discussed above, bear the administrative and criminal responsibility established by Russian law for the divulgence of information comprising a State secret (see Chapter 7 below).

---

94 Confirmed by Decree No. 1003 of 22 August 1998. *СЗ РФ* (1998), no. 35, item 4407.
95 *СЗ РФ* (1997), no. 32, item 3786.

Russian legislation also regulates the status of foreigners *when engaging in activity or filling posts to which their access is limited by a federal law.* Limitations of this type are of the most diverse and sometimes unexpected nature and are widely scattered throughout sundry branches of the Russian economy. The 1993 Constitution of the Russian Federation itself contains limitations on foreign citizens and stateless persons not being elected to the offices of President of the Russian Federation (Article 81), deputy of the State Duma of the Federal Assembly of the Russian Federation (Article 97), or judge (Article 119). The 1997 Constitutional Law on the Government of the Russian Federation (Article 7) requires that the Chairman of the Government be appointed by the President of Russia in the procedure established by the 1993 Constitution from among citizens of the Russian Federation.[96] As already noted, notaries must be Russian citizens. **6.118**

Under the 1993 Fundamental Principles of Legislation of the Russian Federation on Protection of the Health of Citizens, as amended, the rights of foreigners to engage in medical and pharmaceutical activities are limited.[97] Only citizens of Russia have the right to engage in folk medicine (Article 57). **6.119**

In the Arctic regions of Russia foreigners are prohibited from acting as the founders of communities of small-number peoples pursuant to the 2000 Federal Law 'On General Principles of Organising Communities of Small-Number Peoples of the North, Siberia, and the Far East of the Russian Federation', as amended.[98] Only individuals who are part of those peoples classified as existing in small numbers may join such communities, defined as '. . . forms of self-organisation of persons relegated to small-number peoples united by blood relations, carrying on a traditional way of life, effectuating traditional economic management, and engaging in traditional crafts' (Article 1). It is presumed that foreign citizens could not meet this standard, although in principle an individual who otherwise met the test and had acquired a foreign citizenship would not seem to be excluded. **6.120**

Limitations on foreigners extend to the level of legislation of subjects of the Russian Federation. Under the Charter of the City of Moscow in the version of a 2001 Law of the City of Moscow, as amended, only a citizen of the Russian Federation may be elected to the office of Mayor of the City of Moscow (Article 51) or Vice-Mayor.[99] **6.121**

[96] *СЗ РФ* (1997), no. 51, item 5712; (2005), no. 23, item 2197.

[97] *Ведомости Верховного Совета Российской Федерации* (1993), no. 33, item 1318; *СЗ РФ* (1998), no. 10, item 1143; (1999), no. 51, item 6289; (2000), no. 49, item 4770; (2003), no. 2, item 167; no. 9, item 805; no. 27(I), item 2700; (2004), no. 27, item 2711; no. 35, item 3608; no. 49, item 4850; (2005), no. 10, item 763.

[98] *СЗ РФ* (2000), no. 30, item 3122; (2002), no. 12, item 1093; (2004), no. 35, item 3607.

[99] *Ведомости Московской Городской Думы* (2001), no. 8; (2002), no. 12.

6.122 In addition to limitations on holding offices or engaging in labour activities, *special rules exist for foreign citizens and stateless persons when engaging in certain types of labour activity*. In some instances these special rules are in essence a prohibition, whereas in others merely an inconvenience. Sometimes they relate to rights and duties in the performance of work, whereas in others they concern the place or site of work. They may also affect the standard of education or skills of a foreign worker which must be recognised in the Russian Federation.

6.123 The 2003 Federal Law 'On the General Principles of Organisation of Local Self-Government in the Russian Federation', as amended,[100] provides (Article 3) that foreigners permanently or primarily residing on the territory of a municipal formation have rights when effectuating local self-government in accordance with international treaties of the Russian Federation and federal laws. Among such rights would be participation in elective and other agencies of local self-government.

6.124 Foreign citizens engaging in outer space activity under the jurisdiction of the Russian Federation enjoy the 'legal regime' established for citizens of Russia on the basis of reciprocity; that is, to the extent that such regime is granted by the respective foreign State to citizens of the Russian Federation. The 'legal regime' includes the legal protection of technologies and commercial secrets of foreign citizens engaged in such activity under Russian jurisdiction in accordance with legislation of the Russian Federation (which is accorded without the requirement of reciprocity) and other necessary protection which is granted under reciprocity.[101]

6.125 The element of reciprocity also is present in the 1995 Federal Law on Pedigree Livestock, as amended (Article 45):[102] foreigners may effectuate activity in the domain of pedigree livestock to the extent the said regime is granted to Russian citizens in the respective country.

6.126 Foreign architects are subject to special requirements if they wish to engage in architectural activity in the Russian Federation under the 1995 Federal Law on Architectural Activity (Article 3^1), as amended.[103] In this case the requirement is in practice prohibitive. Foreign citizens and stateless persons may engage in architectural activity equally with Russian citizens if this is provided for by an

[100] *СЗ РФ* (2003), no. 40, item 3822; (2004), no. 2, item 2484; no. 33, item 3368; (2005), no. 1(I), items 9, 12, 25, and 37.

[101] See Article 27, 1993 Law on Outer Space Activity; transl. in *СЗ РФ* (1996), no. 50, item 5609; (2003), no. 2, item 167; (2004), no. 10, item 834; no. 35, item 3607.

[102] *СЗ РФ* (1995), no. 32, item 3199; (2003), no. 2, item 167; (2005), no. 19, item 1752.

[103] *СЗ РФ* (1995), no. 47, item 4473; (2001), no. 2, item 167; (2002), no. 1(I), item 2; (2004), no. 35, item 3607; excerpts transl. in W E Butler, *Intellectual Property Law in the Russian Federation* (4th ed.; 2004), pp. 72–5.

international treaty of the Russian Federation. In the absence of a treaty, foreign architects may take part in architectural activity on the territory of the Russian Federation only with an architect who is a Russian citizen or juridical person. This limitation is readily addressed through appropriate structuring under Russian legislation.

As noted above, foreign citizens may become Russian advokats. Foreign jurists **6.127** who do not wish to become members of the Russian advokatura may engage in advokat activity on the territory of the Russian Federation by registering with the Ministry of Justice of the Russian Federation. Without such registration, the effectuation of advokat activity by jurists of foreign States is prohibited in Russia. The 2003 Statute on Keeping the Register of Advokats of Foreign States Effectuating Activity on the Territory of the Russian Federation[104] provides that the following documents must be submitted by an advokat of a foreign State: (a) completion of an application and questionnaire in the Russian language; (b) a document confirming the status of advokat of a foreign State, which must be legalised unless provided otherwise by international treaties of the Russian Federation; (c) an identity document; (d) documents confirming the legality of sojourn on the territory of the Russian Federation regulating the legal status of foreign citizens in the Russian Federation and copies of these documents certified by a notary; and (e) two photographs 4×5 cm in dimension. These documents must be submitted in the original and copies translated into the Russian language, and any translations must be notarially certified or the genuineness of the translation attested if the notary does not command the relevant foreign language. The failure to submit the necessary documents or the submission of unreliable information is grounds for refusal of registration.

The Ministry of Justice has three months in which to verify the reliability of the **6.128** documents submitted, including recourse to law enforcement and other State agencies with a request to assist in the verification. These agencies are required to report the results of the verification or confirm their reliability within a month from the day of receiving the request from the Ministry of Justice. If reliability is confirmed, the Ministry issues a regulation to register the jurist. On the basis of the registration, the foreign jurist is issued a numbered certificate of registration. The registration number may not be conferred on any other person, even if the certificate were later to be annulled (although a duplicate certificate would be issued if the original were lost). An issued certificate is subject to annulment by the Ministry of Justice in the event of: (a) establishing the unreliability of documents submitted for registration; (b) deportation of the jurist from Russia in the established procedure; or (c) entry into legal force of the

[104] *СЗ РФ* (2003), no. 39, item 3768.

judgment of a court deeming the jurist to be guilty of the commission of a crime. If a certificate is annulled, the jurist concerned must return it to the Ministry.

6.129 Information contained in the register may be provided to others upon payment of an established charge, except for agencies of State power and agencies of local self-government, who may obtain the information free of charge. Such information is provided in the form of extracts relating to individual jurists under a 2004 Order of the Ministry of Justice confirming the procedure for the provision of such information.[105]

6.130 *Special rules may apply to the labour activity of foreign citizens in connection with the place where work is to be performed.* An example is the conditions and procedure for conducting marine scientific research by foreigners in the internal sea waters and territorial sea of the Russian Federation established by the 1998 Federal Law 'On Internal Sea Waters, Territorial Sea, and Contiguous Zone of the Russian Federation', as amended.[106] Foreigners may conduct marine scientific research in internal sea waters and territorial sea, including from on board flying apparatus and weather balloons, in the procedure provided by Russian laws or international treaties subject to ratification. An authorization to carry on such marine scientific research must be sought through diplomatic channels not less than six months before the proposed date of commencing the research from the federal agency of executive power for science and technologies. The Rules for conducting marine scientific research are established by the Government of the Russian Federation. Foreign applicants (who may be foreign citizens) must submit information concerning all forms and the extent of planned participation of Russian citizens in the research and indicate within the framework of which international treaty it is intended to carry on the research. If authorization is granted, the labour rights and duties thereafter of foreigners within the said spaces are virtually undistinguishable from those of Russian citizens (see Chapter 10).

6.131 There are *special rules for foreigners when working in foreign organisations.* The 1991 Law on Foreign Investments in the RSFSR, as amended,[107] contained a special provision (Article 33) devoted to labour relations. Although that Law was repealed in July 1999 and the 1999 Law on Foreign Investments in

---

[105] *БНА РФ*, no. 9 (2004).

[106] *СЗ РФ* (1998), no. 31, item 3833; (2003), no. 17, item 1556; no. 27(I), item 2700; no. 46(I), item 4444; (2004), no. 35, item 3607; (2005), no. 1(I), item 25.

[107] *Ведомости Верховного Совета РСФСР* (1991), no. 29, item 1008; *САПП РФ* (1993), no. 52, item 5086; *СЗ РФ* (1995), no. 26, item 2397; no. 47, item 5341; (1999), no. 7, item 879; transl. in W E Butler, *Foreign Investment Law in the Commonwealth of Independent States* (2002), pp. 613–31.

the Russian Federation did not contain an equivalent provision, the legacy of practice based on the 1991 legislation remains influential. Article 33 provided that labour relations, including questions of hire and dismissal, the regime of labour and leisure, conditions for the payment of labour, guarantees, and contributory compensations at an enterprise with foreign investments, are regulated by the collective contract and individual labour contracts. Such collective and individual labour contracts could not, however, worsen the position of workers of the enterprise in comparison with the conditions provided for by legislation in force on the territory of Russia. It was expressly provided that foreigners might be members of the management organs of enterprises with foreign investments and that the conditions of hire, labour, and leisure, as well as pension security, of foreign workers are to be agreed in an individual labour contract with each of them.

This formulation in the eyes of many Russian jurists made it possible for the employer and foreign employee to choose the law applicable to the labour contract, including the law of the country of origin of the foreign worker.[108] Since the 1991 law on foreign investments offered no further guidance concerning the conditions and procedure for concluding labour contracts with foreign workers and the 1999 law is silent on the point, the general view is that the 'parties are obliged to follow imperative norms of legislation of the Russian Federation and by mutual consent resolve in contracts those questions which have been left by this legislation to the discretion of the parties'.[109] This leads Boguslavskii to the view that, although there is no general conflicts principle formulated in Russian legislation with regard to labour relations, 'it originates from the principle of the application of the law of the country of the place of fulfilment of work (*lex loci laboris*) even if the contract is concluded between foreign subjects abroad. No exceptions are made from this principle'.[110] Russian jurists in fact understand the Latin expression differently: some believe it means the 'law of the country of the place of the fulfilment of work', whereas others suggest it means the location of the enterprise or organization where the working person is employed. If the enterprise is 'located' outside Russia, an employee performing duties inside Russia for the representation office or branch of a foreign firm may, as a matter of Russian law, be regarded as employed outside Russia because neither the representation office nor the branch are juridical persons in their own right. The employer under this concept is actually outside Russia. If, however, one understands work being physically performed on **6.132**

[108] See I Ia Kiselev, *Международный труд*: *Практическое пособие* [International Labour: Practical Manual] (1997), p. 92.

[109] Boguslavskii, *Международное частное право*: *Учебник* [International Private Law: Textbook] (4th rev. edn 2003), p. 382.

[110] Boguslavskii, ibid., p. 382.

Russian territory by this expression, the site of the employer is secondary to where the work is actually performed.

6.133 It would appear that Russian legal doctrine is partial to the first view. Kiselev argued that:

> . . . from the standpoint of Russian doctrine of international private law a State may agree to an exception from the rules concerning the application of its internal law to a particular contract and permit the application of foreign law to it. The last must have a close link with the particular labour relations, not worsen the position of the worker in comparison with Russian legislation, and not violate imperative norms of labour law of the Russian Federation.[111]

6.134 Labour contracts with foreign workers tend to be more specific and individually-tailored than Russian labour contracts. Clauses commonplace in Russia include the provision of housing or a housing allowance, use of a car, tutoring in the Russian language, and the like.[112]

6.135 The numbers of foreign personnel in the representation office of foreign firms and organisations are determined by the authorization issued to open the said office.[113] As a rule, the number is five unless a special case is made for more. Branches are opened on the basis of the 1999 Provisional Statute 'On the Procedure for Accrediting Branches of Foreign Juridical Persons Created on the Territory of the Russian Federation', confirmed by Order of the Ministry of Justice of the Russian Federation (unpublished). The Ministry of Justice has explained that because representation offices and branches are not juridical persons and therefore not employers, the confirmation of the right of labour activity issued on the basis of an authorisation received by Russian employers is not required in this situation.[114]

6.136 A major concern arising out of the legal status of foreign citizens and stateless persons is the *equivalence of documents of foreign States concerning higher and postgraduate vocational education and learned degrees.* This is especially so when a certain level of education or skill is required as a precondition of employment. The 1996 Federal Law on Higher and Postgraduate Vocational Education, as

[111] Kiselev, *Труд с иностранным участием (правовые аспекты)* [Labour With Foreign Participation (Legal Aspects)], p. 128.

[112] See Kiselev, *Трудовое право России и зарубежных стран. Международные нормы труда* [Labour Law of Russia and Foreign Countries. International Norms of Labour] (2005), pp. 241–3.

[113] The procedure for opening such an office is regulated by the Decree of the USSR Council of Ministers, No. 1074, of 30 November 1989, which confirmed the 'Statute on the Procedure for Opening and Activity in the USSR of Representations of Foreign Firms, Banks, and Organizations'; transl. as amended in W E Butler, *Basic Documents on the Soviet Legal System* (3rd edn, 1992), pp. 461–7.

[114] Letter of Ministry of Justice of Russia, 9 March 2000, No. 1596-EC, 'On the Results of Consideration of a Recourse of the Ministry of Trade of the Russian Federation' (unpublished).

amended,[115] is devoted to the recognition and establishment of the equivalence of documents of foreign States concerning higher and postgraduate vocational education and learned degrees to the respective documents of the Russian Federation. Under Article 23, 'recognition' of documents of foreign States means the consent of the respective agencies of State power to the legal force of these documents on the territory of the Russian Federation. Equivalence in this context means that the respective agencies of State power grant to the possessors of the said documents the same academic and/or vocational rights that the possessors of Russian Federation documents have.

However, recognition and equivalence does not exempt possessors of the said documents from compliance with the general requirements for admission to educational institutions or from being employed (including knowledge of the Russian language). **6.137**

The relevant procedures are regulated by the 1997 Order of the Ministry of Education of Russia 'On Confirmation of the Procedure for the Recognition and Establishment of Equivalence (Nostrification) of Documents of Foreign States on Education and Learned Titles and Forms of the Respective Certificates'.[116] It is the Ministry of Education which recognizes and establishes the equivalence of documents of foreign States on education and learned titles and issues certificates concerning this unless such equivalence has been established by an intergovernmental or interdepartmental agreement or protocol. A foreign citizen or stateless person seeking recognition of such documents must submit an application with the following appended: (a) a duly legalized document on education or learned title, either original or notarized copy; (b) a duly legalized annex to the document on education, either an original or notarized copy, specifying the instructional courses completed and the number thereof, the grades received, and a list of practical, course, or graduating qualifications and others which are part of the instructional process; and (c) an attested translation of the document and annexes thereto. **6.138**

An applicant also has the right to submit other evidence of his training, including documents on subsequent education, access to vocational or professional activity, and practical experience. When necessary, clarifying documentation may be requested either from the applicant or from the respective Russian or foreign educational institution. Materials and documents used in the recognition procedure must be submitted in an attested translation. **6.139**

---

[115] *СЗ РФ* (1996), no. 35, item 4135; (2000), no. 29, item 3001; no. 33, item 3348; (2001), no. 1(I), item 2; no. 53(I), item 5030; (2002), no. 26, item 2517; (2003), no. 2, item 165; no. 14, item 1254; no. 28, item 2892; no. 52(I), item 5038; (2004), no. 35, item 3607; (2005), no. 17, item 1481.

[116] *БНА РФ*, no. 6 (1997).

6.140 For recognition of a document concerning education or a learned title, it is necessary that: (a) the educational institution which issued the document on education or learned title be recognised by competent agencies of the country in which the document is issued; (b) the document on education or learned title be recognized in the country of issuance; and (c) the recognition of a document on education or learned title be provided for by an international treaty of the Russian Federation. As a rule, the period for consideration of the documents submitted by the applicant should not exceed three weeks from the day of receipt of all the necessary materials, including the clarifying information. Non-recognised documents concerning education and learned titles of foreign States are returned to the applicant with an explanation of the reasons for refusal. If they are recognised, a certificate concerning recognition of the document on education is issued personally to the applicant or on his behalf to his representative or sent by registered post.

6.141 A certificate on recognition of a document concerning education issued by an educational institution of a foreign State gives the right to enrol in an educational institution offering the educational programmes of the respective level on the territory of the Russian Federation, giving credit for or setting off the disciplines already passed successfully. The document on education of the foreign State is regarded as an academic reference.

6.142 The conformity of documents concerning education and learned titles of foreign States to Russian documents for the purposes of access to professional or vocational activity is determined by establishing equivalence. A certain procedure must be followed for this purpose. To the application for equivalence must be appended the same documents as for an application concerning recognition of education documents. Additional documentation may be requested when necessary from the applicant. The procedure for establishing equivalence involves: (a) the conducting of an expert examination; (b) the adoption of a decision; and (c) the formalization and issuance of a certificate of equivalence.

6.143 The expert examination has regard to the content and evolution of instructional plans and syllabi; whether there were entry examinations; the system of examinations and marking; the marks received by the student; the number of subjects studied; the existence and duration of practical experience; the existence and standard of the final degree examinations; the existence and topic of the final dissertation; the form of study; and the existence of additional education. The applicant has the right to see the reasoned expert opinion submitted to the Ministry of Education of Russia.

6.144 A negative decision with regard to equivalence of education documents of a foreign State may be adopted on the grounds of: (a) the total period of study after completing secondary education for receiving a document on vocational education in a foreign State is at least a half-year less than provided by the Russian State educational standard; (b) in the country where the documents were issued their recipient has materially fewer academic and professional rights to enter higher educational institutions or the master or doctoral programmes, or does not have the right to engage in vocational activity, than in Russia; (c) the area of training does not correspond to the Russian list of orientations and specializations for primary, secondary, and higher vocational education (e.g. chiropractic medicine, cosmetology, and the like); or (d) the education document gives evidence of completing external study for specializations and orientations for which this form of study is not permitted in the Russian Federation.

The period for establishing equivalence should not, as a rule, exceed one **6.145**
month from the day of receipt of the necessary materials, including clarifying information.

The decision to recognize and establish the equivalence of higher and post- **6.146**
graduate documents of foreign States is taken on the basis of international treaties of the Russian Federation, where applicable. The Russian Federation is party to the 1997 Convention on the Recognition of Qualifications Concerning Higher Education in the European Region;[117] the 1953 European Convention on the Equivalence of Diplomas Leading to Admission to Universities and 1964 Protocol thereto;[118] the 1956 European Convention on the Equivalence of Periods of University Study;[119] and the 1959 European Convention on the Academic Recognition of University Qualifications.[120] The Russian Federation has a number of bilateral treaties concluded to the same end: Georgia (15 September 1995); Moldova (3 March 2003), and within the framework of the CIS, the 1993 Agreement on Principles of Recognition and Nostrification of Documents on Learned Degrees[121] and the 1998 Agreement on the Mutual Recognition and Equivalence of Documents on Education, Learned Degrees, and Titles.[122]

Special requirements attend the *determination of the level of education and skills of* **6.147**
foreigners with regard to medical and pharmaceutical activity in the Russian Federation. Special rules apply to foreign citizens who have received their medical or pharmaceutical training outside the Russian Federation. Under the 1993 Fundamental Principles on the Protection of Health of Citizens (Article 54),

[117] Ratified by Russia 4 May 2000. *СЗ РФ* (2000), no. 19, item 2031.
[118] Ratified by Russia 8 July 1999. *СЗ РФ* (1999), no. 28, item 3480.
[119] Ratified by Russia 8 July 1999. *СЗ РФ* (1999), no. 28, item 3481.
[120] Ratified by Russia 8 July 1999. *СЗ РФ* (1999), no. 28, item 3482.
[121] *БМД*, no. 7 (2000). The parties are Azerbaidzhan, Belarus, Kazakhstan, Kyrgyzia, Moldova, Russia, Turkmenistan, Uzbekistan, and Ukraine.
[122] *БМД*, no. 3 (1998). The parties are Belarus, Kazakhstan, Kyrgyzia, Russia, and Tadzhikistan.

individuals trained in medicine or pharmacy in foreign States are admitted to engage in such activity in the Russian Federation after an examination in the respective educational institutions of Russia in the procedure established by the Government of the Russian Federation and after receiving a license to effectuate medical or pharmaceutical activity, unless provided otherwise by international treaties of the Russian Federation.

6.148 The 1995 Statute on the Procedure for Admittance to Medical and Pharmaceutical Activity in the Russian Federation of Persons Who Received Medical and Pharmaceutical Training in Foreign States, confirmed by Decree of the Government of the Russian Federation, as amended,[123] provides that documents certifying the right to engage in medical and pharmaceutical activity in the former Soviet Union and RSFSR issued to persons prior to the date of the said Decree who, receiving their medical and pharmaceutical training in foreign States, retain legal force in the Russian Federation and are not subject to exchange.

6.149 Persons trained outside Russia in medicine and pharmacy may be admitted to such activity in the Russian Federation on condition that the Ministry of Education of Russia jointly with the Ministry of Public Health and Social Development establishes the equivalence of education. An application requires the submission by the applicant of: (a) documents on education; (b) information concerning previous work in the specialization; and (c) photographs. The Ministry of Public Health and Social Development then considers whether to subject the applicant to special examinations and issue a specialist certificate, the last, if issued, giving the right to engage in medical and pharmaceutical activity throughout the Russian Federation. If the applicant has for some reason not worked in his specialization for more than five years, he may be required to undergo retraining in Russian educational institutions at his own expense.[124]

Social benefits for foreigners working in Russia

6.150 Foreigners who engage in labour activity in the Russian Federation may be eligible for certain social benefits, sometimes characterized as 'guarantees' by Russian jurists. These may be reflected in the documentation which a foreign citizen or stateless person is required to carry and submit, or in the establishment of legislative minimums.

---

[123] *СЗ РФ* (1995), no. 7, item 548; (2005), no. 7, item 560.

[124] On 26 July 2000 the Ministry of Public Health and Social Development confirmed a number of relevant documents, including an Instruction on the procedure for conducting the necessary special examinations, a List of educational institutions in Russia where special examination commissions are formed to administer the examinations, and the form of the protocol of the special examination. See *БНА РФ*, no. 34 (2000).

Under the 1996 Federal Law on exit and entry into the Russian Federation (Article 27[6]) a foreign citizen or stateless person applying for a visa or seeking entry to Russia may be refused if he is unable to confirm that he has the means to live on the territory of the Russian Federation and subsequently leave Russia, or to present a guarantee that such means will be provided, in the procedure established by the Government of the Russian Federation. The 'procedure' established by the Government is contained in the Statute on Confirmation by a Foreign Citizen or Stateless Person of the Existence of Means for Living on the Territory of the Russian Federation and Exit from the Russian Federation or Presentation of a Guarantee of Such Means Being Provided When Applying for a Visa or at an Admittance Point Across the State Boundary of the Russian Federation, confirmed by Decree of 24 April 2003.[125] Foreigners entering Russia to engage in labour activity must submit in this connection: (a) a letter of guarantee from the inviting party formalized in the established procedure; and (b) an invitation of a foreigner to Russia issued in the established procedure by internal affairs agencies of the Russian Federation. **6.151**

The letter of guarantee or other confirmation of means to subsist is not required for persons on a business trip to a foreign diplomatic or consular mission, international organization or a representation or subdivision thereof, or other purposes provided by the business trip, or for a family coming to Russia of a foreigner who is working in Russia, or for a person travelling to Russia who is deemed to be a refugee.

The Decree of 24 April 2003 would appear to have de facto superseded Decree No. 167, adopted a month earlier, 'On the Procedure for the Provision of Guarantees of Material, Medical, and Housing Provision of Foreign Citizens and Stateless Persons for the Period of Their Sojourn in the Russian Federation',[126] adopted pursuant to Article 16 of the 2002 Federal Law on the Legal Status of Foreign Citizens. Under this Decree an 'inviting party' may be federal agencies of State power; diplomatic or consular missions of foreign States in Russia; international organizations or their representations in Russia or representations of foreign States attached to international organizations located in Russia, or agencies of State power of subjects of the Russian Federation; or agencies of local self-government, or juridical persons, or citizens of Russia and foreign citizens permanently residing in Russia. Decree No 167 sets out in greater detail the guarantees to be provided than does the April Decree No.241. **6.152**

Under Decree No. 167 the inviting party must assume the following obligations: (a) provide monetary means for the foreigner to subsist during the period of his sojourn in Russia in an amount not lower than the living minimum **6.153**

[125] *СЗ РФ* (2003), no. 17, item 1622.

[126] *СЗ РФ* (2003), no. 13, item 1240.

established in the respective subject of the Russian Federation and monetary means necessary for the exit of the foreigner from Russia when the period of his sojourn ends; (b) payment by the inviting party to the invited foreigner of earnings not lower than the minimum amount for the payment of labour established by a federal law; (c) provision by the inviting party to the invited foreigner of a medical insurance policy duly formalized unless provided otherwise by an international treaty of the Russian Federation or necessary monetary means for the foreign invitee to receive medical care; and (d) provision by the inviting party of housing to the foreign invitee for the period of his sojourn in Russia which conforms to the social norm of dwelling space established by the respective subject of the Russian Federation.

6.154 A natural person who enters Russia as an invitee should attach to the letters of guarantee information on his revenues or monetary means that would enable him to perform the aforesaid obligations, and the inviting party when making application to the Ministry of Foreign Affairs or the Ministry of Internal Affairs also submits simultaneously the guarantees of material, medical, and housing provision.

Material and housing provision

6.155 Under the Decree of 24 April 2003 confirmation of having means to subsist and exit from Russia or a guarantee of the provision thereof may take the form of: (a) a letter of guarantee from the inviting party duly formalized; (b) an invitation of the foreigner to Russia issued by the Ministry of Foreign Affairs, Ministry of Internal Affairs, or representations thereof in Russia; or (c) travel tickets valid for departure from Russia or a document confirming a guarantee to acquire them at a transfer point in Russia in the event of transit passage through Russia.

6.156 Of relevance to the provision of guarantees to foreign citizens of material provision is an unpublished Letter of the Ministry of Taxes and Charges of Russia dated 19 September 2003 'On the Application of Individual Provisions of the Federal Law No. 115-ФЗ of 25 July 2002', having in view the 2002 Federal Law on the Legal Status of Foreign Citizens. Among the documents confirming the existence of means to subsist in Russia is a reference concerning revenues of a natural person, a declaration of revenues with a notation of the relevant tax agency, a reference from the place of work, labour book, pension certificate, reference of a social defence agency on the receipt of benefits, confirmation of the receipt of alimony, reference concerning deposits in a credit institution specifying the account number, certificate of the right to an inheritance, reference concerning the revenues of a person on whom the foreigner is dependent, or other document confirming the receipt of revenues from activity not prohibited by law or the lack of labour capacity.

In order to verify whether the requisite documents and information is appropriate the passport-visa administration or the Ministry of Internal Affairs or other internal affairs agency may send written requests to tax and bailiff agencies, social security agencies, public health agencies, migration subdivisions, and other interested agencies to determine whether grounds exist that would obstruct the issuance of an authorization to the foreign citizen or stateless person. **6.157**

Medical insurance

Under the 1991 Law 'On Medical Insurance of Citizens in the Russian Federation', as amended, foreign citizens permanently residing in the Russian Federation have the same rights and duties as Russian citizens with respect to medical insurance unless provided otherwise by an international treaty (Article 8).[127] **6.158**

For foreigners temporarily in the Russian Federation medical insurance is acquired in the procedure determined by a 1998 Decree of the Government of the Russian Federation, No. 1488, 'On the Medical Insurance of Foreign Citizens Temporarily Situated in the Russian Federation and Russian Citizens in the Event of Exit from the Russian Federation', which confirmed the 'Statute on Medical Insurance of Foreign Citizens Temporarily Situated in the Russian Federation'.[128] This Statute does not extend to foreign citizens (a) residing in the Russian Federation for more than 183 days in the calendar year; (b) working in the Russian Federation under labour contracts; (c) on official business trips in foreign diplomatic and consular missions or international organizations accredited to the Ministry of Foreign Affairs of Russia; (d) in the Russian Federation on an official visit; (e) in Russian on the invitation of workers of foreign diplomatic or consular missions or international organizations accredited to the Ministry of Foreign Affairs of Russia; and (f) having the right to free medical care under international treaties of the Russian Federation (including medical transport services). **6.159**

Medical insurance of citizens from other CIS countries who are temporarily in Russia is available under international treaties with those countries.[129]

Russian insurance companies offer medical insurance to foreigners temporarily in the Russian Federation on the basis of licences. The extent of coverage varies, but may not be less than the minimum list of medical services, including **6.160**

[127] *Ведомости Верховного Совета Российской Федерации* (1991), no. 27, item 920; *САПП РФ* (1993), no. 52, item 5086; *СЗ РФ* (1994), no. 10, item 1108; (2002), no. 22, item 2026; (2003), no. 52(I), item 5037.

[128] *СЗ РФ* (1998), no. 51, item 6305.

[129] Such as, for example, the Russo-Ukrainian Agreement of 28 October 1999. *БМД*, no. 4 (2000).

medical transport services, confirmed by the Ministry of Public Health and Social Development and set out in Decree No. 1488. Pursuant to that Decree, the Ministry of Public Health adopted Order No. 315 'On the Minimum List of Medical Services (Including Medical Transport Services) to be Rendered in the Medical Insurance System to Insured Foreign Citizens Temporarily Situated in the Russian Federation'.[130] Among those services are: (a) medical care offered by out-patient first aid stations; (b) medical care at in-patient and out-patient medical institutions in the event of a sudden impairment of health or accident to the extent necessary to eliminate the threat to the health of the patient and/or the elimination of sharp pain; (c) medical transport, including medical accompaniment from the place of illness or incident to a medical institution; and (d) posthumous repatriation of remains.

6.161 The extent to which foreign citizens are covered by obligatory medical insurance has been addressed in a 1995 Letter of the Federal Obligatory Medical Insurance Fund, No. 3–1146, 'On the Legal Status of Foreign Citizens in the System of Obligatory Medical Insurance'. Whether foreigners are eligible under this programme turns upon the basis upon which they are present in the Russian Federation, that is, permanently or temporarily, and upon their right to work in enterprises located on Russian territory. Foreign citizens permanently residing in Russia have the same rights and duties in the domain of medical insurance as do Russian citizens unless provided otherwise by international treaties. A residence permit is considered to be satisfactory documentary confirmation of this status, and foreigners having such permit are issued with an obligatory medical insurance policy in order to receive care within the programme.

6.162 An employer who makes contributions to the obligatory medical insurance fund submits to the insurance organization with which the contract to provide medical insurance is concluded a list of foreign citizens, indicating the period of operation of their permit. The foreigner is then issued a policy on the basis of confirmation of his right to engage in labour activity. The validity of the medical insurance policy must correspond to the validity of the authorization issued for his presence in Russia by the Federal Migration Service.

6.163 A 1999 Letter of the Federal Obligatory Medical Insurance Fund 'On Medical Insurance of Foreign Citizens' clarified that those who pay obligatory medical insurance contributions are organizations, institutions, and enterprises, irrespective of forms of ownership and organizational-legal forms of activity, including enterprises with foreign investments. As payers to this fund, such enterprises must be registered with territorial obligatory medical insurance funds. Workers, including foreign citizens, who validly conclude a labour

---

[130] *БНА РФ*, no. 41 (1999).

contract with any of the said employers, are automatically covered by obligatory medical insurance. In this respect the principle of national regime extends to foreigners and stateless persons.

Apart from these general provisions on the provision of medical care and insurance to foreigners, there are detailed provisions which turn upon whether the foreigner is a citizen of a CIS country or otherwise. The 1993 Fundamental Principles on the Protection of the Health of Citizens (Articles 18 and 19), as amended, are the foundation for Order No. 280 of the Ministry of Public Health of Russia 'On the Procedure for Rendering Medical Assistance to Citizens of the CIS, Other Citizens of the Former USSR, and Citizens of the Far Abroad' (unpublished). Order No. 280 instructs public health institutions to proceed from the circumstances set out in intergovernmental and interdepartmental agreements concluded with the respective countries. Ambulance and other urgent medical assistance needed because of accidents, poisonings, and acute illnesses is rendered free of charge at the expense of the budget of the relevant territorial-administrative unit. Scheduled medical care by appointment is given on a commercial basis at the expense of the individual concerned or the organizations which sponsored their travel to Russia. **6.164**

Of key importance for foreigners in Russia is the 2005 Decree of the Government of the Russian Federation 'On Confirmation of the Rules for Rendering Medical Assistance to Foreign Citizens on the Territory of the Russian Federation'.[131] These Rules confirm the position that emergency medical treatment is rendered by treatment-prophylactic institutions irrespective of organizational-legal form to foreigners temporarily sojourning or residing or permanently residing in Russia. Emergency medical assistance is given free of charge and urgently by State and municipal public health institutions or by medical workers or persons obliged by law or special rules to give first aid when circumstances arise which are an immediate threat to life or require urgent medical intervention (accidents, traumas, poisonings). Thereafter, such care is available for payment either under a medical insurance scheme or by contract. **6.165**

What is called scheduled medical care (by appointment) is available on condition that the foreign citizen provides the requisite medical documentation, such as personal medical history, and either prepayment for care or a guarantee obligation for payment. Each patient is supplied with a document when treatment is completed that sets out the history of the treatment given and any diagnostic or other measures taken. The official language for such a document is Russian. The account for actual medical care given is sent within ten days after **6.166**

[131] *СЗ РФ* (2005), no. 36, item 3708.

treatment is completed to the foreigner or to the juridical or natural persons representing the interests of the foreigner.

6.167 The above are rules of general applicability which give way to treaty provisions should an international treaty be relevant to the matter. Various intergovernmental and interdepartmental treaties are in place with respect to citizens of CIS countries, the most fundamental being the 1997 Agreement on Rendering Medical Assistance to Citizens of States-Participants of the Commonwealth of Independent States and accompanying Protocol (unpublished officially). These documents set out in great detail the precise procedures for rendering medical care, including the imposition of a forfeit per day for delay in making payment for services rendered. Also material are the 1998 Agreement on the Mutual Provision to Citizens of the Republic Belarus, Republic Kazakhstan, Kyrgyz Republic, and the Russian Federation of Equal Rights to Receive Emergency and Urgent Medical Assistance,[132] and the 1996 Statute on the Procedure for the Provision of Medical Assistance to Citizens of the Republic Belarus in Public Health Institutions of the Russian Federation and Citizens of the Russian Federation in Institutions of the Republic Belarus, confirmed by Decision of the Executive Committee of the Commonwealth of Belarus and Russia.[133]

Social insurance

6.168 Under the 1999 Federal Law 'On the Fundamental Principles of Obligatory Social Insurance',[134] social insurance extends to foreign citizens and stateless persons working under labour contracts irrespective of when they arrived on the territory of the Russian Federation and to foreign individual entrepreneurs who made contributions to the Social Insurance Fund of the Russian Federation. The categories of foreigners who have the right to receive social insurance benefits are: (a) employed foreigners who reside in Russia on the basis of a residence permit; (b) employed foreigners who are residing in Russia on the basis of an authorization for temporary residing; (c) foreigners temporarily in Russia and employed on the basis of an authorization for work; and (d) foreign individual entrepreneurs who have an authorization for work in Russia and who pay insurance contributions to the Social Insurance Fund.

6.169 State social insurance benefits encompass, subject to eligibility: payment of expenses to a medical institution connected with the provision of necessary medical care to the insured person in the event of production accidents or vocational illnesses; disability pension; loss of breadwinner pension; temporary benefit for lack of capacity to labour; benefit for labour injury and vocational illness; pregnancy and birth benefits; monthly benefit for care of a child until it

[132] *Российская газета*, 20 March 1999.

[133] *Российская газета*, 24 May 1997.

[134] *СЗ РФ* (1999), no. 29, item 3686.

reaches 18 months of age; unemployment benefit; lump sum benefit to women registered in medical institutions in early stages of pregnancy; lump sum benefit for birth of child; benefit for sanatorium and resort treatment; social benefit for burial; and payment for passes for sanatorium and resort treatment and recreation for workers and their families.

The 1998 Federal Law on Obligatory Social Insurance Against Accidents in Production and Vocational Illnesses, as amended,[135] extends to foreign citizens and stateless persons, unless provided otherwise by federal laws or international treaties of the Russian Federation. The national regime thus extends in this domain to foreigners who work in Russia on the basis of a labour contract or civil-law contract. **6.170**

Payment for education

Under the 1992 Law on Education, as amended, study, training, and raising the qualifications of foreign citizens and stateless persons in educational institutions of the Russian Federation is effectuated on the basis of direct contracts concluded between the provider of education and the recipient of education or benefactor thereof in accordance with international treaties of the Russian Federation (Article 57). Education, in the absence of private stipends or scholarships, is therefore provided on a fee basis unless treaties stipulate to the contrary. Citizens of Belarus have access to tuition-free general education in the Russian Federation pursuant to the 1998 Treaty on Equal Rights of Citizens (Article 4) between Russia and Belarus.[136] **6.171**

The same is in principle true of institutions of higher education in the Russian Federation. It is expressly stipulated, however, that payment of tuition may be made either by the applicant for enrolment himself or by an enterprise, institution, or organization sending the student to Russia for study, or by a foreign State. Under the 2002 Russian-Vietnamese Agreement on Study of Vietnamese Citizens in Educational Institutions of Higher Vocational Education of the Russian Federation,[137] the relevant Vietnamese ministry concludes contracts directly with Russian higher educational institutions and arranges for the payment of tuition. It goes without saying that the applicant must satisfy the qualitative conditions for admission to the programme being applied for. **6.172**

The Russian Government does finance or support higher education for certain categories of foreigners. As noted above, under the 1998 Belarus-Russian Treaty **6.173**

[135] *СЗ РФ* (1998), no. 31, item 3803; (1999), no. 29, item 3702; (2001), no. 44, item 4152; (2002), no. 1(I), items 2 and 3; no. 7, item 628; no. 48, item 4737; (2003), no. 6, item 508; no. 28, item 2887; no. 43, item 4108; no. 50, item 4852; no. 52(I), item 5037; (2004), no. 35, item 3607.

[136] *СЗ РФ* (1999), no. 47, item 5625.

[137] *БМД*, no. 10 (2002).

citizens of Belarus may enrol in a Russian higher educational institution on an equal basis with citizens of Russia and compete for places supported by the Russian federal budget equally with Russians if they are receiving their first degree. Persons who hold citizenship of the USSR and who reside in the former union republics of the Soviet Union and have taken the citizenship of those Independent States, or who have become stateless persons are, under Russian legislation, treated as 'compatriots'. Under the 1999 Federal Law 'On State Policy of the Russian Federation With Respect to Compatriots Abroad',[138] agencies of State power are obliged to assist compatriots equally with Russian citizens in receiving secondary and higher vocational education on a competitive basis for places financed by the budget in accordance with admission requirements, provided they are seeking to obtain a first degree (Article 17).

6.174 The Russian Federation is expanding its network of intergovernmental and interdepartmental agreements with reference to secondary and higher education. The 2003 Decree of the Government of the Russian Federation, No. 668, 'On Cooperation with Foreign Countries in the Domain of Education'[139] provides a quota of up to 7,000 foreign citizens and compatriots abroad per year who may be accepted to study in State institutions of higher education on a tuition-free basis. Annually prior to 1 May of the calendar year, the Ministry of Education and Science of the Russian Federation confirms a plan for the admission and distribution of foreign citizens to Russian higher educational institutions irrespective of departmental subordination within the quota fixed. Any admissions in excess of the quota are solely on a tuition fee basis.

6.175 Each educational institution in Russia determines its own rules for admission of foreign citizens and stateless persons on condition that these rules are not contrary to: (a) the 2003 Procedure for Admission to State Educational Institutions of Higher Vocational Education, confirmed by Order of the Ministry of Education of Russia, as amended;[140] (b) the 2002 Procedure for Admission to State and Municipal Educational Institutions of Secondary Vocation Education (or Secondary Specialised Educational Institutions) of the Russian Federation, confirmed by Order of the Ministry of Education of Russia;[141] and (c) the 1996 Procedure for the Admission and Study of Foreign Citizens in Educational Institutions of Higher Secondary Vocational Education of the Russian Federation, confirmed by Decree of the State Committee of Higher Education of Russia, No. 5.[142] This last enactment provides that foreigners may enrol in Russian higher educational institutions of all forms on the basis of a referral of an international cooperation subdivision of the Ministry of Education and

[138] *СЗ РФ* (1999), no. 22, item 2670.

[139] *СЗ РФ* (2003), no. 35, item 4387.

[140] *Российская газета*, no. 28 (2003).

[141] *Российская газета*, no. 30 (2003).

[142] *БНА РФ*, no. 5 (1996).

Science of the Russian Federation. The Russian Federation has acceded to the relevant document associated with the Bologna Process.

6.176 Foreign citizens not having a command of the Russian language are first enrolled in a preparatory faculty for one year, where they study Russian and other subjects in the specialization which they intend to pursue. Those who graduate successfully at the end of this preparatory year receive a certificate of completion and move on to study in the institution of their chosen specialization. The Russian side will propose a city and an educational institution in that city to the foreigner in accordance with the distribution plan. Those wishing to pursue a bachelor's degree in Russia will need to give evidence of having completed the equivalent of the Russian secondary general or specialized vocational education.

6.177 Those who have a bachelor's degree or the equivalent may apply to enrol for the magister degree by submitting: (a) a completed application form in the Russian, English, French, or Spanish languages, which comprises a questionnaire; copies of the certificates or documents of prior education, including marks achieved (transcript); a medical report attested by a public health agency of the sending country; a certificate confirming the absence of HIV; copy of birth certificate; and six photographs. These documents are submitted to the international cooperation subdivision of the Ministry of Education and Science of the Russian Federation. Entry examinations for a foreigner are mandatory if enrolment is based on a stipend.

Rights of ownership

6.178 The 1993 Russian Constitution provides that 'each' has the right to have property in ownership and to possess, use, and dispose of property both as one person and jointly with other persons (Article 35). Although the formulation extends to foreign citizens and stateless persons, there are in fact certain limitations on the right of ownership for foreigners.

6.179 Under the Land Code of the Russian Federation (Article 15), foreign citizens, stateless persons, and foreign juridical persons may not possess by right of ownership land plots on frontier territories.[143] A List of frontier territories is to be established by the President of the Russian Federation, but so far this has not been done. In the interim the 2001 Federal Law on the Introduction into Operation of the Land Code of the Russian Federation (Article 5) does not permit land plots located on the said territories to be granted to foreign citizens,

[143] *СЗ РФ* (2001), no. 44, item 4147; transl. in W E Butler, *Russian Company and Commercial Legislation* (2003), p. 81.

stateless persons, and foreign juridical persons.[144] Frontier territories comprise the frontier zone, the territories of admittance points across the State boundary of the Russian Federation, and also the territories of administrative districts and cities, sanitary and resort zones, specially-protected nature territories, objects, and other territories adjacent to the State boundary of the Russian Federation, frontier zone, shores of frontier rivers, lakes, and other waters, sea coast, or other admittance points.

6.180 Lands of agricultural designation are treated specially. Foreign citizens, foreign juridical persons, stateless persons, and juridical persons in whose charter or contributed capital the participatory share of foreigners comprises more than 50%, may not own land plots on lands of agricultural designation. They have such land plots in possession only by right of lease pursuant to the 2002 Federal Law on the Turnover of Lands of Agricultural Designation (Article 3).[145] Land plots in State or municipal ownership of any designation other than agricultural may be transferred to the ownership of foreign citizens, stateless persons, and foreign juridical persons only for payment, the amounts of which are established by the Land Code (Article 28); Russian citizens, on the other hand, have the right to acquire free of charge land in State or municipal ownership but allotted to them for use in perpetuity.

6.181 Foreign individual entrepreneurs who conclude concession agreements under the 2005 Federal Law on Concession Agreements (Article 11) as concessionaires do not have the right to transfer their rights under a contract of lease or sublease of a land plot to other persons, nor to sublease out the land plot, unless provided otherwise by the contract of lease for the land plot.

6.182 Foreign citizens, stateless persons, and foreign juridical persons who are the owners of buildings, structures, and installations situated on someone else's land plot have a preferential right to purchase or lease the land plot under prescribed provisions of the Land Code (Article 35). However, the President of the Russian Federation may establish a List of buildings, structures, and installations to which this provision does not extend.

D. Citizenship

6.183 The law of citizenship in the Russian Federation is very much a subject of its own. We are concerned with citizenship here primarily insofar as foreign citizens

[144] *СЗ РФ* (2001), no. 44, item 4148; transl. in Butler, *Russian Company and Commercial Legislation* (2003), pp. 145–6.

[145] *СЗ РФ* (2002), no. 30, item 3018; transl. in Butler, *Russian Company and Commercial Legislation* (2003), p. 153.

and stateless persons may be able to acquire Russian citizenship, or, in the technical language of Russian law, be admitted to Russian citizenship. These are individuals who have no right to Russian citizenship, but who wish the Russian State in its discretion to admit them as citizens.[146] In this respect there is substantial continuity in Russian legal history. As one Russian jurist observed, 'there can be no doubt that during the [sixteenth to eighteenth centuries] *jus soli* remains alien to Russian legislation: the children of foreigners born in Russia remain foreigners; children born of subjects are "natural" subjects. This principle did not receive definite expression in a law; however, in essence it is incontestable'.[147] In the eighteenth century naturalization by oath came to be recognised, replacing conversion to the Russian Orthodox faith. With naturalization came access to trade rights and membership in the merchant guilds. There emerged a key distinction between naturalized foreigners and Russians: a 'naturalized foreigner remained a foreigner, albeit a privileged one . . . as such he possessed rights which a native-born subject was deprived of but lacked those rights which a native-born Russian possessed'.[148] The equalization of these rights came in 1864 with the enactment of appropriate legislation.

The concept of 'subjecthood' disappeared with the coming to power of the Soviet Government in October 1917. The term 'citizen' emerged in a number of the earliest legislative acts. In the early months of Soviet power, every foreigner residing within the limits of the RSFSR could acquire the rights of Russian citizenship and, in certain instances, even those residing outside Russia. Some Soviet jurists went so far as to suggest that the concept of 'foreigner' had outlived itself; that the concept of foreigner had been theoretically abolished because political rights had been recognised for all toiling people irrespective of their subjecthood.[149] This situation did not last, and in the course of time the Soviet authorities introduced an oath of allegiance and eventually more formalities for the process of becoming a Soviet citizen.[150] **6.184**

[146] Between January 1992 and September 2002 the Russian Federation admitted 4,836,900 persons to Russian citizenship, of which 85,800 were by the President of Russia, 2,936,200 by the Ministry of Internal Affairs, and 1,814,900 by the Ministry of Foreign Affairs. See O E Kutafin, *Российское гражданство* [Russian Citizenship] (2003), p. 295.

[147] V M Gessen, *Подданство, его установление и прекращение* [Subjecthood, Establishment and Termination Thereof] (1909), p. 209.

[148] Gessen, *Подданство, его установление и прекращение* [Subjecthood, Establishment and Termination Thereof] (1909), p. 227.

[149] See A V Sabanin, in *Международная жизнь*, no. 15 (1928), p. 11.

[150] These are addressed in authoritative detail by G Ginsburgs, *Soviet Citizenship Law* (1968) and Ginsburgs, *The Citizenship Law of the USSR* (1983).

Acquisition of Russian citizenship

6.185 There are four grounds upon which citizenship of the Russian Federation may be acquired: (1) by birth; (2) as a result of admittance to Russian citizenship; (3) as a result of the restoration of Russian citizenship; or (4) on other grounds provided for by the 2002 Federal Law on Citizenship or by an international treaty of the Russian Federation.

6.186 A child acquires citizenship of the Russian Federation by birth if on the day on which the child is born: (1) both parents or his sole parent have citizenship of the Russian Federation irrespective of where the child is born; (2) one parent has citizenship of the Russian Federation and the other is a stateless person or has been deemed to be missing, or his whereabouts is unknown, irrespective of where the child is born; (3) one parent has citizenship of the Russian Federation and the other parent is a foreign citizen, provided that the child was born on the territory of the Russian Federation or otherwise becomes a stateless person; or (4) both parents or the sole parent residing on the territory of the Russian Federation are foreign citizens or stateless persons, provided that the child was born on the territory of the Russian Federation and the State of which his parents or sole parent is a citizen does not grant its citizenship to the child. A child born on the territory of the Russian Federation and whose parents are unknown becomes a citizen of the Russian Federation if the parents do not declare within six months from the day of discovery thereof.

6.187 Under the 2002 Federal Law on Citizenship in the Russian Federation,[151] a person seeking Russian citizenship must satisfy certain conditions. In establishing these conditions the State is concerned not to accept undesirable persons who seek a change of citizenship in order to escape criminal prosecution in their own country, or other unworthy purposes. The general procedure for being admitted to Russian citizenship is as follows. A foreign citizen or stateless person who is at least eighteen years of age and who has dispositive legal capacity has the right to apply for Russian citizenship. The right to apply, of course, is not the same as the right to receive such citizenship.

6.188 Applicants must meet the following basic requirements: (1) have a residence permit issued in confirmation of their right to permanently reside on the territory of the Russian Federation and to freely leave and return to the Russian Federation; (2) reside on the territory of the Russian Federation from the day of receipt of the residence permit until the day of application for citizenship for five years without interruption. For these purposes the term 'without interruption' means that the individual did not leave the Russian Federation for more

[151] *СЗ РФ* (2002), no. 22, item 2031; (2003), no. 46(II), item 4447; (2004), no. 45, item 4377; (2006), no. 2, item 170.

than three months within one year; (3) assume the obligation to comply with the Constitution and legislation of the Russian Federation; (4) have a legal source of means for existence; (5) apply to an empowered agency of the foreign State of which he is a citizen and renounce the citizenship of that country, unless an international treaty of the Russian Federation or Russian legislation provides otherwise or if renunciation of the other citizenship is impossible for reasons beyond his control; and (6) have a command of the Russian language, the procedure for determining which is established by a statute on the procedure for considering questions of citizenship of the Russian Federation.

An individual who has made or is making special services to the Russian Federation may be admitted to citizenship without complying with all of the aforesaid conditions.[152] **6.189**

Under stipulated circumstances the five-year residency requirement is reduced to one year, namely: (1) the applicant has high achievements in the domain of science, technology, and culture or has a profession or skills of interest to the Russian Federation; (2) the applicant has been granted political asylum on the territory of the Russian Federation; or (3) the applicant has been recognized as a refugee in the procedure established by the Federal Law on Refugees. Citizens of States which were part of the former Soviet Union and who served not less than three years in the Armed Forces of the Russian Federation under contract or in other forces or military formations may apply for citizenship without having lived five years without interruption in Russia and without the submission of a residence permit. **6.190**

A simplified procedure for being admitted to Russian citizenship exists for those who qualify for the preferential conditions established by Russian legislation. Under this procedure it is not necessary to reside on the territory of the Russian Federation. The simplified procedure extends to foreign citizens and stateless persons who: (1) have at least one parent who has citizenship of the Russian Federation and resides on the territory of the Russian Federation; (2) had USSR citizenship, resided or reside in States which were part of the former Soviet Union, did not receive citizenship of those States, and remain as a result stateless persons; (3) are citizens of States within the former Soviet Union and received secondary vocational or higher vocational education in educational institutions of the Russian Federation after 1 July 2002. The simplified procedure also extends to foreign citizens and stateless persons who are residing on the territory **6.191**

[152] One individual who obtained Russian citizenship on this basis was a basketball player from Pennsylvania who played professionally in the Russian Federation and was selected for the Russian national team. Without Russian citizenship, he would have been unable to play for the national team in European competitions. His application for citizenship was approved with record speed.

of the Russian Federation and who: (1) have citizenship of the former USSR; (2) have been married to a citizen of the Russian Federation for not less than three years; (3) lack labour capacity and have a son or daughter who has dispositive legal capacity, is eighteen years of age or more, and is a citizen of the Russian Federation. These individuals need not have been in Russia for five years, but do require a residence permit.

6.192 Foreign citizens and stateless persons who lack labour capacity and who arrived in the Russian Federation from States of the former Soviet Union and were registered at a place of residence in the Russian Federation as of 1 July 2002 may use the simplified procedure without complying with either the five-year residence period or the submission of a residence permit.

6.193 Yet another category enjoying the simplified procedure consists of foreign citizens and stateless persons who had citizenship of the former USSR, arrived in the Russian Federation from States which were part of the former Soviet Union, and registered at a place of residence in the Russian Federation as of 1 July 2002 or had received an authorization for temporary residing in the Russian Federation or a residence permit, provided that they apply for citizenship before 1 January 2008. Veterans of the Second World War who had USSR citizenship and reside on the territory of the Russian Federation may apply in the simplified procedure without the five-year residence requirement and residence permit.

6.194 As for children and persons who lack dispositive legal capacity who are foreign citizens and stateless persons, under the simplified procedure they do not need to have resided in the Russian Federation, or have a legal source of means for existence, or have a command of the Russian language, assume an obligation to comply with the Russian Constitution, or renounce another citizenship. Those who qualify for Russian citizenship under these conditions include: (1) a child, one of whose parents has citizenship of the Russian Federation, upon the application of this parent and with the consent of the other parent for the child to acquire Russian citizenship, such consent not being essential if the child lives on the territory of the Russian Federation; (2) a child whose sole parent has citizenship of the Russian Federation, upon the application of the parent; and (3) a child or person who lacks dispositive legal capacity over whom a trusteeship or guardianship has been established, upon the application of the trustee or guardian who has citizenship of the Russian Federation.

6.195 Restoration of Russian citizenship is possible for foreign citizens and stateless persons who previously had such citizenship. In this event the residence period on the territory of the Russian Federation is reduced to three years.

Rejection of application for Russian citizenship

Under the 2002 Law on Citizenship there are a number of grounds on which applications for being admitted to Russian citizenship are subject to rejection, irrespective of whether the general or the simplified procedure is being used. These include applications by persons: (1) who favour the forcible change of the foundations of the constitutional system of the Russian Federation or other actions which create a threat to the security of Russia; (2) who within five years which preceded the day of application were deported beyond the limits of the Russian Federation; (3) who used false documents or communicated information known to be false; (4) who are in military service or in the service of security agencies or law enforcement agencies of a foreign State, unless provided otherwise by an international treaty of the Russian Federation; (5) who have an unremoved or uncancelled record of conviction for the commission of intentional crimes on the territory of the Russian Federation or beyond the limits thereof, recognized as such by a federal law; (6) who are being prosecuted in a criminal proceeding by competent agencies of the Russian Federation or competent agencies of a foreign State for a crime recognized to be such in accordance with a federal law; or (7) who have been convicted and are serving punishment in the form of deprivation of freedom for actions prosecuted in accordance with a federal law until the period of punishment expires. **6.196**

Termination of Russian citizenship

There are a number of grounds on which Russian citizenship terminates or may be terminated. Among them are withdrawal, optation, revocation, or change. Withdrawal arises when a citizen of Russia residing on the territory of the Russian Federation expresses a voluntary wish to withdraw by using the general procedure. A simplified procedure is available if the Russian citizen is residing on the territory of a foreign State, including the situation of a child when one parent is a Russian citizen and the other a foreign citizen, or a sole parent is a foreign citizen and both parents or the sole parent apply for withdrawal on behalf of the child. **6.197**

Withdrawal may be refused if the citizen of the Russian Federation: (1) has an obligation established by a federal law to the Russian Federation which has not been fulfilled (e.g. taxes); (2) the citizen has been brought by competent agencies of the Russian Federation as an accused or with respect to whom there is a judgment of conviction of a court which has entered into legal force and is subject to execution; or (3) the citizen has no other citizenship or guarantee of acquiring such. Accordingly, an applicant for withdrawal from Russian citizenship must submit: (1) an application to withdraw in the established form; (2) a document from the empowered agency of the relevant foreign State confirming **6.198** that the applicant has another citizenship or the possibility of him being granted another citizenship in the event of withdrawal from Russian citizenship; and (3) a document of a tax agency of the Russian Federation that the applicant has no indebtedness with regard to the payment of taxes.[153]

6.199 Optation is available in the event of territorial transformations in accordance with an international treaty of the Russian Federation. If the State boundary changes and citizens of the Russian Federation are subjected to the said transformations, they have the right to retain or to change their citizenship in accordance with the treaty.

6.200 Revocation arises in connection with either the acquisition or termination of citizenship if it is determined that the decision was adopted on the basis of false documents submitted by the applicant or was adopted on the basis of false information known to be false. The fact of using false documents or communicating false information must be established in a judicial proceeding. If the court so decides, the President of the Russian Federation or other empowered agency revokes the decision; the revocation takes effect from the day of adopting the original decision.

6.201 A child acquires Russian citizenship if both of its parents or the sole parent acquires Russian citizenship, and the same applies if the Russian citizenship of both parents or sole parent terminates, provided that the child does not become stateless as a result thereof. The rules become more complex if only one parent changes citizenship. Thus, if one parent who had a foreign citizenship acquired Russian citizenship, a child thereof residing on the territory of the Russian Federation may acquire Russian citizenship upon the application of the parent who acquired Russian citizenship. If the child resides outside Russia, citizenship of the Russian Federation for him may be acquired upon the application of both parents. If one parent acquires Russian citizenship and the other is a stateless person, the child may acquire Russian citizenship upon the application of the parent acquiring Russian citizenship. The application of both parents is required for a child to acquire Russian citizenship if one parent has foreign citizenship and the other is a stateless person.

6.202 If the Russian citizenship of one parent terminates and the other parent remains a citizen of the Russian Federation, their child retains Russian citizenship. However, the Russian citizenship of a child may be terminated simultaneously with the termination of one parent's Russian citizenship with the consent in writing

[153] See point 24, Statute on the Procedure for the Consideration of Questions of Citizenship of the Russian Federation, confirmed by Edict of the President of the Russian Federation, 14 November 2002, No. 1325. *СЗ РФ* (2002), no. 46, item 4571; (2004), no. 1, item 16.

of the other parent who is a Russian citizen, provided that the child would not become stateless.

In the event of adoption of a child who is a Russian citizen by a foreign citizen(s), the child retains Russian citizenship. The child's Russian citizenship may be changed in the event of adoption by foreign citizen(s) in the general procedure upon the application of both adoptive parents or sole parent, provided that the child would not become stateless. A child who is adopted by a citizen of Russia, or by spouses who are Russian citizens, or by spouses, one of whom is a Russian citizen and the other a stateless person, acquires Russian citizenship from the day of adoption irrespective of the child's place of residence, upon the application of the adoptive parent who is a Russian citizen. If a child is adopted by spouses, one of whom is a Russian citizen and the other has foreign citizenship, the child may acquire Russian citizenship in a simplified procedure upon the application of both adoptive parents, irrespective of the child's place of residence; if the adoptive parents fail to make an application within one year from the day of adoption and the child and adoptive parents live on the territory of other Russian Federation, the child acquires Russian citizenship from the day of adoption. Analogous rules apply for the citizenship of children and persons who lack dispositive legal capacity and are under trusteeship or guardianship. **6.203**

7

DUTIES AND PROCEDURAL RIGHTS OF FOREIGNERS

The principal duty of foreign citizens and stateless persons in the Russian Federation is to comply with the 1993 Constitution and legislation of the Russian Federation. This is a duty they share equally with Russian citizens. Nonetheless, there are duties of compliance that fall especially on foreigners and sanctions imposed for violations applicable solely to foreigners. They form the subject of **7.01** the present Chapter, together with an account of the special concomitant procedural rights and duties that apply to foreigners in certain situations.

A. Criminal Responsibility of Foreigners

7.02 Russian law bases the spatial domain of its criminal law on the 'territorial principle'. All 'persons', irrespective of citizenship, who have committed crimes on the territory of the Russian Federation are 'equal before the law and subject to criminal responsibility'. The extent and nature of criminal responsibility is determined by the 1996 Criminal Code of the Russian Federation, as amended.[1] The 'territory' of the Russian Federation for these purposes includes, in addition to the land territory of the Russian Federation within its State boundary, the territorial waters, airspace, continental shelf, and exclusive economic zone of the Russian Federation (Article 11). In addition, a person who has committed a crime on a vessel or aircraft registered in the Russian Federation and which is situated on the high seas or airspace beyond the limits of the Russian Federation is subject to criminal responsibility under the Russian Criminal Code, unless provided otherwise by an international treaty of the Russian Federation. A person who has committed a crime on a warship or military aircraft of the Russian Federation, irrespective of where it is situated, also bears responsibility under the Criminal Code.

7.03 Stateless persons permanently residing in the Russian Federation who have committed a crime beyond the limits of the Russian Federation are subject to responsibility under the Russian Criminal Code if the act they have committed is deemed to be a crime in the State on whose territory it was committed and if those persons were not convicted in the foreign State. If the said persons were convicted in Russia, the punishment may not exceed the upper limit of the sanction provided for by the law of the foreign State on whose territory the crime was committed (Article 12).

7.04 Given that foreign citizens may serve under contract in the Armed Forces of the Russian Federation, they are affected by the provision that military servicemen of military units of the Russian Federation stationed beyond the limits of the Russian Federation bear criminal responsibility for crimes committed on the territory of the foreign State under the Russian Criminal Code, unless provided otherwise by an international treaty of the Russian Federation.

7.05 Foreign citizens and stateless persons who do not reside permanently in the Russian Federation and who have committed a crime beyond the limits of the

[1] Transl. in W E Butler, *Criminal Code of the Russian Federation* (4th edn, 2004), p. 2.

Russian Federation are subject to criminal responsibility under the 1996 Russian Criminal Code if the crime was directed against the interests of the Russian Federation and, in instances provided for by an international treaty of the Russian Federation, if they were not convicted in the foreign State and are brought to criminal responsibility on the territory of the Russian Federation.

Russian citizens who commit a crime on the territory of a foreign State are not subject to extradition to that State. Foreign citizens and stateless persons, however, who have committed a crime beyond the limits of the Russian Federation and are situated on the territory of the Russian Federation, may be extradited to a foreign State to be brought to criminal responsibility there or to serve punishment there in accordance with an international treaty of the Russian Federation. **7.06**

The criminal jurisdiction of the Russian Federation will not be exercised on board a foreign vessel passing through the territorial sea to arrest any person or to perform an investigation in connection with any crime committed on board the foreign vessel during its passage unless: the consequences of the crime extend to the territory of the Russian Federation; the crime has such a character that it disturbs the quiet in the Russian Federation or good order in the territorial sea, and the master of the foreign vessel, diplomatic agent, or consular officer of the flag State of the vessel requests officials of federal agencies of executive power or similar agencies of a subject of the Russian Federation to render assistance; or such measures are necessary in order to suppress illegal trade in narcotic means or psychotropic substances; or to suppress other crimes of an international character provided for by international treaties of the Russian Federation.[2] This rule does not affect crimes allegedly committed with respect to a foreign ship passing through the territorial sea after having departed from Russian internal sea waters. **7.07**

Crossing the protected State boundary of the Russian Federation without valid documents for the right of entry into or exit from the Russian Federation or without proper authorization received in the procedure established by legislation of the Russian Federation is one of the crimes against the administrative order under the Criminal Code (Article 322). Upon conviction, this crime is punishable by a fine in an amount of up to two hundred thousand rubles, or in the amount of earnings or other revenue of the convicted person for a period of up to eighteen months, or by deprivation of freedom for a term of up to two years. **7.08**

If the illegal crossing of the State boundary is committed by a group of persons by prior collusion, or by an organised group, or with the use or threat of force, **7.09**

[2] Article 17, 1998 Federal Law on Internal Sea Waters, the Territorial Sea, and Contiguous Zone. *СЗ РФ* (1998), no. 31, item 3833.

the applicable sanction is deprivation of freedom for a term of up to five years. However, in a Note to Article 322, the operation of these provisions with respect to foreign citizens or stateless persons who have violated the State boundary in order to take advantage of the right of political asylum in accordance with the Constitution of the Russian Federation is expressly excluded, unless the actions of these foreign citizens and stateless persons contain another constituent element of a crime.

7.10 Moreover, it is accepted that foreign citizens or stateless persons who have crossed the Russian State boundary without the established documents or proper authorizations as a result of a forced crossing by reason of extraordinary circumstances (forced landing of aircraft, shipwreck, natural disaster, ice conditions, towage of damaged ships, delivery of rescued people, urgent medical assistance for crew or passenger, and the like) would not constitute the constituent elements of Article 322.[3]

7.11 One criminal offence in the code can be committed only by a foreign citizen or stateless person: espionage. By definition, a Russian citizen can not commit this crime. Espionage is the transfer, collecting, stealing, or keeping for the purpose of passing to a foreign State, foreign organization, or representatives thereof, any information constituting a State secret, or the transfer and collecting in accordance with an 'assignment' of foreign intelligence of other information for the use thereof to the prejudice of the foreign security of the Russian Federation if these acts were committed by a foreign citizen or stateless person. Punishment under the Criminal Code is deprivation of freedom for a term of from ten to twenty years (Article 276).[4]

7.12 This provision in fact has in view two types of espionage which differ one from the other by the subject of the espionage. The first type is espionage whose subject is merely information comprising a State secret, whereas the subject of the second type is 'other information' intended for use to the prejudice of the foreign security of the Russian Federation. The 'transfer' of information is its communication to a foreign State, foreign organization, or representatives thereof. Such communication may be by any means: orally, in writing, by telephone, through other persons, and so on. The collecting of the information may be done variously, through personal observation, photographing of secret objects, use of tape recordings, acquisition for money, and so on. The stealing of

[3] See A V Naumov, *Практика применения Уголовного кодекса Российской Федерации; комментарий судебной практики и доктринальное толкование* [Practice of Application of Criminal Code of the Russian Federation: Commentary on Judicial Practice and Doctrinal Interpretation] (2005), p. 842.

[4] Butler, *Criminal Code of the Russian Federation* (4th edn, 2004), p. 218.

information is the removal from institutions, enterprises, organizations, or individuals of certain documents containing a State secret, such as plans, drawings, reports, and the like. The keeping of information[5] may be accomplished in a premise belonging to, occupied by, or used by the guilty person or in another place, such as a garden, dacha, forest, and so on.

The transfer or collecting of 'other information' which, although not containing a State secret, is intended for use to the prejudice of the foreign security of the Russian Federation, qualifies as espionage only if this is done upon the instructions of a foreign intelligence service. **7.13**

Any foreign citizen or stateless person aged sixteen or above may be deemed guilty of committing espionage. Direct intent is required to commit this crime; that is, the guilty person is aware that he is transferring, collecting, stealing, or keeping for the purpose of transfer to a foreign State, foreign organization, or representatives thereof respective information for use thereof to the prejudice of the foreign security of the Russian Federation and wishes this.[6] **7.14**

What constitutes a 'State secret' is determined not by the Criminal Code, but by the 1993 Law on State Secrecy. A State secret is defined as 'information defended by the State in the domain of its military, foreign policy, economic, intelligence, counter-intelligence, and operational-search activity, the dissemination of which could prejudice the security of the Russian Federation' (Article 2). Such information is divided by the 1993 Law into four categories, as follows: **7.15**

(1) *information in the military domain* concerning (a) the content of strategic and operational plans; combat management documents for the preparation and carrying out of operations; strategic, operational, and mobilization development of the Armed Forces of the Russian Federation, other forces, military formations, and agencies provided by the Federal Law 'On Defence', their combat and mobilization readiness; and the creation and use of mobilization resources; (b) construction plans of the Armed Forces of the Russian Federation or other forces of the Russian Federation; orientations of development of armaments and military technology; the content and results of fulfilling special-purpose programmes; scientific-research and experimental-construction design work with regard to the creation and modernization of models of armaments and military technology; (c) the working out,

[5] The definition of espionage is essentially that of the 1960 RSFSR Criminal Code; however, criminal responsibility for the keeping of espionage materials is new to the 1996 Criminal Code.

[6] See Naumov, *Практика применения Уголовного кодекса Российской Федерации: комментарий судебной практики и доктринальное толкование* [Practice of Application of Criminal Code of the Russian Federation: Commentary on Judicial Practice and Doctrinal Interpretation] (2005), pp. 732–733.

technology, production, production volumes, keeping, and utilization of nuclear missiles; technical means and/or methods of defence of nuclear missiles against unsanctioned use; and nuclear power and special physical installations of defence significance; (d) the placement, purpose, and degree of readiness and defensibility of regime and especially important objects; the designing, construction, and operation thereof; and also allotment of land, subsoil, and aquatories of these objects; and (e) the placement, actual names, organizational structures, armaments, force numbers and state of their combat provision; and also military-political and/or operational situation;

(2) *information in the domain of the economy, science, and technology* concerning: (a) the content of plans of the readiness of the Russian Federation and individual regions thereof for possible military actions; mobilization capacities of industry for the manufacture and repair of armaments and military technology; production volumes, deliveries, and reserves of strategic types of raw material and materials; and also the placement, actual amounts, and use of State material reserves; (b) the use of the infrastructure of the Russian Federation for the purpose of ensuring defence capacity and security of the State; (c) the forces and means of civil defence; the site, designation, and degree of defensibility of objects of administrative management; the degree of provision of security for the population; the functioning of transport and communications in the Russian Federation for the purpose of ensuring the security of the State; (d) the amounts, plans (or planning tasks) of the State defence budget; issue and deliveries (in money or in kind) of armaments, military technology, and other defence products; the existence and growth of capacities for the issue thereof; links of enterprises for cooperation production; designers or manufacturers of the said armaments, military technology, and other defence products; (e) the achievements of science and technology; scientific-research, experimental-construction design; and design work and technologies having important defence or economic significance affecting the security of the State; and (f) the reserves of platinum, metals of the platinum group, natural diamonds in the State Precious Metals and Precious Stones Fund of the Russian Federation; and also the amounts of reserves in the subsoil, extraction, production, and consumption of strategic types of minerals of the Russian Federation (according to a List determined by the Government of the Russian Federation);

(3) *information in the domain of foreign policy and the economy* concerning (a) the foreign policy and foreign economic activity of the Russian Federation, the premature dissemination of which may prejudice the security of the State; and (b) the financial policy with respect to foreign States (except for generalized indicators for foreign indebtedness); and also the financial or monetary-credit activity, the premature dissemination of which may prejudice the security of the State;

(4) *information in the domain of intelligence, counter-intelligence, and operational-search activity* concerning (a) the forces, means, sources, methods, plans, and results of intelligence, counter-intelligence, and operational-search activity; and also data concerning the financing of this activity if this data discloses the enumerated information; (b) the persons cooperating or who have cooperated on a confidential basis with agencies effectuating intelligence, counter-intelligence, and operational-search activity; (c) the organization, forces, means, and methods of ensuring the security of objects of State protection; and also data concerning the financing of this activity if this data disclosed the enumerated information; (d) the system of presidential, governmental, encoded (including coded and classified) communications, cyphers, working out and manufacture of cyphers and provision thereof; methods and means of analysis of cypher means and means of special defence; and informational-analytical systems of special purpose; (e) the methods and means of defence of secret information; (f) the organization and actual state of defence of a State secret; (g) the defence of the State boundary of the Russian Federation, exclusive economic zone, and continental shelf of the Russian Federation; (h) expenditures of the federal budget connected with the provision of defence and security of the State and law enforcement activity in the Russian Federation; and (i) the training of cadres which disclose measures being conducted for the purpose of ensuring the security of the State.

Certain information is as a matter of law not subject to being considered or **7.16** classified as a State secret; that is, information concerning: (a) extraordinary incidents and catastrophes threatening the security and health of citizens and the consequences thereof, as well as natural calamities and the official forecasts and consequences thereof; (b) the state of the ecology, public health, sanitation, demography, education, culture, agriculture, and the state of criminality; (c) the privileges, contributory compensations, and social guarantees granted by the State to citizens, officials, enterprises, institutions, and organisations; (d) the facts of a violation of the rights and freedoms of man and citizen; (e) the amounts of the gold reserve and State hard currency reserves of the Russian Federation; (f) the state of health of the highest officials of the Russian Federation; and (g) the facts of a violation of legality by agencies of State power and officials thereof (Article 7, Law on State Secrecy).

The categories of State secrets are elaborated in the List on Information Relegated **7.17** to a State Secret, confirmed by Edict of the President of the Russian Federation in its 2006 version.[7] In the field of law, for example, the list includes: 'information

[7] *СЗ РФ* (1995), no. 49, item 4775; (1998), no. 5, item 561; (2001), no. 24, item 2418; no. 38, item 3724; (2002), no. 22, item 2074; (2005), no. 10, item 807; (2006), no. 8, item 892.

concerning the preparation, conclusion, ratification, preparation for denunciation, content, or fulfilment of treaties, conventions, and agreement with foreign States, the premature dissemination of which may prejudice the security of the State' (point 71); and in the field of international relations: 'information concerning negotiations between representatives of the Russian Federation and representatives of other States on working out a unified position of principle in international relations if, in the opinion of participants of the negotiations, divulgence of this information may prejudice the security of the Russian Federation and other States' (point 70).

7.18 Under certain circumstances foreign citizens and stateless persons may be given access to a State secret (for these purposes, persons having dual citizenship, emigrants, and re-emigrants are equated to foreign citizens). Persons having dual citizenship are given access to State secrets in the procedure for officials and citizens of the Russian Federation. Stateless persons obtain access to State secrets solely on the basis of a decision of the Government of the Russian Federation, and not, as a rule, to information of special importance or top secret. Foreign citizens are given access to State secrets pursuant to an international treaty of the Russian Federation.

7.19 The Russian Federation is a party to a number of international treaties which require persons to be prosecuted for the commission of certain crimes irrespective of their citizenship, place of commission of the crime, or whether the crime was directed against the Russian Federation or not. Examples of such crimes are terrorism, counterfeiting, hijacking of aircraft, and certain narcotics offences.

B. Administrative Responsibility

7.20 Foreign citizens and stateless persons also are subject specifically in their own capacities to other duties which, if not fulfilled, engage administrative responsibility either under the Code of the Russian Federation on Administrative Violations or under individual legislative acts. Just as Russian criminal law, so too does administrative responsibility operate spatially on the territorial principle. Foreign citizens, stateless persons, and foreign juridical persons who have committed on the territory of the Russian Federation an administrative violation are subject to administrative responsibility on the general grounds (Article 2.6).[8]

[8] See A B Agapov, *Кодекс Российской Федерации об административных правонарушениях: постатейный комментарий* [Code of Russian Federation on Administrative Violations: Article-by-Article Commentary] (2nd rev. edn, 2004), p. 3. Agapov argues that under this Code the term 'foreign citizen' also includes Russian citizens who have dual citizenship. His view is supported by the 1997 'Statute on the Preparation for Transfer of

For these purposes the 'territory' of the Russian Federation also includes the territorial waters, continental shelf, and exclusive economic zone of Russia.

First and foremost among the individual acts is the 2002 Law on the Legal Status of Foreign Citizens, which establishes the general rule that a 'foreign citizen guilty of a violation of legislation in the Russian Federation shall be brought to responsibility in accordance with legislation of the Russian Federation' (Article 33). This formulation applies to all violations and all types of responsibility, and insofar as foreigners and stateless persons are capable of committing crimes or violations which do not extend to Russian citizens, or vice versa, their responsibility under the law differs from that of Russian citizens and the principle of national regime does not fully operate. **7.21**

Foreign citizens who are in the Russian Federation illegally are subject to being recorded as such, photographed, and fingerprinted. All of this information is then placed in a Central Data Bank specially created to record foreign citizens who temporarily sojourn or who reside temporarily or permanently in the Russian Federation. The dissemination of information concerning a foreign citizen contained in the Central Data Bank is prohibited pursuant to the 2005 Decree of the Government of the Russian Federation, No. 186.[9] **7.22**

In addition to establishing the general grounds of responsibility of foreign citizens, the 2002 Law on the Legal Status of Foreigners elaborates the procedure for imposing two special sanctions applicable only to foreign citizens: deportation [депортация] and administrative deportation [административное выдворение]. Deportation is defined as the 'compulsory banishment' of a foreign citizen from the Russian Federation in the event of the loss or termination of legal grounds for the further sojourn or residing of that individual in the Russian Federation (Article 2) and is not provided for in the Code on Administrative Violations.[10] The procedures attending both sanctions are quite similar. **7.23**

The definition of administrative deportation is to be found in the Code on Administrative Violations (Article 3.10): '. . . the compulsory and controlled movement of [foreign citizens or stateless persons] across the State boundary of the Russian Federation beyond the limits of the Russian Federation, and in **7.24**

Information Comprising a State Secret to Other States and by the 1998 Statute on the Procedure for the Admittance of Persons Having Dual Citizenship, Stateless Persons, and also Persons from Among Foreign Citizens, Emigrants, and Re-Emigrants to a State Secret', both of which effectively treat these categories of individuals apart from Russian citizens.

[9] *СЗ РФ* (2005), no. 15, item 348.

[10] However, deportation is also an administrative sanction in the 1993 Federal Law on Refugees (Article 13).

instances provided for by legislation of the Russian Federation—the controlled autonomous exit of foreign citizens and stateless persons from the Russian Federation'. As a measure of administrative punishment, administrative deportation is assigned by a judge, but if the administrative violation was committed when entering the Russian Federation, the respective officials assign this sanction.

7.25 Deportation is engaged as a sanction when the period of sojourn or temporary residing for a particular foreign citizen is reduced, in which event the foreigner must leave Russia within three days; or when an authorization for temporary residing or a residence permit has been annulled, in which case the foreigner must leave Russia within fifteen days. If these periods are not complied with, the foreigner is subject to deportation; that is, compulsory banishment, by internal affairs agencies.

7.26 The implementation of deportation and administrative deportation is linked directly with the invitation procedure for issuing visas to foreigners. The expenses associated with deportation are to be borne first by the deportee himself. If the foreign citizen being deported has no funds to pay for this or if the foreigner was hired in violation of the procedure for the recruitment and use of foreign workers, the expenses then fall in succession on the agency which invited the deportee to the Russian Federation, the diplomatic or consular representation of the foreign State of which the foreigner is a citizen, international organization, or representation thereof, or the natural or juridical person who supported the invitation. If it is impossible to ascertain who the inviting party was, the Russian Federation itself must pay the expenses of the deportation.

7.27 The procedure for incurring expenditures for the purposes of deportation or administrative deportation is determined by the 2002 Decree of the Government of the Russian Federation, No 769, 'On Confirmation of the Rules for the Expenditure of Means for Measures Relating to Deportation or Administrative Deportation of Foreign Citizens and Stateless Persons Beyond the Limits of the Russian Federation in the Event of the Impossibility of Establishing the Inviting Party', as amended.[11] Expenditures may be for: (a) the acquisition of travel documents for foreigners subject to deportation or administrative deportation and, in instances established by legislation of the Russian Federation, travel documents for internal affairs agency officials accompanying the foreigner being deported; (b) the maintenance of the foreigner in a specially-allotted premise of an internal affairs agency or border guard or special institution created in the procedure established by a law of a subject of the Russian Federation until the decision concerning deportation or administrative deportation is

[11] *СЗ РФ* (2002), no. 43, item 4275; (2004), no. 52(I), item 5501.

executed; (c) the formalization of documents needed to effectuate deportation or administrative deportation; or (d) the performance of other actions directly connected with deportation or administrative deportation of the foreigner.

The agencies principally responsible for deportation and administrative deportation are the Ministry of Internal Affairs or the border guard, depending upon which articles of the Code on Administrative Violations have been violated (Article 32.09). When either is carried out, the Ministry of Foreign Affairs of the Russian Federation must be informed. Notification is then sent by the Ministry of Foreign Affairs to the diplomatic mission or consulate of the foreign State in Russia of which the deportee is a citizen. **7.28**

While a foreign citizen awaits deportation he is subject to being confined, by decision of a court, in a specially-allotted premise of the internal affairs agencies or in special institutions created in a subject of the Russian Federation until the deportation process is completed. These are the same premises, as a rule, in which persons detailed for an administrative violation are confined (Article 27.6, Code on Administrative Violations). **7.29**

Example: There has been constitutional litigation in the Russian Federation arising out of the practice of deportation as follows: a stateless person, J D Gafur, who arrived in the Russian Federation on 18 February 1997, was detained in a proceeding sanctioned by the procurator of the City of Moscow for deportation from the Russian Federation under escort. For more than two months he was confined under guard in Social Rehabilitation Centre No. 1 of the Chief Administration of Internal Affairs of the City of Moscow and on 29 April 1997 was compulsorily deported to Sweden. The decree to deport Gafur was rendered on the basis of Article 31, paragraph two, of the 1981 USSR Law on the Legal Status of Foreigners in the USSR, which at the time remained in force on the territory of the Russian Federation. Under that provision of Article 31, a foreign citizen or stateless person was obliged to leave the country within the period specified in the decision to deport. A person evading that order was subject with the sanction of a procurator to detention and deportation in a compulsory procedure, and detention was permitted for the period necessary for the deportation. Counsel for Gafur argued that the provision of Article 31 allowing detention of a foreign citizen or stateless person for the period needed for the deportation violated Article 22 of the 1993 Russian Constitution, which provided in relevant part: '2. Arrest, confinement under guard, and maintenance under guard shall be permitted only according to a judicial decision. Before a judicial decision a person may not be subjected to detention for a period of more than 48 hours'.[12] **7.30**

[12] Butler, *Russian Public Law* (2005), p. 9.

7.31 The Constitutional Court of the Russian Federation held in a Decree of 17 February 1998 as follows: First, in the sense of Article 22 of the 1993 Russian Constitution the provision extends to a detention undertaken to ensure the execution of a decree on deportation from the Russian Federation in an administrative proceeding. Second, under Article 62(3) of the Constitution foreign citizens and stateless persons enjoy in the Russian Federation the rights and bear duties equally with citizens of the Russian Federation unless provided otherwise by a federal law or international treaty of the Russian Federation. Read against Article 17 and other provisions of the Constitution concerning the rights and freedoms of man and citizen, it follows that the reference is only to rights and freedoms which belong to a citizen of the Russian Federation; that is, which arise and are effectuated by virtue of the special link between the State and its citizens. Both from the literal meaning of Articles 22 and 46 of the 1993 Russian Constitution (having regard to the words 'each' and 'person') and the meaning arising from the interlinkage of these articles with other provisions of Chapter 2, 'Rights and Freedoms of Man and Citizen', of the Russian Constitution, and also with generally-recognized principles and norms of international law, the right to freedom and personal inviolability and the right to judicial defence are personal inalienable rights of each person, irrespective of whether he has the citizenship of any State and, consequently, must be guaranteed to foreign citizens and stateless persons equally with citizens of the Russian Federation.

7.32 Furthermore, the Court continued, the 1948 Universal Declaration on Human Rights proclaims that each person has the right to liberty and security of the person (Article 3), no one may be subjected to arbitrary arrest or detention (Article 9), and each person has the right to an effective remedy by the competent national tribunals for acts violating the fundamental rights granted him by the constitution or by law (Article 8). Under Article 5(1)(a) of the 1985 Declaration of Human Rights with Respect to Persons Who Are Not Citizens of the Country in Which They Reside, aliens enjoy in accordance with domestic law and subject to the relevant international obligation of the State in which they are present the right to security of the person; no alien shall be subjected to arbitrary arrest or detention. The 1966 International Covenant on Civil and Political Rights provides that every person has the right to liberty and security of the person, and no one may be subjected to arbitrary arrest or detention (Article 9); anyone who is deprived of his liberty by arrest or detention is entitled to take proceedings before a court, in order that the court may decide without delay on the lawfulness of his detention and order his release if the detention is unlawful (Article 9); and each State-party to the Covenant is obliged to develop the possibilities of judicial remedy (Article 2).

7.33 Thus, the Constitutional Court concluded, the right of each, irrespective of citizenship, to freedom and personal inviolability and to judicial defence in the event of detention is among the generally-recognized principles and norms of international law which, in accordance with Article 15(4) of the 1993 Russian Constitution, are an integral part of the legal system of the Russian Federation. By virtue of Article 22(2) of the 1993 Russian Constitution, a foreign citizen or stateless person in the event of deportation from the Russian Federation in a compulsory proceeding may be subjected until a judicial decision to detention for the period necessary for deportation, but not exceeding 48 hours. A person may remain detained in excess of the said period only by a judicial decision and only on condition that without such detention can the decision on deportation be executed. Moreover, the judicial decision is to guarantee to the person the defence not only of the arbitrary extension of the period of detention above 48 hours but also against the unlawful detention as such, since the court in any event evaluates the legality and substantiation of the application of detention to the specific person.

It follows from Article 22 of the 1993 Constitution in connection with Article 55(2) and (3)[13] that detention for an indeterminate period may not be regarded as a permissible limitation of the right of each to freedom and personal inviolability and is, in essence, a diminution of the said right. Therefore, the provision of the 1981 USSR Law on the Legal Status of Foreign Citizens in the USSR being contested by the applicant concerning detention for a period necessary for deportation should not be regarded as grounds for detention for an indeterminate period even when the decision on the question concerning deportation of a stateless person may drag out because no State agrees to accept the person being deported. Otherwise, detention as a necessary measure to ensure the fulfilment of a decision on deportation would be transformed into an autonomous type of punishment not provided for by legislation of the Russian Federation and would be contrary to the said norms of the 1993 Russian Constitution. The Constitutional Court ruled that Article 31, paragraph two, of the said 1981 USSR Law did not correspond to the Constitution to the extent that it permits extension of the period of detention of the stateless persons in excess of 48 hours without a judicial decision.[14] **7.34**

[13] '2. Laws abolishing or diminishing the rights and freedoms of man and citizen must not be issued in the Russian Federation. 3. The rights and freedoms of man and citizen may be limited by a federal law only in the extent to which this is necessary for the purposes of defence of the foundations of the constitutional system, morality, health, rights, and legal interests of other persons and ensuring the defence of the country and security of the State'. Article 55, 1993 Russian Constitution, in Butler, *Russian Public Law* (2005), p. 15.

[14] For the text of the decision, see V F Mironov and A V Mironov, *Гражданство в Российской Федерации. Российские и международные акты. Комментарии законодательства* [Citizenship in the Russian Federation. Russian and International Acts. Commentaries on Legislation] (2003), pp. 458–63.

7.35 The actual organization of deportation and administrative deportation is arranged on the basis of the Code of Administrative Violations (Article 32.10) in accordance with a 2004 Order of the Ministry of Internal Affairs of the Russian Federation, No. 533, 'On Organization of the Activity of Internal Affairs Agencies of the Russian Federation and Federal Migration Service With Regard to Deportation or Administrative Deportation Beyond the Limits of the Russian Federation of Foreign Citizens or Stateless Persons' which confirmed the 'Directions' [наставление] to be followed for this purpose.[15] The foreigners subject to deportation fall into three categories; (a) those whose period of sojourn or temporary residing has been reduced or the authorization for temporary residing or residence permit has been annulled; (b) those with respect to whom a decision has been adopted concerning the undesirability of sojourn or residing in Russia; and (c) those who, with their families, have been refused or deprived of refugee status at any stage of that process.

7.36 The Federal Migration Service, under the 2004 Direction (point 5), takes a decision to deport on the basis of a reasoned recommendation from the subdivision head of the passport-visa service of the Ministry of Internal Affairs or the head of the subdivision for migration affairs of the internal affairs agency. A recording file is then set up for the foreigner concerned which contains copies of the recommendation and the decision taken, copies of identity and citizenship documents of the foreigner being deported, a copy of the visa, and, when necessary, copies of other documents connected with the entry, sojourn, and exit of the foreigner from the Russian Federation. The Federal Migration Service then informs the internal affairs agency which submitted the recommendation in writing about the decision taken.

7.37 The decision to deport is then disclosed by personnel of the internal affairs agency to the foreign citizen at a personal meeting with him under signature while simultaneously handing over to the foreigner a copy of the opinion to deport. If the foreigner does not have a command of the Russian language, the decision is announced to him with the participation of an interpreter. The identity document of the foreigner is then stamped. The head of the internal affairs agency executing the decision to deport may render a decision to send the materials concerning deportation of the foreigner to a court with a view to considering whether to confine the foreigner in specially-allotted premises of internal affairs agencies or in special institutions until the decision to deport is executed. The decision to deport with the notation concerning his exit from Russia is attached to the materials of the recording file of the deportee.

---

[15] *БНА РФ*, no. 40 (2004).

When the matter concerns administrative deportation to be assigned by a judge, the proceedings are arranged in accordance with the Code of Administrative Violations and the agencies executing a decree to administratively deport are guided by the procedural requirements of the same Code. When it is determined by personnel of internal affairs agencies that a foreigner is guilty of committing actions for which administrative deportation may be applied as a sanction, a report is submitted to the head or deputy head of the internal affairs agency setting out the circumstances connected with the sojourn of the foreigner in Russia and the legal grounds for consideration of whether he should be deported. **7.38**

When the foreigner is delivered for administrative deportation and held in administrative detention, his identity is verified against the Central Data Bank. If an international treaty of the Russian Federation so provides, the diplomatic or consular mission of the foreign State of which the foreigner is a citizen or permanent resident is informed about the administrative detention. At the request of the detained foreigner, this information must be sent without delay. If the foreigner has no identity documents, the information about the detention is accompanied by a request for assistance in establishing the detainee's identity and providing documentation. **7.39**

If there are no grounds preventing the exit of the foreigner from the Russian Federation, the head or deputy head of the internal affairs agency will send the case to a court after the formalization of all necessary materials and ensure the personal presence of the foreigner in court so that the question of administrative deportation may be considered. The materials of the case for these purposes are the report of the personnel of the internal affairs agency, protocols concerning the delivery and administrative detention and the protocol concerning the administrative violation, the results of verifications carried out, and other necessary documents. They are sent by decision of the head of the internal affairs agency or his deputy for consideration of the court within twenty-four hours from the moment of drawing up the protocol on the administrative violation. **7.40**

If the court issues a decree on administrative deportation which has entered into legal force, the internal affairs agency responsible for the execution of this decree determines the State to which the foreign citizen is to be deported (if necessary, by agreement with the Ministry of Foreign Affairs of Russia) and sets about organizing the deportation. The identity document of the foreign citizen is stamped as required; if the foreigner has no identity document, a request is made by the internal affairs agency to the diplomatic or consular mission for an identity document to be supplied as soon as possible. If the appropriate documents are missing or there are no financial resources for the deportation or there **7.41** are other circumstances preventing execution of the decree on administrative deportation, the head of the internal affairs agency responsible for execution of the decree or his deputy sends the respective materials to the judge who rendered the decree for consideration of the question of whether to extend the maintenance of the foreigner in special institutions. Once executed, the decree on administrative deportation is returned to the judge who rendered the decree. A copy of the decree with the notation concerning execution thereof is attached to the recording file of the foreigner.

7.42 The Russian Federation has international treaties with three countries (Armenia, Georgia, and Turkmenistan) which preclude the administrative deportation of citizens who reside permanently on the territory of Russia. The 1995 Treaty with Turkmenistan, for example, provides that to citizens of both States permanently residing on the territory of the other Contracting Party '. . . shall not extend limitations in rights or additional duties which have been established or may be established for foreign citizens in the Party of residing, including conditions and procedure for entry, sojourn, deportation, and exit'.[16] There are analogous provisions in the treaties with Armenia[17] and Georgia.[18] There is also a 1997 Treaty within the CIS which provides that citizens of parties who have arrived at an admittance point without the necessary documents from States which are not within the CIS may not be deported back or transferred to the authorities of States not within the CIS without the consent of the party of which the person concerned is a citizen. Thus, if a citizen of Moldova arrived by air from Germany at an international airport in Russia and had no documents for entry into Russia, the border agencies would not have the right to deport him back to Germany, but rather he must be transferred to Moldova.[19]

7.43 Chapter 18 of the Code on Administrative Violations is devoted to 'Administrative Violations in the Domain of Defence of the State Boundary of the Russian Federation and Ensuring the Regime of Sojourn of Foreign Citizens or Stateless Persons on the Territory of the Russian Federation'. Within this Chapter there are fourteen articles, some of which overlap with the discussion of the administrative responsibility of foreigners above. We consider each in succession insofar as they involve natural persons who are foreign citizens or stateless persons.

A *violation of the regime of the State boundary of the Russian Federation* (Article 18.1) consists of crossing the State boundary of the Russian Federation by persons and/or means of transport or a violation of the procedure for the route of such persons and/or means of transport from the State boundary of the

[16] *СЗ РФ* (1997), no. 32, item 3748. [17] *СЗ РФ* (2002), no. 8, item 747.
[18] *Российская газета*, 14 October 1995. [19] *Содружество*, no. 1 (1997)

Russian Federation up to the admittance point across the State boundary of the Russian Federation or return, excluding innocent passage and overflight. These actions, if committed by a foreign citizen or stateless person, entail an administrative fine of up to ten minimum amounts of payment for labour with or without administrative deportation beyond the limits of the Russian Federation.

The second type of violation under Article 18.1 is the conducting on the State boundary or nearby economic, fishery, or other activity without informing border agencies and forces or, having given such notification, in violation of the established procedure for conducting such activity on or near the State boundary. The sanction for a violation is an administrative fine, which may be applied to natural persons, officials, or juridical persons. **7.44**

The State boundary is defined by the 1993 Law on the State Boundary of the Russian Federation as the 'line and vertical surface passing along this line which determines the limits of State territory (land, waters, subsoil, and air-space) of the Russian Federation', that is, the spatial limit of the operation of State sovereignty of the Russian Federation. An 'admittance point' across the State boundary is a territory within the limits of a railway or motor vehicle station or a sea port or river port or an airport or aerodrome that is open to international traffic or flights and other specially-equipped place where border or other types of control and admittance across the State boundary is carried out for persons, means of transport, cargo, goods, or livestock (see Chapter 10). **7.45**

Under the 1993 Law on the State Boundary (Article 14) foreign citizens and stateless persons who do not have the status of persons residing or sojourning on the territory of the Russian Federation and who have crossed the State boundary from the territory of a foreign State, when there are the indicia of either a crime or an administrative violation, bear responsibility under Russian criminal or administrative law. If there are no grounds for instituting criminal or administrative proceedings and the individuals concerned do not seek political asylum, the border guard may officially turn them over to the authorities of the foreign State from which they crossed into Russia if there is an international treaty to this effect. In the absence of such a treaty, the individuals concerned may be deported to the neighbouring State, the officials thereof being informed. Much will turn upon whether the Russian officials consider the actions of the foreign citizen or stateless person in crossing the State boundary without proper documents to constitute a crime under Article 322 of the Criminal Code, or to justify formal administrative proceedings leading to administrative deportation (in which case the matter is referred to the judge of a district court), or an administrative fine is appropriate (in which event the matter is referred to a justice of the peace). **7.46**

7.47 Insofar as the case involves the conducting of economic or other activity on or near the State boundary, the general requirements for doing so are that the activity should not cause harm to the population or ecological or other security of the Russian Federation or to other foreign States, nor should the activity create hindrances to any maintenance of the State boundary and the fulfilment by border agencies and forces of their tasks. For the purposes of this Article individual entrepreneurs who commit such a violation are equated under the Code on Administrative Violations to officials, and not to ordinary natural persons.

7.48 A *violation of the frontier regime in the border zone* (Article 18.2) constitutes a violation of the rules for entry or passage into a border zone or the temporary sojourn, movement of persons, and/or means of transport into a border zone. It is punishable by a warning or an administrative fine. A 'border zone' or 'frontier zone' is defined in the 1993 Law on the State Boundary of the Russian Federation as a zone of up to five kilometres in breadth along the State boundary on land or seashore of the Russian Federation, Russian shores of frontier rivers, lakes, and other waters and islands on the said waters. The border zone may not include the territories of population centres, sanatoriums, houses of leisure, and other recreational institutions, objects or institutions of culture, or places of mass leisure, active water use, performance of religious rites, or other sites where citizens traditionally gather in large numbers. The entrances to a border zone are marked with warning signs.

7.49 Within a border zone a 'frontier regime' involves the introduction of special rules for entry or passage, temporary sojourn, movement of persons or means of transport or the effectuation of economic or other activities and the conducting of mass socio-political, cultural, and other measures. Entry is based on individual or collective passes issued by border agencies or border guards on the basis of personal applications of citizens or petitions of enterprises and organizations. There is an established place of entry and possibly time schedules when entry is permitted. The maintenance and pasturing of livestock in the border zone may be restricted in the interests of public health.

7.50 A *violation of the frontier regime in the territorial sea and internal sea waters of the Russian Federation* (Article 18.3) consists of a violation of the rules for recording, keeping, departure, and return and sojourn in water or ice of small Russian self-propelled or non-self-propelled surface or submarine ships or means of movement on ice in the territorial sea or internal sea waters of the Russian Federation, or the Russian part of frontier rivers, lakes, or other waters, for which an administrative fine is applicable. A violation also may comprise the conducting in the said waters or ice of any commercial, research, survey, or other activities without authorization or notification of border agencies and forces.

A *violation of the regime at admittance points across the State Boundary of the Russian Federation* (Article 18.4) entails a breach of the rules for admittance, including rules for entry into those points, sojourn therein, or exit therefrom, of persons, means of transport, the bringing in and bringing out of cargoes, goods, and livestock, these rules being laid down in the interests of creating conditions for effectuating border, customs, and other types of control. The regime in admittance points is established by an order or instruction of the head of the airport, aerodrome, sea or river port, railway or motor vehicle station, or executive of other transport enterprise, having regard to local conditions and by agreement with the respective officials of border guard, customs, and other agencies. If the actions amounting to a violation are committed by a foreign citizen or stateless person, the sanction is an administrative fine of from one to three minimum amounts of payment for labour with or without administrative deportation. **7.51**

A *violation by a foreign citizen or stateless person of the regime of sojourn in the Russian Federation* (Article 18.8) as expressed in the failure to comply with the established procedure for registration or movement or the procedure for choice of place of residence, or evading exit from the Russian Federation upon the expiry of the determined period of sojourn, or the failure to comply with the rules for transit passage through the territory of the Russian Federation, entails an administrative fine of from five to ten minimum amounts of payment for labour with or without administrative deportation. This provision of the Code on Administrative Violations is aimed particularly at enforcing the 2002 Law on the Legal Status of Foreigners. **7.52**

A *violation of the rules for recruitment and use in the Russian Federation of foreign work force* (Article 18.10) involves a violation by an employer of the relevant rules. If a violation is committed by a foreign citizen or stateless person, the sanction is an administrative fine with or without administrative deportation. An employer and a customer for work or services have the right to recruit and use foreign workers only if they have an authorization for this; certain categories of foreigners are exempted from this requirement, but not all (see Chapter 5). **7.53**

A *violation of immigration rules* (Article 18.11) is the evasion by the immigrant of the duty to reside in a place of temporary confinement attached to an immigration control post, temporary placement centre for immigrants, or the place determined by the territorial agency of the Federal Migration Service or a violation of the rules for residing in the said places while the status of an immigrant in the Russian Federation is being determined. The sanction is an administrative fine with or without administrative deportation. An immigrant for the purposes of this provision is a foreign natural person, including refugee, **7.54** who has settled permanently or for a determined period on the territory of the Russian Federation.

7.55 The system of immigration control at admittance points on the State boundary of the Russian Federation was introduced by a 1993 Edict of the President of the Russian Federation, No. 2145. A 1994 Decree of the Government of the Russian Federation confirmed the Statute on Immigration Control. Immigration control is the effectuation by the Federal Migration Service and its territorial agencies of activity with regard to the regulation of migration and of measures to prevent uncontrolled migration of foreign citizens and stateless persons to the territory of Russia. Immigration control posts established at admittance points on the State boundary are structural subdivisions of migration service agencies.

7.56 A *violation by a refugee or forced resettler of rules of residing* (Article 18.12) constitutes the failure of a refugee or forced resettler in the event of a change of place of sojourn or place of residence to perform the duty to remove himself from the records of the Federal Migration Service agency or to be recorded at his new place of sojourn or place of residence, or to notify a change of name, family status, composition of status, or change of citizenship. The sanction is an administrative fine.

C. Extradition

7.57 The transfer of a person from one State to another for trial or to serve a sentence is a form of legal assistance by one country to another effectuated in accordance with international treaties and national legislation. In the Russian Federation extradition is regulated by the 1993 Russian Constitution, the Criminal Code of the Russian Federation, the Code of Criminal Procedure of the Russian Federation, and international treaties of Russia. For Russian citizens the constitutional position is unequivocal: a Russian citizen may not be extradited to another State, a position reiterated in the Criminal Code of Russia (Article 13). When the Russian Federation acceded in 2000 to the 1957 European Convention on Extradition,[20] a reservation was entered to this effect.[21]

7.58 Foreign citizens are another matter entirely. Excluding situations when foreign citizens or stateless persons in Russia are being persecuted for their political

[20] *СЗ РФ* (2000), no. 23, item 2348.

[21] For the reservations entered upon signature of the Convention in 1996, see the Regulation of the President of the Russian Federation, No. 458-рп, of 3 September 1996. *СЗ РФ* (1996), no. 37, item 4286.

views or for an action or failure to act which is not a crime in the Russian Federation—extradition not being possible in these situations—persons accused of committing a crime are extradited on the basis of a federal law or an international treaty of the Russian Federation. The same applies to the transfer of convicted persons to serve punishment in other States (Article 63, 1993 Russian Constitution).

In addition to the 1957 European Convention mentioned above, of relevance are the 2002 Convention on Legal Assistance and Legal Relations With Regard to Civil, Family, and Criminal Cases,[22] bilateral treaties devoted to legal assistance, including extradition (such as the 1996 Russian-Iranian Treaty on Legal Assistance and Legal Relations With Regard to Civil and Criminal Cases)[23] or solely to extradition (for example, the 1998 Treaty on Extradition between Russia and India).[24] **7.59**

The Code of Criminal Procedure of the Russian Federation permits extradition on the basis of reciprocity: on the basis of assurances of a foreign State who has sent a request for extradition it would be expected that in an analogous situation extradition would be made at the request of the Russian Federation. The decision to extradite is taken by the Procurator General of the Russian Federation or his deputy. The conditions for extradition established by the Code of Criminal Procedure (Article 462) are as follows: (a) the act committed by the person whose extradition is requested must be deemed to be criminally punishable both under Russian legislation and legislation of the foreign State (the principle of 'dual criminality'); (b) the criminal law must provide punishment for the commission of these acts in the form of deprivation of freedom for a term exceeding one year or a graver punishment, such as deprivation for a longer period, life imprisonment, or the death penalty; (c) the person to be extradited must be sentenced to deprivation of freedom for a term of not less than six months or a graver punishment if extradition is sought to serve punishment; and (d) the foreign State requesting extradition must guarantee that the person to be extradited will be prosecuted only for a crime specified in the request and after the end of the judicial examination and serving of punishment may freely leave the territory of the said State, and also will not be banished, transferred, or extradited to a third State without the consent of the Russian Federation. **7.60**

The circumstances under which extradition will not be made also are set out in the Code of Criminal Procedure (Article 464). They fall into two groups, the first of which comprises absolute grounds for refusing extradition and the second, discretionary grounds on which extradition may be refused. The first **7.61**

[22] Russia has signed, but not ratified, this Convention.

[23] *СЗ РФ* (2000), no. 47, item 4579.

[24] *СЗ РФ* (2000), no. 28, item 2883.

group consists of: (a) the person to be extradited has Russian citizenship; (b) the person to be extradited is deemed to be a refugee or has been given political asylum; (c) a judgment has entered into legal force for the same crime on Russian territory with respect to the person to be extradited or the proceedings in the criminal case have been terminated; (d) a criminal case may not be instituted under Russian legislation or a judgment may not be enforced if any of the following periods have lapsed: (i) two years after the commission of a crime of small gravity; (ii) six years after the commission of a crime of average gravity; (iii) ten years after the commission of a grave crime; (iv) fifteen years after the commission of an especially grave crime.

7.62 The periods of limitation commence in this connection from the day of the commission of the crime until the moment of the entry of the judgment of the court into legal force. If a person commits a new crime, the period of limitation for each crime is calculated autonomously. *Example:* If a British citizen committed theft in the United Kingdom eleven years ago, he could not be extradited from Russia because the most severe punishment for theft under Article 158(3) of the Criminal Code of the Russian Federation is six years. This crime would be regarded as a grave crime in Russia, and extradition for a grave crime must take place within not more than ten years after the commission of the crime (assuming there were no grounds for suspension of the period of limitations).

7.63 Moreover, if pursuant to Article 83 of the Criminal Code a judgment of guilty was not brought into execution within the period stipulated by the Criminal Code, extradition would be refused. *Example:* A British citizen is found guilty of committing open stealing without aggravating circumstances, which in Russia is regarded as a crime of average gravity for which the maximum punishment is deprivation of freedom for a term of up to four years. For some reason the judgment was never executed, and if the British citizen were on Russian territory six years or later after the judgment should have been executed, the British citizen would not be extradited to the United Kingdom to serve punishment on condition that the periods for execution of the punishment had not been suspended.

7.64 A criminal case cannot be instituted under Russian legislation if there are no legal grounds for doing so. An application for extradition which fails to specify the occasion with regard to which the criminal case is instituted is grounds for refusal of extradition. Moreover, there must be sufficient data or evidence indicating the indicia of the crime. The absence of grounds to institute a criminal case should result in a refusal to do so and a refusal of extradition. *Example:* An eighteen-year old British citizen accused of having committed homicide five years previously would not be extradited from Russia to the United Kingdom since under the Russian Criminal Code the causing of death to a human being by an individual who was less than fourteen years of age at the time does not contain the constituent elements of a crime. A person may be brought to criminal responsibility in Russia only from the age of fourteen years.

Extradition also would be refused if there is a decision of a court of the Russian Federation which has entered into legal force that indicated there were obstacles to the extradition of a particular foreign citizen. Such a court decision might exist if the foreigner concerned appealed the decision of the Procurator General to extradite under Article 463 of the Code of Criminal Procedure of the Russian Federation. The Procurator General may grant or refuse extradition as follows: (a) the act which is grounds for the request to extradite was committed on the territory of Russia or beyond the limits of the Russian Federation but against Russian interests. As a rule, the foreigner would be subject to criminal responsibility in Russia under Russian legislation; (b) a foreigner is prosecuted in Russia for the same act for which extradition is requested; and (c) the criminal prosecution of a foreigner whose extradition is requested has been instituted privately; that is, in the case of the Russian Criminal Code prosecutions for causing light harm to health, beatings, slander, or insult are instituted only upon the application of the victim or his legal representative and may be terminated by reconciliation of the victim with the accused. Extradition would not be granted in such cases. **7.65**

The Russian Federation would also refuse extradition of a foreigner who would be brought to responsibility abroad in an extraordinary court or by way of simplified proceedings, or to execute a judgment rendered by an extraordinary court when there are grounds to suppose that minimum due process would not be ensured (right to counsel, right to submit evidence, and so on). The same would result if there were serious grounds to suppose that the person to be extradited was or would be subjected to torture or other cruel, inhumane, or humiliating treatment. If extradition would entail serious complications by reason of advanced age or state of health, it would be likely to be refused. These considerations in exercising discretion with respect to extradition were reflected in the reservations made by the Russian Federation on 25 October 1999 when acceding to the 1957 European Convention on Extradition.[25] In addition, the Russian Federation reserves the right not to extradite persons whose extradition may prejudice its sovereignty, security, public order, or other vital interests. A foreigner who had knowledge of Russian State secrets would probably fall into this category. **7.66**

The procedure for the extradition of foreigners is set out in the Code of **7.67**

[25] See the Federal Law on Ratification of the European Convention on Extradition, Additional Protocol, and Second Additional Protocol Thereto. *СЗ РФ* (1999), no. 43, item 5129.

Criminal Procedure of the Russian Federation. The Procurator General of the Russian Federation or his deputy takes the decision to extradite a foreign citizen or stateless person, who is then informed in writing about the decision. The decision to extradite enters into legal force ten days from the moment of receipt of the notification thereof. If the decision is appealed, the extradition does not proceed until the judicial decision regarding the appeal enters into legal force.

7.68 If attached to the extradition request there is a decision of a court of a foreign State to confine the person under guard, the procurator has the right to subject the foreign citizen to house arrest or to confine him under guard without the confirmation of the said foreign court decision by a court of the Russian Federation. An extradition request without confinement under guard designated is referred by the procurator to a district court with a petition to choose the measure of restraint.

7.69 Appeal against the procurator's decision to extradite within ten days from the receipt of notification of the decision is made by a simple written application to the court. It is not necessary to set out the reasons and grounds why the person to be extradited considers the decision to be illegal. The burden of proof to demonstrate the legality and well-foundedness of the decision to extradite lies on the officials who took the decision. Verification by the court of the legality and well-foundedness of the procurator's decision to extradite must be completed within one month from the day of receipt of the appeal. If the foreigner to be extradited is being held under guard, the administration of his place of confinement immediately sends his appeal to the respective court and notifies the procurator thereof. The procurator within ten days from receipt of the appeal at the court sends the materials confirming the legality and substantiation of his decision to extradite to the court.

7.70 A bench consisting of three judges verifies the legality and substantiation of the decision to extradite within one month from the day of receipt of the appeal in open judicial session with the participation of the procurator, the person to be extradited, and the defender of the last, if there is one. The court is not concerned with whether the person to be extradited is guilty or not. The hearing is limited to whether the procurator's decision conforms to Russian legislation and international treaties of the Russian Federation. The court issues a ruling on whether the appeal should be left without satisfaction or should be deemed to be illegal or unsubstantiated and vacated. If the decision to extradite is vacated, the court also removes the measure of restraint with respect to the appellant. In either event, the ruling of the court may be appealed within seven days from the day of issuance to the Supreme Court of the Russian Federation.

7.71 Once the decision to extradite enters into legal force, the Russian Federation informs the foreign State about the place, date, and time for transferring the person to be extradited. If the person is not accepted within fifteen days from the day established for transfer, he may be released from under guard. If for reasons beyond its control the foreign State cannot accept the person subject to extradition and so informs the Russian Federation, the date for transfer may be changed. The same procedure of changing the date applies if the Russian Federation is for reasons beyond its control unable to transfer the person to be extradited. In any event the person being extradited is subject to release thirty days from the day established for his transfer.

A number of international judicial organs have been created, including the international tribunals for Rwanda and Yugoslavia, on the basis of decisions of the United Nations Security Council or, in the case of the International Criminal Court, a multilateral treaty. Russian legal doctrine takes the view that if tribunals established by the Security Council of the United Nations were to request the extradition of a foreign citizen or stateless person officially, all members of the United Nations would be obliged to comply, including the Russian Federation. *Example:* If the international tribunal for Yugoslavia requested Russia to extradite a specific foreign citizen suspected of war crimes on the territory of the former Yugoslavia, the Russian law enforcement agencies would be obliged to detain this person and pursue extradition proceedings in the same procedure as though the request were from a foreign State. **7.72**

The Russian Federation has signed, but not ratified, the treaty creating the International Criminal Court in Rome. **7.73**

D. Law of Criminal, Civil, and Arbitrazh Procedure

Section 1. Criminal procedure

Unlike the codes of procedure which follow below, the Code of Criminal Procedure of the Russian Federation imposes on foreign citizens and stateless persons the greatest measure of 'national regime'. The Code of Criminal Procedure contains no special sections and only one chapter related to the citizenship or lack thereof on the part of natural persons. Proceedings in criminal cases concerning crimes committed by foreign citizens or stateless persons on the territory of the Russian Federation are considered and conducted in accordance with the Code of Criminal Procedure (Article 3). **7.74**

There are, however, individual criminal procedure provisions that reflect citizenship status. If a foreign citizen fails to appear in court as a victim or witness, the court has the right upon the petition of a party or upon its own initiative to read out testimony previously given by the foreign citizen (Article 281, Code of Criminal Procedure). If a foreign citizen is convicted by a Russian court, one of **7.75** the questions which the court must consider when deliberating about the execution of the criminal judgment is whether the citizen of a foreign State sentenced to deprivation of freedom in Russia might be transferred to serve the punishment in the State of which he is a citizen (Article 397).

7.76 The Russian authorities have two possibilities when faced with a situation in which a foreign citizen who has committed a crime in Russia proves to be outside Russia. One is to refer all the materials relating to the criminal case to the General Procuracy of the Russian Federation for possible referral of the materials to the competent agencies of the foreign State in order to pursue a criminal prosecution. The second is to seek extradition of the foreign citizen from the foreign State, either on the basis of reciprocity or in accordance with an international treaty of the Russian Federation, provided that the acts concerned are criminally punishable both in Russia and in the foreign State. The decision to extradite or not lies with the Procurator General of the Russian Federation or his deputy. The decision to extradite can be appealed to a Russian court.

7.77 Extradition is not permitted if: (1) the person whose extradition is requested proves to be a citizen of the Russian Federation; (2) the person to be extradited has been granted political asylum in Russia in connection with persecution by reason of race, profession of faith, citizenship, nationality, affiliation to a particular social group, or political beliefs; (3) a judgment which has entered into legal force has been rendered by a Russian court for the same act or the proceedings in a criminal case have been terminated; (4) the period of limitations has expired or other legal grounds exist which means a criminal case can not be instituted in Russia or a judgment executed; or (5) there are obstacles to extradition which preclude extradition in accordance with Russian legislation or an international treaty of the Russian Federation.

7.78 Extradition may be refused if: (1) the act which serves as grounds for the request to extradite is not a crime; (2) the act concerned was committed on the territory of Russia or against the interests of Russia, albeit outside the Russian Federation; (3) a criminal prosecution is being effectuated in Russia for the same act; or (4) a criminal prosecution has been instituted in Russia for the act concerned by private accusation.

7.79 Extradition may be deferred or postponed in accordance with the Code of Criminal Procedure. If an extradition request is received, the Procurator General or his deputy decides whether the individual concerned should be held in custody or not pending resolution of the request. Articles connected with the alleged crime, such as implements of the crime, or articles bearing traces of the crime, or articles extracted by criminal means, also may be transferred.

7.80 The Code of Criminal Procedure also addresses the circumstances under which a foreign citizen may be transferred abroad to serve punishment in the form of deprivation of freedom to the State of which he is a citizen (Chapter 55).

Section 2. Civil procedure

The courts of ordinary jurisdiction of the Russian Federation, headed by the Supreme Court, consider, in addition to criminal cases (see above), cases with the participation of foreign citizens, stateless persons, foreign organizations, organizations with foreign investments, and international organizations concerning the defence of violated or contested rights, freedoms, and legal interests and disputes arising from civil, family, labour, housing, land, ecological, and other legal relations, as well as other cases determined by the Russian Code of Civil Procedure to be within the ambit of courts of ordinary jurisdiction (Article 22). In general, one may say that the courts of ordinary jurisdiction handle all cases not within the jurisdiction of arbitrazh courts. **7.81**

Section V of the Code of Civil Procedure is devoted to Proceedings with Regard to Cases with the Participation of Foreign Persons. The term 'foreign persons' means foreign citizens, stateless persons, foreign organizations, and international organizations, all of whom have the right to apply to courts of the Russian Federation in order to defend their violated or contested rights, freedoms, and legal interests. The principle of national regime applies: foreign persons enjoy procedural rights and fulfil procedural duties equally with Russian citizens and organizations (Article 398). However, the Government of the Russian Federation may establish retaliatory limitations with respect to foreign persons of those States in whose courts such limitations are permitted with respect to the procedural rights and Russian citizens and organizations. **7.82**

Civil procedural legal capacity

The legal capacity and dispositive legal capacity of foreign citizens and stateless persons with respect to civil procedure is determined by their personal law; that is, the law of the country of which they are a citizen. If an individual has both Russian citizenship and a foreign citizenship, Russian law is considered to be his personal law. If a person has several foreign citizenships, his personal law is the law of the country in which the citizen has a place of residence (Article 399, Code of Civil Procedure). However, if a foreign citizen has a place of residence in the Russian Federation, his personal law is Russian law. **7.83**

A stateless person has the personal law of the country in which he has a place of residence. If under his personal law a foreign person does not have procedural dispositive legal capacity, he may nonetheless be deemed to have such if in accordance with Russian law this person has dispositive procedural legal capacity. **7.84**

7.85 The personal law of a foreign organization is the law of the country in which the organization was founded, and its procedural legal capacity is determined on the basis of that personal law. However, a foreign organization not possessing procedural legal capacity under its personal law may be deemed to have such on the territory of the Russian Federation in accordance with Russian law (Article 400, Code of Civil Procedure).

7.86 With respect to an international organization, procedural legal capacity is established on the basis of the international treaty in accordance with which it was created or its constitutive documents, or by an agreement with the competent agency of the Russian Federation.

Rules of jurisdiction

7.87 Under the Code of Civil Procedure (Article 402), the national regime applies to jurisdictional aspects of cases with the participation of foreign persons. Russian courts consider cases with the participation of foreign persons if the defendant organization is situated on the territory of the Russian Federation or the defendant citizen has a place of residence in the Russian Federation. In addition, Russian courts have the right to consider cases with the participation of foreign persons under the following circumstances: (1) a management organ, branch, or representation of a foreign juridical person is situated on the territory of the Russian Federation; (2) the defendant has property on the territory of the Russian Federation; (3) with regard to the recovery of alimony or establishment of paternity the plaintiff has a place of residence in the Russian Federation; (4) with regard to compensation of harm caused by injury, other impairment of health, or death of breadwinner, the harm was caused on the territory of the Russian Federation or the plaintiff has a place of residence in the Russian Federation; (5) with regard to compensation of harm caused to property, the action or other circumstance which served as grounds for presenting the demand concerning compensation of harm occurred on the territory of Russia; (6) the suit arises from a contract under which full or partial performance should have occurred or did occur on the territory of the Russian Federation; (7) the suit arises from unsubstantiated enrichment which occurred on the territory of the Russian Federation; (8) with regard to dissolution of marriage the plaintiff had a place of residence in the Russian Federation or one of the spouses is a Russian citizen; and (9) with regard to defence of honour, dignity, and business reputation the plaintiff has a place of residence in the Russian Federation.

7.88 Russian courts have exclusive jurisdiction in cases: (1) concerning the right to immoveable property situated on the territory of the Russian Federation; (2) relating to disputes arising from a contract of carriage if the carriers are situated on the territory of the Russian Federation; (3) concerning dissolution of marriage of Russian citizens with foreign citizens or stateless persons if both spouses have a place of residence in the Russian Federation; and (4) other cases provided for by designated chapters of the Code of Civil Procedure. Also in specific instances Russian courts consider cases by way of special proceedings.

Jurisdiction by agreement is permitted until a court accepts a case for proceedings, except that jurisdiction over certain cases may not be altered by agreement. Once a case is accepted by a Russian court for proceedings in compliance with the jurisdictional rules, the case will be decided by that court even if there should occur a change of citizenship, place of residence, location of the parties, or other circumstances by virtue of which the case would be within the jurisdiction of the court of another country (Article 405, Code of Civil Procedure). **7.89**

The officials of federal agencies of executive power would not stop a foreign vessel passing through the territorial sea nor change its course in order to exercise civil jurisdiction of the Russian Federation with respect to a person on board the foreign vessel pursuant to the 1998 Federal Law on Internal Sea Waters, the Territorial Sea, and Contiguous Zone (Article 18). Measures of recovery or arrest with regard to any civil case would be applied only in respect of obligations or by reason of responsibility accepted or assumed by the foreign vessel during or for the passage through the territorial sea. This provision does not extend to a foreign vessel at anchor in the territorial sea or passing through the territorial sea after having departed from the internal sea waters of the Russian Federation. **7.90**

Procedural consequences of cases considered by foreign court

If a suit is being considered by a foreign court and there is a decision of the court with regard to a dispute between the same parties, on the same subject, and on the same grounds, and there is an international treaty of the Russian Federation between the country of the court providing for the mutual recognition and enforcement of the court decision, the Russian court will refuse to accept the petition to sue or terminate the proceedings in the case. The Russian court will return the petition to sue or leave the application without consideration if, in the foreign court whose decision is subject to recognition and enforcement on the territory of the Russian Federation, a case has been instituted with regard to such a dispute. **7.91**

Judicial commissions

Russian courts perform commission of foreign courts transferred to them in the procedure established by an international treaty of the Russian Federation or a federal law if the commissions concern the performance of individual **7.92** procedural actions such as handing over notices and other documents, obtaining explanations of parties, testimony of witnesses, opinions of experts, a view on the spot, and the like. Such commissions will not be performed if they would prejudice the sovereignty of the Russian Federation or threaten the security of the country, or are not within the competence of the court. They are performed in accordance with Russian law unless provided otherwise by an international treaty.

Recognition of documents

7.93 Documents issued, drawn up, or certified in accordance with foreign law by competent agencies of foreign States outside the Russian Federation with respect to Russian citizens or organizations or foreign persons are accepted by Russian courts, provided that they have been duly legalized, unless an international treaty or federal law of the Russian Federation provides otherwise. If the documents are in a foreign language they must be submitted to the Russian court together with a duly attested translation into the Russian language.

7.94 Judicial notices and summonses issued by Russian courts also apply to foreign citizens and foreign juridical persons unless established otherwise by an international treaty (Article 113, Code of Civil Procedure).

Adoption proceedings

7.95 The Russian authorities have taken a number of steps in recent years to impose greater supervision on the adoption of Russian children by foreign persons. Some of these changes are reflected in the Code of Civil Procedure. Citizens of the Russian Federation, for example, who reside permanently outside Russia, foreign citizens, and stateless persons who wish to adopt a child that is a Russian citizen, file the application to adopt with the supreme court of the republic, territory, or regional court, court of a city of federal significance (Moscow or St. Petersburg), court of an autonomous region, or court of an autonomous national area at the place of residence or location of the child.

7.96 The documents to be filed with the application to the court include those which normally apply for an adopting Russian citizen in Russia, together with the opinion of a competent agency of the State of which the adopting parents are citizens concerning the living conditions and the possibility of the individuals to be adoptive parents, as well as the authorization of the competent agency of the foreign State for the child, if adopted, to enter the country and take up permanent residence on the territory of that State. These documents must be legalized, translated into the Russian language, and the translation duly notarized.

7.97 When preparing an adoption case involving foreign persons for consideration, there must be submitted to the Russian court a document confirming that in the State data bank on children there is information confirming that the child or children concerned have been left without the care of parents and that it is impossible to transfer the child for care to a family of Russian citizens or for relatives of the child to adopt, irrespective of the citizenship or place of residence of the relatives.

Section 3. Arbitrazh procedure

The system of arbitrazh courts in the Russian Federation operates on the basis of legislation on the arbitrazh courts and the 2002 Code of Arbitrazh Procedure of the Russian Federation, as amended.[26] The national regime of arbitrazh procedure applies to foreigners and stateless persons subject to the special provisions of Section V of the Code of Arbitrazh Procedure, 'Proceedings with Regard to Cases with the Participation of Foreign Persons'. Section V addresses the competence of the arbitrazh courts in cases in which foreigners participate and the distinctive aspects of the consideration of such cases. **7.98**

Competence of arbitrazh courts to consider cases

Competence of arbitrazh courts

The Code of Arbitrazh Procedure establishes ten circumstances under which the arbitrazh courts in the Russian Federation are competent to consider cases with regard to economic disputes and other cases connected with the effectuation of entrepreneurial activity with the participation of foreign organizations, international organizations, foreign citizens, and stateless persons effectuating entrepreneurial and other economic activity. They are as follows: (1) the defendant is situated or resides on the territory of the Russian Federation, or property of the defendant is situated on the territory of the Russian Federation; (2) a management organ, branch, or representation of a foreign person is on the territory of the Russian Federation; (3) the dispute arose from a contract under which performance should have occurred or did occur on the territory of the Russian Federation; (4) a demand arose from the causing of harm to the property by an action or other circumstances which occurred on the territory of the Russian Federation, or harm ensued on the territory of the Russian Federation; (5) the dispute arose from unsubstantiated enrichment which occurred on the territory of the Russian Federation; (6) the plaintiff with regard to a case concerning defence of business reputation is situated in the Russian Federation; (7) the dispute arose from relations connected with the circulation of securities whose **7.99**

[26] On the arbitrazh courts, see Butler, *Russian Law* (2nd edn, 2003), pp. 166–71. For the basic legislation on the arbitrazh courts, see Butler, *Russian Public Law* (2005), pp. 543–72.

issuance occurred on the territory of the Russian Federation; (8) the application with regard to a case concerning the establishment of a fact having legal significance indicates the existence of this fact on the territory of the Russian Federation; (9) the dispute arose from relations connected with the State registration of names and other objects and the rendering of services on the Internet on the territory of the Russian Federation; and (10) other instances when the legal relation in dispute is closely connected with the territory of the Russian Federation (Article 247, Code of Arbitrazh Procedure).

7.100 The above criteria for arbitrazh court competence are broad and, as such, considered as one of the 'merits of Russian law'.[27] The place of residence or the location of a defendant are determined under the Civil Code of the Russian Federation (Articles 20 and 54 respectively). The plaintiff has considerable latitude of choice in deciding whether to bring suit in the Russian Federation, having regard to the ten points enumerated above.

Exclusive competence of arbitrazh courts

7.101 There are five categories of cases within the competence of Russian arbitrazh courts, provided that they are cases with foreign participation: (1) disputes with respect to property in State ownership of the Russian Federation, including cases connected with the privatization of State property and compulsory alienation of property for State needs; (2) disputes whose subject is immoveable property or rights to such property situated on the territory of the Russian Federation; (3) disputes connected with the registration or issuance of patents, the registration and issuance of certificates for trademarks, industrial designs, utility models, or other results of intellectual activity which require registration or issuance of a patent or certificate in the Russian Federation; (4) disputes regarding the recognition of invalid entries in State registers or cadastres made by a competent agency of the Russian Federation keeping such register or cadastre; and (5) disputes connected with the founding, liquidation, or registration on the territory of the Russian Federation of juridical persons and individual entrepreneurs, and with the contesting of decisions of organs of these juridical persons. In addition, all cases involving foreign participation and falling under or arising out of administrative and other public law relations set out in Section III of the Code of Arbitrazh Procedure are within the exclusive competence of arbitrazh courts of the Russian Federation (Article 248, Code of Arbitrazh Procedure).

The rules governing exclusive competence of arbitrazh courts are imperative and may not be altered by agreement of the parties.

[27] See T N Neshataeva, in V F Iakovlev and M K Iukov (eds.), *Комментарий к Арбитражному процессуальному кодексу Российской Федерации* [Commentary to Code of Arbitrazh Procedure of the Russian Federation] (2003), p. 652.

Agreement on competence of arbitrazh courts

If a foreign person has concluded an agreement in which it is provided that an arbitrazh court of the Russian Federation possesses competence with regard to a dispute which has arisen or which might arise and such dispute is connected with the effectuation by the party(ies) of entrepreneurial or other economic activity, the Russian arbitrazh court will have exclusive competence to consider the dispute on condition that such agreement does not change the exclusive competence of a foreign court. An agreement to determine competence must be concluded in written form. **7.102**

It is common commercial practice for foreign parties to choose the Russian arbitrazh court system by contract for the settlement of their disputes. Confusion is not uncommon either between the arbitrazh courts and the arbitration courts. Foreign parties who make a choice of judicial system or arbitration need to be clear as to which is which in the Russian Federation. **7.103**

Security measures

A Russian arbitrazh court may, in cases involving foreign persons, upon the application of an organization or natural person impose preliminary and other security measures with a view to securing the property interests of the applicant or plaintiff in a proceeding (Article 250, Code of Arbitrazh Procedure). The preliminary measures bear a certain analogy to, but should not be confused with or translated as, preliminary injunctions as known in the Anglo-American legal system. They are elaborated in Chapter 8 of the Code of Arbitrazh Procedure, which means in effect that the national regime applies to foreign persons for these purposes. **7.104**

Procedural consequences of res judicata

Unless a dispute has been referred to the exclusive jurisdiction of an arbitrazh court in the Russian Federation, the said court shall leave a suit without consideration if there is a case under proceedings in a foreign court between the same persons, on the same subject, and on the same grounds. It would follow that the arbitrazh court would terminate proceedings if a decision of a foreign court has entered into legal force which was adopted in a dispute between the same persons, on the same subject, and on the same grounds unless the consideration of the case was within the exclusive jurisdiction of an arbitrazh court of the Russian Federation or the foreign court decision cannot be enforced in the Russian Federation. **7.105**

Russian legal assistance treaties commonly resolve these issues by giving preference to the court where proceedings were engaged in earlier under the dispute. In the absence of a treaty, however, the approach set out above will prevail. **7.106**

Consideration of cases with foreign persons

Procedure for consideration of cases

7.107 Unless an international treaty of the Russian Federation provides otherwise, arbitrazh cases with the participation of foreign persons are considered in accordance with the Code of Arbitrazh Procedure, subject to the distinctive provisions contained in that Code. Whether the presence of a foreign person in a case should alter the procedural periods within which the case is to be considered is dealt with as follows. If the foreign persons or their management organs, branches, representation offices, or empowered representatives are situated on or reside on the territory of the Russian Federation, the usual periods laid down in the Code of Arbitrazh Procedure apply. However, if the foreign person participating in a case being considered by an arbitrazh court is situated or resides outside the Russian Federation, these persons are notified of arbitrazh proceedings through the justice or other competent agencies of the foreign State, in which case the periods apply as stipulated in legal assistance treaties with the Russian Federation or in the absence of such a treaty, a period not exceeding six months.

7.108 The Code of Arbitrazh Procedure thus starts in this respect from the principle of national regime and that all cases with the participation of foreign persons are considered according to the provisions of that Code. The procedural periods for considering cases are rather brief and presuppose that the parties to a case are present in the Russian Federation. Only when the foreign participant is abroad do special rules come into play. The Russian Federation is party to the 1965 Hague Convention on the Service Abroad of Judicial and Extrajudicial Documents in Civil and Commercial Matters since the year 2000. Other bilateral treaties of the Russian Federation establish various periods for documents and notices to be served.

Procedural rights and duties of foreign persons

7.109 The national regime of arbitrazh procedural rights and duties extends to foreign persons, including juridical and natural persons. Procedural privileges are granted to foreigners only on the basis of international treaties. Foreign persons participating in a case must submit evidence to the arbitrazh court confirming their legal status and their right to effectuate entrepreneurial and other activity, and in the event of the failure to submit such evidence the arbitrazh court has the right to demand and obtain this at its own initiative.

7.110 The Code of Arbitrazh Procedure contains no provisions under which court costs of foreign participants in an arbitrazh proceeding can be secured. State duty associated with the filing of a suit may be paid from Russian bank accounts of juridical persons located in Russia, or paid by third persons contractually linked with the foreign participant and representing that participant in the arbitrazh proceeding, or failing the first two alternatives, the arbitrazh court may issue a decision to recover State duty from the accounts of the foreign participant abroad. In this event the Russian tax service would send the demand to a foreign court.

A foreign participant of an arbitrazh proceeding may petition the arbitrazh court to defer payment of State duty or to allow payment by instalments. In deciding whether to accept the petition, the arbitrazh court needs to determine whether granting the petition would be tantamount to allowing procedural privileges to the foreign participant; these normally being granted on the basis of reciprocity. **7.111**

The evidentiary requirement that a foreign participant prove its legal capacity is the logical counterpart to the Civil Code provisions which make the personal law of a juridical person or entrepreneur the law of the country where the relevant foreign person is registered. **7.112**

The Code of Arbitrazh Procedure (Article 254) confirms that the Government of the Russian Federation may establish retaliatory limitations (retorsion) with respect to foreign persons of those foreign States in which limitations with respect to Russian organizations and citizens have been established. **7.113**

Documents of foreign origin

Documents issued, drawn up, or certified by competent agencies of foreign States beyond the limits of the Russian Federation according to the rules of foreign law with respect to Russian organizations and citizens or foreign persons are accepted by arbitrazh courts in Russia, provided that they have been legalized or apostilled unless provided otherwise by an international treaty of the Russian Federation. If drawn up in a foreign language, they must, when submitted to an arbitrazh court, be accompanied by an attested translation into the Russian language. **7.114**

In effect, three alternatives are available with respect to documents of foreign origin. The most complex and expensive is to have the documents legalized by a Russian embassy or consulate abroad in accordance with the 1976 Consular Statute of the USSR. The second alternative is to take advantage of the 1961 Hague Convention Abolishing the Requirement of Legalisation of Foreign Public Documents under which States-parties accept documents duly supplied with an apostille. Official documents emanating from the Russian Federation with an apostille are so recognized by other countries as from 31 May 1992. The third alternative requires neither legalization nor apostille, but is available only in those countries who have appropriate bilateral legal assistance treaties with the Russian Federation and who have ratified the 1993 Minsk Convention. **7.115**

Under the Minsk Convention, appropriately issued and sealed documents in the originating country require no further special certification, and a translation need only be notarially attested.

7.116 In principle, documents submitted for the notarization of a translation into Russian may be translated by anyone who knows the respective language, although notaries are in practice sometimes unwilling to certify work by someone unknown to them. In fact the notary is guaranteeing only the signature of the translator and not the accuracy of the translation. Whether the translation is in fact accurate will normally deserve careful due diligence. The fact that in certain situations the translation may be supplied by the Ministry of Foreign Affairs or the Ministry of Justice adds nothing. Within the CIS, documents in the Russian language do not require translation in States-parties to the 1993 Minsk Convention.

Individual procedural actions

7.117 Cases with the involvement of a foreign element commonly require in an arbitrazh court the need to request a foreign State to render legal assistance in the form of 'judicial commissions' to perform certain procedural actions. These may include the serving of writs or other documents, gathering written evidence, performing an expert examination, conducting a view on the spot, and so on. Both the request for such actions to be undertaken and the performance or refusal to perform a judicial commission from a foreign court require consideration in a judicial session of the arbitrazh court.

7.118 Whether a judicial commission originating in a Russian arbitrazh court and sent to a foreign court will be executed or not, and how, will be determined by foreign procedural legislation, and *vice versa.* When a Russian arbitrazh court receives such a request, the court will be guided by federal laws and international treaties of the Russian Federation.

7.119 Legal assistance may be refused to a foreign court for several reasons: public policy; failure to comply with technicalities; improper court system; and documents whose genuineness is in doubt.

Example: A foreign court requested an arbitrazh court to serve a copy of a petition to sue on a Russian defendant entrepreneur. Without formalizing any judicial documents, the arbitrazh court sent the documents by post to the address indicated in Russia. Several months later the documents were returned to the arbitrazh court with a notation that the entrepreneur had died. The arbitrazh court returned by post all the documents to the foreign court which had requested foreign assistance. The foreign court regarded these actions as a refusal of legal assistance, and without ascertaining the reason for the return of the documents, applied to the Supreme Arbitrazh Court of the Russian

Federation for an explanation. While the Russian arbitrazh court was in fact unable to perform the judicial commission from the foreign court, its failure to adopt a ruling which explained the reasons for the failure to give legal assistance had complicated the foreign legal proceeding.

Enforcement of foreign court decisions and arbitral awards

7.120 The possibility of enforcing foreign judicial decisions and arbitral awards in the Russian Federation, and *vice versa*, is commonly a major consideration in foreign investor decisions and strategies. The general rule is that a foreign judicial decision and a foreign arbitral award is subject to recognition and enforcement in the Russian Federation on condition that there is an international treaty between the Russian Federation and the country of the court or tribunal issuing the decision or award. The reality is that the Russian Federation is a party to the 1958 New York Convention on the Recognition and Enforcement of Arbitral Awards, which means that in principle foreign arbitral awards enjoy a greater likelihood of being enforced in Russia simply because few countries outside Central Europe, Mongolia, China, Vietnam, and Cuba have bilateral treaties with Russia regulating the recognition and enforcement of judicial decisions.

Recognition and enforcement of decisions and awards

7.121 The Code of Arbitrazh Procedure (Article 241) confirms the general rule: decisions of courts of foreign States adopted by them with regard to disputes and other matters arising when effectuating entrepreneurial and other economic activity (foreign courts) and awards of arbitration courts and international commercial arbitral tribunals adopted by them on the territory of foreign States with regard to disputes and other matters arising when effectuating entrepreneurial and other economic activity (foreign arbitral awards) are recognized and enforced in the Russian Federation by arbitrazh courts unless provided otherwise by an international treaty of the Russian Federation and a federal law. Questions of the recognition and enforcement of decisions of a foreign court and of a foreign arbitral award are settled by an arbitrazh court upon the application of the parties to the dispute considered by the foreign court or parties to the arbitration.

7.122 The requirement of an international treaty was laid down unequivocally by the Edict of the Presidium of the Supreme Soviet of the USSR on 21 June 1988, which continues to be in force except insofar as contrary to the Code of Arbitrazh Procedure.

7.123 Arbitrazh courts are characterized by some Russian jurists as issuing an exequatur, although that term is not used in Russian legislation, for the recognition and enforcement of a foreign judicial decision or arbitral award if this is provided for by (a) an international treaty; or (b) a federal law. As noted above, the 1958 New York Convention is one such treaty, and the 1992 Kiev Agreement on the Procedure for the Settlement of Disputes Connected with the Effectuation of Economic Activity is another. The 1993 Minsk Convention is a third. In all, the Russian Federation is party to more than thirty treaties on legal assistance in civil, family, and criminal cases, many of which contain a section on the recognition and mutual execution of judicial arbitrazh decisions.

7.124 An exequatur may be issued for a foreign decision without an international treaty in pursuance of the generally-recognized legal principle of comity and reciprocity. It has been suggested that the United States and the Russian Federation have grounds to act on this basis in their relations with one another.[28] The procedure for the issuance of an exequatur for a foreign judicial decision or arbitral award commences from the moment of filing an application for the recognition and enforcement by an interested party. This party may be a Russian or foreign juridical or natural person, international organization, foreign State, or the Russian Federation.

Application for recognition and enforcement

7.125 The party to a dispute in whose favour the judicial decision or arbitral award was rendered may apply for recognition and enforcement thereof at an arbitrazh court of a subject of the Russian Federation where the debtor is located or has a place of residence, and if this is unknown, at the location of property of the debtor. The application must be filed in written form and signed by the debtor or his representative. The application must specify: (1) the name of the arbitrazh court in which application is filed; (2) the name and location of the foreign court or name and composition of the arbitration court or international arbitral tribunal and its location; (3) the name of the recovering party and its location or his place of residence; (4) the name of the debtor and its location or his place of residence; (5) information concerning the decision of the foreign court or foreign arbitral award whose recognition and enforcement is being sought; (6) the petition of the recovering party for recognition and enforcement; and (7) the list of documents appended. The telephone, fax, and e-mail addresses of the recovering party, debtor, their representatives, and other information may be indicated.

7.126 To the application for recognition and enforcement of a foreign judicial decision must be appended: (1) a duly certified copy of the decision of the foreign court or foreign arbitral award for which recognition and enforcement is being

[28] Neshataeva, in Iakovlev and Iukov (eds.), *Комментарий к Арбитражному процессуальному кодексу Российской Федерации* [Commentary to Code of Arbitrazh Procedure of the Russian Federation] (2003), p. 640.

sought; (2) a document duly certifying and confirming the entry of the decision of the foreign court into legal force if this is not indicated in the text of the decision itself; (3) a document duly certifying and confirming that the debtor was properly and timely notified about the consideration of the case in the foreign court whose decision is to be recognized and enforced; (4) a power of attorney or other document duly certified and confirming the powers of the person who signed the application to the arbitrazh court; (5) a document confirming that a copy of the application to recognize and enforce the decision of the foreign court was sent to the debtor; and (6) a duly attested translation of all the foregoing the documents into the Russian language.

In the case of a foreign arbitral award, unless an international treaty provides otherwise, there must be appended to the application for recognition and enforcement: (1) a duly attested original foreign arbitral award or duly attested copy; (2) an original agreement concerning the arbitral examination or duly attested copy thereof; and (3) a duly attested translation into the Russian language of the said documents. **7.127**

Both applications must be accompanied by a document confirming that State duty has been paid. If the documents submitted have been certified as documents of foreign origin (see above), this is sufficient for the Russian arbitrazh court. **7.128**

Procedure for consideration of application for recognition and enforcement

An application for the recognition and enforcement of a foreign judicial decision or arbitral award is considered by a single judge in a judicial session within not more than a month from the day of receipt of the application at the court in accordance with the rules of the Code of Arbitrazh Procedure, unless provided otherwise by an international treaty of the Russian Federation. The arbitrazh court notifies the persons participating in the case about the time and place of the judicial session. The failure of persons duly notified to appear is not an obstruction to consideration of the case. **7.129**

When considering the case, the arbitrazh court establishes in the judicial session whether the grounds for recognition and enforcement exist or not on the basis of investigating the evidence submitted to the arbitrazh court, the grounds set out by the applicant, and the objections thereto. The arbitrazh court does not have the right to reconsider the decision of the foreign court in substance. **7.130**

Under some procedures established by treaty, the recovering party has the right without seeking an exequatur to file the foreign court decision directly with a Russian bank where the debtor has an account, or with the court bailiff. In this event the debtor takes the initiative by petitioning the arbitrazh court not to enforce the foreign decision in the Russian Federation. Under the 1992 **7.131**

Kiev Agreement, for example, the national regime for enforcement is granted to natural and juridical persons of States-parties to the Agreement (Article 3). The debtor will petition the court in which enforcement is sought to refuse enforcement if the grounds provided for by the Agreement (Article 8) are absent. Legal assistance treaties commonly provide for yet another procedure.[29]

Grounds for refusal of recognition and enforcement

7.132 The Code of Arbitrazh Procedure sets out seven grounds for the refusal to recognize and enforce a foreign court decision: (1) the decision according to the law of the State on whose territory the decision was adopted did not enter into legal force; (2) the party against whom the decision was adopted was not duly and timely notified about the time and place of consideration of the case or for other reasons could not submit its explanations to the court; (3) the consideration of the case is in accordance with an international treaty of the Russian Federation or a federal law within the exclusive competence of a court in the Russian Federation; (4) there is a decision of the court in the Russian Federation which has entered into legal force and been adopted with regard to a dispute between the same persons, on the same subject, and on the same grounds; (5) there is a case instituted for consideration of a court in the Russian Federation with regard to a dispute by the same persons, on the same subject, and on the same grounds, the proceedings regarding which were instituted before the proceedings regarding the case in a foreign court, or a court in the Russian Federation was to first to accept an application for proceedings with regard to a dispute between the same persons, the same subject, and on the same grounds; (6) the period of limitation expired for enforcing the decision of a foreign court and was not reinstated by an arbitrazh court; or (7) enforcement of the decision of a foreign court would be contrary to the public policy of the Russian Federation.

7.133 The rules in the Code of Arbitrazh Procedure differ with respect to enforcement of a foreign arbitral award. They include public policy only from the enumeration above, plus a refusal to issue a writ for enforcement against an award of an international commercial arbitral tribunal on the grounds provided for by an international treaty of the Russian Federation (which means, *inter alia*, the 1958 New York Convention and any relevant regional treaties) and by the 1993 Federal Law on International Commercial Arbitration. In substance, the grounds for refusal to enforce an international arbitral award are identical to those for refusal to enforce a domestic Russian arbitral award (see Article 233, Code of Arbitrazh Procedure).

[29] Among recent treaties, see the 2002 Treaty between Russia and Belarus 'On the Procedure for the Mutual Execution of Judicial Acts'.

Ruling of arbitrazh court to recognize and enforce

An arbitrazh court issues a ruling with regard to the recognition and enforcement, or not, of a foreign court decision or arbitral award according to the general rules in the Code of Arbitrazh Procedure. The ruling must contain: (1) the name and location of the foreign court or the name and composition of the arbitration court or international arbitral tribunal which issued the award; (2) the name of the recovering party and debtor; (3) information concerning the decision of the foreign court or foreign arbitral award for whose recognition and enforcement the recovering party is petitioning; and (4) confirmation as to whether recognition and enforcement is being granted or refused. The ruling of the arbitrazh court may be appealed within one month to the arbitrazh court of cassational instance. **7.134**

Enforcement of decision or award

The actual enforcement of a decision or an award is based on a writ of execution issued by the arbitrazh court which rendered the ruling. The procedure for enforcing the writ is regulated by the Code of Arbitrazh Procedure and the Federal Law on an Execution Proceeding.[30] A three-year period of limitation applies during which the foreign court decision or arbitral award may be submitted for recognition and enforcement. The period begins to run from the day of entry into force of the respective decision or award. If the three-year period has lapsed, it remains open to petition the arbitrazh court to reinstate the period of limitations in accordance with the Code of Arbitrazh Procedure (Chapter 10). **7.135**

[30] Transl. in Butler, *Russian Public Law* (2005), pp. 417–53.

8

FOREIGN JURIDICAL PERSONS AND ENTITIES IN RUSSIA

Foreign juridical persons and entities enjoy the principle of 'national regime' in the Russian Federation, just as natural persons, in three senses. First, they are equated in rights and duties to Russian juridical persons, except insofar as Russian legislation and international treaties of the Russian Federation provide otherwise. Second, insofar as foreign juridical and natural persons may create Russian juridical persons and entities on the territory of the Russian Federation, by virtue of foreign ownership or creation, these Russian juridical persons may be subject to a special legal regime. And third, by virtue of a decision of the Constitutional Court of the Russian Federation, juridical persons in Russia have, as appropriate to their status, constitutional rights similar to those of natural persons, including foreign citizens and stateless persons. **8.01**

Russian law in practice draws a distinction similar to that of Anglo-American legal systems between 'juridical' persons and 'legal entities'. All juridical persons are legal entities, but not all legal entities are juridical persons. The example in Anglo-American law is the classic partnership; in Russian law the concept of 'legal entities' would encompass the 'representation office', the 'branch', and the 'simple partnership', among others. **8.02**

A. Criminal Responsibility

Juridical persons are not subject to criminal responsibility under Russian law. The Criminal Code provides (Article 19): 'Only a putable natural person who **8.03** has attained the age established by the present Code shall be subject to criminal responsibility'.[1]

B. Administrative Responsibility

8.04 Foreign juridical persons which have committed administrative violations on the territory of the Russian Federation are subject to administrative responsibility on the general grounds; the same applies to administrative violations committed on the continental shelf or in the exclusive economic zone of the Russian Federation. Any immunities against the administrative jurisdiction of the Russian Federation extend only to foreign natural persons and not to foreign juridical persons.[2]

C. Civil Responsibility

8.05 Foreign juridical persons enjoy legal personality and legal capacity under Russian civil legislation in accordance with its provisions. They may be the owners of property, enter into transactions, sue and be sued in courts and arbitral tribunals, and otherwise exercise their rights and fulfil their duties in accordance with the Russian Constitution and all relevant branches of the Russian legal system. They may be foreign investors (see Chapter 4) and enter into foreign trade transactions (see Chapter 3).

D. Taxation

8.06 For the principal investing jurisdictions of the world there is a double taxation treaty in place with the Russian Federation, whether concluded during the existence of the former Soviet Union or subsequently (see Annex 5 below). Most foreigners, whether natural or juridical persons or legal entities, will be guided in their tax planning and structuring by the relevant treaty provisions. Absent a treaty, the full force of the Russian national regime of taxation will apply.

Permanent representation

8.07 A key concept in international taxation is that of the 'permanent representation'. Unfortunately, in the case of the Russian Federation that term was first used in Soviet legislation to refer to something completely different: the creation of a foreign presence on the territory of the Soviet Union in the form of a legal

[1] W E Butler, *Criminal Code of the Russian Federation* (4th edn, 2004), pp. 10–11.

[2] See A B Agapov, *Постатейный комментарий к Кодексу Российской Федерации об административных правонарушениях, Расширенный, с использованием материалов судебной практики* [Article-by-Article Commentary to Code of Russian Federation on Administrative Violations. Enlarged with Use of Materials of Judicial Practice] (2d ed.; 2004), I, pp. 53–5.

entity which was not a juridical person. The Soviet concept of a 'representation' or 'representative office' had nothing to do with taxation.[3] As the Soviet Union came to be involved increasingly in market relations with the rest of the world and to negotiate double taxation conventions, the terminologies crossed and remain a source of confusion. One must therefore distinguish with care in Russia between the concept of the 'representation' or 'representative office'—which may have tax implications—and the 'permanent establishment' for the purposes of taxation.

The term 'permanent establishment' also appears in the Tax Code of the Russian Federation (Chapter 25) and in the 'Methods Recommendations to Tax Agencies With Regard to the Application of Individual Provisions of Chapter 25 of the Tax Code of the Russian Federation Concerning the Peculiarities of Taxation of Profit (or Revenues) of Foreign Organizations' [hereinafter: Methods Recommendations].[4] The definition of a 'permanent establishment' in the Tax Code differs materially from that first introduced into the legislation of the Russian Federation[5] and has been revised to bring the legislative definition into accordance with the network of Russian tax treaties. Under the treaty supremacy clause of the 1993 Russian Constitution (Article 15) and Tax Code (Article 7), treaty rules apply in the event that they establish rules and norms other than those provided for by legislation on taxes and charges and thereby constitute an exception from the rules established by law. Insofar as there is no divergence, the rules of tax legislation apply. **8.08**

In Russian tax law the concept of 'permanent establishment' is used '. . . to evaluate the character of activity (including the types and permanence thereof) of a person on the territory of another State'.[6] Some Russian tax specialists regard the term as synonymous with 'permanent place of business', or 'permanent business establishment', or 'permanent place of conducting business', and others; although this view is not unanimously accepted. Without ascribing **8.09**

[3] See the relevant 1989 Decree of the USSR Council of Ministers in W E Butler, *Basic Documents on the Soviet Legal System* (3rd edn, 1992), pp. 461–7. The same applies to contemporary Russian legislation. The term 'representation' used in the Civil Code of the Russian Federation (Article 55) has nothing to do with the term used in the Tax Code of the Russian Federation.

[4] Confirmed by Order of the Ministry of Taxes and Charges of Russia, 28 March 2003, No. БГ-3-23/150. The word 'permanent' is not a source of difficulty. The only plausible term for 'establishment' in the Russian language in this context is 'representation', which means that a precise translation of the Anglo-American concept is not possible. The same Russian word for 'representation' also applies to a diplomatic representation.

[5] See the Law on the Tax on Profit of Enterprises and Organizations, 27 December 1991.

[6] See V V Poliakova, «Налоговые обязанности представительств иностранных фирм» [Tax Duties of Representations of Foreign Firms], *Ваш налоговый адвокат*, no. 3(9) (1999), p. 63.

synonymy, the Methods Recommendations (point 2.1) provide that the term 'permanent establishment' does not have 'organizational-legal meaning' classifying the activity of a foreign organization with which the duty of that organization arises to pay tax on profit in the Russian Federation is linked. One Russian jurist has distinguished between two autonomous types of permanent representations as follows: what he calls the 'first' or 'principal' type is formed when a foreign person carries on activity directed towards deriving revenue in a permanent place, whereas the 'second' is formed if a foreign person has representatives with a determined status and powers in a State. This second type he calls 'agency', although that term is not intended to imply that the representation operates under an 'agency relationship' pursuant to the Russian Civil Code.[7]

8.10 It follows that whether a foreign organization creates a 'representation office' in Russia on the basis of Soviet and post-Soviet Russian legislation is not in and of itself decisive as to whether a 'permanent establishment' exists for the purposes of Russian tax legislation. Whether a foreign presence constitutes a permanent establishment for taxation purposes turns upon whether the 'presence' carries on activity of a preparatory or auxiliary character, such as keeping stocks of goods and manufactures for the purpose of storage, exhibition, or delivery, or purchases goods and articles, or collects information to the benefit of the head company, and so on. If the country of a foreign organization has a tax treaty with Russia which contains a List determining the types of activity not leading to the formation of a permanent establishment, that List is an exhaustive exception to national legislation. Double taxation or other agreements not containing such a List or not clarifying the concept of preparatory and auxiliary activity automatically fall back on national legislation of the respective parties. The Methods Recommendations assume that preparatory or auxiliary activity by its nature may not comprise the entire principal activity or part thereof. The Supreme Arbitrazh Court of the Russian Federation concluded in an individual case that 'the construction of an object is impossible in principle without conducting design work, and therefore such work is preparatory with respect to the principal activity—the construction of a business-centre'.[8]

8.11 Also of relevance is the extent to which preparatory or auxiliary activity coincides or not with the principal activity of the foreign organization. Activity of a division in Russia whose purpose coincides directly with the entrepreneurial purpose of the enterprise itself by deriving revenues in Russia would not be

[7] See O Iu Konnov, *Понятие постоянного представительства в налоговом праве* [Concept of Permanent Establishment in Tax Law] (2001), p. 18 (abstract of kand. iurid. nauk dissertation).

[8] Decree of Presidium of Supreme Arbitrazh Court of Russian Federation, 17 December 2002, No. 897/02.

regarded as preparatory or auxiliary activity. Russian tax agencies usually base their decision as to whether the profit tax is due from a representation office on whether revenues have been received by a foreign organization in Russia and are connected with the activity of its representation. The profit tax is applicable when the activity of a representation of a foreign firm goes beyond the limits of representative functions. Common representative functions include seeking business partners in the interests of the foreign parent, facilitating the conclusion of transactions, undertaking market research, and advertising the services and activities of the company. Exceeding the representative function occurs when the representation office carries on activity that is expressly directed towards the foreign firm receiving entrepreneurial revenues, in which event the Russian division of the foreign firm becomes a taxpayer with respect to the tax on profit.

Neither the Tax Code of the Russian Federation nor judicial practice offers a **8.12** complete answer to the question of what constitutes activity being carried on 'through' a permanent establishment. It has been suggested that this criterion would be satisfied by any activity of a foreign organization with the use of a permanent base on the territory of Russia which is directed expressly towards the receipt by the foreign organization of revenues and directly connected with those revenues.[9]

Since the tax concept of a 'permanent establishment' is not linked with the **8.13** organizational-legal form of a juridical person or legal entity, this characterization is based on recognizing the activity of a foreign organization to be analogous to the activity of a Russian juridical person. However, the permanent establishment does not thereby become a taxpayer; it is the foreign organization itself that is the taxpayer in the person of its Russian divisions. The object of taxation is profit derived from the activity of foreign organizations who have formed a permanent establishment in Russia; for these purposes profit is defined in the Tax Code of the Russian Federation (Article 247) as 'revenues received through a permanent establishment reduced by expenses made by it'.

A permanent establishment acts in tax relations as a resident. The place where **8.14** profit is actually received and from whom is irrelevant: bank accounts in Russia or abroad, Russian or foreign contracting parties. The same applies to expenses for the activity of the permanent establishment. Generally speaking, profit received by a foreign organization through a permanent establishment is

[9] See M A Denisaev, «Налоговые аспекты деятельности иностранных компаний в России» [Urgent Problems of Classification of Activity of Foreign Organization in Russia When Taxing Profit], in M V Ivlieva (ed.), *Налогообложение иностранных компаний в России: Сборник материалов правоприменительной практики* [Taxation of Foreign Companies in Russia: Collection of Materials of Law Enforcement Practice] (2004), p. 17.

determined by the direct method; that is, the foreign subject determines the tax base while being guided by the general provisions of the Tax Code (Article 54) and the special provisions of Chapter 25 of the Tax Code, just as in the procedure for a Russian juridical person. Further to these general provisions profit is attributed to a permanent establishment by using either the 'independent enterprise' approach (the permanent establishment revenues are calculated as though it were an autonomous juridical person) or the 'fractional' approach (the revenue of the permanent establishment is calculated on the basis of the aggregate revenue of the foreign juridical person depending upon the economic role of the permanent establishment in deriving such revenue).

8.15 Accrued revenues of foreign organizations in Russia, especially arising from differences in exchange rates, have been treated variously. The Constitutional Court of the Russian Federation (Decree of 28 October 1999) took the legal position that revenues not actually received could not be included in the taxable base. The arbitrazh courts ruled that whatever bookkeeping rules may provide, the exchange rate difference should be calculated for tax purposes at the moment of performing the specific payment operation. When the Tax Code of the Russian Federation was adopted, a different procedure was introduced (Article 271). Revenues in the form of a positive exchange rate difference are recognized on the date of the transfer of the right of ownership to foreign currency, and a positive difference with regard to property and demands or obligations expressed in foreign currency, as of the last day of the current month. The same rule applies to a negative exchange rate difference arising out of expenses, with special procedures used to recalculate exchange rates of hard currency when applicable. The overall result is that only those nonrealised revenues subject to Russian profit tax are those which were received by the permanent establishment and relegated to its entrepreneurial activity.

8.16 The Tax Code is silent about the transfer of means to a permanent establishment by the head office of a foreign organization. Relevant Methods Recommendations stipulate that if expenses were incurred by a foreign organization in favour of its divisions located in various countries, the share of a Russian permanent establishment must be substantiated by the foreign organization in a procedure analogous to that used for distributing revenues. Double taxation agreements commonly provide for a way to offset revenues with expenses in these situation.

8.17 In practice it can be difficult to determine the financial result of the Russian permanent establishment, and especially when a foreign organization may have several within the Russian Federation. In principle the Tax Code of the Russian Federation is sympathetic to treating an entire group of permanent representations as a single permanent establishment that happens to carry on activity at several different sites in Russia.

Currency control

8.18 Juridical persons and enterprises and organizations which are not juridical persons but were created in accordance with the legislation of foreign States and have a location beyond the limits of the Russian Federation, or branches and representations of these entities which are nonresidents, are for the purposes of currency control and regulation nonresidents in the Russian Federation. Under the 2003 Law on Currency Regulation and Currency Control,[10] they have the right without limitation to transfer, bring in, or send currency valuables to the Russian Federation, and to purchase and sell foreign currency for Russian currency in the procedure established by the Central Bank. Currency valuables include foreign currency, securities denominated in foreign currency, payment documents such as cheques, bills of exchange, and the like, emission securities such as stocks and bonds, derivatives of emission securities, security options, and debt obligations expressed in foreign currency, precious metals, and natural precious stones. The term 'foreign currency' encompasses both foreign banknotes and coins, treasury notes, and the like, and foreign currency accounts.

E. International Nongovernmental Organizations

8.19 So-called international nongovernmental organizations (NGOs) represent something of a conundrum for Russian law. First, they are not 'international'. Rather, they are created and registered under the legislation of one State or another; that is, they are juridical persons national in origin. Second, they are not 'nongovernmental', but rather 'non-State'. In the Russian legal system, as in many others, the government and the State are quite distinct legally, and under Russian law the former is a legal entity without autonomous legal personality; whereas the second has a full-fledged legal identity, personality, and capacity in the Russian legal system.

8.20 Whether NGOs should be deemed to have international legal personality is beginning to be considered in Russian international legal doctrine. The majority of Russian international lawyers certainly consider NGOs to be 'subjects of international relations'. The elements of legal capacity required to have international legal personality have been characterized as: personification; external solitariness; autonomy of will; and participation in the creation of international legal norms.[11] Some these criteria are satisfied by an NGO. Personification is present; that is, the NGO participates in international relations as a single juridical person. External solitariness exists: the NGO has it own name, charter,

[10] *СЗ РФ* (2003), no. 50, item 4859.

[11] See K A Bekiashev, *Международное право* [International] (1999), p. 98.

State affiliation by way of registration, and so on. There is autonomy of will as well, but only what is characterized in Russian legal doctrine as 'law-realising' or 'right-realising' will, not 'law-formative' or 'right-formative' will. Some would distinguish NGOs on the basis of whether they have been recognized to have consultative status with the United Nations or not. In this view, the conferment of consultative status is a form of international recognition originating in the United Nations Charter (Article 71).[12]

8.21 Insofar as NGOs have an approximate equivalent in the Russian Federation, it would be the social association, governed by the 1995 Federal Law on Social Associations, as amended.[13] These exist in Russia pursuant to the 1993 Constitution of the Russian Federation (Article 30): 'Each shall have the right to association, including the right to create trade unions in order to defend their interests. The freedom of activity of social associations shall be guaranteed.'[14] Foreign citizens and stateless persons have equal rights with citizens of the Russian Federation 'in the sphere of relations regulated by' the 1995 Federal Law on Social Associations unless established otherwise by federal laws or international treaties of the Russian Federation.

8.22 But these are Russian social associations. They have certain duties in respect of their relations with foreign citizens and stateless persons: for example, they are required to inform the federal agency of State registration about the amount of monetary means and other property received from international and foreign organizations, foreign citizens, and stateless persons, the purposes for the expenditure and use thereof, and the actual expenditure or use according to a form and within the periods established by the Government of the Russian Federation. Russian social associations have the right to join international social associations, acquire rights and bear duties corresponding to the status of these international social associations, and maintain direct international contacts and communications and conclude agreements with noncommercial non-governmental organizations. And they may create their own organizations, divisions, branches, or representations in foreign States on the basis of generally-recognized principles of international law, international treaties of the Russian Federation, and the legislation of those States.

8.23 The question remains as to the status, rights, and duties of NGOs registered

---

12 For a recent discussion of doctrinal views, see S A Podshibiakin, *Правовой статус международных неправительственных организаций* [Legal Status of International Non-governmental Organisations] (2006), pp. 31–7.

13 *СЗ РФ* (1995), no. 21, item 1930; (1997), no. 20, item 2231; (1998), no. 30, item 3608; (2002), no. 11, item 1018; no. 12, item 1093; no. 30, item 3029; (2003), no. 50, item 4844; (2004), no. 27, item 2711; (2006), no. 3, item 282; no. 6, item 636.

14 Transl. in Butler, *Russian Public Law* (2005), p. 10.

outside the Russian Federation. The answer is to be found not in the 1995 Federal Law on Social Associations, but rather in the 1996 Federal Law on Noncommercial Organizations, as amended. The provisions of the said Law determine the procedure for the creation and activity on the territory of the Russian Federation of structural subdivisions of foreign noncommercial non-governmental organizations and apply to structural subdivisions of international organizations or associations insofar as not contrary to international treaties of the Russian Federation.

A foreign noncommercial NGO carries out its activity in the Russian Federation **8.24**
through its structural subdivisions (divisions, branches, and representations). A structural subdivision which is a division of a foreign NGO is deemed to be a form of noncommercial organization and is subject to State registration. Structural subdivisions which are branches and representations of foreign NGOs acquire legal capacity on the territory of the Russian Federation from the day of their entry in the register of branches and representations of international organizations and foreign NGOs of information concerning the respective subdivision.

If a foreign NGO intends to create a division in the Russian Federation, the **8.25**
following documents must be submitted in the State language of the respective foreign State with a translation, duly certified, into the Russian language: (1) application signed by an empowered person indicating his full name, place of residence, and contact telephone numbers; (2) constitutive documents of the noncommercial organization in three examples; (3) the decision to create a noncommercial organization and confirmation of the constitutive documents thereof, indicating the membership of the elected or appointed organs in two examples; (4) information concerning the founders in two copies; and (5) a document concerning the payment of State duty.

The decision concerning the State registration of a division of a foreign NGO is **8.26**
adopted by the Ministry of Justice on the basis of the documents submitted. The registration itself proceeds in accordance with the 2001 Federal Law on the State Registration of Juridical Persons.[15] State duty is recovered for the State registration of the division of an NGO.

With respect to the creation of a branch or representation of a foreign noncom- **8.27**
mercial NGO, a notification system operates. Within three months from the day of adoption of a decision by a foreign noncommercial NGO to create a branch or representation in Russia, the Ministry of Justice of the Russian Federation must be notified. The notification must be attested by the empowered organ of

[15] Transl. in Butler, *Russian Company and Commercial Legislation* (2003), pp. 1–16.

the foreign noncommercial NGO and contain information about the founders and the address or location of the permanently operating executive organ. The form of the notification is established by the Ministry of Justice.

8.28 To the notification must be appended the following documents: (1) the constitutive documents of the foreign noncommercial NGO; (2) the decision of the executive organ of the foreign noncommercial NGO to create a branch or representation; (3) the Statute on the branch or representation; (4) the decision to appoint the executive of the branch or representation; and (5) the document setting out the purposes and tasks of creating the branch or representation. These documents must be submitted in the State language of the respective foreign State with a duly attested translation into the Russian language. The confirmation contained in the notification and appendices constitutes the register of branches and representations of international organizations and foreign noncommercial NGOs kept by the Ministry of Justice.

8.29 Within thirty days from the day of receipt of the notification, the Ministry of Justice issues to the executive of the branch or representation an extract from the register.

8.30 A foreign noncommercial NGO may be refused entry of the information in the register on the following grounds: (1) the information and documents have not been submitted in full or the documents have not been duly formalized; (2) it is established that the documents submitted contain unreliable information; (3) the purposes and tasks of creating the branch or representation of the foreign noncommercial NGO are contrary to the Russian Constitution or to legislation of the Russian Federation; (4) the purposes and tasks of creating the branch or representation create a threat to the sovereignty, political independence, territorial integrity, national unity and identity, cultural legacy, and national interests of the Russian Federation; or (5) if a branch or representation of a foreign noncommercial NGO previously entered in the register was excluded from the register in connection with a flagrant violation of the Russian Constitution or legislation. In the event of a refusal, the applicant is notified in writing with an indication of the specific provisions of the Constitution and legislation, a violation of which entailed the said refusal, or the reasons for the refusal. The refusal may be appealed to the superior agency or to a court.

8.31 A refusal to enter information in the register is not a barrier to a second notification provided that the grounds which gave rise to the refusal have been eliminated.

8.32 The legal capacity of a branch or representation of a foreign noncommercial NGO arises from the day of entry of information concerning the structural subdivision into the register. Within not more than twenty days from the day of entering the information in the register, the executive of the structural subdivision is obliged to notify the Ministry of Justice about the address or location of the branch or representation and contact telephone numbers. Changes of information are filed in the same procedure.

The structural subdivision of a foreign commercial NGO is obliged to notify **8.33** the Ministry of Justice about the amounts of monetary means and other property received, the proposed distribution thereof, the purposes of the expenditure or use thereof, and the actual expenditure or use thereof, programmes proposed for effectuation on the territory of the Russian Federation, the expenditure of monetary means provided to natural and juridical persons, and the use of other property provided to them in the form and within the periods established by the Government of the Russian Federation. If a violation of legislation of the Russian Federation is uncovered or the commission of actions by a branch or representation of a foreign noncommercial NGO which are contrary to the declared purposes and tasks thereof, the Ministry of Justice has the right to issue a written warning to the executive of the respective structural subdivision specifying the violation permitted and the period for eliminating it, which must be not less than a month. The warning may be appealed to the superior agency or to a court.

If the branch or representation of a foreign noncommercial NGO fails to sub- **8.34** mit the information concerning revenues, it may be excluded from the register of branches and representations of noncommercial NGOs by decision of the Ministry of Justice. The same sanction applies if the activity of the branch or representation does not conform to the purposes declared in its notification. The Ministry of Justice also adopts a decision to exclude the branch or representation from the register in the event of its liquidation.

The Ministry of Justice may send to the structural subdivision of a foreign **8.35** noncommercial NGO in written form a reasoned decision to prohibit the effectuation of the programme or part thereof of the NGO on the territory of the Russian Federation. A structural subdivision which has received such a decision is obliged to terminate the activity connected with the effectuation of this programme to the extent specified in the decision. The failure to comply with this decision entails exclusion from the register and liquidation of the division of the foreign noncommercial NGO. Moreover, the Ministry of Justice may issue a written reasoned decision prohibiting the direction of monetary means and other property to specified recipients.

Foreign noncommercial NGOs are subject to verifications by federal agencies of **8.36** State financial control, the Ministry of Taxes and Charges, and the federal agency of executive power concerned with money laundering and the financing of terrorism in order to establish whether the activities of branches and representations are consistent with the declared purposes and tasks and communicate the results of these verifications to the Ministry of Justice. A foreign noncommercial NGO has the right to appeal the actions or failure to act of State agencies to a court at the location of the State agency concerned.

8.37 It has been assumed in Russian legal doctrine that the branches and representations, at least, of foreign noncommercial NGOs are created, accredited, and registered under the 1989 USSR Statute on the Procedure for Opening and Activity in the USSR of Representations of Foreign Firms, Banks, and Organisations.[16] The amendments to the 1996 Federal Law on Noncommercial Organisations of 10 January 2006 appear to have resolved the issue by placing, for the first time, foreign noncommercial NGOs completely and unequivocally under the law on noncommercial organizations. In some measure this removes the national regime for foreign noncommercial NGOs, which by default many Russian jurists considered to be applicable. The Russian Federation has not ratified the European Convention on recognition of the legal personality of international nongovernmental organizations.

[16] Podshibiakin, *Правовой статус международных неправительственных организаций* [Legal Status of International Nongovernmental Organisations] (2006), pp. 95–6. For the text of the Statute, see Butler, *Basic Documents on the Soviet Legal System* (3rd edn, 1992), pp. 461–6.

9

PRIVATE INTERNATIONAL LAW

In the conventional understanding many chapters of this volume would fall within the traditional scope of private international law. Here, however, we use the expression as employed in Part Three of the Civil Code of the Russian Federation, with minor adjustments. **9.01**

A. General Provisions Concerning Applicable Law

9.02 Section VI of the Civil Code of the Russian Federation is principally concerned with what in the Anglo-American family of legal systems is called conflicts of law; that is, conflicts rules or more general norms which do not resolve conflicts issues, but nonetheless ensure the application of conflicts norms. Although not an exhaustive codification of these rules, Section VI of the Civil Code does constitute the principal statement of conflicts law in the Russian Federation.

9.03 The point of departure is that the law subject to being applied to civil-law relations with the participation of foreign citizens (including stateless persons) or foreign juridical persons, or civil-law relations complicated by another foreign element, including when the object of civil rights is situated abroad, is determined on the basis of international treaties of the Russian Federation, the Civil Code itself, other laws, and customs recognized in the Russian Federation. The 'foreign element', it is clear, may be expressed either in the participation of foreign citizens or foreign juridical persons in civil-law relations, or otherwise, including when the object of civil rights (especially property) is physically located abroad. More abstractly, but in the mainstream of Russian private international law doctrine, the 'foreign elements' characterize the classic triad: the subject, object, and legal fact; although it is universally recognized that other categories exist where complications with a foreign element may arise.[1]

9.04 These are sweeping characterizations, but not necessarily exhaustive in defining how a foreign element may be manifested. Civil-law relations may arise as a consequence of the occurrence of a legal fact; for example, the causing of harm (tort, delict). On the other hand, in the absence of a foreign element, the issue of applicable law does not arise.

9.05 The mere fact that a foreign element exists does not in and of itself predetermine that foreign law will necessarily be the applicable law. Conflicts rules may require the application of Russian material, or substantive law. International treaties of the Russian Federation which contain conflicts rules include the 1992 Kiev Agreement, the 1993 Minsk Convention, the 1988 Ottawa UNIDROIT Convention on International Finance Leasing,[2] and various bilateral legal assistance treaties, among others. Under Article 15(4) of the 1993 Russian Constitution and Article 7 of the Civil Code, if '. . . other rules have been established by an international treaty of the Russian Federation than those which have been

---

[1] L P Anufrieva, in Anufrieva (ed.), *Комментарий к Гражданскому кодексу Российской Федерации. Часть третья (постатейный)* [Commentary to the Civil Code of the Russian Federation. Part Three (Article-by-Article)] (2004), p. 368.

[2] *СЗ РФ* (1999), no. 32, item 4040.

provided for by civil legislation, the rules of the international treaty shall apply'. This is further clarified by Article 1186 of the Civil Code: 'If an international treaty of the Russian Federation contains material law norms subject to application to a respective relation, the determination on the basis of conflicts norms of the law applicable to questions fully regulated by such material law norms shall be excluded'. This is understood to mean that determining the law applicable to a legal relation is excluded if: (1) there is an international treaty of the Russian Federation in force; and (2) that international treaty contains material law norms subject to application to the said legal relation. The use of conflicts rules is excluded when their application would be necessary; that is, the parties did not themselves use their right to make a choice of law. Certain treaties may exclude the priority of a material law provision in the treaty by way of a special stipulation providing when the material law provision may be applied. An example is the 1980 Vienna Convention on the Sale of Goods, which expressly allows the parties to a contract to exclude the application of the Convention in whole or in part, except the provision concerning the form of the contract. Moreover, if the Vienna Convention were applicable in general to a dispute but the matters in specific dispute were not regulated by the Convention, the court could then turn to national conflicts rules in order to determine the national material law to be applied.

Although sometimes formulated with variations, the principle of treaty supremacy over national legislation is incorporated in most Russian codes of law and major federal laws, including family law, labour law, civil and criminal procedure, and international commercial arbitration. Material law provisions of an international treaty have priority, in the opinion of most Russian jurists, over Russian domestic imperative material law norms. **9.06**

Other federal laws regulating aspects of civil-law relations contain conflicts rules; for example, the laws on pledge and on finance leasing. However, these laws must not, in this respect in particular, be inconsistent with the Civil Code. Moreover, the Family Code of the Russian Federation also permits the Civil Code to be applied to certain nonproperty family relations not regulated by civil legislation, which in turn has implications for conflict rules, as does the Merchant Shipping Code with respect to property relations arising from merchant shipping. Although reference also is made to 'customs', their role in practice is minor, if not minimal. These customs should not be confused with the 'customs of business turnover' (see Chapter 2 above). Here the term would appear to mean customs whose operation is connected with the basic principles of public and private international law. **9.07**

The Federal Law on International Commercial Arbitration applies to conflicts issues when the parties to the arbitration have not made a choice of law, following **9.08** the model of the 1985 UNCITRAL Model Law on International Commercial Arbitration. The arbitrators are given relatively large freedom to determine the applicable conflicts rules.

9.09 If the applicable law cannot be determined on the basis of an international treaty, federal law, or customs, the reserve position is the principle of the closest link. In this event the court should look to the aggregate of circumstances, and not any single circumstance, when determining the closest link to the law of the respective State. The influence of the closest link doctrine is to be seen in a number of conflicts provisions of the Civil Code.

9.10 Because the 'closest link' doctrine is new to Russian civil legislation, having been introduced only from 1 March 2002, its prior application has been confined to arbitration practice. *Example:* A Russian juridical person brought suit in the International Commercial Arbitration Court in Moscow against an Algerian organization. The Plaintiff based its demands on the Civil Code of the Algerian People's Democratic Republic, although the contract between the parties did not contain an applicable law clause. The arbitrators applied Algerian law on the principle of closest link, since the seller was a firm founded and operating on the territory of Algeria and the obligations under the contract were subject to performance in Algeria.[3]

Interpretation and classification

9.11 The problem of what is sometimes called 'concealed conflicts' is addressed as follows in the Russian Civil Code (Article 1187): if, when determining what law is subject to application, an interpretation of legal concepts is necessary, this will be done in accordance with Russian law unless provided otherwise by a law. However, if the legal concepts requiring classification, or qualification, are unknown to Russian law or are known with another verbal designation or have a different content and cannot be determined by means of interpretation in accordance with Russian law, then foreign law may be applied when classifying or qualifying them.

9.12 The Supreme Arbitrazh Court of the Russian Federation has determined that in order to determine the applicable law one must first establish the nature of the respective legal relation, which may depend upon classifying that legal relation as being foreign, economic, or otherwise, and the nature of the contract which binds the parties. Having established the nature of the legal relation, one must

[3] Reported in M G Rozenberg, *Международный договор и иностранное право в практике Международного коммерческого арбитражного суда* [International Contract and Foreign Law in the Practice of the International Commercial Arbitration Court] (1999), pp. 149–55.

then choose the conflicts norm applicable to the legal relation, and on the basis of the conflicts norm, determine the law applicable to the legal relation. The nature of the legal relation and its content will be determined by classifying the concept used to designate the elements of which the legal relation is actually comprised.[4] A 'concealed conflict' arises when legal concepts bearing the same name in the law of different States have a different content, or a concept known in the legal system of a foreign State is unknown to Russian law, or is known to Russian law in words but the substance is different and cannot be ascertained by an interpretation in accordance with Russian law.

An example commonly cited in Russian doctrinal writings is the Common Law concept of 'trust', which does not exist as such in Russian law, although the expression 'trust' exists in the Russian language. The Anglo-American concept of trust permits the 'fractionalization' of the right of ownership: the grantor acts as the founder of a trust and passes title to his property to a trustee, who will administer the property in the interests of third-person beneficiaries. Although the concept of trust management is part of the Civil Code of the Russian Federation, the Russian understanding of trust management does not permit transfer of the right of ownership to property placed in trust from the owner to the trustee, and indeed is part of the law of obligations under Russian law. It would not be appropriate to apply Russian law to the Anglo-American trust. **9.13**

The various approaches to resolving concealed conflicts have been described as follows in Russian legal sources:[5] **9.14**

> First, the primary classification of legal concepts may be effectuated on the basis of the content which these concepts have in the country of the Court (*lex fori*). Second, the legal concepts may be classified in accordance with concepts of that law which is subject to application by virtue of the respective conflicts norm (*lex causae*). Third, the primary classification may be effectuated on the basis of 'generalized' legal concepts. Since any conflicts norm emanates from recognition of the possibility of the application of an indeterminate group of foreign legal systems, such a norm may be expressed only by means of concepts which by their content are common to various legal systems. This means of classification has received the name in doctrine of 'autonomous classification'. It is based on comparative law as a method of research and comparison of the norms of various legal systems. Finally, in foreign doctrine yet another means is proposed, namely: international private-law classification. It is based on the fact that a particular concept may have different

[4] See Decree No. 911/96, 17 September 1996, of the Supreme Arbitrazh Court of the Russian Federation. *Вестник Высшего Арбитражного Суда Российской Федерации*, no. 12 (1996).

[5] See G M Vel'iaminov, in T E Abova, M M Boguslavskii, A Iu Kabalkin, and A G Lisitsyn-Svetlanov (eds.), *Постатейный комментарий к Гражданскому кодексу Российской Федерации, части первой, второй, третьей* [Article-by-Article Commentary to the Civil Code of the Russian Federation. Parts One, Two, and Three] (2005), Article 1187.

meaning in conflicts and material law. For example, the concept of 'marriage' from the standpoint of conflicts law criteria is broader than the concept having the same name in the material-law aspect. The fact is that the situation is entirely possible when the applicable law (*lex causae*), unlike that legal sysem whose conflicts norm is used when determining the applicable law, equates 'cohabitation' with 'marriage' and thereby expands the last. In the view of proponents of this theory, the conflicts-law framework of classification should be broader than the material-law. Therefore, establishing the nature of a legal relation and the interpretation of conflicts norms should be effectuated on the basis of conflicts-law and not material-law criteria.

9.15 Russian legal doctrine on the whole has traditionally preferred the 'autonomy of classification' approach. As for the classification of the concepts of a conflicts link, under the traditionally-preferred Russian approach this classification should be undertaken only under the *lex fori* basis, even though it is acknowledged that this approach does not always and necessarily satisfactorily resolve the issue of a 'conflict of classifications'. In any event, in Russian legislation there is an exception to this approach with respect to the distinction to be made between moveable and immoveable property. Under the Russian Civil Code (Article 1205), whether property is one or the other is determined according to the law of the country where the property is situated.

Multiplicity of legal systems

9.16 Some countries, including the Russian Federation itself, contain several legal systems based on subdivisions into which the country is divided or based on the historical coexistence of more than one system of law operating on the territory of the country concerned. The United States, exemplified by federal law and the law of the fifty States, and the United Kingdom, exemplified by English and Scottish law, are two examples of the first. Countries where canon law, the law merchant, admiralty law, or customary law operate side by side with statutory law are examples of the second.

9.17 When a Russian court is faced with the choice of law of a foreign State in which several legal systems operate, the basic principle is that the legal system is chosen according to the law of that country. If it is impossible to make this determination in accordance with the law of the country, then the legal system most closely connected with the legal relation is chosen. In Russian practice if the parties to a contract have not agreed as to the applicable law, the court may take the initiative to resolve the issue. Thus, if a contract were concluded by a company registered in the state of Delaware but headquartered in the state of New York and the contract contained no applicable law clause, the Russian court would determine whether to apply Delaware or New York law. Russian courts experience more difficulty when the conflicts link referring the court to a particular jurisdiction does not resolve the problem of which legal system within the country concerned. For example, if the Russian court has to determine the dispositive legal capacity of a non-Russian citizen and is referred by the country of the individual's citizenship to the United States of America (which has a unified citizenship), this does not assist the court in determining the law of which state of the United States should apply to this question, the more so since United States federal law will not resolve the issue. While conflicts rules in the United States might readily resolve the issue, the Russian court cannot avoid the problems of choosing not only the relevant material law but also the relevant conflicts rules. Russian legislation equips the Russian court to choose between Russian and foreign legal orders, but not to make choices within foreign legal orders. In all likelihood the Russian court will fall back in such instances on the factual circumstances of the matter and make a determination based on the legal system with which the particular legal relation is most closely linked.

Reciprocity

The principle of reciprocity is very much a two-edged sword. By insisting on reciprocity as a precondition of cooperation, a State in fact places in the hands of other States the decision as to whether there should be cooperation or not, for by withholding reciprocity or declining to conclude a treaty on the issue, the foreign State in practice defeats the possibility of cooperation at all levels, both State and non-State. **9.18**

The Russian Federation has neatly avoided this situation with respect to applicable law. Foreign law is subject to application in the Russian Federation irrespective of whether Russian law is applied in the respective foreign State at all or with respect to legal relations of a particular nature unless provided otherwise by a law. When reciprocity is relevant, it is presumed that reciprocity exists unless proved otherwise. This provision has been included for the first time in Russian civil legislation (Article 1189). **9.19**

Russian legal doctrine takes the position that in the broad sense of the word reciprocity is '. . . one of the principles of international cooperation enabling the rights and interests of States and their citizens and organizations to be ensured on the basis of equality and mutual advantage'.[6] The essence of the Civil Code provision is that the application of foreign law to which a conflicts rule refers is not preconditioned by reciprocity, and the Russian court does not need to determine whether Russian law is applied or not in a foreign country whose conflicts rule is relevant. There is no federal law of the Russian **9.20**

[6] See V P Zvekov, *Международное частное право: Учебник* [International Private Law: Textbook] (2nd ed.; 2004), p. 175.

Federation which invokes reciprocity as a condition of the application of foreign law.

9.21 Nonetheless, Russian private international law doctrine distinguishes between 'formal' and 'material' reciprocity, and it is not entirely clear which of the two the legislator had in view under Article 1189. Material reciprocity presupposes that there is an identical amount of powers and the same character of powers between natural and juridical persons of two or more States.

9.22 *Example:* A treaty signed on 25 December 1998 between the Russian Federation and the Republic Belarus provided for the equal rights of citizens within the Union of States being created by the two countries. This meant that if citizens of Belarus have the right without any obstruction or any conditions to acquire houses, apartments, and other immoveables in ownership on the territory of Russia, then citizens of the Russian Federation have an analogous right in Belarus. Before the 1998 treaty was ratified, a Decision of the Supreme Council of the Soviet of the Union of Belarus and Russia adopted 2 April 1997 'On Ensuring the Equal Rights of Citizens of the Republic Belarus and Russia to Acquire Property in Ownership, Possession, Use, and Disposition' required the two States to ensure to one another's citizens this right on their respective territories. Decisions of the Supreme Council of the Union are subject to execution by agencies of the Union in compliance with legislation of the States-parties. The agencies of State power of the States-participants are required to bring their legal acts into conformity with decisions of the Union or issue legal acts ensuring the realization of those decisions. On 25 March 1997 the Belarus Constitutional Court issued a decision 'On Interpretation of the Opinion of the Constitutional Court of the Republic Belarus of 26 June 1996 "On the Conformity to Laws of the Republic Belarus of the Decree of the Supreme Soviet of 11 June 1993 'On the Procedure for the Purchase-Sale of Apartments (or Houses) in the Republic Belarus' " and the Provisional Statute on the Procedure for the Purchase-Sale of Apartments (or Houses), confirmed by decree of the Council of Ministers of 31 August 1993, No. 589'. This decision acknowledged that foreign citizens and stateless persons not residing on its territory have the right to acquire apartments and houses in the Republic Belarus only on the basis of international treaties and in accordance with the procedure for the realization of their norms. As a result, Russian citizens not residing on the territory of Belarus were, until the introduction into operation of the procedure for the realization of the norms of the decision of the Supreme Council of the Union of 2 April 1997 or Treaty of 25 December 1998, deprived of the right to acquire immoveable property on the territory of Belarus even though in Russia citizens of Belarus had this right on the basis of the 1993 Constitution of Russia (Article 62) and other international treaties (1993 Minsk Convention).

This was 'material reciprocity' in contrast with the 'formal reciprocity' that usually takes the form of national regime or most-favoured-nation regime.

Renvoi

Under the Russian Civil Code (Article 1190) any reference to foreign law in accordance with Section VI of that Code is regarded as a reference to material law and not to the conflicts law of the country except when the reference is to Russian law determining the legal status of a natural person. This rule was introduced into civil legislation for the first time in the present Civil Code and prior to its introduction was the subject of divergent views in Russian legal doctrine.[7] However, its legislative consolidation initially emerged in the 1993 Law on International Commercial Arbitration (Article 28): '. . . Any specification of the law or system of law of any State must be interpreted as directly referring to the material law of that State and not to its conflicts of law norms'.[8] **9.23**

The reference in these provisions to a 'conflicts norm' has in view not an isolated prescription of foreign law, but the material law of the foreign legal system as a whole. When parties to a contract make a choice of the applicable law, this is part of their exercise of the autonomy of will of the parties, and their choice encompasses solely the material law and not the conflicts rules of the foreign law chosen. The sole exception relates to two categories of instances: first, when norms of foreign law refer specifically to Russian law and not to the law of any third country, in which event a reference to the law of a third country is not permitted under the Russian Civil Code; and second, when a reference to Russian law establishes that renvoi may apply only to provisions determining the legal status of a natural person. In the last instance such legal status involves the personal law of a natural person, the law determining his civil law capacity or dispositive legal capacity, or the rights of a natural person to a name, or the law subject to application with regard to trusteeship or guardianship, or the law subject to application when deeming a person to be missing. Russian jurists regard this approach as encouraging stability and clarity in determining the rights of an individual and simplifying the task of the Russian court. This approach also is consistent with the modern trend towards emphasizing the close link between the individual concerned and the applicable law. **9.24**

---

[7] For a discussion, see L A Lunts, *Курс международного частного права. В 3 т.* [Cours of International Private Law. In 3 Volumes] (2002), pp. 303–6; M M Boguslavskii (ed.), *Международное частное право: современные проблемы* [International Private Law: Contemporary Problems] (1994), pp. 460–62.

[8] *Ведомости СНД и ВС Российской Федерации* (1993), no. 32, item 1240; transl. in W E Butler, *Russian Company and Commercial Legislation* (2003), p. 849.

9.25 Where international treaties of the Russian Federation override this approach to renvoi, the provisions of the treaty would apply.

Substance of foreign law

9.26 It is generally accepted in Russian legal doctrine that the process of applying conflicts rules requires two stages: in the first stage one determines whether a conflict rule applies and, if so, to the law of which country does the conflicts rule refer one. During the second stage, the law to which the conflicts rule points is applied. The question then arises as to how one correctly ascertains what the content of foreign law is. Under the Russian Civil Code (Article 1191), the content of the norms of foreign law are to be established in accordance with their official interpretation and their application in practice and doctrine in the respective foreign State.

9.27 Unlike the general position in Anglo-American legal systems, where foreign law is one of the factual circumstances subject to proof, the predominant view in Russian legal doctrine and that adopted in the Russian Civil Code is that foreign law is a 'legal category'. Under this approach the Russian court has the duty to determine *ex officio* the content of foreign law. If the Russian court finds this impossible to do, this is not grounds for rejection of the suit; a superior court has the right to review the conclusions of the inferior court with regard to foreign law.

9.28 This approach does not simplify the task of establishing, or proving, what the substance of foreign law is. Assistance is sought through procedural means. The Civil Code suggests various 'sources' through which the meaning of foreign law may be determined, among them the Ministry of Justice of the Russian Federation, Russian and foreign competent agencies and organizations, and the use of experts. The Russian Federation is a party to the European Convention on Information on Foreign Law,[9] although most acknowledge the Convention is not an effective means of establishing the content of foreign law.

9.29 An expert is a person who possesses special knowledge under the Code of Civil Procedure (Article 79) and Code of Arbitrazh Procedure (Article 55). There remains controversy, however, in Russian legal doctrine as to whether knowledge in the domain of law constitutes special knowledge which can be ascertained by way of an expert examination. In judicial practice experts commonly assist the Russian court by providing the texts of foreign legislation and legal opinions on foreign law and judicial practice. When a suit is concerned with demands related to entrepreneurial activity, the court may place the burden of

[9] *БМД*, no. 1 (2000).

proof with respect to foreign law on the parties, which in effect comes close to approximating the Anglo-American approach.

If it is ultimately impossible to establish the content of applicable foreign law, the Russian court is authorized by the Civil Code to apply the *lex fori.* Russian legal doctrine holds that this outcome applies even if the parties assume the burden of proof to establish the content of foreign law; that is, if the evidence submitted is not satisfactory with regard to foreign law, the court will not reject the suit, but rather will decide the dispute on the basis of Russian law. 9.30

The Russian Federation is party to a number of treaties intended to facilitate international cooperation in the exchange of legal information. Among them are the 1968 European Convention on Information on Foreign Law,[10] the 1993 Minsk Convention and 1997 Protocol thereto, the 2002 Kishinev Convention on Legal Assistance and Legal Relations with Regard to Civil, Family, and Criminal Cases (intended to supplant the 1993 Minsk Convention), and the 1994 CIS Agreement on the Exchange of Legal Information.[11] In 2001 the Russian Federation acceded to the 1970 Hague Convention on the Taking of Evidence Abroad in Civil and Commercial Matters.[12] 9.31

Imperative norms of Russian law

The Russian Civil Code (Article 1192) has incorporated a doctrine originally developed in France during the late 1950s of super-imperative norms in private international law. These are imperative norms which, by virtue of their special significance, must be applied always, irrespective of the applicable law determined by the parties in a contract exercising their autonomy of will or by a court as a result of the application of conflicts rules. In Russian legal doctrine, following foreign practices, the super-imperative norms are sometimes described as norms of direct application or imperative norms in private international law. 9.32

Example: When building a sanatorium in Russia, a foreign contractor, referring to the choice of law made by the parties when concluding the contract, ignored prohibitory norms of Russian construction norms and rules which did not permit the design and siting of boilers in basement premises of treatment and sanatorium institutions. The customer, having reinstalled new equipment at his own expense, brought suit in an arbitrazh court against the contractor for compensation of losses connected with the reinstallation and reassembly in the basement. The court satisfied the suit, accepting the plaintiff's argument that the construction rules and norms were imperative and of direct application. 9.33

[10] *СДД*, XLVII (1993), pp. 415–420.
[11] *БМД*, no. 2 (1994).
[12] *СЗ РФ* (2001), no. 7, item 616.

9.34 In practice Russian courts experience difficulty in distinguishing super-imperative norms from ordinary imperative norms. The Civil Code offers several criteria for drawing the distinction: an indication in the norm itself that it is super-imperative; ensuring the rights of participants of civil turnover; and ensuring the interests protected by a law of the participants of civil turnover. A classic example is Article 162(3) of the Civil Code provisions regulating the consequences of the failure to comply with the simple written form of a transaction. If it is a foreign economic transaction, the consequences are invalidity of the transaction. This imperative norm of Russian legislation cannot be changed either by agreement of the parties, including by an agreement on the applicable law. Consequently, irrespective of the law chosen by the parties or the applicable law determined by a court on the basis of conflicts rules, the provision concerning the form of a foreign economic transaction is always applied. There are suggestions in some Russian doctrinal writings that certain norms of joint-stock legislation, such as the right to participate in a general stockholder meeting, alienate stocks, receive dividends, and receive information on the activity of a joint-stock society, may in some situations be regarded as super-imperative norms whose operation is not affected by foreign law applicable in a specific instance.

9.35 Russian jurists note the inevitable relationship between super-imperative norms, on the one hand, and doctrines of public policy (see below), on the other. Both operate to impose provisions of Russian legislation irrespective of choices of applicable law. The principal difference is that public policy is less concerned with specific norms of law and more with underlying principles of the Russian legal system.

9.36 The Russian Civil Code distinguishes between two types of situation: the first is the application of super-imperative norms of the country of the court, and the second, the application of super-imperative norms of a third country with which a particular legal relation has a close connection. In the first instance the Russian court would be obliged to apply Russian super-imperative norms. In the second instance it would be in the discretion of the Russian court to apply these norms or not.[13] The principle of super-imperative norms has enabled 'circumventions of the law' through choice of law clauses to be reduced.

9.37 Imperative norms of another country may be applied in the discretion of a Russian court if the court comes to the conclusion that the legal relation concerned is closely connected with the other country. The Russian court therefore should determine whether (1) a close connection exists between the legal relation concerned and the law of another country (and not whose law

[13] The approach of the Russian Civil Code is based on the 1980 Rome Convention (Article 7).

should apply by reason of autonomy of will of the parties or the application of a conflicts rule), and (2) what imperative norms of that legal system should be taken into account. The existence of a close link may turn on such factors as the place of performance of a contract, among others. The overall approach is flexible and gives the court the possibility to assess the circumstances in each situation.

Public policy

Although the public policy clause in Soviet civil legislation was aggressively and ideologically formulated, it was apparently not extensively used in practice. The more neutrally drafted public policy clause of the Russian Civil Code is extensively used in practice, and often to the disadvantage of foreign parties seeking to enforce foreign arbitration awards in Russian courts when, in the opinion of Russian courts, arbitrators have failed to apply imperative provisions of Russian legislation or otherwise 'misunderstood' applicable Russian law. The principle of public policy also appears in the 1993 Law on International Commercial Arbitration, the Family Code, the Code of Arbitrazh Procedure, the Code of Civil Procedure, and the 2002 Federal Law on Arbitration Courts in the Russian Federation. **9.38**

The essence of the position is that norms of foreign law subject to application in accordance with the Russian Civil Code are not applied when the consequences of the application thereof would be clearly contrary to the foundations of the legal order (public policy) of the Russian Federation. Russian law would be applied in their stead. A refusal to apply norms of foreign law may not be based only on differences of the legal, political, or economic system of the respective foreign State from that of the Russian Federation. **9.39**

An example of public policy being debated in Russian legal doctrine is whether Russian courts would recognize and give effect to the legal consequences of single-sex marriages, which have been legalized in some countries but not in the Russian Federation. There is no clear answer, although it is recognized that in the twenty-first century there is greater tolerance of 'legal innovation' in other countries, which should lead to a reduction in the instances when the public policy clause would be applied. **9.40**

When a Russian court comes to the conclusion that the application of a rule of foreign law would lead to consequences contrary to public policy, the question remains as to what norm the court should apply in place of the foreign rule. Russian courts as a rule turn to the *lex fori.* The Civil Code of the Russian Federation, however, does not compel this result and the Russian court could in fact apply a different and inoffensive norm of foreign law. Russian legal doctrine holds that the court must be convinced of the impossibility of finding other **9.41** norms of foreign law in place of the unacceptable norms and only if that is impossible turning to Russian law.

9.42 In Russian judicial practice, decisions of the Supreme Court of the Russian Federation have indicated that 'public policy' means the basic principles consolidated in the 1993 Russian Constitution and federal laws of the Russian Federation.[14] In another Ruling of the Judicial Division for Civil Cases of the Supreme Court the public policy clause was construed to mean: '. . . the foundations of the social system of the Russian State. The public policy clause is possible only in those individual instances when the application of a foreign law might give rise to a result inadmissible from the standpoint of the Russian legal consciousness'.[15] Russian courts also have considered public policy to be relevant when refusing to enforce an arbitral award based on the behaviour of parties not in good faith and abuse of right in the proceeding.[16]

9.43 *Example:* A Russian juridical person appealed against the decision of the St. Petersburg City Court of 25 September 1998 allowing the recognition and enforcement of an arbitral award rendered in Stockholm, Sweden on the grounds that the award was contrary to the public policy of the Russian Federation. The arbitrators had failed to give effect to the imperative provisions concerning the signature of a foreign trade contract set out in the Decree of the USSR Council of Ministers of 14 February 1978, No. 122, on the procedure for the signature of foreign trade transactions. Under the 1978 decree, two signatures were required from the Soviet side. Under the 1958 New York Convention, it was admissible not to enforce an arbitral award which was contrary to public policy. The Supreme Court of the Russian Federation determined in deciding the appeal that '. . . the court does not find that the recognition and enforcement of this decision is contrary to the public policy of the Russian Federation', thereby upholding the decision of the St. Petersburg court.[17]

Retorsion

9.44 The principle of retaliatory reprisals against another country is found in several Russian legislative acts, including legislation on foreign trade (see Chapter 3) and on civil procedure (Article 398) and arbitrazh procedure (Article 254). Retorsion is defined as the lawful actions of one State adopted in response

[14] *Бюллетень Верховного Суда Российской Федерации*, no. 7 (1999).

[15] *Бюллетень Верховного Суда Российской Федерации*, no. 3 (1998).

[16] The case is discussed by Iu G Bogatina, «Оговорка о публичном порядке: *Теория и судебна япрактика*» [Clause on Public Policy: Theory and Judicial Practice], in Erpyleva, Gashi-Butler, and Henderson (eds.), *Forging a Common Legal Destiny: Liber Amicorum in honour of William E. Butler* (2005), pp. 441–2.

[17] *Бюллетень Верховного Суда Российской Федерации*, no. 3 (1999).

to discriminatory limitations established by another State with respect to the natural or juridical persons of the State lawfully responding. In the Civil Code (Article 1194) the possibility of retorsion exists with respect to property and personal nonproperty rights of Russian citizens and juridical persons. General limitations adopted by foreign States on the rights of all foreign citizens or juridical persons would not qualify.

Russian legal doctrine holds that such retaliation, if introduced, must be commensurate to those limitations enacted with respect to Russian citizens and juridical persons. In effect, this provision of the Civil Code gives effect to the 1993 Constitution of the Russian Federation, which vests the right to introduce retorsion in the Government of the Russian Federation (Article 114). In a sense the provision on retorsion is the logical consequence of the approach to reciprocity set out in the Civil Code (Article 1189). Since reciprocity is not required with regard to the application of foreign law, it is applicable in individual instances with regard to limitations introduced abroad on the legal status of natural and juridical persons. Retorsion enables measures to be taken against discrimination without compromising the principle of national regime as such, which underlies the status of foreign citizens in the Russian Federation. Retorsion also may be used if the rights and interests of compatriots residing abroad are infringed by the State in which they reside. **9.45**

Example: In response to discriminatory measures adopted in a number of foreign States against Soviet citizens, the Council of People's Commissars of the USSR on 26 November 1937 adopted a Decree which provided that **9.46**

> . . . houses and any type of other structures situated on the territory of the USSR and belonging by right of ownership or by right of building to foreigners not residing in the USSR who are citizens of States which do not recognize for Soviet citizens not residing on the territories of these States the rights of ownership to property situated on the territories of these States—shall be subject to transfer to local soviets of people's deputies of toilers at the location of this property.[18]

B. Applicable Law and the Legal Status of Persons

Personal law of natural person

The Russian Federation is among those countries of the world, principally in continental Europe and the CIS, in which the personal status of a natural person is determined by the law of the country whose citizenship the individual holds (*lex patriae*). A stateless person has his status determined according to the law of **9.47**

[18] *C3 CCCP* (1937), no. 75, item 368.

the country in which this person has a place of residence. The link with place of residence also is used when persons have dual or multiple citizenships and none of them is the citizenship of the country of the court. Territorial links, in other words, are secondary and operate only where citizenship requires replacement or augmentation as the criterion for personal law. The Russian legislator has avoided the term 'domicile', although it is sometimes used in doctrinal writings.

9.48 The traditional Russian preference for citizenship as the determining factor in personal law is attributed to two factors. First, this approach offers a high degree of certitude since for most persons the fact of affiliation to a particular citizenship is usually formalized. Second, as a rule citizenship is subject to fewer changes than place of residence. The factor of citizenship is extensively used in Russian legal assistance treaties.

9.49 When dual or multiple citizenships exist, the Russian approach falls back to the need to make a choice in favour of one of the legal systems with which the natural person concerned has a legal link. If one of the two or multiple citizenships is Russian citizenship, then Russian law will be the personal law of the individual. This position follows from the Russian approach to the law of citizenship under which a Russian citizen may have dual citizenship in accordance with a federal law or an international treaty of the Russian Federation. However, unless dual citizenship does arise from a federal law or treaty, the Russian citizen who has dual citizenship is regarded as having only Russian citizenship. The result is that a Russian citizen who acquires a foreign citizenship does not violate Russian law, but the relationship between this individual and the Russian State, including his personal status, is regulated solely by Russian legislation and the fact that he has a foreign citizenship is irrelevant.

9.50 If an individual has several citizenships, none of which is Russian, his personal law is the law of the country in which this person has a place of residence. This approach, which stresses territorial linkage, replaces that used in Russian family legislation, which required a person having multiple citizenships and entering marriage to choose the law of one of the States of which he was a citizen.

9.51 The exception from the general approach above is that a foreign citizen who has a place of residence in Russia falls under Russian law so far as personal status is concerned, with the obvious result that the Russian legal system places a considerable premium on expanding the sphere of application of the *lex fori.* The 'place of residence' is defined in the Civil Code (Article 20) as the '. . . place where a citizen permanently or primarily resides . . .'. The conjunction 'or' is used without determining any priority between a permanent or primary place of residence. Moreover, there is no indication as to whether Article 20 is to be construed against the background of Russian administrative law formulations concerning the legal status of foreigners, such as 'permanently residing'. It would not be uncommon for a foreigner to have a permanent place of residence abroad, yet also qualify for a resident permit or other extended-sojourn status in Russia.

Russian legal doctrine suggests that Article 20 of the Civil Code may be approached in two ways. The first would emphasise that Russian law does not apply to a foreigner primarily residing in Russia if he has a permanent place of residence in another country. This approach accentuates a search for the closest link between the foreigner and a particular legal system, and in the opinion of many Russian jurists is preferable. The difficulty is that Article 1195(3) is directed towards enlarging the domain of the *lex fori*, and the closest link approach is not consistent with that approach. Under the second approach the fact of primary residence of a foreigner in Russia would be sufficient for Russian law to be the personal law of that individual even if he did have a permanent place of residence outside the Russian Federation. While this approach satisfies the logic of Article 1195(3) and a literal reading of Article 20, it does not necessarily meet the requirements or legal interests of the individual concerned. **9.52**

The position that the personal law of a stateless person is considered to be the law of the country in which that person has a place of residence is long established in Russian law and avoids the issues arising in Article 20 of the Civil Code with respect to permanent or primary residence. The rule with respect to refugees is an exception to both the principles of citizenship and place of residence. The assumption is that refugees forced to leave their country of citizenship or permanent residence have lost their link with that country, and therefore the law of the country which has accepted them should be their personal law. **9.53**

Civil law capacity of natural person

Under the Universal Declaration of Human Rights (Article 6), a provision widely accepted as a generally-recognized norm of international law, every person, irrespective of where located, has the right to his legal personality being recognized. In the Russian Federation an individual's legal capacity arises from the moment of birth and terminates with death (Article 17, Civil Code). The civil legal capacity of a natural person is determined in Russia by his personal law (unless an international treaty of the Russian Federation provides otherwise),[19] provided that the principle of national regime extends to foreign citizens and stateless persons such that their civil legal capacity will be equal to that of Russian citizens, unless a law of the Russian Federation establishes otherwise **9.54**

[19] The Russian Federation has treaties with a number of countries (Georgia, Kazakhstan, Kyrgyzia, and others) providing that the legal capacity of citizens of one State permanently residing on the territory of another State is determined by the law of the country of residence.

(Article 1196, Civil Code). Certain federal laws do establish otherwise, among them legislation in the sphere of foreign trade, investment, production cooperation, and the exchange of information, work, services, and so on. In some instances the principle of national regime operates only if that right is expressly provided for in an international treaty or on the basis of reciprocity; e.g. the Patent Law of the Russian Federation.[20] Citizens of Kyrgyzia enjoy the principle of national regime in the Russian Federation with respect to the protection of industrial property by virtue of a 1995 Agreement on Cooperation in the Domain of the Protection of Industrial Property.

9.55 Moreover, although the Civil Code recognizes civil law capacity as being equal for all citizens, whether a natural person actually has the right to own property, inherit or bequeath property, engage in entrepreneurial or other activity, create juridical persons, and conclude transactions will depend upon the legal status of the natural person. Foreigners, for example, may not own land plots in frontier territories of the Russian Federation, nor engage in architectural activity in the absence of an international treaty except in collaboration with a Russian architect. On the other hand, certain federal laws may enlarge the civil capacity of foreigners to, for example, receive compensation in the event of the expropriation of investments.

9.56 The personal law of a natural person also determines his dispositive legal capacity. However, a natural person who lacks dispositive legal capacity under his personal law may not refer to this if he has such capacity under the law of the place of conclusion of a transaction unless it is proved that the other party knew or should have known about the lack of dispositive legal capacity. Recognition in the Russian Federation of a natural person to lack or to be limited in dispositive legal capacity is subordinate to Russian law.

9.57 Civil dispositive legal capacity is the ability of a natural person by his actions to acquire and effectuate civil rights, to create civil duties for himself, and to perform them (Article 21, Civil Code). The six means of determining the personal law of a natural person (Article 1195, Civil Code) apply when determining civil dispositive legal capacity, unless an international treaty of the Russian Federation establishes other rules. The 1993 Minsk Convention and a number of bilateral treaties concluded with the Russian Federation use the law of the person's citizenship for this purpose, whereas others use the law of the place of residence.

9.58 The Civil Code, in comparison with earlier Soviet legislation, introduces greater differentiation in the conflicts of law principles applicable to various types of

[20] Transl. in W E Butler, *Intellectual Property Law in the Russian Federation* (4th edn, 2005), pp. 128–88.

civil dispositive legal capacity, such as the capacity to engage in entrepreneurial activity, tort capacity, the capacity to inherit and bequeath property, and the autonomy of will of parties to contracts. Each of these is subject to special conflicts rules (see below). Insofar as these are *lex specialis*, they have priority over the general conflicts rules (Article 1197, Civil Code). The same applies to special rules contained in treaties (for example, in legal assistance treaties concluded by the Russian Federation with Bulgaria, Cuba, Mongolia, and Vietnam the civil dispositive legal capacity of persons to conclude domestic petty transactions is determined by the legislation of the country on whose territory the transaction is concluded and not by the personal law of the individual). Similarly as in the case for general legal capacity, Russian legislation on export control and foreign investments contains different rules for foreign citizens and stateless persons with regard to their dispositive legal capacity to enter into respective foreign economic or investment transactions.

The Russian Civil Code contains a unilateral conflicts norm pursuant to which the recognition of a natural person in the Russian Federation to lack or be limited in dispositive legal capacity is subordinate to Russian law unless an international treaty of the Russian Federation provides otherwise. Several bilateral treaties of the Russian Federation do stipulate otherwise, including with Bulgaria, Cuba, Lithuania, and Poland, among others. **9.59**

Right to name

Under Russian law a natural person has a personal nonproperty right to a name. **9.60** This right is linked directly with his person and arises from the moment of birth. Registration or re-registration of a name carries with it the right to use that name in order to participate in legal relations. A 'name' in Russia encompasses the surname and forename conferred on birth and a patronymic, unless it arises otherwise from a law or national custom (Article 19, Civil Code), as well as a change of name or a fictitious name. The conflicts rule encompasses both the right to use and to defend the name (Article 1198). However, the right to a name under the General Part of the Civil Code should not be confused with the author's right to a name, which has rather a more territorial character than a personal character and would be defended under intellectual property legislation and conflicts rules.

Example: A defendant residing on the territory of the Russian Federation used **9.61** the name of a foreign citizen residing beyond the limits of Russia without his consent and contrary to his wish. In so doing the name was distorted: instead of 'Gashi' it was written 'Gashli'. In this situation the foreigner has the right to bring suit in a Russian court at the defendant's place of residence to defend his name and demand compensation for moral harm. In this event under

Article 1198 of the Russian Civil Code foreign law would apply—the law of the country of which the plaintiff is a citizen.[21]

Trusteeship and guardianship

9.62 The personal law of the person with respect to whom a trusteeship or guardianship is established or revoked applies to minors, persons who have reached majority and lack or are limited in dispositive legal capacity. This is a rule of Russian civil legislation (Article 1199, Civil Code), although in the past it was considered part of family law. The formulation of the rule brings Russian legislation closer to the rules contained in the 1993 Minsk Convention and virtually all bilateral treaties of the Russian Federation concerning trusteeship and guardianship, although there is not complete coincidence of the legislative and treaty provisions. The treaties establish the link to the law of the country of citizenship of the natural person over whom a trusteeship or guardianship is being established. Moreover, the treaties, although the precise formulations differ, generally allow the possibility of the transfer of trusteeship or guardianship to the competent agency of the other contracting party if the person limited or lacking in dispositive legal capacity has a place of residence, whereabouts, or property on the territory of the last. The agency which accepts the trusteeship or guardianship usually manage it in accordance with national legislation, although some treaties stipulate that the role of the receiving State is to manage or administer, and not establish or terminate, the trusteeship or guardianship.

9.63 The duty of a person to accept the duties of a trustee or guardian placed on him is determined by his personal law. Although the Family Code of the Russian Federation and its predecessor did not contain such a rule, many bilateral legal assistance treaties of the Russian Federation did so, subject to the qualification that they referred to the law of citizenship of the individual rather than the personal law.

9.64 Relations between the trustee or guardian and the person under the trusteeship or guardianship are determined according to the law of the country whose institution appointed the trustee or guardian, unless the person under trusteeship or guardianship has a place of residence in the Russian Federation, in which case Russian law applies if it is more favourable for this person. This position coincides with that taken in Russian bilateral treaty practice. Although the link is not dependent upon a direct choice of law or upon the citizenship or personal

---

[21] The general example is given by G Iu Fedoseeva, in Anufrieva (ed.), *Комментарий к Гражданскому кодексу Российской Федерации. Часть третья (постатейный)* [Commentary to the Civil Code of the Russian Federation. Part Three (Article-by-Article)] (2004), p. 438.

law of one of the participants, in practice these factors play a role when courts or other competent agencies establish or revoke a trusteeship or guardianship.

Recognition of person to be missing or deceased

The deeming in the Russian Federation of a natural person to be missing (Article 42, Civil Code) or declared to be deceased is subordinate to Russian law (Article 45, Civil Code). If a matter of either nature is complicated by a foreign element, the Russian court must determine which law is the applicable law. The Russian Civil Code (Article 1200) operates in this situation from the unilateral principle of *lex fori.* Under the Code of Civil Procedure of the Russian Federation (Article 403), Russian courts are competent to consider applications where the following conditions are simultaneously present: the person who is to be declared missing or deceased is a Russian citizen or had a last place of residence in Russia and on the resolution of this question depends the establishment of the rights and duties of citizens and organizations having respectively a place of residence or location in the Russian Federation. **9.65**

The 1993 Minsk Convention and the majority of Russian bilateral treaties work from the principle of citizenship of the person at the time when he was last known to be alive, although institutions of one contracting party may deem a person to be missing or deceased upon the petition of persons residing on their territory if their rights and interests are based on the legislation of that contracting party. Justice agencies considering the matter would apply the *lex fori.* **9.66**

Russian legislation does not regulate the applicable law and jurisdiction with respect to cases concerning the establishment of the fact of death of a foreign person at a determined time or circumstances. By analogy of *lex* some Russian jurists consider that Article 1200 of the Civil Code would apply to these situations. **9.67**

Entrepreneurial activity

Since the advent of perestroika, the Russian legal system has exhibited a certain naivete about the manner in which individuals in the rest of the world engage in entrepreneurial activity. USSR and RSFSR legislation initially failed to recognize the classic Anglo-American partnerships, so commonly used for auditing and legal services, as potential investors, and they assumed that in order to engage in entrepreneurial activity, that is, to start up and conduct a business in their individual capacity, some form of State registration was required. This placed some foreign investors in an impossible position because as a matter of Soviet or Russian law they were required to produce evidence of a legal capacity which they could not produce. **9.68**

9.69 The Russian Civil Code (Article 1201) has declined to see the right to engage in entrepreneurial activity as a natural human right and contains a conflicts rule as follows: the right of a natural person to engage in entrepreneurial activity without the formation of a juridical person as an individual entrepreneur is determined according to the law where this natural person has registered as an individual entrepreneur. If there is no obligatory registration, the law of the country of the principal place of effectuating entrepreneurial activity applies. While this formulation recognizes that the entire world outside the Russian Federation does not necessarily register individual entrepreneurs, it does make at least three false assumptions: (1) that the foreign legal system concerned has the category of an individual entrepreneur; (2) that the foreign citizen concerned is already engaging in entrepreneurial activity; and (3) the foreign citizen has a principal place where he does so.

9.70 The rationale in Russian legal doctrine for this approach is that situations arise in modern business practice when the place of residence and place of engaging in entrepreneurial activity of a natural person-entrepreneur may be in different countries, and even that the individual concerned may have the citizenship of a third country. Whether a natural person has the right to engage in entrepreneurship or not may be decided variously in different legal orders. The dilemma is, which law to apply in order to determine the 'entrepreneurial status' of a natural person. However, as Russian jurists have acknowledged, 'special regulation of this question is lacking in the conflicts law of a majority of States of the world'.

9.71 It is worthy of remark that in this case the Russian legal system no longer applies the personal law of the individual concerned, but rather introduces a special criterion: the existence of a special right and dispositive legal capacity of natural persons with respect to the possibility of their participating in individual entrepreneurial activity. Construed literally, if a foreign citizen or stateless person who does not have Russian citizenship or a place of residence in the Russian Federation has registered as an entrepreneur in Russia without the formation of a juridical person, the legal possibilities to engage in individual entrepreneurship will be determined under Russian law, and likewise if the individual concerned has registered in a foreign State. Whether this is an issue of priority or not the Civil Code does not address.

9.72 Under the Russian Civil Code (Article 2[1]), the ability of a natural person to engage in entrepreneurial activity is a component of his legal capacity (Articles 17 and 18, Civil Code), to realize which he need merely register as an entrepreneur (Article 23(1), Civil Code). The consequence of the failure to register as an entrepreneur is that the natural person concerned does not have the right to refer with respect to transactions concluded by him to the fact that he is not an entrepreneur. As from 1 January 2004 the registration of entrepreneurs is effectuated under the 2001 Law on State Registration, as amended (Chapter VIII–1). However, the full implications of the position for a foreign citizen have not been addressed by the Russian legislator. While foreign citizens enjoy the right under the 2002 Federal Law on the Legal Status of Foreign Citizens to freely dispose of their capacities for labour, choose the nature of activity and profession, and to the free use of their capacities and property for entrepreneurial and other economic activity not prohibited by a law (Article 13), it is far from evident that a foreigner who has registered in his own country as an entrepreneur is required or not to so register in the Russian Federation. Moreover, such registration of a foreigner in Russia has implications for receiving a work authorization which have not been fully considered by the legislator.

Personal law of juridical person

The personal law of a juridical person is the law of the country where the juridical person is founded (Article 1202, Civil Code). Russian legal doctrine, judicial, legislative, and law enforcement practice use the term 'juridical person' to designate the 'affiliation' of the juridical person to a State and the term 'personal law' to designate affiliation to a legal system. It is suggested by some Russian jurists that the expression 'nationality' of a juridical person reflects the public law and private law status of the juridical person, whereas the term 'personal law' has in view the private law status thereof. **9.73**

The position of the Civil Code in linking 'juridical person' with place of 'founding' was also traditional for Soviet law. Russian courts and law enforcement agencies have applied this concept in accordance with the principles of classification and qualification set out above (Article 1187, Civil Code). The 'place' is the State where a respective legal system operates. In the event of multiple jurisdiction, as in the case of the United States, the principles of the Civil Code discussed above (Article 1188) would apply. A number of Russian bilateral treaties also proceed from the principle of founding, creation, or registration. Russian legal doctrine regards the provision on the personal law of a juridical person as applicable to the juridical persons of all countries and a general rule that precludes the possibility of using other criteria to determine the personal law of a juridical person. **9.74**

Certain international treaties of the Russian Federation contain exceptions, however, to this rule. The 1998 Agreement on Air Transport between Russia and Croatia uses the 'control theory'; that is, the law of the country whose persons control the juridical person, as the personal law of juridical persons.[22] The Russia-Kazakhstan 1995 Agreement on the status of Baikonur contains **9.75**

[22] *БМД*, no. 3 (2002).

an interesting clause whereby juridical persons of Kazakhstan registered in Baikonur during the period while the city is under Russian lease are registered just as Russian juridical persons. Formally the Republic Kazakhstan is considered to be the place of founding, but Russian law is the personal law of these juridical persons.[23] A number of criteria for determining the personal law of companies are set out in the 1994 Agreement on Partnership and Cooperation between Russia and the European Communities.[24]

9.76 Insofar as 'customs' may be relevant under Article 1186 of the Civil Code in determining the law applicable to civil-law relations with foreign persons (see above), codes of corporate conduct may qualify in those countries where these codes have become customs, in which event these codes might be drawn upon when considering disputes.

9.77 The Civil Code of the Russian Federation (Article 1202) contains an exemplary list of questions internal to a juridical person which should be resolved under the personal law of a juridical person. However, the personal law of the juridical person is relevant only to the extent that these questions do not exceed the framework of the legal status of the juridical person. Thus, the internal relations of a juridical person are regulated on the basis of the personal law of a juridical person insofar as they are not resolved on the basis of a contract between the founders or stockholders, or even with the juridical person itself. When there is a contract, the law applicable to the contract resolves these issues (Article 1214, Civil Code).

9.78 A juridical person may not refer to a limitation on the powers of its organs or a representative to conclude a transaction unknown to the law of the country in which the organ or representative of the juridical person has done so, unless it is proved that the other party knew or knowingly should have known about the said limitation.

Personal law of foreign organization not a juridical person

9.79 Organizations which are not juridical persons are 'legal entities'. Although the Russian language does readily accommodate the term 'legal entity' (and often wrongly translates the term as 'juridical person', thereby losing the distinction between the two),[25] the concept of an organization or entity which is not a juridical person is well-known to the Russian legal system; e.g. branch, representation, simple partnership. The partnership and the trust are classic legal entities in Anglo-American legal systems.

[23] *БМД*, no. 5 (1999). [24] *БМД*, no. 8 (1998).

[25] 'All juridical persons are legal entities, but not all legal entities are juridical persons'.

As used in the Civil Code of the Russian Federation (Article 1203), a foreign 'organization' which is not a juridical person under foreign law is broadly understood to encompass any organized association of persons (e.g. partnership) and any organized property complex (e.g. trust). Insofar as the creation of such organizations is based on contract, the place of concluding the constitutive contract may be considered the place of founding. If State registration is required after the constitutive contract is concluded, the place of founding may be considered the place of State registration. Insofar as such organizations may be created under foreign law without a fully-fledged corporative structure, their status under the law of obligations may be decisive. Where registration is required in the foreign legal system, Russian law is likely to consider the place of founding to be the place of registration. **9.80**

If Russian law is applicable to such organizations, the rules of the Civil Code which regulate the activity of juridical persons will be applied unless it arises otherwise from a law, other legal acts, or the essence of the relation. Although it would be possible for the founders of a foreign organization which is not a juridical person to choose Russian law as the law applicable to the constitutive contract, such a choice is unlikely. Similarly, it would be unlikely that a trust created under foreign law could properly function if the Civil Code norms that regulate the activity of Russian juridical persons were made applicable to the trust. It is noteworthy that the Civil Code does not offer an enumeration of exemplary questions to be decided on the basis of personal law for a foreign organization which is not a juridical person under foreign law. A Russian court might apply analogy of *lex* under Article 1202(2) of the Civil Code by way of guidance. **9.81**

Participation of state in civil-law relations complicated by foreign element

The Civil Code of the Russian Federation (Article 1204) provides that the rules of Section VI of the Code apply on the general grounds, unless established otherwise by a law, to civil-law relations complicated by a foreign element with the participation of a State. Few legal systems contain such a rule. **9.82**

This provision does not extend to jurisdictional immunities of a foreign State, which in the Russian Federation are regulated by the Code of Civil Procedure (Article 401) and the Code of Arbitrazh Procedure (Article 251). The provision does extend to any State, whether Russian or foreign, in its contractual relations with private persons which, exercising autonomy of will, determine a choice of law having due regard to relevant imperative norms. The effect of Article 1204 is that if the parties do not take advantage of the right to choose an applicable law provided for by legislation, the consequences will ensue when a State is a party that would otherwise ensue under the Civil Code in the absence of a **9.83** choice of law clause if only natural and juridical persons were parties to the agreement.

9.84 Most of the links enumerated in Article 1211 of the Civil Code (see below) would be unlikely to be relevant to contracts to which the State is a party for the purposes of determining applicable law. Complications have arisen in judicial practice in disputes involving construction work performed on the territory of a foreign embassy in the Russian Federation, for example.

9.85 *Example:* (1) A foreign embassy in the Russian Federation concluded an independent-work contract with a Russian joint-stock society to erect a hotel on the territory of the embassy. Under Russian law, the territory of an embassy is considered to be the territory of a foreign State. The contract did not contain an applicable law clause. Under Article 1211(4)(1) of the Civil Code, the law of the country with which a contract is most closely connected is considered with respect to a contract of construction independent-work to be the '. . . law of the country where the results provided for by the respective contract are basically created'. Since the hotel was being built on the embassy land plot, the place of creation of the result would not be the Russian Federation, but the foreign State. It would follow that foreign law would apply to the construction contract.[26]

9.86 (2) A foreign consulate in the Russian Federation is not an 'institution' or 'establishment' in the organizational-legal meaning of the term as used in the Civil Code of the Russian Federation (Article 125): '. . . an organization created by the owner in order to effectuate management, socio-cultural, or other functions of a non-commercial character and financed by it wholly or partially', but rather a general term for an entity which represents the State as such. In the meaning of civil legislation, a consulate is not an agency of the State.[27]

9.87 Although laws are adopted at various levels of the Russian state system, in the meaning of Article 1204 of the Civil Code Russian legal writers understand the term 'law' to mean only a federal law.

9.88 The Russian Federation continues to be party to a number of treaties which contain special provisions concerning the immunity of trade representations abroad.

---

[26] See the Information Letter of the Supreme Arbitrazh Court of the Russian Federation, No. 58, of 18 January 2001. *Вестник Высшего Арбитражного Суда Российской Федерации*, nos. 3, 4, and 7 (2001).

[27] See the Decree of the Federal Arbitrazh Court of the Northwestern District, 20 February 2002, No. A56–20526/01; No. A56–20527/01, available on ConsultantPlus data base.

C. Applicable Law and Property and Personal Nonproperty Relations

General provisions on rights to a thing

Under Russian conflicts rules, the content of the right of ownership and other rights to things in immoveable and moveable property and the effectuation of these rights and defence of such rights is determined according to the law of the country where the property is situated. The affiliation of property to the categories of immoveable and moveable likewise is determined by the same law. **9.89**

The scope of these rules is considerable. They extend not only to issues of title and the powers of an owner, but also to rights of use, servitudes, economic jurisdiction, operative management, and others. However, these provisions should not be confused with applicable law issues arising out of contracts for immoveable property, addressed in Article 1213 of the Civil Code. **9.90**

The law of the country where property is situated at the moment when the action or other circumstance occurred which served as grounds for the arising and termination of the right of ownership and other rights to a thing, unless provided otherwise by a law, determines when rights of ownership and other rights to a thing in property arise or terminate. If moveable property is in transit and a transaction is concluded with respect to that property, the law of the country from which the property was despatched governs the arising and termination of the right of ownership and other rights to a thing to such property unless provided otherwise by a law. Under these provisions a Russian court is required to evaluate the legal significance and consequences of the respective actions and circumstances, being guided not by the law of the place where the transactions were concluded or actions performed, but by the law of the location of the thing at the moment when they were concluded or performed. The parties to the transaction have no discretion to make a choice of law in these instances. In many legal systems, including Russia, transactions with immoveable property are subject to State registration, which predetermines the regulation of questions connected with the arising and termination of rights thereto by the legislation of the country where the property is situated. **9.91**

Issues arise with some frequency in judicial and arbitral practice with respect to property in transit. The operation of the transit provision (Article 1206) extends both to foreign economic transactions and to noncommercial transactions complicated by a foreign element. The object of the property rights must be en route, crossing the boundaries of different States or situated beyond State boundaries (for example, on the high seas). The principle of point of dispatch is used because situations arise when several transactions are concluded while **9.92** property is en route and it is impossible to determine precisely where the property is situated when a particular transaction occurs.

9.93 With respect to vessels, aircraft, and space objects the law of the country where these vessels and objects have been registered applies to the rights of ownership and other rights to things (Article 1207, Civil Code). All of these objects are equated with immoveables under the Russian Civil Code (Article 130) and therefore subject to registration. The term 'other rights to a thing' would include the right of pledge or mortgage, the right of economic jurisdiction, and the right of operative management. Vessels are registered in accordance with the Merchant Shipping Code of the Russian Federation; aircraft are registered under the Air Code of the Russian Federation; river vessels are registered under the Code of Internal Water Transport of the Russian Federation; and satellites and other space objects are registered under the 1993 Law on outer space activity; international treaties of the Russian Federation affect the registration of all these objects.

Limitations

9.94 Periods of limitation are determined according to the law of the country which is subject to being applied to the respective legal relation (Article 1208, Civil Code).

9.95 The Russian Federation thus with respect to limitations follows the law of the *lex causae*; that is, the law applicable to the rights and duties of the parties arising from either contractual or extra-contractual relations also governs the periods of limitation applicable to demands arising from those relations. The periods of limitation under Russian law are set out in Chapter 12 of the Civil Code and in dozens of other legislative acts relating to other branches of law. From the standpoint of conflicts of law, the Russian court must determine whose law regulated the essence of relations between the parties and then decide the question of limitations. In effect, therefore, when parties make a choice of law they also choose the applicable periods of limitation on the principle that having selected a legal order whose rules regulate their relations, the parties must accept the imperative periods of limitation that accompany that legal order.

9.96 If international treaties of the Russian Federation contain different conflicts rules relating to periods of limitation, the rules of the treaty prevail. The Russian Federation is party to a number of such treaties.[28]

[28] See M G Rozenberg, *Исковая давность в международном коммерческом обороте*: *Практика применения* [Periods of Limitation in International Commercial Turnover: Practice of Application] (1999), pp. 3–66.

Form of transactions

The general rule with respect to transactions complicated by a foreign element is that the form of a transaction is subordinated to the law of the place where the transaction is concluded (*lex locus actus*) on condition that a transaction concluded abroad may not be deemed to be invalid as a consequence of the failure to comply with form if the requirements of Russian law have been complied with. A power of attorney, which is a unilateral transaction, falls under these rules (see below). **9.97**

These provisions extend to unilateral, bilateral, and multipartite transactions. The form of a will and acts of revocation thereof are also regulated by Article 1224 of the Civil Code, and conflicts aspects of pledge are regulated by the 1992 Law on Pledge (Article 10[5]). The Civil Code does not give to parties the right to choose an applicable law for the form of a transaction. **9.98**

The 'form' of a transaction is a conceptual category which engages the rules regulating the interpretation or classification of a legal concept (see above). The Civil Code of the Russian Federation devotes several articles to the forms of transactions (Articles 158–165, 434) and the consequences of failure to comply. In the sense of Article 1209 the 'form' of a transaction has to do with the requirements for the formalization of a transaction, including standard model contracts, affixing of a seal, signature requirements, and the like. Practically speaking, if questions concerning the invalidity of a transaction arise solely because of defects of form and the transaction is deemed to be invalid under the law applicable to the form of the transaction, then having recourse to another law in order to ascertain the consequences of invalidity (that is, a law regulating the essence of an obligation and subject to determination under other provisions of the Civil Code) creates additional complications. Some Russian jurists suggest that for the purposes of Article 1209 it may be sufficient to be guided by Article 444 of the Civil Code, which provides that unless the place of conclusion has been specified in a contract, a 'contract shall be deemed to be concluded at the place of residence of a citizen or location of the juridical person which sent the offer'. The place of residence of a citizen is determined pursuant to Article 20 of the Civil Code, and the location of a juridical person, pursuant to Article 54. However, Article 444 does not assist with unilateral transactions, nor is it always clear who is the party which sent the offer. **9.99**

The Civil Code (Article 1209[2]) contains a unilateral conflicts rule *lex specialis* concerning the form of foreign economic transactions. If one of the parties to such a transaction is a Russian juridical person, the form of the foreign economic transaction is subordinated, irrespective of where the transaction is concluded, to Russian law. The same rule applies when one party to a foreign economic transaction is a natural person effectuating entrepreneurial activity **9.100** whose personal law is Russian law. Under Article 162 of the Civil Code, the simple written form is obligatory for a foreign economic transaction.

9.101 There is no definition of a 'foreign economic transaction' in Russian legislation. Russian legal doctrine defines such a transaction as contracts between persons whose commercial enterprises are situated in different States and concluded in the course of entrepreneurial activity as understood in the meaning of the Civil Code (see Article 2). The concept of a foreign economic transaction is narrower than a 'transaction with a foreign element'; to put it another way, a foreign economic transaction is a species of transaction with a foreign element. To qualify as a foreign economic transaction for conflicts purposes, one party must be a Russian juridical person, a Russian citizen, or a foreign citizen or stateless person having a place of residence in the Russian Federation (their personal law is Russian law pursuant to Article 1195, Civil Code). The form of a contract of pledge which is a foreign economic transaction as defined in Russian legal doctrine also must meet the requirements of Article 1209(2) of the Civil Code.

9.102 Also *lex specialis*, the form of a transaction with respect to immoveable property, is subordinated to the law of the country where the property is situated, and if such property has been entered in a State register in the Russian Federation, to Russian law. The provision concerning the State register is essential because Russian legislation equates certain property that is physically moveable with immoveable property: aircraft, space objects, vessels. The concept of a 'transaction with respect to immoveable property' (Article 1209) and a narrower concept of 'contract with respect to immoveable property' (Article 1213, Civil Code) are concerned principally with the subject of the contract. The phrase 'with respect to' should not be understood broadly.

9.103 International treaties of the Russian Federation would take precedence over the imperative provisions discussed above. Conflicts norms are found in the 1992 Kiev Agreement and 1993 Minsk Convention, as well as in a number of bilateral mutual assistance treaties. The USSR (and therefore the Russian Federation) ratified the 1980 Vienna Convention on the Sale of Goods, which does not require that a contract of sale be concluded in written form and permits witness testimony to be used to prove the existence and content of such a contract (Article 11). The Soviet Union entered a reservation when acceding to the Vienna Convention excluding provisions which permitted contracts in other than written form if any contracting party was a commercial enterprise in the USSR.[29] The Russian Federation also is party to a number of conventions

[29] See *Ведомости Верховного Совета СССР* (1990), no. 23, item 428. The reservation has not been withdrawn by the Russian Federation and is regarded by Russian jurists as being in force.

concerning bills of exchange and international transport which contain provisions on the form of contracts. Article 1209 of the Civil Code does not extend to arbitration agreements or clauses.

Choice of law by parties to contract

This subject tests the true understanding of a legal system with regard to the autonomy of will of the parties to a contract. In the Russian Civil Code (Article 1210) the formulation is dispositive: the parties of a contract may, when concluding a contract or subsequently, choose by agreement between them the law which is subject to application to their rights and duties under the contract. The Code goes on to establish a hierarchy of norms with regard to autonomy of will, establishing that the law chosen by the parties applies to the arising and termination of the right of ownership and other rights to a thing to moveable property without prejudice to the rights of third persons. This formulation sets out the means by which the parties may make their choice as to the applicable law. The parties may express their will in the contract itself, in a separate document(s), or during the arbitral or judicial consideration of a dispute which is recorded in the protocol of the judicial or arbitral session.[30] **9.104**

The provision that an agreement of the parties concerning the choice of law must be either directly expressed or should definitely arise from the conditions of the contract or from the aggregate circumstances of the case is based upon an analogous clause in the 1980 Rome Convention. There are elements of a Common Law approach in this formulation uncharacteristic of the Russian legal tradition. Russian jurists observe that the court or arbitral tribunal must look into all the circumstances accompanying the conclusion and performance of the contract, including negotiations, correspondence, place and time of **9.105**

[30] See M G Rozenberg, *Международный договор и иностранное право в практике Международного коммерческого арбитражного суда* [International Treaty and Foreign Law in the Practice of the International Commercial Arbitration Court] (2nd edn, 2000), pp. 16, 18–19. Doubts have been expressed by some Russian jurists as to whether applicable law can be chosen in an arbitral or judicial session. They regard the choice of law as a foreign economic transaction which must be in written form and to which all requirements of the foreign economic transaction apply. The protocol of an arbitral or judicial session in which the agreement on applicable law would be recorded is not signed by the parties and therefore is not properly concluded. See A V Pokrovskaia, «Соглашение о праве, применимом к гражданско-правовым сделкам, осложненным иностранным элементом» [Agreement on Law Applicable to Civil-Law Transactions Complied by Foreign Element], in *Актуальные проблемы гражданского права* [Urgent Problems of Civil Law] (2002), V, p. 355. For the contrary view that an agreement on applicable law is an agreement of a special nature whose validity does not turn on the requirements of form for a foreign economic contract, see Rozenberg, *Международная купля-продажа товаров: Комментарий к правовому регулированию и практике разрешения споров* [International Purchase-Sale of Goods: Commentary to Legal Regulation and Practice of Settlement of Disputes] (2nd edn 2003).

preparation of the text, signature and performance, currency of the contract and payment, and other relevant factors in order to determine the true intention of the parties with regard to applicable law. References to specific clauses of legislation or the use of particular terminology may assist the court or tribunal. Although they regard the result in these situations as less predictable, it is observed that this method of determining the applicable law is extensively used in practice, which testifies to its usefulness, adequacy, and effectiveness.

9.106 A choice of law made by the parties after a contract is concluded operates retroactively and is considered to be valid without prejudice to the rights of third persons from the moment the contract is concluded. The parties may choose a law applicable either to the contract as a whole or to individual parts thereof. The last formulation, which permits the 'fractionalization of a conflicts link', was frowned upon for many years in private international legal doctrine, but has been accepted into Russian law and practice principally because a number of international treaties unifying or harmonizing norms of private international law have included this principle. The intention of the principle is not to juxtapose legal systems which take a profoundly different view of certain legal principles, but perhaps rather to address issues that may arise out of a contract being performed partly in one country and partly in another.

9.107 The Russian Civil Code also gives the parties to a contract not complicated by a foreign element the right to make a choice of law. This is a genuine innovation in Russian civil legislation, never before addressed in Russian legal doctrine but, given the provision, used with some frequency in commercial practice. If, from the aggregate of circumstances which existed when the choice of law was made, it follows that the contract is actually connected only with one country, the choice by the parties of the law of another country may not affect the operation of imperative norms of the country with which the contract is actually connected. Thus, if Russian persons have concluded a contract to be performed on the territory of the Russian Federation that contains no element connected with any other country, it was always assumed in Russian international legal doctrine that Russian law would apply. Under Article 1210(5) of the Civil Code, when a foreign element is absent in a contract the parties nonetheless may at their discretion choose an applicable law.

9.108 Russian jurists regard these provisions as reflective of modern trends in private international law generally: 'Given today's level of internationalization of commercial relations it makes no sense to deprive the parties of the possibility to take advantage of those advantages which a particular foreign legal system provides'.[31]

[31] Vel'iaminov, in T E Abova, M M Boguslavskii, A Iu Kabalkin, and A G Lisitsyn-Svetlanov (eds.), *Постатейный комментарий к Гражданскому кодексу Российской Федерации*,

The limitations on the choice are that the parties may not change imperative norms of the law of the country with which the contract is actually connected. It should be noted, though, that this formulation leaves unclear whether all 'imperative' norms are intended, or only 'super-imperative' norms.

Applicable law in absence of choice of law by parties

Having given the parties to a contract broad discretion to make a choice of law, the Civil Code of the Russian Federation contains detailed rules regarding the applicable law if they fail to exercise that discretion. The basic rule is that in the absence of an agreement of the parties concerning applicable law, the law of the country with which the contract is most closely connected applies (Article 1211, Civil Code). This formulation eliminates the 'dualism' present in prior Soviet-era legislation, which distinguished between contractual obligations in general and foreign economic transactions in this regard. **9.109**

'Close connection' has in view the law of the country where the place of residence or principal place of activity of the party is situated which effectuates the performance having decisive significance for the content of the contract. This is a rebuttable presumption which may be altered by a law, the conditions or essence of the contract, or the aggregate of circumstances of the matter. The Civil Code then elaborates a further set of presumptions, nineteen in all, which designate a particular party as effectuating performance having decisive significance for the content of a contract. This approach places a considerable burden on the Russian court or arbitral tribunal. No specific legal system is named as being applicable; the court or tribunal must make this determination on the basis of the specific dispute. In Russian legislation there is no definition of the 'principal place of activity', although there is a definition of 'place of residence' (Article 20, Civil Code). Taken as a whole, it cannot be excluded that under Article 1211 a Russian court may not, in being guided by a presumption rather than a firm conflicts rule, assess the aggregate of circumstances or the essence of the contract differently and in effect decline to apply the close connection criterion. **9.110**

Special presumptions operate with respect to contracts of construction independent-work, the contract of simple partnership, and contracts concluded at an auction, competition, or exchange. The Civil Code also recognized the concept of 'mixed contract' (Article 421); the applicable law in this event is the law of the country with which the contract, considered as a whole, is most closely connected unless it arises otherwise from a law or the conditions or essence of **9.111**

части первой, второй, третьей [Article-by-Article Commentary to the Civil Code of the Russian Federation. Parts One, Two, and Three] (2005), Article 1210.

the contract, or the aggregate of circumstances of the matter. The intention of the legislator is, of course, to reduce the possibility that the provisions of a mixed contract may become subject to the applicable law of quite different legal systems. The Russian court must therefore seek the 'close connection' of the contract as a whole.

9.112 If trade terms have been used in a contract accepted in international turnover (for example, Incoterms), in the absence in the contract of indications to the contrary it is considered that the application of customs of business turnover to their relations designated by the trade terms has been agreed by the parties. 'Customs of business turnover' are a source of law in the Russian Federation (see Chapter 2). Under this approach a custom of business turnover is accorded priority over a dispositive norm of a law or international treaty since the parties may in their discretion agree otherwise. This provision of Article 1211(6) also reverses or at least narrows the application of Article 421(5), which seeks to establish the predominance of a dispositive norm of a law over customs of business turnover. By Decree of the Board of the Chamber of Commerce and Industry of the Russian Federation of 28 June 2001, No. 117–13, the Incoterms–2000 were deemed to be a trade custom in the Russian Federation. These trade customs fall within the concept of customs of business turnover. The authorization for their adoption by the Chamber of Commerce and Industry is set out in the 1993 Law of the Russian Federation 'On Chambers of Commerce and Industry of the Russian Federation', as amended.[32]

Applicable law in contract with consumer

9.113 Russian legal doctrine has traditionally regarded consumer protection rules as falling into the category of 'super-imperative'. The Civil Code of the Russian Federation (Article 1212) confirms the super-imperative status of consumer protection by providing that an applicable law clause to which a natural person is a party in a contract under which the individual uses, acquires, or orders moveable things or work or services for personal, family, household, and other needs unconnected with entrepreneurial activity cannot deprive this individual of the legal protections granted by imperative norms of law of the country in which the individual has a place of residence, on condition that certain conditions are met.

9.114 *Example:* Russian arbitrazh courts have taken jurisdiction over cases in which a natural person purchased a tour to a foreign country for the purpose of

[32] *Ведомости СНД и ВС Российской Федерации* (1993), no. 33, item 1309; *СЗ РФ* (1995), no. 21, item 1930; (2002), no. 12, item 1093; (2003), no. 50, item 4855.

purchasing goods for subsequent resale and deriving profit and these goods were damaged during carriage by air; the individual sued the tour company for damage to the goods acquired. Although Article 1212 was not applicable in this case, doctrinal commentary suggests that had the individual under these circumstances experienced difficulties with hotel accommodation on the same trip, the individual's status as an entrepreneur should not necessarily prejudice his status as a consumer.

It has been suggested that, notwithstanding the super-imperative character of Article 1212, it is in essence a dispositive provision insofar as, first, it merely provides that the choice of law may not deprive a consumer of the defence granted him by national legislation and not that a choice of law is per se inadmissible; and second, a number of conditions are laid down under which the law of the country of the consumer's place of residence may be applicable to the contract, including those instances when agreement on the applicable law is absent. **9.115**

Applicable law to contract for immoveable property

The 'close connection' test is applied when the parties fail to exercise a choice of law with respect to immoveable property. What property is deemed to be immoveable has been determined by Articles 432 and 1205 of the Civil Code (see above), including property equated to an immoveable. Contracts related to an immoveable do not necessarily qualify; for example, a contract of commission concluded with a view to acquiring immoveable property would not be classified as a 'contract with respect to immoveable property' because the subject of the contract is services related to the conclusion of the transaction but the rights of the parties to the arising, change, or termination of rights in the property itself are not affected. Article 1213 of the Civil Code represents *lex specialis* with respect to Article 1211 (law of country of lessor), such that if a contract concerns the lease of immoveable property, the provisions of Article 1213 (law of country of location of property) will apply in preference to those of Article 1211. **9.116**

Although the *lex rei sitae* is the general rule, situations could arise when Russian law would nonetheless be the applicable law to a contract for the sale of immoveable property situated abroad if the aggregate of circumstances or essence of the contract persuaded a Russian court to so decide. If a foreign citizen who had a permanent residence in the Russian Federation sold immoveable property in a foreign country to a citizen of the Russian Federation also residing in Russia, considering that the personal law of both parties to the contract is Russian law and the place of residence of both parties is Russia, the court might conclude Russian law is applicable to the contract of sale for the property even **9.117** though the property is located outside Russia. The law applicable to the form of a transaction with respect to immoveable property is governed by Article 1209 of the Civil Code (see above).

Applicable law to creation of juridical person with foreign participation

9.118 Under Russian conflicts law, the law of the country in which according to the contract a juridical person is subject to founding applies to the contract concerning the creation of a juridical person with foreign participation (Article 1214, Civil Code). This is an imperative provision which places the law applicable to the creation of a juridical person with foreign participation beyond the discretion of the parties. The reasons for this are attributed in Russian doctrinal writings to historical considerations.

9.119 When it became possible from January 1987 to create joint enterprises with foreign participation in the former Soviet Union, there was no corporative legislation in place other than the governmental decrees on the joint enterprises themselves. Foreign investors commonly decided to conclude the contracts with applicable law clauses which were also related to arbitral clauses for the settlement of disputes in third countries. The Soviet response and then the Russian Federation response was to subordinate such contracts respectively to Soviet and Russian law and then to extend the provisions to all juridical persons, not merely joint enterprises. The provision is interpreted formally to mean the existence of a foreign element in the person of the State affiliation of the founder(s) place of registration.

9.120 Whether a constitutive contract is essential or not depends upon the type of juridical person being created. Such a contract is required for the creation of a limited responsibility society, limited partnership, and full partnership, but is optional for the creation of a joint-stock society, production or consumer cooperative, foundations, social organization, noncommercial partnership, and autonomous noncommercial organization. Under no circumstances does the charter of an organization constitute a constitutive contract. Russian legal doctrine classifies the charter of a juridical person as a local normative act regulating the legal status of a juridical person. Accordingly, the Civil Code contains different conflicts rules with respect to the legal status of a juridical person (Article 1202) and a contract to create a juridical person (Article 1214). Some Russian jurists contend that it should be impossible to split the personal law applicable to the charter and to the contract creating the juridical person.

Operation of law subject to application to contract

9.121 What precisely the law applicable to a contract should extend to is determined by a special provision of the Civil Code of the Russian Federation (Article 1215).

The provision enumerates six circumstances by way of example: (1) interpretation of the contract, which is understood in doctrinal writings to mean both the legal nature of and the conditions contained in the contract; (2) the rights and duties of the parties to the contract; (3) performance of the contract; (4) the consequences of failure to perform or of improper performance of the contract; (5) termination of the contract; and (6) the consequences of invalidity of the contract. Although the list may be considered to be quite minimal, the sphere of the operation of law applicable to a contract is not without limitation; issues of the legal personality and legal capacity of the parties to the contract are determined by personal status and not by contract, as are issues relating to rights to a thing and to requirements for the form of a contract.

Law applicable to assignment of demand

Under the Civil Code (Article 382), the right or demand belonging to a creditor on the basis of an obligation may be transferred by him to another person with regard to the transaction (assignment of demand) or pass to another person on the basis of a law, excluding regressive demands. Unless a law or contract provides otherwise, the consent of the debtor shall not be required to transfer the rights of a creditor to another person. Accordingly, when assignment occurs, relations arise between the initial creditor, and the new creditor and between the new creditor with the debtor, which may raise conflicts of law issues. **9.122**

The general conflicts rules concerning contracts are applicable to the agreement between the initial and the new creditors concerning the assignment of a demand (Article 1216, Civil Code). This would suggest the parties are at liberty to choose an applicable law, and if they fail to exercise this discretion, the law of the country with which the agreement to assign the demand is most closely connected will be the applicable law. Unless it arises otherwise from a law or the essence of conditions of the contract or the aggregate of circumstances of the matter, the law of the country where the place of residence or principal place of activity of the party which makes performance having decisive significance for the content of the contract will be the applicable law. In the case of an assignment, the creditor making the cession would seem to be making the performance having decisive significance. **9.123**

The admissibility of assigning a demand, either contractual or non-contractual, the relations between the new creditor and the debtor, the conditions under which this demand may be presented to the debtor by the new creditor, and whether the debtor has performed his obligation properly are all governed by the law applicable to the demand which is being assigned. The form of the agreement to assign the demand is regulated by Article 1209 of the Civil Code (see above). Russian law would not recognize the assignment of a demand which **9.124** is inextricably linked with the person of the creditor, and in certain instances the consent of the debtor to the assignment is required (Articles 382 and 388, Civil Code). To the extent that after the assignment relations continue to exist between the initial creditor and the debtor, these would be regulated by the law applicable to the assignment of the demand.

Applicable law to unilateral transactions

9.125 A transaction for whose conclusion in accordance with a law, other legal acts, or by agreement of the parties the expression of will of one party is necessary and sufficient is considered to be a unilateral transaction (Article 154, Civil Code). Unless it arises otherwise from a law, the conditions or essence of the transaction, or aggregate of circumstances of the matter, the law of the country applies to unilateral transactions where the place of residence or principal place of activity assuming the obligation under the said unilateral transaction is situated (Article 1217, Civil Code).

9.126 The formulation is controversial in Russian legal doctrine, although its flexibility is widely applauded. Individuals often conclude transactions outside their place of residence or principal place of activity. Unilateral transactions, especially on the Internet, may actually be concluded on no identifiable territory. Powers of attorney, acknowledgements of debt, and testamentary directions may have minimal links with a particular territory, which leads some Russian jurists to prefer an approach based on the law to which the contract or transaction is subordinate. The difficulty with this view is that most unilateral transactions are not a 'contract'. The reference to a 'law' in Article 1217 is regarded by some commentators as a reference not to a law in general, but to a conflicts law.

9.127 The period of operation of a power of attorney and grounds for the termination thereof are determined according to the law of the country where the power of attorney was issued.

Applicable law to payment of interest

9.128 The payment of interest on monetary obligations is subordinated to the imperative rule of the Russian Civil Code (Article 1218) that the applicable law is the law of the country subject to application to the respective obligation. On the one hand, some Russian jurists query why the legislator singled out the payment of interest for special treatment when the Civil Code already contained conflicts rules relating to the applicable law of contracts, unilateral transactions, and obligations in general. On the other hand, having decided to introduce special treatment, the legislator confined such treatment to the grounds for recovery, procedure for calculating, and amount of interest on monetary obligations.

Nothing was said about the means of paying interest, or the legal nature of interest, the impact of insuperable force or force majeure on the calculation of interest, who is at fault in failure to pay interest, and the relationship between interest and penalties, forfeits, and fines.

Russian legal doctrine accordingly suggests that conflicts norms have, as a rule, more general significance than material norms of law and should accordingly be construed more broadly than material norms. In this instance the approach to 'interest' would encompass sanctions for a violation under a law, for the use of a commercial credit, and any variety of contractual interest. **9.129**

Applicable law to delictual obligations

Tort or delict, what Russian law calls obligations arising as a consequence of the causing of harm, are classified as extra-contractual or non-contractual obligations. When conflicts issues arise in this connection, the Russian legal system has long preferred and continues to prefer the principle *lex loci delicti commissii*, the law of the country where the action or other circumstance occurred serving as grounds for the demand concerning compensation of harm. However, in a world with modern technologies, advanced systems of rapid international transport, mass media, and the Internet, it is not uncommon for an act to be committed in one place and the harm caused by this action to ensue in another place, creating the duality of *locus delicti*. Accordingly, Russian law also provides that when, as a result of an action or other circumstance, harm has occurred in another country, the law of that country may apply if the person who caused the harm foresaw or should have foreseen the ensuing of harm in that country. **9.130**

The place where harm ensued is understood to be the location of the victim at the moment when harm ensued to the person of the victim, or the location of the victim's property if harm was caused to his property. The requirement of foreseeability is present to protect the good-faith causer of harm who did not and could not foresee that harm would ensue in the country concerned. The provisions are so formulated that the Russian court has discretion to apply foreign law or not and may exercise initiative in doing so rather than depend upon the parties to the suit to raise the issue. **9.131**

However, if with respect to obligations arising as a consequence of the causing of harm abroad the parties are citizens or juridical persons of the same country, the law of that country should apply. If the parties to such obligations are not citizens of the same country but have a place of residence in the same country, the law of that country applies. This approach is an exception to the territorial principle by giving priority to the personal law of the parties to the delictual obligation in the event of common citizenship, place of residence, or affiliation of juridical persons to the same State. **9.132**

9.133 If a delictual action occurs or other circumstances which entailed the causing of harm, the parties may agree between themselves what should be the applicable law to the obligations that arose. In effect, the parties are granted a certain autonomy of will to make a choice of law. This autonomy of will is limited in time; that is, may be exercised only after the harm has been caused. And their autonomy is confined to deciding whether to choose the law of the country where the court is hearing the dispute. In practice, it would be a rare situation in which Russian law were not the applicable law given relevant Russian conflicts rules.

Operation of law with respect to delict

9.134 The Civil Code (Article 1220) also determines the sphere of operation of law subject to obligations arising as a consequence of the causing of harm. Six consequences are enumerated as examples: (1) the capacity of the person to bear responsibility for harm caused; (2) the placing of responsibility for harm on a person who did not cause harm; (3) the grounds of responsibility; (4) the grounds of limitation of responsibility and relief therefrom; (5) the means of compensation of harm; and (6) the extent and amount of compensation of harm.

9.135 This approach is based not on the personal law of the person who caused harm, but on his delictual capacity in accordance with the status of the delictual obligation.

Applicable law to harm caused by defects of goods, work, or services

9.136 Russian law applies special conflicts rules to consumer protection issues arising out of defects in goods, work, or services, or to demands for compensation of harm caused as a consequence of unreliable or insufficient information concerning the said goods, work, or services. The victim of harm caused by such defects is at liberty to make certain choices of law, with distinctions being drawn between responsibility of the producer for damage caused by his products and responsibility of the producer for introducing poor-quality goods into turnover. The last situation falls into the domain of contractual obligations rather than delictual.

9.137 The victim is given a choice among the law of the country where the seller or manufacturer of the good or other person causing harm has a place of residence or principal place of activity; the law of the country where the victim has a place of residence or principal place of activity; and the law of the country where work was fulfilled, service rendered, or where the good was acquired. The last two choices may be recognized only if the causer of harm does not prove that the good came to the respective country without its consent. And there is a fallback position: if the victim does not take advantage of the choice of law available to him, the applicable law is determined under Article 1219 of the Civil Code (see above).

There are no indications when the choice of law has to be made, which suggests the choice may be made at any time until the court actually renders a decision in the case. **9.138**

Applicable law to obligations arising from unfair competition

Unless it arises otherwise from a law or the essence of the obligation, the law of the country whose market is affected by unfair competition applies to obligations arising as a consequence of such competition (Article 1222, Civil Code). This formulation does not extend to actions violating antimonopoly legislation of the Russian Federation, which would need to be addressed either under the general rules applying to delict or would require an expansive interpretation of unfair competition. **9.139**

The definitions of unfair competition would need to be sought in other Russian legislation, such as the 1991 Law on Competition and Limitation of Monopolistic Activity on Goods Markets, as amended,[33] the 1999 Law on the Defence of Competition in the Financial Services Markets,[34] the Patent Law, the Law on Trademarks, and the 1995 Federal Law on Advertising, as amended.[35] Moreover, the formulation of Article 1222 is not interested in the territory of the country where unfair competition has occurred, but the market where such competition took place, that is, where the negative result occurred or arose as a result of such actions. **9.140**

Law applicable to unfounded enrichment

The law of the country where enrichment occurred applies to obligations arising as a consequence of unfounded enrichment. However, the law of the country where this dispute is being considered may be chosen as the applicable law by agreement of the parties (Article 1223, Civil Code). In the majority of instances the place where enrichment occurred will be known to the creditor and the **9.141**

[33] *Ведомости СНД и ВС Российской Федерации* (1991), no. 16, item 499; (1992), no. 32, item 1882; *СЗ РФ* (1995), no. 22, item 1977; (1998), no. 19, item 2066; (2000), no. 2, item 124; (2001), no. 1(I), item 2; (2002), no. 12, item 1093; no. 41, item 3969; (2005), no. 10, item 761.

[34] *СЗ РФ* (1999), no. 26, item 3174; (2002), no. 1(I), item 2.

[35] *СЗ РФ* (1995), no. 30, item 2864; (2001), no. 26, item 2580; no. 51, item 4827; (2002), no. 1(I), item 2; (2004), no. 34, item 3530; no. 35, item 3607; no. 45, item 4377; (2005), no. 19, item 1752.

debtor. Accordingly, the Civil Code commences with a link to where the enrichment took place. The place of enrichment will be where the debtor entered into actual possession of property, including through a representative. It may be the place where there is a bank account, or the location of a thing that was received, or the principal place of activity of a debtor who acquired a right of demand unfoundedly, or the place where property determined by generic indicia is mixed with the debtor's property. Often the size of the debt rather than the justness of property claims is the subject of a dispute, and much depends upon the intent and the good faith of the parties. Accordingly, the parties have been given the discretion to choose the law of the country where the court is located that will resolve their disagreement.

9.142 Often enrichment occurs through a breach of the principle of equivalence as a result of a misunderstanding or actions leading to an interruption in performance of an obligation. If unfounded enrichment arose in connection with an existing or proposed legal relation under which property was acquired or saved, to obligations arising as a consequence of such unfounded enrichment applies the law of the country to which this legal relation was or could be subordinated.

Law applicable with regard to inheriting

9.143 The point of departure in determining conflicts issues relating to inheriting is the law of the country where the decedent has his last place of residence, except with respect to immoveable property when the applicable law is the law of the country where this property is situated, and if the said immoveable property has been entered in a State register in the Russian Federation, the applicable law is Russian law. In Russian legislation a distinction is drawn between the 'place of residence' of a citizen and the 'place of sojourn of a citizen'. The place of residence is defined for these purposes in the Civil Code (Article 20). If a citizen had a last place of residence on the territory of the Russian Federation, Russian law is applicable to the status of the inheriting, since this classification of the concept is determined according to Russian law (Article 1187, Civil Code).

9.144 The place of residence of a foreign citizen is the criterion for determining his personal law. If a foreign citizen had a place of residence in the Russian Federation, his personal law is Russian law (Article 1195, Civil Code). A 'normative correlation' thus exists between Articles 1115, 1195, and 1224 of the Civil Code.

9.145 Since the inheriting of immoveable property is determined by the law of the country where such property is located, foreign citizens are limited in the extent to which they may inherit land plots. The general rule is that land plots may be alienated or pass from one person to another by other means to the extent that their turnover is permitted by land legislation. The Land Code of the

Russian Federation essentially reproduces the provision of the 1993 Russian Constitution (Article 62) that foreign citizens and stateless persons enjoy in the Russian Federation rights and bear duties equally with citizens of the Russian Federation except for instances provided by a federal law or international treaty. The Land Code includes foreign citizens and stateless persons in the group of participants of land relations (Article 5) and determines the rights of foreign citizens and stateless persons to acquire land plots in ownership (Articles 15, 22, 28, 30, 35, and 36, Land Code). However, the limitations on foreigners in owning land also extend to inheritance relations. Foreigners may not own nor inherit land plots located in frontier territories and other special territories of the Russian Federation, nor land plots granted for personal subsidiary or dacha husbandry, gardening, or individual construction, or land plots of agricultural designation or a participatory share in the common ownership thereof.

The capacity of a person to draw up and revoke a will, including with respect to immoveable property, and also the form of such will or act of revocation thereof, is determined according to the law of the country where the testator had a place of residence at the moment of drawing up such will or act. However, the will or revocation thereof may not be deemed invalid as a consequence to comply with the form if it satisfies the requirements of the place where the will or act of revocation was drawn up or the requirements of Russian law. **9.146**

The Russian Federation is not a party to any of the general multilateral international treaties which further the unification of inheritance relations. However, the 1993 Minsk Convention furthers regional unification to some extent. A number of bilateral treaties of the Russian Federation on legal assistance or on consular relations address inheritance relations. **9.147**

Part IV

THE STATE AND FOREIGN RELATIONS

10

INTERNATIONAL LAW AND THE RUSSIAN LEGAL SYSTEM

Having dealt briefly (Chapter 2) with the role of international law, including international treaties of the Russian Federation, as sources of Russian law, we turn to the general dialogue in Russian legal doctrine about the relationship between international law and the Russian legal system and then consider specific Russian legislation addressed to traditional domains or branches of international law: diplomatic and consular law, the law of treaties, the law of territory, and others. **10.01**

A. International Law and the Russian Legal System

The point of departure is the provision of the 1993 Russian Constitution (Article 15[4]) stipulating that 'generally-recognized principles and norms of international law and international treaties of the Russian Federation' are an 'integral part' of its legal system. The literature on what constitutes a 'legal **10.02** system' and how it may or may not differ from a 'system of law' is truly vast in the Russian Federation, mostly as part of an abstract jurisprudential discussion, but inconclusive. Given the fact that the term 'legal system' is a term of constitutional law, Russian jurists consider the category of legal system to be inadequately and unsatisfactorily analysed.[1] Some jurists insist upon the necessity to define and distinguish a 'legal system' from a 'system of law';[2] whereas others have doubted whether the term 'legal system', being a theoretical scholarly conception, is an appropriate term for a constitution.[3] Some are beginning to distinguish among a 'constitutional' understanding of a legal system and that term as used in the theory of law.

10.03 A number of writers emphasise that a 'legal system' consists of a number of inter-related elements connected with the legal realities existing within a particular State, among them legal norms, institutions, and principles, legal institutions, legal consciousness, and legal culture. A 'legal system is a complex collective, multi-tiered phenomenon which does not coincide either with the system of law or the system of legislation, but rather combines these and other concepts'.[4] Talalaev identified 'system of law' with the structure of law as a normative formation comprised of the branches and institutions of law, whereas a 'legal system' is a broader, more expansive concept reflecting the distinctive features of a country's legal reality in the family of national legal systems of the world.[5] There seems to be a consensus among most jurists that a 'legal system' is something more than the aggregate of normative legal acts.

10.04 The place of international legal norms in the legal system is the subject of no less a diversity of doctrinal views. Those who believe a 'legal system' and a 'system of law' are the same emphasize that norms of international law are an integral part of municipal law. An international treaty of the Russian Federation is a source of

[1] See the observations of S Iu Marochkin, *Действие норм международного права в правовой системе Российской Федерации* [Operation of Norms of International Law in the Legal System of the Russian Federation] (Tiumen, 1998), p. 31.

[2] See L P Anufrieva, *Соотношение международного публичного и международного частного права: правовые категории* [Correlation of Public International Law and International Private Law: Legal Categories] (2002), pp. 110–11.

[3] E T Usenko, «Соотношение и взаимодействие международного и национального права и российская конституция» [Correlation and Interaction of International and National Law and the Russian Constitution], *Московский журнал международного права*, no. 2 (1995), p. 18.

[4] G N Manov, *Теория государства и права* [Theory of State and Law] (1995), p. 180.

[5] A N Talalaev, «Соотношение международного и внутригосударственного права и Конституция Российской Федерации» [Correlation of International and Municipal Law and the Constitution of the Russian Federation], *Московский журнал международного права*, no. 4 (1994), p. 4.

Russian law.[6] Danilenko referred to generally-recognized principles and norms of international law and international treaties of the Russian Federation as 'an integral part of the law of Russia'.[7] Lukashuk has written that 'when we speak of the "application of norms of international law", then bear in mind that we speak about norms of internal law created in accordance with norms of international law'.[8] Perhaps a more persuasive view has been expressed by Khlestova: 'the introduction of international law into the Russian legal system means that it is incorporated in all elements of the legal system, including the application of law and legal consciousness'.[9] Sandutsa concurs, taking the position that norms of international law are part of the legal system, and the system of law, and the system of legislation, but disagrees with Lukashuk and maintains that norms of international law included in the legal system do not become municipal norms.[10] It is suggested that international law remains distinct within the Russian legal system because the Constitution did not provide that international law is part of the 'law' of Russia.[11]

The range of doctrinal opinion as to whether international legal rules need **10.05**
to be received by way of being transformed, incorporated, or in some way reprocessed, and whether such processes may be implicit or explicit, or whether international legal rules are of direct application unless their content indicates otherwise, is considerable.[12]

[6] M N Marchenko (ed.), *Теория государства и права: Учебник* [Theory of State and Law: Textbook] (2004), pp. 659–74; A B Vengerov, *Теория государства и права: Учебник* [Theory of State and Law: Textbook] (1998), pp. 427–8.

[7] G M Danilenko, «Применение международного права во внутренней правовой системе России: практика Конституционного Суда» [Application of International Law in the Internal Legal System of Russia: Practice of the Constitutional Court], *Государство и право*, no. 11 (1995), pp. 119–20.

[8] I I Lukashuk, *Нормы международного права в правовой системе России* [Norms of International Law in the Legal System of Russia] (1997), p. 24.

[9] I O Khlestova, «Соотношение международного и внутригосударственного права и Конституция Российской Федерации» [Correlation of International and Municipal Law and the Constitution of the Russian Federation], *Журнал российского права*, no. 2 (1997), p. 23; also see V A Tolstik, «Общепризнанные принципы и нормы международного права в правовой системе России» [Generally-Recognised Principles and Norms of International Law in the Legal System of Russia], *Журнал российского права*, no. 8 (2000), p. 76.

[10] See G I Sandutsa, «Применение общепризнанных принципов и норм международного права в правовой системе России» [Application of Generally-Recognised Principles and Norms of International Law in the Legal System of Russia], *Международное публичное и частное право*, no. 3 (2001), pp. 9, 11, 13.

[11] See V A Kanashevskii, *Международные нормы и гражданское законодательство* [International Norms and Civil Legislation] (2004), p. 31.

[12] For an extensive summary of the views, see B L Zimnenko, *Международное право и правовая система Российской Федерации* [International Law and the Legal System of the Russian Federation] (2006), pp. 176–82.

Generally-recognized principles and norms of international law

10.06 Various views exist as to what generally-recognized principles and norms of international law are, what the distinction is between principles and norms, what constitutes being 'generally-recognized' for the purposes of Russian law, and what the sources of such principles and norms are. Although some believe that international treaties and international custom are sources of the existence of generally-recognized norms of international law,[13] greater emphasis is placed in the post-Soviet era on 'international custom recognized by all or by the majority of States of the world community' as constituting such general principles.[14] It has been observed that the formulation of the 1993 Russian Constitution in Article 15(4) is illogical in that it 'mixes categories of different orders: norms as rules of behaviour and international treaties, which are one of the sources of international law'.[15] If the Constitution is to speak of 'norms', it should 'at least have referred not to international treaties, but to treaty norms'.[16] Be that as it may, the expression 'generally-recognized principles and norms of international law' has been used in United Nations General Assembly resolutions and declarations, documents of international conferences, Russian treaty practice and foreign policy statements, and Russian legislative acts, including besides the 1993 Constitution, the Criminal Code (Article 1[2]), the Code of Criminal Procedure (Article 1[3]), and others. Despite extensive usage, however, there is no international or domestic act which defines the phrase. Russian legal doctrine offers some guidance, but not a great deal.

10.07 Chernichenko approaches the issue as follows. 'Generally-recognized norms' are considered to be such because 'virtually all members of the inter-State community directly or indirectly have agreed to consider them binding upon themselves'. These norms form the body, the carcass, of international law. A 'norm providing for the inviolability of the person of a diplomatic representative, or a norm consolidating the freedom of navigation on the high seas, is generally-recognized. These norms may be reproduced, or confirmed, or clarified in bilateral and multilateral treaties, but this does not diminish their significance as

---

13 L N Shestakov, *Императивные нормы в системе современного международного права* [Imperative Norms in the System of Contemporary International Law] (1981), pp. 33–4.

14 Zimnenko, *Международное право и правовая система Российской Федерации* [International Law and the Legal System of the Russian Federation] (2006), p. 206.

15 Usenko, «Соотношение и взаимодействие международного и национального права и российская конституция» [Correlation and Interaction of International and National Law and the Russian Constitution], *Московский журнал международного права*, no. 2 (1995), p. 17.

16 S V Chernichenko, *Теория международного права* [Theory of International Law] (1999), II, p. 344.

generally-recognized'.[17] Principles of international law, Chernichenko continues, are 'generally-recognized norms of international law of the most general character'.

Other writers have fallen back on slightly different terms without offering a comprehensive definition. Vel'iaminov speaks of 'international legal principles' being especially important in principle norms of international law such as *pacta sunt servanda* or so-called 'complex norms' grouped around a 'basic conceptual rule-principle and clarifying this rule, such as the principle of sovereign equality and respect for rights inherent in sovereignty'.[18] Usenko in an earlier work likewise refers to 'principles of international law' which are the '. . . basic, most general norms thereof and express the ideas underlying the entire system of international law'.[19] In a later work 'generally-recognized principles of international law' are said to be identical with 'basic principles of international law', and such principles not only possess 'legal, but also political and moral authority. The principles are universal, that is, generally-binding norms; the said principles are relegated to imperative norms'.[20] **10.08**

Yet another standard textbook prefers the concept of a 'universal norm of international law', understood to be a norm 'regulating relations whose object represents universal interest and is recognized by the overwhelming majority or by all States'. Principles of international law have the following characteristics: they are the most important fundamental norms of international law constituting the normative basis of the entire international legal system; they are the most general norms; they are generally-recognized norms binding upon all States; they are imperative norms *jus cogens* having the highest legal force; they have a universal sphere of operation and determine the content and methods of cooperation of States in various spheres; and they are mutually related and of a complex character.[21] **10.09**

Taking Russian international legal doctrine as a whole, as Zimnenko aptly puts it, the position would seem to be that 'any generally-recognized principle **10.10**

[17] Chernichenko, *Нормы и принципы международного права* [Norms and Principles of International Law] (1998), pp. 9, 13.

[18] G M Vel'iaminov, *Международное экономическое право и процесс: академический курс* [International Economic Law and Procedure: Academic Cours] (2004), p. 101.

[19] Usenko, «Соотношение категорий международного и национального (внутригосударственного) права» [Correlation of Categories of International and National (Municipal) Law], *Советское государство и право*, no. 10 (1983), pp. 49–50.

[20] E T Usenko and G G Shinkaretskaia (eds.), *Международное право* [International Law] (2003), p. 41.

[21] G V Ignatenko and O I Tiunov (eds.), *Международное право: Учебник* [International Law: Textbook] (1999), pp. 93–95.

is a generally-recognized norm of international law, but not every generally-recognized norm is a generally-recognized principle of international law'.[22] Lukashuk has observed that: 'in ascertaining the status of generally-recognized principles and norms of international law in the legal system of a State one should take into account that custom serves as the basic form of their existence'.[23]

10.11 *Example:* The Supreme Court of the Russian Federation, leaving in force a decision of the court of first instance, noted in a Ruling of 28 April 2000 that

> in discussing the question of the possible adoption of R by foreign citizens—the spouses G, the court well-foundedly came to the conclusion that such adoption was unlawful since in violation of the provisions of international law—Articles 16 and 17 of the Declaration on Social and Legal Principles Relating to the Protection and Welfare of Children [generally-recognized principle of international law, the source of which is international custom—WEB], especially when transferring children for nurturing and adoption on the national and international levels, the 1989 Convention on the Rights of the Child [law of treaties—WEB], and of Russian legislation—Articles 122, 123, and 124 of the Family Code of the Russian Federation [State practice—WEB] . . . the principle of priority arrangement of the child for nurturing in a family of Russian citizens was not complied with . . . Consequently, when deciding the question of adoption of R by foreign citizens the norms of international law defending the interests of children were not fulfilled and Russian legislation on the priority arrangement thereof for nurturing in a family of origin—citizens of the Russian Federation and the procedure provided for these purposes for recording children left without the care of parents was not complied with.[24]

International Treaties of the Russian Federation

10.12 The definition of a treaty set out in the 1969 Vienna Convention on the Law of Treaties has been incorporated virtually verbatim in the 1995 Federal Law on International Treaties of the Russian Federation.[25] In a case which could arise only in the Russian language, where the term *договор* depending upon context could be translated either as 'contract' or 'treaty' (one reason why in the Russian language the term 'international treaty' is so widely used,

[22] Zimnenko, *Международное право и правовая система Российской Федерации* [International Law and the Legal System of the Russian Federation] (2006), p. 212.

[23] I I Lukashuk, in «Всероссийская научно-практическая конференция. Нижегородский юридический институт, сентябрь 1995 года: Российская правовая система и международое право: современные проблемы взаимодействия», *Государство и право*, no. 3 (1996), p. 25.

[24] Case cited in Zimnenko, *Международное право и правовая система Российской Федерации* [International Law and the Legal System of the Russian Federation] (2006), p. 238.

[25] *СЗ РФ* (1995), no. 29, item 2757. The Vienna Convention entered into force for the USSR on 29 May 1986.

although in principle the same could mean 'international contract'), the Supreme Arbitrazh Court held:

> In a Decree of 24 December 2002 in Case No. 6018/02 the Supreme Arbitrazh Court of the Russian Federation noted that the 'court of cassational instance rightly pointed out that the contract of international carriage of goods can not be regarded as carriage provided for by an international treaty (or agreement), the definition of the concept of which was given in Article 2(a) of the Federal Law 'On International Treaties of the Russian Federation'.[26]

Although the 1995 Federal Law on International Treaties distinguishes among inter-State treaties concluded in the name of the Russian Federation, inter-governmental treaties in the name of the Russian Government, and inter-departmental treaties in the name of federal agencies of executive power, all such treaties are in equal measure international legal obligations of the State as a whole, irrespective of what agency of the State concluded the treaty. Treaties become binding upon the Russian Federation after the completion of any formalities of ratification, accession, or approval and the entry of the treaty formally into force.[27] **10.13**

Example: In a Decision of 5 March 2003 the Supreme Court of the Russian Federation investigated norms of international law whose provisions might be applicable in the case; however, in connection with the absence thereof the demands of the applicant to deem illegal point 10(c) of the 1998 Rules for Recording Military Servicemen Subject to Discharge from Military Service and Citizens Discharged from Military Service into the Reserve or Retirement and Service in Internal Affairs Agencies Who Need to Receive Dwelling Premises or Improvement of Housing Conditions in a Selected Permanent Place of Residence, confirmed by Decree of the Government of the Russian Federation, No. 1054, were not satisfied. In the decision of the Court it was noted that **10.14**

> Article 3 of the Agreement on the Provision with Dwelling Premises of Military Servicemen, Citizens Discharged from Military Service, and Members of their Families in States-Participants of the Commonwealth of Independent States of 28 March 1997 provided that the said category of persons when moving to a permanent place of residence from the territory of one to the territory of another State-participant are provided at the chosen place of residence with dwelling premises according to norms established for citizens of the State on whose territory they arrived. The said Agreement extends its operation to military servicemen (except

[26] *Вестник Высшего Арбитражного Суда Российской Федерации*, no. 5 (2003), p. 6.

[27] But see Tikhomirov, who argued that 'all international legal acts "enter" the legal system of Russia only after their ratification, approval, or accession'. Iu A Tikhomirov, «Реализация международно-правовых актов в российской правовой системе» [Realisation of International Legal Acts in the Russian Legal System], *Журнал российского права*, no. 3 (1999), p. 90.

military servicemen on active service) undergoing military service in States-participants of the CIS who were previously in military service in the Armed Forces of the former USSR, in the United Armed Forces of the CIS, and also citizens from among the said servicemen discharged from military service after 31 December 1991 and members of their families and who are foreign citizens with respect to the State of their sojourn or who have the right to acquire citizenship of the State-participant on whose territory the permanent place of residence was selected. This Agreement was signed by Armenia, Belarus, Kazakhstan, Kyrgyzia, Russia, and Tadzhikistan. So far the said Agreement has not entered into force for Russia. On the basis of the foregoing, it is necessary to conclude that in the event of the fulfilment of municipal procedures and ratification of the Agreement, the Russian Federation will assume the duty with regard to providing dwelling premises on the conditions of social rental only of military servicemen and citizens discharged from military service who underwent military service in States-participants of the CIS, were previously in military service in the Armed Forces of the former USSR or United Armed Forces of the CIS and moved from Armenia, Belarus, Kazakhstan, Kyrgyzia, and Tazhikistan for a permanent place of residence in Russia.[28]

10.15 The view has been expressed in Russian international legal doctrine that only ratified international treaties are an integral part of the legal system of Russia. Danilenko observed: 'Article 15(4) of the Constitution does not speak of treaties ratified by the Russian Federation; obviously it had in view precisely such treaties'.[29] However, this is not what the Constitution says.[30]

10.16 The 1995 Federal Law on International Treaties provides, based on Article 25 of the 1969 Vienna Convention on the Law of Treaties, that an international treaty or part thereof may before its entry into force be applied provisionally by the Russian Federation if this is provided in the treaty, or an arrangement about this was reached with the parties who signed the treaty (Article 23). It would follow to some that the State not only has the right but is obliged to implement the respective treaty provisions, including in municipal relations. Talalaev was of a different opinion,[31] pointing out that provisionally-applied international treaties are not subject to obligatory publication and therefore do not become part of

---

[28] Unpublished decision; reported in Zimnenko, *Международное право и правовая система Российской Федерации* [International Law and the Legal System of the Russian Federation] (2006), pp. 252–3.

[29] See G M Danilenko, «Применение международного права во внутренней правовой системе России: практика Конституционного Суда» [Application of International Law in the Internal Legal System of Russia: Practice of the Constitutional Court], *Государство и право* no. 11 (1995), pp. 116–17.

[30] See W E Butler, *The Law of Treaties in Russia and the Commonwealth of Independent States: Text and Commentary* (2002).

[31] A N Talalaev, «Два вопроса международного права в связи с Конституцией РФ» [Two Questions of International Law in Connection with the Constitution of the Russian Federation], *Государство и право*, no. 3 (1998), p. 70.

the legal system of Russia. If the parties intend a treaty to be provisionally applied, official publication of the treaty must be arranged.

International law does not require that treaties be in written form, although the 1969 Vienna Convention does not apply to oral treaties. Official publication of an oral treaty would appear to require reduction to written form if the treaty is to be regarded as an integral part of the Russian legal system. At the inter-State level 'international treaties are binding irrespective of form and the principle *pacta sunt servanda* extends to all treaties'.[32] Whether, however, particular oral, or gentlemen's, agreements are treaties is questioned in doctrinal writings. Two examples commonly cited are the London Gentlemen's Agreement between the USSR, the United States, and the United Kingdom and other countries concerning the principle of just geographic distribution of seats for nonpermanent members of the United Nations Security Council and the so-called Gentleman's Agreement on the voting rules at the United Nations Conference on the Law of the Sea. Lukashuk regards both as a simplified form of international agreement in oral form having moral and political, but not legally, binding force, whereas Talalaev regards gentlemen's agreements as international treaties which are legally binding.[33] **10.17**

The official publication of treaties depends in part upon whether they are inter-State, intergovernmental, or interdepartmental. An international treaty, consent to which is expressed in the form of a federal law (ratification, accession, confirmation), is subject to publication in the *СЗ РФ* and *БМД*. Intergovernmental treaties are published in the *БМД*. Interdepartmental treaties are published in the designated official gazettes of the respective departments. The publication of treaties of the Russian Federation which have entered into force in other sources which are not official will not be used by Russian courts. The 2003 Decree of the Plenum of the Supreme Court of the Russian Federation, No. 5, provides that: **10.18**

> . . . proceeding from the meaning of Article 15(3) and (4) of the Constitution of the Russian Federation and Article 5(3) of the Federal Law on International Treaties of the Russian Federation those international treaties which have entered into force and which have been officially published in the *Собрание законодательства Российской Федерации* or in the *Бюллетень международных договоров* in the procedure established by Article 30 of the said Federal Law may be applied directly by courts. International treaties of the

[32] Talalaev, *Венская конвенция о праве международных договоров. Комментарий* [Vienna Convention on the Law of Treaties. Commentary] (1997), p. 19.

[33] Lukashuk, *Современное международное право международных договоров* [Contemporary Law of International Treaties] (2004), I, p. 540; Talalaev, *Венская конвенция о праве международных договоров. Комментарий* [Vienna Convention on the Law of Treaties. Commentary] (1997), p. 19.

Russian Federation of an interdepartmental character shall be published by decision of federal agencies of executive power in the name of which such treaties have been concluded in the official publications of those agencies.

International treaties of the USSR which are binding upon the Russian Federation as the State-continuer of the USSR have been published in official publications of the Supreme Soviet of the USSR and Council of Ministers (or Cabinet of Ministers) of the USSR. The texts of the said treaties also have been published in the collections of international treaties of the USSR, but this publication was not official.

Official communications of the Ministry of Foreign Affairs of the Russian Federation concerning the entry into force of international treaties concluded in the name of the Russian Federation and in the name of the Government of the Russian Federation shall be subject to publication in the same procedure as international treaties (Article 30, Federal Law 'On International Treaties of the Russian Federation').

10.19 The 1995 Federal Law on International Treaties entered into force on 15 July 1995, from which date the requirement for official publication commences. Between the period from 1 January 1992 to 15 July 1995 an international treaty of the Russian Federation was published in the procedure established by the Edict of the President of the Russian Federation 'On International Treaties of the Russian Federation' of 11 January 1993; this publication also is considered to be official. In its capacity as the State-continuer of the former Soviet Union, the Russian Federation also considers to be official the texts of treaties published in the official gazettes of the USSR.

10.20 *Example:* The regional State unitary enterprise 'Vichug Cotton Depot' brought suit in the Arbitrazh Court of Ivanovo Region against the Ivanovo Customs Office to deem invalid a demand for customs payments of 15 February 2001, No. 1, in the amount of 5,188,853.43 rubles. By a decision of 23 April 2001 the suit was satisfied. By Decree of the appellate instance of 18 June 2001 the decision was left without change. Not agreeing with the judicial acts adopted, the Ivanovo Customs Office brought a cassational appeal to the Federal Arbitrazh Court of the Volga-Viatka District requesting the decision and decree of the Arbitrazh Court of Ivanovo Region be vacated. In refusing to satisfy the cassational appeal the arbitrazh court emphasized that 'in accordance with Article 15 of the Constitution of the Russian Federation international treaties of the Russian Federation are an integral part of its legal system and subject to official publication. This requirement of the Constitution of the Russian Federation was consolidated in Articles 24 and 30 of the Federal Law of 15 July 1995, No. 101-ФЗ 'On International Treaties of the Russian Federation'. Since an agreement of 10 October 2000 at the moment of imposing the customs demands was not published, the value-added tax from the enterprise must be paid in accordance with Part Two of the Tax Code of the Russian Federation. On 10 October 2000 an Agreement on the Principles of Recovering Indirect

Taxes in Mutual Trade was concluded between the Government of the Russian Federation and the Government of the Kyrgyz Republic. The said Agreement was ratified by the Russian Federation by a Law of 27 December 2000, No. 154-ФЗ. In accordance with Article 9 of the Agreement, it enters into force from 1 January of the year following the year of the fulfilment by the parties of the necessary municipal procedures. After the fulfilment by the parties of the necessary municipal procedures, the Agreement entered into force from 1 January 2001. In accordance with Article 15(4) of the Constitution of the Russian Federation, generally-recognized principles and norms of international law and international treaties of the Russian Federation are an integral part of its legal system, and if other rules have been established by an international treaty than provided for by a law, the rules of the international treaty shall apply. In accordance with Article 30(1) of the Federal Law of the Russian Federation 'On International Treaties of the Russian Federation', international treaties which have entered into force for the Russian Federation, decisions concerning the consent to which have been adopted in the form of a federal law, are subject to official publication upon the recommendation of the Ministry of Foreign Affairs of the Russian Federation in the *Собрание законодательства Российской Федерации*. International treaties which have entered into force for the Russian Federation (except for treaties of an interdepartmental character) are officially published upon the recommendation of the Ministry of Foreign Affairs of the Russian Federation also in the *Бюллетень международных договоров* (Article 30(2), Federal Law on treaties). Thus, an international treaty of the Russian Federation must be brought to general information by means of publication. The arbitrazh court applies international treaties of the Russian Federation—international-legal agreements concluded by the Russian Federation with a foreign State(s)—which have entered into force and been duly brought to general information. In the contested instance the Agreement between the Government of the Russian Federation and the Government of the Kyrgyz Republic on the principles of recovery of indirect taxes in mutual trade of 10 October 2000 was not published in January–February 2001 and therefore the said agreement is not subject to application.[34]

The same treaty apparently provoked litigation in Moscow. On 5 December 2001 the Federal Arbitrazh Court of Moscow District issued a decree which, it has been argued, should have become a 'turning point' on the path towards the reform of Russian legislation on the procedure for the publication of **10.21**

[34] Unpublished Case No. 490/5-K, Decree of 28 August 2001, Archive of Federal Arbitrazh Court, Volga-Viatka District, as reported in Zimnenko, *Международное право и правовая система Российской Федерации* [International Law and the Legal System of the Russian Federation] (2006), pp. 265–6.

international treaties. The facts were similar to those in the preceding example. The customs agency believed the Russo-Kyrgyz treaty was in force, referring to a 'teletype' message circulated to Russian customs houses on 7 February 2001. The Russian arbitrazh courts, however, held that although the treaty may have entered into force for Russia, until it was official published it was not subject to application within the Russian legal system. One jurist commented that this decision would be greeted with 'enthusiasm' by Russian commercial interests: 'Russia by reason of its own delays in the publication of international treaties not substantiated by any objective reasons will frequently bear the risk of loss of reputation as a good-faith participant of international relations fulfilling international treaties which have entered into force'.[35]

10.22 *Example:* When considering a case concerning the deeming of demands of the Voronezh Customs House to be illegal, the Arbitrazh Court of the Voronezh Region unfoundedly applied the Protocol of 29 May 2001 on Making Changes and Additions to the Protocol to the Agreement Between the Council of Ministers-Government of the Russian Federation and the Government of Moldova on Free Trade of 9 February 1993 (hereinafter: Protocol of 29 May 2001), which served in turn as the grounds for the calculation of customs payments. The Supreme Arbitrazh Court, in vacating the respective judicial acts, in a Decree of 21 December 2004 with regard to Case No. 9366/04 pointed out:

> in leaving the said decision without change the court of appellate and cassational instances indicated that the moment of entry into legal force of the said Protocol is the date of publication of its text in the *Бюллетень международных договоров*, in connection with which the Protocol of 29 May 2001 should be considered to have entered into legal force at the moment of bringing in the good by the society. The conclusions of the judicial instances on the procedure and period of entry into legal force of the Protocol of 29 May 2001 were made on the basis of an incomplete investigation of the circumstances of the case and an incorrect interpretation of the norms of law. In accordance with Article 1(1) of the Agreement on Free Trade of 9 February 1993, the Contracting Parties do not apply customs duties, taxes, and charges having equivalent operation on the export and/or import of goods originating from the customs territory of one of the Contracting Parties and destined for the customs territory of the other Contracting Party. Exceptions from the said trade regime for an agreed nomenclature of goods are formalized by bilateral documents which are an integral part of this Agreement. Later, on 29 May 2001, a Protocol was signed on making changes in and additions to the Protocol to the said Agreement which provided that the parties will inform one another about the introduction of exceptions from the free trade regime in goods specified in Annexes 1 and 2 (white sugar was included on this list) not less

[35] See O D Antsiferov, «Опубликование международных договоров: теория и практика» [Publication of International Treaties: Theory and Practice], in N Iu Erpyleva, M E Gashi-Butler, and J E Henderson (eds.), *Forging a Common Legal Destiny* (2005), p. 624.

than two months before the introduction thereof (Article 1(3), Protocol of 29 May 2001). In accordance with Article 24 of the Vienna Convention on the Law of Treaties, a treaty enters into force in the procedure and within the period provided for in the treaty itself. Moreover, Article 39 of the Convention provides that a treaty may be changed by agreement between the participants and in that procedure which was agreed either in the text of the basic treaty or directly in the agreement itself by which amendments are inserted in the text of the basic treaty. It was provided by articles of the Protocol of 29 May 2001 that the said Protocol enters into force from the moment of receipt by the last of written notification concerning the fulfilment by the parties of municipal procedures necessary for its entry into force. In the materials of the file of the case there is a Letter of the Ministry of Economic Development and Trade of the Russian Federation signed by the deputy head of the legal department in which it is indicated that the Protocol of 29 May 2001 was signed on the basis of Decrees of the Government of the Russian Federation of 9 October 1999, No. 1139, and 27 October 2000, No. 827, by which the text was approved of the Model Protocol on Making Changes in and Additions to the Protocol to the Agreement on Free Trade concluded by the Government of the Russian Federation with States-participants of the CIS . . . The Protocol was signed on 29 May 2001, and published in the *Бюллетень международных договоров*, no. 7 (2002) for July indicating that it entered into force 15 April 2002. In accordance with Article 1(3) of the Protocol of 29 May 2001 the parties inform one another about the introduction of exceptions from the free trade regime in goods specified in Annexes 1 and 2 . . . not less than two months before the introduction thereof. Thus, in order to establish exceptions a special notification is necessary of the Contracting Parties concerning the introduction of exceptions, and also compliance with the two-month period on condition of bringing the new rules to general information. Since the Protocol of 29 May 2001 entered into force only on 15 April 2002, until that moment the 1993 Agreement on Free Trade operated, which provided in Article 1 that exceptions from the free trade regime must be formalized by bilateral documents which are an integral part of the said Agreement. The establishment of exceptions in the procedure agreed by the Contracting Parties in the Protocol of 29 May 2001 might be effectuated only after the entry of the last into force, that is, after 15 April 2002. In the materials of the file of the case there is a statement of the Ministry of Economic Development and Trade of Russia of 17 January 2002 which might be regarded as notification concerning exceptions from the free trade regime; however, the said exceptions could be introduced only after the expiry of the two-month period calculated with respect to the Russian side from 15 April 2002. Information concerning publication of the statement of 17 January 2002 is absent in the materials of the file of the case; this question was not investigated by the court. So that an international treaty could create legal consequences for natural and juridical persons to whose activity its operation extends, in accordance with Article 5 of the Federal Law on International Treaties it is essential to adopt respective legal acts. An international protocol enters into force only from the moment of the publication of such acts. The Protocol of 29 May 2001 provides only for the possibility of introducing exceptions; however, it does not establish them directly. Therefore, the fact of official publication cannot testify that the information concerning the introduction by the Russian side of exceptions from the free trade regime was brought to general notice from 29 January 2002. Consequently, the reference of the State Customs Committee of the Russian Federation in the Letter of 21 January 2003, No. 01–06/1843, to the fact that exceptions from the free trade regime are being introduced from the said date are not subject to application . . . Proceeding from the meaning of legal definitude so that a legal act may directly create rights and duties of natural and juridical persons, it should be accessible to an interested person. Only in this event can the person coordinate his conduct with the respective legal norm and foresee for himself the consequences which the failure to perform entail. When considering the present case the courts did not investigate the question of the fulfilment by the Russian Federation of the internal procedures with a view to bringing to general notice the information on the introduction of exceptions from the free trade regime in goods with the Republic Moldova and the application of customs duties, taxes, and charges, in connection with which the date of the bringing in of the good was not duly compared with the date of the arising with the public of the duty to pay customs duties, taxes, and charges.[36]

10.23 It is not uncommon in Russian State practice for treaties which have entered into legal force to be officially published at a considerably later date, often several years. Notice of the termination or suspension of a treaty can be more problematic; in this case official publication of such notice does not become the official date of termination or suspension. The *Бюллетень международных договоров*, no. 6 (2004) carried an official communication of the Ministry of Foreign Affairs notifying the termination from 18 January 2002 of the 1957 Treaty on legal assistance and legal relations between the USSR and Poland. The termination was notified because the Russo-Polish Treaty of 16 September 1996 on the same subject had entered into force on 18 January 2002.[37] Notwithstanding the fact that Russian courts could not have been aware of the termination of the treaty until mid-2004, the provisions of the 1957 treaty could not have been applied after 18 January 2002; that is, after the fact of termination.

Decisions of international intergovernmental organisations

10.24 Article 15(4) of the 1993 Russian Constitution does not expressly mention the decisions of international intergovernmental organizations as part of the rules of international law which are part of the Russian legal system. It is widely accepted in Russian international legal doctrine that such decisions may be a source of international law and that, as a rule, such decisions are of a recommendatory character.[38] Insofar as such decisions may become or incorporate generally-recognized principles of international law, they would fall under

[36] *Вестник Высшего Арбитражного Суда Российской Федерации*, no. 5 (2005), pp. 28–34.

[37] *БМД*, no. 5 (2002), pp. 56–86.

[38] I I Lukashuk, *Международное право в судах государств* [International Law in the Courts of States] (1993), p. 172.

Article 15(4); otherwise, the Russian Federation must by means of municipal law-creation incorporate the decisions or the substance of the decisions of organs of international intergovernmental organizations into Russian law.

Decisions of European Court of Human Rights

On 30 March 1998 the Russian Federation ratified the Convention for the Protection of Human Rights and Fundamental Freedoms (the European Human Rights Convention) (Rome, 4 November 1950; TS 71 (1953); Cmd 8969) with the changes introduced by Protocols 3, 5, and 8 and additions contained in Protocol 2 and the Protocols thereto, Nos. 1, 4, 7, 9, 10, and 11. These all entered into force for the Russian Federation from 5 May 1998, except for Protocol No. 7, which entered into force for Russia from 1 August 1998 and Protocol No. 11, in force from 1 November 1998. As of 1 January 2006 the European Court of Human Rights had considered in substance more than sixty cases involving the Russian Federation. **10.25**

The Federal Law on the ratification of the 1950 European Human Rights Convention provides the basis for treating judgments of the European Court of Human Rights (ECHR) directed against the Russian Federation as binding in the Russian legal system with respect to the interpretation and application of international acts. Interpretation encompasses those legal positions (precedents of interpretation) set out by the ECHR in its judgment. Questions of application of the 1950 Convention include the execution of judgments rendered against the Russian Federation or the renewal of arbitral or criminal proceedings. **10.26**

There are various theories in Russian legal doctrine about the relationship between decisions and judgments of the ECHR and the Russian legal system. Zimnenko observes that judgments of the ECHR perform two basic functions. The first is the consolidation of the Court's legal position in the text of the judgment, and this becomes part of the legal system, but not the system of law, of Russia because precedents of interpretation are not themselves legal norms and consequently do not become incorporated into municipal law. Russian State agencies are required to have regard to those legal positions consolidated in judgments of the ECHR. Although other decisions and judgments of the ECHR are rendered with regard to other States-parties to the 1950 Convention, these judicial acts, Zimnenko contends, are not part of the legal system of Russia and therefore not binding upon Russia. However, Russian State agencies may be guided by these decisions and judgments, having regard to their precedential nature, and also being guided by the generally-accepted principle of international law—the good faith performance of international obligations. Moreover, 'interpretative evolution' may occur in the jurisprudence of the ECHR. **10.27**

However, in his view the fact that Russia is bound by decisions of the ECHR rendered against her and that these have become part of the legal system of Russia does not mean that these judgments '. . . are sources of a law of precedent of Russia'.[39] Other Russian jurists argued that every decision of the ECHR, irrespective of whether it was adopted with respect to Russia, becomes part of the system of law of the Russian Federation.[40] It is believed that Russian legislation and judicial practice both under the European Convention and the Russian Constitution may not diverge from the provisions and standards of the Convention, nor '. . . may Russian laws diverge from the case law created by the principal official interpreter of the European Convention—the European Court of Human Rights'.[41]

10.28 Russian judicial practice does have regard to ECHR decisions and judgments which are considered by some Russian jurists not to be binding upon Russia. The Constitutional Court of the Russian Federation has on several occasions invoked specific decisions of the ECHR when deciding its own cases and the Russian Federation was not a party to the said cases. In other words, the Russian Constitutional Court has drawn upon, cited, and relied upon decisions of the ECHR even though the cases involved other countries. Moreover, the cases referred to were decided by the ECHR prior to 5 May 1998; that is, prior to the date when the Convention entered into force for the Russian Federation.[42]

10.29 *Example:* In a decision of 17 October 2003 the Supreme Court of the Russian Federation pointed out that Article 1 of Protocol No. 1 to the European Human Rights Convention does not impute the duty of the State to maintain the purchasing power of monies placed in financial institutions. To confirm this legal position the Supreme Court referred to the decision of the ECHR of 29 August 2002 in the Case of Appolonov v. Russian Federation, the decision of the European Commission of 6 March 1980 in the Case of X v. the Federal Republic of Germany, the decision of the ECHR of 7 September 1999 in the

---

[39] Zimnenko, *Международное право и правовая система Российской Федерации* [International Law and the Legal System of the Russian Federation] (2006), pp. 315–16, 319.

[40] See K N Ratsiborinskaia, «Применение международного права российскими судами» [Application of International Law by Russian Courts], *Международное публичное и частное право*, no. 1 (2004), p. 26.

[41] See P Laptev and G Gadzhiev, «Предисловие» [Preface], in Iu. Iu. Berestnev (ed.), *Европейские правовые стандарты в постановлениях Конституционного Суда Российской Федерации* [European Legal Standards in Decrees of the Constitutional Court of the Russian Federation] (2003), p. 7.

[42] A new version of the official Russian text of the European Convention was published in *СЗ РФ* (2001), no. 2, item 163. Decisions of the ECHR are issued in the monthly *Бюллетень Европейского Суда по правам человека* [Bulletin of the European Court of Human Rights] (Moscow, 2004–).

Case of Rudzinska v. Poland, and the decision of the ECHR of 2 July 2002 in the Case of Haiduk v. Ukraine.[43]

A 2005 Decree of the Plenum of the Supreme Court of the Russian Federation, No. 3 'On Judicial Practice With Regard to Cases on the Defence of Honour and Dignity of Citizens, and also Business Reputation of Citizens and Juridical Persons' drew the attention of Russian courts of ordinary jurisdiction to the fact that when settling disputes in this domain they should be guided not only by norms of Russian legislation (Article 152, Civil Code of Russian Federation), but also by reason of Article 1 of the Federal Law on the ratification of the European Human Rights Convention to take into account the legal position of the ECHR expressed in its judgments and concerning the interpretation and application of that Convention. In particular, said the Supreme Court, the concept of defamation used by the ECHR is identical to the concept of the dissemination of defaming information which does not correspond to reality as set out in Article 152 of the Civil Code. And Russian courts must do so not only when implementing the Convention, but also when applying norms of national legislation.[44] **10.30**

Insofar as a judgment of the ECHR creates a legal fact, it affects both material and procedural Russian law. If by judgment of the ECHR the Russian Federation is obliged to pay compensation to a private individual, for example, since that judgment is part of the legal system of the Russian Federation municipal legal relations arise between the State in its person of its financial agencies and the private individual pursuant to which the State has a duty to pay the sums due. These would be relations of material law. **10.31**

Procedural legal relations would arise especially in connection with the Code of Criminal Procedure (Article 413) or the Code of Arbitrazh Procedure (Article 311). Under the Code of Criminal Procedure the grounds for instituting a criminal proceeding is a violation established by the ECHR of the provisions of the European Human Rights Convention in the event of the consideration by a court of the Russian Federation of a criminal case connected with: (a) the application of a federal law not corresponding to the provisions of the European Human Rights Convention; or (b) other violations of the European Human Rights Convention.[45] Under the Code of Arbitrazh Procedure a violation established by the ECHR of the provisions of the European Human Rights Convention in the event of the consideration by an arbitrazh court of a specific case in connection with the adoption of a decision with regard to which **10.32**

[43] *Бюллетень Верховного Суда Российской Федерации*, no. 12 (2004), pp. 13–14.

[44] *Бюллетень Верховного Суда Российской Федерации*, no. 4 (2005), p. 3.

[45] *СЗ РФ* (2002), no. 22, item 2027.

the applicant has applied to the ECHR also is grounds for a review of judicial acts on the basis of newly discovered circumstances. The Code of Civil Procedure does not contain analogous provisions, although the judges in courts of ordinary jurisdiction might be guided by analogy of lex as a means of filling the gap.

Conflicts of precedence between international and national law in Russia

10.33 In theory, according to some jurists, a conflict between a norm of international law and a norm contained in sources of national law is impossible because they are by definition norms of different legal systems which may interact but not collide with one another. Chernichenko believes that 'when one speaks of the priority of international legal norms, treaty or treaty and customary . . . in the event of their divergence from norms of municipal law, we understand by this if one adheres to the dualist conception, the priority of "readdressed", transformed norms which have become municipal, that is, the priority of some norms of municipal law over others in the event conflicts arise between them'.[46] Mironov shared the same view: 'being autonomous and independent legal categories, national and international law and norms thereof may not be in hierarchical dependence on one another'.[47] Conflicts may arise, however, between legal norms if those norms regulate the same category of social relations, either relations between subjects of international law or relations between subjects of municipal law. The conflict, as a rule, lies in the existence of contradictions between norms forming the legal system of the State such that when one norm is applied there is automatically a violation of another norm which cannot be resolved by interpretation.

10.34 *Example:* An enterprise brought suit in the arbitrazh court of the Maritime Territory against the State Tax Inspectorate in the City of Nakhodka to deem the decision thereof partly invalid. The Tax Inspectorate had been guided when rendering a decision by the Instruction of the State Tax Service of Russia of 16 June 1995, No. 34, 'On the Taxation of Profit and Revenues of Foreign Juridical Persons'. According to this Instruction taxes are withheld from the revenues of foreign juridical persons at source in the Russian Federation for all types of revenues in all instances of the payment of such revenues, and when there is an international treaty in which lower rates of taxes or complete exemption from taxation in the Russian Federation has been established, the excess withheld is refunded in accordance with point 6.2 of the Instruction. Thus, the

[46] S V Chernichenko, *Теория международного права* [Theory of International Law] (1999), I, p. 342.

[47] N V Mironov, *Международное право: нормы и их юридическая сила* [International Law: Norms and the Legal Force Thereof] (1980), p. 95.

Instruction established the duty to pay taxes in all instances. However, by virtue of Article 11(1) of the Convention between the Government of the Russian Federation and the Government of the United Kingdom of Great Britain and Northern Ireland of 15 February 1994 for the Avoidance of Double Taxation and the Prevention of Fiscal Evasion with Respect to Taxes on Income and Capital Gains, which entered into force on 18 April 1997, 'interest arising in a Contracting State and paid to a resident of the other Contracting State shall be taxable in that other State if such resident is the beneficial owner of the interest'. Thus, unlike the aforesaid Instruction, the provisions of the international treaty provided for the right of a private person not to pay certain taxes on revenues in the Russian Federation and, as a consequence, the Russian Federation had no right to recover such taxes from the private person. Taking into account that the provisions of the said international treaty were not taken into account by the court of first instance, the Supreme Arbitrazh Court by a Decree of 25 April 2000 with regard to Case No. 5029/99 vacated the judicial acts of inferior instances, and the case was sent for consideration to the court of first instance.[48]

The conflict between the Instruction of the State Tax Inspectorate and the treaty provision was resolved in favour of the treaty, which has greater hierarchical force within the Russian legal system than the subordinate normative legal act of an administrative department. **10.35**

Whereas the 1993 Constitution of the Russian Federation explicitly gives priority to treaties which contain rules that differ from norms of national legislation, the legal force of generally-recognized principles of international law within the legal system of the Russian Federation is not regulated. Chernichenko observed that 'it would be natural and logical to believe that all international-legal customary norms recognized by Russia . . . in transformed form have priority over laws of Russia in the event of their divergence from the last'.[49] Khlestova considers that 'generally-recognized principles and norms of international law have priority over national law since Russia favours undeviating compliance with international treaty and customary norms, adhering to the principle of good-faith fulfilment of treaty obligations which have been consolidated in the preamble of the Law on International Treaties'; however, she believes that the 1993 Russian Constitution has hierarchical priority over the said international legal norms.[50] Danilenko argued that 'generally-recognized principles and norms of **10.36**

[48] *Вестник Высшего Арбитражного Суда Российской Федерации*, no. 8 (2000).

[49] Chernichenko, *Теория международного права* [Theory of International Law] (1999), II, pp. 345–6.

[50] I O Khlestova, «Соотношение международного и внутригосударственного права и Конституция Российской Федерации» [Correlation of International and Municipal Law and the Constitution of the Russian Federation], *Журнал российского права*, no. 12 (1997), p. 24. Marchenko shares this view: '. . . it follows that the Constitution of the Russian

international law do not have priority with regard to internal legal acts contrary to them', and adds that one should have recourse to such norms only '. . . when an international treaty subject to application is lacking'.[51]

10.37 Tiunov would give preference to generally-recognized principles and norms of international law expressed in the form of an international custom as '. . . having unlike the rules of many treaties, a universal and fundamental character, and in a number of instances are even endowed with the properties of imperativeness. The priority of such norms over a municipal act in the form of a law by a Constitution recognizing the subordination of a law to an international treaty—is presumed'.[52]

10.38 Neither Russian international legal doctrine, nor Russian legislation and judicial practice offer an unequivocal answer to the issue. Individual Russian legislative acts which enumerate what sources of law a court or State agency is to apply in its activity are inconsistent in the sequence in which these acts are listed. The 1996 Federal Constitutional Law on the Judicial System of the Russian Federation refers, for example, to the '. . . unity of the judicial system of the Russian Federation being ensured by means of: . . . the application by all courts of the Constitution of the Russian Federation, federal constitutional laws, federal laws, generally-recognized principles and norms of international law and international treaties of the Russian Federation . . .' (Article 3).[53] The 2002 Federal Constitutional Law on a Military Situation refers to '. . . the Constitution of the Russian Federation, present Federal Constitutional Law, federal laws adopted on the basis thereof, and other normative legal acts of the Russian Federation, and also generally-recognized principles and norms of international law and international treaties of the Russian Federation in this domain' (Article 2).[54] However in the 1996 Federal Law on Defence reference is made to acting '. . . in

Federation with respect to ratified and all other international treaty acts of Russia has absolute priority'. See M N Marchenko, «Международный договор в правовой системе современной России» [The International Treaty in the Legal System of Contemporary Russia], in Erpyleva, Gashi-Butler, and Henderson, *Forging a Common Legal Destiny* (2005), p. 598. For a contrary view, see M P Avdeenkova and Iu A Dmitriev, *Конституционное право Российской Федерации Курс лекций* [Constitutional Law of Russia. Cours of Lectures] (2002), I, p. 120.

[51] Danilenko, «Материалы Научно-практической конференции по применению международного права правоохранительными органами Российской Федерации, состоявшейся в г. Москве с 7 по 9 февраля 1996 года» [Materials of Scientific-Practical Conference With Regard to Application of International Law by Law Enforcement Agencies of the Russian Federation Held in the City of Moscow from 7 to 9 February 1996], *Государство и право*, no. 5 (1996), p. 139.

[52] O I Tiunov, «Конституционный Суд и международно-правовые акты об обеспечении прав человека» [Constitutional Court and International Legal Acts on Ensuring Human Rights], *Журнал российского права*, no. 7 (1997), p. 9.

[53] *СЗ РФ* (1997), no. 1, item 1; transl. in Butler, *Russian Public Law* (2005), pp. 361–2.

[54] *СЗ РФ* (2002), no. 5, item 375.

accordance with generally-recognized principles and norms of international law and international treaties of the Russian Federation, federal constitutional laws, federal laws, and normative legal acts of the President of the Russian Federation and other normative legal acts of the Russian Federation' (Article 19).[55]

The 2001 Labour Code of the Russian Federation and 2003 Customs Code of the Russian Federation use different and noncommittal formulations. The Labour Code entitles the relevant provision 'Laws, Other Normative Legal Acts Containing Norms of Labour Law, and Norms of International Law' (Article 10), which indicates the legislator did not distinguish between generally-recognized principles and norms of international law and international treaties.[56] In the Customs Code the relevant provision was entitled 'Operation of International Treaties of the Russian Federation in the Domain of Customs Matters' (Article 8), where the legislator either ignored generally-recognized principles of international law or assimilated them to treaties. **10.39**

Sometimes doctrinal writings become so preoccupied with legal logic that they lose sight of what is being analysed. If international law recognizes any hierarchy in the world of treaties, that hierarchy turns primarily on the universality of the treaty and the generality of its provisions. In the domain of customary rules of international law, generally-recognized rules should be categorized as super-imperative, imperative, and dispositive. The category of super-imperative would embrace rules *jus cogens.*[57] Imperative norms are those which States may not contract out of but which nonetheless do not command the degree of imperativeness or fundamentalness characteristic of super-imperative rules. Dispositive norms are those which by agreement the parties are able to choose or not as the case may be. Generally-recognized dispositive norms would include the rules concerning diplomatic immunity, which may be modified by individual States by agreement between themselves. Not all Russian jurists accept the distinction between super-imperative and imperative rules. **10.40**

Turning to hierarchy, it would follow that an international treaty whose provisions are contrary to *jus cogens* is void. Zimnenko would go further: '. . . within the framework of the legal system of Russia provisions of imperative customary law norms must be a hierarchical force greater than an international treaty of the Russian Federation and a law'.[58] However, **10.41**

[55] *СЗ РФ* (1996), no. 23, item 2750.

[56] *СЗ РФ* (2002), no. 1, item 3; transl. in W E Butler, *Labour Code of the Russian Federation* (2004).

[57] See T N Neshataeva, 'The Court and Generally-Recognized Principles of International Law', in Erpyleva, Gashi-Butler, and Henderson, *Forging a Common Legal Destiny* (2005), p. 570.

[58] Zimnenko, *Международное право и правовая система Российской Федерации* [International Law and the Legal System of the Russian Federation] (2006), p. 366.

> . . . the Constitution of the Russian Federation within the framework of the legal system of Russia has higher legal force with regard to all municipal normative acts, and also provisions provided for by imperative norms of international law. In the event of a conflict between constitutional provisions and the aforesaid international legal provisions, a State agency must, according to the Constitution of the Russian Federation, be guided by the rules consolidated in the Constitution of the Russian Federation.[59]

Neshataeva takes the opposite view: '. . . in the event of a divergence between a generally-recognized principle of international law and a principle of any national Constitution in the domain of human rights, the generally-recognized principles of international law have priority'.[60]

10.42 As regards dispositive generally-recognized norms of international law which have become part of the Russian legal system, these should be applied if other norms have not been provided for by sources of Russian national law and if with respect to such municipal norms there have not been protests on the part of other subjects of inter-State relations regulated by the respective dispositive norm.[61]

10.43 If more than one treaty is concluded between the same States on the same subject, '. . . they must take into account the hierarchical level of the treaties already concluded and to be concluded with regard to the same questions'.[62]

10.44 *Example:* Zhumurov and Konnov were accused of intentional homicide committed with special cruelty by a group of persons by prior arrangement for hooligan motives. The Third District Military Court returned the criminal case to the procuracy of the 'Baikonur' Complex to separate the case with respect to citizen of the Republic Kazakhstan Zhumurov and resolution of the question of

[59] Zimnenko, (2006), p. 367. Tumanov wrote: '. . . generally-recognized principles and norms of international law . . . in its legal system occupy a subordinate place with respect to the Constitution of the Russian Federation as the highest law of the country. They may not operate contrary to it'. V A Tumanov, «Российская правовая система и международное право: современные проблемы взаимодействия» [The Russian Legal System and International Law: Contemporary Problems of Interaction], *Государство и право*, no. 2 (1996), p. 4.

[60] T N Neshataeva, «Арбитражные суды и некоторые вопросы применения международного права в Российской Федерации» [Arbitrazh Courts and Certain Questions of the Application of International Law in the Russian Federation], *Российский ежегодник международного права 1998–1999* (1999), p. 221. Also see Lukashuk: '. . . one may with every reason speak about the primacy of generally-recognized norms on human rights in the legal system'. Lukashuk, *Нормы международного права в правовой системе России* [Norms of International Law in the Legal System of Russia] (1997), p. 54.

[61] Zimnenko, *Международное право и правовая система Российской Федерации* [International Law and the Legal System of the Russian Federation] (2006), pp. 375–6.

[62] N V Mironov, «О соотношении юридической силы норм международного права» [On the Correlation of the Legal Force of Norms of International Law], *Советское государство и право*, no. 9 (1979), p. 136.

his transfer to law enforcement agencies of the Republic Kazakhstan. To substantiate its decision the Court referred to point 6.12 of the Treaty of Lease of the 'Baikonur' Complex concluded 10 December 1994 between the Russian Federation and the Republic Kazakhstan, according to which the jurisdiction of the Russian Federation extends solely to its citizen military servicemen, civilian personnel of the Russian Federation, and members of their families. The question was raised in the protest of the procurator of the 'Baikonur' Complex of vacating the decree of the judge of the district military court since the court should have been guided not by the said Treaty, but by the Agreement concluded on the basis thereof between the Governments of the Russian Federation and the Republic Kazakhstan of 4 October 1997 'On the Interaction of Law Enforcement Agencies in Ensuring Legal Order on the Territory of the "Baikonur" Complex', ratified by the Federal Law of 8 October 2000, No. 123-ФЗ. Article 5 of the Agreement relegates to the jurisdiction of Russia the consideration of all cases concerning violations of law committed on the territory of the Complex, except for crimes committed by citizens of the Republic Kazakhstan against the Republic Kazakhstan or its natural and juridical persons. By virtue of Article 59 of the 1969 Vienna Convention on the Law of Treaties a prior treaty is applied only to the extent that its provisions are compatible with the provisions of the subsequent treaty, and in the event of the incompatibility of provisions excluding the simultaneous application of the treaties, the prior treaty in this part is considered to be terminated. Thus, in this situation the Agreement of 4 October 1997 is subject to application since it treats questions of jurisdiction differently from the Treaty of 10 December 1994.[63]

Thus, in resolving conflicts arising directly between treaty provisions which have become part of the legal system of Russia the principles of hierarchy and of priority are applied while having regard to the rules operating in the Russian legal system; in particular, the hierarchical position of the State agency which expressed consent in the name of the State to the said treaty being binding. **10.45**

B. Organs of Foreign Relations

Under the 1993 Russian Constitution (Article 71[l]) the foreign policy and international relations of Russia are within the jurisdiction of the Federation. By an Edict of the President of the Russian Federation of 12 March 1996 the Ministry of Foreign Affairs was given the coordinating role in conducting a unified foreign policy line for the Russian Federation.[64] In July 2000 the **10.46**

[63] *Бюллетень Верховного Суда Российской Федерации*, no. 7 (2001), pp. 18–19.
[64] *СЗ РФ* (1996), no. 12, item 1061.

Conception of Foreign Policy of the Russian Federation[65] set out the legal basis of the Conception as comprising the Russian Constitution, federal laws, other normative legal acts of the Russian Federation regulating the activity of federal agencies of State power in the sphere of foreign policy, generally-recognized principles and norms of international law and international treaties of the Russian Federation, as well as the Conception of National Security of the Russian Federation, confirmed by Edict of the President of the Russian Federation on 10 January 2000.[66]

President of Russian Federation

10.47 In his capacity as the Head of State, the President of the Russian Federation represents the Russian Federation in international relations (Article 80(4), Russian Constitution), directs foreign policy, confirms the military doctrine and foreign policy doctrine, conducts negotiations, and signs international treaties. After consultations with relevant committees and commissions of the Federal Assembly of the Russian Federation, the President appoints diplomatic representatives to foreign States and international organizations and accepts the credentials and letters of recall of foreign diplomatic representatives.

10.48 As Commander-in-Chief of the Armed Forces of the Russian Federation, the President exercises the rights provided for by international law in the event of war.

Federal Assembly of Russian Federation

10.49 The parliament or principal legislative body of a country is not traditionally classified as an agency of foreign relations by either international legal doctrine or by the domestic law of a country. Foreign policy is routinely regarded as the responsibility primarily of the executive branch and the Head of State.

10.50 In the Russian Federation, both chambers of the Federal Assembly nonetheless exercise significant foreign relations functions. The Federal Assembly has constitutional responsibility for the ratification of certain categories of international treaties. From time to time the chambers will hold hearings on foreign policy questions or enact resolutions, declarations, or appeals on individual foreign policy issues, or determine in certain situations when the Armed Forces of the Russian Federation may be used. In 1995 the State Duma adopted a law which would have terminated Russian participation in international sanctions against Yugoslavia and thereby breached Russian obligations under the United Nations Charter, prompting a veto from the President of Russia and a reminder that it

[65] *Российская газета*, 11 July 2000.

[66] *СЗ РФ* (2000), no. 2, item 170.

was desirable that the State speak with a single voice in foreign policy matters.[67] When Russia reached agreement with Ukraine over boundaries and jurisdiction in the Sea of Azov and connecting straits, the Russian parliament sought to impose additional reservations and criteria for compliance.

The Federal Assembly, just as most other parliaments of the world, maintains links, including treaty links, with other parliaments and with international parliamentary organizations.[68] Delegations are sent and received, and experience exchanged. Insofar as the Federal Assembly approves the State budget which finances the foreign relations functions of all ministries and departments and of the State as a whole, it also performs a foreign relations function. **10.51**

Judicial system

Although the courts are not organs of foreign relations in the classical sense, they are extensively involved in relations with a foreign element, as discussed several places elsewhere in this study. We merely observe here that the judiciary as such maintains relations with the judiciary in foreign countries and with international organizations. **10.52**

Government of Russian Federation

The powers of the Government of the Russian Federation in the domain of foreign policy are set out in the most general form by the 1993 Russian Constitution: to effectuate measures with regard to ensuring the realization of foreign policy (Article 114). In effect, the Government implements the foreign policy determined by the President of the Russian Federation; that is, as stipulated in the Federal Constitutional Law on the Government of the Russian Federation, effectuates direction in the sphere of ensuring the relations of Russia with foreign States and international organizations.[69] **10.53**

Ministry of Foreign Affairs

The departments of foreign affairs are agencies of executive power which manage the foreign relations of the Russian Federation. Chief among these is the Ministry of Foreign Affairs of the Russian Federation, whose activities are governed by the 2004 Statute on the Ministry confirmed by Edict of the President **10.54**

---

[67] President Eltsyn complained: 'Deputies regularly and without qualification intrude into foreign policy questions. This seriously complicates the relations of Russia with other States and undermines the authority of our country'. See *Российская газета*, 4 October 1997.

[68] See A Kh Saidov, *Национальные парламенты мира* [National Parliaments of the World] (2005).

[69] *СЗ РФ* (1997), no. 51, item 5712; (1998), no. 1, item 1; (2004), no. 25, item 2478; no. 45, item 4376; transl. in Butler, *Russian Public Law* (2005), pp. 181–97.

of the Russian Federation.[70] The principal tasks of the Ministry are as follows: (1) working out the general foreign policy strategy of the Russian Federation and submitting respective proposals to the President of Russia; (2) implementing the foreign policy of Russia in accordance with the 2000 Conception of Foreign Policy; (3) ensuring diplomatic and consular relations with foreign States and international organizations; (4) providing diplomatic and international legal protection of the sovereignty, security, and territorial integrity of the Russian Federation and its other interests in the international arena; (5) defending by diplomatic and international legal means the rights, freedoms, and interests of citizens and juridical persons of the Russian Federation abroad; (6) facilitating the interaction of State agencies at the federal level and level of subjects of the Russian Federation in international activity and ensuring that the principle of the unity of foreign policy of Russia and realization of its international rights and obligations is ensured; (7) coordinating the international activity of other federal agencies of executive power and of subjects of the Russian Federation; and (8) facilitating the development of links and contacts with compatriots abroad.

10.55 The Ministry of Foreign Affairs contains within its system four organs and agencies: the central apparatus, foreign institutions (e.g. embassies, consulates), territorial agencies, and organizations within the jurisdiction of the Ministry which enable it to operate on the territory of the Russian Federation. The Statute enumerates no less than forty-nine various powers of the Ministry and thirteen 'rights' which the Ministry may exercise when fulfilling its functions. Within the legal domain, the Ministry of Foreign Affairs submits draft legislation on questions within its jurisdiction; adopts its own normative legal acts with regard to its sphere of activity; prepares draft treaties and submits them in the established procedure as well as proposals concerning the suspension or termination of treaties, concludes interdepartmental treaties within its competence, submits treaty texts for official publication; formalizes powers to conduct negotiations and sign treaties; gives explanations on questions of international law perform; the functions of treaty depositary; watches over compliance with international obligations of the Russian Federation; and registers and records treaties of the Russian Federation, among other functions.

10.56 The Ministry of Foreign Affairs is headed by a minister appointed by the President of the Russian Federation upon the recommendation of the Chairman of the Government of Russia. The minister may in turn have deputy ministers

[70] *СЗ РФ* (2004), no. 28, item 2880; transl. in Butler, *Russian Public Law* (2005), pp. 230–6. This Statute replaced the version of 14 March 1995.

appointed by the President of Russia. The President also appoints the Director General of the Ministry.

The central apparatus of the Ministry is composed principally of departments for the principal orientations of ministry activities and is governed by the Statute on the Central Apparatus of the Ministry of Foreign Affairs. The minister distributes duties among his deputies and the Director General, confirms statutes on the structural subdivisions of the central apparatus and appoints the principal executives of those subdivisions, confirms the structure and personnel establishment of the central apparatus and territorial agencies within the budget,[71] and confers certain levels of diplomatic ranks, among other functions. **10.57**

The Ministry of Foreign Affairs is a juridical person located in Moscow and has its own seal, stamps, and letterheads and other attributes of legal personality. **10.58**

Embassy

An embassy is, under the Statute on an Embassy of the Russian Federation,[72] a State agency of foreign relations which effectuates the representation of the Russian Federation in the receiving State and is founded by decision of the Government of the Russian Federation on the basis of an edict of the President of the Russian Federation to establish diplomatic relations with a foreign State at the level of embassies (point 1). The embassy is to ensure that the Russian Federation conducts a unified political line in the receiving State by coordinating the activities and control over the work in the receiving State of federal agencies of executive power, Russian State institutions, organizations and enterprises, delegations and groups of specialists, and representations of subjects of the Russian Federation. The embassy and its personnel and family members are required to respect the laws, administrative rules, and the traditions and customs of the receiving State and to refrain from any actions which may be construed as interference in the internal affairs of the receiving State. All enjoy privileges and immunities in accordance with international law and legislation of the receiving State. **10.59**

An embassy is headed by the Extraordinary and Plenipotentiary Ambassador of the Russian Federation in the foreign State, who is the highest official representative of the Russian Federation accredited to the receiving State. The personnel establishment of an embassy is confirmed by the Ministry of Foreign Affairs of the Russian Federation. Sections or groups may be created in the embassy for **10.60**

[71] Financing of the Ministry of Foreign Affairs is regulated in part by the 1995 Decree of the Government of the Russian Federation, No. 1029, 'Questions of Financial and Material Provision for the Ministry of Foreign Affairs of the Russian Federation', as amended. *СЗ РФ* (1995), no. 44, item 4183.

[72] *СЗ РФ* (1996), no. 45, item 5090.

foreign policy, domestic policy, bilateral relations, economic work, science and technology, press and information, culture, consular, and others. The embassy work is structured on the basis of quarterly or semi-annual plans drawn up by taking into account the instructions of the Ministry of Foreign Affairs.

10.61 The opinion of the ambassador is taken into account when the Ministry of Foreign Affairs appoints to senior positions in the embassy (counsellor or higher).

10.62 An embassy is a juridical person and has a seal, stamps and the like, and bank accounts. Land plots, buildings, installations, and other property of an embassy consolidated to it in the procedure established by Russian legislation is the ownership of the Russian Federation. The rights of possession, use, and disposition to embassy property are effectuated by taking into account the legislation of the receiving State.

Ambassador

10.63 Ambassadorial functions are for Russian diplomatic personnel set out in the 1999 Statute on the Extraordinary and Plenipotentiary Ambassador of the Russian Federation in a Foreign State.[73] The Ambassador is the highest official representative of the Russian Federation accredited to a receiving State, where his responsibilities are to carry out the foreign policy of the Russian Federation by diplomatic means and defend the national interests, sovereignty, security, and territorial integrity of the Russian Federation and the rights and interests of its citizens and of Russian juridical persons in the receiving State. The Ambassador is appointed to office and recalled upon the proposal of the Minister of Foreign Affairs by the President of the Russian Federation after consultations with committees and commissions of the Federal Assembly of the Russian Federation. A citizen of the Russian Federation capable of performing by reason of his professional and personal qualities, education, and health may be an ambassador.

10.64 The Ambassador heads the Embassy of the Russian Federation in the receiving State, directly guides its work and determines its structure in accordance with normative acts of the Ministry of Foreign Affairs, and distributes duties among Embassy personnel. He is personally accountable in accordance with the Statute on the Embassy to the Ministry of Foreign Affairs for the proper performance of instructions and missions. During the ambassador's absence in the receiving State, his functions are performed by a chargé d'affaires designated from among the senior diplomatic personnel of the Embassy.

[73] *СЗ РФ* (2000), no. 1(II), item 101. Certain provisions of this Statute are classified.

The ambassador has responsibility for conducting a unified policy line of the Russian Federation in the receiving State and accordingly coordinates the activities and supervises the work of other representations of the Russian Federation in the receiving country, including representations of other ministries and departments, Russian State institutions, organizations, and enterprises, and their delegations and groups of specialists, and representations of subjects of the Russian Federation. The heads of these representations, delegations, and groups are obliged to coordinate their activities with the ambassador as the official accredited representative of the Russian Federation and to assist the ambassador in exercising his powers and inform the ambassador about their activities. **10.65**

An ambassador has the right, *inter alia*, to conduct negotiations on behalf of the President, Government, or Ministry of Foreign Affairs to sign international treaties of the Russian Federation with the receiving State and to participate in international conferences and meetings, and to make proposals with regard to bilateral relations with the receiving State and to Embassy activities. He also may suspend the execution of decisions and prevent actions in the receiving State of representatives of federal agencies of executive power and similar agencies of subjects of the Russian Federation, Russian State institutions, organizations, and enterprises if such decisions and actions are not in the interests of the Russian Federation. **10.66**

Consulates

Russian consulates principally operate in accordance with the 1963 Vienna Convention on Consular Relations, the 1976 Consular Statute of the USSR,[74] and the 1998 Statute on a Consular Institution of the Russian Federation.[75] The 1998 Statute does not extend to honorary consuls. A consulate is a State agency of foreign relations of the Russian Federation which, within its consular district on the territory of the receiving State, exercises consular functions in the name of the Russian Federation. A consulate is opened by decision of the Government of the Russian Federation on the basis of a treaty between Russia and the respective foreign State. A consulate is within the system of the Ministry of Foreign Affairs and subordinate in the receiving State to the head of the diplomatic representation of the Russian Federation. **10.67**

Consulates are subdivided into general consulates, consulates, vice consulates, and consular agencies. The class or category of consulate and the consular district is determined by the Government of the Russian Federation with the **10.68**

[74] *Ведомости Верховного Совета СССР* (1976), no. 27, item 404 (1981), no. 7, item 156; *Свод законов СССР*, IX, p. 24; transl. in W E Butler, *Collected Legislation of the USSR and Union Republics*, pp. 1–21; *International Legal Materials*, XV (1976), 1178–90.

[75] *СЗ РФ* (1998), no. 45, item 5509.

consent of the receiving State. Consular sections also may be opened within a consular district on the same basis, and consular sections may be created within diplomatic representations of the Russian Federation in order to perform consular functions. On the building or territory of a consulate the State flag and State arms of the Russian Federation are displayed, together with the name of the consulate in the Russian language and State language(s) of the receiving State. The State symbols of the Russian Federation are used by taking into account the protocol practice of the receiving State. The consulate and its personnel and members of their families enjoy privileges and immunities in the receiving State in accordance with international law and the legislation of the receiving State (see Chapter 8 above).

10.69 The legal functions of a consulate are substantial and significant. Among them are: to offer passport and visa services in the receiving country; to perform notarial actions; the registration of acts of civil status; the legalization of documents; representation of citizens in courts and other institutions of the receiving State; to provide legal assistance in civil, family, and criminal cases; to take measures to locate missing Russian citizens within the consular district; and to participate in preparing draft treaties of the Russian Federation with the receiving State.

10.70 Depending upon its class or category, a consulate is headed by a consul general, consul, vice consul, or consular agent. The head of the consulate, appointed by the Ministry of Foreign Affairs, bears personal responsibility for the performance of his functions, distributes duties among consulate personnel, and determines in accordance with Ministry normative acts the structure of the consulate. The personnel establishment of the consulate is determined by the Ministry of Foreign Affairs. Only a citizen of the Russian Federation may be a consular official.

10.71 With the consent of the receiving State, the Ministry of Foreign Affairs of the Russian Federation may entrust the performance of individual consular functions to honorary consuls of the Russian Federation, pursuant to the Statute on the Honorary Consul of the Russian Federation, confirmed by Order of the Ministry of Foreign Affairs of 13 October 1998. Either a citizen of the Russian Federation or a citizen of a foreign State chosen from among individuals who have a prominent social position in the receiving State and who possess the requisite personal qualities may be an honorary consul. An honorary consul is not considered to be a Russian civil servant. His task is to defend the rights and interests of the Russian Federation and the citizens and juridical persons thereof in his consular district.

10.72 Honorary consuls are subdivided into the following classes: Honorary Consul General, Honorary Consul, Honorary Vice Consul, and Honorary Consular

Agent. The location of the residence and chancellery of the honorary consul and his class and consular district are determined by agreement with the receiving State. The honorary consul has what is called the 'consular requisite': a State flag of the Russian Federation and the consular shield bearing the State arms of the Russian Federation and a seal depicting the State arms of the Russian Federation and name of the consulate in the Russian language, together with stamps and letterheads. The consular requisite is in the State ownership of the Russian Federation. The chancellery of a consulate headed by an honorary consul is kept separate from the clerical work, having no relation to consular duties, and mixing or combining such is not permitted.

An honorary consul is appointed by the Minister of Foreign Affairs of the Russian Federation or person replacing him upon the proposal of the diplomatic mission or consulate of Russia and with the consent of the authorities of the receiving State. An honorary consul receives a patent certifying his powers and indicating his full name, citizenship, class, consular district, and location of the consulate. The patent is signed by the Minister of Foreign Affairs. A person appointed honorary consul gives a written undertaking that he will properly perform the consular functions placed on him and not require any remuneration; however, the actual expenses connected with the performance of consular actions may be reimbursed from revenues received by the honorary consul as fees for consular services according to the rates fixed by the Russian Government. **10.73**

Representation of Ministry of Foreign Affairs in Russia

The Ministry of Foreign Affairs maintains representations on the territory of the Russian Federation which are known as the 'territorial agency' of the Ministry. The territories on which they operate are determined by the Ministry. Such representations are divided into two categories: (a) representations in centres of federal districts; and (b) representations in subjects of the Russian Federation. Those within subjects of the Russian Federation may have sections which perform primarily consular functions. They all operate on the basis of the 2002 Statute on the Representation of the Ministry of Foreign Affairs of the Russian Federation on the Territory of the Russian Federation confirmed by Order of the Ministry of Foreign Affairs, No. 2792.[76] **10.74**

The principal tasks of these representations are: (1) to ensure the interaction of the Ministry of Foreign Affairs with agencies of State power of subjects of the Russian Federation; (2) to assist the plenipotentiary representative of the President of the Russian Federation in the federal district and his apparatus with **10.75**

[76] *БНА РФ*, no. 19 (2002).

regard to questions within the competence of the representation; (3) to participate within the limits of their competence in ensuring control over compliance with norms of international law and international obligations of the Russian Federation when subjects of the Russian Federation effectuate their powers in the domain of international links; (4) to render assistance to subjects of the Russian Federation in preparing and effectuating measures of an international character; (5) to inform on a regular basis the agencies of State power of the subjects of the Russian Federation about basic issues of Russian foreign policy; (6) to assist agencies of local self-government, social associations, and other nongovernmental organizations when they effectuate international links; (7) to participate in resolving questions connected with foreign labour migration of citizens of the Russian Federation and the use of foreign work force in Russia; (8) passport and visa servicing of Russian citizens and juridical persons; (9) visa provision for entry into and exit from the Russian Federation by foreign citizens and stateless persons; and (10) interaction with foreign diplomatic representations in Russia and consulates and representations of international organizations on the territory of their activity.

10.76 A representation is headed by the Representative of the Ministry of Foreign Affairs of the Russian Federation appointed to and relieved from office by Order of the Ministry on the basis of a decision of the College of the Ministry of Foreign Affairs by agreement with the plenipotentiary representative of the President in the Russian Federation in the respective federal district. The powers of the Representative are determined by the Statute on the representation and a special power of attorney issued by the Ministry. The structure and personnel establishment of the representation are determined by the Ministry.

10.77 Representations of the Ministry of Foreign Affairs are not juridical persons, and the fees and charges they recover for formalizing documents are not regarded by the Russian tax authorities as the proceeds of entrepreneurial activity. However, revenues received by a representation from rendering other types of services are subject to taxation in the generally-established procedure.[77]

Trade representations

10.78 Pursuant to the Federal Law on the State Regulation of Foreign Trade, the entire system of trade representations of the Russian Federation was reorganized in 2005 pursuant to the 2005 Decree of the Government of the Russian Federation 'On the Optimization of the System of Trade Representations of the

[77] See the Letter of the Ministry of Finances of the Russian Federation, No. 26, and State Tax Service of the Russian Federation, dated 11 March 1994 'On the Taxation of Representations of the Ministry of Foreign Affairs of the Russian Federation on the Territory of Russia'. *БНА РФ*, no. 6 (1994).

Russian Federation in Foreign States'.[78] The 2005 Decree also confirmed the Statute on the Trade Representation of the Russian Federation in a Foreign State.

With the reorganization of trade representations, it was decided to maintain them in forty-two States, to establish them in eight (all CIS countries), and to eliminate them in fifty-two States as from 1 January 2006. **10.79**

A trade representation is a State agency ensuring the foreign economic interests of the Russian Federation in the receiving State and is founded on the basis of a treaty between Russia and the receiving State. The trade representation is an integral part of the diplomatic representation of the Russian Federation in the receiving State and operates under the direct guidance of the Russian ambassador in that State. The principal tasks of a trade representation are nine: (1) to ensure that the foreign economic policy of the Russian Federation is conducted in the receiving State and promote the expansion and diversification of the Russian export of goods and services and create conditions in the receiving State for realizing the competitive advantages of the Russian Federation and to analyse and forecast the state of foreign economic relations in the receiving State; (2) to participate in ensuring the realization of Russian trade policies and the development of economic links between Russia and the receiving State, and participate in working out and realizing measures to ensure favourable conditions for the integration of the Russian economy into the world economy; (3) to not permit complications to arise in trade and economic relations of Russia with the receiving State; (4) to participate in working out and ensuring the positions of the Russian Federation in international economic organizations; (5) to disseminate information in the receiving State on the Russian economy and investment climate in the Russian Federation; (6) to provide information on tenders to erect objects and to deliver goods and services in the receiving State to interested agencies of the central Russian authorities and subjects of the Russian Federation and to Russian participants in foreign trade turnover; (7) to assist the interests of participants in foreign trade activity in obtaining orders for the delivery of goods, work, and services, including trade information and objects of intellectual property, and the promotion of Russian investment projects abroad; (8) to render assistance in the promotion of Russian goods, services, and objects of intellectual property on the markets of the receiving State and attracting investments to the Russian Federation, and to create favourable conditions in the receiving State for participants in foreign trade activity to obtain credit; and (9) to render assistance in the establishment and development of trade links between natural and juridical persons of the Russian Federation and the receiving State. **10.80**

[78] *СЗ РФ* (2005), no. 27, item 2761.

10.81 The decision whether to establish, reorganize, or liquidate a trade representation or divisions thereof in a receiving State is adopted by the Government of the Russian Federation in accordance with international treaties. A trade representation may conclude in its own name and in the established procedure transactions and other legal actions necessary to effectuate the tasks placed on it and to act as a plaintiff or representative of a plaintiff in courts. However, the trade representation may act as a defendant or respondent in courts only with regard to disputes arising from transactions and other legal actions concluded or performed by the trade representation in the receiving State, and only when the Russian Federation in an international treaty with the receiving State or by means of a statement in a court or written notification within the framework of the examination of a case has expressed consent to subordination of the trade representation to the jurisdiction of the court of the receiving State with regard to the said disputes.

10.82 Although the trade representation is subordinate to the Russian ambassador in the receiving State, general guidance over the activity of the trade representation is effectuated by the Ministry of Economic Development and Trade of the Russian Federation. The structure and personnel establishment of the trade representation is confirmed by this Ministry within the limits of the total personnel establishment of the foreign apparatus of that Ministry. However, the Trade Representative and his deputy are members of diplomatic personnel and enjoy, together with workers of the representation and members of their families, privileges and immunities in accordance with international law. The moveable and immoveable property of the Trade Representation are in the federal ownership of the Russian Federation which the trade representation uses without payment in order to fulfil its functions.

10.83 A trade representation is headed by the Trade Representative of the Russian Federation, who is appointed to and dismissed from office by the Government of the Russian Federation upon the recommendation of the Ministry of Economic Development and Trade agreed with the Ministry of Foreign Affairs. While abroad, the Trade Representative and workers of the trade representation have labour and service relations with the Ministry of Economic Development and Trade.

10.84 The trade representation is a juridical person and has its own seal, stamp, and letterheads and may open settlement and other accounts in banks in the procedure and on the conditions determined by legislation of the Russian Federation and the receiving State. The information and analytical materials having principled significance for the development of relations between the Russian Federation and the receiving State to be sent by the Trade Representation, including through special communications channels, are submitted to the Russian ambassador for familiarization.

Other departments

In its capacity as one of the great powers in the international system, the Russian Federation has found it necessary to disperse foreign relations functions among a vast variety of departments and agencies and to devolve some upon the 87 or so subjects of the Russian Federation. Although the Ministry of Foreign Affairs is first among equals in this respect, the 1995 Federal Law on International Treaties provides specifically for the possibility of interdepartmental treaties that may be concluded by ministries and departments other than the Ministry of Foreign Affairs. Moreover, some foreign relations powers are included in virtually every Statute on an individual ministry or department. The 2004 Statute on the Ministry of Justice, for example, gives the Ministry the right to 'conclude in accordance with legislation of the Russian Federation international treaties of the Russian Federation of an interdepartmental character with regard to questions relegated to the established sphere of activity' (point 8(6), Statute).[79] In fact the Ministry of Justice has extensive cooperation and liaison functions with international organizations and foreign States concerned with crime prevention, narcotics control, extradition, and other matters. The Ministry of Economic Development and Trade, the Ministry of Defence, the Procuracy of the Russian Federation, the Federal Security Service, and a number of other ministries, departments, services, and agencies have extensive foreign relations activities. 10.85

[79] *СЗ РФ* (2004), no. 42, item 4108; transl. in Butler, *Russian Public Law* (2005), pp. 703–10.

11

TERRITORY OF THE RUSSIAN FEDERATION

The territory of the Russian Federation consists of land space within the State boundary of the Russian Federation, subjacent subsoil, superjacent airspace, internal sea waters and the territorial sea of the Russian Federation, navigable rivers which adjoin a neighbouring State along the thalweg, and as designated on non-navigable rivers, on lakes and other waters, water reservoirs of hydro-installations and other artificial water bodies, and on bridges, dams, and other installations. Historically speaking, these boundaries are those of the former RSFSR as consolidated by international treaties and legislative acts of the former Soviet Union as adjusted by international treaties of the Russian Federation. In some locations the adjustment by treaty remains to be accomplished. The legal regime of the State boundary is regulated principally by the 1993 Law on the State Boundary of the Russian Federation, as amended.[1] **11.01**

[1] *Ведомости СНД и ВС Российской Федерации* (1993), no. 17, item 594.

A. Border Relations and Cooperation

11.02 The 1993 Law on the State Boundary requires that the Russian Federation, when regulating legal relations in frontier areas or aquatories and on international transport routes adjacent to Russian territory, be guided by the following principles: (1) ensuring the security of the Russian Federation and international security; (2) mutually-advantageous comprehensive cooperation with foreign States; (3) mutual respect for the sovereignty and territorial integrity of States and the inviolability of State boundaries; and (4) the peaceful settlement of frontier questions (Article 2). For some years the Russian Federation had an Interdepartmental Commission for the Development of Frontier Cooperation; however, it was abolished by Decree of the Russian Government, No. 215, on 16 April 2004.

11.03 There nonetheless remains in place the Conception of Frontier Cooperation in the Russian Federation, confirmed by Regulation of the Government of the Russian Federation, No. 196-p, on 9 February 2001.[2] The Conception sets out the purposes, principles, and priorities in the activities of federal agencies of executive power, agencies of executive power of subjects of the Russian Federation, and agencies of local self-government and citizens in the domain of frontier cooperation. The term 'frontier cooperation' means the coordinated or agreed actions of all the aforesaid agencies and individuals directed towards strengthening the interaction of the Russian Federation with neighbouring countries in encouraging the stable development of frontier territories, enhancing the well-being of the population of frontier territories, and strengthening friendship and good-neighbourliness with those States. In addition to the four principles enumerated in the 1993 Law on the State Boundary, the Conception adds the principles of: (1) mutual respect for the legislation of States effectuating frontier cooperation and respective international treaties; (2) ensuring the interests of Russia in frontier cooperation; (3) not prejudicing the economic and other interests of States effectuating frontier cooperation; (4) taking into account the peculiarities of frontier territories of the Russian Federation and neighbouring States, including their different natures, the character of inter-State relations and historically-formed links with neighbouring States; the natural resource, socio-economic, urban construction, and transport conditions for developing frontier territories; and the nature of threats to the national security of Russia on the frontier territory; and (5) compliance with the 1980 European Outline Convention on Transfrontier Cooperation between Territorial Communities or Authorities.

[2] *СЗ РФ* (2001), no. 8, item 764.

The 'frontier territory' for these purposes encompasses the frontier or border zone the Russian portion of the waters of frontier rivers, lakes and other waters; internal sea waters; territorial sea of the Russian Federation where a frontier or border regime has been established; admittance points across the State boundary of the Russian Federation; the territories of administrative districts and cities; sanatorium-resort zones; especially protested nature territories; objects, and other territories adjacent to the State boundary of the Russian Federation; frontier zone; shores of frontier rivers, lakes, and other waters; sea coast; and admittance points. The territory with regard to which frontier cooperation is being effectuated may be determined either by international treaties of the Russian Federation or in agreements of subjects of the Russian Federation with foreign partners in the procedure determined by Russian Federation legislation. At the federal level such treaties or agreements may be interdepartmental, and juridical or natural persons, including agencies of local self-government, may be participants. **11.04**

The principal tasks of frontier cooperation are several. They include the creation of a situation of confidence, mutual understanding, and good-neighbourliness between agencies of power, business circles, and the population of the frontier territory; the development and strengthening of economic, cultural, and humanitarian links between Russian frontier territories and neighbouring States; the promotion of mutual understanding and friendship between the peoples populating the frontier territories; the simplification of mutual communion of interested agencies of power, business circles, and groups of the population, including ethnic communities separated by the State boundary, and support for compatriots abroad who reside in the frontier territory; the joint creation and effective development of the economic and social infrastructure on frontier territories; the joint resolution of economic, transport, electric power, municipal, ecological, socio-demographic, humanitarian, and other problems of frontier territories; supporting agencies of State power and local government in arranging the public amenities of the frontier territory; creating conditions promoting the movement of export and import goods across the frontier territory and developing frontier cooperation, including public amenities at admittance points on the State boundary, transportation infrastructure, customs houses, terminals, and the like; enchancing the effective use of the production and social base of the frontier territory; effectuating an agreed urban construction policy on the frontier territory; creating conditions for the integration of warning systems and eliminating extraordinary situations of neighbouring States in order to improve the reaction to such situations having transfrontier consequences; the creation of conditions encouraging the population to avoid strategically important and sparsely populated frontier territory; and resistance to manifestations of nationalism, chauvinism, ethnic and religious separatism, and inter-ethnic enmity in the frontier territory. **11.05**

11.06 When Russian State agencies engage in frontier cooperation, they are to take into account the following 'basic factors' determining the distinctive features of frontier territories of the Russian Federation with neighbouring States: the general character of inter-State, including military and political relations, of the Russian Federation with the neighbouring States; the historically-formed links with the neighbouring States and the traditions and customs of the population residing on the frontier territories; the character of the influence of frontier cooperation on the development of inter-regional economic cooperation with the neighbouring States; the peculiarities of the regime of the State boundary of the Russian Federation; the influence of the 'migration factor' on social processes in the frontier territories connected with external, including illegal, migration; ethno-political factors; the state of the protection of public order on the frontier territories and peculiarities of maintaining it; the existence of natural or technogenic conditions for extraordinary situations to arise which have transfrontier consequences; and the peculiarities of ensuring national security on the frontier territory.

11.07 Several types of frontier cooperation are identified in legislation, although the enumeration is not exhaustive. They include: creating joint coordinating agencies for frontier cooperation and working groups attached thereto; holding meetings of empowered agencies of State power on questions of frontier cooperation; concluding agreements on frontier cooperation at whatever level of State cooperation is advisable; and creating working groups for the development of frontier cooperation within the framework of intergovernmental commission for trade and economic and scientific-technical cooperation. Recommended areas of frontier cooperation include frontier trade between Russian juridical and natural persons having a permanent location or place of residence in the frontier territory with neighbouring counterparts; cooperative investment projects, including for the creation of joint enterprises, provision of information to attract investments, formation of joint chambers of commerce and industry, and the conclusion of contracts to attract investments in favoured areas; joint urban construction planning; uniform requirements for the certification of livestock and agricultural products; and the like.

Frontier representatives

11.08 The 1993 Law on the State Boundary makes provision for the appointment, pursuant to international treaties of the Russian Federation, of frontier representatives for certain sectors of the State boundary. These representatives are appointed to settle questions arising out of compliance with the regime of the State boundary and to resolve frontier incidents. There are various designations for such officials: frontier representative, frontier commissar, frontier plenipotentiary, and deputies thereof. They are appointed by the head of the Federal

Security Service of the Russian Federation by agreement with the Ministry of Foreign Affairs.

The settlement of frontier incidents connected with the actions of Russian or foreign military aircraft or warships, other military objects, or military servicemen involves representatives of the Ministry of Defence of the Russian Federation directly unless the participation of frontier representatives is necessary. If such incidents concern objects or servicemen of border guards and the interests of averting the danger of military activity are not involved, the frontier representatives may deal with them. Incidents not involving frontier representatives or the Ministry of Defence are settled through diplomatic channels. **11.09**

Frontier representatives act in accordance with the Statute on Frontier Representatives of the Russian Federation, confirmed by a 1995 Decree of the Government of the Russian Federation.[3] Such representatives have the right, *inter alia*, to cross the State boundary of the Russian Federation in the procedure established by the relevant international treaty; to hold meetings with frontier representatives of neighbouring States on Russian or foreign territories, and to sign acts, protocols, and other documents arising from such meetings; to involve when necessary specialists for the investigation of frontier incidents; to correspond with counterpart frontier representatives in neighbouring States; and to require officials and citizens of the Russian Federation and foreign citizens and stateless persons to comply with legislation of the Russian Federation and international treaties on the State boundary. **11.10**

Defence and protection of State boundary

Under the 1993 Law on the State Boundary, the defence of the State boundary is regarded as a component of ensuring the security of the Russian Federation as a whole and in implementing the State frontier policy of the Russian Federation through the coordinated activities of federal agencies of State power, similar agencies of subjects of the Russian Federation and agencies of local self-government, and organizations and citizens of the Russian Federation. Measures regarding the defence of the State boundary are taken in accordance with the status of the boundary determined by international treaties of the Russian Federation and legislation of Russia. The Russian Federation cooperates with foreign States in this domain on the basis of generally-recognized principles and norms of international law and international treaties of the Russian Federation. **11.11**

There is a distinction between 'defence' and 'protection' drawn in Russian **11.12**

[3] *СЗ РФ* (1995), no. 21, item 1971.

legislation in this connection. 'Defence' of the State boundary has as its purpose to secure the vitally important interests of the individual, society, and the State within the limits of the frontier territories as defined in the Law on the State Boundary. Whereas 'defence' is the duty of all federal agencies of executive power of the Russian Federation, 'protection' is the duty of specially designated agencies within the Federal Security Service.[4] 'Protection' of the State boundary is part of 'defence', and is effected by frontier agencies so as not to permit an unlawful change of the course of the State boundary, and to ensure compliance by natural and juridical persons with the regime of the State boundary, the frontier regime, and the regime at admittance points across the State boundary. In other words 'protection' is a narrower and more specialized term.

11.13 The powers of individual components of the Russian Armed Forces—border guard agencies, anti-aircraft defence forces, naval forces—are laid out in basic form in the 1993[5] Law on the State Boundary. The procedure for the use of weapons and combat technology when defending the State boundary is laid down in a special document confirmed by 1998 Decree of the Government of the Russian Federation, No. 20: 'Procedure for the Use of Weapons and Combat Technology When Defending the State Boundary of the Russian Federation'.[6] The Procedure extends to incidents on land, at sea, on rivers, lakes or other waters, and at admittance points across the State boundary of the Russian Federation. These are in effect rules of engagement that set out in detail precisely under what circumstances weaponry may be used, after what kind of warnings, and who may give the order, and under what circumstances a military serviceman may act autonomously. Russian aircraft are in addition subject to a special 1994 Decree of the Government of the Russian Federation, No. 977, 'On the Procedure for the Use of Weapons and Combat Technology When Protecting the State Boundary of the Russian Federation in Air Space'.[7]

11.14 Special regulations apply to defence of the State boundary in the northern Caucasus pursuant to treaties concluded with Azerbaidzhan and Georgia: the 1999 Decree of the Government of the Russian Federation, No. 1223, 'On Measures With Regard to the Prevention of Penetration on the Territory of the Russian Federation of Members of Foreign Terrorist Organizations, Bringing in

[4] In March 2004 the system of Russian State agencies involved in ensuring the security of Russia was substantially reorganized, and the Federal Frontier Service abolished; its functions were transferred to the Federal Security Service. See the Edict of the President of the Russian Federation, No. 308, 'On Measures With Regard to Improvement of State Administration in the Domain of Security of the Russian Federation'. *СЗ РФ* (2004), no. 12, item 1101.

[5] *СЗ РФ* (1999), no. 45, item 5439.

[6] *СЗ РФ* (1998), no. 2, item 273.

[7] *СЗ РФ* (1997), no. 43, item 4982. The Decree was not published until 1997. It replaced a joint Decree of the Central Committee of the Communist Party and USSR Council of Ministers dated 26 April 1961, No. 392–166, also unpublished.

of Weapons and Means of Sabotage at Established Admittance Points Across the State Boundary of the Russian Federation Within the Northern Caucasus Area'.[8]

Citizens are directly involved in a voluntary basis in the defence of the State boundary within frontier territories. There are several possible capacities: members of social associations, voluntary people's guards, and non-establishment personnel of frontier agencies, among others. The procedure for involving citizens has been established by a 1995 Decree of the Government of the Russian Federation, No. 339.[9] The tasks of volunteers include ensuring control over compliance with the regime of the State boundary, frontier regime, and regime at admittance points; participating in the search for persons attempting to illegally cross or who have illegally crossed the State boundary, and explaining to citizens the rules for the regime of the State boundary, frontier regime, and regime of admittance points. This is an exhaustive list of tasks; others may not be imposed. **11.15**

Volunteers have the right to assist border detachments in verifying documents which persons have and help inspect means of transport and goods carried on them, help detain persons suspected of violating the regime of the State boundary and deliver persons detained to structural subdivisions of the border guard, headquarters of the people's guard, or other places to determine their identity and circumstances of the violation, take measures to ensure the preservation of material evidence when border guards suppress violations; and assist border guards when a temporary limitation or prohibition of traffic of citizens or means of transport is imposed. **11.16**

Admittance points

The 1993 Law on the State Boundary provides that persons, means of transport, cargoes, goods, and fauna are admitted across the State boundary at 'admittance points' in established sites. 'Admittance' consists of recognition of the legality of crossing the State boundary by persons and means of transport which have arrived on the territory of the Russian Federation or of authorization of such persons or means of transport to leave the Russian Federation by crossing the State boundary. Foreign citizens and stateless persons who have not been authorized entry into the Russian Federation or who have been prohibited entry are not subject to admittance to Russia (see Chapter 5 above). **11.17**

The organizational, financial, economic, and other grounds for the establishment, opening, functioning, and closure of admittance points, which are **11.18**

[8] *СЗ РФ* (1999), no. 45, item 5439.

[9] *СЗ РФ* (1995), no. 17, item 1545.

intended to ensure international communication of the Russian Federation with other States, are regulated by the 1998 Statute on Admittance Points Across the State Boundary of the Russian Federation, confirmed by a 1998 Decree of the Government of the Russian Federation, No. 60.[10] The territory of an admittance point consists of a complex of buildings, premises, installations, and appropriate technological equipment to carry on the official activities of the border guard, customs, and other types of control, internal affairs agencies, and transport and other enterprises and organizations which enable the work of the admittance point to be carried out. The precise means of control are set out in the 2005 Statute on the Application of Means and Methods of Control When Effectuating the Admittance of Persons, Means of Transport, Cargoes, Goods, and Fauna Across the State Boundary of the Russian Federation.[11] Motor vehicles are subject to special regulations confirmed by the Ministry of Transport of the Russian Federation.[12]

11.19 The locations of admittance points are various: airports, seaports, river and fishing ports, aerodromes, frontier railway stations, and specially-designated sites near frontier localities; In addition, where appropriate State inspectorates may be created, or State supervision or control agencies for such matters as aviation safety, immigration, quarantine, navigability of vessels, and so on.

11.20 Admittance points are classified into: (1) sea, river, air, motor vehicle, railway, and pedestrian, by type of international transport; (2) passenger, cargo, and cargo-passenger, by type of international transport; and (3) permanent, temporary, and seasonal, by work regime. Admittance points may be multilateral (for natural persons irrespective of citizenship) or bilateral (for inhabitants or citizens of the Russian Federation and of the neighbouring State, including in a simplified procedure). Decisions of the Government of the Russian Federation to establish admittance points, indicating the classification thereof, are published in the official press and, when necessary, brought to the attention of diplomatic missions or consulates of foreign States in the Russian Federation and abroad, and interested international organizations by the Ministry of Foreign Affairs.

11.21 The 'initiators' of establishing an admittance point may be federal agencies of executive power and agencies of executive power of subjects of the Russian Federation. They follow a formal petitioning process, with supporting documentation, set out in the 1998 Decree No. 60. Expenses for an admittance point may be shared between the federal and inferior budgets.

---

[10] *СЗ РФ* (1998), no. 4, item 485. [11] *СЗ РФ* (2005), no. 6, item 462.

[12] Order of the Ministry of Transport of the Russian Federation, No. 3, of 9 January 1997, as amended 17 June 2003. See *БНА РФ*, no. 5 (1997).

Admittance points may be closed by reason of international treaties to terminate transport across the State boundary at designated points, or a unilateral decision of the Russian Federation or another State to terminate relevant international treaties, or the submissions of interested federal agencies of executive power of the Russian Federation or subjects of the Russian Federation on the inadvisability or impossibility of continuing to operate the admittance point. Temporary closure may be directed by decision of the Government of the Russian Federation because of a natural disaster or other factors that make transport or the functioning of State control agencies impossible, or for reasons of a sanitary-quarantine nature. **11.22**

B. Maritime Territory and Jurisdiction

The Russian Federation is a party to the United Nations Convention on the Law of the Sea, concluded at Montego Bay on 10 December 1982,[13] and to the four 1958 Geneva Conventions on the law of the sea. The 1982 Convention entered into force on 16 November 1994 and for the Russian Federation on 11 April 1997. On the eve of ratification of the Convention, the Russian Federation adopted by Edict of the President of the Russian Federation a federal special-purpose programme, 'World Ocean', which defined the position of Russia with respect to the principal questions concerning that Convention, including legal questions. In furtherance of its obligations under the 1982 Law of the Sea Convention, the Russian Federation has enacted a substantial body of legislation intended to implement and elaborate the Convention provisions. **11.23**

Internal sea waters

Under the 1958 Geneva Convention on the Territorial Sea and Contiguous Zone (Article 5), the 1982 Law of the Sea Convention (Article 8), and the 1998 Federal Law on Internal Sea Waters, Territorial Sea, and Contiguous Zone of the Russian Federation (Article 1)[14] the internal sea waters of the Russian Federation are those '. . . situated landward of straight baselines from which the breadth of the territorial sea of the Russian Federation is measured'. Internal sea waters are an integral part of the territory of the Russian Federation. There are relegated to the internal sea waters of Russia: (1) ports of the Russian **11.24**

[13] For background see W E Butler, *The Soviet Union and the Law of the Sea* (1971). On recent Russian approaches, see A A Kovalev, *Contemporary Issues of the Law of the Sea: Modern Russian Approaches*, transl. W E Butler (2004).

[14] *СЗ РФ* (1998), no. 31, item 3833.

Federation delimited by a line passing through the furthest point seaward of hydro-engineering and other permanent port installations; (2) gulfs, bays, inlets, and reefs whose coasts belong entirely to the Russian Federation up to a straight line passing from coast to coast at the place of lowest ebb tide where seaward there are first formed one or several passages if the breadth of each does not exceed 24 nautical miles; (3) gulfs, bays, inlets, and reefs, seas and straits, the breadth of whose entry does exceed 24 nautical miles which historically belong to the Russian Federation, a list of which is established by the Government of the Russian Federation and published in *Notices to Mariners.*

11.25 The legal regime of seaports of the Russian Federation, whether commercial, fishing, or specialized, is uniform for all ports on Russian territory irrespective of their form of ownership or departmental affiliation. Sea ports are declared to be open to foreign vessels on the basis of a decision of the Government of the Russian Federation, and the List of such sea ports is published in *Notices to Mariners.* All Russian and foreign vessels are required to comply with the legal regime of a sea port.

11.26 All foreign vessels except warships and other State vessels operated for noncommercial purposes, irrespective of their designation and form of ownership, may enter Russian sea ports open to foreign vessels. The Government of the Russian Federation may establish retaliatory limitations with respect to foreign ships of States in which there exist special limitations on the entry of Russian vessels to their ports. The criminal, civil, and administrative jurisdiction of the Russian Federation extends to foreign ships and to passengers and crew members on board while they are in Russian ports. A foreign vessel may leave a Russian port only with the authorization of the port master by agreement with safety and customs officials of the port.

11.27 Foreign warships and other State vessels operated for noncommercial purposes may enter Russian ports only if they have received prior authorization requested through diplomatic channels 30 days in advance of the proposed entry unless provided otherwise by an international treaty of the Russian Federation. The procedure for foreign warships and other State vessels to enter Russian ports is laid down in the 1999 Rules for the Navigation and Sojourn of Foreign Warships and Other State Vessels Operated for Noncommercial Purposes in the Territorial Sea, Internal Sea Waters, Naval Bases, Points for Basing Warships, and Seaports of the Russian Federation, confirmed by Decree of the Government of the Russian Federation.[15]

11.28 The requirement of prior authorization is subject to an exception: forced entry

[15] *СЗ РФ* (1999), no. 42, item 5030.

by reason of: (1) accident, natural calamity, or strong storm threatening the safety of the foreign vessel, foreign warship, or other State vessel; (2) ice drift or ice conditions threatening the safety of a foreign vessel; (3) toward of a damaged foreign vessel; (4) delivery of rescued people or (5) need to render urgent medical assistance to a member of the crew or passenger, or by virtue of other extraordinary circumstances. All foreign vessels, foreign warships, and other State vessels enjoy without discrimination the right of forced entry in accordance with norms of international law.

Territorial sea

The territorial sea of the Russian Federation extends for twelve nautical miles from the land territory, including islands, or outward limit of internal sea waters measured from baselines. The low-water line along the coast is as specified on maritime charts officially published in the Russian Federation, or straight baseline joining the points of islands, reefs, and cliffs farthest seaward, or straight baseline across the mouth of a river directly flowing into the sea between points on its shores maximally seaward at lowest ebb tide, or a straight baseline not exceeding 24 nautical miles joining points of the natural entrance into a gulf or strait between islands, or between islands and the mainland whose coasts belong to the Russian Federation; or a system of straight baselines of more than 24 miles in length joining points of natural entrance into a gulf or strait between islands, or between islands and the mainland historically belonging to the Russian Federation. The List of geographic coordinates determining the placement of straight baselines is confirmed by the Government and published in *Notices to Mariners.* **11.29**

Innocent passage

The 1998 Federal Law on Internal Sea Waters, the Territorial Sea, and Contiguous Zone incorporates the definition of 'passage' set out in the 1982 Law of the Sea Convention (Article 18): '. . . passage through the territorial sea' is understood as navigation for the purpose of traversing the territorial sea without entering into internal waters or calling at a roadstead or port facility beyond the limits of internal waters, or proceeding to or from internal waters or a call as such roadstead or port facility. The passage must be uninterrupted and expeditious. It may include stopping or anchoring, but only insofar as they are connected with ordinary navigation or are necessary as a consequence of insuperable force or distress or in order to render assistance to people, vessels, or flying apparatus in danger or distress (Article 10). **11.30**

Passage through the territorial sea is innocent if it does not disturb the peace, good order, or security of the Russian Federation. Such disturbance occurs in the event of: (1) the threat or use of force against the sovereignty, territorial **11.31** integrity, or independence of the Russian Federation or in any other manner in violation of the principles of international law embodied in the Charter of the United Nations; (2) any manoeuvers or training with weapons of any type; (3) any act directed towards the collecting of information to the prejudice of the defence or security of the Russian Federation; (4) any act of propaganda having the purpose of infringing the defence or security of the Russian Federation; (5) the launching, landing, or taking on board of any aircraft; (6) the launching, landing, or taking on board of any military device; (7) the loading or unloading of any good or currency or disembarkation of any person contrary to the customs, tax (fiscal), sanitary, immigration, veterinary, phytosanitary, navigation, and other rules established by laws of the Russian Federation and other normative legal acts of the Russian Federation; (8) any act of deliberate and serious pollution of the environment contrary to the requirements of legislation of the Russian Federation and norms of international law; (9) any fishing activities; (10) the carrying out of research or hydrographic activity; any act directed towards the creation of obstacles to the functioning of any systems of communication or any other facilities or installations of the Russian Federation; and (11) any other activity not having a direct relation to passage through the territorial sea unless provided otherwise by international treaties of the Russian Federation.

11.32 Foreign ships, including warships and other State vessels, enjoy the right of innocent passage through the territorial sea provided they comply with the 1998 Federal Law on Internal Sea Waters, Territorial Sea, and Contiguous Zone and with generally-recognized principles and norms of international law and international treaties of the Russian Federation. In the interests of security of the Russian Federation or in order to carry on exercises with weapons of any type, the Ministry of Defence or the Federal Security Agency may temporarily suspend innocent passage in certain areas of the territorial sea for any foreign vessels, provided that the suspension is notified in good time in the *Notices to Mariners*.

11.33 When exercising their right of innocent passage through the Russian territorial sea, foreign vessels must comply with the rules relating to innocent passage with respect to the safety of navigation and regulation of maritime traffic, including the use of marine corridors and traffic separation schemes, the protection of navigation and other equipment and other installations and devices, the protection of submerged cables and pipelines, the conservation of living resources of the sea, fishing laws and rules, the preservation of the environment and the prevention, reduction, and control of pollution, marine scientific research and hydrographic surveys, and the prevention of violations of border, customs, tax (fiscal), sanitary, immigration, veterinary, phytosanitary, navigation, and other rules.

Foreign warships

Not more than three foreign warships and other State vessels of a single foreign State may pass through the territorial sea for the purpose of putting in to a sea port of the Russian Federation unless provided otherwise by an international treaty of the Russian Federation or by special decision of the Government of the Russian Federation on the occasion of a holiday or commemorative date. Submarines must navigate on the surface under their own flag when exercising innocent passage. **11.34**

If a foreign warship does not comply with Russian legislation concerning passage through the territorial sea or sojourn in internal sea waters or a seaport and ignores a request to comply with such legislation, the vessel may be required to leave the respective waters immediately. Disputes between Russian officials and the commander of the foreign warship in peacetime not resolved on the spot are decided solely through diplomatic channels. If a foreign warship uses weapons against the Russian Federation, ships, vessels, or aircraft thereof, or citizens, the retaliatory measures to repulse the attack are taken in accordance with the 1993 Law on the State Boundary and the United Nations Charter. **11.35**

The 1999 Rules for foreign warships set out the duty to comply with navigation and other rules, radio communications between the vessel and coastal posts or Russian warships, pilotage, areas prohibited for navigation, passage by nuclear-powered vessels or vessels carrying nuclear or other hazardous cargoes, and sea corridors. Russian legislation distinguishes among types of visits by warships: official visits (associated with international events or national holidays, visits by heads of State, and the like), unofficial visits (arrangements to enhance cooperation, or unofficial training, scientific, or analogous purposes without ceremony), and business visits (for material-technical provision, crew leave, and so on). **11.36**

Northern sea route

Passage along the Northeast Passage from Norway through the Bering Strait to the Pacific Ocean also embraces in part the domestic cabotage route of the Russian Federation from roughly the White Sea to Vladivostok and other far eastern ports of the Russian Federation. The 1998 Federal Law on Internal Sea Waters, the Territorial Sea, and Contiguous Zone (Article 15) provides that navigation along the lanes of the Northern Sea Route—the 'historically-formed national unified transport communication of the Russian Federation in the Arctic'—including the Vilkitskii, Shokalskii, Dmitrii Laptev, and Sannikov Straits is effectuated in accordance with the said 1998 Federal Law, other federal laws, international treaties of the Russian Federation, and 'rules for navigation along lanes of the Northern Sea Route confirmed by the Government of the Russian Federation and published in *Notices to Mariners*'. **11.37**

11.38 The Rules for Navigation Along the Lanes of the Northern Sea Route and the Rules for Icebreaker and Pilot Escort of Vessels Along the Northern Sea Route, confirmed by the USSR Ministry of the Maritime Fleet on 14 September 1990, remain in force; they were enacted pursuant to Decree 565 of the USSR Council of Ministers of 1 June 1990.[16] The 'Northern Sea Route' is defined in the Rules as the

> national transport communication located in the internal sea waters, territorial sea (or territorial waters), or economic zone of the USSR adjacent to the northern coast of the USSR, including lanes suitable for the icebreaker escort of vessels, the extreme points of which are limited in the east by the western entrances to the Novaia Zemlia straits and the meridian passing northward from Cape Zhelania and eastward to the Bering Strait to parallel 66° N. lat. and the meridian 168°58′37″ W. long.

The Rules on a 'basis nondiscriminatory for the vessels of all States' regulate navigation along the Northern Sea Route for the 'purposes of ensuring navigation safety, the prevention, reduction, and preservation of the marine environment from vessels' since the 'especially severe climatic conditions existing in the Arctic and the presence of ice during the greater part of the year create obstacles or a heightened danger for navigation', and 'pollution of the sea or the northern coast of the USSR may cause grave harm to the ecological equilibrium or irretrievably disturb it, and also prejudice the interests and well-being of the peoples of the Far North' (point 2, Rules).

11.39 A shipowner or the master of a vessel which intends to pass along the Northern Sea Route applies to the Northern Sea Route Administration and also supplies information concerning a guarantee for icebreaker escort. The vessel must meet the physical standards for passage and the master or person replacing him must have experience of ice navigation. In the absence of such experience, the Northern Sea Route may supply a State pilot to assist. A vessel must possess a certificate of proper financial coverage for civil responsibility of a shipowner against damage from pollution of the marine environment and northern coast of the USSR. Vessels may pass along the Northern Sea Route during the navigation period, whose commencement and end is determined by the Northern Sea Route Administration by having regard to the forecast and actual state of the ice, navigation, hydrographic, meteorological, and other conditions. The lanes used, route followed, and adjustments thereto must be followed by the master of the vessel.

11.40 State icebreaker escort and pilotage is obligatory in the Vilkitskii, Shokalskii,

[16] Each set of Rules was published respectively as a separate booklet in 1991 and 1995 by the Chief Administration of Navigation and Oceanography of the USSR Ministry of Defence, later the Ministry of Defense of the Russian Federation.

Dmitrii Laptev, and Sannikov straits in light of the complex navigational and ice situation and in order to ensure navigation safety.

The List of Arctic Ports open to foreign flag vessels in practice has been confirmed at two-year intervals by Regulation of the Government of the Russian Federation. The List comprises two parts for the years 2005 and 2006: the List of Arctic Ports and Points Open for the Entry in 2005 and 2006 of Cargo Ships Under a Foreign Flag (forty ports are enumerated) and the List of Arctic Ports and Points Located on the Territory of the Russian Federation with a Regulated Visit for Foreign Citizens Open for Entry in 2005 and 2006 of Cargo Ships Under a Foreign Flag with Crews Made up of Citizens of the Russian Federation (twenty-seven ports are enumerated).[17] **11.41**

The Russian Federation has begun to encourage greater foreign use of the Northern Sea Route. What may or may not be enduring climate change has nonetheless witnessed a retreat of the Arctic icepack and lengthened the shipping season. The Ministry of Transport of the Russian Federation has developed standards for the escort of vessels to port in ice conditions and is encouraging the introduction of an 'ice passport' for vessels to certify their 'ice-worthiness'.[18] **11.42**

Provisional Rules adopted by the former Soviet Union to regulate the issuance of authorizations for conducting scientific and expedition activities and tourism in the marine areas adjacent to the northern coast of the Russian Federation remain in force, as amended on 28 March 2001.[19] **11.43**

Marine research

Foreign citizens, stateless persons, foreign juridical persons, and associations of juridical persons of foreign States not having the status of a juridical person, and international organizations may carry on research or may explore for and exploit or extract aquatic biological resources and other natural resources of internal sea waters and the territorial sea, including from on board aircraft, provided that the **11.44**

[17] Vessels in these categories are admitted across the State boundary of the Russian Federation, and maritime pilots are provided with the necessary sea charts and manuals by the Ministry of Defence of the Russian Federation. See the Regulation of the Government of the Russian Federation, No. 137-p, of 8 February 2005. *СЗ РФ* (2005), no. 7, item 584. Similar Lists were confirmed for the years 1995, 1996, 1997, 1998 individually and thereafter for two year periods: 2001–2, 2003–4, and 2005–6.

[18] See the Regulation of the Ministry of Transport of the Russian Federation, No. BP-30-p, of 17 February 2003 'On Measures With Regard to Ensuring Safety of Navigation of Transport Vessels in Frozen Ports of the Russian Federation'. (Unpublished).

[19] See the Decree of the USSR Council of Ministers, No. 400, of 15 July 1991 'On the Confirmation of Provisional Rules for the Issuance of Authorizations for Conducting Scientific and Expedition Activities, and also the Effectuation of Tourism in Marine Areas Adjacent to the Northern Coast of the USSR', as amended by Decree of the Government of the Russian Federation, 28 March 2001, No. 249 (unpublished).

research has a peaceful character solely and does not threaten the defence or security of the Russian Federation. Marine scientific research, whether fundamental or applied, is to be directed towards obtaining knowledge with regard to all aspects of the natural processes which occur on the seabed, subsoil thereof, water column, and atmosphere. The basis for conducting marine research is an authorization issued by the relevant federal agency; other licenses issued in connection with particular activity do not substitute for the research authorization required.

11.45 Applications for permission to use the subsoil for the purposes of geological study of subsoil plots are filed in accordance with the Order of the Ministry of Natural Resources of the Russian Federation, No. 62, of 15 March 2005, as amended 29 August 2005.[20] These applications are distinct from those filed to receive the right to use the subsoil when a mineral deposit has been discovered by a subsoil user who has undertaken the geological study of subsoil plots beneath internal sea waters, the territorial sea, or continental shelf at his own expense.[21]

11.46 The Rules for conducting marine research in the said waters were confirmed on 30 July 2004,[22] but do not extend to applied marine research of living and nonliving resources. Foreign applicants make an application not later than six months in advance through diplomatic channels to conduct the marine research, appending to the application drawn up in the Russian language and the language of the applicant a detailed map or diagram of each area where marine research is to be conducted, the route of the vessel or other means of transport to be used when the research is conducted, and the points for setting autonomous measurement devices to be used for the research, and other data required. The grounds for refusal to issue an authorization include: doubt as to the exclusively peaceful character of the research; the research relates directly to the study, exploration, or exploitation of nonliving resources or living resources of the sea; the research is incompatible with the requirements for protection of the marine environment or living or nonliving resources; and the research includes drilling on the continental shelf or the use of explosives or pneumatic devices or the injection of harmful substances into the marine environment, among others.

---

[20] *БНА РФ*, no. 20 (2005).

[21] See the Decree of the Government of the Russian Federation, No. 27, of 18 January 2005 'On Confirmation of the Statute Concerning the Consideration of Applications to Receive the Right to Use the Subsoil When Establishing the Fact of a Discovery of a Mineral Deposit by a Subsoil User Who Conducted Work With Regard to the Geological Study of Subsoil Plots of Internal Sea Waters, Territorial Sea, and Continental Shelf of the Russian Federation at the Expense of Own (including Borrowed) Means for the Purpose of the Exploitation and Extraction of Minerals of This Deposit'. *СЗ РФ* (2005), no. 4, item 302.

[22] *СЗ РФ* (2004), no. 32, item 3338.

Search, rescue, and salvage operations

The basic presumption is that search, rescue, and salvage operations in internal sea waters and the territorial sea of the Russian Federation will be carried out, as a rule, by rescue vessels of the Russian Federation. Foreign vessels exercising their right of innocent passage may engage in such operations without acting inconsistently with their right of passage; that is, such actions are incidental to the right of passage. **11.47**

Otherwise, the procedure for foreign vessels to cross the State boundary of the Russian Federation in order to perform rescue and salvage services is regulated by the 2000 Decree of the Government of the Russian Federation, No. 654, 'On Confirmation of the Statute on Crossing the State Boundary of the Russian Federation by Foreign Rescue Units and the Sojourn Thereof on the Territory of the Russian Federation for the Purpose of the Search and Rescue of People'.[23] Unless provided otherwise by a treaty, a foreign rescue unit will usually request authorization to cross the State boundary of the Russian Federation in order to search for and rescue people at sea from the State Maritime Accident and Rescue Coordination Service of the Russian Federation or the Russian sea rescue coordination centre in the area where the operation is to be conducted. The request should indicate the reason for crossing the State boundary, the type and name of the rescue unit, call signals of the rescue unit, the State affiliation of the rescue unit and its affiliation to a specific organization, the surname of the rescue unit commander, the number of crew members and number of people rescued if there are any, the name of the sea port or airport where the rescue unit proposes to go, and route and altitude of air rescue units, the proposed place and time of crossing the State boundary, and the coordinates of the proposed search and rescue operation. The Russian authorities are required to give a positive or negative reply to the request as soon as possible. **11.48**

Artificial islands, cables, and pipelines

The 1998 Federal Law on Internal Sea Waters, Territorial Sea, and Contiguous Zone laconically provides (Article 16[4]) that the creation, operation, and use of artificial islands, installations, and devices for any purposes, and also the laying of underwater cables and pipelines for any purposes, in the internal sea waters and territorial sea is effectuated in the procedure determined by the Government of the Russian Federation. By Decree No. 44, of 19 January 2000, as amended 30 July 2004, the Government of the Russian Federation confirmed the 'Procedure for the Creation, Operation, and Use of Artificial Islands, Installations, and Devices in the Internal Sea Waters and Territorial Sea of **11.49**

[23] *СЗ РФ* (2000), no. 37, item 3722.

the Russian Federation'[24] and on 12 November 2004 the Ministry of Natural Resources of the Russian Federation confirmed the 'Reglement for the Consideration of Requests (or Applications) and Preparation of Decisions for the Possibility of the Creation, Operation, and Use of Artificial Islands, Installations, and Devices, Performance of Drilling Work, Laying of Underwater Cables and Pipelines in the Internal Sea Waters, Territorial Sea, and Continental Shelf of the Russian Federation' (unpublished).

11.50 Such islands, installations, and devices may be created for any purposes which are not contrary to laws and other normative legal acts or international treaties of the Russian Federation, provided they are not created on recognized sea routes having material significance for shipping or in localities having especially important significance for fishing and the regeneration of marine biological resources, and that a safety zone of not more than 500 metres encircles the said islands, installations, and devices. Foreign citizens and stateless persons, foreign juridical persons, and associations of foreign juridical persons not having the status of a juridical person are among those who may carry out work with regard to the creation, operation, and use of the said islands, installations, and devices provided that they have authorizations issued by the relevant designated federal agencies of executive power of the Russian Federation.

11.51 Requests to engage in such work must contain the information set out in normative legal acts and, in the case of foreign applicants, the request must be sent through diplomatic channels. Which Russian agency issues the relevant authorization depends upon whether the artificial islands, installations, and devices are to be used for geological study of the seabed and subsoil, or in connection with the conservation and protection of living resources of the sea, or in connection with shipping safety, reloading of cargoes, or otherwise linked with maritime transport, or with national security. Decree No. 44 contains an exhaustive list of grounds for refusal of an authorization: (1) a threat to the security of the Russian Federation will or may be created; (2) the creation of the artificial islands, installations, or devices is incompatible with shipping safety or environmental requirements; (3) they are orientated towards preserve zones or specially-protected territories having important significance for the preservation, regeneration, and migration of valuable species of living resources; (4) they have direct significance for the regional geological study of the seabed and subsoil or the prospecting, exploration, or exploitation of mineral and other nonliving resources or the taking of living resources; or (5) the information submitted in the request does not correspond to the purposes of creating and the designation of the artificial islands, installations, and devices or the applicant

[24] *СЗ РФ* (2000), no. 4, item 396.

has obligations unfulfilled from prior work undertaken. It is prohibited to transfer or assign authorizations.

Foreign applicants are required to ensure the presence on artificial islands, installations, and devices of representatives of the Russian Federation who are specially empowered by relevant Russian agencies, including accommodation and provision equally with the command staff of the foreign participants. Such representatives must have access to all premises and all objects on the artificial island, installation, or device. Foreign applicants may commence work to create, operate, or use the islands only in the presence of the said representatives. **11.52**

Applications are filed with the Federal Agency for Supervision in the Sphere of Nature Use (Rosprirodnadzor), which in turn refers them to the Administration of Maritime, Water, and Forestry Supervision for consideration and processing. **11.53**

The laying of pipelines and underwater cables in the internal sea waters and territorial sea is regulated by the Decree No. 68 of the Government of the Russian Federation 'On Confirmation of the Procedure for Laying Underground Cables and Pipelines in Internal Sea Waters and Territorial Sea of the Russian Federation',[25] as amended 9 November 2004. Foreign natural and juridical persons are entitled to engage in work of this nature on essentially the same basis as in the case of artificial islands. Communications lines may be laid in accordance with the 2004 Statute on the Construction and Operation of Communications Lines When Crossing the State Boundary of the Russian Federation, on Frontier Territory, in Internal Sea Waters, and Territorial Sea of the Russian Federation.[26] **11.54**

Marine environment

Protection and preservation of the marine environment is addressed principally through the creation of State monitoring and supervision agencies charged with this responsibility. Provision is made for assessing the quality of the marine environment by establishing the maximum admissible norms for impact on the environment of pollutants and discharges, for State ecological expert examination of economic and other activities in internal sea waters and the territorial sea, and for State ecological monitoring[27] of the state of the waters. The burial of wastes and other materials and the discharge of harmful substances into the internal sea waters and territorial sea is prohibited. **11.55**

[25] *СЗ РФ* (2000), no. 5, item 534. [26] *СЗ РФ* (2004), no. 46(II), item 4531.

[27] A unified integrated system of State ecological monitoring has been established which includes within its mandate the internal sea waters and territorial sea of the Russian Federation. See the 2003 Statute on the Organisation and Effectuation of State Monitoring of the Environment (State Ecological Monitoring). *СЗ РФ* (2003), no. 12, item 1287.

11.56 A 'branch system' for monitoring aquatic biological resources and for observation and control over fishing vessels in the internal sea waters, territorial sea, continental shelf, exclusive economic zone, and in the Caspian Sea and the Sea of Azov, as well as on the high seas and in the economic zones of foreign States, is being introduced. Foreign fishing vessels operating in these waters have been required from 1 January 2000 to be equipped with the appropriate technical devices for such control to be exercised.[28] The requirement extends to 'all foreign fishing vessels carrying on trade in aquatic biological resources and marine resource research in the maritime waters of the Russian Federation'.[29]

11.57 Conservation is pursued, *inter alia*, through the establishment of total admissible catches of aquatic and biological resources. The procedure for determining these is regulated by the 2005 'Statute on the Determination and Confirmation of Total Admissible Catches of Aquatic Biological Resources and also the Making of Changes Therein'.[30] Total catches are determined by weight or by piece (crabs, and others). The distribution of the catch quotas is governed by the 2005 Statute on the Distribution of Total Admissible Catches of Aquatic Biological Resources With Regard to Types of Quotas for the Extraction (or Catch) Thereof'.[31] The Federal Agency for Fishing annually prepares and sends to the Ministry of Agriculture of the Russian Federation the draft distribution plan.

Contiguous zone

11.58 The contiguous zone of the Russian Federation is a sea belt extending from the outer boundary of the territorial sea for twenty-four nautical miles measured from the same baseline as the territorial sea itself. If the contiguous zone overlaps the zones of opposite or adjacent States, the delimitation of the zone is effectuated in accordance with 'generally-recognized principles and norms of international law and international treaties of the Russian Federation' (Article 22, 1998 Law on Internal Sea Waters, Territorial Sea, and Contiguous Zone).

11.59 Within its contiguous zone the Russian Federation exercises the control necessary in order to prevent violations of customs, fiscal, immigration, or sanitary rules established by normative legal acts of the Russian Federation, including

[28] See the Decree No. 226 of 26 February 1999 'On the Creation of a Branch System of Monitoring Aquatic Biological Resources and Observation and Control Over the Activity of Fishing Vessels'. *СЗ РФ* (1999), no. 10, item 1243.

[29] See the Provisional Statute on Satellite Position Control of Foreign Fishing Vessels, confirmed by Order No. 330, 22 November 1999, of the State Committee of the Russian Federation for Fisheries. *БНА РФ*, no. 4 (2000).

[30] Confirmed by Decree of the Government of the Russian Federation, No. 583, of 26 September 2005. *СЗ РФ* (2005), no. 40, item 4036.

[31] Confirmed by Decree of the Government of the Russian Federation, No. 768, of 15 December 2005. *СЗ РФ* (2005), no. 52(III), item 5734.

violations in the territorial sea and to punish such violations committed on the territory of the Russian Federation, including the territorial sea. Measures may be taken within the zone, including the right of hot pursuit, to detain guilty persons and to stop, inspect, and detail offending foreign ships (excluding warships and other State vessels operated for noncommercial purposes). The rights exercised in the contiguous zone are without prejudice to the rights of the Russian Federation in the exclusive economic zone or on the continental shelf.

Exclusive economic zone

The legal regime of the Russian exclusive economic zone is based on the 1982 Law of the Sea Convention as set out in the 1998 Federal Law on the Exclusive Economic Zone of the Russian Federation.[32] The exclusive economic zone is the sea area beyond the limits of and adjacent to the territorial sea of the Russian Federation, the outer boundary of which extends to a distance of 200 nautical miles from the baselines of the territorial sea unless provided otherwise by an international treaty of the Russian Federation. All islands of the Russian Federation excluding rocks not suitable for human life or for the effectuation of autonomous economic activity have their own exclusive economic zone. **11.60**

The legal regime of the exclusive economic zone has been described as follows in Russian international legal doctrine: **11.61**

> the maritime area beyond the limits of the territorial sea and adjacent thereto, called the exclusive economic zone, is high seas with respect to the exercise therein of freedom of the high seas and other legal types of use of the sea, as is established by this [1982] Convention. However, it is not considered to be high seas with respect to the exercise therein of sovereign rights and jurisdiction of the coastal State granted to it under this [1982] Convention.[33]

This has been described as the 'optimal definition' of the legal status of the exclusive economic zone.[34]

Living resources

The obligations of the Russian Federation with respect to specific activities within the exclusive economic zone have been elaborated in a number of subordinate normative legal acts. The regulations concerning total admissible catches and the distribution of catch quotas have been discussed above. Although in the post-Soviet era the role of the State in foreign trade transactions has been **11.62**

---

[32] *СЗ РФ* (1998), no. 51, item 6273.

[33] S V Molodtsov, *Правовой режим морских вод* [Legal Regime of Maritime Waters] (1982), p. 108.

[34] Kovalev, *Contemporary Issues of the Law of the Sea* (2004), p. 64.

materially reduced, there is State regulation of foreign trade operations in the domain of fisheries. No less than twelve federal agencies of executive power are involved in preventing violations of law connected with foreign trade in fishery products (Federal Border Service, Ministry of Internal Affairs, Ministry of Foreign Affairs, Ministry for Taxes and Charges, Ministry of Natural Resources, Ministry of Finances, Ministry of Economic Development and Trade, State Customs Committee, Federal Security Service, Federal Tax Police Service, and Central Bank—the names of some having been changed as a result of reforms introduced in March 2004). They are required to 'interact' and 'coordinate' their activities pursuant to a joint Order of 14 November 2000 (unpublished).

11.63 The right to use living resources of the exclusive economic zone may be granted, *inter alia*, to foreign citizens, foreign juridical persons, foreign States, and competent international organizations; however, a preferential right to use living resources belongs to representatives of native small-number peoples and ethnic communities of the North and Far East of the Russian Federation; the population of the North and Far East and the population permanently residing on the territories adjacent to the sea coast whose way of life, employment, and economy is traditionally based on the living resources; Russian applicants engaged in marine scientific research of a biological character and/or measures for the artificial regeneration of living resources; and Russian applicants engaged in fishing for living resources for the purpose of delivery of the products for federal and regional needs. Foreign applicants may use living resources for scientific, commercial, and other purposes after the satisfaction of all applications of Russian applicants and on condition that the Russian applicants do not have the possibility to catch the entire admissible limit for specific living resources in specific areas and only in accordance with international treaties of the Russian Federation with the States of which the foreign applicants are citizens, or in which they have registered in compliance with Russian legislation. Foreign applicants must submit their application to receive a licence or authorization to take living resources in the exclusive economic zone. The licence, if issued, is then subject to registration by the agency which issued it.[35]

11.64 The 'List of Commercial Species of Living Resources for Individual Seas and Oceans of the Russian Federation' was confirmed by Order No. 299 of the State Committee of the Russian Federation for Fisheries on 14 November 2000 (Barents Sea, Black Sea, Caspian Sea, Sea of Japan, and others). Each species is identified in Russian and Latin (unpublished).

[35] See the 'Rules for the Registration of Licences (or Registrations) to Take Aquatic Biological Resources in the Exclusive Economic Zone of the Russian Federation Issued to Russian and Foreign Juridical persons and Citizens', confirmed by Decree of the Government of the Russian Federation, No. 102, 12 February 2001. *СЗ РФ* (2003), no. 18, item 1721.

Marine environment

As in the case of internal sea waters, the territorial sea, and the contiguous zone, State ecological control and supervision extends to the exclusive economic zone. The norms, rules, and measures relating to the prevention, reduction, and control of pollution from vessels, aircraft, artificial islands, devices, and installations also extend to the exclusive economic zone, with due regard to international norms and standards and international treaties of the Russian Federation. **11.65**

Pursuant to the 1998 Federal Law on the Exclusive Economic Zone (Article 30), the Government of the Russian Federation confirmed the List of Harmful Substances Whose Discharge in the Exclusive Economic Zone of the Russian Federation from Vessels, Other Floating Means, Aircraft, Artificial Islands, Devices, and Installations is Prohibited.[36] In addition, the Government confirmed the ceilings of admissible concentrations and conditions of discharge of harmful substances into the exclusive economic zone,[37] implementing in so doing the 1973 International Convention for the Prevention of Pollution from Ships. **11.66**

Protection of zone

The protection of the exclusive economic zone falls principally upon three State agencies concerned with security, environmental protection, and customs, collectively called 'protection agencies' under the 1998 Federal Law on the Exclusive Economic Zone (Article 35). The Russian border forces are empowered to use force to protect the exclusive economic zone and continental shelf against offending vessels in response to the use of force by them or in other exceptional instances when pursuing offending vessels by right of hot pursuit when all measures under the circumstances have been exhausted which are necessary to terminate the violation and detain the offending vessel.[38] **11.67**

Before using force, the commander of the Russian warship or aircraft must: (1) give signals used in international practice to the offending vessel to stop, the signals being given from a distance enabling the offending vessel to see or hear the signals; (2) during the pursuit warn the offending vessel by signals used in international practice at a distance enabling the offending vessel to see or hear the signals that unless the vessel stops, force will be used against it; and (3) be **11.68**

[36] Confirmed by Decree of the Government of the Russian Federation, No. 251, of 24 March 2000. *СЗ РФ* (2000), no. 14, item 1490.

[37] *СЗ РФ* (2000), no. 41, item 4087.

[38] Decree of the Government of the Russian Federation, No. 1208, of 14 October 1996, as amended 9 September 1999, 'On Confirmation of the Procedure for the Use of a Weapon by Warships and Aircraft of the Federal Border Service of the Russian Federation When Protecting the Exclusive Economic Zone and Continental Shelf of the Russian Federation'. *СЗ РФ* (1996), no. 43, item 4921.

convinced that the offending vessel will not comply with the request to stop and will attempt to conceal itself despite the signals and warning shots. The decision to use a weapon against an offending vessel is taken by the head of the regional administration of the Federal Border Service of the Russian Federation.

Continental shelf

11.69 Under international law the continental shelf is the natural prolongation of land territory up to the seaward boundary of the underwater extension of the mainland, or up to 200 nautical miles if the boundaries of the underwater extension do not reach to that distance. The shelf includes the continental slope and rise, together with the seabed and subsoil thereof. The Imperial Russian Government in 1916 laid claim to certain islands in the Northern Arctic Ocean on the grounds that the islands were a continuation northward of the Siberian continental platform.[39]

11.70 For most of its coastline the Russian Federation enjoys a substantial continental shelf rich in living resources, oil, and gas. The provisions of the 1982 Law of the Sea Convention regulating the continental shelf have been replicated and elaborated by the 1995 Federal Law on the Continental Shelf of the Russian Federation,[40] as amended. The precise seaward boundary of the continental shelf has been delimited on the basis of coordinates confirmed by the Government of the Russian Federation.[41] Certain segments of the Russian continental shelf are subject to special programmes intended to encourage the exploitation of shelf resources. Within the overall Federal special-purpose programme 'World Ocean', for example, a subprogramme has been adopted for the 'Creation of Advanced Technology Devices, Machines, and Equipment for the Marine Extraction of Oil and Gas and the Mastery of Hydrocarbon Deposits on the Continental Shelf of the Arctic for the Years 2003 to 2012' (Subprogramme 'Shelf') of the Federal Special-Purpose Programme 'World Ocean'.[42]

Living resources

11.71 The living organisms of the Russian continental shelf, sometimes called sedentary species, have been enumerated in the 'List of Species of Living Organisms Which Are Living Resources of the Continental Shelf of the Russian Federation', confirmed by Order No. 169 of the State Committee of the Russian Federation

[39] See Butler, *The Soviet Union and the Law of the Sea* (1971).

[40] *СЗ РФ* (1995), no. 49, item 4694.

[41] See the Decree No. 717, of 16 June 1997. *СЗ РФ* (1997), no. 25, item 2939, as amended 9 March 2005.

[42] See the Decree No. 623 of 20 August 2002, as amended 21 September 2004, No. 491. *СЗ РФ* (2002), no. 34, item 3310.

for Fisheries on 10 September 1996 pursuant to the 1995 Federal Law on the Continental Shelf (Article 4). There are 53 species in all (including one misnumbered) (unpublished).

Mineral resources

Exploitation of the nonliving resources of the continental shelf sometimes requires as part of international scientific or scientific-technical programmes and projects that foreign technical means of observation and control be placed on the Russian continental shelf. These include devices produced outside Russia, or technical means of Russian production but devised with the participation of representatives of the foreign side, intended to perform measurements or register various parameters in the physical milieu, or to conduct chemical or biological studies or determine the location or identity of objects. The siting and maintenance of such means on the continental shelf or in the exclusive economic zone is regulated by Decree No. 633 of the Government of the Russian Federation, adopted 29 August 2001, 'On the Procedure for the Siting and Use on the Territory of the Russian Federation, on the Continental Shelf, and in the Exclusive Economic Zone of the Russian Federation of Foreign Technical Means of Observation and Control',[43] as amended 23 May 2005. **11.72**

The Russian Federation exercises State control over the geological study and the rational use and protection of the subsoil, including the subsoil of the continental shelf. What is characterized as 'State geological control' is intended to ensure compliance by all subsoil users with the established procedure for subsoil use and the requirements of Russian legislation.[44] **11.73**

Oil and gas exploration and exploitation on the continental shelf of the Russian Federation are subject to special safety rules binding upon all enterprises, organizations, scientific-research, and project-survey and other subdivisions whose activity is connected with exploration and exploitation on the continental shelf. They also extend to activities with regard to oil, gas, and gas condensate deposits beyond the Russian continental shelf in those '. . . instances when this follows from international law or from an agreement with a foreign State' (point 1.1.1.)[45] and to stationary installations and floating objects, including drilling ships. A licence is required for an enterprise, organization, joint enterprise, firm, or design organization to undertake work relating to the exploration and exploitation of oil, gas, and gas condensate fields on the continental shelf. **11.74**

[43] *СЗ РФ* (2001), no. 36, item 3580.
[44] *СЗ РФ* (2005), no. 20, item 1885.
[45] *Российская газета*, 21 June 2003.

12

FOREIGN PERSONNEL ENJOYING SPECIAL LEGAL STATUS

Although it is common in doctrinal writings to refer to 'diplomatic and consular' law in its collective meaning, they are actually distinct. In Russian legal doctrine, diplomatic law refers to the aggregate of norms regulating the legal status and activity of diplomatic missions or representations of States and international organizations, whereas consular law is the aggregate of norms regulating consular relations, including the status and functions of consuls. The rupture of diplomatic relations between States does not necessarily mean an automatic rupture of consular relations, although the establishment of diplomatic relations will normally presume consent in principle to opening consular relations. **12.01**

A. Diplomatic and Consular Personnel

Privileges and immunities accorded under international law extend both to the diplomatic and consular missions in a foreign country and to the personnel of the mission. The premises of the representation or mission are inviolate and the authorities of the receiving country may enter only with the consent of the head of the representation. If a crime is committed on the territory of the diplomatic **12.02** mission, it is investigated by the personnel of the embassy or consulate and/or by specialists from the sending country that may be specially invited for this purpose.

12.03 *Example:* In March 2002 a large sum of money was stolen from the safe in the consular section of the Embassy of Mongolia in the Russian Federation. The Embassy invited law enforcement personnel from Mongolia to investigate the crime. The Chief Administration for Internal Affairs in the City of Moscow declared that it had received no information from the Embassy concerning the theft.[1]

12.04 Full immunity is granted to diplomatic personnel; that is, individuals who have diplomatic rank. The immunity extends to the person, his housing or dwelling premise (including hotel accommodation or sanatorium), and his property. There are nonetheless limitations sometimes imposed on diplomats in the Russian Federation by the sending country. For many years the United States Department of State prohibited service personnel of the United States Embassy in Moscow from entering into 'intimate and romantic relations' with Russian citizens, this stricture finally being removed in 1995 except for personnel having access to classified information. The USSR Ministry of Foreign Affairs did not publish similar instructions, but nonetheless enforced unpublished prohibitions until the early 1990s against Soviet diplomats who entered into close relations with citizens of the receiving country. The unofficial prohibition was unofficially withdrawn and now extends only to those who have possession of State secrets.[2]

12.05 The administrative and technical personnel of an embassy—bookkeepers, cryptographers, chancellery workers, interpreters, and the like—have privileges and immunities approximating those of diplomatic personnel, subject to certain exceptions. Immunity against civil and administrative jurisdiction does not extend to actions committed outside the performance of employment or official duties, and although this category of individuals enjoys customs exemptions, they are not exempt from customs inspection.

12.06 So-called 'service personnel' of an Embassy—the gardener, cook, security personnel, driver, and the like—have certain fiscal immunities and immunity with respect to actions committed when performing their employment or official duties, unless they are citizens of the receiving State.

---

[1] The example is cited in I I Lukashuk, *Международное право: Особенная часть* [International Law: Special Part] (2005), II, p. 83.

[2] Ibid., p. 85.

Currency control

Foreign natural persons who hold diplomatic and consular posts and personnel of international organizations of branches and representations thereof are subject to the same currency control requirements in principle as other natural persons (see Chapter 6). **12.07**

Immunity from criminal jurisdiction

Russian legal doctrine distinguishes between general immunity and functional immunity from criminal jurisdiction. Functional immunity extends only to actions connected with the performance of employment duties or functions by a person, whereas an individual enjoying general immunity comes close to having absolute immunity based on his status. **12.08**

With respect to Russian criminal law, a foreign citizen who commits actions which fall within his employment duties that would engage prosecution under the Criminal Code of the Russian Federation will not be brought to criminal responsibility in Russia unless the State of which he is a citizen or where he is permanently resident (for stateless persons) gives consent to his being prosecuted. For example, if the driver of an embassy was involved in a motor vehicle accident in Russia which constituted a crime under the Criminal Code, there would be no prosecution if the driver was on embassy business because the incident occurred as part of the performance of his employment duties, unless the embassy consented to prosecution. However, if the same driver committed robbery, there would be a prosecution because these actions were not part of his employment duties. In September 1995 the driver of a vehicle of the Embassy of Saudi Arabia was arrested and bound over for trial for having taken and conveyed a hostage in the car to a suburban Moscow destination. **12.09**

Even though prosecution may not be possible in the State where a diplomat has committed a crime, the sending State may recall the diplomat from his posting and apply sanctions of its own, either at the request of the receiving State or at its own initiative. **12.10**

Example: On 25 January 2001 the First Secretary of the Russian Embassy in Canada killed two pedestrians while driving apparently under the influence of alcohol. Although the Canadian police did not have the right to perform a blood test, in their opinion the driver showed external signs of intoxication and drew up a protocol to this effect, after which the driver returned to the Russian Embassy. Several days later the diplomat was recalled and dismissed from the Russian diplomatic service. Upon the recommendation of the Canadian Government, the General Procuracy of the Russian Federation instituted a criminal proceeding against the former First Secretary, and in March 2002 he was **12.11** found guilty by a Moscow court and sentenced to four years' deprivation of freedom. Counsel for relatives of the victims brought suit against the Canadian Government for $2 million for failing to ensure the safety of Canadian citizens. The Canadian Government agreed to pay the sum so as to thereafter receive compensation from Russia.[3]

12.12 General immunity is accorded most commonly to diplomatic representatives of foreign States pursuant to the 1961 Vienna Convention on Diplomatic Relations.[4] The heads of diplomatic missions and other personnel of the embassy having diplomatic rank, administrative-technical personnel, and family members of the said persons residing jointly with them enjoy absolute immunity. Service personnel of the diplomatic mission have functional immunity only with respect to actions committed by them in the performance of their duties.

12.13 Russian international legal doctrine recognises that on the basis of international customary law the heads of foreign States, ministers of foreign affairs, and other senior individuals of high rank coming to the Russian Federation on special missions have absolute immunity.

12.14 Consular officials and consular administrative-technical personnel have functional immunity against criminal jurisdiction in the Russian Federation pursuant to the 1963 Vienna Convention on Consular Relations. On the basis of reciprocity, however, more extensive immunities are granted to consular officials under bilateral consular agreements concluded by the Russian Federation. The 1964 United States-USSR Consular Convention is based on functional immunity but also granted to consular personnel absolute immunity against consular jurisdiction.[5]

12.15 *Example:* In 1996 the Ukrainian Vice Consul in Toronto was accused of driving while intoxicated and, when apprehended by a policeman, offered a bribe. The Canadian authorities requested Ukraine to deprive the Vice Consul of diplomatic immunity. When Ukraine refused to do so, the Vice Consul was declared *persona non grata* and required to leave the country within forty-eight hours.

12.16 International civil servants in the Russian Federation enjoy immunity from criminal jurisdiction, or not, as determined in the treaties defining their privileges and immunities concluded between the receiving State and international organization concerned. The 2001 Convention on Privileges and Immunities of the Eurasian Economic Community[6] grants functional immunity against

[3] Ibid., p. 86. [4] *Ведомости Верховного Совета СССР* (1964), no. 18, item 221.
[5] *Ведомости Верховного Совета СССР* (1968), no. 29, item 261.
[6] *БМД*, no. 2 (2006), pp. 6–18. The Convention entered into force for Russia on 15 December 2002.

personal arrest or detention, and also the jurisdiction of judicial and administrative authorities with respect to all actions which may be performed by them in this capacity to the Secretary-General and officials of the Community and members of their families residing with them and certain other categories of individuals (Articles 11 and 19).

Immunity from administrative responsibility

The 2001 Code of the Russian Federation on Administrative Violations **12.17** provides (Article 2.6[3]) that the question of administrative responsibility of a foreign citizen enjoying immunity against the administrative jurisdiction of the Russian Federation in accordance with federal laws and international treaties of the Russian Federation and an administrative violation committed on the territory of the Russian Federation is resolved in accordance with the norms of international law. This is understood by Russian jurists to mean that 'only those foreign natural persons who do not enjoy immunity against administrative jurisdiction of the Russian Federation are subject to administrative responsibility on the general grounds with citizens of the Russian Federation'.[7]

Since administrative violations are committed far more frequently than crimes, **12.18** the issue of granting immunity or not arises often. The view is widely held in Russian legal doctrine that immunity against administrative jurisdiction is functional, and not absolute.

Immunity from civil suit

Under Section V of the Code of Civil Procedure of the Russian Federation, the **12.19** filing of suit against a foreign State, or involving a foreign State in a suit as a defendant or third person, or the imposition of arrest on property belonging to the foreign State and situated on the territory of the Russian Federation, or the taking of other measures to secure the suit with regard to such property, or the levy of execution against this property by way of executing decisions of a court, is permitted only with the consent of competent agencies of the respective State unless provided otherwise by an international treaty of the Russian Federation or a federal law.

An international organization is subject to the jurisdiction of Russian courts **12.20**

[7] See A B Agapov, *Постатейный комментарий к Кодексу Российской Федерации об административных правонарушениях. Расширенный, с использованием материалов судебной практики* [Article-by-Article Commentary to Code of Russian Federation on Administrative Violations. Enlarged with Use of Materials of Judicial Practice] (2nd edn, 2004), I, p. 54.

with regard to civil cases within the limits determined by international treaties of the Russian Federation and federal laws.

12.21 Diplomatic representatives of foreign States accredited in the Russian Federation and other persons specified in international treaties of the Russian Federation or federal laws are subject to the jurisdiction of courts of the Russian Federation with regard to civil cases within the limits determined by generally-recognized principles and norms of international law or by international treaties of the Russian Federation (Article 401, Code of Civil Procedure).

Judicial immunity in arbitrazh courts

12.22 A foreign State in its capacity as the bearer of power has judicial immunity in the Russian Federation with respect to a suit brought against it in an arbitrazh court, or being involved in a case as a third person, or against the imposition of arrest on property belonging to the foreign State and situated on the territory of the Russian Federation, and against measures taken by a court to secure the suit and property interests. Compulsory enforcement of a judicial act against the property of a foreign State by an arbitrazh court is permitted only with the consent of competent agencies of the foreign State unless provided otherwise by a federal law or an international treaty of the Russian Federation (Article 251, Code of Arbitrazh Procedure).

12.23 The judicial immunity of an international organization is determined by an international treaty and federal law. Judicial immunity may be waived only in the procedure provided for by a law of a foreign State or rules of the international organization. If immunity is waived, the arbitrazh court considers the case before it in the usual procedure established by the Code of Arbitrazh Procedure.

12.24 State immunity is considered in Russian doctrinal writings to be a customary norm of international law which finds a measure of support in regional and bilateral treaties and national legislation. This is a further expression of the Russian inclination towards functional State immunity and a withdrawal of prior doctrines of absolute immunity.

12.25 *Example:* Suit was filed in an arbitrazh court against the embassy of a foreign State which was building a small guest house on Russian territory. The embassy pleaded judicial immunity in reply to the suit. The arbitrazh court of first instance did not recognize judicial immunity under these circumstances because the operation of the guest house could bring profit and was in its view a form of commercial activity. The arbitrazh court of cassational instance recognized judicial immunity in this situation on the grounds that the guest house was being built to perform sovereign functions—to receive delegations during political negotiations on the territory of the Russian Federation.

A waiver of immunity may be made in whole or in part and may be expressed when concluding a foreign economic transaction or when a dispute arises and a decision is made with regard to the appropriate means for the settlement of a dispute. Russian law does not determine the procedure for waiver. Some Russian jurists seem to believe that waiver is governed by the national legislation of foreign States.[8] In the case of international organizations, it is assumed that the senior officials of the organization have the right to waive immunities, usually the secretary-general and, by his power of attorney, other senior officials. The powers to waive immunity are also assumed to be the same as those to conclude treaties. In fact, few States have legislation on this issue. **12.26**

Example: An intergovernmental international organization (IGO) with headquarters in Moscow brought suit against a Russian juridical person in an arbitrazh court. The Russian defendant filed a counterclaim. The IGO pleaded judicial immunity against the counterclaim, and the arbitrazh court of first instance refused to accept the counterclaim. The arbitrazh court of superior instance deemed this refusal to accept the counterclaim to be unlawful and reversed the ruling, holding that after filing suit demands in the arbitrazh court the IGO had lost its right to immunity against Russian court proceedings in the specific dispute. **12.27**

Customs immunity

A foreign diplomat in Russia enjoys immunity against the imposition of customs duty on articles intended for personal use and his personal baggage is not subject to inspection. Under the 1961 Vienna Convention on Diplomatic Relations, there is an exception if the customs authorities have serious grounds to believe that diplomatic baggage contains articles prohibited to be brought in or taken out of the country. If a search is performed under these circumstances, it must be in the presence of the diplomat or his representative, or the person responsible for the diplomat's baggage. **12.28**

Example: In April 1996 at Butovo the Russian customs authorities inspected the personal baggage of three Italian diplomats being transported by an Italian transport company. During the inspection a large number of art objects were found whose export was prohibited. The articles were confiscated. According to Russian customs officers, diplomatic baggage is inspected only when they have reason to believe smuggling is taking place.[9] **12.29**

[8] Neshataeva, in Iakovlev and Iukov (eds.), *Комментарий к Арбитражному процессуальному кодексу Российской Федерации* [Commentary to Code of Arbitrazh Procedure of the Russian Federation] (2003), p. 659.

[9] Lukashuk, *Международное право: Особенная часть* [International Law: Special Part] (2005), II, p. 87.

Fiscal immunity

12.30 Diplomatic personnel in Russia enjoy immunity against direct taxes, as do members of the diplomat's family residing with him unless the family members are citizens of the Russian Federation.

B. International Civil Servants

12.31 There are substantial numbers of international organizations who maintain headquarters or offices and missions on the territory of the Russian Federation. The privileges and immunities of these organizations and their personnel are determined by the individual charters of the organizations themselves and by multilateral and bilateral treaties concluded with the receiving country. Customary rules of international law play a significant role.

12.32 In addition to the organizations and their personnel, many members of an international organization located in Russia establish missions manned by representatives and their staffs attached to the international organization. The Russian Federation is party to the 1975 Vienna Convention on the Representation of States in Their Relations with International Organizations of a Universal Character, which has not yet entered into force, and to the 1973 Convention for the Protection and Punishment of Crimes Against Internationally-Protected Persons, Including Diplomatic Agents.

C. Journalists

12.33 A journalist under the 1991 Russian Law 'On the Mass Media' is a '. . . person who engages in the editing, creation, collecting, or preparation of communications and materials for the editorial board of a registered mass media and connected with it by labour or other contractual relations or engaging in such activity upon the empowerment thereof'. Not all journalists are accredited. A Russian editorial board has the right to make an application to a State agency, organization, institution, or an organ of a social association for the accreditation of its journalists to the entity concerned (Article 48). Under Article 55 of the same Law, the Ministry of Foreign Affairs of the Russian Federation accredits foreign correspondents in the Russian Federation.

12.34 The virtue of accreditation lies in the different status between an accredited and a non-accredited foreign correspondent. Foreign correspondents not accredited in the Russian Federation '. . . enjoy the rights and bear the duties as representatives of a foreign juridical person'. To correspondents accredited in the Russian

Federation, irrespective of their citizenship, extends the '. . . professional status of a journalist' established by the Law on Mass Media (Article 55).

Journalists, irrespective of their citizenship, and representatives of periodical printed publications, radio, television, video and cinema chronicle programmes and other forms of the periodical dissemination of the mass media, may be accredited as correspondents of foreign mass media in Russia. A request for the accreditation of a correspondent of foreign mass media is sent by the executives of the foreign mass media to the Ministry of Foreign Affairs directly or through the diplomatic representation of the Russian Federation in the respective country. The decision to accredit the correspondent is adopted within two months from the day of receipt of the application. **12.35**

An accredited correspondent is issued a foreign correspondent certificate which is valid for two years. Family members of the correspondent are issued a card valid for the same period. **12.36**

Journalists, irrespective of their citizenship, may be accredited temporarily as special correspondents in order to complete assignments of their editors with visa support from the Ministry of Foreign Affairs. Journalists who have arrived in the Russian Federation with the visa support of any other Russian organizations are accredited to the Ministry of Foreign Affairs at the request of the leadership of those organizations. Journalists who have come to Russia to replace the principal correspondent by reason of leave, illness, or business trips to other countries also may be treated as special correspondents temporarily accredited to the Ministry of Foreign Affairs. Entry visas are to be issued promptly to persons replacing the principal correspondent who is on leave, ill, or on a business trip. Special correspondents are issued a card valid for up to three months with possible extension to six months. **12.37**

Technical personnel of correspondent points of foreign mass media may be persons who, irrespective of their citizenship, work as producers, editors, secretaries, interpreters, and specialists who service television and cinema equipment or means of communication. Other persons who perform other types of activity at correspondent points are treated as servicing personnel and are not subject to registration as technical personnel. The request to register technical personnel is sent to the Ministry of Foreign Affairs by the executives of the foreign mass media or correspondent thereof accredited to the Ministry in the same procedure as for a correspondent. The decision to register technical personnel is taken within not more than two months from the day of receipt of the application. Those registered receive a certificate which is valid for up to two years. **12.38**

Upon arrival in Russia a foreign correspondent, technical personnel, and **12.39** members of their families are required to register within three days, excluding days off and holidays, at the agencies of the Ministry of Internal Affairs.

12.40 Certain categories of individuals may not be accredited as correspondents nor registered as technical personnel of correspondent points; among these are personnel of foreign diplomatic and consular representations, the apparatus of military attachés or of representative offices of airlines, banks, trade, industrial, and intermediary firms registered in Russia, or persons who are personnel of Russian mass media.

12.41 The Ministry of Foreign Affairs may terminate the accreditation or registration of correspondents if there is a violation by them of legislation of the Russian Federation. A journalist may be deprived of his accreditation if the established accreditation rules have been violated by him or by his editorial board or he has disseminated information not corresponding to reality which defames the honour and dignity of the organization which accredited the journalist as confirmed by the decision of a court which has entered into legal force.

12.42 Retaliatory measures may be undertaken by the Russian Federation with respect to correspondents of the mass media of those countries where limitations with respect to Russian journalists operate. If an extraordinary situation is introduced throughout the entire territory of the Russian Federation, a special procedure for the accreditation of correspondents of foreign mass media may be instituted in accordance with the Constitutional Law on an Extraordinary Situation (Article 12). Should an extraordinary situation be instituted in individual localities of the Russian Federation, the commandant of the territory where the extraordinary situation is introduced may establish a special procedure for the accreditation of correspondents of foreign mass media and for the procedure of their work (Article 18).

12.43 Under Article 13(4) of the 2002 Law on the Legal Status of Citizens, journalists accredited to the Russian Federation are excluded from the requirement that their employer must have a valid authorization for work. Journalists have the right to be in the Russian Federation on condition of compliance with the rules of their accreditation and sojourn, as confirmed by a 1994 Decree of the Government of the Russian Federation 'On Confirmation of the Rules of Accreditation and Sojourn of Correspondents of Foreign Mass Media on the Territory of the Russian Federation', as amended.[10]

12.44 Entry to the Russian Federation of newly appointed correspondents, special correspondents, or technical personnel who are foreigners, is on the basis of

[10] *СЗ РФ* (1994), no. 21, item 2399; (1999), no. 32, item 4098; (2002), no. 23, item 2189.

passports or identity documents replacing them and an entry visa issued by a consulate of the Russian Federation, unless a different procedure is established by an international treaty of the Russian Federation. Consular institutions are to issue entry visa within five working days on the basis of reciprocity. Foreign journalists are issued a single-entry ordinary work visa for a period of up to three months; that is, permanent correspondents working in foreign representation offices of mass media accredited to the diplomatic and protocol section (DIP) of the Ministry of Foreign Affairs of Russia. This category of foreign citizens is first accredited to the Ministry with subsequent registration at the territorial agency of the Ministry of Internal Affairs of Russia where the foreigner lives and extension by the formalization of a multi-entry visa for a period of up to one year at the said territorial agency.

Technical personnel of the mass media; that is, foreigners coming to Russia to work as permanent technical personnel of representations of foreign mass media accredited to DIP of the Ministry of Foreign Affairs, also receive an ordinary single-entry work visa for a period of up to three months. Their accreditation and subsequent registration is the same as that for journalists. **12.45**

Rights of journalists

Accredited foreign correspondents have, irrespective of their citizenship, the rights and duties of a journalist as provided by international treaties and legislation of the Russian Federation. The 1991 Law on the Mass Media enumerates (Article 47) twelve rights of a journalist: (1) to seek, ask for, receive, and disseminate information; (2) to visit State agencies and organizations, enterprises, and institutions and organs of social associations and the press services thereof; (3) to be received by officials in connection with a request for information; (4) to receive access to documents and materials, except for fragments thereof containing information comprising a State, commercial, or other secret specially protected by a law; (5) to copy, publish, divulge, or by other means reproduce documents and materials on condition of compliance with the confidentiality requirements of the Law on Mass Media; (6) to make recordings, including with the use of audio and video equipment and cinema and photographic equipment, except for instances provided for by a law; (7) to visit specially-protected sites of natural disasters, wrecks, catastrophes, mass disorders, and mass concentrations of citizens, and also localities in which an extraordinary situation has been declared, and be present at meetings and demonstrations; (8) to verify the reliability of information communicated to him; (9) to set out his personal judgments and assessments in communications and materials intended for dissemination over his signature; (10) to refuse to prepare communications or materials over his signature which are contrary to his convictions; (11) to remove his signature from a communication or materials whose content, in his **12.46** opinion, was distorted in the process of editorial preparation, or to prohibit or otherwise stipulate conditions and the character of the use of the communication or material author's rights; and (12) to disseminate communications and materials prepared by him over his signature or under a pseudonym, or without a signature.

12.47 Among these is the right to create on the territory of the Russian Federation a professional organization of journalists operating on the basis of a charter confirmed by its members, the provisions of which may not be contrary to Russian legislation.

12.48 Accredited representatives of foreign mass media and members of their families may invite as personal guests the citizens of foreign States. Visa questions and the legalization of their sojourn in Russia are handled through the Ministry of Foreign Affairs. They may also take advantage of the services provided by various subdivisions of the Ministry of Foreign Affairs which service the diplomatic corps.

12.49 The freedom of movement of journalists about the territory of the Russian Federation is granted on the basis of reciprocity, with the exception of closed objects for which a special authorization is required to visit.

Customs regulations

12.50 Accredited representatives of foreign mass media and foreign personnel of correspondent points may bring in and take out in order to effectuate their professional activities office equipment, computer, radio, and television equipment, professional audio, video, cinema, and photo equipment, spare parts and materials for this property, informational materials on various carriers, articles of domestic designation, and personal motor vehicles (not exceeding one for each correspondent and foreign personnel of the correspondent point) during the period of their accreditation in the Russian Federation with exemption from customs duties and taxes on condition that the said property is taken out of the Russian Federation when the period of accreditation ends.[11]

Duties of journalists

12.51 The 1991 Law on Mass Media contains thirteen duties of a journalist, as follows: (1) to comply with the charter of the editorial board with which he is in labour relations; (2) to verify the reliability of information communicated by

[11] By a Regulation No. 258-p, 22 March 2001, the State Customs Committee of the Russian Federation directed that foreign correspondents be ensured their rights to duty-free imports and that past violations of this exemption be rectified.

him; (3) to satisfy the request of persons who have provided information to specify the source thereof, and also authorisation of expressions to be quoted if it is divulged for the first time; (4) to preserve the confidentiality of information and/or the source thereof; (5) to receive the consent to the dissemination in the mass media of information concerning the personal life of a citizen from the citizen himself or his legal representatives except for instances when this is necessary to defend the public interest; (6) when obtaining information from citizens and officials, to make them aware an audio or video recording or cinema or photography is being carried out; (7) to inform the editor-in-chief about possible suits and presentation of other demands provided for by law in connection with the dissemination of a communication or material prepared by him; (8) to refuse an assignment given to him by the editor-in-chief or editorial board if it or the fulfilment thereof is connection with a violation of law; (9) to present when effectuating professional activity at first request the editorial card or other document certifying the identity and powers of a journalist; (10) to comply with the prohibition against conducting any pre-election agitation, or agitation with regard to a referendum when effectuating professional activities; (11) to respect the rights, legal interests, honour, and dignity of citizens and organizations; (12) to not permit the use of the rights of a journalist for the purpose of concealing or falsifying socially significant information, the dissemination of rumours under the guise of reliable information, collecting information to the benefit of an outside person or organization which is not part of the mass media; and (13) to prohibit the use of the right of a journalist to disseminate information for the purpose of defaming a citizen or individual categories of citizens solely by reason of sex, age, racial or nationality affiliation, language, attitude towards religion, vocation, place of residence and work, or political convictions.

Within the framework of the CIS, a multilateral Convention on the Status **12.52**
of a Correspondent Representing the Mass Media of a State-Participant of the Commonwealth of Independent States in Other States of the Commonwealth has been drafted and approved for signature by the Russian Federation on 17 April 2004. The Convention would extend to a 'correspondent', defined as a 'person (irrespective of his citizenship) representing the mass media' of one of the Parties and '. . . accredited in another State-Participant of the Commonwealth of Independent States'. The Convention would grant to correspondents the 'most favoured conditions' for the effectuation of professional activity and the receipt and dissemination of objective information about the political, socio-economic, and cultural life of the accrediting State. Under the Convention the 'legal status of a correspondent is regulated by generally-recognized principles and norms of international law, international treaties, the provisions of the present Convention, and national legislation of the Parties'

(Article 3). On the other hand, the 'professional activity' of a correspondent is to be carried on '. . . in accordance with legislation of the accrediting State and generally-recognized rules and norms of journalist ethics'.

12.53 The Parties agree to render assistance to correspondents by facilitating access to official sources of information, press conferences, and similar measures on conditions analogous to those provided to mass media representatives of the accrediting State. Correspondents are granted the right of free movement about the territory of the accrediting State unless a special procedure has been introduced for access to those territories. The right of correspondents to free transmission of information to the mass media they represent is guaranteed, provided they use means not prohibited by legislation of the accrediting State.

12.54 Applications to accredit correspondents are to be considered within not more than two months from the day of receipt. Where a visa regime operates, the Parties agree to issue a entry/exit visa to the correspondent and members of his family. Assistance is even to be given in leasing or acquiring employment and dwelling premises and to extend assistance in the event of unforeseen circumstances, such as natural calamities. And the Parties agree to refrain from taking restrictive measures, including deprivation of accreditation or deportation from the accrediting State by reason of the content of information transmitted by him and disseminated by the mass media which the correspondent represents, unless there has been a violation of legislation of the accrediting State.

12.55 In addition to the draft CIS Convention, the Russian Federation has authorized the signature of a series of bilateral agreements concerning the status of correspondents: Armenia (signature authorized: 27 May 2000); Azerbaidzhan (signature authorized: 5 January 2001); Georgia (signature authorized: 17 November 1994); Kazakhstan (signature authorized: 17 January 2000); Kyrgyz Republic (signature authorized: 29 June 1995); Moldova (signature authorized: 22 April 1997); Tadzhikistan (signature authorized: 26 September 2000); Turkmenistan (signature authorized: 17 May 1995); Uzbekistan (signature authorized: 14 February 1997). The bilateral agreements are substantially similar in substance to the draft CIS Convention.

ANNEXES

FEDERAL LAW ON THE LEGAL STATUS OF FOREIGN CITIZENS IN THE RUSSIAN FEDERATION

[Federal Law of 25 July 2002, No. 115-ФЗ, as amended by Federal Laws of 30 June 2003, No. 86-ФЗ, 11 November 2003, No. 141-ФЗ, 22 August 2004, No. 122-ФЗ, and 2 November 2004, No. 127-ФЗ. *СЗ РФ* (2002), no. 30, item 3032; (2003), no. 27(I), item 2700; no. 46(I), item 4437; (2004), no. 35, item 3607; no. 45, item 4377; (2006), no. 30, item 3587]

Chapter I. General Provisions

Article 1. Subject of Regulation of Present Federal Law

The present Federal Law shall determine the legal status of foreign citizens in the Russian Federation, and also regulate relations between foreign citizens, on one hand, and agencies of State power, agencies of local self-government, and officials of the said agencies, on the other, arising in connection with the sojourn (or residing) of foreign citizens in the Russian Federation and effectuation by them on the territory of the Russian Federation of labor, entrepreneurial, and other activity.

Article 2. Basic Concepts

1. For the purposes of the present Federal Law the following basic concepts shall apply:

foreign citizen—natural person who is not a citizen of the Russian Federation and who has evidence of the existence of citizenship (or subject-ship) of a foreign State;

stateless person—natural person who is not a citizen of the Russian Federation and who has not evidence of the existence of citizenship (or subjectship) of a foreign State;

invitation for entry into the Russian Federation—document which is the grounds for issuance of a visa to a foreign citizen either for entry into the Russian Federation in a procedure not requiring receipt of a visa in instances provided for by a federal law or international treaty of the Russian Federation;

migration card—document containing information concerning a foreign citizen or stateless person arriving or who has arrived in the Russian Federation and the period of the temporary sojourn thereof in the Russian Federation, confirming the right of a foreign citizen or stateless person who has arrived in the Russian Federation in a procedure not requiring receipt of a visa to temporary sojourn in the Russian Federation, and also serving for control over the temporary sojourn of a foreign citizen or stateless person in the Russian Federation [as amended by Federal Law of 18 July 2006, No. 110-ФЗ];

authorization for temporary residing—confirmation of the right of a foreign citizen or stateless person to reside temporarily in the Russian Federation until receipt of a residence permit formalized in the form of a notation on a document certifying the identity of a foreign citizen or stateless person, or in the form of a document of the established form issued in the Russian Federation to a stateless person not having a document certifying his identity;

residence permit—document issued to a foreign citizen or stateless person and confirmation of their right for permanent residing in the Russian Federation, and also their right to free exit from the Russian Federation and entry into the Russian Federation. A residence permit issued to a stateless person shall be simultaneously a document confirming his identity;

foreign citizen legally situated in the Russian Federation—person having a valid residence permit, or authorization for temporary residing, or visa and/or migration card, or other documents provided by a federal law or international treaty of the Russian Federation confirming the right of a foreign citizen to sojourn (or residing) in the Russian Federation [as amended by Federal Law of 18 July 2006, No. 110-ФЗ];

foreign citizen temporarily sojourning in the Russian Federation—person who arrived in the Russian Federation on the basis of a visa or in a procedure not requiring receipt of a visa and having received a migration but not having a residence permit or authorization for temporary residing [as amended by Federal Law of 18 July 2006, No. 110-ФЗ];

foreign citizen temporarily residing in the Russian Federation—person who received authorization for temporary residing;

foreign citizen permanently residing in the Russian Federation—person who received a residence permit;

labor activity of foreign citizen—work of foreign citizen in the Russian Federation on the basis of a labour contract or civil-law contract for the fulfillment of work (or rendering of services);

foreign worker—foreign citizen temporarily sojourning in the Russian Federation and effectuating labour activity in the established procedure;

foreign citizen registered as individual entrepreneur—foreign citizen registered in the Russian Federation as an individual entrepreneur effectuating activity without the formation of a juridical person;

authorization for work—document confirming the right of a foreign worker to effectuate temporarily on the territory of the Russian Federation labour activity or the right of a foreign citizen to register in the Russian Federation a an individual entrepreneur for the effectuation of entrepreneurial activity;

deportation—compulsory banishment of a foreign citizen from the Russian Federation in the event of the loss or termination of legal grounds for the further sojourn (or residing) thereof in the Russian Federation;

foreign citizen who has arrived in the Russian Federation in a procedure not requiring receipt of a visa—a foreign citizen who has arrived in the Russian Federation in the procedure not requiring receipt of a visa (except for a foreign citizen who has arrived in the Russian Federation without a visa in the procedure established for certain categories of foreign citizens (including possessors of diplomatic or employment (or official) passports, passengers of cruise ships, members of the crew of sea-going and river vessels or other means of transport, persons who have performed transit passage across the territory of the Russian Federation, and inhabitants of frontier territories), and also a foreign citizen who has arrived in the Russian Federation without a visa in the procedure established for special purposes, including trade and economic activity in frontier territories, tourism, and construction) [added by Federal Law of 18 July 2006, No. 110-ФЗ].

2. For the purposes of the present Federal Law the concept "foreign citizen" incorporates the concept "stateless person", except for instances when special rules distinctive from rules established for foreign citizens are established by a federal law for stateless persons.

Article 3. Legislation on Legal Status of Foreign Citizens in Russian Federation

Legislation on the legal status of foreign citizens in the Russian Federation shall be based on the Constitution of the Russian Federation and consist of the present Federal Law and other federal laws. Together with this the legal status of foreign citizens in the Russian Federation shall be determined by international treaties of the Russian Federation.

Article 4. Foundations of Legal Status of Foreign Citizens in Russian Federation

Foreign citizens shall enjoy in the Russian Federation rights and bear duties equally with citizens of the Russian Federation, except for instances provided for by a federal law.

Article 5. Temporary Sojourn of Foreign Citizens in Russian Federation

1. The period of temporary sojourn of a foreign citizen in the Russian Federation shall be determined by the period of operation of the visa issued to him.

The period of temporary sojourn in the Russian Federation of a foreign citizen who arrived in the Russian Federation in a procedure not requiring receipt of a visa may not exceed ninety days, except for instances provided by the present Federal Law.

2. A foreign citizen temporarily sojourning in the Russian Federation shall be obliged to exit from the Russian Federation upon the expiry of the period of operation of his visa or other period of temporary sojourn established by the present Federal Law or international treaty of the Russian Federation, except for instances when on the day of expiry of the said periods the period of operation of the visa or period of temporary sojourn was extended for him, or a new visa was issued to him, or authorization for temporary residing, or residence permit, or an application and other documents have been accepted from him necessary for the receipt by him of an authorization for temporary residing in the procedure provided for by Article 6^1 of the present Federal Law [as amended by Federal Law of 18 July 2006, No. 110-ФЗ].

3. The period of temporary sojourn of a foreign citizen in the Russian Federation may be respectively extended or reduced in instances when conditions have changed or circumstances ceased to exist in connection with which entry into the Russian Federation was authorized to him.

4. A decision concerning the extension or reduction of the period of temporary sojourn of a foreign citizen in the Russian Federation shall be adopted by the federal agency of executive power concerned with questions of foreign affairs or federal agency of executive power effectuating law-application functions and functions for control, supervision, and rendering State services in the sphere of migration (hereinafter – federal agency of executive power in the sphere of migration), or territorial agencies thereof [as amended by Federal Law of 18 July 2006, No. 110-ФЗ].

5. The period of temporary sojourn in the Russian Federation of a foreign citizen who arrived in the Russian Federation in a procedure not requiring receipt of a visa and who concluded a labor contract or civil-law contract for

the fulfillment of work (or rendering of services) in compliance with the requirements of the present Federal Law shall be extended for the period of operation of the concluded contract but not more than one year, calculated from the day of entry of the foreign citizen into the Russian Federation. A decision concerning extension of the period of temporary sojourn of a foreign citizen in the Russian Federation shall be adopted by the territorial agency of the federal agency of executive power in the sphere of migration, of which a notation shall be made on the migration card [as amended by Federal Law of 18 July 2006, No. 110-ФЗ].

6. The period of temporary sojourn in the Russian Federation of a foreign citizen who arrived in the Russian Federation and entered military service under a contract shall be established in the procedure determined by the Government of the Russian Federation [added by Federal Law of 11 November 2003, No. 141-ФЗ].

Article 5[1]. Change of Period of Temporary Sojourn [added by Federal Law of 18 July 2006, No. 110-ФЗ]

1. For the purposes of ensuring national security, maintenance of an optimal balance of labour resources, facilitating by way of priority the arrangement of labour of citizens of the Russian Federation, and also for the purpose of resolving other tasks of internal and foreign policy of the State, the Government of the Russian Federation shall have the right to increase up to one hundred eighty days or reduce the period of temporary sojourn of a foreign citizen established by article 5(1), paragraph two, of the present Federal Law both on the territory of one or several subjects of the Russian Federation and throughout the territory of the Russian Federation—with respect to individual categories of foreign citizens temporarily sojourning in the Russian Federation.

2. When adopting a decision concerning the reduction of a period established by Article 5(1), paragraph two of the present Federal Law in accordance with point 1 of the present Article, the Government of the Russian Federation also shall establish the period during which foreign citizens temporarily sojourning in the Russian Federation at the moment of adoption by the Government of the Russian Federation of the said decision shall be obliged to depart from the Russian Federation.

Article 6. Temporary Residing of Foreign Citizen in Russian Federation

1. An authorization for temporary residing may be issued to a foreign citizen within the limits of a quota confirmed by the Government of the Russian Federation unless established otherwise by the present Federal Law. The period of operation of an authorization for temporary residing shall comprise three years [as amended by Federal Law of 18 July 2006, No. 110-ФЗ].

2. The quota for the issuance to foreign citizens of authorizations for temporary residing annually shall be confirmed by the Government of the Russian Federation upon the proposals of executive agencies of State power of subjects of the Russian Federation, taking into account the demographic situation in the respective subject of the Russian Federation and possibilities of the particular subject with regard to the arrangement of foreign citizens.

3. Without taking into account quotas confirmed by the Government of the Russian Federation an authorization for temporary residing may be issued to a foreign citizen:

(1) born on the territory of the RSFSR and in the past in citizenship of the USSR or born on the territory of the Russian Federation;

(2) deemed to lack labor capacity and having a son or daughter who have dispositive legal capacity and in citizenship of the Russian Federation;

(3) having even one parent lacking labor capacity who is in citizenship of the Russian Federation;

(4) in marriage with a citizen of the Russian Federation who has a place of residence in the Russian Federation;

(5) effectuated investments in the Russian Federation in an amount established by the Government of the Russian Federation;

(6) enrolled in military service, for the period of military service thereof [added by Federal Law of 11 November 2003, No. 141-ФЗ];

(6^1) who has arrived in the Russian Federation in the procedure not requiring receipt of a visa [added by Federal Law of 18 July 2006, No. 110-ФЗ];

(7) in other instances provided for by a federal law.

4. A territorial agency of a federal agency of executive power in the sphere of migration shall upon an application filed at the said agency by a foreign citizen temporarily sojourning in the Russian Federation, or upon an application filed by a foreign citizen in a diplomatic representation or consular institution of the Russian Federation in the State of residing of this citizen issue within a six-month period to a foreign citizen an authorization for temporary residing or refuse the issuance to him of such an authorization [as amended by Federal Law of 18 July 2006, No. 110-ФЗ].

5. A territorial agency of a federal agency of executive power in the sphere of migration shall when considering an application of a foreign citizen concerning the issuance of an authorization for temporary residing send queries to security agencies, bailiff service, tax agencies, social security agencies, public health agencies, internal affairs agencies, and other interested agencies which within a two-month period from the day of receipt of the query submit information concerning the existence or absence of circumstances obstructing the issuance to a foreign citizen of an authorization for temporary residing [as amended by Federal Law of 18 July 2006, No. 110-ФЗ].

6. If a foreign citizen was refused issuance of an authorization for temporary residing, or an authorization previously issued to him for temporary residing was annulled, he shall have the right a second time to file an application in the same procedure concerning issuance of an authorization for temporary residing not earlier than one year from the day of rejection of the preceding application concerning the issue of an authorization for temporary residing or annulment of the authorization for temporary residing previously issued to him [as amended by Federal Law of 18 July 2006, No. 110-ФЗ].

7. An authorization for temporary residing shall contain the following information: surname, forename (written in letters of the Russian and Latin alphabets), date and place of birth, sex, citizenship of foreign State, number and date of adoption of decision concerning issuance of authorization, period of operation of authorization, and name of agency of executive power which issued the authorization.

8. The procedure for the issuance of an authorization for temporary residing and list of documents to be submitted simultaneously with an application concerning issuance of an authorization for temporary residing shall be confirmed by the Government of the Russian Federation;

9. A foreign citizen temporarily residing in the Russian Federation for two months from the day of expiry of the next year from the day of receipt by him of an authorization for temporary residing shall be obliged personally to file at the territorial agency of the federal agency of executive power in the sphere of migration at the place of receiving the authorization for temporary residing a notification concerning confirmation of his residing in the Russian Federation with a reference appended concerning revenues, copies of the tax declaration or other document confirming the amount and source of revenue of this foreign citizen for the next year from the day of receipt by him of the authorization for temporary residing [added by Federal Law of 18 July 2006, No. 110-ФЗ].

When there are justifiable reasons, the said notification may be filed by a foreign citizen within a later period, but not later than six months from the day of expiry of the next year from the day of receipt of the authorization for temporary residing, with the documents appended enumerated in paragraph one of the present point, and also documents confirming the impossibility of filing the said notification within the established period [as amended by Federal Law of 18 July 2006, No. 110-ФЗ].

10. The following information shall be entered in the notification specified in point 9 of the present Article:

(1) name of the foreign citizen temporarily residing in the Russian Federation, including his surname, forename, and patronymic (the last—if there is such):

(2) place of residing of the particular foreign citizen;

(3) place(s) of work and duration of effectuation by his foreign citizen of labour activity during the next year from the day of receipt by him of the authorization for temporary residing;

(4) period of the particular foreign citizen being beyond the limits of the Russian Federation during the next year from the day of receipt by him of authorization for temporary residing (specifying the State of exit).

11. Acceptance of a notification in a territorial agency of the federal agency of executive power in the sphere of migration shall be effectuated upon the submission by the foreign citizen of a document certifying his identity and recognized by the Russian Federation in this capacity and the authorization for temporary residing [added by Federal Law of 18 July 2006, No. 110-ФЗ].

12. The requirement of the submission by a foreign citizen of other documents or other information besides that specified in the present Article shall not be permitted. The form and procedure for filing the said notification shall be established by the Government of the Russian Federation [added by Federal Law of 18 July 2006, No. 110-ФЗ].

Article 6[1]. Temporary Residing of Foreign Citizens Who Have Arrived in Russian Federation in Procedure Not Requiring Receipt of Visa [added by Federal Law of 18 July 2006, No. 110-ФЗ]

1. To a foreign citizen who has arrived in the Russian Federation in the procedure not requiring receipt of a visa an authorization for temporary residing shall be issued without taking into account the quota established by the Government of the Russian Federation in accordance with Article 6(2) of the present Federal Law.

2. In order to receive an authorization for temporary residing a foreign citizen who has arrived in the Russian Federation in the procedure not requiring receipt of a visa shall file at the territorial agency of the federal agency of executive power in the sphere of migration:

(1) an application concerning the issuance of an authorization for temporary residing;

(2) a document certifying the identity of the particular foreign citizen and recognized by the Russian Federation in this capacity;

(3) a migration card with a notation of the border control agency concerning entry of the particular foreign citizen into the Russian Federation or with a notation of the territorial agency of the federal agency of executive power in the sphere of migration concerning the issuance to the particular foreign citizen of the said migration card;

(4) a receipt concerning payment of State duty for the issuance to the particular foreign citizen of an authorization for temporary residing.

3. The form of the application specified in point 2(1) of the present Article and the List of information which should be contained therein shall be established by the Government of the Russian Federation.

4. A notation concerning the acceptance from a foreign citizen who has arrived in the Russian Federation in the procedure not requiring a visa of an application concerning the issuance to him of an authorization for temporary residing shall be placed on his migration card. A refusal to accept a particular application shall not be permitted except for instances when any of the documents specified in point 2 of the present Article is not submitted.

5. A foreign citizen who has arrived in the Russian Federation in the procedure not requiring receipt of a visa shall be obliged to submit to the territorial agency of the federal agency of executive power in the sphere of migration which has accepted his application concerning the issuance to him of an authorization for temporary residing:

(1) documents confirming that he has no illness of narcotics addiction and infectious diseases which represent a danger for surrounding persons provided for by a List confirmed by the Government of the Russian Federation, and also a certificate that he has no illness caused by the human immunodeficiency virus (HIV-infection)—within thirty days from the day of filing an application concerning the issuance to him of an authorization for temporary residing;

(2) a certificate (or notification) concerning the placing of the particular foreign citizen on the records of the tax agency—within one year from the day of his entry into the Russian Federation.

6. The executive of the territorial agency of the federal agency of executive power in the sphere of migration shall have the right when a foreign citizen who has arrived in the Russian Federation in a procedure not requiring receipt of a visa has documentarily confirmed justifiable reasons to adopt a decision to extend the period for him to submit the documents specified in point 5 of the present Article.

7. A territorial agency of the federal agency of executive power in the sphere of migration when receiving an application of a foreign citizen who has arrived in the Russian Federation in the procedure not requiring receipt of a visa concerning the issuance to him of an authorization for temporary residing shall send queries to the security agency, tax agency, and public health agency, which shall be obliged within one month from the day of receipt of the respective query to provide information to the said territorial agency concerning the presence or absence of circumstances preventing the issuance to the particular foreign citizen of an authorization for temporary residing or which are grounds for the annulment of an authorization for temporary residing previously issued to him.

8. Not later than sixty days from the day of acceptance from a foreign citizen who has arrived in the Russian Federation in a procedure not requiring receipt of a visa of an application concerning the issuance to him of an authorization for temporary residing on condition of the submission by him of the documents specified in point 5(1) of the present Article, the territorial agency of the federal agency of executive power in the sphere of migration shall be obliged to issue to the said foreign citizen the authorization for temporary residing according to the form established by the Government of the Russian Federation or the notification provided for by Article 7(1)(2) of the present Federal Law concerning a refusal to issue to the particular foreign citizen of an authorization for temporary residing.

Article 7. Grounds for Refusal to Issue or Annulment of Authorization for Temporary Residing

1. An authorization for temporary residing shall not be issued to a foreign citizen, and authorization previously issued shall be annulled, if the particular foreign citizen [as amended by Federal Law of 18 July 2006, No. 110-ФЗ]:

(1) favours the forcible change of the foundations of the constitutional system of the Russian Federation or by other actions creates a threat to the security of the Russian Federation or citizens of the Russian Federation;

(2) finances and plans terrorist (or extremist) acts, renders assistance in the commission of such acts or commits them, and likewise by other actions supports terrorist (or extremist) activity;

(3) within five years which preceded the day of filing an application concerning the issuance of an authorization for temporary residing was subjected to administrative deportation beyond the limits of the Russian Federation or deportation;

(4) submitted forged or false documents or communicated information about himself known to be false;

(5) was convicted by judgment of a court which has entered into legal force for the commission of a grave or especially grave crime or a crime, the recidivism of which was deemed to be dangerous;

(6) has an uncancelled or unremoved record of conviction for the commission of a grave or especially grave crime on the territory of the Russian Federation or beyond the limits thereof deemed to be such in accordance with a federal law;

(7) repeatedly (two or more times) within one year was brought to administrative responsibility for a violation of legislation of the Russian Federation with respect to ensuring the regime of sojourn (or residing) of foreign citizens in the Russian Federation;

(8) during the next year from the day of issuance of an authorization for temporary residing has not effectuated labor activity in the procedure

established by legislation of the Russian Federation for one hundred eighty days or has not received revenues or does not have sufficient means in amounts permitted him to maintain himself and members of his family dependent on him without resorting to assistance of the State at a level not lower than the living minimum established by a law of a subject of the Russian Federation on whose territory temporary residing has been authorized to him. The operation of the present provision shall not extend to a foreign citizen:

the amount of whose average monthly revenue or amount of average monthly per capita revenue of a member of the family is not lower than the living minimum established by a law of a subject of the Russian Federation on whose territory temporary residing has been authorized to the said foreign citizen. The average monthly revenue of a foreign citizen and average monthly per capita revenue of a member of the family of a foreign citizen shall be determined in the procedure established by the Government of the Russian Federation;

studying in day form at a secondary specialized educational institution of the Russian Federation;

students or postgraduates of the day form of study in a higher educational institution of the Russian Federation;

pensioner or disabled person;

relegated to other categories of persons, a List of which shall be established by the Government of the Russian Federation [point (8) as amended by Federal Law of 18 July 2006, No. 110-ФЗ];

(9) upon the expiry of three years from the day of entry has no dwelling premise in the Russian Federation on grounds provided for by legislation of the Russian Federation;

(10) departed from the Russian Federation to a foreign State for permanent residing;

(11) is beyond the limits of the Russian Federation for more than six months;

(12) concluded marriage with a citizen of the Russian Federation which served as grounds for receipt of an authorization for temporary residing and this marriage was deemed by a court to be invalid;

(13) is ill with narcotics addiction, or has no certificate concerning the absence in him of the disease caused by human immuno-deficiency virus (HIV-infection) or suffers from one of the contagious diseases which represent a danger for surrounding persons. A list of such diseases and the procedure for confirming the existence or absence thereof shall be confirmed by the Government of the Russian Federation;

(14) arrived in the Russian Federation in the procedure not requiring receipt of a visa and did not submit the documents within the established period specified in Article $6^1(5)$ of the present Federal Law [added by Federal Law of 18 July 2006, No. 110-ФЗ].

2. In the event of the adoption of a decision concerning a refusal to issue to a foreign citizen an authorization for temporary residing or annulment of an authorization previously issued to him for temporary residing, the territorial agency of the federal agency of executive power in the sphere of migration which adopted such a decision shall issue a respective notification to the said foreign citizen [added by Federal Law of 18 July 2006, No. 110-ФЗ].

3. A decision concerning a refusal to issue to a foreign citizen who has arrived in the Russian Federation in a procedure not requiring receipt of a visa an authorization for temporary residing or annulment of an authorization previously issued to him for temporary residing shall be adopted when there are circumstances provided for by point 1(1)-(8), (10), (11), (13), and (14) of the present Article [as amended by Federal Law of 18 July 2006, No. 110-ФЗ].

4. A decision of a territorial agency of the federal agency of executive power in the sphere of migration concerning a refusal to issue to a foreign citizen an authorization for temporary residing or annulment of an authorization previously issued to him for temporary residing may be appealed by the particular foreign citizen to the federal agency of executive power in the sphere of migration or to a court within three work days from the day of receipt by the particular foreign citizen of notification concerning the adoption of the respective decision. In the period of consideration of the appeal of the particular foreign citizen he shall not lose the right to temporary sojourn in the Russian Federation, except for instances provided for by a federal law. Copies of the decision of the federal agency of executive power in the sphere of migration upon the appeal of the particular foreign citizen within three work days from the day of adoption of such decision shall be sent to the territorial agency of the federal agency of executive power in the sphere of migration which rendered the decision appealed and to the particular foreign citizen [added by Federal Law of 18 July 2006, No. 110-ФЗ].

5. If the federal agency of executive power in the sphere of migration vacated the decision of its territorial agency concerning a refusal to issue to a foreign citizen an authorization for temporary residing or annulment of an authorization previously issued to him for temporary residing, the said territorial agency within three work days from the day of vacating the respective decision shall issue (or restore) the authorization for temporary residing to the particular foreign citizen [added by Federal Law of 18 July 2006, No. 110-ФЗ].

Article 8. Permanent Residing of Foreign Citizens in Russian Federation

1. Within the period of operation of an authorization for temporary residing and when there are legal grounds a residence permit may be issued to a foreign citizen upon the application thereof. An application concerning the issuance of a residence permit shall be filed by a foreign citizen at the territorial agency of

the federal agency of executive power in the sphere of migration not later than six months before expiry of the period of operation of the authorization for temporary residing [as amended by Federal Law of 18 July 2006, No. 110-ФЗ].

2. Before receiving a residence permit a foreign citizen shall be obliged to live in the Russian Federation not less than one year on the basis of an authorization for temporary residing.

3. A residence permit shall be issued to a foreign citizen for five years. Upon the end of the period of operation of a residence permit the said period upon the application of a foreign citizen may be extended for five years. The number of extensions of the period of operation shall not be limited.

4. A residence permit shall contain the following information: surname, forename (written in letters of the Russian and Latin alphabets), date and place of birth, sex, citizenship of foreign citizen, number and date of adoption of decision concerning issuance of residence permit, period of operation of residence permit, name of agency of executive power which issued the residence permit, and shall be formalized in the form of a document of the established form.

5. The procedure for the issuance of a residence permit and list of documents to be submitted simultaneously with the application concerning the issuance of a residence permit shall be confirmed by the Government of the Russian Federation [as amended by Federal Law of 18 July 2006, No. 110-ФЗ].

6. A foreign citizen permanently residing in the Russian Federation shall be obliged annually to inform the territorial agency of the federal agency of executive power in the sphere of migration about confirmation of his residing in the Russian Federation at the place of receipt by the particular foreign citizen of a residence permit. The filing by the particular foreign citizen of the notification shall be effectuated by him personally or in the established procedure by post when submitting the document certifying the identity of the particular foreign citizen and recognized by the Russian Federation in this capacity, and also his residence permit. The requirement of the provision by a foreign citizen of other documents or other information besides those subject to insertion in the said notification shall not be permitted. The following information shall be inserted in the said notification:

(1) name of the particular foreign citizen permanently residing in the Russian Federation, including the surname, forename, and patronymic (the last—if there be such);

(2) the place of residing of the particular foreign citizen;

(3) the place(s) of work and duration of the effectuation by the particular foreign citizen of labour activity during the next year from the day of receipt by him of a residence permit;

(4) period of the particular foreign citizen being beyond the limits of the Russian Federation during the next year from the day of receipt by him of the residence permit (specifying the States of exit);

(5) the amount and sources of revenue of the particular foreign citizen for the next yer from the day of receipt by him of the residence permit [point 6 added by Federal Law of 18 July 2006, No. 110-ФЗ].

7. The form and procedure for filing the notification specified in point 6 of the present Article shall be established by the Government of the Russian Federation [added by Federal Law of 18 July 2006, No. 110-ФЗ].

Article 9. Grounds for Refusal to Issue or Annulment of Residence Permit

A residence permit shall not be issued to a foreign citizen, and residence permit previously issued shall be annulled, if the particular foreign citizen:

(1) favours the forcible change of the foundations of the constitutional system of the Russian Federation or by other actions creates a threat to the security of the Russian Federation or citizens of the Russian Federation;

(2) finances and plans terrorist (or extremist) acts, renders assistance in the commission of such acts or commits them, and likewise by other actions supports terrorist (or extremist) activity;

(3) was subjected to administrative deportation beyond the limits of the Russian Federation or deportation;

(4) submitted forged or false documents or communications information about himself known to be false;

(5) was convicted by judgment of a court which has entered into legal force for the commission of a grave or especially grave crime or a crime, the recidivism of which was deemed to be dangerous;

(6) has an uncancelled or unremoved record of conviction for the commission of a grave or especially grave crime on the territory of the Russian Federation or beyond the limits thereof deemed to be such in accordance with a federal law;

(7) repeatedly (two or more times) within one year was brought to administrative responsibility for a violation of legislation of the Russian Federation with respect to ensuring the regime of sojourn (or residing) of foreign citizens in the Russian Federation;

(8) can not submit evidence of the possibility to maintain himself and members of his family in the Russian Federation within the limits of the living minimum without resorting to assistance of the State, except for instances when the foreign citizen is deemed to lack labor capacity;

(9) upon the expiry of three years from the day of entry has no dwelling premise in the Russian Federation on grounds provided for by legislation of the Russian Federation;

(10) departed from the Russian Federation to a foreign State for permanent residing;

(11) is beyond the limits of the Russian Federation for more than six months;

(12) concluded marriage with a citizen of the Russian Federation which served as grounds for receipt of an authorization for temporary residing and this marriage was deemed by a court to be invalid;

(13) is ill with narcotics addiction, or has no certificate concerning the absence in him of the disease caused by human immuno-deficiency virus (HIV-infection) or suffers from one of the contagious diseases which represent a danger for surrounding persons. A list of such diseases and the procedure for confirming the existence or absence thereof shall be confirmed by the Government of the Russian Federation.

Article 10. Documents Certifying Identity of Foreign Citizen in Russian Federation

1. The passport of a foreign citizen or other document established by a federal law or recognized in accordance with an international treaty of the Russian Federation as a document certifying the identity of a foreign citizen shall be documents certifying identity of a foreign citizen.

2. Documents certifying the identity of a stateless person in the Russian Federation shall be:

(1) document issued by a foreign State and recognized in accordance with an international treaty of the Russian Federation as a document certifying the identity of a stateless person;

(2) authorization for temporary residing;

(3) residence permit;

(4) other documents provided for by a federal law or recognized in accordance with an international treaty of the Russian Federation as documents certifying the identity of a stateless person.

Article 11. Movement of Foreign Citizens Within Limits of Russian Federation

1. Foreign citizens shall have the right to freedom of movement for personal or business purposes within the limits of the Russian Federation on the basis of documents issued to them or formalized in accordance with the present Federal Law, except for visiting territories, organizations, and objects for the entry to which a special authorization is required in accordance with federal laws.

A list of territories, organizations, and objects for entry to which by foreign citizens a special authorization is required shall be confirmed by the Government of the Russian Federation.

2. A foreign citizen temporarily residing in the Russian Federation shall not have the right at own wish to change the place of his residing within the limits of a subject of the Russian Federation on whose territory temporary residing has been authorized to him or to choose the place of his residing outside the limits of the said subject of the Russian Federation.

3. The right to freedom of movement within the limits of the Russian Federation shall be granted to foreign citizens—personnel of diplomatic representations and workers of consular institutions of foreign States in the Russian Federation, personnel of international organizations, and also foreign journalists accredited in the Russian Federation, on the basis of the principle of reciprocity, except for limitations provided for by point 1 of the present Article.

Article 12. Relation of Foreign Citizens to Electoral Law

1. Foreign citizens in the Russian Federation shall not have the right to elect or to be elected to federal agencies of State power, agencies of State power of subjects of the Russian Federation, and also to participate in a referendum of the Russian Federation and referendums of subjects of the Russian Federation.

2. Foreign citizens permanently residing in the Russian Federation shall in the instances and procedure provided for by federal laws have the right to elect and to be elected to agencies of local self-government, and also participate in a local referendum.

Article 13. Conditions of Participation of Foreign Citizens in Labour Relations

1. Foreign citizens shall enjoy the right to freely dispose of their capacities for labour, choose the nature of activity and profession, and also the right to free use of their capacities and property for entrepreneurial and other economic activity not prohibited by a law, taking into account the limitations provided by a federal law.

2. A natural or juridical person who has received in the established procedure an authorization to recruit and use foreign workers and who uses the labor of foreign workers on the basis of labor contracts concluded with them shall be an employer in accordance with the present Federal Law. A foreign citizen registered as an individual entrepreneur may act, inter alia, as an employer.

3. A natural or juridical person who has received an authorization in the established procedure for the recruitment and use of foreign workers and who uses the labor of foreign workers on the basis of civil-law contracts concluded with them for the fulfilment of work (or rendering of services) shall be the customer of work (or services) in accordance with the present Federal Law. A foreign citizen registered as an individual entrepreneur may act, inter alia, as a customer of work (or services).

4. An employer and customer of work (or services) shall have the right to recruit and use foreign workers only when there is an authorization to recruit and use foreign workers.

A foreign citizen shall have the right to effectuate labor activity only when there is an authorization for work. The said procedure shall not extend to foreign citizens who:

(1) permanently reside in the Russian Federation;

(2) temporarily reside in the Russian Federation;

(3) are personnel of diplomatic representations, workers of consular institutions of foreign States in the Russian Federation, personnel of international organizations, and also private domestic workers of the said persons;

(4) are workers of foreign juridical persons (producers or suppliers) fulfilling assembly (or chief assembly) work, service and guarantee servicing, and also post-guarantee repair of technical equipment delivered to the Russian Federation;

(5) are journalists accredited to the Russian Federation;

(6) are studying in the Russian Federation in educational institutions of vocational education and fulfilling work (or rendering services) during vacation;

(7) are studying in the Russian Federation in educational institutions of vocational education and working in time free from study as auxiliary instructional personnel in those educational institutions in which they are studying;

(8) are invited to the Russian Federation as teachers in order to conduct lessons in educational institutions, except for persons entering the Russian Federation in order to engage in teaching activity in institutions of vocational religious education (or theological educational institutions).

4^1. The peculiarities of effectuating labour activity by a foreign citizen who has arrived in the Russian Federation in a procedure not requiring receipt of a visa shall be determined by Article 13^1 of the present Federal Law [added by Federal Law of 18 July 2006, No. 110-ФЗ].

4^2. A foreign citizen temporarily sojourning in the Russian Federation shall not have the right to effectuate labour activity beyond the limits of the subject of the Russian Federation on whose territory the authorization for work was issued to him [added by Federal Law of 18 July 2006, No. 110-ФЗ].

5. A foreign citizen temporarily residing in the Russian Federation shall not have the right to effectuate labour activity beyond the limits of a subject of the Russian Federation on whose territory temporary residing has been authorized for him.

6. Taking into account the peculiarities of regional economic links, the Government of the Russian Federation may establish instances of the effectuation of labour activity:

(1) by a foreign citizen temporarily sojourning in the Russian Federation—beyond the limits of a subject of the Russian Federation on whose territory an authorization for work was issued to him;

(2) by a foreign citizen temporarily residing in the Russian Federation—beyond the limits of the subject of the Russian Federation on whose territory the authorization for work was issued to him [point 6 added by Federal Law of 18 July 2006, No. 110-ФЗ].

Article 13[1]. Labour Activity of Foreign Citizens Who Have Arrived in Russian Federation in Procedure Not Requiring Receipt of Visa

1. An authorization for work shall be issued to a foreign citizen who has arrived in the Russian Federation in a procedure not requiring receipt of a visa, except for instances provided by Article 18(4) of the present Federal Law, by the federal agency of executive power in the sphere of migration or territorial agency thereof on the basis of an application of the particular foreign citizen concerning the issuance to him of an authorization for work.

2. A foreign citizen who has arrived in the Russian Federation in a procedure not requiring receipt of a visa shall file an application concerning the issuance to him of an authorization for work personally or through an organization in the established procedure effectuating the arrangement of labor of foreign citizens in the Russian Federation or through a person acting in accordance with civil legislation of the Russian Federation as a representative of the particular foreign citizen.

3. Simultaneously with the application specified in point 2 of the present Article a foreign citizen shall submit:

(1) a document certifying the identity of the particular foreign citizen and recognized by the Russian Federation in this capacity;

(2) a migration card with a notation of the border control agency concerning the entry of the particular foreign citizen in the Russian Federation or with a notation of the territorial agency of the federal agency of executive power in the sphere of migration concerning the issuance to the particular foreign citizen of the said migration card;

(3) a receipt concerning the payment of State duty for the issuance to the particular foreign citizen of an authorization for work.

4. The federal agency of executive power in the sphere of migration or its territorial agency shall send information concerning the authorizations for work issued to foreign citizens to the agency of executive power concerning with questions of employment of the population to the respective subject of the Russian Federation.

5. A refusal to accept from a foreign citizen who has arrived in the Russian

Federation in the procedure not requiring receipt of a visa of an application concerning the issuance to him of an authorization for work shall not be permitted, except for instances of the failure to submit the documents specified in point 3 of the present Article by the particular foreign citizen.

6. A territorial agency of the federal agency of executive power in the sphere of migration shall consider the application of the foreign citizen concerning the issuance to him of an authorization for work, taking into account the quota for the issuance of such authorizations if the said quotas have been established by the Government of the Russian Federation.

7. The federal agency of executive power in the sphere of migration or its territorial agency not later than ten work days from the day of acceptance from the foreign citizen who arrived in the Russian Federation in a procedure not requiring receipt of a visa of an application concerning the issuance to him of an authorization for work shall be obliged to issue to the particular foreign citizen an authorization for work or notification concerning a refusal to issue such authorization. An authorization for work shall be issued to the particular foreign citizen personally upon the submission by him of a document certifying his identity and recognized by the Russian Federation in this capacity. A decision concerning refusal to issue to the particular foreign citizen an authorization for work may be appealed to the federal agency of executive power in the sphere of migration or to a court within three work days from the day of receipt by the particular foreign citizen of the said notification.

8. If an authorization for work was issued to a foreign citizen who arrived in the Russian Federation in a procedure not requiring receipt of a visa for a period of more than ninety days, he shall be obliged within thirty days from the day of receipt of such authorization to submit to the territorial agency of the federal agency of executive power in the sphere of migration documents confirming that he has no illness of narcotics addiction and infectious diseases which represent a danger for surrounding persons provided for by a List confirmed by the Government of the Russian Federation, and also a certificate that he has no illness caused by the human immunodeficiency virus (HIV-infection).

9. Employers or customers of work (or services) shall have the right to recruit and use for the effectuation of labour activity of foreign citizens who have arrived in the Russian Federation in a procedure not requiring receipt of a visa and having an authorization for work without receiving an authorization for the recruitment and use of foreign workers, but with obligatory notification about such recruitment and use to the territorial agency of the federal agency of executive power in the sphere of migration and the agency of executive power concerned with question of employment of the population in the

respective subject of the Russian Federation. The form and procedure for filing the said notification shall be established by the Government of the Russian Federation.

Article 14. Relation of Foreign Citizens to State or Municipal Service and Individual Types of Activity

1. A foreign citizen shall not have the right to:

(1) be in municipal service [as amended by Federal Law of 11 November 2003, No. 141-ФЗ].

The relation of foreign citizens to State service shall be determined by a federal law [added by Federal Law of 11 November 2003, No. 141-ФЗ];

(2) fill offices in the crew of a vessel flying under the State Flag of the Russian Federation in accordance with limitations provided by the Merchant Shipping Code of the Russian Federation;

(3) be a member of the crew of a warship of the Russian Federation or other vessel to be operated for noncommercial purposes, and also a flying apparatus of State or experimental aviation;

(4) be the captain of a civil aviation aircraft;

(5) be hired for work at objects and in organizations whose activity is connected with ensuring the security of the Russian Federation. A list of such objects and organizations shall be confirmed by the Government of the Russian Federation;

(6) engage in other activity and fill other offices, access of foreign citizens to which is limited by a federal law.

2. The procedure for the filling by foreign citizens of executive offices in organizations in whose charter capital more than 50% of the stocks or participatory shares belong to the Russian Federation shall be established by the Government of the Russian Federation.

Article 15. Relation of Foreign Citizens to Military Service

1. Foreign citizens may not be called up to military service (or alternative military service).

2. Foreign citizens may enter military service under a contract and may be hired for work in the Armed Forces of the Russian Federation, other forces, military formations, and agencies as civilian personnel in accordance with federal laws and other normative legal acts of the Russian Federation [as amended by Federal Law of 11 November 2003, No. 141-ФЗ].

Chapter II. Procedure for Formalization of Invitations for Entry into Russian Federation

Article 16. Procedure for Formalization of Invitation for Entry into Russian Federation

1. An invitation for entry into the Russian Federation (hereinafter also—invitation) shall be issued by a federal agency of executive power concerned with questions of foreign affairs, or federal agency of executive power in the sphere of migration, or territorial agency thereof [as amended by Federal Law of 18 July 2006, No. 110-ФЗ].

2. An invitation shall contain the following information: surname, forename (written in letters of the Russian and Latin alphabets), date and place of birth, sex, citizenship of the invited person, State of residing thereof, number and date of issuance of document certifying identity thereof, purpose of trip, proposed period of sojourn in the Russian federation, proposed destination points in the Russian Federation, name of inviting organization and location thereof, or surname and forename of inviting natural person and address of place of residence thereof, number and date of adoption of decision concerning issuance of invitation and period of operation of invitation.

3. The federal agency of executive power concerned with questions of foreign affairs shall issue invitations upon the petition of:

(1) federal agencies of State power;

(2) diplomatic representations and consular institutions of foreign States in the Russian Federation;

(3) international organizations and their representations in the Russian Federation, and also representations of foreign States attached to international organizations situated in the Russian Federation;

(4) agencies of State power of subjects of the Russian Federation.

4. The territorial agency of a federal agency of executive power in the sphere of migration shall issue an invitation upon the petition of [as amended by Federal Law of 18 July 2006, No. 110-ФЗ]:

(1) agencies of local self-government;

(2) juridical persons;

(3) citizens of the Russian Federation and foreign citizens permanently residing in the Russian Federation.

5. Simultaneously with a petition concerning the issuance of an invitation guarantees shall be provided by the inviting party of material, medical, and housing provision for the foreign citizen for the period of his sojourn in the Russian Federation.

The procedure for granting the said guarantees shall be established by the Government of the Russian Federation.

Article 17. Invitation for Entry into Russian Federation of Foreign Citizen for Purposes of Study in Educational Institution

1. An invitation for entry into the Russian Federation of a foreign citizen for the purposes of study in an educational institution shall be issued by the territorial agency of the federal agency of executive power in the sphere of migration upon the petition of the particular educational institution [as amended by Federal Law of 18 July 2006, No. 110-ФЗ].

2. An invitation for the purposes of study in educational institutions of vocational education shall be issued by a federal agency of executive power in the sphere of migration upon the petition of the federal agency of executive power concerned with questions respectively or defense, or security, or internal affairs, or customs, or the prevention and liquidation of the consequences of extraordinary situations and natural calamities if the said agencies have in their structure an educational institution of vocational education of the corresponding types and varieties [as amended by Federal Law of 30 June 2003, No. 86-ФЗ and by Federal Law of 18 July 2006, No. 110-ФЗ].

3. The educational institution which invited the foreign citizen to the Russian Federation for the purposes of study shall:

(1) guarantee to the foreign citizen the possibility to receive education in the particular educational institution, facilitate the timely registration thereof at the place of sojourn, and also ensure his departure from the Russian Federation upon the completion or termination of study;

(2) within three work days from the day of arrival of a foreign citizen in the particular educational institution send information concerning this to the agency of executive power of the subject of the Russian Federation concerned with questions of education;

(3) within three work days from the day of establishing the fact of the arbitrary departure of the foreign citizen from the particular educational institution send information concerning this to the agency of executive power of the subject of the Russian Federation concerned with questions of education, territorial agency of the federal agency of executive power in the sphere of migration, and territorial agency of the federal agency of executive power concerned with questions of security [as amended by Federal Law of 18 July 2006, No. 110-ФЗ].

Article 18. Invitation for Entry into Russian Federation of Foreign Citizen for Purposes of Effectuation of Labor Activity

1. The quota for the issuance to foreign citizens, except foreign citizens who have arrived in the Russian Federation in a procedure not requiring receipt of a visa, of invitations for entry into the Russian Federation for the purposes of the effectuation of labor activity annually shall be confirmed by the Government

of the Russian Federation upon the proposals of executive agencies of State power of subjects of the Russian Federation, taking into account the demographic situation in the respective subject of the Russian Federation and possibilities of the particular subject with regard to the arrangement of foreign citizens [as amended by Federal Law of 18 July 2006, No. 110-ФЗ].

The said proposals of executive agencies of State power of subjects of the Russian Federation shall be formed on the basis of the principle of priority use of national labor resources taking into account the situation on the labor market.

2. An invitation for entry into the Russian Federation of a foreign worker, except for a foreign citizen who arrived in the Russian Federation in the procedure not requiring receipt of a visa, for the purposes of the effectuation of labor activity shall be issued by the federal agency of executive power in the sphere of migration or territorial agency thereof upon a petition concerning the issuance of an invitation filed by the employer or customer of work (or services) at the respective agency [as amended by Federal Law of 18 July 2006, No. 110-ФЗ].

Simultaneously with the petition concerning the issuance of an invitation for the purposes of the effectuation of labor activity an employer or customer of work (or services) shall submit to the territorial agency of the federal agency of executive power in the sphere of migration or directly at the federal agency of executive power in the sphere of migration if the issuance of an invitation is effectuated by the said federal agency [as amended by Federal Law of 18 July 2006, No. 110-ФЗ]:

(1) authorization for recruitment and use of foreign workers;

(2) documents necessary for the issuance of an authorization for work for each foreign worker. Simultaneously with the invitation an authorization for work for each foreign worker shall be issued for the purposes of the effectuation of labor to an employer or customer of work (or services).

3. An authorization for the recruitment and use of foreign workers, except for the instance provided by point 4 of the present Article, shall be issued by the federal agency of executive power in the sphere of migration or territorial agencies thereof when there is an opinion of the respective territorial agency of the federal agency of executive power concerned with questions of employment of the population [as amended by Federal Law of 18 July 2006, No. 110-ФЗ].

4. An authorization for the recruitment and use of foreign workers in the composition of crews of Russian maritime vessels shall be issued by the federal agency of executive power in the sphere of migration when there is an opinion of a federal agency of executive power concerned with questions of transport in the procedure established by the Government of the Russian Federation in

accordance with the present Federal Law [as amended by Federal Law of 18 July 2006, No. 110-ФЗ].

5. An authorization for work issued to a foreign citizen temporarily sojourning in the Russian Federation shall be issued by the territorial agency of the federal agency of executive power in the sphere of migration on condition of the deposit by the employer or customer of work (or services) of means to an account specially opened by the federal agency of executive power in the sphere of migration necessary to ensure the exit of the foreign worker by a respective type of transport from the Russian Federation [as amended by Federal Law of 18 July 2006, No. 110-ФЗ].

In the event of the administrative deportation of a foreign citizen effectuating labor activity in the Russian Federation without an authorization for work, the means spent from the federal budget for ensuring the exit of the foreign citizen by the respective type of transport from the Russian Federation shall be subject to recovery in a judicial proceeding from the employer or customer for work (or services) who recruited the said foreign citizen for labor activity upon the suit of the agency which executed the decree on administrative deportation of the said foreign citizen [added by Federal Law of 18 July 2006, No. 110-ФЗ].

6. The procedure for issuance of an authorization for work and list of documents to be submitted simultaneously with an application concerning issuance of an authorization for work shall be confirmed by the Government of the Russian Federation.

7. After the exit of a foreign worker from the Russian Federation the means specified in point 5 of the present Article shall be returned to the employer or customer of work (or services) upon the expiry of the period of the contract, and to a foreign citizen registered as an individual entrepreneur—upon the presentation of travel documents confirming payment of exit of the foreign worker from the Russian Federation.

8. An employer or customer of work (or services) who has invited a foreign citizen to the Russian Federation for the purposes of the effectuation of labor activity or conclusion with a foreign worker in the Russian Federation of a new labor contract or civil-law contract for the fulfillment of work (or rendering of services) shall be obliged to:

(1) have an authorization for the recruitment and use of foreign workers, unless provided otherwise by the present Federal Law [as amended by Federal Law of 18 July 2006, No. 110-ФЗ];

(2) ensure the receipt of an authorization for work by a foreign citizen;

(3) submit documents necessary for registration of the foreign citizen at the place of sojourn in the Russian Federation;

(4) inform the tax agency at the place of recording concerning recruitment and use of foreign workers within ten days from the day of filing a petition concerning the issuance to a foreign citizen of an invitation for the purposes of the effectuation of labor activity, or arrival of a foreign citizen at the place of work or place of sojourn, or receipt by a foreign citizen of an authorization for work, or conclusion with a foreign citizen in the Russian Federation of a new labor contract or civil-law contract for the fulfilment of work (or rendering of services), or suspension of the operation or annulment or an authorization for the recruitment and use of foreign workers, or suspension of the operation or annulment of authorization for work to a foreign citizen registered as an individual entrepreneur, or annulment of an authorization for work to a foreign worker;

(5) facilitate the exit of a foreign worker from the Russian Federation upon the expiry of the period of the labor contract concluded with him or civil-law contract for the fulfillment of work (or services);

(6) pay expenses connected with administrative deportation beyond the limits of the Russian Federation or deportation of a foreign citizen hired for work in violation of the procedure established by the present Federal Law for the recruitment and use of foreign workers;

(7) send to the federal agency of executive power in the sphere of migration or territorial agency thereof information concerning a violation by a foreign worker of conditions of the labor contract or civil-law contract for the fulfillment of work (or rendering of services), and also the dissolution of such contracts before time [as amended by Federal Law of 18 July 2006, No. 110-ФЗ];

(8) send to the federal agency of executive power in the sphere of migration or territorial agency thereof and territorial agency of the federal agency of executive power concerned with questions of security information concerning the arbitrary leaving by a foreign worker of the place of work or place of staying [as amended by Federal Law of 18 July 2006, No. 110-ФЗ].

9. An authorization for work shall not be issued to a foreign citizen, and an issued authorization for work shall be annulled, by the territorial agency of the federal agency of executive power in the sphere of migration if the particular foreign citizen [as amended by Federal Law of 18 July 2006, No. 110-ФЗ]:

(1) favors the forcible change of the foundations of the constitutional system of the Russian Federation or by other actions creates a threat to the security of the Russian Federation or citizens of the Russian Federation;

(2) finances and plans terrorist (or extremist) acts, renders assistance in the commission of such acts or commits them, and likewise by other actions supports terrorist (or extremist) activity;

(3) within five years preceding the day of filing an application concerning

issuance of an authorization for work was subjected to administrative deportation beyond the limits of the Russian Federation or deportation;

(4) submitted forged or false documents or communications information about himself known to be false;

(5) was convicted by judgment of a court which has entered into legal force for the commission of a grave or especially grave crime or a crime, the recidivism of which was deemed to be dangerous;

(6) has an uncancelled or unremoved record of conviction for the commission of a grave or especially grave crime on the territory of the Russian Federation or beyond the limits thereof deemed to be such in accordance with a federal law;

(7) repeatedly (two or more times) within one year was brought to administrative responsibility for a violation of legislation of the Russian Federation with respect to ensuring the regime of sojourn (or residing) of foreign citizens in the Russian Federation;

(8) departed from the Russian Federation to a foreign State for permanent residing;

(9) is beyond the limits of the Russian Federation for more than six months;

(10) is ill with narcotics addiction, or has no certificate concerning the absence in him of the disease caused by human immuno-deficiency virus (HIV-infection) or suffers from one of the contagious diseases which represent a danger for surrounding persons. A list of such diseases and the procedure for confirming the existence or absence thereof shall be confirmed by the Government of the Russian Federation;

(11) within thirty days from the day of receipt of the authorization for work in the procedure provided by Article 13^1 of the present Federal Law not submit to the territorial agency of the federal agency of executive power in the sphere of migration documents confirming that he no illness of narcotics addiction and infectious diseases which represent a danger for surrounding persons provided for by a List confirmed by the Government of the Russian Federation, and also a certificate that he has no illness caused by the human immunodeficiency virus (HIV-infection) [added by Federal Law of 18 July 2006, No. 110-ФЗ].

10. The procedure for the contribution of means by an employer or customer of work (or services) necessary in order to ensure by a respective type of transport the departure of foreign workers from the Russian Federation and the return of such means to an employer or customer of work (or services) shall be established by the Government of the Russian Federation.

11. If an employer or customer of work (or services) has violated provisions of the present Federal Law, the federal agency of executive power in the sphere of migration, or the territorial agency thereof, may suspend the operation of the authorization for the recruitment and use of foreign workers, and also author-

ization for work to a foreign citizen who is registered as an individual entrepreneur, issued to an employer or customer of work (or services) or foreign citizen registered as an individual entrepreneur until the elimination by the said persons of violations permitted within the established period [as amended by Federal Law of 18 July 2006, No. 110-ФЗ].

12. If an employer or customer of work (or services) has not eliminated violations permitted within the established period, the authorization for the recruitment and use of foreign workers issued to an employer or customer of work (or services), and also an authorization for work issued to a foreign citizen who is registered as an individual entrepreneur, shall be annulled by the federal agency of executive power in the sphere of migration of the territorial agency thereof [as amended by Federal Law of 18 July 2006, No. 110-ФЗ].

13. In the event of the annulment of an authorization for the recruitment and use of foreign workers, and also in the event of termination of the activity of an employer or customer of work (or services), a foreign worker shall have the right to conclude a new contract with another employer or customer of work (or services) for the period remaining before expiry of the period of operation of an authorization for work on condition that not less than three months remains before the expiry of this period and the new employer or customer of work (or services) has an authorization for the recruitment and use of foreign workers.

Article 18[1]. Peculiarities of Regulation of Labor Market of Foreign Workers [added by Federal Law of 18 July 2006, No. 110-ФЗ]

1. The Government of the Russian Federation annually shall determine the requirement for recruiting foreign workers, including for priority vocational-skills groups, taking into account the political, economic, social, and demographic situation, and also for the purpose of assessing the effectiveness of the use of foreign work force.

2. Executive agencies of State power of a subject of the Russian Federation annually shall determine the requirement for recruiting foreign workers, assess the effectiveness of the use of the foreign work force and contribution of foreign workers to the socio-economic development of the particular subject of the Russian Federation. The determination by agencies of State power of a subject of the Russian Federation of the requirement for recruiting foreign workers shall be effectuated in accordance with the rules established by the Government of the Russian Federation.

3. For the purpose of ensuring national security, maintenance of the optimal balance of labor resources, facilitating in a priority procedure the arrangement of labor of citizens of the Russian Federation, and also for the purpose of resolving other tasks of internal and foreign policy of the State, the Government

of the Russian Federation shall have the right to establish quotas for the issuance to foreign citizens who have arrived in the Russian Federation in a procedure not requiring receipt of a visa of authorizations for work both on the territory of one or several subjects of the Russian Federation and throughout the entire territory of the Russian Federation.

4. Quotas provided for by point 3 of the present Article may be established depending on vocation, speciality, and skills of foreign citizens, countries of origin, and also depending on other economic and/or social criteria, taking into account regional peculiarities of the labor market. The said quotas shall not extend to foreign citizens who are skilled specialists whose labor is arranged for their vocation (or speciality) in accordance with a List of vocations (or specialities, posts), confirmed by the federal agency of executive power effectuating functions with regard to working out State policy and normative legal regulation of employment of the population by agreement with the federal agency of executive power effectuating functions with regard to working out State policy and normative legal regulation in the sphere of socio-economic development and trade.

5. The Government of the Russian Federation shall have the right annually, taking into account regional peculiarities of the labor market and need by way of priority for the arrangement of labor of citizens of the Russian Federation to establish the admissible share of foreign workers to be used in various branches of the economy by economic subjects effectuating activity both on the territory of one or several subjects of the Russian Federation and throughout the entire territory of the Russian Federation. When establishing the said admissible share, the Government of the Russian Federation shall determine the period for bringing into conformity with it by economic subjects the number of foreign workers to be used by them. This period shall be established by taking into account the need for compliance by employers with the procedure for dissolution of a labor contract established by labor legislation of the Russian Federation.

Article 19. State Duty to be Recovered for Actions Performed in Accordance with Present Federal Law

1. State duty shall be recovered for:

(1) issuance to a foreign citizen of an authorization for temporary residing; for issuance of a residence permit to a foreign citizen;

(2) issuance of an invitation for entry into the Russian Federation of a foreign citizen, except for the instance provided for by point 2(1) of the present Article;

(3) issuance of an authorization for the recruitment and use of foreign workers; for issuance to a foreign citizen of an authorization for work, unless

established otherwise by the present Federal Law [as amended by Federal Law of 18 July 2006, No. 110-ФЗ];

(4) extension of a period of temporary sojourn of a foreign citizen to the Russian Federation, except for the instance provided for by point 2(2) of the present Article;

(5) registration of a foreign citizen in the Russian Federation at the place or residence or place of sojourn.

2. State duty shall not be recovered for:

(1) issuance of an invitation for entry into the Russian Federation of a foreign citizen for the purposes of study in a State or municipal educational institution;

(2) extension of a period of temporary sojourn in the Russian Federation of a foreign citizen who arrived in the Russian Federation for the purposes of effectuation of philanthropic activity or delivery of humanitarian assistance or circumstances connected with the necessity of urgent treatment, grave illness, or death of a close relative.

3. The amount of State duty to be recovered in accordance with the present Article and procedure for payment thereof shall be established by a federal law.

Chapter III. Registration of Foreign Citizens in Russian Federation
[Chapter III lost force: by Federal Law of 18 July 2006, No. 110-ФЗ]

Article 20. Registration of Foreign Citizens [lost force: by Federal Law of 18 July 2006, No. 110-ФЗ]

Article 21. Procedure for Registration of Foreign Citizens [lost force: by Federal Law of 18 July 2006, No. 110-ФЗ]

Article 22. Registration of Foreign Citizens Having Diplomatic Privileges and Immunities and Members of Their Families [lost force: by Federal Law of 18 July 2006, No. 110-ФЗ]

Article 23. Documents Necessary for Registration of Foreign Citizen [lost force: by Federal Law of 18 July 2006, No. 110-ФЗ]

Article 24. Registration of Foreign Citizens in Hotel [lost force: by Federal Law of 18 July 2006, No. 110-ФЗ]

Article 24^1. Registration of Foreign Citizens Who Have Applied for Acceptance into Military Service Under Contract [lost force: by Federal Law of 18 July 2006, No. 110-ФЗ]

Article 25. Exemption of Foreign Citizens from Registration [lost force: by Federal Law of 18 July 2006, No. 110-ФЗ]

Chapter IV. Recording of Foreign Citizens Temporarily Sojourning and Residing in Russian Federation

[lost force: by Federal Law of 18 July 2006, No. 110-ФЗ]

Article 26. Centralized Recording of Foreign Citizens [lost force: by Federal Law of 18 July 2006, No. 110-ФЗ]

Article 27. Recording of Foreign Citizens Studying in Russian Federation in Educational Institutions [lost force: by Federal Law of 18 July 2006, No. 110-ФЗ]

Article 28. Recording of Foreign Workers in Russian Federation [lost force: by Federal Law of 18 July 2006, No. 110-ФЗ]

Article 28[1]. Recording of Foreign Citizens Entering Military Service Under Contract and Undergoing Military Service [lost force: by Federal Law of 18 July 2006, No. 110-ФЗ]

Article 29. Recording of Foreign Citizens Having Diplomatic Privileges and Immunities and Members of Their Families [lost force: by Federal Law of 18 July 2006, No. 110-ФЗ]

Chapter V. Migration Recording of Foreign Citizens and Control Over Sojourn (or Residing) of Foreign Citizens in Russian Federation

[as amended by Federal Law of 18 July 2006, No. 110-ФЗ]

Article 29[1]. Migration Recording of Foreign Citizens [added by Federal Law of 18 July 2006, No. 110-ФЗ]

The migration recording of foreign citizens in the Russian Federation shall be effectuated in accordance with the Federal Law on Migration Recording of Foreign Citizens and Stateless Persons in the Russian Federation.

Article 30. Control Over Sojourn and Residing of Foreign Citizens in Russian Federation

1. Control over the residing and temporary sojourn in the Russian Federation and transit movement within the limits of the Russian Federation of foreign citizens, except for citizens specified in point 2 of the present Article, shall be effectuated by the federal agency of executive power in the sphere of migration and by the federal agency of executive power concerned with questions of internal affairs and territorial agencies thereof [as amended by Federal Law of 18 July 2006, No. 110-ФЗ].

2. The federal agency of executive power concerned with questions of foreign affairs shall effectuate control over the temporary sojourn in the Russian Federation of foreign citizens who [are]:

(1) heads of diplomatic representations and heads of consular institutions of foreign States in the Russian Federation, personnel of diplomatic representations and workers of consular institutions of foreign States in the Russian Federation, and also members of families and guests of the said persons if the members of the families or guests reside in residences of the said persons or on the territories of such representations or institutions;

(2) officials of ministries of foreign affairs of foreign States and members of families of the said persons who have entered the Russian Federation on a working visit and have diplomatic or employment passports;

(3) officials of international organizations, officials of representations of the said organizations in the Russian Federation, and officials of international organization s which have headquarters in the Russian Federation, and also members of families and guests of the said persons, if the members of families and guests reside in residences of the said persons or on the territories of such representations, who have entered the Russian Federation on a working visit and enjoy diplomatic privileges and immunities in accordance with an international treaty of the Russian Federation.

3. A foreign citizen shall when entering the Russian Federation fill out a migration card which together with the document certifying the identity of a foreign citizen shall be presented to an official of the border control agency at the admittance point across the State boundary of the Russian Federation. In the event of exit from the Russian Federation the foreign citizen shall be obliged to surrender the migration card to the official of the border control agency at the admittance point across the State boundary of the Russian Federation. The official of the border control agency shall place a notation on the migration card concerning entry of the foreign citizen to the Russian Federation and notation concerning the exit thereof from the Russian Federation.

Article 31. Consequences of Failure to Comply by Foreign Citizen with Period of Sojourn or Staying in Russian Federation

1. If the period of sojourn or temporary staying of a foreign citizen in the Russian Federation is reduced, the particular foreign citizen shall be obliged to exit from the Russian Federation within three days.

2. If an authorization for temporary residing or residence permit issued to a foreign citizen has been annulled, the particular foreign citizen shall be obliged to exit from the Russian Federation within fifteen days.

3. A foreign citizen who has not performed the duty provided for by points 1 or 2 of the present Article shall be subject to deportation.

4. The deportation of foreign citizens in instances provided for by the present Article shall be effectuated by the federal agency of executive power in the

sphere of migration and its territorial agencies in interaction with the federal agency of executive power concerned with questions of internal affairs and its territorial agencies, and also with other federal agencies of executive power and their territorial agencies within the limits of their competence [as amended by Federal Law of 18 July 2006, No. 110-ФЗ].

5. Deportation shall be effectuated at the expense of means of the foreign citizen being deported, and in the absence of such means or if a foreign worker was hired in violation of the procedure established by the present Federal Law for the recruitment and use of foreign workers, at the expense of means of the agency which invited him, diplomatic representation or consular institution of the foreign State of which the foreign citizen being deported is a citizen, international organization or representation thereof, and natural or juridical person specified in Article 16 of the present Federal Law.

6. If establishment of the inviting party is impossible, measures with regard to deportation shall be expense obligations of the Russian Federation. The procedure for the expenditure of means for the said purposes shall be determined by the Government of the Russian Federation [as amended by Federal Law of 22 August 2004, No. 122-ФЗ];

7. The federal agency of executive power in the sphere of migration or territorial agency thereof shall send information concerning deportation of the foreign citizen to the federal agency of executive power concerned with questions of foreign affairs [as amended by Federal Law of 18 July 2006, No. 110-ФЗ].

8. The federal agency of executive power concerned with questions of foreign affairs shall inform about the deportation of a foreign citizen the diplomatic representation or consular institution of the foreign State in the Russian Federation of which the foreign citizen being deported is a citizen.

9. Foreign citizens subject to deportation shall by decision of a court be confined in specially allotted premises of internal affairs agencies or in special institutions created in the procedure established by the law of a subject of the Russian Federation until execution of the decision concerning deportation.

Article 32. Control Over Labor Activity of Foreign Workers

1. Control over the labor activity of foreign workers shall be effectuated by the federal agency of executive power in the sphere of migration and territorial agencies thereof in interaction with other federal agencies of executive power, territorial agencies thereof, and agencies of executive power of subjects of the Russian Federation within the limits of their competence [as amended by Federal Law of 18 July 2006, No. 110-ФЗ].

2. If a foreign worker has violated the conditions of a labor contract or civil-law contract for the fulfillment of work (or rendering of services), the authorization for work issued to the particular foreign worker may be upon the petition of the employer or customer for work (or services) be annulled by the federal agency of executive power within the sphere of migration or territorial agency which issued the particular authorization [as amended by Federal Law of 18 July 2006, No. 110-ФЗ].

Chapter VI. Responsibility for Violation of Present Federal Law

Article 33. Responsibility of Foreign Citizens

A foreign citizen guilty of a violation of legislation of the Russian Federation shall be brought to responsibility in accordance with legislation of the Russian Federation. In so doing a foreign citizen illegally situated in the Russian Federation shall be subject to recording, photographing, and obligatory State fingerprint registration with subsequent placing of the information received in the central data bank to be created in accordance with Article 26 of the present Federal Law.

Article 34. Procedure for Administrative Deportation of Foreign Citizen Beyond Limits of Russian Federation

1. Administrative deportation of a foreign citizen beyond the limits of the Russian Federation shall be effectuated at the expense of means of the foreign citizen being deported, and in the absence of such means or if the foreign citizen was hired in violation of the procedure established by the present Federal Law for the recruitment and use of foreign workers—at the expense of means of the agency which invited him, diplomatic representation or consular institution of the foreign State of which the foreign citizen being deported is a citizen, international organization, or representation thereof, or natural or juridical person specified in Article 16 of the present Federal Law.

2. If establishment of the inviting party is impossible, measures with regard to administrative deportation of a foreign citizen beyond the limits of the Russian Federation shall be expenditure obligations of the Russian Federation. The procedure for the expenditure of means for the said purposes shall be determined by the Government of the Russian Federation [as amended by Federal Law of 22 August 2004, No. 122-ФЗ].

3. The federal agency of executive power concerned with questions of internal affairs or territorial agency thereof or federal agency of executive power concerned with questions of security or agencies thereof shall effectuate the administrative deportation of a foreign citizen beyond the limits of the Russian Federation and send information concerning them to the federal agency of

executive power concerned with questions of foreign affairs, and also to the federal agency of executive power in the sphere of migration [as amended by Federal Law of 30 June 2003, No. 86-ФЗ and by the Federal Law of 18 July 2006, No. 110-ФЗ].

4. The federal agency of executive power concerned with questions of foreign affairs shall notify about the administrative deportation of a foreign citizen beyond the limits of the Russian Federation the diplomatic representation or consular institution of the foreign State in the Russian Federation of which the foreign citizen being deported is a citizen.

5. Foreign citizens subject to administrative deportation beyond the limits of the Russian Federation shall by decision of a court be confined in specially allotted premises of internal affairs or security agencies or in special institutions created in the procedure established by a law of a subject of the Russian Federation until execution of the decision concerning administrative deportation beyond the limits of the Russian Federation [as amended by Federal Law of 30 June 2003, No. 86-ФЗ].

Article 35. Responsibility of Officials

Officials of organizations receiving foreign citizens in the Russian Federation, ensuring the servicing thereof or fulfilling duties connected with compliance with conditions for the sojourn (or residing) of foreign citizens in the Russian Federation, and also the procedure for the registration thereof, formalization of documents for the right of sojourn or residing of foreign citizens in the Russian Federation, movement thereof within the limits of the Russian Federation, and change of place of residence by them in the Russian Federation who are guilty of a violation of legislation of the Russian Federation shall be brought to responsibility in accordance with legislation of the Russian Federation.

Chapter VII. Concluding Provisions

Article 36. Bringing Normative Legal Acts into Conformity with Present Federal Law

1. To propose to the President of the Russian Federation and to charge the Government of the Russian Federation within a three-month period from the day of official publication of the present Federal Law to bring their normative legal acts into conformity with the present Federal Law. To propose to the Government of the Russian Federation to carry on negotiations with the governments of adjacent States concerning the revision of intergovernmental agreements concerning mutual visa-free trips of citizens for the purpose of limiting the list of documents certifying the identity of citizens for entry into the Russian Federation, exit from the Russian Federation, sojourn (or residing) in the Russian Federation, and movement within the limits of the Russian

Federation, and also for the purposes of clarifying the periods of visa-free sojourn of citizens of one State on the territory of another State.

2. From the day of entry into force of the present Federal Law to deem not operating on the territory of the Russian Federation:

Law of the USSR of 24 June 1981, No. 5152-X "On the Legal Status of Foreign Citizens in the USSR" (*Ведомости Верховного Совета СССР* (1981), no. 26, item 836);

Decree of the Supreme Soviet of the USSR of 24 June 1981, No. 5153-X "On the Introduction into Operation of the Law of the USSR 'On the Legal Status of Foreign Citizens in the USSR'" (*Ведомости Верховного Совета СССР* (1981), no. 26, item 837).

3. [lost force – Federal Law of 2 November 2004, No. 127-ФЗ]

4. To insert in Article 7(4) of the Federal Law of 10 December 1995, No. 195-ФЗ, "On the Foundations of Social Servicing of the Population in the Russian Federation" (*Собрание законодательства Российской Федерации* (1995), no. 50, item 4872) a change, setting it out in the following version:

> 'Foreign citizens permanently residing in the Russian Federation shall have rights equal with citizens of the Russian Federation to social servicing unless established otherwise by an international treaty of the Russian Federation'.

5. To make the following change and addition to the Federal Law of 25 July 1999, No. 128-ФЗ, "On State Fingerprint Registration in the Russian Federation" (*Собрание законодательства Российской Федерации* (1998), no. 31, item 3806; (2001), no. 11, item 1002):

(1) Article 9, paragraph one, to add points (l) and (m) of the following content:

> '(l) foreign citizens illegally situated on the territory of the Russian Federation;
> (m) foreign citizens who have received an authorization for temporary residing'.

(2) Article 119, paragraph one, indentation five, to set out in the following version:

> 'persons specified in Article 9, paragraph one, subpoints (i)–(m) of the present Federal Law—internal affairs agencies'.

Article 37. Period of Temporary Sojourn in Russian Federation of Foreign Citizens Who Arrived in Russian Federation Before Entry of Present Federal Law into Force in Procedure Not Requiring Receipt of Visa

1. Foreign citizens who arrived in the Russian Federation before entry of the present Federal Law into force in a procedure not requiring receipt of a visa shall

be obliged to apply concerning receipt of a migration card to the territorial agency of the federal agency of executive power in the sphere of migration at the place of sojourn thereof within sixty days from the day of entry into force of the present Federal Law. The period of temporary sojourn in the Russian Federation of a foreign citizen who received a migration card shall comprise not more than ninety days from the day of receipt of a migration card [as amended by Federal Law of 18 July 2006, No. 110-ФЗ].

2. The period of temporary sojourn in the Russian Federation of a foreign citizen who arrived in the Russian Federation before entry into force of the present Federal Law in a procedure not requiring receipt of a visa and who have not applied concerning receipt of a migration card shall be calculated from the day of entry into force of the present Federal Law.

Article 38. Entry of Present Federal Law into Force

The present Federal Law shall enter into force upon the expiry of three months from the day of official publication thereof.

FEDERAL LAW ON FOREIGN INVESTMENTS IN THE RUSSIAN FEDERATION

[Federal Law No. 160-ФЗ, 9 July 1999, as amended by Federal Law No. 31-ФЗ, 21 March 2002, Federal Law No. 117-ФЗ, 25 July 2002, Federal Law No. 169-ФЗ, 8 December 2003, No. 117-ФЗ, 22 July 2005 and No. 75-ФЗ, 3 June 2006. *СЗ РФ* (1999), no. 28, item 3493; (2002), no. 12, item 1093; no. 30, item 3034; (2003), no. 50, item 4855; (2005), no. 30(II), item 3128; (2006), no. 23, item 2382]

The present Federal Law determines the basic guarantees of the rights of foreign investors to investments and revenues and profit received therefrom and the conditions of entrepreneurial activity of foreign investors on the territory of the Russian Federation.

The present Federal Law is directed towards the attraction and effective use in the economy of the Russian Federation of foreign material and financial resources, progressive techniques and technologies, and management experience and ensuring the stability of the conditions of the activity of foreign investors and compliance with the conformity of the legal regime of foreign investments to the norms of international law and international practice of investment cooperation.

Article 1. Relations Regulated by Present Federal Law and Sphere of Application Thereof

1. The present Federal Law shall regulate relations connected with State guarantees of the rights of foreign investors in the event of the effectuation by them of investments on the territory of the Russian Federation.

2. The present Federal Law shall not extend to relations connected with investments of foreign capital in banks and other credit organizations, nor to insurance organizations, which are regulated respectively by legislation of the Russian Federation on banks and banking activity and by legislation of the Russian Federation on insurance.

The present Federal Law also shall not extend to relations connected with the investment of foreign capital in noncommercial organizations for the achievement of a determined socially useful purpose, including educational, philanthropic, scientific, or religious, which shall be regulated by legislation of the Russian Federation on noncommercial organizations.

The operation of Articles 7 and 16 of the present Federal Law shall not extend to relations connected with the effectuation of industrial-production, technical-introductory or tourist-recreational activity by residents of a special economic zone [added by Federal Law of 22 July 2005, No. 117-ФЗ as amended 3 June 2006].

Article 2. Basic Concepts Used in Present Federal Law

For the purposes of the present Federal Law the following basic concepts shall be used:

foreign investor—foreign juridical person, the civil law capacity of which is determined in accordance with legislation of the State in which it was founded and which has the right in accordance with legislation of the said State to effectuate investments on the territory of the Russian Federation; foreign organization which is not a juridical person, the civil law capacity of which is determined in accordance with legislation of the State in which it was founded and which has the right in accordance with legislation of the said State to effectuate investments on the territory of the Russian Federation; a foreign citizen, the civil law capacity and dispositive legal capacity of whom is determined in accordance with legislation of the State of his citizenship and who has the right in accordance with the legislation of the said State to effectuate investments on the territory of the Russian Federation; a stateless person who permanently resides beyond the limits of the Russian Federation, the civil law capacity and dispositive legal capacity of whom is determined in accordance with legislation of the State of his permanent place of residence and who has the right in accordance with legislation of the said State to effectuate investments on the territory of the Russian Federation; an international organization which has the right in conformity with an international treaty of the Russian Federation to effectuate investments on the territory of the Russian Federation; foreign States in accordance with the procedure determined by federal laws;

foreign investment—the investing of foreign capital in an object of entrepreneurial activity on the territory of the Russian Federation in the form of objects of civil rights which belong to the foreign investor if such objects of civil rights have not been withdrawn from turnover or have not been limited in turnover in the Russian Federation in accordance with federal legislation, including money, securities (in foreign currency and in the currency of the Russian Federation), other property, property rights having the monetary value of exclusive rights to the results of intellectual activity (intellectual property), and also services and information;

direct foreign investment—the acquisition by a foreign investor of not less than 10% of a participatory share(s) (or contribution) in the charter capital of a commercial organization created or newly created on the territory of the Russian Federation in the form of an economic partnership or society in accordance with civil legislation of the Russian Federation; the investing of capital in the basic funds of a branch of a foreign juridical person created on the territory of the Russian Federation; the effectuation on the territory of the Russian Federation by a foreign investor as lessor of a finance lease (finance leasing) of the equipment specified in Section XVI and XVII of the Goods Nomenclature of Foreign Activity of the Commonwealth of Independent States (ТН ВЭД СНГ) with a customs value of not less than 1 million rubles;

investment project—substantiation of the economic advisability and the amount and periods for the effectuation of a direct foreign investment including design-estimate documentation which has been worked out in accordance with standards provided for by legislation of the Russian Federation;

priority investment project—an investment project, the total volume of foreign investments in which constitutes not less than 1 billion rubles (or not less than the equivalent amount in foreign currency at the exchange rate of the Central Bank of the Russian Federation on the day of entry into force of the present Federal Law), or an investment project in which the minimum participatory share (or contribution) of foreign investors in the charter (or contributed) capital comprises not less than 100 million rubles (or not less than the equivalent amount in foreign currency at the exchange rate of the Central Bank of the Russian Federation on the day of entry into force of the present Federal Law) included in a List to be confirmed by the Government of the Russian Federation;

period of recoupment of investment project—the period from the day of commencement of the financing of an investment project with the use of a direct foreign investment until the day when the difference between the accumulated amount of net profit with amortization deductions and the amount of investment expenditures of a commercial organization with foreign investments or the branch of a foreign juridical person or lessor under a contract of finance lease (finance leasing) acquires a positive significance;

reinvestment—the effectuation of capital investments in objects of entrepreneurial activity on the territory of the Russian Federation at the expense of revenues or profit of a foreign investor or commercial organization with foreign investments which have been received by them from the foreign investments;

aggregate tax load—settlement summary amount of monetary means subject to payment in the form of import customs duties (except for customs duties caused by the application of measures relating to the defence of economic interests of the Russian Federation in the event of the effectuation of foreign trade in goods in accordance with legislation of the Russian Federation), federal taxes (except excises and value-added tax on goods produced on the territory of the Russian Federation), and contributions to State extrabudgetary funds (except for contributions to the Pension Fund of the Russian Federation) by a foreign investor and commercial organization with foreign investments effectuating an investment project at the expense of foreign investments at the moment of the commencement of the financing of the investment project.

Article 3. Legal Regulation of Foreign Investments on Territory of Russian Federation

1. The legal regulation of foreign investments on the territory of the Russian Federation shall be effectuated by the present Federal Law, other federal laws, and other normative legal acts of the Russian Federation, and also by international treaties of the Russian Federation.

2. Subjects of the Russian Federation shall have the right to adopt laws and other normative legal acts regulating foreign investments with regard to questions relegated to their jurisdiction, and also to the joint jurisdiction of the Russian Federation and subjects of the Russian Federation, in accordance with the present Federal Law and other federal laws.

Article 4. Legal Regime of Activity of Foreign Investors and Commercial Organizations with Foreign Investments

1. The legal regime of the activity of foreign investors and the use of profit received from investments may not be less favourable than the legal regime of activity and the use of profit received from investments granted to Russian investors, with the exceptions established by federal law.

2. Exceptions of a limited character for foreign investors may be established by federal laws only to the extent that this is necessary for the purposes of defence of the foundations of the constitutional system, morality, public health, and the rights and legal interests of other persons and ensuring the defence of the country and the security of the State.

Exceptions of an incentive character in the form of privileges for foreign investors may be established in the interests of the socio-economic development of the Russian Federation. The types of privileges and procedure for granting them shall be established by legislation of the Russian Federation.

3. A branch of a foreign juridical person created on the territory of the Russian Federation shall fulfill part of the functions or all of the functions, including the function of representation, in the name of the foreign juridical person which created it (hereinafter: head organization) on condition that the purposes of the creation and activity of the head organization shall have a commercial character and the head organization bears direct property

responsibility for obligations accepted by it in connection with the conducting of the said activity on the territory of the Russian Federation.

4. Subsidiary and dependent societies of a commercial organization with foreign investments shall not enjoy the legal defence, guarantees, and privileges established by the present Federal Law in the event of the effectuation by them of entrepreneurial activity on the territory of the Russian Federation.

5. A foreign investor, commercial organization with foreign investments created on the territory of the Russian Federation in which the foreign investor(s) possess not less than 10% of the participatory share(s) (or contribution) in the charter (or contributed) capital of the said organization shall in the event of the effectuation of reinvesting by them enjoy in full the legal defence, guarantees, and privileges established by the present Federal Law.

6. A Russian commercial organization shall receive the status of a commercial organization with foreign investments from the day of the entry of participants of the foreign investor into the composition thereof. From this day the commercial organization with foreign investments and the foreign investor shall enjoy the legal defence, guarantees, and privileges established by the present Federal Law.

A commercial organization shall lose the status of a commercial organization with foreign investments from the day of withdrawal of the foreign investor from the composition of the participants thereof (when there are several foreign investors in the composition of its participants, in the event of the withdrawal of all foreign investors). From this day the said commercial organization shall lose the legal defence, guarantees, and privileges established by the present Federal law.

Article 5. Guarantee of Legal Defence of Activity of Foreign Investors on Territory of Russian Federation

1. Full and unconditional defence of the rights and interests which are ensured by the present Federal Law, other federal laws, and other normative legal acts of the Russian Federation, and also international treaties of the Russian Federation, shall be granted to a foreign investor on the territory of the Russian Federation.

2. A foreign investor shall have the right to compensation of losses caused to it as a result of the illegal actions (or failure to act) of State agencies, agencies of local self-government, or officials of these agencies in accordance with civil legislation of the Russian Federation.

Article 6. Guarantee of Use by Foreign Investor of Various Forms of Effectuation of Investments on Territory of Russian Federation

A foreign investor shall have the right to effectuate investments on the territory of the Russian Federation in any forms not prohibited by legislation of the Russian Federation.

The investing of capital in the charter (or contributed) capital of a commercial organization with foreign investments shall be valued in accordance with legislation of the Russian Federation.

The valuation of the investing of capital shall be effectuated in the currency of the Russian Federation.

Article 7. Guarantee of Transfer of Rights and Duties of Foreign Investor to Another Person

1. A foreign investor by virtue of a contract shall have the right to transfer his rights (or assign demands) and duties (or transfer a debt), and on the basis of a law or decision of a court shall be obliged to transfer his rights (or assign demands) and duties (or transfer a debt) to another person in accordance with civil legislation of the Russian Federation.

2. If a foreign State or State agency empowered by it makes payment to the benefit of a foreign investor under a guarantee (or contract of insurance) granted to a foreign investor with respect to investments effectuated by it on the territory of the Russian Federation, and to this foreign State or State agency empowered by it the rights (or demands) of the foreign investor to the said investments pass (or are assigned), then in the Russian Federation such a transfer of rights (or assignment of demand) shall be deemed to be lawful.

Article 8. Guarantee of Contributory Compensation in Event of Nationalization and Requisition of Property of Foreign Investor or Commercial Organization with Foreign Investments

1. The property of a foreign investor or commercial organization with foreign investments shall not be subject to compulsory seizure, including nationalization or requisition, except for instances and on the grounds which have been established by a federal law or international treaty of the Russian Federation.

2. In the event of the requisition to a foreign investor or commercial organization with foreign investments shall be paid the value of the requisitioned property. In the event of the termination of the operation of the circumstances in connection with which the requisition was performed, the foreign investor or commercial organization with foreign investments shall have the right to demand in a judicial proceeding the return of the preserved property, but in so doing shall be obliged to return the amount of contributory compensation

received by them, taking into account the loss from the reduction of the value of the property.

In the event of nationalization to a foreign investor or commercial organization with foreign investments shall be compensated the value of the property nationalized and other losses. Disputes concerning compensation of losses shall be settled in the procedure provided for by Article 10 of the present Federal Law.

Article 9. Guarantee Against Unfavourable Change for Foreign Investor or Commercial Organization with Foreign Investments of Legislation of Russian Federation

1. In the event new federal laws and other normative legal acts of the Russian Federation enter into force which change the amounts of import customs duties (except for customs duties caused by the application of measures relating to the defence of the economic interests of the Russian Federation when effectuating foreign trade in goods in accordance with legislation of the Russian Federation), federal taxes (except for excises and value-added tax on goods produced on the territory of the Russian Federation) and contributions to State extrabudgetary funds (except for contributions to the Pension Fund of the Russian Federation), or changes and additions are made in prevailing federal laws and other normative legal acts of the Russian Federation which lead to an increase of the aggregate tax load on the activity of a foreign investor or commercial organization with foreign investments with regard to the realization of priority investment projects, or they establish a regime of prohibitions and limitations with respect to foreign investments in the Russian Federation in comparison with the aggregate tax load and regime which operated in accordance with federal laws and other normative legal acts of the Russian Federation on the day of commencement of the financing of a priority investment project at the expense of foreign investments, then such new federal laws and other normative legal acts of the Russian Federation, and also the changes in and additions made in prevailing federal laws and other normative legal acts of the Russian Federation, shall not be applied during the periods specified in point 2 of the present Article with respect to the foreign investor and commercial organization with foreign investments on condition that the goods imported to the customs territory of the Russian Federation by the foreign investor and commercial organization with foreign investments are used for the special-purpose designation in order to realize the priority investment projects.

The provisions of paragraph one of the present point shall extend to a commercial organization with foreign investments if the participatory share(s) (or contribution) of foreign investors in the charter (or contributed) capital of such organization comprise more than 25%, and also to a commercial organization with foreign investments realizing a priority investment project irrespective of the participatory share(s) (or contribution) of foreign investors to the charter (or contributed) capital of such organization.

2. Stability for a foreign investor effectuating an investment project and the conditions and regime specified in point 1 of the present Article shall be guaranteed for the period of recoupment of the investment project, but not more than seven years from the day of commencement of the financing of the said project at the expense of foreign investments. Differentiation of the period of recoupment of investment projects shall, depending upon their types, be determined in the procedure established by the Government of the Russian Federation.

3. In exceptional instances in the event of the realization by a foreign investor and commercial organization with foreign investments of priority investment projects in the sphere of production or creation of a transport or other infrastructure with a total amount of foreign investments of not less than 1 billion rubles (or not less than the equivalent amount in foreign currency at the exchange rate of the Central Bank of the Russian Federation on the day of entry into force of the present Federal Law), the period of recoupment of which exceeds seven years, the Government of the Russian Federation shall adopt a decision concerning extension for the said foreign investor and commercial organization with foreign investments of the period of operation of the conditions and regime specified in point 1 of the present Article.

4. The provisions of point 1 of the present Article shall not extend to changes and additions which are made in legislative acts of the Russian Federation or adopted new federal laws and other normative legal acts of the Russian Federation for the purpose of defence of the foundations of the constitutional system, morality, public health, rights and legal interests of other persons, and ensuring the defence of the country and security of the State.

5. The Government of the Russian Federation shall:

establish the criteria for evaluating changes of conditions for the recovery of import customs duties, federal taxes, and contributions to State extrabudgetary funds, and the regime of prohibitions and limitations for the effectuation of foreign investments on the territory of the Russian Federation which are unfavourable for a foreign investor or commercial organization with foreign investments;

confirm the procedure for the registration of priority investment projects by a federal agency of executive power specified in Article 24 of the present Federal Law;

effectuate control over the performance by the foreign investor and commercial organization with foreign investments of obligations assumed by them with regard to the realization of priority investment projects within the periods specified in points 2 and 3 of the present Article.

In the event of the failure of the foreign investor or commercial organization with foreign investments to perform obligations specified in paragraph one of the present point, they shall be deprived of the privileges granted to them in accordance with the present Article. The amount of monetary means not paid as a result of the granting of such privileges shall be subject to return in the procedure established by legislation of the Russian Federation.

Article 10. Guarantee of Ensuring Proper Settlement of Dispute Which Arose in Connection with Effectuation of Investments and Entrepreneurial Activity on Territory of Russian Federation by Foreign Investor

A dispute of a foreign investor which has arisen in connection with the effectuation of investments and entrepreneurial activity on the territory of the Russian Federation shall be settled in accordance with international treaties of the Russian Federation and federal laws in a court or arbitrazh court or in international arbitration (or arbitration court).

Article 11. Guarantee of Use on Territory of Russian Federation and Transfer Beyond Limits of Russian Federation of Revenues, Profit, and Other Lawfully Received Monetary Amounts

A foreign investor shall after payment of the taxes and charges provided for by legislation of the Russian Federation have the right to free use of revenues and profits on the territory of the Russian Federation for reinvesting in compliance with the provisions of Article 4(2) of the present Federal Law or for other purposes which are not contrary to legislation of the Russian Federation and to unhindered transfer beyond the limits of the Russian Federation of revenues and other lawfully received monetary amounts in foreign currency in connection with investments previously effectuated by him, including:

revenues from investments received in the form of profit, dividends, interest, and other revenues;

monetary amounts in performance of obligations of a commercial organization with foreign investments or a foreign juridical person which opened its branch on the territory of the Russian Federation with regard to contracts and other transactions;

monetary amounts received by a foreign investor in connection with the liquidation of a commercial organization with foreign investments or branch of a foreign juridical person or alienation of invested property, property rights, and exclusive rights to the results of intellectual activity;

contributory compensation provided for by Article 8 of the present Federal Law.

Article 12. Guarantee of Right of Foreign Investor to Unhindered Export Beyond Limits of Russian Federation of Property and Information in Documentary Form or in Form of entry of Electronic Carriers Which Were Initially Imported to Territory of Russian Federation as Foreign Investment

A foreign investor which initially imported to the territory of the Russian Federation property and information in documentary form or in the form of entries on electronic carriers as a foreign investment shall have the right to unhindered (without quotas, licensing, and application to it of other measures of nontariff regulation of foreign trade activity) export of the said property and information beyond the limits of the Russian Federation.

Article 13. Guarantee of Right of Foreign Investor to Acquisition of Securities

A foreign investor shall have the right to acquire stocks and other securities of Russian commercial organizations and State securities in accordance with legislation of the Russian Federation on securities.

Article 14. Guarantee of Participation of Foreign Investor in Privatization

A foreign investor may participate in the privatization of objects of State and municipal ownership by means of the acquisition of the rights of ownership to State and municipal property or participatory share(s) (or contribution) to charter (or contributed) capital of an organization being privatized on the conditions and in the procedure which have been established by legislation of the Russian Federation on privatization of State and municipal property.

Article 15. Guarantee of Granting to Foreign Investor of Right to Land Plots, Other Natural Resources, Buildings, Installations, and Other Immoveable Property

The acquisition by a foreign investor of the right to land lots, other natural resources, buildings, installations, and other immoveable property shall be effectuated in accordance with legislation of the Russian Federation and legislation of subjects of the Russian Federation.

The right of lease of a land plot may be acquired by a commercial organization with foreign investments at a public sale (or auction, competition) unless provided otherwise by legislation of the Russian Federation.

Article 16. Privileges to be Granted to Foreign Investor or Commercial Organization with Foreign Investments With Regard to Payment of Customs Payments

Privileges with regard to the payment of customs duties shall be granted to foreign investors and commercial organizations with foreign investments in the event of the effectuation by them of a priority investment project in accordance with customs legislation of the Russian Federation and legislation of the Russian Federation on taxes and charges.

Article 17. Privileges and Guarantees to be Granted to Foreign Investor by Subjects of Russian Federation and Agencies of Local Self-Government

Subjects of the Russian Federation and agencies of local self-government may within the limits of their competence grant to a foreign investor privileges and guarantees to effectuate the financing and render other forms of support for the investment project effectuated by a foreign investor at the expense of means of the budgets of subjects of the Russian Federation and local budgets, and also extrabudgetary means.

Article 18. Anti-Monopoly Legislation of Russian Federation and Compliance with Good-Faith Competition by Foreign Investor

A foreign investor shall be obliged to comply with anti-monopoly legislation of the Russian Federation and not permit unfair competition and restrictive business practices, including by means of the creation on the territory of the Russian Federation of a commercial organization with foreign investments or branch of a foreign juridical person for the production of any good enjoying increased demand and then self-liquidation for the purposes of putting forward on the market an analogous good of foreign origin, and also by means of an ill-intentioned agreement concerning prices or distribution of markets for the sale of the good or concerning participation in a public sale (or auction, competition).

Article 19. Property Insurance Effectuated by Commercial Organization with Foreign Investments and Head Organization of Branch of Foreign Juridical Person

Property insurance of the risk of loss (or perishing), shortage, or damage to property, risk of civil responsibility and entrepreneurial risk shall be effectuated by a commercial organization with foreign investments at its discretion, and by the branch of a foreign juridical person, at the discretion of the head organization, unless provided otherwise by legislation of the Russian Federation.

Article 20. Creation and Liquidation of Commercial Organization with Foreign Investments

1. The creation and liquidation of a commercial organization with foreign investments shall be effectuated on the conditions and in the procedure which has been provided for by the Civil Code of the Russian Federation and other federal laws, with the exceptions which may be established by federal laws in accordance with Article 4(2) of the present Federal Law.

2. Juridical persons which are commercial organizations with foreign investments shall be subject to State registration in the procedure determined by the Federal Law "On the State Registration of Juridical Persons" [as amended by Federal Laws of 21 March 2002, No. 31-ФЗ, 25 July 2002, No. 117-ФЗ and 8 December 2003, No. 169-ФЗ].

Article 21. Creation and Liquidation of Branch of Foreign Juridical Person

The branch of a foreign juridical person shall be created for the purposes of the effectuation on the territory of the Russian Federation of activity which the head organization effectuates beyond the limits of the Russian Federation and shall be liquidated on the basis of a decision of the foreign juridical person-head organization.

State control over the creation, activity, and liquidation of a branch of a foreign juridical person shall be effectuated by means of the accreditation thereof in the procedure determined by the Government of the Russian Federation.

The federal agency of executive power specified in Article 24 of the present Federal Law shall effectuate the accreditation of the branch of a foreign juridical person.

The branch of a foreign juridical person may be refused accreditation for the purposes of defence of the constitutional system, morality, public health, the rights and interests of other persons ensuring defence of the country and the security of the State.

Article 22. Requirements for Statute on Branch of Foreign Juridical Person

1. A head organization shall submit to the federal agency of executive power specified in Article 24 of the present Federal Law the Statute on the branch of the foreign juridical person and other documents, a List of and the requirements for the content of which, taking into account points 2 and 3 of the present Article, shall be confirmed by the Government of the Russian Federation.

2. The Statute on the branch of a foreign juridical person must specify the name of the branch and its head organization, the organizational-legal form of the head organization, the location of the branch on the territory of the Russian Federation and legal address of its head organization, the purposes for the creation and the types of activity of the branch, the composition, amount, and periods for investing capital in the basic funds of the branch, and the procedure for management of the branch. Other information reflecting the peculiarities of the activity of the branch of a foreign juridical person on the territory of the Russian Federation and not contrary to legislation of the Russian Federation may be included in the Statute on the branch of a foreign juridical person.

3. Investing of capital in the basic funds of the branch of a foreign juridical person shall be valued by the head organization on the basis of internal prices or world prices. Valuation of the investing of capital shall be effectuated in the currency of the Russian Federation. The increase of the value valuation of the investing of capital in the basic funds of the branch of a foreign juridical person must be specified in the Statute on the branch of a foreign juridical person.

4. The branch of a foreign juridical person shall have the right to effectuate entrepreneurial activity on the territory of the Russian Federation from the day of its accreditation.

The branch of a foreign juridical person shall terminate entrepreneurial activity on the territory of the Russian Federation from the day of deprivation of the accreditation thereof.

Article 23. Working Out and Realization of State Policy in Domain of Foreign Investments

In accordance with the Federal Constitutional Law on the Government of the Russian Federation, the Government of the Russian Federation shall work out and realize State policy in the sphere of international investment cooperation.

The Government of the Russian Federation shall:

determine the advisability of introducing prohibitions and limitations on the effectuation of foreign investments on the territory of the Russian Federation and work out draft laws concerning lists of the said prohibitions and limitations;

determine the measures relating to control over the activity of foreign investors in the Russian Federation;

confirm the List of priority investment projects specified in Article 2 of the present Federal Law;

work out and ensure the realization of federal programs for attracting foreign investments;

attract investment credits of international financial organizations and foreign States for financing the Development Budget of the Russian Federation and investment projects of federal significance;

effectuate interaction with subjects of the Russian Federation with regard to questions of international investment cooperation;

effectuate control over the preparation and conclusion of investment agreements concerning the realization by them of large-scale investment projects;

effectuate control over the preparation and conclusion of international treaties of the Russian Federation on encouraging and mutual defence of investments.

Article 24. Federal Agency of Executive Power with Regard to Coordination of Attraction of Direct Foreign Investments

The Government of the Russian Federation shall determine the federal agency of executive power responsible for the coordination of attracting direct foreign investments to the economy of the Russian Federation.

Article 25. Deeming to Have Lost Force Previously Adopted Legislative Acts of Russian Federation and Individual Provisions Thereof in Connection with Adoption of Present Federal Law

In connection with the adoption of the present Federal Law, to deem to have lost force:

the Law of the RSFSR on Foreign Investments in the RSFSR (*Ведомости Съезда народных депутатов РСФСР и Верховного Совета РСФСР* (1991), no. 29, item 1008);

the Decree of the Supreme Soviet of the RSFSR 'On the Introduction into Operation of the Law of the RSFSR on Foreign Investments in the RSFSR' (*Ведомости Съезда народных депутатов РСФСР и Верховного Совета РСФСР* (1991), no. 29, item 1009;

Article 6 of the Federal Law 'On Making Changes in and Additions to Legislative Acts of the Russian Federation in Connection with the Adoption of the Laws of the Russian Federation "On Standardization", "On Ensuring the Unity of Measurements", and "On the Certification of Products and Services" ' (*Собрание законодательства Российской Федерации* (1995), no. 26, item 2397);

Article 1(4) of the Federal Law 'On Making Changes in and Additions to Laws and Other Legal Acts of the Russian Federation in Connection with the Adoption of the Federal Constitutional Law "On Arbitrazh Courts in the Russian Federation" and the Code of Arbitrazh Procedure of the Russian Federation' (*Собрание законодательства Российской Федерации* (1997), no. 47, item 5341).

Article 26. Bringing Legislation of Russian Federation into Conformity with Present Federal Law

1. To propose to the President of the Russian Federation and to the Government of the Russian Federation to bring their normative legal acts into conformity with the present Federal Law.

2. The Government of the Russian Federation shall submit proposals in the established procedure to the State Duma of the Federal Assembly of the Russian Federation concerning the making of changes in and additions to legislative acts of the Russian Federation which arise from the present Federal Law.

Article 27. Bringing Statutes of Foreign Juridical Persons Created on Territory of Russian Federation into Conformity with Present Federal Law

Head organizations whose branches have been created on the territory of the Russian Federation before the entry into force of the present Federal Law shall be obliged to:

bring the Statutes on the branches of foreign juridical persons into conformity with the present Law within six months from the day of the entry thereof into force;

conduct the accreditation of branches of foreign juridical persons within one year from the day of entry into force of the present Federal Law.

Article 28. Entry of Present Federal Law into Force

The present Federal Law shall enter into force from the day of official publication thereof.

FEDERAL LAW ON INVESTMENT ACTIVITY IN THE RUSSIAN FEDERATION EFFECTUATED IN THE FORM OF CAPITAL INVESTMENTS

[Federal Law No. 39-ФЗ, 25 February 1999, as amended by Federal Law No. 22-ФЗ, 2 January 2000, Federal Law No. 122-ФЗ, 22 August 2004, and Federal Law No. 19-ФЗ, 2 February 2006. *жСЗ РФ* (1999), no. 9, item 1096; (2000), no. 2, item 143; (2004), no. 35, item 3607; (2006), no. 6, item 636]

The present Federal Law determines the legal and economic foundations of investment activity effectuated in the form of capital investments on the territory of the Russian Federation, and also establishes guarantees of the equal defence of the rights, interests, and property of the subjects of investment activity effectuated in the form of capital investments irrespective of the forms of ownership.

Chapter I. General Provisions

Article 1. Basic Concepts

For the purposes of the present Federal Law the following basic concepts are used:

investments: monetary means, securities, other property, including property rights, other rights having monetary value contributed to objects of entrepreneurial and/or other activity for the purposes of receiving profit and/or achieving another useful effect;

investment activity: the investing of investments and the effectuation of practical actions for the purposes of receiving profit and/or achieving another useful effect;

capital investments: investments in the basic capital (or basic means), including expenditures for new construction, expansion, conversion, and technical re-equipping of operating enterprises, the acquisition of machines, equipment, tools, inventory, and design-prospecting work and other expenditures;

investment project: substantiation of the economic advisability, amount, and periods for the effectuation of capital investments, including necessary design-estimate documentation worked out in accordance with legislation of the Russian Federation and standards (or norms, rules) confirmed in the established procedure, and also a description of the practical actions relating to the effectuation of the investments (business plan);

priority investment project: an investment project, the total amount of capital investments in which corresponds to the requirements of legislation of the Russian Federation included in the List confirmed by the Government of the Russian Federation [added by Federal Law No. 22-AP, 2 January 2000];

period of recoupment of investment project: the period from the day of commencement of the financing of an investment project up to the day when the difference between the accumulation of the amount of net profit with amortization deductions and the amount of investment expenditures acquires positive significance [added by Federal Law No. 22-AP, 2 January 2000];

aggregate tax load: account settlement total amount of monetary means subject to payment in the form of import customs duties (except for special types of duties caused by the application of measures with regard to the defence of the economic interests of the Russian Federation when effectuating foreign trade in goods in accordance with legislation of the Russian Federation), federal taxes (except for excises and value-added tax on goods produced on the territory of the Russian Federation), and contributions to State extrabudgetary funds (except for contributions to the Pension Fund of the Russian Federation) by the investor effectuating the investment project on the day of commencement of the financing of the investment project [added by Federal Law No. 22-AP, 2 January 2000].

Article 2. Relations Regulated by Present Federal Law

The operation of the present Federal Law shall extend to relations connected with investment activity effectuated in the form of capital investments.

The present Federal Law shall not extend to relations connected with the making of investments in banks and other credit organizations, nor also to insurance organizations, which shall be regulated respectively by legislation of the Russian

Federation on banks and banking activity and by legislation of the Russian Federation on insurance [added by Federal Law No. 22-AP, 2 January 2000].

Article 3. Objects of Capital Investments

1. Various types of newly created and/or modernized property, with the exceptions established by federal laws, which are in private, State, municipal and other forms of ownership shall be objects of capital investments in the Russian Federation.

2. Capital investments shall be prohibited in objects whose creation and use does not correspond to legislation of the Russian Federation and to standards (or norms and rules) confirmed in the established procedure.

Article 4. Subjects of Investment Activity Effectuated in Form of Capital Investments

1. Investors, customers, independent-work contractors, and users of the objects of capital investments, and other persons shall be the subjects of investment activity effectuated in the form of capital investments (hereinafter: subjects of investment activity).

2. Investors shall effectuate capital investments on the territory of the Russian Federation with the use of own and/or attracted means in accordance with legislation of the Russian Federation. Natural and juridical persons created on the basis of a contract on joint activity and not having the status of a juridical person, associations of juridical persons, State agencies, agencies of local self-government, and also foreign subjects of entrepreneurial activity (hereinafter: foreign investors) may be investors.

3. Customers shall be natural and juridical persons empowered by investors which effectuate the realization of investment projects. In so doing they shall not interfere in entrepreneurial and/or other activity of other subjects of investment activity unless provided otherwise by the contract between them. Investors may be customers.

A customer who is not an investor shall be endowed with the rights of possession, use, and disposition of capital investments in the period and within the limits of the powers which have been established by the contract and/or State contract in accordance with legislation of the Russian Federation.

4. Independent work contractors—natural and juridical persons who fulfill work under an independent-work contract and/or State or municipal contract to be concluded with customers in accordance with the Civil Code of the Russian Federation. Independent-work contractors shall be obliged to have a license for the effectuation by them of those types of activity which are subject to licensing in accordance with a federal law [as amended by Federal Law No. 19-AP, 2 February 2006].

5. The users of objects of capital investments—natural and juridical persons, including foreign, and also State agencies, agencies of local self-government, foreign States, and international associations and organizations for which the said objects are created. Investors may be the users of objects of capital investments.

6. A subject of investment activity shall have the right to combine the functions of two or more subjects unless established otherwise by the contract and/or State contract concluded between them.

Article 5. Activity of Foreign Investors on Territory of Russian Federation

Relations connected with investment activity effectuated in the form of capital investments by foreign investors on the territory of the Russian Federation shall be regulated by international treaties of the Russian Federation, the Civil Code of the Russian Federation, the present Federal Law, other federal laws and other normative legal acts of the Russian Federation. If other rules than those provided for by the present Federal Law have been established by an international treaty of the Russian Federation, the rules of the international treaty shall apply.

Chapter II. Legal and Economic Foundations of Investment Activity Effectuated in Form of Capital Investments

Article 6. Rights of Investors

Investors shall have equal rights to:

the effectuation of investment activity in the form of capital investments, with the exceptions established by federal laws;

autonomous determination of the amounts and orientations of capital investments, and also the conclusion of contracts with other subjects of investment activity, in accordance with the Civil Code of the Russian Federation;

the possession, use, and disposition of objects of capital investments and the results of the effectuated capital investments;

the transfer under a contract and/or State contract of their rights to the effectuation of capital investments and to the results thereof to natural and juridical persons, State agencies, and agencies of local self-government in accordance with legislation of the Russian Federation;

the effectuation of control over the special-purpose use of means directed towards capital investments;

the combining of own and attracted means with the means of other investors for the purposes of joint effectuation of capital investments on the basis of a contract and in accordance with legislation of the Russian Federation;

the effectuation of other rights provided for by the contract and/or State contract in accordance with legislation of the Russian Federation.

Article 7. Duties of Subjects of Investment Activity

Subjects of investment activity shall be obliged to:

effectuate investment activity in accordance with international treaties of the Russian Federation, federal laws, and other normative legal acts of the Russian Federation, laws of subjects of the Russian Federation, and other normative legal acts of subjects of the Russian Federation and agencies of local self-government, and also with standards (or norms and rules) confirmed in the established procedure [as amended by Federal Law No. 122-AP, 22 August 2004];

execute demands presented by State agencies and officials thereof which are not contrary to norms of legislation of the Russian Federation;

use means directed towards capital investments for their special-purpose designation.

Article 8. Relations Between Subjects of Investment Activity

1. Relations between subjects of investment activity shall be effectuated on the basis of a contract and/or State contract concluded between them in accordance with the Civil Code of the Russian Federation.

2. The conditions of contracts and/or State contracts concluded between subjects of investment activity shall retain their force for the entire period of their operation, except for instances provided for by the present Federal Law and other federal laws.

Article 9. Sources of Financing of Capital Investments

The financing of capital investments shall be effectuated by investors at the expense of own and/or attracted means.

Article 10. Interaction of Agencies of State Power of Russian Federation, Agencies of State Power of Subjects of Russian Federation and Agencies of Local Self-Government in Investment Activity Effectuated in Form of Capital Investments

Agencies of State power of the Russian Federation, agencies of State power of subjects of the Russian Federation, and agencies of local self-government by agreement between them may effectuate interaction in investment activity effectuated in the form of capital investments in accordance with the Constitution of the Russian Federation, the present Federal Law, and other federal laws.

Chapter III. State Regulation of Investment Activity Effectuated in Form of Capital Investments

Article 11. Forms and Methods of State Regulation of Investment Activity Effectuated in Form of Capital Investments

1. State regulation of investment activity effectuated in the form of capital investments shall be effectuated by agencies of State power of the Russian Federation and by agencies of State power of subjects of the Russian Federation.

2. Federal agencies of State power shall in order to regulate investment activity effectuated in the form of capital investments use the following forms and methods [as amended by Federal Law No. 122-AP, 22 August 2004]:

(1) the creation of favourable conditions for the development of investment activity effectuated in the form of capital investments by means of:

improvement of the system of taxes, mechanism of calculating amortization and the use of amortization deductions;

establishment for subjects of investment activity of special tax regimes not of an individual character;

defence of the interests of investors;

granting to subjects of investment activity privileged conditions for the use of land and other natural resources which are not contrary to legislation of the Russian Federation;

expansion of the use of means of the population and other extrabudgetary sources for the financing of housing construction and the construction of objects of socio-cultural designation;

creation and development of the network of informational analytical centres effectuating the regular conducting of ratings and the publication of rating evaluations of subjects of investment activity;

adoption of anti-monopoly measures;

expansion of the possibilities of the use of pledges when effectuating the granting of credits;

development of finance leasing in the Russian Federation;

conducting of the revaluation of basic funds in accordance with the rates of inflation;

creation of possibilities for the formation of own investment funds by subjects of investment activity;

(2) direct participation of the State in investment activity effectuated in the form of capital investments by means of:

working out, confirmation, and financing of investment projects effectuated by the Russian Federation jointly with foreign States, and also investment projects to be financed at the expense of means of the federal budget [as amended by Federal Law No. 122-AP, 22 August 2004];

formation of the List of construction sites and objects of technical re-equipping for federal State needs and financing thereof at the expense of means of the federal budget. The procedure for the forming of the said List shall be determined by the Government of the Russian Federation;

[paragraph lost force by Federal Law No. 122-AP, 22 August 2004].

placement of means of the federal budget for financing investment projects in the procedure provided by legislation of the Russian Federation concerning the placement of orders for the delivery of goods, fulfillment of work, and rendering of services for State and municipal needs. The placement of the said means shall be effectuated on repayment and fixed-term bases with the payment of interest for the use thereof in the amounts determined by a federal law on the federal budget for the respective year or on the conditions of the consolidation in State ownership of the respective part of the stocks of the joint-stock society created which shall be realized within a determined period on the securities market with the proceeds sent from the realization to the revenues of the respective budgets [as amended by Federal Law No. 122-AP, 22 August 2004 and Federal Law No. 19-AP, 2 February 2006];

conducting an expert examination of investment projects in accordance with legislation of the Russian Federation;

defence of Russian organizations against deliveries of morally obsolete and material-intensive, energy-intensive, or nonscientific-intensive technologies, equipment, construction designs, and materials [as amended by Federal Law No. 122-AP, 22 August 2004];

working out and confirmation of standards (or norms and rules) and effectuation of control over compliance therewith;

issuance of bond loans and guaranteed special-purpose loans;

involvement in the investment process of temporarily suspended and shut-down construction sites and objects in State ownership;

granting of concessions to Russian and foreign investors with regard to the results of public sales (or auctions and competitions) in accordance with legislation of the Russian Federation.

(2^1) Agencies of State power of subjects of the Russian Federation may in order to regulate investment activity effectuated in the form of capital investments use the following forms and methods:

working out, confirmation, and effectuation of inter-municipal investment projects and investment projects in objects of State ownership of subjects of the Russian Federation being financed at the expense of means of budgets of subjects of the Russian Federation;

conducting an expert examination of investment projects in accordance with legislation of the Russian Federation;

granting on a competitive basis of State guarantees for investment projects at the expense of means of the budgets of subjects of the Russian Federation. The procedure for granting State guarantees at the expense of means of budgets of subjects of the Russian Federation shall be determined by laws of the respective subjects of the Russian Federation;

the placement of means of budgets of subjects of the Russian Federation for financing investment projects in the procedure provided by legislation of the Russian Federation concerning the placement of orders for the delivery of goods, fulfillment of work, and rendering of services for State and municipal needs. The placement of the said means shall be effectuated on repayment and fixed-term bases with the payment of interest for the use thereof in the amounts determined by a law on the budget of a subject of the Russian Federation or on the conditions of the consolidation in ownership of a subject of the Russian Federation of the respective part of the stocks of the joint-stock society created which shall be realized within a determined period on the securities market with the proceeds sent from the realization to the revenues of the respective budgets [as amended by Federal Law No. 19-AP, 2 February 2006];

issuance of bond loans of subjects of the Russian Federation and guaranteed special-purpose loans;

involvement in the investment process of temporarily suspended and shut-down construction sites and objects in the ownership of subjects of the Russian Federation [point 2^1 added by Federal Law No. 122-AP, 22 August 2004].

3. State regulation of investment activity effectuated in the form of capital investments may be effectuated with the use of other forms and methods in accordance with legislation of the Russian Federation.

Article 12. State Regulation of Investment Activity Effectuated in Form of Capital Investments under Conditions of Arising of Extraordinary Situations

Under conditions of the arising of extraordinary situations on the territory of the Russian Federation the activity of subjects of investment activity which prove to be in the zone of an extraordinary situation shall be effectuated in accordance with legislation of the Russian Federation.

Article 13. Procedure for Adoption of Decisions on Effectuation of State Capital Investments

1. Decisions concerning the effectuation of State capital investments shall be adopted by agencies of State power in accordance with legislation of the Russian Federation.

2. Expenses for the financing of State capital investments shall be provided:

in the federal budget—on condition that these expenses are part of the expenses for the realization of the respective federal special-purpose programs, and also on the basis of proposals of the President of the Russian Federation or Government of the Russian Federation;

in budgets of subjects of the Russian Federation—on condition that these expenses are part of the expenses for the realization of the respective regional special-purpose programs, and also on the basis of proposals of agencies of executive power of the subjects of the Russian Federation.

3. The working out, consideration, and confirmation of investment projects financed at the expense of means of the federal budget shall be in accordance with legislation of the Russian Federation in the procedure provided for federal special-purpose programs. The Lists of investment projects financed at the expense of means of the federal budget shall form federal investment programs.

4. The procedure for financing investment projects at the expense of means of the federal budget shall be determined by the Government of the Russian Federation, and the procedure for financing investment projects at the expense of means of the budgets of subjects of the Russian Federation, by agencies of executive power of the respective subjects of the Russian Federation. The Lists of investment projects financed at the expense of means of the budgets of subjects of the Russian Federation shall form regional investment programs.

5. Decisions concerning the use of means of the federal budget for financing of investment projects and/or investment programs effectuated by the Russian Federation jointly with foreign States shall be adopted after the conclusion by the Russian Federation of the respective inter-State agencies.

6. The placement of orders for independent-work contract construction work for State needs at the expense of means of the federal budget and means of the budgets of subjects of the Russian Federation when realizing the respective investment projects shall be by State customers in the procedure provided for by legislation of the Russian Federation on the placement of orders for the delivery of goods, fulfilment of work, and rendering of services for State and municipal needs [as amended by Federal Law No. 19-AP, 2 February 2006].

7. Control over the special-purpose and effective use of means of the federal budget directed towards capital investments in accordance with legislation of the Russian Federation shall be effectuated by the Counting Chamber of the Russian Federation, and also empowered federal agencies of executive power. Control over the special-purpose and effective use of means of budgets of subjects of the Russian Federation shall be effectuated by empowered agencies of the respective subjects of the Russian Federation.

Article 14. Expert Examination of Investment Projects

1. All investment projects irrespective of the sources of financing and forms of ownership of objects of capital investments shall before the confirmation thereof be subject to expert examination in accordance with legislation of the Russian Federation.

Expert examination of investment projects shall be conducted for the purposes of preventing the creation of objects whose use violates the rights of natural and juridical persons and the interests of the State or does not meet the requirements of standards (or norms and rules) confirmed in the established procedure, and also to assess the effectiveness of the capital investments to be effectuated.

2. Investment projects financed at the expense of means of the federal budget, means of the budgets of subjects of the Russian Federation, and also investment projects having important national economic significance, irrespective of the sources of financing and forms of ownership of objects of capital investments, shall before their confirmation be subject to State expert examination effectuated by empowered State agencies [as amended by Federal Law No. 122-AP, 22 August 2004].

The procedure for conducting State expert examination of investment projects shall be determined by the Government of the Russian Federation.

3. All investment projects shall be subject to ecological expert examination in accordance with legislation of the Russian Federation.

Chapter IV. State Guarantees of Rights of Subjects of Investment Activity and Defence of Capital Investments

Article 15. State Guarantees of Rights of Subjects of Investment Activity

1. The State in accordance with the present Federal Law, other federal laws, and other normative legal acts of the Russian Federation, laws of subjects of the Russian Federation, and other normative legal acts of subjects of the Russian Federation shall guarantee to all subjects of investment activity irrespective of the forms of ownership:

ensuring of equal rights when effectuating investment activity;

glasnost in the discussion of investment projects;

right to appeal to a court the decisions and actions (or failure to act) of agencies of State power, agencies of local self-government, and officials thereof;

defence of capital investments [as amended by Federal Law No. 22-AP, 2 January 2000].

2. If new federal laws and other normative legal acts of the Russian Federation enter into force which change the amounts of import customs duties (except for special types of duties caused by the application of measures with regard to defence of the economic interests of the Russian Federation when effectuating foreign trade in goods in accordance with legislation of the Russian Federation), federal taxes (except for excises, value-added tax on goods produced on the territory of the Russian Federation), and contributions to State extrabudgetary funds (except for contributions to the Pension Fund of the Russian Federation),

or make changes in and additions to prevailing federal laws and other normative legal acts of the Russian Federation which lead to an increase of the aggregate tax load on the activity of the investor with regard to the realization of a priority investment project on the territory of the Russian Federation or establish a regime of prohibitions and limitations with respect to the effectuation of capital investments on the territory of the Russian Federation in comparison with the aggregate tax load and regime which operated in accordance with federal laws and other normative legal acts of the Russian Federation on the day of the commencement of the financing of a priority investment project, then such new federal laws and other normative legal acts of the Russian Federation, and also changes and additions made in prevailing federal laws and other normative legal acts of the Russian Federation, shall not apply during the periods specified in point 3 of the present Article with respect to an investor effectuating a priority investment project, on condition that the goods imported to the customs territory of the Russian Federation by the investor are used for their special-purpose designation in order to realize a priority investment project [added by Federal Law No. 22-AP, 2 January 2002].

3. The stability for an investor effectuating an investment project and the conditions and regime specified in the present Article shall be guaranteed for the period of recoupment of the investment project, but not more than seven years from the day of the commencement of financing of the said project. Differentiation of the periods of recoupment of investment projects depending upon the types thereof shall be determined in the procedure established by the Government of the Russian Federation [added by Federal Law, No. 22-AP, 2 January 2000].

4. In exceptional instances in the event of the realization of a priority investment project by an investor in the sphere of production or the creation of transport or other infrastructure, the period of recoupment of which exceeds seven years, the Government of the Russian Federation shall adopt a decision concerning the extension of the periods of operation of the conditions and regime specified in point 2 of the present Article for the said investor [added by Federal Law, No. 22-AP, 2 January 2000].

5. The provisions of point 2 of the present Article shall not extend to changes and additions which are made in legislative acts of the Russian Federation or new federal laws and other normative legal acts of the Russian Federation adopted for the purposes of the defence of the constitutional system, morality, health, rights and legal interests of other persons, and ensuring the defence of the country and security of the State [added by Federal Law, No. 22-AP, 2 January 2000].

6. The Government of the Russian Federation shall:

establish the criteria for assessing the changes in conditions for the recovery of import customs duties, federal taxes and contributions to the State extra-budgetary funds, regime of prohibitions and limitations with respect to the effectuation of capital investments on the territory of the Russian Federation which are unfavourable for the investor effectuating a priority investment project on the territory of the Russian Federation [added by Federal Law, No. 22-AP, 2 January 2000];

confirm the procedure determining the day of the commencement of financing of an investment project, including with the participation of foreign investors;

confirm the procedure for the registration of priority investment projects;

effectuate control over the performance by the investor of obligations assumed by him with regard to the realization of the priority investment project within the periods specified in points 3 and 4 of the present Article.

In the event of the failure of the investor to perform obligations specified in paragraph one of the present point, he shall be deprived of the privileges granted to him in accordance with the present Article. The amount of monetary means not paid as a result of the granting of the said privileges shall be subject to refund in the procedure established by legislation of the Russian Federation [added by Federal Law, No. 22-AP, 2 January 2000].

Article 16. Defence of Capital Investments

1. Capital investments may be:

nationalized only on condition of the prior and fair compensation by the State of losses caused to subjects of investment activity in accordance with the Constitution of the Russian Federation and the Civil Code of the Russian Federation;

requisitioned by decision of State agencies in the instances, procedure, and conditions which have been determined by the Civil Code of the Russian Federation.

2. Insurance of capital investments shall be effectuated in accordance with legislation of the Russian Federation.

Article 17. Responsibility of Subjects of Investment Activity

1. In the event of a violation of the requirements of legislation of the Russian Federation, conditions of the contract, and/or State contract subjects of investment activity shall bear responsibility in accordance with legislation of the Russian Federation.

2. Disputes connected with investment activity effectuated in the form of capital investments shall be settled in the procedure established by legislation of the Russian Federation and international treaties of the Russian Federation.

Article 18. Termination or Suspension of Investment Activity Effectuated in Form of Capital Investments

1. The termination or suspension of investment activity effectuated in the form of capital investments shall be in the procedure established by legislation of the Russian Federation.

2. The procedure for compensation of losses to subjects of investment activity in the event of the termination or suspension of investment activity effectuated in the form of capital investments shall be determined by legislation of the Russian Federation and contracts and/or State contracts concluded.

Chapter V. Foundations of Regulation of Investment Activity Effectuated in Form of Capital Investments by Agencies of Local Self-Government

Article 19. Forms and Methods of Regulation of Investment Activity Effectuated in Form of Capital Investments by Agencies of Local Self-Government

1. The regulation by agencies of local self-government of investment activity effectuated in the form of capital investments shall provide for:

(1) the creation in municipal formations of favourable conditions for the development of investment activity effectuated in the form of capital investments by means of:

establishment of privileges with regard to the payment of local taxes for subjects of investment activity;

defence of the interests of investors;

granting to subjects of investment activity privileged conditions for the use of land and other natural resources in municipal ownership which are not contrary to legislation of the Russian Federation;

expansion of the use of means of the population and other extrabudgetary sources of financing of housing construction and the construction of objects of socio-cultural designation;

(2) direct participation of agencies of local self-government in investment activity effectuated in the form of capital investments by means of:

the working out, confirmation, and financing of investment projects effectuated by municipal formations;

placement of means of local budgets to finance investment projects in the procedure provided for by legislation of the Russian Federation on the placement of orders for delivery of goods, fulfillment of work, and rendering of services for State and municipal needs. Placement of the said means shall be effectuated on a repayment and fixed-term basis with the payment of interest for the use thereof in the amounts determined by normative legal acts concerning local budgets, or on conditions of consolidation in municipal ownership of the respective part of the stocks of the joint-stock society created which shall be realized within a determined period on the securities market with the proceeds from the realization to be directed to the revenues of the local budgets [as amended by Federal Law, No. 19-AP, 2 February 2006];

conducting of expert examination of investment projects in accordance with legislation of the Russian Federation;

issuance of municipal loans in accordance with legislation of the Russian Federation;

involvement in the investment process of temporarily suspended or shut-down construction sites and objects in municipal ownership.

2. Agencies of local self-government shall grant municipal guarantees on a competitive basis with regard to investment projects at the expense of means of the local budget. The procedure for granting municipal guarantees at the expense of means of the local budgets shall be confirmed by the representative agency of local self-government in accordance with legislation of the Russian Federation.

3. Expenses for financing investment activity effectuated in the form of capital investments by agencies of local self-government shall be provided for by the local budgets. Control over special-purpose and effective use of the means of local budgets directed towards capital investments shall be effectuated by the agencies empowered by representative agencies of local self-government.

4. In the event of the participation of agencies of local self-government in the financing of investment projects effectuated by the Russian Federation and subjects of the Russian Federation, the working out and confirmation of these investment projects shall be effectuated by agreement with the agencies of local self-government.

5. When effectuating investment activity agencies of local self-government shall have the right to interact with agencies of local self-government of other municipal formations, including by means of combining own and attracted means on the basis of a contract between them and in accordance with legislation of the Russian Federation.

6. The regulation by agencies of local self-government of investment activity effectuated in the form of capital investments may be effectuated with the use of other forms and methods in accordance with legislation of the Russian Federation.

Article 20. Municipal Guarantees of Rights of Subjects of Investment Activity

Agencies of local self-government within the limits of their powers in accordance with the present Federal Law, other federal laws, and other normative legal acts of the Russian Federation, laws of subjects of the Russian Federation, and other normative legal acts of subjects of the Russian Federation shall guarantee to all subjects of investment activity:

ensuring of equal rights when effectuating investment activity;

glasnost in the discussion of investment projects;

stability of the rights of subjects of investment activity.

Chapter VI. Concluding Provisions

Article 21. On Deeming Certain Legislative Acts to Have Lost Force in Connection with Adoption of Present Federal Law

In connection with the adoption of the present Federal Law to deem to have lost force in the part of norms which are contrary to the present Federal Law:

Law of the RSFSR 'On Investment Activity in the RSFSR' (*Ведомости Съезда народных депутатов РСФСР и Верховного Совета РСФСР* (1991), no. 29, item 1005);

Decree of the Supreme Soviet of the RSFSR 'On the Introduction into Operation of the Law of the RSFSR on Investment Activity in the RSFSR' (*Ведомости Съезда народных депутатов РСФСР и Верховного Совета РСФСР* (1991), no. 29, item 1006);

Article 5 of the Federal Law 'On Making Changes in and Additions to Legislative Acts of the Russian Federation in Connection with the Adoption of Laws of the Russian Federation "On Standardization", "On Ensuring the Unity of Measurements", and "On the Certification of Products and Services" '(*Ведомости Съезда народных депутатов РСФСР и Верховного Совета РСФСР* (1995), no. 26, item 2937).

Article 22. Entry of Present Federal Law into Force

The present Federal Law shall enter into force from the day of official publication thereof.

Article 23. Bringing Legal Acts into Conformity with Present Federal Law

The President of the Russian Federation and the Government of the Russian Federation shall bring their legal acts into conformity with the present Federal Law.

FEDERAL LAW ON THE FUNDAMENTAL PRINCIPLES OF STATE REGULATION OF FOREIGN TRADE ACTIVITY

[Federal Law No. 164-ФЗ, 8 December 2003; as amended 22 August 2004, 22 July 2005, and 2 February 2006. *СЗ РФ*; (2003), no. 50, item 4850; (2004), no. 35, item 3607; (2005), no. 30(II), item 3128; (2006), no. 5, item 636]

Chapter 1. General Provisions

Article 1. Purposes and Sphere of Application of Present Federal Law

1. The present Federal Law shall determine the fundamental principles of State regulation of foreign trade activity, the powers of the Russian Federation and subjects of the Russian Federation in the domain of foreign trade activity for the purpose of ensuring favourable conditions for foreign trade activity, and also the defence of economic and political interests of the Russian Federation.

2. The present Federal Law shall apply to relations in the domain of the State regulation of foreign trade activity, and also to relations directly connected with such activity.

3. The peculiarities of State regulation of foreign trade activity in the domain connected with the taking out from the Russian Federation and bringing in to the Russian Federation, including with delivery or procurement, of products of military designation, with the development and production of products of military designation, and also the peculiarities of State regulation of foreign trade activity with respect to goods, information, work, services, and results of intellectual activity, may be used when creating a mass strike weapon, means of the delivery thereof, and other types of armaments and military technology, shall be established by international treaties of the Russian Federation, federal laws on military-technical cooperation of the Russian Federation with foreign States, and export control.

4. The provisions of the present Federal Law concerning the State regulation of foreign trade in services shall not apply to:

(1) services to be rendered when performing the functions of agencies of State power not on a commercial basis and not on conditions of competition with one or several performers of services;

(2) services to be rendered when effectuating the activity of the Central Bank of the Russian Federation for the purpose of the performance of functions established by federal laws;

(3) financial services to be rendered when effectuating activity not on conditions of competition with one or several performers of services with regard to social security, including State pension security, and activity under guarantee of the Government of the Russian Federation or with the use of State financial resources.

Article 2. Basic Concepts Used in Present Federal Law

For the purposes of the present Federal Law the following basic concepts are used:

(1) analogous good—good which by functional designation, application, qualitative, and technical characteristics is completely identical to another good or in the absence of such completely identical good, a good having characteristics close to the characteristics of the other good;

(2) reciprocity—the granting by one State (or group of States) to another State (or group of States) of a determined regime of international trade in exchange for the granting by a second State (or group of States) to the first State (or group of States) of this regime;

(3) foreign trade barter transaction—transaction concluded when effectuating foreign trade activity and providing for an exchange of goods, services, work, and intellectual property, including a transaction which together with the said exchange provides for the use in the event of its effectuation of monetary and/or other means of payments;

(4) foreign trade activity—activity with regard to the effectuation of transactions in the domain of foreign trade in goods, services, information, and intellectual property;

(5) foreign trade intellectual property—transfer of exclusive rights to objects of intellectual property or granting of right to use of objects of intellectual property by a Russian person to a foreign person or by a foreign person to a Russian person;

(6) foreign trade information—foreign trade in goods if the information is a component part of these goods, foreign trade in intellectual property if the transfer of information is effectuated as the transfer of rights to objects of intellectual property, or foreign trade in services in other instances;

(7) foreign trade in goods—import and/or export of goods. The movement of goods from one part of the customs territory of the Russian Federation to another part of the customs territory of the Russian Federation, if such parts are not connected by land territory of the Russian Federation, across the customs territory of a foreign State is not foreign trade in goods;

(8) foreign trade in services—rendering of services (or fulfillment of work), including the production, distribution, marketing, and delivery of services (or work) and effectuated by means specified in Article 33 of the present Federal Law;

(9) free trade zone—customs territories on which in accordance with an international treaty with one or several States or groups of States customs duties have been repealed and other measures of the limitation of foreign trade in goods originating from the said customs territories with respect to virtually all foreign trade in such goods within the limits of the said customs territories, except for the possibility of the application, when necessary, of such measures in instances provided for by Articles 21, 32, 38, and 39 of the present Federal Law. Participants of the free trade zone shall not effectuate any material coordination with respect to the application of customs duties and other measures of the regulation of foreign trade in goods with third countries;

(10) import of good—bringing in of a good to the customs territory of the Russian Federation without an obligation of taking the good out;

(11) foreign person—natural person, juridical person, or organization which is not a juridical person under the law of the foreign State who are not Russian persons;

(12) foreign customer of services—foreign person who has ordered services (or work) or uses them;

(13) foreign performer of services—foreign person rendering services (or fulfilling work);

(14) commercial presence—any form or the organization of entrepreneurial and other economic activity of a foreign person on the territory of the Russian Federation or Russian person on the territory of a foreign person permitted by

legislation of the Russian Federation or legislation of the foreign State for the purposes of rendering services, including the creation of a juridical person, branch, or representation of a juridical person or participation in the charter (or contributed) capital of a juridical person. A Russian juridical person through which a commercial presence is effectuated shall be regarded as a foreign performer of services if the foreign person(s) by virtue of overwhelming participation in the charter (or contributed) capital of a Russian juridical person, or in accordance with the contract concluded between them, or otherwise has the possibility to determine the decisions adopted by a Russian juridical person;

(15) international transit—movement across the customs territory of the Russian Federation of goods and means of transport, if such movement is merely part of the route commencing or ending beyond the limits of the customs territory of the Russian Federation;

(16) directly competing good—good which we compare with another good with regard to its purpose, application, qualitative, and technical characteristics, and also other basic properties, so that the recipient replaces or is prepared to replace it with the other good in the process of consumption;

(17) nontariff regulation—method of State regulation of foreign trade in goods effectuated by means of the introduction of quantitative limitations and other prohibitions and limitations of an economic character;

(18) pre-unloading inspection agency—Russian or foreign juridical person determined by the Government of the Russian Federation in accordance with Article 28(4) of the present Federal Law;

(19) passport of foreign trade barter transaction—document necessary for control over foreign trade in goods, services, work, and intellectual property effectuated on the basis of foreign trade barter transactions;

(20) pre-unloading inspection—verification of the quality, quantity, price, including financial conditions thereof, and/or correctness of coding for customs purposes of goods intended for import in the Russian Federation;

(21) Russian customer of services—Russian person who has ordered services (or work) or uses them;

(22) Russian performer of services—Russian person rendering services (or fulfilling work);

(23) Russian person—juridical person created in accordance with legislation of the Russian Federation, natural person having a permanent or primary place of residence on the territory of the Russian Federation who is a citizen of the Russian Federation or has a right of permanent residing in the Russian Federation or registered as an individual entrepreneur in accordance with legislation of the Russian Federation;

(24) customs tariff regulation—method of State regulation of foreign trade in goods effectuated by means of the application of bringing-in and taking-out customs duties;

(25) customs union—unified customs territory which on the basis of an international treaty with one or several States or groups of States replaces two or several customs territories and within whose limits customs duties are abolished and other measures of the limitation of foreign trade in goods originating from the unified customs territories with respect to virtually all trade in such goods within the limits of this customs territory, except for the possibility of the application, when necessary, of such measures in instances provided for by Articles 21, 32, 38, and 39 of the present Federal Law. Each participant of a customs union shall apply identical customs duties and other measures of regulation of foreign trade in goods with third countries;

(26) good—movable property which is an article of foreign trade activity, aircraft, sea-going vessels, vessels of internal navigation, and mixed (river-sea) navigation, and space objects relegated to immoveable property, and also electric power and other types of power. Means of transport used under a contract on international carriages shall not be considered as a good;

(27) participants of foreign trade activity—Russian and foreign persons engaging in foreign trade activity;

(28) export of good—taking out of good from customs territory of the Russian Federation without the obligation of bringing back in.

Article 3. Legislation of Russian Federation on Foreign Trade Activity

State regulation of foreign trade activity shall be based on the Constitution of the Russian Federation and shall be effectuated in accordance with the present Federal Law, other federal laws, and other normative legal acts of the Russian Federation, and also by generally-recognized principles and norms of international law and international treaties of the Russian Federation.

Article 4. Basic Principles of State Regulation of Foreign Trade Activity

The basic principles of State regulation of foreign trade activity shall be:

(1) defence by the State of the rights and legal interests of participants of foreign trade activity, and also the rights and legal interests of Russian producers and consumers of goods and services;

(2) equality and nondiscrimination of participants of foreign trade activity unless provided otherwise by a federal law;

(3) unity of customs territory of Russian Federation;

(4) reciprocity with respect to another State (or group of States);

(5) ensuring the fulfillment of obligations of the Russian Federation under international treaties of the Russian Federation and effectuation of rights of the Russian Federation arising from these treaties;

(6) choice of measures of State regulation of foreign trade activity which are not more burdensome for the participants of foreign trade activity than is necessary for ensuring the effective achievement of the purposes for whose

effectuation it is proposed to apply measures of State regulation of foreign trade activity;

(7) glasnost in working out, adoption, and application of measures of State regulation of foreign trade activity;

(8) well-foundedness and objectivity of application of measures of State regulation of foreign trade activity;

(9) exclusion of unjustified interference of the State or its agencies in foreign trade activity and causing of damage to participants of foreign trade activity and economy of the Russian Federation;

(10) ensuring defence of the country and security of the State;

(11) ensuring the right to appeal in a judicial or other procedure established by a law of illegal actions (or failure to act) of State agencies and officials thereof, and also the right to contest normative legal acts of the Russian Federation impinging the right of a participant of foreign trade activity to effectuate foreign trade activity;

(12) unity of the system of State regulation of foreign trade activity;

(13) unity of application of methods of State regulation of foreign trade activity throughout the entire territory of the Russian Federation.

Article 5. Trade Policy of Russian Federation

1. The trade policy of the Russian Federation shall be an integral part of the economic policy of the Russian Federation. The purpose of the trade policy of the Russian Federation shall be the creation of favourable conditions for Russian exporters, importers, producers, and consumers of goods and services.

2. The trade policy of the Russian Federation shall be built on the basis of compliance with generally-recognized principles and norms of international law, and also obligations arising from international treaties of the Russian Federation.

3. The realization of the trade policy of the Russian Federation shall be effectuated with the use of methods of State regulation of foreign trade activity provided for in Article 12 of the present Federal Law.

Chapter 2. Powers of Federal Agencies of State Power, Agencies of State Power of Subjects of Russian Federation and Agencies of Local Self-Government in Domain of Foreign Trade Activity

[as amended by Federal Law of 22 August 2004, No. 122-ФЗ]

Article 6. Powers of Federal Agencies of State Power in Domain of Foreign Trade Activity [as amended by Federal Law of 22 August 2004, No. 122-ФЗ]

There shall be relegated to the powers of federal agencies of State power in the domain of foreign trade activity: [as amended by Federal Law of 22 August 2004, No. 122-ФЗ]:

(1) forming of the conception and strategy of the development of foreign trade links and basic principles of trade policy of the Russian Federation;

(2) defence of the economic sovereignty and economic interests of the Russian Federation and Russian persons [as amended by Federal Law of 22 August 2004, No. 122-ФЗ];

(3) State regulation of foreign trade activity, including customs tariff and nontariff regulation, and also State regulation of activity in the domain of conformation of the conformity of goods to obligatory requirements in connection with their being brought in to the Russian Federation and taken out of the Russian Federation;

(4) establishment of safety requirements and criteria obligatory throughout the entire territory of the Russian Federation for the life and health of citizens, property of natural or juridical persons, State or municipal property, environment, life or health of flora and fauna in the event of bringing goods into the Russian Federation and rules of control over them;

(5) determination of the procedure for taking out of the Russian Federation and bringing in to the Russian Federation of fissionable nuclear substances, poisonous, explosive, toxic substances, dangerous wastes, virulent and narcotic means, psychotropic substances, and precursors thereof, biologically active materials (donor blood, internal organs, and other materials), genetically active materials (cultures of mushrooms, bacteria, viruses, spermatic material of fauna and humans and other materials), flora and fauna under threat of extinction, parts and derivatives thereof, and also other goods which might exert an unfavourable impact on the life or health of citizens, life or health of flora and fauna, and the environment;

(6) determination of the procedure for bringing in to the Russian Federation and taking out of the Russian Federation of precious metals and precious stones;

(7) coordination of international cooperation of the Russian Federation in the domain of outer space activity and control over the working out and realization of international space projects of the Russian Federation;

(8) establishment of indicators of statistical reports of foreign trade activity binding throughout the entire territory of the Russian Federation;

(9) conclusion of international treaties of the Russian Federation in the domain of foreign economic ties;

(10) founding, maintenance, and liquidation of trade representations of the Russian Federation in foreign States;

(11) participation in the activity of international economic organizations and realization of decisions adopted by these organizations;

(12) determination of the procedure for taking out goods from the Russian Federation, an integral part of which is information comprising a State secret;

(13) information provision for foreign trade activity on the territory of the Russian Federation [added by Federal Law of 22 August 2004, No. 122-ФЗ];

(14) creation of insurance and pledge funds in the domain of foreign trade activity [added by Federal Law of 22 August 2004, No. 122-ФЗ].

Article 7 [lost force—Federal Law of 22 August 2004, No. 122-ФЗ]

Article 8. Powers of Agencies of State Power of Subjects of Russian Federation in Domain of Foreign Trade Activity [as amended by Federal Law of 22 August 2004, No. 122-ФЗ]

There shall be relegated to the powers of agencies of State power of subjects of the Russian Federation in the domain of foreign trade activity:

(1) conducting negotiations and conclusion of agreements on the effectuation of foreign economic links with subjects of foreign federated States, administrative-territorial formations of foreign States, and also the consent of the Government of the Russian Federation with agencies of State power of foreign States [as amended by Federal Law of 22 August 2004, No. 122-ФЗ];

(2) maintenance of their representatives attached to trade representations of the Russian Federation in foreign States at the expense of means of budgets of subjects of the Russian Federation by agreement with the federal agency of executive power specified in Article 13(3) of the present Federal Law and the Ministry of Foreign Affairs of the Russian Federation [as amended by Federal Law of 22 August 2004, No. 122-ФЗ];

(3) opening of representations in foreign States for the purposes of the realization of agreements concerning the effectuation of foreign economic ties in the procedure established by legislation of the Russian Federation [as amended by Federal Law of 22 August 2004, No. 122-ФЗ];

(4) effectuation of the forming and realization of regional programs of foreign trade activity [as amended by Federal Law of 22 August 2004, No. 122-ФЗ];

(5) information provision of foreign trade activity on the territory of a subject of the Russian Federation [added by Federal Law of 22 August 2004, No. 122-ФЗ];

(6) creation of insurance and pledge funds in the domain of foreign trade activity on the territory of a subject of the Russian Federation [added by Federal Law of 22 August 2004, No. 122-ФЗ].

Article 8^{1}. Powers of Agencies of Local Self-Government in Domain of Foreign Trade Activity

Foreign trade activity of agencies of local self-government shall be effectuated in accordance with legislation of the Russian Federation.

Article 9. Interaction of Federal Agencies of Executive Power and Agencies of Executive Power of Subjects of Russian Federation

1. The federal agency of executive power specified in Article 13(3) of the present Federal Law shall be obliged to agree with the respective agencies of executive power of subjects of the Russian Federation draft plans and programs for the development of foreign trade activity affecting the interests of subjects of the Russian Federation and within the limits of its competence.

2. The agency of executive power of a subject of the Russian Federation shall within thirty days after the submission of the respective draft plan or program for agreement send an official opinion to the federal agency of executive power specified in Article 13(3) of the present Federal Law.

3. The failure to submit an official opinion by an agency of executive power of a subject of the Russian Federation shall be considered as its consent with the draft plan and program sent for agreement.

4. Agencies of executive power of a subject of the Russian Federation shall be obliged to inform the federal agency of executive power specified in Article 13(3) of the present Federal Law about all actions undertaken by the subject of the Russian Federation with regard to questions of joint jurisdiction of the Russian Federation and subjects of the Russian Federation in the domain of foreign trade activity.

Chapter 3. Participants of Foreign Trade Activity

Article 10. Russian Persons and Foreign Persons as Participants of Foreign Trade Activity

Any Russian persons and foreign persons shall possess the right to effectuate foreign trade activity. This right may be limited in instances provided for by international treaties of the Russian Federation, present Federal Law, and other federal laws.

Article 11. Participation of Russian Federation, Subjects of Russian Federation, and Municipal Formations in Effectuation of Foreign Trade Activity

The Russian Federation, subjects of the Russian Federation, and municipal formations effectuate foreign trade activity only in instances established by federal laws.

Chapter 4. Basic Provisions of State Regulation of Foreign Trade Activity

Article 12. Methods of State Regulation of Foreign Trade Activity

1. State regulation of foreign trade activity shall be effectuated in accordance with international treaties of the Russian Federation, present Federal Law,

other federal laws, and other normative legal acts of the Russian Federation by means of:

(1) customs tariff regulation;

(2) nontariff regulation;

(3) prohibitions and limitations of foreign trade in services and intellectual property;

(4) measures of an economic and administrative character promoting the development of foreign trade activity and provided for by the present Law.

2. Other methods of State regulation of foreign trade activity shall not be permitted.

Article 13. Powers of Agencies of State Power of Russian Federation in Domain of State Regulation of Foreign Trade Activity

1. The President of the Russian Federation in accordance with the Constitution of the Russian Federation and federal laws shall:

(1) determine the basic orientations of trade policy of the Russian Federation;

(2) determine the procedure for the bringing in to the Russian Federation and taking out of the Russian Federation of precious metals and precious stones;

(3) establish prohibitions and limitations of foreign trade in goods, services, and intellectual property for the purpose of the participation of the Russian Federation in international sanctions;

(4) effectuate other powers.

2. The Government of the Russian Federation shall:

(1) ensure the conducting in the Russian Federation of a unified trade policy and effectuate measures for the realization thereof, adopt respective decisions, and ensure the fulfillment thereof;

(2) apply special defensive measures, anti-dumping measures, and compensatory measures when effectuating foreign trade in goods, and also other measures for the defence of the economic interests of the Russian Federation;

(3) establish the rates of customs tariff within the limits determined by a federal law;

(4) introduce quantitative limitations on export and import of goods in accordance with international treaties of the Russian Federation and federal laws and determine the procedure for the application of quantitative limitations of export and import of goods;

(5) establish an authorization procedure for the export and/or import of individual types of goods which may exert an unfavourable impact on the security of the State, life or health of citizens, property of natural or juridical persons, State or municipal property, environment, life or health of flora and

fauna, and also determine the list of individual types of goods with respect to which such procedure applies;

(6) determine the procedure of licensing in the sphere of foreign trade in goods and procedure for forming and keeping of the federal bank of licenses issued;

(7) upon the recommendation of the federal agency of executive power specified in point 3 of the present Article and determine the list of individual types of goods for the export and/or import of which supervision is established;

(8) determine the procedure for observation over the export and/or import of individual types of goods;

(9) adopt within the limits of its competence decisions concerning the conducting of negotiations and signature of international treaties of the Russian Federation;

(10) adopt decisions concerning the introduction as retaliatory measures with respect to foreign States of limitations in the foreign trade in goods, services, and intellectual property in instances provided for by the present Federal Law;

(11) determine the procedure for bringing in to the Russian Federation and taking out of the Russian Federation of fissionable nuclear substances;

(12) establish the procedure for taking out of the Russian Federation goods of which an integral part is information comprising a State secret;

(13) confirm the goods nomenclature of foreign economic activity;

(14) effectuate other powers placed on it by the Constitution of the Russian Federation, federal laws, and edicts of the President of the Russian Federation in the domain of State regulation of foreign trade activity and State control in this domain.

3. The working out of proposals affecting trade policy of the Russian Federation, State regulation of foreign trade activity, and conclusion of international treaties and other treaties of the Russian federation in the domain of foreign economic links shall be effectuated by the empowered federal agency of executive power which the Government of the Russian Federation within the limits of its competence endowed with the right of State regulation of foreign trade activity. If the interests of subjects of the Russian Federation are affected, the working out of the said proposals shall be effectuated with the participation of respective agencies of executive power of subjects of the Russian Federation.

4. The federal agency of executive power specified in point 3 of the present Article shall submit to the Government of the Russian Federation concerning trade policy of the Russian Federation and ensure the realization of tasks with regard to the defence of economic interests of the Russian Federation, subjects of the Russian Federation, and Russian persons, and also conducting measures connected with the State regulation of foreign trade activity.

5. The federal agency of executive power specified in point 3 of the present Article shall be the sole agency of State power issuing licenses provided for by Article 24 of the present Federal Law.

Article 14. Conclusion of International Trade Treaties and Other Treaties of Russian Federation in Domain of Foreign Economic Ties

1. Proposals concerning the conclusion of international trade treaties and other treaties of the Russian Federation in the domain of foreign economic links shall be submitted in the procedure established by the Federal Law of 15 July 1995, No. 101-ФЗ "On International Treaties of the Russian Federation", to the President of the Russian Federation or Government of the Russian Federation and federal agency of executive power specified in Article 13(3) of the present Federal Law jointly with the Ministry of Foreign Affairs of the Russian Federation or by agreement with it.

2. Proposals submitted by other federal agencies of executive power concerning the conclusion of international treaties of the Russian Federation affecting questions of foreign economic ties shall be agreed with a federal agency of executive power specified in Article 13(3) of the present Federal Law. When consultations are necessary with respective agencies of foreign States or international organizations for the purpose of the preparation of drafts of such international treaties, the said consultations shall be conducted in the procedure established by the Federal Law of 15 July 1995, No. 101-ФЗ "On International Treaties of the Russian Federation" by agreement with the federal agency of executive power specified in Article 13(3) of the present Federal Law.

Article 15. Glasnost in Working Out Measures of State Regulation of Foreign Trade Activity

1. When working out a normative legal act of the Russian Federation affecting the right to effectuate foreign trade activity, the federal agency of executive power responsible for working it out shall propose to subjects of the Russian Federation, Russian organizations, and individual entrepreneurs whose economic interests may be affected by the adoption of such a normative legal act (interested persons) to submit proposals and comments with regard to this question to the said agency.

2. The federal agency of executive power specified in point 1 of the present Article shall adopt a decision concerning the means and form of conducting consultations, and also the means and form of bringing information concerning the course and results of conducting consultations, to interested persons who have submitted their proposals and comments.

3. If this follows from international treaties of the Russian Federation, it shall be proposed to competent agencies of other States (or groups of States) to

submit their opinions by a means provided for by provisions of a respective international treaty of the Russian Federation. It shall be proposed to foreign organizations and entrepreneurs also to submit their opinions by a means provided for by provisions of the respective international treaty of the Russian Federation.

4. The federal agency of executive power specified in point 1 of the present Article may adopt a decision not to conduct consultations in accordance with points 1 and 2 of the present Article when one of the following conditions is present:

(1) the measures provided for by the draft normative legal act of the Russian Federation affecting the right of the effectuation of foreign trade activity should not be known before the moment of entry thereof into force and conducting the consultations leads or may lead to the failure to achieve the purposes provided for by such normative legal act;

(2) the conducting of consultations will lead to a delay of the adoption of a normative legal act of the Russian Federation affecting the right to effectuate foreign trade activity that may lead to causing the material damage to the interests of the Russian Federation.

5. The provisions of points 1 and 2 of the present Article shall not apply to measures provided for by Article 27 of the present Federal Law.

6. The failure to carry on consultations may not be grounds for deeming a normative legal act of the Russian Federation affecting the right to effectuate foreign trade activity to be invalid.

7. The provisions of points 4 and 6 of the present Article shall not apply when working out draft federal laws affecting the right to effectuate foreign trade activity, proposals concerning the conclusion of international trade treaties of the Russian Federation, and also when determining the method of the distribution of quotas in accordance with Article 23 of the present Federal Law.

Article 16. Entry into Force of Normative Legal Acts in Domain of Foreign Trade Activity

Normative legal acts in the domain of foreign trade activity shall enter into force after their official publication within the periods and in the procedure which have been provided by legislation of the Russian Federation.

Article 17. Confidentiality

Agencies of State power of the Russian Federation and officials of agencies of State power of the Russian Federation effectuating activity connected with the State regulation of foreign trade activity must ensure the confidentiality of information comprising a State, commercial, or other secret protected by a law and use it only for the purposes for which such information is provided.

Article 18. Right to Appeal Decisions, Actions (or Failure to Act) of State Agency or Official Thereof

1. A participant of foreign trade activity shall have the right to appeal a decision and action (or failure to act) of a State agency or official thereof if by such decision or action (or failure to act) in the opinion of the participant of foreign trade activity his rights, freedoms, or legal interests have been violated, obstacles have been created for him in the realization thereof or any duty has been placed illegally on him.

2. A decision and action (or failure to act) of a State agency or official thereof may be appealed to a court, arbitrazh court, and in instances established by legislation of the Russian Federation, to a superior State agency.

Chapter 5. State Regulation of Foreign Trade Activity in Domain of Foreign Trade in Goods

Article 19. Customs Tariff Regulation

For the purposes of foreign trade in goods, including defence of the internal market of the Russian Federation and stimulation of structural changes in the economy, bringing-in and taking-out customs duties shall be established in accordance with legislation of the Russian Federation.

Article 20. Nontariff Regulation

Nontariff regulation of foreign trade in goods may be effectuated only in instances provided for by Articles 21–24, 26, and 27 of the present Federal Law in compliance with the requirements specified therein.

Article 21. Quantitative Limitations Established by Government of Russian Federation in Exceptional Instances

1. The import and export of goods shall be effectuated without quantitative limitations, except for instances provided for by point 2 of the present Article, and also by other provisions of the present Federal Law.

2. The Government of the Russian Federation may in exceptional instances establish:

(1) provisional limitations or prohibitions of the export of goods in order to prevent or reduce a critical shortage on the internal market of the Russian Federation of foodstuffs or other goods which are materially important for the internal market of the Russian Federation. The List of goods which are materially important shall be determined by the Government of the Russian Federation;

(2) limitations of the import of agricultural goods or aquatic biological resources brought in to the Russian Federation in any form if it is necessary to:

(a) reduce production or the sale of an analogous good of Russian origin;

(b) reduce production or the sale of a good of Russian origin which may be directly substituted by an imported good if there is no significant production of the Russian Federation of an analogous good;

(c) remove from the market a temporary surplus of an analogous good of Russian origin by means of providing the existing surplus of such good to certain groups of Russian consumers free of charge or at prices lower than market;

(d) remove from the market a temporary surplus of a good of Russian origin which may be directly substituted by an imported good if there is no significant production in the Russian Federation of an analogous good by means of providing the existing surplus of this good to certain groups of Russian consumers free of charge or at prices lower than market;

(e) limit the production of products of animal origin whose production depends upon a good imported into the Russian Federation if the production in the Russian Federation of an analogous good is relatively insignificant.

3. Foodstuffs and agricultural goods for the purposes of the present Article shall be determined by the Government of the Russian Federation.

Article 22. Nondiscriminatory Application of Quantitative Limitations

1. If the establishment of quantitative limitations on the export and/or import of a good are permitted by the present Federal Law, such limitations shall apply irrespective of the countries of the origin of the good unless provided otherwise by the present Federal Law.

2. If when establishing quantitative limitations on the import of a good the shares of the import of the good are distributed between interested foreign States, the previous import of the good from such States shall be taken into account.

3. The provisions of points 1 and 2 of the present Article may not apply with respect to a good originating from a foreign State (or groups of States) with which the Russian Federation has not mutual treaty obligations concerning the granting of the regime no less favourable than the regime granted to other States or groups of States.

4. The provisions of the present Article shall not apply to compensatory measures specified in Article 27 of the present Federal Law.

5. The provisions of points 1 and 2 of the present Article shall not obstruct compliance with obligations in accordance with international treaties of the Russian Federation on frontier trade, customs union, or free trade zone.

Article 23. Distribution of Quota

When adopting a decision concerning the introduction of a quota, the Government of the Russian Federation shall determine the method for the distribution of the quota and in the respective instance shall establish the procedure for conducting a competition or auction. The distribution of a quota shall be based on the equality of participants of foreign trade activity with respect to receiving a quota and nondiscrimination by indicia of form of ownership, place of registration, or position in the market.

Article 24. Licensing in Sphere of Foreign Trade in Goods

1. Licensing in the sphere of foreign trade in goods (hereinafter: licensing) shall be established in the following instances:

(1) introduction of provisional quantitative limitations of export or import of individual types of goods;

(2) realization of an authorization procedure for export and/or import of individual types of goods which may exert an unfavourable impact on the security of the State, life or health of citizens, property of natural or juridical persons, State or municipal property, environment, and life or health of flora and fauna;

(3) granting of exclusive right for the export and/or import of individual types of goods;

(4) fulfillment by Russian Federation of international obligations.

2. A license issued by the federal agency of executive power specified in Article 13(3) of the present Federal Law shall be grounds for the export and/or import of individual types of goods in the instances specified in point 1 of the present Article.

The absence of a license shall be grounds for a refusal to release goods by customs agencies of the Russian Federation.

3. The federal agency of executive power specified in Article 13(3) of the present Federal Law shall form and keep the federal bank of licenses issued. The procedure for the forming and keeping of the federal bank of licenses issued shall be determined by the Government of the Russian Federation.

Article 25. Observation Over Export and/or Import of Individual Types of Goods

1. Observation over the export and/or import of individual types of goods shall be established as a provisional measure for the purposes of monitoring the dynamics of export and/or import of individual types of goods.

2. Observation over the export and/or import of individual types of goods shall be effectuated by means of the issuance of licenses for export and/or

import of individual types of goods. Authorizations shall be issued without limitations to any participants of foreign trade activity on the basis of applications submitted according to the form determined by the federal agency of executive power specified in Article 13(3) of the present Federal Law. The period for the issuance of an authorization may not exceed three work days from the date of filing the application. It shall not be permitted to require the submission of other documents except applications in order to receive an authorization for export and/or import of individual types of goods. The absence of an authorization shall be grounds for the refusal to issue goods by customs agencies of the Russian Federation.

Article 26. Exclusive Right to Export and/or Import of Individual Types of Goods

1. The right to effectuate foreign trade activity may be limited by means of granting the exclusive right to export and/or import individual types of goods.

2. Lists of individual types of goods for whose export and/or import the exclusive right is granted, and also the organization to which the exclusive right is granted for the export and/or import of individual types of goods, shall be determined by federal laws.

3. The exclusive right to export and/or import of individual types of goods shall be effectuated on the basis of a license. Licenses for the effectuation of the exclusive right to export and/or import of individual types of goods shall be issued by a federal agency of executive power specified in Article 13(3) of the present Federal Law.

4. Transactions for the export and/or import of individual types of goods concludes without a license for the effectuation of the exclusive right for the export and/or import of individual types of goods shall be null.

5. Organizations to whom the exclusive right is granted for the export and/or import of individual types of goods shall conclude transactions for export and/or import of individual types of goods, basing themselves on the principle of nondiscrimination and being guided only by commercial considerations.

Article 27. Special Defensive Measures, Anti-Dumping Measures, and Compensatory Measures

In accordance with a federal law special defensive measures, anti-dumping measures, and compensatory measures may be introduced in the event of the import of goods for the defence of the economic interests of Russian producers of goods.

Article 28. Pre-Unloading Inspection

1. For the purposes of defence of the rights and interests of consumers and counteracting the unfair practice of distorting information about goods being imported into the Russian Federation, including a reduction of the value thereof, the Government of the Russian Federation shall have the right to introduce pre-unloading inspection, including the issue of a certificate concerning the undergoing of pre-unloading inspection, with respect to individual goods to be imported into the Russian Federation. The pre-unloading inspection shall be introduced with respect to individual goods for a period not exceeding three years. The Government of the Russian Federation shall when deciding the question of the advisability of extending the period of the effectuation of pre-unloading inspection with respect to individual goods summarize and analyze the practice and results of the application of this measure.

2. The List of goods with respect to which pre-unloading inspection is introduced shall be confirmed by the Government of the Russian Federation.

3. Expenses for the effectuation of pre-unloading inspection shall be borne by the importer of the good with respect to which pre-unloading inspection is introduced. The Government of the Russian Federation simultaneously with the adoption of the decision on the introduction of pre-unloading inspection shall reduce the rate of customs duties on goods with respect to which such inspection is introduced.

4. The pre-unloading inspection agency shall be determined by the Government of the Russian Federation according to the results of a competition for rendering services with regard to pre-unloading inspection and effectuate its activity on the basis of an agreement with the Government of the Russian Federation.

5. The following characteristics should be taken into account when choosing the pre-unloading inspection agency:

(1) professional reputation;

(2) sufficient production and professional resources;

(3) work experience in the domain of rendering services for pre-unloading inspection;

(4) cost of effectuation of pre-unloading inspection.

6. The Statute on Pre-Unloading Inspection shall be confirmed by the Government of the Russian Federation and include the reglament of the effectuation thereof, rights, duties, and responsibility of persons participating in the pre-unloading inspection, procedure for the consideration of disputes between the pre-unloading inspection agency and importer of the good, and procedure for the effectuation of control over the activity of pre-unloading inspection agencies.

7. A pre-unloading inspection shall be effectuated in compliance with the following principles:

(1) glasnost and openness;

(2) application of procedures and criteria to be used in the course of the pre-unloading inspection objectively on an equal basis to all importers of a good;

(3) verification of the quality and quantity of the good in accordance with the requirements of legislation of the Russian Federation;

(4) provision of importers of a good with information concerning requirements in the Russian Federation with respect to the pre-unloading inspection;

(5) ensuring the confidentiality of information received in the course of the pre-unloading inspection.

8. The pre-unloading inspection agency shall effectuate the pre-unloading inspection on the basis of the application of an importer of a good in conformity with the provision specified in point 6 of the present Article and shall issue to the importer of the good with regard to its results a certificate concerning the undergoing of pre-unloading inspection or adopt a decision concerning a reasoned refusal to issue such a certificate.

9. The period for the effectuation of a pre-unloading inspection shall, as a rule, not exceed three work days.

10. The import of goods subject to pre-unloading inspection shall be effectuated only when there is a certificate concerning the undergoing of pre-unloading inspection.

Article 29. National Regime With Respect to Goods Originating from Foreign States

1. In accordance with legislation on taxes and charges it shall not be permitted to establish differential rates of taxes and charges (except for bringing-in customs duties) depending on the country of origin of goods.

2. Technical, pharmacological, sanitary, veterinary, phyto-sanitary, and ecological requirements, and also requirements of obligatory confirmation of the conformity, shall apply to goods originating from a foreign State just as they apply to analogous goods of Russian origin.

3. A regime shall be granted for goods originating from a foreign State or groups of foreign States no less favourable than the regime granted to analogous goods of Russian origin or directly competing goods of Russian origin with respect to the sale, offer for sale, purchase, carriage, distribution, or use on the internal market of the Russian Federation. This provision shall not prevent the application of differential payments connected with carriage and based solely on the cost of operation of means of transport and not on the origin of the good.

4. A different regime of regulation may be granted in accordance with legislation of the Russian Federation for goods originating from a foreign State or groups of foreign States which do not have international treaties with the Russian Federation on granting to goods of Russian origin the regime provided for by points 2 and 3 of the present Article.

5. The provisions of the present Article shall not apply to deliveries of goods for State or municipal needs [as amended by Federal Law of 2 February 2006, No. 19-ФЗ].

Article 30. Payments to be Recovered in Connection with Import and Export of Goods

1. All payments established by normative legal acts of the Russian Federation to be recovered in connection with the import and export of goods and which are not customs duties and other taxes must not exceed the approximate value of services rendered and represent a defence of goods of Russian origin or levy for fiscal purposes.

2. The present Article shall apply to payments to be recovered in connection with the import and export of goods, including those relating to:
(1) quantitative limitations;
(2) licensing;
(3) effectuation of currency control;
(4) statistical services;
(5) confirmation of the conformity of a product to obligatory requirements;
(6) expert examination and inspections;
(7) quarantine, sanitary service, and fumigation.

Article 31. Freedom of International Transit

1. Unless provided otherwise by federal laws, international transit shall be effectuated freely along railway, water, air, and motor vehicle routes most suitable for international carriages. Differences based on flag, place of registration, place of origin of a vessel, place of putting in, place of departure, or point of destination, point of departure, or other circumstances relating to the ownership of a good, vessel, or other means of transport, unless provided otherwise by the present Federal law and other federal laws shall not be permitted in international transit.

2. In accordance with customs legislation of the Russian Federation requirements may be established concerning individual types of goods and means of transport to the customs territory of the Russian Federation or taking out of individual types of goods and means of transport from the customs

territory of the Russian Federation through a determined admittance point across the State boundary of the Russian Federation and the crossing thereof according to determined routes.

3. The present Article shall not apply to international transit traffic of aircraft, except for air transit carriages of goods.

Article 32. Measures Affecting Foreign Trade in Goods and Introduced by Proceeding from National Interests

1. Irrespective of the provisions of the present Chapter measures not having an economic character and affecting foreign trade may be introduced in accordance with international treaties of the Russian Federation and federal laws by proceeding from national interests if these measures:

(1) are necessary for compliance with public morality or public order;

(2) are necessary for the protection of life or health of citizens, environment, and the life or health of flora and fauna;

(3) relate to the import or export of gold or silver;

(4) are applied in order to defend cultural valuables;

(5) are necessary in order to prevent the disappearance of irreplaceable natural resources and are conducted simultaneously with the limitation of internal production or consumption connected with the use of irreplaceable natural resources;

(6) are necessary for the acquisition or distribution of goods in the event of their general or local shortage;

(7) are necessary in order to fulfill international obligations of the Russian Federation;

(8) are necessary to ensure the defence of the country and security of the State;

(9) are necessary in order to ensure compliance with normative legal acts of the Russian Federation which are not contrary to international treaties of the Russian Federation concerning *inter alia*:

(a) the application of customs legislation of the Russian Federation;

(b) the submission to customs agencies of the Russian Federation simultaneously with a cargo customs declaration of documents concerning the conformity of the goods to obligatory requirements;

(c) protection of the environment;

(d) obligations in accordance with legislation of the Russian Federation to take out or destroy goods not corresponding to the technical, pharmacological, sanitary, veterinary, phyto-sanitary, and ecological requirements;

(e) prevention and investigation of crimes, and also court proceedings and execution of judicial decisions with respect to these crimes;

(f) defence of intellectual property;

(g) granting of an exclusive right in conformity with Article 26 of the present Federal Law.

2. The measures specified in point 1 of the present Article should not be applied or be applied by a means which is a means of arbitrary or unfounded discrimination against States or represents covert limitations on foreign trade in goods.

3. The provisions of point 2 of the present Article may not be applied with respect to goods originating from foreign States or groups of foreign States, with which the Russian Federation does not have mutual treaty obligations to grant a regime no less favourable than the regime to be granted to other States or groups of States.

Chapter 6. State Regulation of Foreign Trade Activity in Domain of Foreign Trade in Services

Article 33. Foreign Trade in Services

1. Foreign trade in services shall be effectuated by the following means:

(1) from the territory of the Russian Federation to the territory of a foreign State;

(2) from the territory of a foreign State to the territory of the Russian Federation;

(3) on the territory of the Russian Federation to a foreign customer of services;

(4) on the territory of a foreign State to a Russian customer of services;

(5) by a Russian performer of services not having a commercial presence on the territory of a foreign State by means of the presence thereof or of empowered persons to act in his name on the territory of a foreign State;

(6) by a foreign performer of services not having a commercial presence on the territory of the Russian Federation by means of the presence thereof or of foreign persons empowered to act in this name on the territory of the Russian Federation;

(7) by a Russian performer of services by means of a commercial presence on the territory of a foreign State;

(8) by a foreign performer of services by means of a commercial presence on the territory of the Russian Federation.

2. Unless provided otherwise by international treaties of the Russian Federation, foreign trade in services may be limited by means of the introduction of prohibitions and limitations affecting all or individual sectors of services with respect to the means of rendering services on the basis of federal laws and other normative legal acts of the Russian Federation.

Article 34. National Regime With Respect to Foreign Trade in Services

1. Unless provided otherwise by international treaties of the Russian Federation, the present Federal Law, or other normative legal acts of the Russian Federation with respect to measures concerning foreign trade in services, to foreign performers of services and services rendered by means specified in Article 33(1), points 2, 4, 6, and 8 of the present Federal Law shall be granted a regime no less favourable than the regime granted to analogous Russian performers of services and services rendered by them on the territory of the Russian Federation. A regime shall be considered to be less favourable if it changes the conditions of competition to the benefit of Russian performers of services or services rendered by them on the territory of the Russian Federation in comparison with services by analogous foreign performers or services rendered by means specified in Article 33(1), points 2, 4, 6, and 8 of the present Federal Law.

2. The provisions of point 1 of the present Article shall not apply to the rendering of services (or fulfillment of work) for State or municipal needs [as amended by Federal Law of 2 February 2006, No. 19-ФЗ].

Article 35. Measures Affecting Foreign Trade in Services and Introduced by Proceeding from National Interests

1. Irrespective of the provisions of Article 34 of the present Federal Law, measures affecting foreign trade in services may be introduced in accordance with international treaties of the Russian Federation and federal laws by proceeding from national interests if these measures:

(1) are necessary for compliance with public morality or public order;

(2) are necessary for the protection of life or health of citizens, environment, and the life or health of flora and fauna;

(3) are necessary to fulfill international obligations of the Russian Federation;

(4) are necessary to ensure the defence of the country and security of the State;

(5) are necessary to ensure the integrity and stability of the financial system, defence of the rights and legal interests of investors, depositors, policyholders, and performers of financial services;

(6) are directed towards ensuring the equal or effective establishment or collection of taxes with respect to foreign performers of services and/or means of rendering services specified in Article 33(1), points 2, 4, 6, and 8 of the present Federal Law;

(7) are measures for the realization of the provision of a treaty on the avoidance of double taxation;

(8) are necessary in order to ensure compliance with normative legal acts of the Russian Federation which are not contrary to the provisions of the present Federal Law concerning, *inter alia*:

(a) the prevention and investigation of crimes, and also court proceedings and the execution of judicial decisions with respect to these crimes;

(b) the prevention of an unfair practice or consequences of the failure to fulfill contracts whose subject is the rendering of services;

(c) defence against interference into the private life of individual persons with respect to the processing and dissemination of information of a personal character and defence of confidential information on the individual and personal accounts.

2. The measures specified in point 1 of the present Article should not be applied or be applied by a means which is a means of arbitrary or unfounded discrimination against States or represent covert limitations of foreign trade in services.

3. The provisions of point 2 of the present Article may not be applied with respect to services, foreign performers of services from foreign States or groups of foreign States, with which the Russian Federation does not have mutual treaty obligations to grant a regime no less favourable than the regime to be granted to other States or groups of States.

Chapter 7. State Regulation of Foreign Trade Activity in Domain of Foreign Trade in Intellectual Property

Article 36. Foreign Trade in Intellectual Property

1. State regulation of foreign trade activity in the domain of foreign trade in intellectual property shall be effectuated in accordance with the present Federal Law.

2. In accordance with international treaties of the Russian Federation and federal laws, measures may be introduced affecting foreign trade in intellectual activity if these measures are necessary for compliance of public morality or legal order, protection of the life or health of citizens, environment, life or health of flora and fauna, fulfilment of international obligations of the Russian Federation, ensuring the defence and security of the State, and in other instances provided for by the present Federal Law.

Chapter 8. Special Types of Prohibitions and Limitations of Foreign Trade in Goods, Services, and Intellectual Property

Article 37. Prohibitions and Limitations of Foreign Trade in Goods, Services, and Intellectual Property for Purposes of Participation of Russian Federation in International Sanctions

In accordance with edicts of the President of the Russian Federation, foreign trade in goods, services, and intellectual property may be limited by measures whose adoption is necessary for the participation of the Russian Federation in international sanctions in accordance with the United Nations Charter, including measures departing from the provisions of Article 21(1) and Articles 22, 29–31, and 34 of the present Federal Law.

Article 38. Limitation of Foreign Trade in Goods, Services, and Intellectual Property for Purpose of Maintenance of Equilibrium of Balance of Payments of Russian Federation

1. For the purposes of defence of the external financial position and maintenance of equilibrium of the balance of payments of the Russian Federation, the Government of the Russian Federation may adopt a decision to introduce measures of limitation of foreign trade in goods, services, and intellectual property, including measures departing from the provisions of Article 21(1) and Articles 22, 29, 30, and 34 of the present Federal law. Such measures shall be introduced or intensified if it is necessary to:

(1) stop a serious reduction of hard currency reserves of the Russian Federation or prevent a threat of serious reduction of hard currency reserves of the Russian Federation;

(2) reach a reasonable rate of increase of the hard currency reserves of the Russian Federation (or if hard currency reserves are very low).

2. The measures specified in point 1 of the present Article shall be introduced for the period which is necessary in order to achieve the purposes put, taking into account the international obligations of the Russian Federation.

3. The Government of the Russian Federation when introducing measures of limitation of foreign trade in goods, services, and intellectual property specified in point 1 of the present Article shall determine the federal agency of executive power responsible for the realization of such measures.

4. A decision concerning the introduction of measures of limitation of foreign trade in goods, services, and intellectual property specified in point 1 of the present Article shall be adopted by the Government of the Russian Federation upon the recommendation of the Central Bank of the Russian Federation.

Article 39. Limitation of Foreign Trade in Goods, Services, and Intellectual Property Connected with Measures of Currency Regulation

Foreign trade in goods, services, and intellectual property may be limited by measures of currency regulation or currency control in accordance with articles of the Agreement of the International Monetary Fund and with legislation of the Russian Federation.

Article 40. Retaliatory Measures

1. The Government of the Russian Federation may introduce measures of limitation of foreign trade in goods, services, and intellectual property (retaliatory measures) if a foreign State:

(1) does not fulfill obligations assumed by it under international treaties with respect to the Russian Federation;

(2) undertakes measures which violate the economic interests of the Russian Federation, subjects of the Russian Federation, municipal formations, or Russian persons or political interests of the Russian Federation, including measures which unfoundedly close access to Russian persons to the market of the foreign State or otherwise unfoundedly discriminate against Russian persons;

(3) does not provide to Russian persons adequate and effective defence of their legal interests in that State, for example, defence against anti-competitive activity of other persons;

(4) does not undertake reasonable actions to struggle against unlawful activity of natural persons or judicial persons of that State on the territory of the Russian Federation.

2. Measures of the limitation of foreign trade in goods, services, and intellectual property specified in point 1 of the present Article shall be introduced in accordance with generally-recognized principles and norms of international law and international treaties of the Russian Federation within the limits necessary for the effective defense of economic interests of the Russian Federation, subjects of the Russian Federation, municipal formations, and Russian persons. The said measures may depart from provisions of Article 21(1) and Articles 22, 29–31, and 34 of the present Federal Law.

3. The federal agency of executive power specified in Article 13(3) of the present Federal Law shall collect and summarize information connected with a violation by a foreign State of the rights and legal interests of the Russian Federation, subjects of the Russian Federation, municipal formations, and Russian persons in the instances specified in point 1 of the present Article. If as a result of the consideration of information received this federal agency of executive power draws a conclusion concerning the advisability of introducing retaliatory measures in connection with the violations specified in point 1 of the present Article, it shall submit to the Government of the Russian Federation a report containing proposals concerning the introduction of retaliatory measures agreed with the Ministry of Foreign Affairs of the Russian Federation.

4. A decision concerning the introduction of retaliatory measures shall be adopted by the Government of the Russian Federation. Before the introduction of retaliatory measures the Government of the Russian Federation may adopt a decision to conduct negotiations with the respective foreign State.

Chapter 9. Special Regimes of Effectuation of Foreign Trade Activity

Article 41. Frontier Trade

1. Frontier trade shall be effectuated, as a rule, on the basis of an international treaty of the Russian Federation with a neighbouring foreign State or group of neighbouring foreign States providing for the provision of an especially favourable regime of foreign trade activity with respect to foreign trade in goods and services effectuated exclusively for the satisfaction of local requirements in goods and services produced within the limits of the respective frontier territories and intended for consumption by natural persons having a permanent place of residence on these territories and by juridical persons having a location on these territories. The said special favourable regime shall not extend to other foreign States or groups of foreign States with which the Russian Federation has concluded international treaties provided for the granting of a regime no less favourable than the regime granted to any other foreign State.

2. Frontier trade may be effectuated between Russian persons having a permanent location (or place of residence) on the frontier territory of the Russian Federation and foreign persons having a permanent location (or place of residence) on the respective frontier territory determined in an international treaty of the Russian Federation with the neighbouring foreign State solely for the satisfaction of local needs in goods and services produced within the limits of respective frontier territories and intended for consumption within the limits of the respective frontier territories.

3. The procedure for the effectuation of frontier trade and respective frontier territories on which special regimes are established for the effectuation of foreign trade activity shall be determined by the Government of the Russian Federation in accordance with international treaties of the Russian Federation with neighbouring foreign States and by federal laws.

Article 42. Special Economic Zones

The special regime of economic, including foreign trade, activity on the territories of special economic zones shall be established by the Federal Law "On Special Economic Zones in the Russian Federation" [as amended by Federal Law of 22 July 2005, No. 117-ФЗ].

Chapter 10. State Regulation of Foreign Trade Barter Transactions

Article 43. Measures With Respect to Foreign Trade Barter Transactions

1. In the event of the establishment in accordance with the present Federal Law of prohibitions and limitations of foreign trade in goods, services, and intellectual property such prohibitions and limitations also shall apply with

respect to foreign trade in goods, services, and intellectual property effectuated with the use of foreign trade barter transactions.

2. On the grounds specified in Article 38(1) of the present Federal Law, the Government of the Russian Federation may establish limitations with respect to the use of foreign trade barter transactions when effectuating foreign trade in goods, services, and intellectual property.

Article 44. Procedure for Control for Effectuation of Foreign Trade Barter Transactions and Recording Thereof

1. Foreign trade in goods, services, and intellectual property with the use of foreign trade barter transactions may be effectuated only on condition that such transactions provide for the exchange of goods, service, work, and intellectual property of equal value, and also the duty of the respective party to pay the difference in the value thereof if such transaction provides for the unequal exchange of goods, services, work, and intellectual property.

2. The procedure for the effectuation of control over foreign trade barter transactions and the recording thereof shall be established by the Government of the Russian Federation. If foreign trade barter transactions provide for the partial use of monetary and/or other means of payment, the procedure for the effectuation of control over such transactions, and the recording thereof shall be established by the Government of the Russian Federation and Central Bank of the Russian Federation in accordance with legislation of the Russian Federation.

Article 45. Peculiarities of Effectuation of Foreign Trade Barter Transactions

1. There must be specified in the document formalizing a foreign trade barter transaction:

(1) the date of conclusion and number of the foreign trade barter transaction;

(2) the nomenclature, quantity, quality, and price of the good for each goods position, periods and conditions of the export and import of the good. In a contract for delivery of sets of equipment (or rendering of services and fulfillment of work) in the event of installing sets of objects in a foreign State the cost of the goods shall be specified (hereinafter: counter goods) provided for exchange as of equal value to the goods being exported from the Russian Federation, and the nomenclature, quantity, quality, and price of counter goods shall be specified in additional protocols, which must be a part of such contracts;

(3) the list of services, work, and intellectual property, the value thereof, periods for rendering services, fulfillment of work, transfer of exclusive rights to

objects of intellectual property, or granting of the right to use objects of intellectual property;

(4) the list of documents to be submitted to the Russian person for confirmation of the fact of rendering services, fulfilment of work, transfer of exclusive rights to objects of intellectual property, or granting of the right to the use of objects of intellectual property.

2. Russian persons who have concluded foreign trade barter transactions or in whose name such transactions have been concluded shall within the periods established by legislation of the Russian Federation for the effectuation of current currency operations and calculated from the date of actual crossing of the customs boundary of the Russian Federation by goods to be exported from the Russian Federation, from the moment of rendering of services, fulfilment of work, transfer of exclusive rights to objects of intellectual activity, or granting of the right to the use of objects of intellectual activity be obliged to ensure the bringing in to the customs territory of the Russian Federation of goods equal in value provided for by such transactions, rendering by foreign persons of services of equal value, fulfillment of work of equal value, transfer of executive rights of equal value to objects of intellectual property or granting of the right to the use of objects of intellectual property with confirmation of the fact of the bringing in of the goods, rendering of services, fulfilment of work, transfer of exclusive rights to objects of intellectual property, or granting of the right to the use of objects of intellectual property by respective documents, and also the receipt of means of payment and crediting to the accounts of the said Russian persons in empowered banks of the respective monetary means, if the foreign trade barter transactions provide for the partial use of monetary and/or other means of payment.

3. Exceeding the periods provided for in point 2 of the present Article and the fulfillment by a foreign person of an obligation under the foreign trade barter transaction by a means not providing for the bringing in to the customs territory of the Russian Federation of goods, rendering by a foreign person of services, fulfilment of work, transfer of exclusive rights to objects of intellectual property, or granting of rights for the use of objects of intellectual property shall be permitted only on condition of the receipt of the authorization issued in the procedure determined by the Government of the Russian Federation.

4. In the event of the export of goods the fulfillment by Russian persons of the duties provided for in point 2 of the present Article shall be a requirement of the customs regime of export.

5. When effectuating foreign trade barter transactions under a contract for the delivery of sets of equipment (or rendering services and fulfillment of

work) in the event of installing sets of objects in a foreign State, counter goods may be realized without bringing them in to the customs territory of the Russian Federation. In so doing:

(1) the actual receipt of counter goods must be confirmed by respective documents;

(2) Russian persons not later than 90 days from the day of actual receipt of the counter goods shall be obliged to ensure their realization at market prices prevailing in the country of their realization and the crediting to their accounts in empowered banks of other monetary means on the territory of the Russian Federation received from their realization or the receipt of means of payment.

6. Foreign trade in goods, services, and intellectual property with the use of foreign trade barter transactions may be effectuated only after the formalization of the respective passport of a foreign trade barter transaction in which, inter alia, information is specified concerning payments with the use of money and/or other means of payment if the foreign trade barter transaction is effectuated with the partial use of money and/or other means of payment.

7. When declaring goods to be moved across the customs boundary of the Russian Federation at the expense of the performance of a foreign trade barter transaction, the passport of the foreign trade barter transaction shall be submitted to customs agencies of the Russian Federation.

Chapter 11. Promotion of Development of Foreign Trade Activity

Article 46. Measures Promoting Development of Foreign Trade Activity

The Government of the Russian Federation and agencies of executive power of subjects of the Russian Federation shall within the framework of their competence effectuate in accordance with international treaties of the Russian Federation and legislation of the Russian Federation measures (including the necessary financing thereof) promoting the development of foreign trade activity, including ensure:

(1) the granting of credits to participants of foreign trade activity;

(2) the functioning of the systems of guarantees and insurance of export credits;

(3) the organization of trade exhibitions and fairs, specialized symposia and conferences, and participation therein;

(4) the conducting of campaigns (including advertising) promoting Russian goods, services, and intellectual property on world markets.

Article 47. Information Provision of Foreign Trade Activity

1. For the purpose of the development and raising the effectiveness of foreign trade activity a system of foreign trade information shall be created, the

administration of which shall be effectuated by the federal agency of executive power specified in Article 13(3) of the present Federal Law.

2. The system of foreign trade information shall include the following information concerning:

(1) Russian persons and foreign persons effectuating foreign trade activity on the Russian market;

(2) Russian persons and foreign persons who have received quotas and licenses;

(3) international trade treaties and other treaties of the Russian Federation in the domain of foreign economic ties;

(4) Russian and foreign legislation in the domain of foreign trade activity;

(5) activity of trade representations of the Russian Federation in foreign States;

(6) activity of the Russian Export-Import Bank and other organizations rendering services with regard to granting credits and insurance in the domain of foreign trade activity;

(7) customs statistics of foreign trade of the Russian Federation;

(8) position on foreign markets with regard to basic goods groups;

(9) legislation of the Russian Federation in the domain of technical regulation;

(10) violations in the domain of foreign trade activity;

(11) list of goods whose bringing in to the territory of the Russian Federation or taking out of which from the territory thereof is prohibited;

(12) other information useful for the effectuation of foreign trade activity.

3. The federal agency of executive power specified in Article 13(3) of the present Federal Law shall be obliged within a reasonable period to provide necessary information in the domain of foreign trade activity to a Russian person or foreign person participating in foreign trade activity for payment not exceeding the cost of the services rendered for the provision of such information. The monetary means received shall go in full to the federal budget.

4. In accordance with obligations from international treaties of the Russian Federation the federal agency of executive power specified in Article 13(3) of the present Federal Law shall provide to foreign States and international organizations information concerning the measures of State regulation of foreign trade activity.

Article 48. Foreign Trade Statistics

1. The Government of the Russian Federation shall jointly with the Central Bank of the Russian Federation ensure the creation of the federal system of statistical reports and the collection and working out of a unified method com-

patible with statistical data used in international practice. To such data shall be relegated data concerning:

(1) foreign trade of the Russian Federation received on the basis of State statistical reporting and customs statistics of foreign trade of the Russian Federation, including trade balances of the Russian Federation;

(2) the balance of payments of the Russian Federation, including statistics of foreign trade in goods, services, intellectual property, and capital movement.

2. The Government of the Russian Federation jointly with the Central Bank of the Russian Federation shall ensure monthly, quarterly, and annual official publication of the statistical data specified in paragraph 1(1) of the present Article.

Article 49. Ensuring Favourable Conditions for Access of Russian Persons to Foreign Markets

The Government of the Russian Federation shall adopt measures with regard to the creation of favourable conditions for access of Russian persons to the markets of foreign States and shall enter for these purposes into bilateral and multilateral negotiations, conclude international treaties of the Russian Federation, and also participate in the creation and activity of international organizations and intergovernmental commissions called upon to promote the development of foreign economic ties of the Russian Federation.

Article 50. Ensuring Foreign Economic Interests of Russian Federation in Foreign States

1. Foreign economic interests of the Russian Federation in foreign States shall be ensured by diplomatic representations and consulates of the Russian Federation, and also trade representations of the Russian Federation created on the basis of international treaties of the Russian Federation.

2. Decisions connected with the founding of trade representations of the Russian Federation in foreign States shall be adopted by the Government of the Russian Federation.

Article 51. Representations of Foreign States for Trade and Economic Questions in Russian Federation

Representations of foreign States for trade and economic questions shall be founded in the Russian Federation on the basis of international treaties concluded by the Russian Federation with respective foreign States.

Chapter 12. Control Over Effectuation of Foreign Trade Activity, Responsibility for Violation of Legislation of Russian Federation on Foreign Trade Activity

Article 52. Control Over Effectuation of Foreign Trade Activity

Control over the effectuation of foreign trade activity shall be effectuated by respective agencies of State power of the Russian Federation and agencies of State power of subjects of the Russian Federation within the limits of their competence for the purpose of ensuring compliance with the provisions of the present Federal Law, other federal laws and other normative legal acts of the Russian Federation on foreign trade activity, ensuring and defence of economic and political interests of the Russian Federation and subjects of the Russian Federation, and also the defence of economic interests of municipal formations and Russian persons.

Article 53. Responsibility of Persons Guilty of Violation of Legislation of Russian Federation on Foreign Trade Activity

Persons guilty of a violation of legislation of the Russian Federation on foreign trade activity shall bear civil-law, administrative, or criminal responsibility in accordance with legislation of the Russian Federation.

Chapter 13. Concluding and Transitional Provisions

Article 54. Entry of Present Federal Law into Force

1. The present Federal Law shall enter into force upon the expiry of six months from the day of official publication thereof, except for Article 45(4) of the present Federal Law.

2. Article 45(4) of the present Federal Law shall enter into force from the day of entry into force of the Customs Code of the Russian Federation of 28 May 2003, No. 61-ФЗ, but not earlier than the entry of the present Federal Law into force.

3. From the day of entry into force of the present Federal Law there shall be deemed to have lost force:

Federal Law of 13 October 1995, No. 157-ФЗ "On State Regulation of Foreign Trade Activity" (*СЗ РФ*; (1995), no. 42, item 3923);

Federal Law of 8 July 1997, No. 96-ФЗ "On Making Changes in the Federal Law 'On State Regulation of Foreign Trade Activity' " (*СЗ РФ*; (1997), no. 28, item 3305);

Article 1(1), paragraphs four and five, Article 1(2), Article 2, paragraphs nine and ten, and Chapters V and VI, Federal Law of 14 April 1998, No. 63-ФЗ "On Measures With Regard to the Defence of Economic Interests of the Russian

Federation When Effectuating Foreign Trade in Goods" (*СЗ РФ*; (1998), no. 16, item 1798).

Article 3, Federal Law of 10 February 1999, No. 32-ФЗ "On Making Changes in and Additions to Legislative Acts of the Russian Federation Arising from the Federal Law 'On Production Sharing Agreements' " (*СЗ РФ*; (1999), no. 7, item 879);

Article 13 of the Federal Law of 24 June 2002, No. 110-ФЗ "On Making Changes in and Additions to Part Two of the Tax Code of the Russian Federation and Certain Other Acts of Legislation of the Russian Federation" (*СЗ РФ*; (2002), no. 30, item 3027).

4. Until normative legal acts of the Russian Federation are brought into conformity in the domain of the State regulation of foreign trade activity with the present Federal Law, the said normative legal acts shall apply in the part not contrary to the present Federal Law.

TABLE OF RUSSIAN DOUBLE TAXATION TREATIES, CONVENTIONS, AND AGREEMENTS

The Table is ordered by country with which the Russian Federation (or the USSR) concluded the treaty, convention, or agreement, followed by date of entry into force and, where appropriate, the date from which the treaty is applicable.

Albania: Convention of 11 April 1995. In force: 1 January 1998
Armenia: Agreement of 28 December 1996. In force: 1 January 1999
Australia: Agreement of 7 September 2000. In force: 1 January 2004. Applicable: 1 July 2004
Austria: Convention of 13 April 2000. In force: 1 January 2003
Azerbaidzhan: Agreement of 3 July 1997. In force: 1 January 1999
Belarus: Agreement of 21 April 1995. In force: 1 January 1998
Belgium: Convention of 16 June 1995. In force: 1 January 2001
Bulgaria: Agreement of 8 June 1993. In force: 1 January 1996
Canada: Agreement of 5 October 1995. In force: 1 January 1998
China: Agreement of 27 May 1994. In force: 1 January 1998
Croatia: Agreement of 2 October 1995. In force: 1 January 1998
Cyprus: Agreement of December 1998. In force: 1 January 2000
Czech Republic: Convention of 17 November 1995. In force: 1 January 1998
Denmark: Convention of 8 February 1996. In force: 1 January 1998
Egypt: Agreement of 23 September 1997. In force: 1 January 2001
Finland: Agreement of 4 May 1996. In force: 1 January 2003
France: Convention of 26 November 1996. In force: 1 January 2000
Germany: Agreement of 29 May 1996. In force: 1 January 1997
Hungary: Convention of 1 April 1994. In force: 1 January 1998
Iceland: Convention of 26 November 1999. In force: 1 January 2004
India: Agreement of 25 March 1997. In force: 1 January 1999
Indonesia: Agreement of 12 March 1999. In force: 1 January 2003
Iran: Agreement of 6 March 1998. In force: 1 January 2003

Ireland: Agreement of 29 April 1994. In force: 1 January 1996. Applicable: 6 April 1996 for income tax and tax on revenues from alienation of property, and from 1 January 1996 for tax on revenues of corporations
Israel: Convention of 25 April 1994. In force: 1 January 2001
Italy: Convention of 9 April 1996. In force: 1 January 1999
Japan: Convention of 18 January 1986. In force: 27 November 1986
Kazakhstan: Convention of 18 October 1996. In force: 1 January 1998
Korea: Convention of 19 January 1992. In force: 1 January 1996
Korean People's Democratic Republic: Agreement of 26 September 1997. In force: 1 January 2001
Kuwait: Agreement of 9 February 1999. In force: 1 January 2004
Kyrgyzia: Agreement of 13 January 1999. In force: 1 January 2001
Lebanon: Convention of 8 April 1997. In force 1 January 2001
Lithuania: Agreement of 26 June 1999, with Protocol of same date. In force: 29 April 2005
Luxembourg: Agreement of 28 June 1998. In force: 1 January 1998
Macedonia: Agreement of 21 October 1997. In force: 1 January 2001
Malaysia: Agreement of 31 July 1987. In force: 1 July 1988
Mali: Convention of 2 June 1996. In force: 1 January 2000
Moldova: Agreement of 12 April 1996. In force: 1 January 1998
Mongolia: Agreement of 5 April 1995. In force: 1 January 1998
Morocco: Agreement of 4 September 1997. In force: 1 January 2000
Namibia: Convention of 31 March 1998. In force: 1 January 2001
Netherlands: Agreement of 16 December 1996. In force: 1 January 1999
New Zealand: Agreement of 5 September 2000. In force: 1 January 2004 (in New Zealand with respect to taxes other than those taxes withheld at source on payment of revenues for revenues for the financial year commencing from 1 April 2004)
Norway: Convention of 26 March 1996. In force: 1 January 2003
Philippines: Convention of 26 April 1995. In force: 1 January 1998
Poland: Agreement of 22 May 1992. In force: 1 January 1994
Portugal: Convention of 29 May 2000. In force: 1 January 2003
Qatar: Agreement of 20 April 1998. In force: 1 January 2001
Romania: Convention of 27 September 1993. In force: 1 January 1996
Slovakia: Agreement of 24 June 1994. In force: 1 January 1998
Slovenia: Convention of 29 September 1995. In force: 1 January 1998
South African Republic: Agreement of 27 November 1995. In force: 1 January 2001 or thereafter (or from 1 September 2000 with respect to taxes recovered at source from amounts to be paid or accrued)
Spain: Convention of 16 December 1999. In force: 1 January 2001
Sri Lanka: Agreement of 2 March 1999. In force: 1 January 2003
Sweden: Convention of 15 June 1993. In force: 1 January 1996

Switzerland: Agreement of 1 November 1995. In force: 1 January 1998
Syrian Arab Republic: Agreement of 17 September 2000. In force: 1 January 2004
Tadzhikistan: Agreement of 31 March 1997. In force: 1 January 2004
Turkey: Agreement of 15 December 1997. In force: 1 January 2000
Turkmenistan: Agreement of 14 January 1998. In force: 1 January 2000
Ukraine: Agreement of 8 February 1995. In force: 1 January 2000
United Kingdom: Convention of 15 February 1994. In force: 1 January 1998
United States of America: Treaty of 17 June 1992. In force: 1 January 1994 (from 1 February 1995 with respect to taxes recovered at source)
Uzbekistan: Agreement of 2 March 1994. In force: 1 January 1996
Vietnam: Agreement of 27 May 1993. In force: 1 January 1997
Yugoslavia: Convention of 12 October 1995. In force: 1 January 1998

TABLE OF FOREIGN INVESTMENT PROTECTION TREATIES AND AGREEMENTS

The Table is ordered by country with which the Russian Federation (or the USSR) concluded the treaty, convention, or agreement, followed by date of entry into force and, where appropriate, the date from which the treaty is applicable. In some instances the date of ratification by the Russian Federation is given instead. Such treaties and agreements are commonly entitled: Agreement on the Encouragement and Mutual Defence of Capital Investments.

Albania: Agreement of 11 April 1995. In force: 29 May 1996
Argentina: Agreement of 2 June 1998. In force: 20 November 2000
Armenia: Agreement of 15 September 2001. In force: 8 February 2006
Bulgaria: Treaty of 8 June 1993 and Protocol of 2 March 2003. In force: 19 December 2005
Cuba: Agreement of 7 July1993. In force: 8 July 1996
Czech Republic: Agreement of 5 April 1994. In force: 6 June 1996
Denmark: Agreement of 4 November 1993. In force: 29 August 1996
Egypt: Agreement of 23 September 1997. In force: 12 June 2000
Greece: Agreement of 30 June 1993. In force: 23 February 1997
Hungary: Agreement of 6 March 1995. In force: 29 May 1996
India: Agreement of 23 December 1994. Ratified by Russia: 23 May 1996
Italy: Agreement of 9 April 1996. In force: 7 July 1997
Korean People's Democratic Republic: Agreement of 28 November 1996. Ratified by Russia: 26 December 2005
Kuwait: Agreement of 21 November 1994. In force: 30 May 1996
Laotian People's Democratic Republic: Agreement of 6 December 1996. Ratified by Russia: 26 December 2005
Lebanon: Agreement of 8 April 1997. In force: 11 March 2003
Lithuania: Agreement of 29 March 1999. In force: 24 May 2004
Macedonia: Agreement of 21 October 1997. In force: 9 July 1998

Moldova: Agreement of 17 March 1998. Ratified by Russia: 28 May 2001
Mongolia: Agreement of 29 November 1995. Ratified by Russia: 26 December 2005
Norway: Agreement of 4 October 1995. In force: 21 May 1998
Philippines: Agreement of 12 September 1997. Ratified by Russia: 29 October 1998
Romania: Agreement of 29 September 1993. In force: 19 July 1996
Slovakia: Agreement of 30 November 1993. Ratified by Russia: 8 July 1996
South African Republic: Agreement of 23 November 1998. In force: 12 April 2000
Sweden: Agreement of 19 April 1995. In force: 7 July 1996
Syrian Arab Republic: Agreement of 26 January 2005. No data on ratification or entry into force
Turkey: Agreement of 15 December 1997. Ratified by Russia: 30 December 1999
Vietnam: Agreement of 16 June 1994. In force: 3 July 1996
Yemen: Agreement of 17 December 2002. In force: 21 July 2005
Yugoslavia: Agreement of 11 October 1995. Ratified by Russia: 8 July 1996

TABLE OF CONVENTIONS OF THE INTERNATIONAL LABOUR ORGANIZATION RATIFIED BY THE RUSSIAN FEDERATION

[as of 1 July 2005]

Convention No. 10: "On Minimum Age (Agriculture)" (1921)
Convention No. 11: "On the Right of Association (Agriculture)" (1921)
Convention No. 13: "On White Lead Painting" (1921)
Convention No. 14: "On Weekly Rest (Industry)" (1921)
Convention No. 15: "On Minimum Age (Trimmers and Stokers)" (1921)
Convention No. 16: "On Medical Examination of Young Persons (Sea)" (1921)
Convention No. 23: "On Repatriation of Seamen" (1926)
Convention No. 27: "On Marking of Weight (Packages Transported by Vessels)" (1929)
Convention No. 29: "On Forced Labour" (1930)
Convention No. 32: "On Protection Against Accidents (Dockers)" (1932)
Convention No. 45: "On Underground Work (Women)" (1935)
Convention No. 47: "On Forty-Hour Week" (1935)
Convention No. 52: "On Holidays With Pay" (1936)
Convention No. 58: "On Minimum Age (Sea)" (Revised) (1936)
Convention No. 59: "On Minimum Age (Industry)" (1937)
Convention No. 60: "On Minimum Age (Non-Industrial Employment)" (1937)
Convention No. 69: "Certification of Ships' Cooks" (1946)
Convention No. 73: "On Medical Examination (Seafarers)" (1946)
Convention No. 77: "On Medical Examination of Young Persons (Industry)" (1946)
Convention No. 78: "On Medical Examination of Young Persons (Non-Industrial Occupations)" (1946)
Convention No. 79: "On Night Work of Young Persons (Non-Industrial Occupations)" (1946)

Convention No. 81: "On Labour Inspection" (1947)
Convention No. 87: "On Freedom of Association and Protection of the Right to Organize" (1948)
Convention No. 90: "On Night Work of Young Persons (Industry)" (revised 1948)
Convention No. 92: "On Accommodation of Crews" (Revised) (1949)
Convention No. 95: "On the Protection of Wages" (1949)
Convention No. 98: "On the Right to Organize and Collective Bargaining" (1949)
Convention No. 100: "On Equal Remuneration" (1951)
Convention No. 103: "On Maternity Protection" (1962)
Convention No. 105: "On the Abolition of Forced Labour" (1957)
Convention No. 106: "On Weekly Rest (Commerce and Offices)" (1957)
Convention No. 108: "On Seafarers' Identity Document" (1958)
Convention No. 111: "On Discrimination (Employment and Occupation)" (1958)
Convention No. 112: "On Minimum Age for Admission to Employment as Fishermen" (1959)
Convention No. 113: "On Medical Examination of Fishermen" (1959)
Convention No. 115: "On Radiation Protection" (1960)
Convention No. 116: "On Final Articles Revision" (1961)
Convention No. 119: "On Guarding of Machinery" (1963)
Convention No. 120: "On Hygiene (Commerce and Offices)" (1964)
Convention No. 122: "On Employment Policy" (1964)
Convention No. 123: "On Minimum Age (Underground Work)" (1965)
Convention No. 124: "On Medical Examination of Young Persons (Underground Work)" (1965)
Convention No. 126: "On Accommodation of Crews (Fishermen)" (1966)
Convention No. 133: "On Accommodation of Crews (Supplementary Provisions)" (1970)
Convention No. 134: "On Prevention of Accidents (Seafarers)" (1970)
Convention No. 137: "On Dock Work" (1973)
Convention No. 138: "On Minimum Age" (1973)
Convention No. 142: "On Human Resources Development" (1975)
Convention No. 147: "On Merchant Shipping (Minimum Standards)" (1976)
Convention No. 148: "On Working Environment (Air Pollution, Noise and Vibration)" (1977)
Convention No. 149: "On Nursing Personnel" (1977)
Convention No. 150: "On Labour Administration" (1978)
Convention No. 152: "On Occupational Safety and Health (Dock Worker)" (1979)
Convention No. 155: "On Occupational Safety and Health" (1981)

Convention No. 156: "On Workers with Family Responsibilities" (1981)
Convention No. 159: "On Vocational Rehabilitation and Employment (Disabled Persons)" (1983)
Convention No. 160: "On Labour Statistics" (1985)
Convention No. 162: "On Asbestos" (1986)
Convention No. 179: "On Recruitment and Placement of Seafarers" (1996)
Convention No. 182: "On Worst Forms of Child Labour" (1999)

SELECT BIBLIOGRAPHY

A. G. «О праве иностранцев усыновлять русских подданных» [On the Right of Foreigners to Adopt Russian Subjects], *Журнал Министерства Юстиции*, № 3 (1897), pp. 223–6.

Agaev, F.A. and Galuzo, V. N. *Иммунитеты в российском уголовном процессе* [Immunities in Russian Criminal Procedure]. M., TEIS, 1998. 135 p.

Aleksandrenko, A. N. «О высылке иностранцев» [On the Banishment of Foreigners], *Журнал Министерства Юстиции*, № 5, ч. 2 (1905), pp. 35–69.

——. *О подданстве и натурализации* [On Citizenship and Naturalization] (Варшава, *Тип. Варшавского учебного округа*, 1904). 42 стр.

Andreevskii, I. E. *О правах иностранцев в России до вступления Иоанна III Васильевича на престол Великого Княжества Московского* [On the Rights of Foreigners in Russia Before the Accession of Ivan III Vasil'evich to the Throne of the Grand Duchy of Muscovy] (Спб., Тип. Якова Трея, 1854). iv, 142 стр.

Averin, D. D. *Положение иностранцев в советском гражданском процессе* [Status of Foreigners in Soviet Civil Procedure]. M., izd-vo Moskovskogo universiteta, 1966. 188 p.

Barkovskii, N. «К вопросу о праве наследования после иностранцев в России» [On the Question of the Right of Inheritance After Foreigners in Russia], *Журнал гражданского и уголовного права*, № 1 (1888), стр. 26–48.

Bilibin, D. *Foreign Students in the USSR.* M., Novosti Press Agency Publishing Agency, 1984. 72 p.

Bogolepov, A. A. *Die Rechtsstellung der Ausländer in Sowjetrussland.* Berlin, 1927. 194 p.

Boguslavskii, M. M. *Правовое положение иностранных инвестиций* [Legal Status of Foreign Investments]. M., Vneshneekonomicheskii tsentr 'Sovinteriur', 1993. 176 p.

——. *Situacion Juridica de los Extranjeros en la URSS.* M., Foreign Languages Publishing House, 1961. 141 p.

Boguslavskii, M. M. and Rubanov, A. A. *The Legal Status of Foreigners in the U.S.S.R.* M., Foreign Languages Publishing House, 1961. 122 p.

——. *Правовое положение иностранцев в СССР* [Legal Status of Foreigners in the USSR]. 2nd. rev. edn. M., Institut mezhdunarodnykh otnoshenii, 1962. 144 p.

Borodin, A. V. «Иноземцы – ратные люди на службе в Московском государстве» [Foreigners – Soldiers in the Service of the Muscovite State], *ВОРИ*, II, стр. 185–201.

Bouve, C. L. 'Some Observations on the Status of Foreigners Under Soviet Treaties', *Proceedings of the American Society of International Law*, XVIII (1934), 92–104.

Brikner, A. G. 'Die Ausländer in Russland im 17.Jahrhundert', *BM*, xxxv (1877), pp. 652–704, 723–65.

Brikner, A. G. 'Zur Geschichte der Ausländer in Russland', *Russische Revue*, xxvi (1886), pp. 274–317.

Budde, Dirk. *Die Rechtsstellung des Auslanders in der Sowjetunion.* Baden-Baden, Nomos Verlagsgesellschaft, 1981. 328 p.

Bulmerincq, August von. *Das Asylrecht und Auslieferung flüchtiger Verbrecher: Eine Abhandlung aus dem Begiete des universellen Rechtsgeschichte und des positiven Völkerrechts* (Dorpat, J. C. Schünmann's Wittwe & C. Mattiesen, 1853). iv, 161 pp.

Butler, W. E. (comp., transl. & ed.). *Basic Documents on the Soviet Legal System.* 3rd edn.; Dobbs Ferry, New York, Oceana Publications Inc., 1992. viii, 557 p.

——. (comp., transl. & ed.). *Basic Legal Documents of the Russian Federation.* Dobbs Ferry, New York, Oceana Publications Inc., 1992.

——. *Foreign Investment Law in the Commonwealth of Independent States* (London, Simmonds & Hill Publishing Ltd., 2002). xxiii, 1116 p.

——. *The Law of Treaties in Russia and the Commonwealth of Independent States: Text and Commentary.* Cambridge, Cambridge University Press, 2002. xiii, 548 p.

—— (ed. & transl.). *Russian Civil Legislation.* The Hague, Kluwer Law International, 1999. lxviii, 676 p.

—— (comp., ed., & transl.). *Russian Company and Commercial Legislation.* Oxford, Oxford University Press, 2003. xxxvii, 880 p.

——. *Russian Law.* 2nd edn. Oxford, Oxford University Press, 2003. lxi, 761 p.

——. *Russian Public Law: The Foundations of a Rule-of-Law State: Legislation and Documents.* London, Wildy, Simmonds & Hill, 2005. xi, 926 p.

Cleinow, G. *Das Recht der Ausländer in der Union der S.S.R.* Erfurt, 1925. 143 p.

'La condition des étrangers dans la république des soviets', Journal de droit international, LIV (1927), 572–81.

Dmitriev, Iu. A. and Korsik, K. A. *Правовое положение иностранцев в Российской Федерации* [Legal Status of Foreigners in the Russian Federation]. M., Manuskript, 1997. 112 p.

Egor'ev, V. V., et al. *Законодательство и международные договоры СССР и союзных республик о правовом положении иностранных физических и юридических лиц* [Legislation and International Treaties of the USSR and Union Republics on the Legal Status of Foreign Natural and Juridical Persons]. M., 1926. 592 p.

Erpyleva, N. Iu., Gashi-Butler, M. E. and Henderson, J. E. (eds.), *Forging a Common Legal Destiny: Liber Amicorum in honour of William E. Butler*, General Ed. A. L. Kolodkin. London, Wildy, Simmonds & Hill Publishing, 2005. xix, 880 p.

Esaian, A. A. *Некоторые вопросы советского гражданства* [Some Questions of Soviet Citizenship]. Erevan, 1966. 115 p.

Farkhutdinov, I. Z. and Trapeznikov, V. A. *Инвестиционное право* [Investment Law]. M., Wolters Kluwer, 2006. 432 p.

Galenskaia, L. N. *Правовое положение иностранцев в СССР* [Legal Status of Foreigners in the USSR]. M., Mezhdunarodnye otnosheniia, 1982. 160 p.

Gessen, V. M. «Иностранцы» [Foreigners], *НЭСл*, xix, столб. 489–92.

——. «О влиянии натупализации на семью иностранца» [On the Influence of Naturalization on the Family of a Foreigner], *Журнал министерства юстиции*, № 7, ч. 2 (сентябрь 1896), стр. 35–58.

——. «О прекращении подданства» [On the Termination of Citizenship],

ЖЮОбСпб, XXVI, № 8 (август 1896), стр. 1–40; № 9 (сентябрь 1896), стр. 31–66.

——. *Подданство, его установление и прекращение* [Subjecthood, Establishment and Termination Thereof] (Спбю, Тип. *Правда, 1909)ю 448* стр.

Ginsburgs, G. *The Citizenship Law of the USSR.* The Hague, Martinus Nijhoff, 1983. xii, 394 p.

——. 'Inheritance by Foreigners Under Soviet Law', *Iowa Law Review*, LI (1965), 16–74.

——. *Soviet Citizenship Law.* Leyden, A. W. Sijthoff, 1968. 270 p.

Golovistikova, A. N. *Иностранцы и граждане России: особенности правового положения, регистрация, учет* [Foreigners and Citizens of Russia: Peculiarities of Legal Status, Registration, and Recording]. M., Eksmo Education, 2006. 432 p.

«Гражданские права иностранцев в России» [Civil Rights of Foreigners in Russia], *Русский Вестник*, xxviii (июль 1860), современная летопись, pp. 129–31.

Gubin, V. F. «Новая Советская конституция и статус иностранцев в СССР», [New Soviet Constitution and the Status of Foreigners in the USSR], *Советский ежегодник международного права 1979* (M., 1980), pp. —.

I. G. «Судебные решения иностранных государств» [Judicial Decisions of Foreign States], *ЖМЮ*, № 10 (октябрь 1895), pp. 214–21.

Ivanov, N. I. *Законы об иностранцах, подданных воюющих с Россиею держав и Сенатская практика* [Laws on Foreigners, Subjects of Foreign Powers Belligerent Against Russia and Senate Practice] (Одесса, М. С. Бершадский, 1914). 65 p.

——. *Лишение права судебную защиту враждебных иностранцев* [Deprivation of Enemy Aliens of Right of Judicial Defense] (Одесса, *Тип. Спорт и наука*, 1915). 30 p.

——. *Новый закон о землевладении и землепользовании подданных воюющих с Россиею держав, а также австрийских, венгерских или германских выходцев* [New Law on Land Possession and Land Use of Subjects of Powers Belligerent Against Russia, and also Austrian, Hungarian, or German Emigrants] (Одесса, *Спорт и наука*, 1916). 52 p.

Ivanovskii, I. A. «О значении в России иностранных судебных приговоров по Уголовным делам» [On the Significance in Russia of Foreign Judicial Judgments With Regard to Criminal Cases], *Право*, № 1 (1898), cols. 16–19; № 2 (1898), cols. 9–16.

Ivechko, V. V. and Samoilova, L. B. *Свободные экономические зоны в зарубежных странах и России: Учебное пособие* [Free Economic Zones in Foreign Countries and Russia: Instructional Manual]. Kaliningrad, Iantarnyi skaz, 1999. 168 p.

Ivlieva, M. V. (ed.). *Налогообложение иностранных компаний в России: Сборник материалов правоприменительной практики* [Taxation of Foreign Companies in Russia: Collection of Materials of Law Enforcement Practice]. Comp. E. V. Ovcharova. M., Status, 2004). 204 p. (Vyp. 1)

Kabalkin, A. Iu., «Правовой статус иностранных инвесторов в Российской Федерации» [Legal Status of Foreign Investors in the Russian Federation], in A. A. Rubanov and N. I. Solovianenko (eds.), *Иностранные инвестиции в странах СНГ и Великобритании* [Foreign Investments in Countries of the CIS and Great

Britain] (M., 1992), pp. 25–35 (Institute of State and Law. Russian Academy of Sciences).

Kamarovskii, L. A. «О допущении и изгнании иностранцев (читано в заседании Московского Юридического Общества 23 октября 1889 г.)» [On Admittance and Expulsion of Foreigners (Delivered at Session of Moscow Law Society, 23 October 1889)], *ЮВ*, III, № 3 (декабрь 1889), pp. 519–33.

Kapustin, M. N. «О значении национальности в международном праве: *Речь, произнесенная в торжественном собрании Имп. Московского университета* 12-го января 1863 года» [On the Significance of Nationality in International Law: Address Delivered at Solemn Meeting of Imperial Moscow University on 12 January 1863], *Краткий отчет о состоянии Императорского Московского университета за 1862 год* (M., 1863). 14, 21 p.

——. «Теория национальности в международном праве» [Theory of Nationality in International Law], *Русский вестник*, XLIII, № 1 (1863), pp. 297–312.

Karadze-Iskrov, N. P. 'Die juristischen personen des öffentlichen rechts nach sovjetrecht', *Zeitschrift für Ostrecht*, VII (1933), 999–1023.

Kazanskii, P. E. 'Aperçu sur la condition des étrangers en Russie', Journal de droit international, xxv (1898), pp. 225–33.

——. «Выдача преступников в России» [Extradition of Criminals to Russia], *Судебная газетаб* № 32 (10 август 1903), pp. 5–7; № 33 (17 август 1903), pp. 5–6.

——. 'L'extradition en Russie', *Journal de droit international*, XXIX (1902), pp. 718–45.

Korkunov, N. M. «Укорение иностранцев и прекрашение подданства» [Taking Root of Foreigners and Termination of Citizenship], *Журнал министерства юстиции*, № 10 (октябрь 1895), стр. 69–120.

Krasnozhen, M. E. *Иноверцы на Руси* [Persons of Other Faiths in Rus] (Юрьев, Тип. К. Маттисен, 1900). 206 стр. (только т. 1); 3-е изд. 1903. 202 стр.

Kuznetsov, V. V. *Предприятие во внешне-экономических связях* [The Enterprise in Foreign Economic Links] (M., Mezhdunarodnye otnosheniia, 1990). 272 p.

Kvachakhiia, A. A. *Гражданство. Вид на жительство. Временное проживание в Российской Федерации: решение проблем* [Citizenship. Residence Permit, Temporary Residing in the Russian Federation. Resolution of Problems]. 3rd edn M., Iurisprudentsiia, 2005 160 p.

Lane, A. M. *Die Rechtslage der deutschen Spezialisten in der Sowjetunion.* [n.p.], 1933. 53 p.

Lazarev, L. V., Marysheva and N. I., Panteleeva, I. V. *Иностранные граждане (Правовое положение)* [Foreign Citizens (Legal Status)]. M., Rossiiskoe pravo, 1992. 320 p.

'Legal Position of Concessionaires in Russia', Journal of Co-National Law, III, no. 1 (1922), pp. 1–3.

Leshkov, V. N. «Взгляд на состояние права иностранцев, *по началам Европейского народного права вообще, и в особенности по законам отечественным*» [View on State of Rights of Foreigners According to Principles of European Law of Nations in General and in Particular According to Fatherland Laws], *Юридические записки, издаваемые Петром Редкином* (М. *Университеоекая тип.*, 1841), II, стр. 1–29.

Lukashuk, I. I. *Международное право в судах государств* [International Law in the Courts of States]. M., SKF 'Rossia-Neva', 1993).

Lunts, L. A. 'Die Rechtsstellung der ausländer in der UdSSR nach dem neuen sowjetische zivilrecht', *Jahrbuch für Ostrecht*, no. 3/2 (1962), pp. 43–8.

——. 'Legal Position of Foreigners in the USSR Under the New Civil Legislation', *Soviet Law and Government*, I, no. 3 (1962/1963), pp. 29–32.

Makarov, A. N. 'Die Rechtslage der ausländer in der Union der S. S. R.', in G. Cleinow (ed.), *Das Recht der Ausländer in der Union der S.S.R.* (Erfurt, 1925), pp. 71–136.

Marysheva, N. I. *Иностранец: правовая защита* [Foreigner: Legal Defense]. M., Izvestia, 1993. 136 p.

Metelev, S. E. *Международная трудовая миграция и нелегальная миграция в России* [International Labour Migration and Illegal Migration in Russia]. M., Iuniti-Dana, 2006. 175 p.

Mukhanov, P. A. «О судебнойзащите иностранных акционерных обществ в России» [On Judicial Defense of Foreign Joint-Stock Societies in Russia], *ЖГУПр*, № 10 (1883), pp. 1–18.

——. *Об иностранцах в России: Сборник узаконений трактатов и конвенций, с относящимся к ним правительственными и судебными разъяснениями* [On Foreigners in Russia: Collection of Legislation, Treaties, and Conventions with Governmental and Judicial Explanations Relating Thereto] (Спб., А. Бенке, 1888; доп., 1894; 2-е изд. *Спб.*, А. *Бенке*, 1911). xxvi, 458 p.

——. «Право наследования после иностранцев в России» [Right of Inheritance After Foreigners in Russia], *ЖГУПр*, № 8 (1887), pp. 1–53.

Muliukin, A. S. «Иностранцы свободных профессий в Московском гоударстве» [Foreigners of Free Professions in the Muscovite State], *ЖМНПр*, XVII (NS), № 10 (1908), отд. *наук*, pp. 307–52.

——. *Очерки по истории юридического положния иностранных купцов в Московском государстве* [Surveys With Regard to History of Legal Status of Foreign Merchants in Muscovy State] (Одесса, *Тип. Техника*, 1912). 394 p.

——. *Приезд иностранцев в древнюю Русь* [Arrival of Foreigners in Mediaeval Rus] (Спб., Сенатская тип., 1907). 35 p.

——. *Приезд иностранцев в Московское государство: Из истории русского права XVI и XVII веков* [Arrival of Foreigners in Muscovy State: From the History of Russian Law of Sixteenth and Seventeenth Centuries] (Спб., Тип. Спб. Т-во «Труд», 1909). 285 p.

Muranov, A. I. *Международный договор и взаимность как основания приведения в исполнение в России иностранных суебльх решений* [International Treaty and Reciprocity as Gounds for Enforcement of Foreign Judicial Decisions in Russia]. M., Statut, 2003. 192 p.

Nemirovskii, M. D. «О силе решений иностранных судов» [On the Force of Decisions of Foreign Courts], *ЖМЮ*, № 3, ч. 2 (1910), pp. 103–46.

——. «Об исполнении иностранных судебных решений» [On the Execution of Foreign Court Decisions], *ЖМЮ*, № 5, ч. 2 (май 1908), pp. 275–86.

Nesteroff, P. 'La situation juridique des étrangers en Russie', Revue critique de droit international privé, XXI (1926), 521–34; XXII (1927), 37–43.

Nolde, B. E. «История русского коллизионного права» [History of Russian Conflicts Law], *Труды русских ученых за-границей*, II (1923), pp. 126–48.

Pergament, O. Ia. *De la condition légale des sociétés étrangères en Russie, avec un appendice contenant les déclarations, traités, lois et décrets qui régissent la condition légale des sociétés étrangères en Russie* (Paris, Larose, 1899). 54 p.

——. «Начало 'locus regit actum' и ст. 1068 т. X» [Principle 'locus regit actum' and Article 1068, Vol. X], *Право*, № 14 (1904), cols. 809–21.

Petchorine, D. *Questions concernant la condition des Russes en France et celle des étrangers (specialement les français) dans l'URSS* Paris, 1929. 298 p.

Pilenko, A. A. *La législation soviétique et la Conférence de la Haye*. Paris, M. Giard, 1922. 52 p.

Pisarevskii, G. G. *Из истории иностранной колонизации в России в XVIII в. (По неиз. Архивным документам)* [From History of Foreign Colonization in Russia in Eighteenth Century] (M., *А. И. Снегирев*, 1909). xii, 340, 84 p.

Plotkin, M. A. *Legal Status of Foreigners in the U.S.S.R.*, transl. R. Biske. M., 1934. 89 p.

Podshibiakin, S. A. *Правовой статус международных неправительственных организаций* [Legal Status of International Nongovernmental Organisations]. M., izd-vo Iurlitinform, 2006. 128 p.

Правовое положение иностранцев в России: Сборник нормативных актов [Legal Status of Foreigners in Russia: Collection of Normative Acts]. Intro. A. L. Makovskii. M., izd-vo BEK, 1996. 242 p.

Правовое положение иностранцев в России: Сборник нормативных актов [Legal Status of Foreigners in Russia: Collection of Normative Acts]. Comp. V. V. Riakhovskii. M., Iurisprudentsia, 2003. 128 p.

Prudhomme, A. 'La révolution bolchevique et le status juridique des russes', Journal de droit international, LI (1924), 5–8.

Prudnikov, A. S. and Tiurkin, M. L. (eds.). *Государственно-правовые основы миграции населения в Российской Федерации* [State-Law Foundations of Migration of the Population in the Russian Federation]. M., Iuniti-Dana, 2006. 480 p.

Rastorgoueff, L. P. *The Legal Position of English Companies in Russia* (London, Jordan & Sons Ltd., 1911). xi, 91 p.

Riakhovskii, V. V. (comp.). *Правовое положение иностранных граждан в России: Сборник нормативных актов* [Legal Status of Foreign Citizens in Russia: Collection of Normative Acts]. M., Iurisprudentsiia, 2003. 128 p.

Rozenberg, M. G. *Международный договор и иностранное право в практике Международного коммерческого арбитражного суда* [International Contract and Foreign Law in the Practice of the International Commercial Arbitration Court]. M., Statut, 1998. 211 p.

Rzepka, W. 'Die rechtsstellung der ausländer in der UdSSR', *Recht in Ost und West*, VIII (1964), 49–55.

Shalland, L. A. «Юридическое положение иностранных акционерных обществ в России» [Legal Status of Foreign Joint-Stock Societies in Russia], *Право*, № 1 (1902), cols. 16–26; № 5 (1902), cols. 219–25; № 16 (1902), cols. 835–40.

Shcherbinin, S. S. *Комментарий к закону «Об инвестиционной деятельности в Российской Федерации, осуществляемой в форме капительных вложений* [Commentary to Law on Investment Activity in the Russian Federation Effectuated in the Form of Capital Investments]. M., Iuridicheskii dom 'Iustitsinform', 2003. 272 p.

Shkatulla, V. I. (ed.). *Комментарий к федеральному закону «О правовом положении иностранных граждан в Российской Федерации* [Commentary to Federal Law on the Legal Status of Foreign Citizens in the Russian Federation]. M., ZAO Iustitsinform, 2004. 176 p.

Skachkova, G. S. *Регулирование труда лиц гражданского персонала федеральных органов исполнительных власти Российской Федерациив выполняющих задачи в области обороны, правооранительной деятельности и безопасности государства. Научно-практическое пособие* [Regulation of Labour of Civilian Personnel of Federal Agencies of Executive Power of Russian Federation Fulfilling Tasks in Domain of Defence, Law Enforcement Activity, and Security of the State]. M., Wolters Kluwer, 2005. 384 p.

Skachkova, G. S. *Труд иностранцев в России: правовое регулирование* [Labour of Foreigners in Russia: Legal Regulation]. M., Wolters Kluwer, 2006. 264 p.

Smirnova. E. S. *Проблемы правового статуса иностранцев в условиях глобализации* [Problems of Legal Status of Foreigners Under Conditions of Globalization]. M., n.p., 2003. ii, 463 p.

'Les sociétés étrangères en Russie', *Journal de droit international*, xxxi (1904), pp. 1044–6.

Статус иностранцев в СССР [Status of Foreigners in the USSR], ed. M. M. Boguslavskii. M., Akademiia nauk SSSR, Redaktsiia 'Obshchestvennye nauki i sovremennost', 1984. 104 p.

Tager, P. *La condition des étrangers dans l'Union des Republiques Soviétiques* (Paris, Clunet, 1925).

Tarel, J. *Essai sur la condition juridique des sociétés russes en France.* Grenoble, 1938. 241 p.

Vitte, Fedor Fedorovich, *Die Rechtsverhältnisse der Ausländer in Russland.* Dorpat, J. C. Schünmann, 1847. 94 p.

Внешнеэкономическая деятельность: Сборник нормативных актов [Foreign Economic Activity: Collection of Normative Acts]. M., GrossMedia, 2005. 304 p.

Всероссийская научно-практическая конференция *Нижегородский юридический институтб сентябрь* 1995 года: *Российская правовая система и международое право: современные проблемы взаимодействия»*, *Государство и право*, nos. 2 and 3 (1996).

Wahl, Albert. «Правовое положение граждан враждебных государств во Франции во время войны» [Legal Status of Citizens of Hostile States in France During Wartime], *ВГП*, № 5 (1915), стр. 13–40.

Zaitseff, L. M. 'The Legal Position of Foreigners in Soviet Russia', *Michigan Law Review*, XXIV (1926), 441–60.

——. *Подданные враждебного государства и русские суды* [Subjects of Enemy State and Russian Courts] (Киев, Тип. Петр Барский, 1915). 16 отр.

——. 'La situacion juridica de los extranjeros en la rusia de los soviets', Revista general de legislacion y jurisprudencia, CXLVIII (1926), 543–62.

——. 'Взаимное исполнение иностранных судебных решений и русско-германской торговый договор' [Mutual Execution of Foreign Judicial Decisions and Russo-German Trade Treaty], *Труды Юго-Западного Отделения Российской Экспортной палаты*, xviii (1914), стр. 1–16.

Zimnenko, B. L. *Международное право и правовая система Российской Федерации* [International Law and the Legal System of the Russian Federation]. M., Statut, 2006. 454 p.

Zmirlov, K. P. *Лишение неприятельских подданных прав на судебную защиту на время войны* [Deprivation of Enemy Subjects of Rights to Judicial Defense During War] (Пг., Сенатская тип., 1915). 25 p.

INDEX OF NAMES

SUBJECT INDEX